THE WELL-MANAGED HEALTHCARE ORGANIZATION

THE WELL-MANAGED HEALTHCARE ORGANIZATION

Seventh Edition

KENNETH R. WHITE

JOHN R. GRIFFITH

AUPHA

Chicago, Illinois

Your board, staff, or clients may also benefit from this book's insight. For more information on quantity discounts, contact the Health Administration Press Marketing Manager at (312) 424-9470.

This publication is intended to provide accurate and authoritative information in regard to the subject matter covered. It is sold, or otherwise provided, with the understanding that the publisher is not engaged in rendering professional services. If professional advice or other expert assistance is required, the services of a competent professional should be sought.

The statements and opinions contained in this book are strictly those of the authors and do not represent the official positions of the American College of Healthcare Executives, of the Foundation of the American College of Healthcare Executives, or of the Association of University Programs in Health Administration.

Reprinting August 2013

Library of Congress Cataloging-in-Publication Data

White, Kenneth R. (Kenneth Ray), 1956-
 The well-managed healthcare organization / Kenneth R. White, John R. Griffith. -- 7th ed.
   p. ; cm.
 Griffith's name appears first on the earlier ed.
 Includes bibliographical references and index.
 ISBN 978-1-56793-357-4 (alk. paper)
 1. Health services administration. I. Griffith, John R. II. Title.
 [DNLM: 1. Health Services Administration--United States. W 84 AA1 W585w 2010]
 RA971.G77 2010
 362.1068--dc22
                          2010014186

The paper used in this publication meets the minimum requirements of American National Standard for Information Sciences—Permanence of Paper for Printed Library Materials, ANSI Z39.48-1984.⊗™

Project manager and editor: Jane Calayag; Acquisitions editor: Janet Davis; Book design: Scott Miller; Cover design: Gloria Chantell; Layout: BookComp, Inc.

Health Administration Press
A division of the Foundation
   of the American College of
   Healthcare Executives
One North Franklin Street
Suite 1700
Chicago, IL 60606
(312) 424-2800

Association of University Programs
   in Health Administration
2000 14th Street North
Suite 780
Arlington, VA 22201
(703) 894-0940

CONTENTS

DETAILED CONTENTS

EXHIBITS

Chapter 6

Chapter 7

Chapter 8

Chapter 9

PREFACE

The Well-Managed Healthcare Organization, now in its 7th edition, is a text for students pursuing professional careers in managing healthcare organizations (HCOs). It describes actual practices that lead to high performance, based on our careful analysis of a small but reasonably representative set of HCOs that have been studied by competent peers and have produced auditable evidence of excellence. We believe the evidence of the superiority of these practices passes both academic and professional challenge. The footnotes in each chapter support our belief. There may be other ways to achieve excellence, but they have not been documented and quite possibly have not been discovered. Healthcare organizations that follow the methods we describe are well-prepared for health reform. We expect them to continue to thrive. Indirectly, health reform initiatives reinforce our message and are consistent with managing and leading excellent HCOs on the basis of evidence, best practices, benchmarks, and a culture of continuous improvement.

The common theme in these organizations is that a specific culture (transformational and evidence-based management) and certain management activities (listening, measurement, benchmarking, negotiated goal setting, and continuous improvement) are essential to high performance. Specialized teams must complete specified tasks correctly to measured standards. These teams include not only those involved in patient care but also clinical support (e.g., laboratory, pharmacy, imaging), logistics (e.g., information, personnel, training, supplies), or strategic (e.g., finance, internal consulting, enterprise level goals). Each chapter, after Chapter 1, has the following structure: Purpose, Functions, People, Measures, and Managerial Issues. The Functions section describes the unit's essential contribution to the whole, and the Measures section identifies opportunities to improve that contribution.

The challenge in managing HCOs is to sustain excellence over all the teams, and the solution to this challenge lies in two core thrusts:

1. Maintaining a culture that empowers each associate (transformational management)
2. Supporting continuous improvement with measurement, process analysis, negotiated goals, and rewards (evidence-based management)

In excellent HCOs, measurement is central, improvement is constant, leaders respond to associates and patients, professionals communicate as equals, everyone is treated with respect, and authority is derived from knowledge rather than rank. These are the foundations of high performance. The record of excellent HCOs shows quite clearly that the new management approach produces excellence in all the sites that now constitute the healthcare industry. High-performing HCOs successfully operate the full gamut of healthcare, including doctors' offices, general and special hospitals, continuing care, home care, and hospices.

Using *The Well-Managed Healthcare Organization*

Any organization is a collaboration to do what an individual alone cannot do. This collaboration succeeds by division of labor—assigning tasks for individuals and small teams to complete to achieve the goals of collaboration. The text begins (chapters 1 and 2) with a description of the collaborators, called *stakeholders.*

Performance excellence is built on a comprehensive and well-supported theory of management (Chapter 2). The elements of that theory are as follows:

1. An HCO is supported by many stakeholders who, in turn, benefit from its success. In general, stakeholders are either "customers" or "providers," and a key organizational issue is balancing and optimizing the rewards to each group.
2. The goals of the HCO are stated in its mission. Missions of HCOs are similar because all stakeholders share a common purpose of extending the length and quality of life and providing safe, effective, patient-centered, timely, efficient, and equitable care.
3. Goal achievement is evidence-based, using objective measures of performance, comparison to competitors and best practices, goal setting, and continuous improvement.
4. The rewards of improvement are shared among the stakeholders so that both customer and provider stakeholders view the organization as their preferred affiliation.

These elements constitute cross-cutting themes that recur throughout the text.

From chapter 3 to 15, the text describes the activities of an HCO in three divisions—corporate, clinical, and technical/logistic. Each chapter identifies an activity and the functions it must perform for the whole to succeed, its organization structures and personnel, its measures of performance, and some of the critical areas in which it needs managerial support. Each chapter addresses (1) "what this activity must do well for the whole to succeed" and (2) "how this activity measures and improves its performance."

Each chapter begins with In a Few Words, a précis of the activity addressed in the chapter; Critical Issues, an outline that emphasizes the distinctions associated with excellence; and Questions for Discussion, five important and easily misunderstood application topics.

Chapter 2 describes leadership and the activities required of senior management to build and sustain the HCO's cultural foundations. Chapter 3 expands the discussion on the operational foundation, exploring the activities that identify opportunities for improvement (OFIs) and lead to improved work processes. Chapter 4 addresses governance, the strategic decision making that provides effective long-term response to stakeholder needs. Chapters 5 through 9 describe the operation of the various clinical and clinical support teams. Chapters 10 through 15 discuss the logistic and strategic support activities.

Each chapter addresses purpose, functions, people, measures, and managerial issues associated with the activity. The content of these chapters gives the student the ability to engage in meaningful dialogue with members of any activity or team, to understand how well a team or activity is currently performing and what its current OFIs are, and to assist in translating those OFIs to actual improvement. That pattern of listening, learning, and supporting improvement is what twenty-first century healthcare managers do for a living.

HCO managers build excellent organizations by ensuring that the functions are carried out as a whole. The theory demands comprehensiveness, as failure in one activity contributes to failure in another. The three divisions must all perform; an HCO cannot have clinical excellence without corporate excellence and logistic excellence. The learning manager, therefore, must grasp the totality and interdependence of the HCO as well as the contributions expected of each activity. He or she must also understand the application of the cross-cutting themes—the role of the mission, evidence-based decisions, measured performance, continuous improvement, and reward. The test of learning is the ability to explain these issues to others, such as customer stakeholders, beginning supervisors, and new employees.

We believe one effective path to mastery is to use the book partly as a text and partly as a reference. Some of the detail should be memorized, for immediate recall in conversations with others. The functions of the governing board (Chapter 4), the way budgets are developed (primarily chapters 3, 4, 7, and 12), and the use of the epidemiologic planning model (every chapter from 4 to 15) are prime examples. Other matters are not unimportant, but when they arise, they can be reviewed through the index and the table of contents.

A beginning student might best master the text, not by reading from page 1 to page 600 but rather by interacting with each chapter:

1. Read In a Few Words to focus on the contribution of the activity.
2. Study the Critical Issues, making an effort to relate them to her prior experience.

Online Learning System

The text offers a two-part online learning system designed to help students and instructors.

The **Companion Website** is designed for students and is available at ache.org/books/Well-Managed7. It contains the following:

- An overview of how to use the text to become an effective healthcare organization manager

- A glossary of all the technical terms identified in the text

- A folder for each chapter that contains (1) a one-page guide to mastering the chapter; (2) "Chapter Learning Goals and Milestones," a list of the questions a professional should be able to answer and guides to where in the chapter the answers can be found; and (3) "Additional Questions for Discussion" to supplement the questions in the text. The questions are in addition to the five given in each chapter. They illustrate the issues managers must think about as they respond to associates' questions and opportunities for improvement.

Instructor Resources are available only to qualified instructors. They contain all the Companion Website elements plus chapter-by-chapter teaching tips, guides for leading the Questions for Discussion, slides for classroom presentations, and gradable questions with answer rubrics. (For access, please apply at hap1@ache.org and include your course, university, and department names.)

3. Review the details of the functions to understand how each element contributes to the whole and how each is best implemented.
4. Study the exhibit that shows the performance measures, and review the Measures section to understand how the measures are defined and used.
5. Check the Managerial Issues section for important elements that relate the activity to management in the organization as a whole and to sustaining high performance.
6. Review the Questions for Discussion in relation to her or his prior experience, striving to understand both the importance of the question and the best way it can be answered in real HCOs.
7. Consider how the material in the chapter can be effectively conveyed to the right people in an HCO—that is, how can it be best summarized in formal policies and procedures, in training programs, and in day-to-day interactions.

The text can certainly be mastered in self-study. We believe a class or discussion group and a mentor or teacher can help substantially, particularly in the latter steps.

Acknowledgments

As the editions of *The Well-Managed Healthcare Organization* mount, keeping track of all who have contributed to this text by their examples becomes difficult. The applications of the HCO recipients of the Malcolm Baldrige National Quality Award are the most comprehensive documentation of the transformational and evidence-based approach. Our visits to Catholic Health Initiatives, Henry Ford Health System, Intermountain Healthcare, Legacy Health System, Medicorp Health System, MedStar Health, Moses Cone Health System, and Sentara Healthcare have helped us understand how leading practices are designed and implemented.

Over a period of time, both of us have worked with specific organizations, including Summa Health System in Akron, Ohio; Allegiance Corporation (a physician hospital organization) in Ann Arbor, Michigan; Mercy Health Center in Oklahoma City, Oklahoma; Mercy International Health Services in Farmington Hills, Michigan; and Bon Secours Health System in Marriottsville, Maryland. We are grateful to these HCOs. We are also grateful for the assistance of our colleagues at the University of Michigan and Virginia Commonwealth University.

Kenneth R. White, PhD, FACHE
Virginia Commonwealth University
Richmond, Virginia

John R. Griffith, MBA, FACHE
The University of Michigan
Ann Arbor, Michigan

1

FOUNDATIONS OF HIGH-PERFORMING HEALTHCARE ORGANIZATIONS

In a Few Words

Healthcare organizations (HCOs) include all organizations that provide healthcare. *The Well-Managed Healthcare Organization* focuses on excellent HCOs—those that delight their patients, families, caregivers, and other associates and that provide care that is safe, effective, patient-centered, timely, efficient, and equitable. To achieve excellence, HCOs build a culture around their mission, vision, and values. They empower their associates, encourage them to meet patient and customer needs, measure their performance, and reward them for improvement. They use evidence-based medicine and systematic analysis of work processes. Extensive boundary-spanning and strong internal relationships allow them to meet strategic challenges. They carefully protect their organizational resources from any kind of loss or diversion.

Critical Issues in Excellence

1. *Emphasizing mission, vision, and values.* Make the contribution and importance of care itself a shared value.

2. *Building a culture that listens, empowers, trains, and rewards.* Begin a program that identifies what people see as barriers to their work and remove them.

3. *Measuring performance, seeking benchmarks, and negotiating realistic goals.* Add quality, customer satisfaction, and associated satisfaction measures for every work unit.

4. *Maintaining close relations with all stakeholders.* Extend the listening activities so that every major affiliate has a point of contact and is assured of fairness and responsiveness.

Consider these questions as you read the chapter.

1. This chapter outlines a *transformational* style of management, emphasizing values, empowerment, communication, trust/accountability, and rewards. Why do high-performing HCOs strive for transformational styles? Some people say that transformational is completely unrealistic; you must enforce order, they say, to have accountability. How is accountability achieved in high-performing, transformational HCOs? How comfortable would you be working in a high-performing, transformational organization?

2. The history and current activities of HCOs are strongly oriented to healing the sick. The first word of this chapter—"patients"—is consistent with that tradition. Some say that the real role of HCOs is community health, including but going well beyond healing the sick. (Contrast the missions of SSM, Bronson, and Saint Luke's with those of Baptist, Robert Wood Johnson, and North Mississippi in Exhibit 1.7.) Should the text have started with, "Building healthy communities is the focus of HCOs, including patient care but going well beyond"?

3. *Systematic change* (page 29) is a four-step process: identify, analyze, test, evaluate. What is new about that? Could you achieve systematic change without measurement and benchmarking? Think of your last encounter with a service organization (e.g., HCO, university, restaurant). What would be different if the organization practiced continuous improvement and systematic change?

4. What happens to an organization that fails in its strategic positioning (see Exhibit 1.14)? Can you name an example or two, and then identify with hindsight where they failed?

5. Ben Franklin founded The Pennsylvania Hospital in 1760, before the American Revolution. His fund-raising arguments were as follows:[49]
   - We need a refuge for the unfortunate, and Christianity will reward you for your generosity to this cause. (Although Franklin did not say so, Islam, Buddhism, and Judaism also praise charitable behavior.)
   - You might need it yourself this very night.
   - Among other things, we can keep contagious people off the streets.
   - We can certainly handle this better as a community than as individuals.
   - Grants from the Crown and the Commonwealth will lower the out-of-pocket costs. (He might have added that the grants were "new money" that would eventually end up in Philadelphians' purses.)
   Are these still valid appeals to gain support for a community HCO? What would you change or add to Franklin's arguments?

Patients are the focus of healthcare, and in the twenty-first century patients are commonly treated by teams. A single caregiver working alone soon must seek support for clinical needs like laboratory, imaging, and pharmacy, or for logistic ones, like information, facilities, and supplies. For a serious problem, such as heart surgery or recovery from stroke, several different caregiving teams will be required. Cure will result from the coordinated efforts of close to 100 people bringing highly specialized skills and using an array of diverse equipment and an extensive set of drugs and supplies. Continuing management of the underlying cardiovascular disease will require a different team that will support the patient for months or years. The **healthcare organization** (HCO) creates, supports, and coordinates those teams. It is a formal legal entity that reaches across the panorama of medicine, other clinical disciplines, and business to identify and deliver care to its community.

Healthcare organization (HCO)
A formal legal entity that reaches across the panorama of medicine, other clinical disciplines, and business to identify and deliver care to its community

Activities

An HCO supports individualized patient care with an array of teams, as shown in Exhibit 1.1. The caregiving teams differ according to patients' needs. They are backed by three levels of support—clinical, logistic, and strategic—that are themselves composed of specialized teams. Each patient care team performs an activity that is essential to a specific group of patients, and each support team performs an activity that is essential to the work of some or all patient care teams. A small HCO has few patient care activities and contracts with other organizations for support; a large one has a broad array of patient care and support. A healthcare system has many patient care activities in several geographic locations.

Teams are usually housed in purpose-built spaces (e.g., clinics, operating rooms, business offices) so that HCO facilities reflect the activities depicted in Exhibit 1.1. With the growth of electronic communication, however, many teams can be geographically remote. A primary care team needs a process that yields timely laboratory results, but that might be a centralized laboratory. All care teams require strategic capability, but it might be provided from the system headquarters in another state.

Exhibit 1.1 is static. Any real HCO is highly dynamic in three senses:

1. The HCO constantly responds to the changing array of patients and their changing needs. This makes most HCOs a 24/7/365 operation.
2. The HCO evolves as medicine and management change, reflecting both the latest scientifically proven treatments and new developments in management practices and information technology.
3. The HCO adjusts to the changes in its community's needs.

As the population grows, shrinks, and changes in age and ethnic diversity, the epidemiology of disease changes and the HCO must respond. One function of the strategic activities is to manage these changes. While the focus of the clinical and support activities is "this patient, now," the strategic focus is "all patients, into the future."

Contribution

The mission HCOs fulfill is one of humanity's highest callings: to assist others in the "beginning of life, the end of life, and the shadows of life."[1] HCOs are essential treatment resources for heart disease, cancer, stroke, obstetrics, major trauma, and several hundred other conditions, providing preventive and episodic care, emergency care, surgery, intensive care, rehabilitation, chronic disease maintenance, and end-of-life care. At least one large HCO exists in virtually every county in the United States and is usually surrounded by several smaller ones such as doctors' offices. About 60 percent of Americans use HCOs in a given year. Although most contacts are relatively simple office visits, one in ten Americans is hospitalized and about three in ten require major outpatient care.[2] It is a rare family who has not had recent contact with an HCO. That contact is often lifesaving, but it is also often intimate, expensive, life threatening, and frightening.

EXHIBIT 1.1 Components of Healthcare Organizations

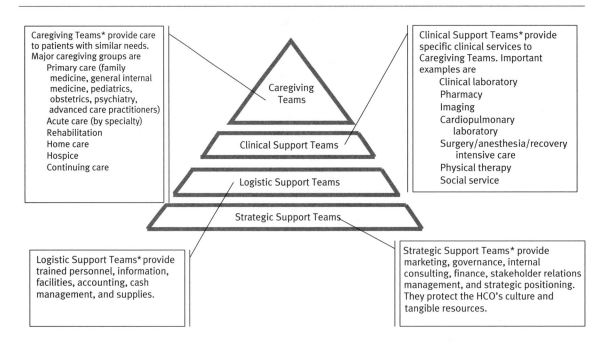

*HCOs have varying sets of clinical or clinical support activities. The logistic support and many strategic support activities are required for any clinical activities.

The nation's HCOs are the point of implementation for a healthcare system that has grown from its commitment to "promote the general welfare" (as stated in the Preamble to the Constitution) to be one of America's largest collective endeavors. The U.S. per capita cost of healthcare is the highest in the world, consuming about one-fifth of the gross domestic product. HCOs and their physician affiliates consume about half of the cost. They justify their cost by meeting powerful individual drives for health and longevity, by making a substantial direct contribution to their local economies, and by implementing a widespread commitment to Samaritanism and social justice. The American healthcare system can be viewed as an investment, contributing to national productivity by adding years of healthy life. Despite its cost, the investment is highly profitable.[3] Much of the cost is returned to the community through employment,[4] as an HCO is often the community's largest employer.

Stakeholders

Formal organizations exist because they fulfill a need that individuals working alone cannot meet,[5] and they thrive because they fulfill that need better than competing alternatives.[6] By definition, any organization serves many masters or **stakeholders**—individuals or groups who have a direct interest in its success. Organizations are economic entities shaped by stakeholder needs. Stakeholders are buyers, workers, suppliers, regulators, and owners who cooperate through economic exchanges as shown in Exhibit 1.2. In a free society, stakeholders can choose to participate in the organization or not, and a shortage caused by some stakeholders

Stakeholders
Individuals or groups (buyers, workers, suppliers, regulators, and owners) who have a direct interest in an organization's success

EXHIBIT 1.2 General Model of Stakeholder–Organization Interaction

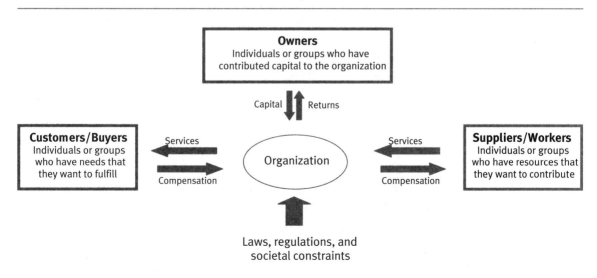

selecting alternative sources is disabling for the organization. Organizational excellence begins with and is measured by stakeholder satisfaction.

Exhibit 1.2 reflects most of the world's economic activity, but reality is not as simple as it suggests. Stakeholders' desires are inherently conflicting. The buyer wants to buy inexpensively; the supplier to sell dear. Each of us is a stakeholder in many organizations. Most of us are alternately buyer (i.e., **customer**) stakeholders and seller (i.e., **provider**) stakeholders, and we and our organizations exist in networks of negotiated solutions to those conflicting desires. The most fundamental element is neither our organization nor our stakeholder desires; it is our ability to negotiate. An important way to understand organizations is as devices to negotiate solutions.

Because of the cost, financing structure, importance, and the intimate and life-changing nature of healthcare services, American HCOs represent one of the most complex applications of Exhibit 1.2. Several levels of complexity are added. The stakeholder environment for HCOs is shown in Exhibit 1.3; the complexity of HCOs arises from the multiplicity of HCO stakeholders and from the nature of healthcare services.

Customers
Patients and others who use the services of the organization and generally compensate the organization for those services; also, by extension, other units within the HCO that rely on a particular unit for service

Providers
Institutional and personal caregivers such as physicians, hospitals, and nurses

Customer Partners

Patients and Families

Patients are the most important stakeholders. They expect, and deserve, care that meets the goals summarized in the Institute of Medicine's report *Crossing the Quality Chasm*: safe, effective, patient-centered, timely, efficient, and equitable.[7] They also expect reasonably comfortable amenities and confidentiality. Friends and family accompany most patients, and many family members serve as informal caregivers, so HCOs must establish close and direct relations with them.

Patients' expectations include a major element of trust. *Information asymmetry*—the organization and its caregivers possess substantially more knowledge about the patient's needs than the patient does—makes it impossible for many patients and families to articulate their needs. Instead, they expect the HCO to do that for them, thoroughly and fairly. Much of the failure in patient relations comes from difficulties with managing that trust.

Health Insurers and Payment Agencies

Patients rely on a variety of mechanisms to pay for care, which can easily cost a large fraction of a family's annual income. Health insurers and fiscal intermediaries provide most of the revenue to HCOs, making them essential exchange partners. Private health insurers are agents for buyers, which include governments, employers, and citizens at large. Two large governmental insurance programs—Medicare and Medicaid—are exchange partners with most HCOs. The federal Medicare program deals with HCOs through its **intermediaries**.[8] Medicaid, a combination state and federal program that finances care for the poor, is run by the state **Medicaid agency** or an intermediary. Representing the buyers, payment organizations use contractual requirements, regulatory support, and incentive payments to improve the quality, safety, and cost of care.

Intermediary
A payment or management agent for healthcare insurance (e.g., Medicare intermediaries that pay providers as agents for CMS)

Medicaid agency
The state agency handling claims and payments for Medicaid

Much health insurance is provided through employment, making employers important exchange partners. Historically, unions played a major role in establishing health insurance as an employee benefit. Federal, state, and local governments purchase care for special groups of citizens and also buy insurance as employers do. Buyers, who must meet the demands of their own exchange networks, have taken action to restrict the growth of costs, acting principally through payment organizations. Their pressure is likely to continue.

Buyers

EXHIBIT 1.3 Model of Stakeholder–HCO Interaction

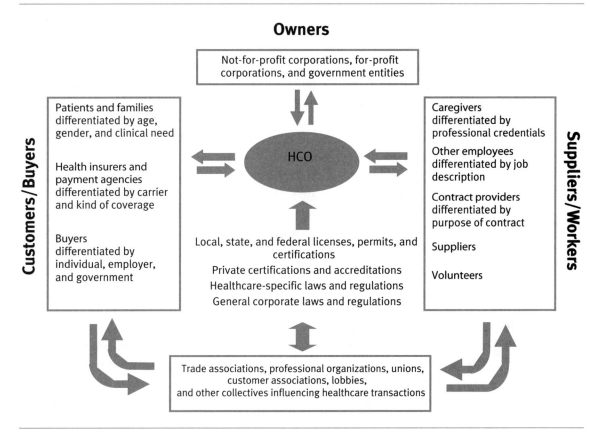

Regulatory Agencies

Most payment organizations mandate two outside audits of HCO performance—accreditation by The Joint Commission or its osteopathic counterpart the American Osteopathic Association and audit by a public accounting firm of the HCO's choice. Some insurance plans are accredited by the National Commission on Quality Assurance (NCQA), which also accredits ambulatory care and disease management. Medicare and Medicaid—contracts that are essential to most HCOs—are monitored through *deemed status*, a determination of conformance usually established through the accreditation agencies.

Government regulatory agencies
Agencies with established authority over healthcare activities; licensing agencies and rate-regulating commissions are examples

Certificate of need (CON)
Certificates or approvals for new services and construction or renovation of hospitals or related facilities; issued by many states

Quality improvement organizations (QIOs)
External agencies that review the quality of care and use of insurance benefits by individual physicians and patients for Medicare and other insurers

Health Insurance Portability and Accountability Act (HIPAA)
A 1996 federal act that establishes standards of privacy for patient information

Government regulatory agencies are exchange partners that at least nominally act on behalf of the patient and buyer. State licensing agencies are common, not only for hospitals and healthcare professionals but sometimes also for other facilities such as ambulatory care centers. Many states have **certificate-of-need** laws, requiring HCOs to seek permission for construction or expansion. **Quality improvement organizations** (QIOs) are external agencies that review the quality of care and use of insurance benefits by individual physicians and patients for Medicare and other insurers. HCOs are subject to many consumer-protection laws, including the **Health Insurance Portability and Accountability Act** (HIPAA), which addresses major issues of patient-record confidentiality.

HCOs require land-use and zoning permits; they use water, sewer, traffic, electronic communications, fire protection, and police services and thus are subject to environmental regulations. HCOs often present unique needs in these areas that must be negotiated with their local government.

The courts can also be viewed as regulatory agencies. HCOs may be sued for malpractice or negligence—harmful conduct that is unintentional but avoidable with reasonable care. Suits are brought by individuals in specific cases, but the court findings establish the rules of conduct for future actions. Thus the courts can also be viewed as regulatory organizations.

Community Groups

HCOs make numerous, varied, and far-reaching exchanges with community agencies and groups. They facilitate infant adoption; receive the victims of accidents, violence, rape, and family abuse; and attract the homeless, the mentally incompetent, and the chronically alcoholic. These activities draw them into exchange relationships with law enforcement and social service agencies.

In addition, HCOs work with United Way charities. They facilitate baptisms, ritual circumcisions, group religious observances, individual spiritual activity, and rites for the dying. They provide educational facilities for caregivers and services to the community such as health education and disease prevention programs, assistance to support groups, and mobile clinics. These activities often make HCOs partners of cultural, religious, educational, and charitable organizations. Prevention and outreach activities draw HCOs into alliances with governmental organizations, such as public health departments and school boards, and with local employers, churches, and civic organizations.

Not-for-profit HCOs often occupy facilities that, if taxed, would add noticeably to local tax revenues. The community may hold the organization to certain conditions, such as a certain level of charity care, in return for nonprofit status.[9] As a result, the electorate and the local government are stakeholders collectively, and the electorate contains many of the HCO's stakeholders individually. Communication with stakeholders often involves the media—print, radio, television, and Internet coverage—and purchased advertising. Web-based public sources such as HealthGrades and Why Not the Best are increasingly influential in forming customer opinion, although they do not give consistent results.[10]

Provider Partners

The second most fundamental exchange, next to patients, is between the HCO and its **associates**—people who give their time and energy to the organization. HCO associates are employees, trustees and other volunteers, and medical staff members.

Associates

Employees are compensated by salary and wages. Trustees and a great many others volunteer their time to the organization; their only compensation is the satisfaction they achieve from the work. Medical staff members receive monetary compensation from either patients and insurance intermediaries or the HCO. **Primary care practitioners**—physicians in family practice, general internal medicine, pediatrics, obstetrics, and psychiatry; nurse practitioners; and midwives—are the most common initial contacts for healthcare. **Referral specialist physicians** tend to see patients referred by primary care practitioners and to care for these patients on a more limited and transient basis. They are more likely to manage episodes of inpatient hospital care. **Hospitalists**, a recently established referral specialty, accept relatively broad

Associates
People (employees, trustees and other volunteers, and medical staff members) who give their time and energy to the HCO

Primary care practitioners
Initial contact providers, including physicians in family practice, general internal medicine, pediatrics, obstetrics, and psychiatry; nurse practitioners; and midwives

Referral specialist physicians
Doctors who care for patients referred by primary care practitioners on a limited or transient basis; likely to manage episodes of inpatient care

categories of patients and manage inpatient care only. Other professional caregivers (e.g., dentists, psychologists, podiatrists) may also be members of the medical staff.

Hospitalists
Physicians who manage broad categories of hospitalized patients

Associate Organizations

Associates are often organized into groups that manage their exchanges to varying extent. Unions, or collective bargaining units, sometimes represent employed associates. Physicians often form professional associations and practice groups. Neurologists, for example, can become a group to represent their interests to the organization as a whole. Group membership is itself an organization; individuals choose it because a group can meet some needs that would otherwise go unmet. The success of the group depends on the exchanges that commit the individuals to the group.

Licensure
Government approval to perform specified activities

Government agencies of various kinds monitor the rights of associate groups. Occupational safety, professional **licensure**, and **equal employment opportunity agencies** are among those entitled access to the HCO and its records. The National Labor Relations Board and various state agencies define which organizations are unions and establish rules for their relations with employers. The HCO is obligated to collect Social Security and income tax withholding.

Equal employment opportunity agencies
Government agencies that monitor the rights of associate groups; these are among those entitled access to the HCO and its records

Suppliers and Financing Agencies

HCOs use goods and services—from artificial implants to food to banking to utilities—purchased from outside suppliers. Financing partners help HCOs acquire capital through a variety of equity, loan, and lease arrangements. HCOs often enter into **strategic partnerships** with suppliers and other provider partners.

Other Providers

In the course of meeting patient needs, HCOs have considerable contact with other providers, including organizations and agencies whose service lines may be either competing or complementary, such as primary care clinics, mental health and substance abuse services, home care agencies, **hospices**, and long-term-care facilities. Many large HCOs have formal relationships with these organizations, such as referral agreements, strategic partnerships, **joint ventures**, and acquisition and ownership. It is not uncommon for two HCOs to collaborate on some activities, such as medical education or care of the poor, and to compete on others. Even competitors with almost exactly the same services negotiate contracts with each other. Federal and state antitrust laws regulate the negotiation between competitors, but these prohibitions are specific and other communication is permitted.

Strategic partnerships
Commitments with long-term obligations

Joint ventures
Formal, long-term collaborative contracts usually involving equity investment

Hospice
A model of caregiving that assists with physical, emotional, spiritual, psychological, social, financial, and legal needs of the dying patient and his family; the service may be provided in the patient's home or in an HCO

Sources of Stakeholder Influence

The ultimate source of stakeholders' power is the marketplace—their ability to participate in the exchange. In reality, influence is exercised through ongoing negotiation rather than discontinued participation. Stakeholders form coalitions and networks to enhance their influence and facilitate negotiation. The results of negotiation are embedded in marketplace contracts and reinforced through government regulation. Ultimately, but rarely, the courts resolve disputes in relationships.

Successful HCOs work steadily and systematically to increase the loyalty of their stakeholders. Their efforts are proactive and extensive. Their goal is to identify stakeholder needs and design effective responses before unmet needs become points of contention.

Participation and Market Pressure

Stakeholder participation is carefully measured. Customer participation is measured by market share, and provider participation is measured by retention and shortages. Satisfaction of participants is also monitored. The goal here is to acquire and retain **loyal** or **secure customers** and associates.

Loyal/secure customers
Customers whose opinions of the organization are so positive that they will return for further interaction and will recommend or refer the organization to others

Rather than discontinue their participation, stakeholders usually present their concerns for negotiation. The stakeholders' desires frequently conflict and can easily become adversarial, as in the traditional relationship between unions and management. Successful HCOs strive to minimize adversarial relationships by building a record of responsiveness and truth telling, making a diligent effort to find and understand relevant facts, maintaining respect and decorum in the debate, and searching diligently for solutions. The goal is to have the stakeholders leave the discussion feeling that their concerns were heard, that the decision was fair, and that no realistic opportunity to improve the decision exists. "My (or our) concerns have been heard and met as well as possible" is the feeling that results from successful negotiation.

Negotiation

Each exchange partner of the HCO has relationships with exchange partners of their own. Individuals and families affiliate with employers, businesses, schools, churches, and community groups. Stakeholder coalitions form among these relationships based on shared values or common needs. Many are more or less permanent, while others are temporary alliances to forward a specific goal.

Networking and Coalition Building

Similar networks exist for other social issues. They are the essence of "community" because they facilitate our living together harmoniously. Nurturing these networks is fundamental to the social fabric.[11] HCOs that deal effectively with these networks contribute to their communities in two ways: (1) they provide and improve healthcare, and (2) they strengthen the social fabric.

A small group of essential caregivers, such as the obstetricians in the community, can challenge how the HCO meets specific needs, such as the care of low-income mothers. Unions or associations that represent doctors, nurses, or patients are more permanent stakeholder coalitions. Buyer- and consumer-oriented networks, such as the National Business Group on Health, CalPERS, and AARP, are coalitions that allow stakeholders to address complicated social problems, such as healthcare's uninsured and health promotion.

Many coalitions become permanent to forward their stakeholder agendas. An important example is **The Joint Commission**. A successful example is the National Quality Forum (NQF), which was created in 1999 "to improve the quality of American healthcare by setting national priorities and goals for performance improvement, endorsing national consensus standards for measuring and publicly reporting on performance, and promoting the attainment of national goals through education and outreach."[12] NQF has a board of 25 members, including 7 organizations that directly represent healthcare providers and 18 that represent buyer coalitions. NQF has established a mechanism to evaluate and standardize measures of quality. These measures are recorded for public use and posted on the website by the Agency for Healthcare Research and Quality (see www.qualitymeasures.ahrq.gov).[13]

The Joint Commission
A voluntary consortium of HCOs and professional provider organizations that ensures a minimum level of safety and quality in HCOs

Social Controls   Stakeholders can imbed their viewpoint into law, regulation, and contract. They can also sue in courts. These actions are social controls on HCOs. They create the various regulatory mechanisms. For example, The Joint Commission has been given extraordinary power by Medicare and Medicaid, which withhold payment unless its standards are met. As a result, it can effectively shut down any HCO by denying accreditation. Medicare and private insurance programs now use the NQF measures in pay-for-performance programs to improve quality,[14] and The Joint Commission has added the measures to its criteria.[15]

Social controls almost always reflect good intentions—safety, quality, individual rights, equity, and efficiency. Accomplishment is another matter. It is fair to conclude that both the regulatory agencies dealing with healthcare delivery and the contracts of the health insurers and intermediaries have generally fallen short of expectations. Safety, quality, healthcare disparities, and cost remain problems despite decades of activity in these areas. In part, this reflects the complexity of the goal and the difficulty of measurement. In part, it reflects the limitations of the market and governmental systems.

The use of objective measures of performance may provide an improvement. Many observers agree that "The U.S. health care delivery system is in need of overhaul. Care is fragmented, unsafe, and inefficient. . . . [S]tronger organizational capabilities and supports are urgently needed to achieve high levels of performance."[16] Pressures to build these capabilities and achieve performance are likely to mount. By the start of the Obama administration, many experts argued that broad changes in the overall system of healthcare are essential. One group of experts from 13 different stakeholder organizations advocated "to create a national center for effectiveness research, develop models of accountable healthcare entities capable of providing integrated and coordinated care, develop payment models to reward high-value care, develop a national strategy for performance measurement, and pursue a multi-stakeholder approach to improving population health."[17] The model described in this text is consistent with such a program. It is based on actual HCOs that have documented their success in meeting multiple stakeholder needs.

Ownership

Not-for-Profit, For-Profit, and Government Owners

Acute care hospitals are the largest single group of HCOs. They are also the largest and oldest components of most large HCOs. They are licensed corporate entities and easily identified for statistics and therefore provide a convenient, though incomplete, description of twenty-first century HCOs.

Most hospitals are **community hospitals**.[18] Historically, they were controlled by either the local government or not-for-profit organizations owned by the community and expected to fulfill community needs. The not-for-profit corporations were given substantial tax advantages, recognizing that their services would otherwise be required of government.[19] In the 1970s, a movement to for-profit ownership quickly reached about 10 percent of all community hospitals, and increased sporadically thereafter. As of 2007, the formal organization of hospitals, shown in Exhibit 1.4, was dominated by not-for-profit corporations. The local government and for-profit sectors were smaller in total, and concentrated among smaller hospitals. In addition, a small number of federal hospitals serve military, veterans, Native American, and federal prison needs. (Federal hospitals are excluded from counts of community hospitals.)

Community hospital
A short-stay general or specialty (e.g., women's, children's, eye, orthopedic) hospital, excluding those owned by the federal government

Healthcare Systems

As Exhibit 1.4 shows, most hospitals are relatively small HCOs. A hospital has about eight full-time employees per million dollars in expenses. The median hospital has only about 300 full-time employees. In the 1980s, HCOs began to organize multiple hospitals and other healthcare activities into a **healthcare system**. By 2007, more than half of all hospitals and almost two-thirds of healthcare expenditures were in systems. Although many systems are large interstate operations that often include a broad spectrum of

Healthcare system
Healthcare organizations that operate multiple service units under a single ownership

EXHIBIT 1.4 Ownership and Size of U.S. Community and Federal Hospitals

Ownership	Number of Hospitals	Percent of All Hospitals	Total Expenditures (in millions)	Percent of Total Expenditures	Average Expenditures per Hospital (in millions)	Median Expenditures per Hospital (in millions)
State and local government	1,110	22%	$ 77,914	14%	$ 70	$ 16
Religious not-for-profit	533	10	70,728	13	133	99
Other not-for-profit	2,425	47	315,265	57	130	62
For-profit	868	17	51,833	9	60	36
Federal	226	4	36,830	7	163	141
Total	5,161	100%	$ 552,570	100%	$ 107	$ 35

SOURCE: Data from American Hospital Association Annual Survey Database, Fiscal Year 2005.

care, the most common system structure is simply a few hospitals and related patient care activities such as primary care operating with one management structure within a single community. The median size of systems was about $500 million expenses per year, or 4,000 employees.

Like the hospitals from which they arose, not-for-profit and governmental systems dominate the market. There are five federal systems, four large for-profit systems, and a number of small for-profit systems. Although many hospitals owned by local governments remain independent, many others have joined not-for-profit or for-profit systems. Exhibit 1.5 shows the system affiliation of community hospitals.

Designing Excellence in an HCO

The better an HCO is managed, the greater the total advantages it produces. Excellence is achieved when these needs of both customer and provider stakeholders are optimally met:

- Patient care is safe, effective, patient-centered, timely, efficient, and equitable.[20]
- The community's health and healthcare needs are met.
- Caregivers and other associates are attracted to the HCO, and they are given support to do their best.
- Expenditures are controlled so that the total cost is within the community's economic reach.

The Well-Managed Healthcare Organization describes how excellence is achieved by large HCOs. It identifies the essential functions, their organization, and the measures that document their performance. It is based not

EXHIBIT 1.5 System Affiliations of U.S. Hospitals

System Affiliation*	Number of Hospitals				Total Expenditures (in millions)				
Ownership	Number of Systems	In Systems	Not in Systems	Percent in Systems	System Members	Not in Systems	Percent in Systems	Average Size of System	Median Size of System
State and local government	31	289	821	26%	$ 30,032	$ 47,882	39%	$ 869	$ 452
Religious not-for-profit	51	472	61	89	63,458	7,270	90	1,551	923
Other not-for-profit	211	1,190	1,235	49	179,009	136,256	57	785	518
For-profit	54	765	103	88	47,953	3,880	93	926	152
Federal	5	226	4	98	36,422	408	99	7,284	143
Total	352	2,942	2,224	57%	$356,874	$195,696	65%	$ 1,014	$ 483

*Many systems include hospitals of differing ownership. The systems are assigned to their largest ownership share.

SOURCE: Data from American Hospital Association Annual Survey Database, Fiscal Year 2005.

on average or typical HCOs, but on the work of HCOs that have achieved excellence and documented it with objective measures.

The teams shown in Exhibit 1.1 can work as independent units, a marketplace where each team is a vendor, selling either to the patient or to another vendor. Much of American healthcare is essentially that. Small HCOs—doctors' offices, pharmacies, hospitals, equipment vendors, nursing homes, etc.—operate without any permanent relationship to each other. They buy logistic services from other vendors. There is no overarching strategy; the patients and the care teams will select each vendor as they need them. Large HCOs and healthcare systems have a very different vision, called **vertical integration**. They will integrate and support a large group of the care teams, most commonly in acute care and rehabilitation, but increasingly also primary care and long-term care. Many also pursue the same kinds of care teams in multiple sites, or **horizontal integration.**

Vertical integration
The affiliation of organizations that provide different kinds of service, such as hospital care, ambulatory care, long-term care, and social services

Horizontal integration
Integration of organizations that provide the same kind of service, such as two hospitals or two clinics

As shown in Exhibit 1.6, excellence has three major foundations:

1. *Cultural,* a commitment to values that attract the respect and support of stakeholders as individuals;
2. *Operational,* a system that seeks out, evaluates, and implements opportunities to improve stakeholder returns; and
3. *Strategic,* a system that deliberately monitors the long-term relationship between stakeholders and responds to changing needs.

EXHIBIT 1.6
Foundations
of Excellence
in Healthcare
Organizations

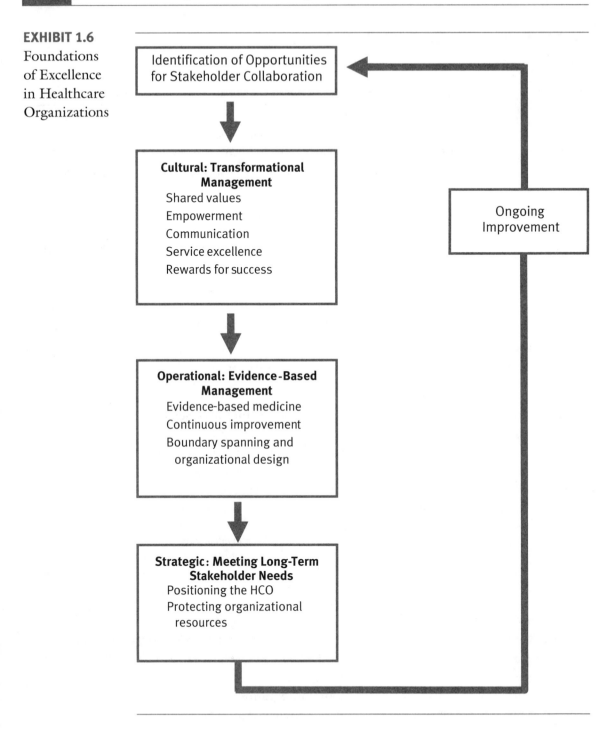

Cultural Foundation of Excellence: Transformational Management

The history of organizations in all industries suggests that stakeholders must build a cultural foundation that consists of five major elements: shared values, empowerment, communication, service excellence, and rewards for success. Excellent HCOs make major investments in clarifying, publicizing, and implementing their commitments to these elements. Their investments create a culture sometimes called *transformational management* that is highly satisfactory to both customer and associate stakeholders.

The transformational culture provides team members with important but intangible rewards—a sense of contribution to critical values, empowerment to shape the work, and partnership with like-minded individuals. The power of transformational management has been extensively documented.[21,22,23] It produces substantially better performance for two reasons:

1. Associates' insights about the job frequently improve the processes used, eliminating waste and inefficiency.
2. Associates are psychologically committed to the goal, rather than simply sellers of their services. Also, when they are well trained, they can adjust to changes that arise, enabling them to avoid many causes of failure.[24]

Shared Values

HCOs state that their **mission** is the central purpose of stakeholder collaboration. The fact that that mission is one of humanity's highest callings makes work in an HCO inherently attractive to many people. The mission to serve the sick provides a common bond that crosses many of the usual separations in society, and it is strongly endorsed by most of the world's religions. It is consistent with the ethical foundation of the caregiving professions. It is frequently mentioned as a personal commitment and source of satisfaction by HCO associates at all levels. Excellent HCOs build deliberately on a strong, visible commitment to this mission.

The mission is supplemented with a shared **vision**, an idealistic goal such as universal healthcare. Evidence from other industrial sectors suggests that *BHAGs*—big, hairy, aggressive goals—challenge associates and lead to better overall performance.[25] The mission and vision are, in turn, supplemented by commitment to **values** shared rules of conduct. Values reflect the humanistic consensus of American thought: respect for all, compassion, honesty, trust, stewardship, and improvement.

The mission, vision, and values of an HCO are usually written by multiple teams with broad stakeholder representation so that many associates and customers can take part in the discussion and commit to the concepts. As a result, the wording of mission, vision, and values differs from HCO to HCO, but common threads are obvious between them.[26] The moral concepts behind the mission, vision, and values are often stated as *autonomy* (commitment to the patient's right to decide his or her own course), *beneficence* (commitment to serve the patient's needs),

Mission
A statement of purpose—the good or benefit the HCO intends to contribute—couched in terms of an identified community, a set of services, and a specific level of cost or finance

Vision
An expansion of the mission that expresses intentions, philosophy, and organizational self-image

Values
An expansion of the mission that expresses basic rules of acceptable conduct, such as respect for human dignity or acceptance of equality

non-maleficence (commitment to "do no harm"), and *justice* (commitment to equity and respect for all).[27] Exhibit 1.7 shows the mission, vision, and value statements of HCOs that have documented their excellence for the Malcolm Baldrige National Quality Award.

Excellent HCOs publicize and display their mission, vision, and values widely, often on every associate's badge and always on every major entrance path, including the website. The mission, vision, and values are extensively advertised to the community at large and are an attractive statement to customers, communicating that "This HCO is here to meet your health needs." They also serve to guide potential associates at all levels.

Empowerment

One purpose of transformational management is to create an environment where every associate can feel comfortable to think: "I will treat patients with compassion and be confident that members of my team and those in other teams will do the same. I will do my job, and I can trust others to do theirs. I can rely on what I'm told. My needs will be met. I won't be ignored, let alone harassed. And we will get better over time." This comfort level reflects **empowerment**.

Empowerment
The ability of an associate to control his or her work situation in ways consistent with the mission

---

Empowerment is particularly important in healthcare, where caregiving professionals must make rapid and correct responses to patient needs. It improves overall performance because associates (1) are not distracted or frustrated by their work situation and (2) feel empowered to meet patient needs. Empowered workers are known to be more effective.[28] Empowerment has long been a concern of the caregiving profession. Excellent HCOs ensure that their doctors, nurses, and other caregivers are empowered, but they also extend the same support to all associates.

Communication

Failures of communication are an obvious source of difficulty. "I didn't know you needed that" is a clear and frequent example. Transformational management addresses communication in several ways, some of which are discussed in this section. Excellent HCOs pursue all such methods, making frequent, candid, and useful communication a hallmark of their organizations and a strength in improving performance.

Listening

Much of modern healthcare (more than most people think) can be quantified, but much remains subjective. Excellent HCOs formally and informally listen to all stakeholders to complement and strengthen their measured performance. Listening means deliberately soliciting stakeholder input through various communication methods, such as surveys, positive and negative event reports, group and individual interviews, direct conversations, e-mails, and blogs. The results of listening are systematically described, tallied, and analyzed to identify trends and opportunities for improvement.

Organization	Mission	Vision	Values
SSM Health Care (OK, IL, MO, WI)	Through our exceptional health care services, we reveal the healing presence of God.	Communities, especially those that are ... marginalized, will experience improved health in mind, body, spirit and environment	Compassion Respect Excellence Stewardship Community
Baptist Hospital (FL)	To provide superior service based on Christian values to improve the quality of life for people and communities served.	To become the best health system in America	Integrity Vision Innovation Superior service Stewardship Teamwork
Saint Luke's Hospital (MO)	Highest levels of excellence in ... health services to all patients in a caring environment	Best place to get care, best place to give care	Quality excellence Customer focus Resource management Teamwork
Robert Wood Johnson University Hospital (NJ)	Excellence through service. We exist to promote, preserve and restore the health of our community	To passionately pursue the health and well-being of our patients, employees and the community	Quality Understanding Excellence Service Teamwork
Bronson Methodist Hospital (MI)	Provide excellent healthcare services	A national leader in healthcare quality	Care and respect Teamwork Stewardship Commitment to community Pursuit of excellence
North Mississippi Medical Center (MS)	To continuously improve the health of the people of our region	To be the provider of the best patient-centered care and health services in America	Compassion Accountability Respect Excellence Smile
Mercy Health System (WI)	The mission of Mercy Health System is to provide exceptional healthcare services resulting in healing in the broadest sense.	Quality—Excellence in patient care Service—Exceptional patient and customer service Partnering—Best place to work Cost—Long-term financial success	Healing in its broadest sense Patients come first Treat each other like family Strive for excellence

EXHIBIT 1.7
Mission, Vision, and Values of Baldrige Award Recipients, 2002–2009

continued

EXHIBIT 1.7
continued

Organization	Mission	Vision	Values
Sharp HealthCare (CA)	To improve the health of those we serve with a commitment to excellence in all that we do. Sharp's goal is to offer quality care and services that set community standards, exceed patients' expectations, and are provided in a caring, convenient, cost-effective, and accessible manner.	Sharp will redefine the health care experience through a culture of caring, quality, service, innovation, and excellence. Sharp will be recognized by employees, physicians, patients, volunteers, and the community as: the best place to work, the best place to practice medicine, and the best place to receive care.	Integrity Caring Innovation Excellence
Poudre Valley Health System (CO)	To be an independent, non-profit organization and to provide innovative, comprehensive care of the highest quality, always exceeding customer expectations.	To provide world-class health care	Quality Compassion Confidentiality Dignity/respect Equality Integrity
AtlantiCare (NJ)	... health and healing to all people through trusting relationships	Builds healthy communities	Integrity Respect Service Teamwork Safety
Heartland Health (MO)	To improve the health of individuals and communities ... and provide the right care, at the right time, in the right place, at the right cost with outcomes second to none	The best and safest place in America to receive health care and live a healthy and productive life	Respect Honesty Compassion Trust Integrity Service

SOURCE: Information from Malcolm Baldrige National Quality Award website. [Online information; retrieved 12/8/09.] www.quality.nist.gov/Contacts_Profiles.htm.

For example, Exhibit 1.8 shows the planned communication and training approaches at Bronson Methodist Hospital in Kalamazoo, Michigan. Bronson, a Malcolm Baldrige National Quality Award recipient in 2005, explains in its Baldrige application that managers are expected to dedicate much effort to ensuring that these processes are completed frequently and well. Each senior manager is expected to spend five hours per week listening to caregiving, logistic, and clinical teams.

Negotiating

Empowerment requires that organization goals and plans be discussed in advance to gain widespread understanding and commitment. Understanding and commitment are not automatic. Their achievement requires exploring implications, identifying concerns and barriers, and finding ways to remove those barriers. From the manager's perspective, conflicting stakeholder needs must be negotiated and a mutually acceptable settlement reached.

Negotiation is a major shift in organizational thought. The bureaucratic organization, going back to Machiavelli's time and before that, operated under the command from superior to subordinate. In excellent HCOs, however, commands are used only in extreme emergency situations, where a team leader must coordinate the team quickly through uncharted territory. All other interactions are established by implicit or explicit negotiation.

EXHIBIT 1.8
Bronson Methodist Hospital: Mechanisms for Communication, Skill Sharing, and Knowledge Transfer

Pre-hire and selection process (C, SK, TT)
New hire orientation (C, SK, TT)
Nursing core orientation (C, SK, TT)
Leadership communication process (C)
Leadership communication forums (C)
Knowledge-sharing documents (C, SK)
Department meetings (C, SK, TT)
Bulletin boards (C)
Communication books (C)
E-mail for all employees (C, TT)
Instant messaging (C, TT)
InsideBronson intranet (C, SK, TT)
Department-specific newsletters (C)
Shared directories (C)
Daily huddles (C, SK, TT)
Healthlines newsletter (C)
CEO/CNE open office hours (C, TT)
Leadership (C, SK, TT)

Competency assessments (C, SK, TT)
Workshops and educational courses (C, SK, TT)
Employee forums and focus groups (C, TT)
Employee neighborhood meetings (C, TT)
Computer-based learning modules (C, SK)
Leader rounds (C, SK, TT)
Self-study modules (C, SK)
Skills fairs and learning labs (C, SK, TT)
Safety champions (C, SK, TT)
Preceptors (C, SK, TT)
Externships/internships (C, SK, TT)
Management mentor program (C, SK, TT)
Shared governance (C, SK, TT)
Teams, work groups, councils, and committees (C, SK, TT)
Staff performance management system (C, SK, TT)

C: communication; SK: skill sharing and knowledge; TT: two-way transfer

SOURCE: Information from Bronson Methodist Hospital application to the Malcolm Baldrige National Quality Award. 2006. "Bronson Methodist Hospital." [Online information; retrieved 9/2/08.] www.baldrige.nist.gov/Contacts_Profiles.htm.

Teaching   The activities of Exhibit 1.1 are learned. They follow prescribed scripts that are replicable for every process but can be adapted to individual patient needs and unanticipated events. Patient care follows **protocols**—from greeting a patient ("Good morning, may I check your armband?") to administering an intravenous drip to performing a surgical "timeout" whereby the circulating nurse verifies the patient, procedure, location, and any unusual risks. Specific **procedures** or **processes** are also followed for nonclinical activities, such as cleaning washrooms, posting payments to patient accounts, and conducting meetings of the governing board.

Protocols
Agreed-on procedures for each task in the care process

Procedures or processes
Actions or steps that transform inputs to outputs

All processes are learned, and most are taught by the organization. High-performing organizations invest heavily in teaching (using a variety of approaches), measuring learning, and rewarding correct application. Bronson Methodist, for example, documents an average of more than 100 hours of teaching for each full-time employee.[29]

Modeling   Actions inevitably speak louder than words. Everyone in leadership positions must model the behaviors that support the organizational values. High-performing HCOs expect their managers' professional actions to personify and implement the mission, vision, and values. Training programs help managers understand how to respond to common problems in ways that encourage associates. These programs often include coaching and mentoring to improve skills and counseling when specific problems arise. Managers at all levels are expected to point out to each other anything that falls short of model behavior. Managers undergo a multi-rater review, a system that allows subordinates, coworkers, customers, and supervisors to evaluate the managers anonymously.

Service Excellence   Every team and organization functions under a contract or agreement; that is, team members are agents who agree to carry out individual acts and to share accountability for the results. Caregiving teams are agents for patients who are unable to act for themselves. The concept of **agency** or **accountability** (also called *stewardship*) is essential to build trust within the organization. HCOs reinforce trust and stewardship by building team spirit and by modeling and rewarding correct behaviors.

Agency or accountability
The notion that the organization can rely on an individual or team to fulfill a specific, prearranged expectation

Service excellence
Associates anticipate and meet or exceed customer needs and expectations on the basis of the mission and values

Trust and accountability, agency, and stewardship are difficult to sustain. They are subject to moral hazard; any member can do less than her share, free-riding on the efforts of others. High-performing HCOs build trust and stewardship with a program of **service excellence**, recognizing that associates will work to meet customer needs if their own needs are met.[30] That is, if management shares the values of its workers, listens to them, responds to the issues they raise (empowering them), trains them, and supports them logistically, the workers perform to the extent that customers' needs are satisfied.

Service excellence has gained wide support, particularly in service industries.[31] It is a universal practice among high-performing HCOs.[32] In addition, team evaluations and team pressure help make free-riding unattractive or difficult. An important motivator among workers is the belief that their colleagues will not let them down, so they will not let their colleagues down in return.

The most important reward for most associates is the satisfaction of having done a good job. Excellent HCOs not only provide that reward but also strengthen and complement it. Success at continuous improvement provides measurable gains in achieving stakeholder goals. HCO operations become safer, more pleasant, more responsive, and more efficient. The new processes developed are better than the ones they replaced. The negotiated goals are almost always achieved. Patients and families express their gratitude.

Rewards for Success

High-performing HCOs distribute a substantial portion of the gains back to the associates who helped produce those gains. HCOs do this in two ways—celebrations and incentive pay. Celebrations include parties, meals, various tokens of recognition, and prizes such as gift certificates or small amounts of cash. They are frequent, usually informal, and can be put together quickly. Often, first-line supervisors are given a budget explicitly for celebrations. Incentive compensation links employee performance to the HCO goals. Substantial financial rewards are provided to associates in return for achieving continuous improvement goals.[33]

The reward system of Mercy Health System in Janesville, Wisconsin, is shown in Exhibit 1.9. The six celebrations offer prizes for various individual achievements that embody the organization's vision and values, such as offering extra help to a patient or family, serving on a demanding committee, contributing a useful solution or a new idea, or reaching out to a coworker. The incentive compensation is open to all but is tailored to specific professions and economic situations. Mercy's retirement program is designed to retain its best associates.

Operational Foundation of Excellence: Evidence-Based Management

The operational foundation reflects a major shift in thinking that began in the 1990s[34] and continues today in more than half of the nation's hospitals.[35] This model, often called **evidence-based management**, relies more heavily on performance measurement and formal process specification than on traditional approaches. Evidence-based management deliberately

Evidence-based management
Relies heavily on formal process specification and performance measurement

EXHIBIT 1.9
Mercy Health
System Award/
Incentive
Programs and
Objectives

Reward	Award/Incentive Programs	Objectives
Celebrations	"Above and Beyond the Call of Duty" Partner* Recognition Dinner Quest for the Best Baskets for Champions Partner Idea Program "Someone to Admire and Respect"	Promote excellent services by rewarding/recognizing best practices, quality outcomes, innovation, teamwork, or partnering initiatives
Incentive Compensation	Report cards/performance appraisals; bonuses dependent on organizational and individual achievement of targets Physician incentive program Individual merit increases Matched savings retirement plan	Reward best-practice achievers of individual targets, tied to Four Pillars of Excellence** Reward superior customer service performance

*Partners are all employees, including managers and senior management
**Four Pillars of Excellence is Mercy Health System's dimensions of strategic measurement: Quality—excellence in patient care and service; Exceptional Patient and Customer Service; Partnering—best place to work; and Cost—long-term financial success

SOURCE: Adapted from Mercy Health System's application to the Malcolm Baldrige National Quality Award 2007, p. 22. [Online information; retrieved 9/20/08.] www.baldrige.nist.gov.

parallels *evidence-based medicine*, a similar shift in medical thinking toward the systematic use of science to identify clinical best practices.

The core concept of evidence-based medicine is that scientific knowledge should drive as many clinical decisions as possible.[36] Much of medicine is judgmental, but as the diagnosis is clarified, evidence can be drawn from existing similar cases. **Patient care protocols** or **guidelines** define the scientifically proven steps appropriate for treating most patients with a specific disease or condition. **Functional protocols** detail the specific steps for performing individual clinical procedures, such as admission interviews and subcutaneous injections. These protocols specify what must be done, by whom, and when, making explicit the agency and stewardship obligations behind service excellence. These are not rules; the empowered caregiver has the obligation to depart from the protocol when the patient's condition requires it.

Patient care protocols or guidelines
Formally established expectations that define the normal steps or processes in the care of a clinically related group of patients at a specific institution

Functional protocols
These determine how functional elements of care are carried out

Although evidence-based medicine encountered substantial resistance when it was introduced around 1990, it has become the standard of practice. Many professional organizations and academic medical centers prepare patient care protocols, and more than 2,000 such protocols are listed on guideline.gov.[37] Evidence-based medicine is deeply embedded in both graduate and continuing clinical education.[38] In fact, the Accreditation Council for Graduate Medical Education has made practice-based learning and improvement, interpersonal and communication skills, and systems-based practice three of the six general competencies required for all physicians entering medicine after 2001.[39] The other three general competencies—medical knowledge, clinical skills, and professionalism—trace back to Hippocrates. Practice-based learning and improvement, interpersonal and communication skills, and systems-based practice implement evidence-based medicine and are highly compatible with the values of excellent HCOs.

Evidence-based management applies the scientific method to managing organizations. It is widely recognized in other industrial sectors, and it requires a thoughtful, thorough, and professionally disciplined approach.[40] In HCOs, it is built around the following elements:

1. *Boundary spanning:* establishing and maintaining effective relationships with all stakeholders, and adapting the HCO to the needs of its community
2. *Knowledge management:* maintaining a detailed fact base about the organization, including performance measures, benchmarks, and work processes, and making that fact base accessible to associates through training and communication
3. *Accountability and organizational design:* identifying and integrating the contribution and goals of each HCO component
4. *Continuous improvement:* continually analyzing and improving all work processes, following a systematic cycle of measurement, opportunity identification, analysis, trial, goal setting, and training for implementation

Evidence-based management is a major philosophic change. Like the advances in web communication, it is one of the latest steps in the centuries-long growth of empiricism and science in human enterprise. Used with transformational management and evidence-based medicine, evidence-based management creates HCOs that can achieve performance previously thought to be beyond reach.

An excellent HCO must be able to provide reliable and timely answers to several recurring questions:

Boundary Spanning

1. What are the opportunities for improvement as seen by customer stakeholders?
2. What are the demands and restrictions imposed by regulatory agencies?
3. What services should be available to our customers?
4. Which services should our HCO own and operate, and which should it acquire by contract?
5. How big should each service be?
6. What are the formal links between services and with the enterprise as a whole?
7. How do we acquire capital?

8. How do we acquire new technology and replace outdated facilities?

9. How do we ensure an adequate group of associates?

These questions identify the components of the HCO, relate them to each other, and relate the HCO to external suppliers and stakeholder networks. They are strategic questions, but the operational foundation must include substantial information gathering and analytic activity to ensure that the best alternatives are fully prepared and understood. Listening to customer stakeholders is an important part of this activity. Understanding and influencing the thinking of insurers, buyers, and regulators allow proactive instead of reactive relations. Quantitative analyses and forecasts of external data, such as population trends, economic trends, and epidemiology, support proposals that are economically realistic and that identify and reduce risks.

Knowledge Management

Facts drive evidence-based decisions. Knowledge management is sometimes called the *data warehouse* or the *source of truth* for the organization. Excellent HCOs build and maintain a large library of work processes, protocols, and performance measures; a training system to convey knowledge and skills that associates will retain; and a communication system to relay information relevant to immediate applications.

Library of Work Processes, Protocols, and Measures

There is a "way we do things" for most activities in HCOs—from how the governing board is selected, to how a new patient is greeted, to how a spontaneous obstetric delivery is managed. Many different associates will be involved in most of these processes, and consistency is important. The processes will change, and the changes must be recorded. In evidence-based management, change is deliberately sought, using performance measures.

As shown in Exhibit 1.10, six dimensions of measurement are necessary to guide the individual teams listed in Exhibit 1.1. This set is called **operational measures** or **operational scorecards**. Three of these measures address the inputs or resources: demand for service, physical resources or costs, and the satisfaction and commitment of the unit's human resources or associates. The other three measures address outputs or results: output and productivity (ratio of resource to output), quality of service or product, and customer satisfaction.

Success for the whole is more than the sum of success of individual teams. The measures must be carefully aggregated to progressively higher levels of accountability. Certain measures—chiefly income and financial position—cannot be calculated at the individual team level but are critical for the HCO as a whole. **Strategic measures** are those that assess the enterprise as a whole. As shown in Exhibit 1.11, they

---

Operational measures or operational scorecards
Six dimensions of measurement that include three measures of inputs or resources and three measures of outputs or results

---

Strategic measures or strategic scorecard
Four dimensions of measurement (finance, operations, customer relations, and learning/human resources) appropriate for service lines or the HCO as a whole

---

Input Oriented	Output Oriented
Demand	*Output and productivity*
Requests for service	Counts of services rendered
Market share	Productivity (resources/treatment or
Appropriateness of demand	service)
Unmet need	
Demand logistics	*Quality*
Demand errors	Clinical outcomes
	Procedural quality
Cost and resources	Structural quality
Physical counts	
Costs	*Customer satisfaction*
Resource conditions	Patients
	Referring physicians
Human resources	Other customers
Supply	
Development	
Satisfaction	
Loyalty	

EXHIBIT 1.10
Template of Operational Performance Measures for Individual Teams and Activities

are carefully aggregated from operational measures to reflect the needs of major stakeholder groups. About 30 measures are used, covering four major dimensions—customers, suppliers and associates, operations, and finance.

Strategic measures, sometimes called the **balanced scorecard**,[41] can be grouped as desired. One popular model, called the "Five Pillars," splits operations into quality and service and discusses demand as "Growth."[42] In the next chapters, the templates in exhibits 1.10 and 1.11 are expanded to show the kinds of measures used by excellent HCOs in each activity and in the aggregate. The system of measures described in exhibits 1.10 and 1.11 tracks the stakeholder relations for each unit of the HCO, making clear what the unit's critical contributions are and allowing for negotiated goals with measured achievement. Quantified goals and measures substantially reduce ambiguity and clarify each team's and associate's obligation. Frequently posted results discourage procrastination. When customers frequently post ratings of your work and attitude, the ratings are difficult for you to ignore.

Training

Work processes and protocols must be learned by all users. In healthcare, many such protocols require users to master specific manual, verbal, and observational skills by practicing these processes regularly. Exhibit 1.8 includes a number of training activities or "knowledge transfer" in Bronson's terminology. Bronson and other high-performing hospitals invest about twice as much time—2 to 2½ weeks per associate per year—in training. Much of this training is made available through organized sessions, but much is provided "just in time," supplied on site by coaches, consultants, or leaders.

EXHIBIT 1.11
Template
of Strategic
Measures
of HCO
Performance

Dimension	Major Concepts	Healthcare Examples
Financial performance	Ability to acquire, support, and effectively reinvest essential resources	Profit and cash flow Days' cash on hand Credit rating and financial structure
Internal operations, including quality and safety	Ability to provide competitive service Quality, efficiency, safety, and availability of service	Unit cost of care Measures of safety and quality of care Processes and outcomes of care Timeliness of service
Market performance and customer satisfaction	Reflects all aspects of relationship to customers	Market share Patient and family satisfaction Measures of access for disadvantaged groups
Associate satisfaction and ability to adapt and improve	Ability to attract and retain an effective associate group Learning and motivation of workforce Response to change in technology, customer attitudes, and economic environment	Physician and employee satisfaction Associate safety and retention Training program participation and skill development Availability of emerging methods of care Trends in service and market performance Ability to implement changes in timely fashion

Communications Networks

The culture of high-performing HCOs emphasizes listening, which requires facts and information such as patient orders, patient conditions, supplies used, and hours worked. Part of knowledge management is supplying this information promptly and accurately. Electronic medical records, e-mail, web access, telephone systems, newsletters, posters, and memos create a network through which time-dependent information can be exchanged.

Accountability and Organizational Design

Integrating an HCO requires careful planning to combine the caregiving and support teams into an effective whole. This means creating effective networks of accountability. Each team must know its contribution, and within the team, each member. In a transformational culture, these contributions are negotiated, but they must still be integrated into the whole.

A framework must exist for the negotiation and integration. The framework, called an **accountability hierarchy**, is a communications network that promotes factual exchange among related work teams and links each work team to the governing board. In

---

Accountability hierarchy
A reporting and communication system that links each operating unit to the governing board, usually by grouping similar centers together under middle management

addition to negotiating performance goals, the accountability hierarchy facilitates review of investment opportunities.

Not all patient needs are filled by associates; many are met by contractual partners, and some services are provided by remote organizations. Various legal structures are available to manage these relationships. Most large HCOs now have subsidiary corporations, joint ventures, and long-term contracts, which are sometimes called *strategic partnerships*. The accountability hierarchy of associates is supplemented with a designed array of other relationships.

Continuous Improvement

Continuous improvement depends on performance measurement and commits the HCO to systematic change; what was done last year is no longer the automatic standard for the future. Continuous improvement was recognized in the 1980s, largely as a result of the work of W. Edwards Deming.[43] It had widespread acceptance and is now a foundation for high-performing organizations in all industries. It is universal among excellent HCOs.[44,45,46]

Systematic change is built on establishing goals, reporting actual results, and comparing actual outcome against goal and goal against **benchmark**. This comparison identifies **opportunities for improvement** (OFIs or "oafies") and involves all teams, ideally all associates. OFIs also arise from qualitative assessments, including listening. Systematic change entails determining OFIs to design and implement changes in the work processes to achieve better performance. Exhibit 1.12 shows how processes are analyzed to translate OFIs to actual performance improvement.

The analysis is carried out by a **process improvement team (PIT)**. Successfully translating OFIs to improvement requires finding the **root causes**, the underlying factors that must be changed to yield consistently better outcomes. These root causes almost always lie in the methods, tools, equipment, supplies, information, training, and rewards provided the team, and almost never in issues of individual effort or attitude. The proposition that opportunities to improve performance lie with process rather than with people has been proven countless times in all kinds of organizations.[47]

Benchmark
The best-known value for a specific measure, from any source

Opportunities for improvement (OFIs)
Result of comparing actual outcome against goal and goal against benchmark; also arise from qualitative assessments, including listening

Process improvement team (PIT)
A group that analyzes processes and translates OFIs to actual performance improvement

Root causes
The underlying factors that must be changed to yield consistently better outcomes

Systematic change is a four-step process that applies to any OFI:

1. *Identify*: find improvable processes or OFIs.
2. *Analyze*: uncover root causes or possible corrections.
3. *Test*: develop alternative solutions and select the best for implementation.
4. *Evaluate*: implement the best solution, establish new goals, and monitor progress.

An older version of this concept is the Shewhart cycle, which labels these four steps as Plan, Do, Check, and Act.

The process, shown as the circle in Exhibit 1.12, can be quite elaborate, involving hundreds of associates and steps. A number of formal approaches to analysis are popular, including Lean Management, Six Sigma, and GE Work-Out; these are rigorous, objective, and thorough work processes for continuous improvement.

OFIs that apply to only one team can often be addressed by that team, but most OFIs are complicated and need a formal coordinating structure called the **performance improvement council** (PIC). The PIC is composed of representatives from all major activities or activity groups and is usually closely linked to senior management. The PIC's first job is to prioritize the OFIs, and top priority are the OFIs that have the highest potential impact on mission achievement and strategic performance measures (Exhibit 1.11). The PIC pursues as many OFIs as possible, limited only by the ability of the organization to staff the improvement projects. An important part of PIC activity is coordinating multiple projects and keeping them aligned with the annual goal-setting activity.

Performance improvement council (PIC)
A formal coordinating structure composed of representatives from all major activities or activity groups; the PIC's first job is to prioritize the OFIs

Strategic Foundation of Excellence: Positioning and Protection

Strategy
A systematic response to a specific stakeholder need

Strategic positioning
The set of decisions about mission, ownership, scope of activity, location, and partners that defines the organization and relates it to stakeholder needs

Strategic protection
Safeguards the assets of the organization

An HCO must support its cultural and operational foundations with a **strategy** or process for matching the activities and resources to stakeholder needs. **Strategic positioning** is an integrative activity that seeks maximum return from the resources available. Its success is measured by improvement in the strategic measures (Exhibit 1.11). Decision making provides definitive answers to boundary-spanning questions. **Strategic protection** safeguards the assets of the organization, including ensuring the reliability and validity of the data and information used for patient care and continuous improvement.

Strategic Positioning   Strategic positioning has two major components. The first component is data intensive and analytical. The boundary-spanning and organization-designed activities generate proposals for responding to the most important questions. The second component is the decision to implement specific proposals. Decision making requires experience, imagination, diligence and risk taking.

Excellent HCOs use their governing boards, managers, and internal and external consultants for strategic positioning. Planning committees are established to pursue specific opportunities. They operate much like PITs in that they usually follow an iterative review process, such as the competitive tests for investment opportunities (see Exhibit 1.13). But planning committees have a broader

EXHIBIT 1.12

Process Analysis: Translating OFIs to Improved Performance

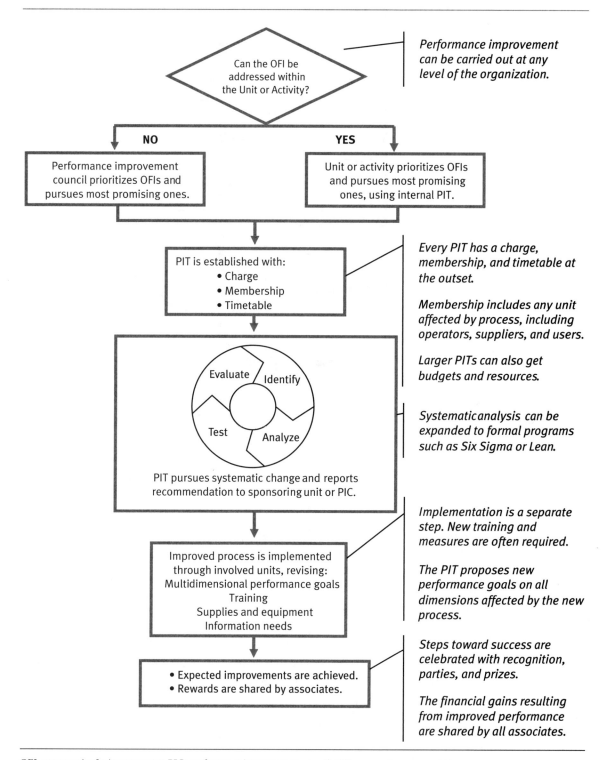

Can the OFI be addressed within the Unit or Activity?

Performance improvement can be carried out at any level of the organization.

NO — Performance improvement council prioritizes OFIs and pursues most promising ones.

YES — Unit or activity prioritizes OFIs and pursues most promising ones, using internal PIT.

PIT is established with:
• Charge
• Membership
• Timetable

Every PIT has a charge, membership, and timetable at the outset.

Membership includes any unit affected by process, including operators, suppliers, and users.

Larger PITs can also get budgets and resources.

Evaluate / Identify / Test / Analyze

PIT pursues systematic change and reports recommendation to sponsoring unit or PIC.

Systematic analysis can be expanded to formal programs such as Six Sigma or Lean.

Improved process is implemented through involved units, revising:
Multidimensional performance goals
Training
Supplies and equipment
Information needs

Implementation is a separate step. New training and measures are often required.

The PIT proposes new performance goals on all dimensions affected by the new process.

• Expected improvements are achieved.
• Rewards are shared by associates.

Steps toward success are celebrated with recognition, parties, and prizes.

The financial gains resulting from improved performance are shared by all associates.

OFI: opportunity for improvement; PIC: performance improvement council; PIT: process improvement team

EXHIBIT 1.13
Competitive
Tests for
Investment
Opportunities

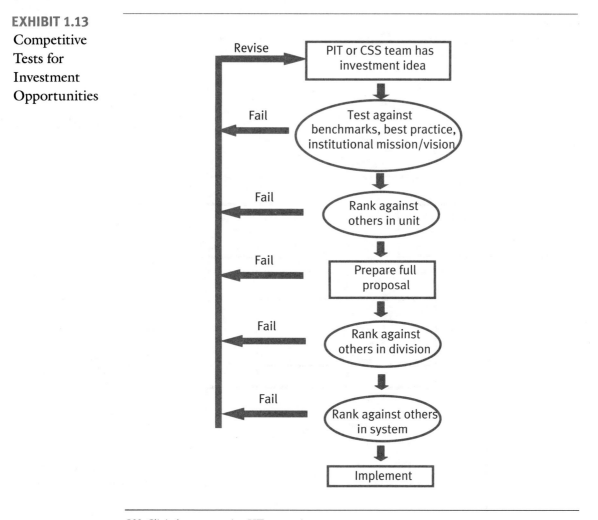

CSS: Clinical support service; PIT: process improvement team

agenda and greater license to consider innovation. They evaluate the impact of alternative actions on the strategic performance measures.

Exhibit 1.14 shows how excellent HCOs coordinate their strategic activity using an annual cycle of review that integrates analysis, proposals, and ongoing operations data to establish specific plans. These plans forecast expectations for the strategic performance measures several years into the future on the basis of the planning committee's analyses. The forecast is refined as time passes, and for the immediate next year it becomes the initial proposal for strategic goals. The governing board and its committees review the forecast and establish the annual goals, which guide internal goal negotiations. Senior management is responsible for forecasting. It participates actively in the discussions and facilitates communications between governance and those in charge of activities.

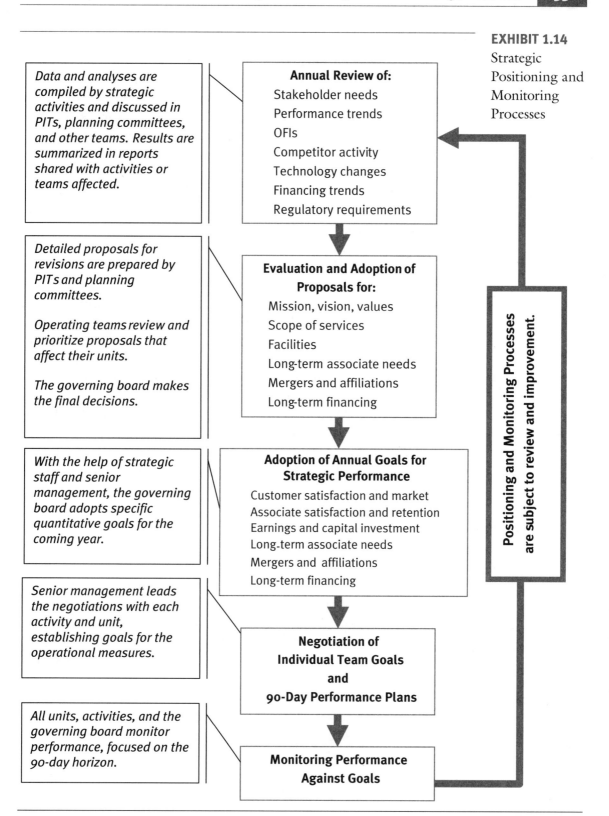

EXHIBIT 1.14
Strategic
Positioning and
Monitoring
Processes

Data and analyses are compiled by strategic activities and discussed in PITs, planning committees, and other teams. Results are summarized in reports shared with activities or teams affected.

Annual Review of:
Stakeholder needs
Performance trends
OFIs
Competitor activity
Technology changes
Financing trends
Regulatory requirements

Detailed proposals for revisions are prepared by PITs and planning committees.

Operating teams review and prioritize proposals that affect their units.

The governing board makes the final decisions.

Evaluation and Adoption of Proposals for:
Mission, vision, values
Scope of services
Facilities
Long-term associate needs
Mergers and affiliations
Long-term financing

With the help of strategic staff and senior management, the governing board adopts specific quantitative goals for the coming year.

Adoption of Annual Goals for Strategic Performance
Customer satisfaction and market
Associate satisfaction and retention
Earnings and capital investment
Long-term associate needs
Mergers and affiliations
Long-term financing

Senior management leads the negotiations with each activity and unit, establishing goals for the operational measures.

**Negotiation of
Individual Team Goals
and
90-Day Performance Plans**

All units, activities, and the governing board monitor performance, focused on the 90-day horizon.

**Monitoring Performance
Against Goals**

**Positioning and Monitoring Processes
are subject to review and improvement.**

OFI: Opportunity for improvement; PIT: process improvement team

Strategic Protection

All the assets of an HCO are subject to known hazards. Money gets stolen; facilities get damaged; people get hurt; information gets distorted. Any kind of asset can be lost. The first line of defense is work processes designed to protect against these risks. Cash is handled in centuries-old processes that make theft and embezzlement rare. Security programs protect facilities and their people. Information handling includes careful attention to accurate inputs, safeguards for appropriate access, and backups for mechanical failure. Excellence must go beyond simply putting these processes in place. It must systematically monitor the security processes and the risks to ensure compliance. Thus, cash and cash processes are examined by external auditors; facilities and security personnel are monitored through video surveillance; data and programs are audited to verify their validity and reliability.

A less-obvious risk inherent in all organizations is the failure of an individual or team to completely carry out their responsibilities. Individuals and teams in HCOs act as agents for patients or internal customers and must be accountable to complete their duties. Other individuals and teams must be able to trust the agents. A high level of trust is essential to sustaining the culture of excellence. As noted, agency, accountability, and trust are inherently subject to moral hazard. Any excellent organization must protect against agency failure, which can occur at all levels—from the temporary employee to the chief executive officer to the governing board. Excellent HCOs have learned to strengthen and protect their agency relationships through six important steps shown in Exhibit 1.15. The first four steps are built into the culture and procedural foundations. The last two—audit and correction—require special attention.

Audits

At least three different kinds of audits go on simultaneously in an evidence-based management system and serve to strengthen accountability:

1. *Transparent performance review.* Each level of the organization has current goals and receives performance data frequently. Excellent HCOs encourage open review of these reports, both within the units and with other units. They use 90-day plans for goal achievement, including corrective plans where necessary. The openness creates an atmosphere that makes it difficult to carry out activities that are contrary to the mission.

2. *Internal audits and reviews.* The fact that audits can be conducted at any time, by auditors deliberately isolated from the activity, on either a random or selective basis serves as a strong deterrent to misfeasance. The processes that ensure reliability of quantitative reports also discourage misrepresentation. The extensive network of listening helps ensure conformance. Reports of difficulty are carefully handled in ways that protect people who report potential problems.

3. *External reviews, audits, and oversight.* The governing board, representing the owners and stakeholders as a whole rather than the organization and its associates, is an ongoing external monitor for the organization. Customer

Values	Mission, vision, and values are collectively developed, prominently displayed, and frequently cited.	**EXHIBIT 1.15** Foundations Reinforcing Agency/ Accountability Relationships
Clarity	Specific desired behaviors are advertised to potential associates and explicitly taught in orientation programs.	
Responsiveness	The responses given by management to associate queries and requests apply the mission, vision, and values.	
Modeling	The behavior of management is consistent with mission, vision, and values.	
Audit	A system of checks and balances assists management and other associates by detecting departures from mission, vision, and values.	
Correction	When necessary, management implements a graduated corrective response that usually includes warning, retraining, second warning, and discharge.	

stakeholders are regularly evaluated by The Joint Commission, external financial auditors, and routine financial and clinical reports. They may pursue criminal or civil redress if they have evidence of difficulty.

High-performing organizations have made the audit structure more robust. They have built reviews into the governance process so that board members evaluate each other and their performance as a team. They have voluntarily implemented the standards of the Sarbanes-Oxley Act, calling for greater protection against fraudulent diversion of assets, fuller disclosure of actual performance, attestation to the accuracy of published results by board members and senior management, increased auditing, and avoidance of conflict of interest in all board decisions.[48]

When failures of accountability, agency, or trust occur, excellent organizations deal with them using a structured program in which managers at all levels have been trained. The program begins with a warning and discussion of causes and corrections. Subsequent failures lead to retraining and a candid discussion about the consequences of failure for the individual as well as the organization. A written record is often created. Continued failure leads to termination or reassignment. When the behavior in question is dangerous, threatening, or deliberate, discharge is often immediate. Deliberate lying, falsification of records, harassment of others, criminal behavior, and violation of community norms usually lead to immediate discharge, regardless of the rank involved.

Correction

The cultural, procedural, and strategic foundations are designed to promote excellence, and they are largely successful. When these foundations are maintained, failures of accountability and agency are rare. If they are not maintained, the entire organization is threatened, and drastic reconstruction is in order. Monitoring and maintaining the foundations is a strategic activity primarily of the governing board and senior management.

Suggested Readings

On the history of healthcare organizations:
Franklin, B. 1760. *Some Account of the Pennsylvania Hospital,* 1954 edition, edited by I. B. Cohen. Baltimore, MD: The Johns Hopkins Press.
Rosenberg, C. E. 1989. *The Care of Strangers: The Rise of America's Health Care System.* New York: Basic Books.
Starr, P. 1982. *The Social Transformation of American Medicine.* New York: Basic Books.
Stevens, R. 1989. *In Sickness and in Wealth: American Hospitals in the Twentieth Century.* New York: Basic Books.

On critical issues facing healthcare organizations:
Andersen, R. M., T. H. Rice, and G. F. Kominski (eds.). 2007. *Changing the U.S. Health Care System: Key Issues in Health Services Policy and Management,* 3rd ed. San Francisco: Jossey-Bass.
Institute of Medicine, Committee on Quality of Health Care in America. 2001. *Crossing the Quality Chasm: A New Health System for the 21st Century.* Washington, DC: National Academies Press.

On organization theory as applied to healthcare organizations:
Kovner, A. R., D. J. Fine, and R. D'Aquila (eds.). 2009. *Evidence-Based Management in Healthcare.* Chicago: Health Administration Press.
Shortell, S. M., and A. D. Kaluzny (eds.). 2006. *Health Care Management: Organizational Design and Behavior,* 5th ed. Clifton Park, NY: Delmar Cengage Learning.

Additional questions for discussion and other teaching aids available from Health Administration Press's Companion Website: ache.org/books/ Well-Managed7.

Notes

1. Attributed to Hubert Humphrey, U.S. senator and vice president.
2. Comprehensive data on the use of healthcare is available from the National Center for Health Statistics. [Online information; retrieved 11/20/08.] www.cdc.gov/ nchs/about/major/hdasd/nhds.htm.
3. Murphy, K. M., and R. H. Topel. 2006. "The Value of Health and Longevity." *Journal of Political Economy* 114 (5): 871–904.
4. Smith, D. G., and J. R. C. Wheeler. 1986. "Multiplier Estimation for Local Economic Impact Analysis." *The Journal of Business Forecasting* 5: 20–22.
5. Shortell, S. M., and A. D. Kaluzny. 2006. "Organization Theory and Health Services Management." In *Health Care Management: Organizational Design and Behavior,* 5th ed., edited by S. M. Shortell and A. D. Kaluzny. Clifton Park, NY: Delmar Cengage Learning.

6. Chandler, A. D. 1977. *The Visible Hand: The Managerial Revolution in American Business.* Cambridge, MA: Belknap Press; R. Coase. 1937. "The Nature of the Firm." *Economica* 4 (16): 386–405.

7. Institute of Medicine, Committee on Quality of Health Care in America. 2001. *Crossing the Quality Chasm: A New Health System for the 21st Century,* p. 39. Washington, DC: National Academies Press.

8. Centers for Medicare & Medicaid Services. [Online information; retrieved 4/20/09.] www.cms.hhs.gov/ContractingGeneralInformation/Downloads/02_ICdirectory.pdf.

9. Singer, L. E. 2008. "Leveraging Tax-Exempt Status of Hospitals." *Journal of Legal Medicine* 29: 1, 41–64.

10. Rothberg, M. B., E. Morsi, and E. M. Benjamin. 2008. "Choosing the Best Hospital: The Limitations of Public Quality Reporting." *Health Affairs* 27 (6): 1680.

11. Putnam, R. D. 1995. "Bowling Alone: America's Declining Social Capital." *Journal of Democracy* 6 (1): 65–78.

12. National Quality Forum. [Online information; retrieved 1/30/09.] www.qualityforum.org/about/mission.asp.

13. National Quality Measures Clearinghouse, Agency for Healthcare Research and Quality. [Online information; retrieved 1/30/09.] www.qualitymeasures.ahrq.gov.

14. Centers for Medicare & Medicaid Services. [Online information; retrieved 1/31/09.] www.cms.hhs.gov/HospitalQualityInits/08_HospitalRHQDAPU.asp#TopOfPage.

15. The Joint Commission. [Online information; retrieved 1/31/09.] www.jointcommission.org/NR/exeres/5A8BFA1C-B844-4A9A-86B2-F16DBE0E20C7.htm.

16. Corrigan, J., and D. McNeill. 2009. "Building Organizational Capacity: A Cornerstone of Health System Reform." *Health Affairs* 28 (2): w205–w215. (Published online January, 27 2009; 10.1377/hlthaff.28.2.w205.)

17. O'Kane, M., et al. 2008. "Crossroads in Quality." *Health Affairs* 27 (3): 749.

18. American Hospital Association. [Online information; retrieved 11/20/08.] www.aha.org/aha/resource-center/Statistics-and-Studies/fast-facts.html.

19. Starr, P. 1982. *The Social Transformation of American Medicine.* New York: Basic Books; Rosenberg, C. E. 1989. *The Care of Strangers: The Rise of America's Health Care System.* New York: Basic Books; Stevens, R. 1989. *In Sickness and in Wealth: American Hospitals in the Twentieth Century.* New York: Basic Books.

20. Institute of Medicine, Committee on Quality of Health Care in America. 2000. *To Err Is Human: Building a Safer Health System,* edited by L. T. Kohn, J. M. Corrigan, and M. S. Donaldson. Washington, DC: National Academies Press.

21. Bass, B. M., B. J. Avolio, D. I. Jung, and Y. Berson. 2003. "Predicting Unit Performance by Assessing Transformational and Transactional Leadership." *Journal of Applied Psychology* 88: 207–18.

22. Srivastava, A., K. M. Bartol, and E. A. Locke. 2006. "Empowering Leadership in Management Teams: Effects on Knowledge Sharing, Efficacy, and Performance." *Academy of Management Journal* 49 (6): 1239–51.

23. Gilmartin, M. J., and T. A. D'Aunno. 2008. "Leadership Research in Healthcare." *Academy of Management Annals* 2: 390–438.

24. Ackerman, A. L., and D. Anderson. 2001. *The Change in Leader's Roadmap: How to Navigate Your Organization's Transformation.* San Francisco: Jossey-Bass/Pfeiffer.

25. Collins, J. 2001. *Good to Great.* New York: Harper.

26. White, K. R., and R. Dandi. 2009. "Intrasectoral Variation in Mission and Values:

The Case of the Catholic Health Systems." *Health Care Management Review* 34 (1): 68–79.

27. Beauchamp, T. L., and J. F. Childress. 2009. *Principles of Biomedical Ethics,* 6th ed. New York: Oxford University Press.

28. Pfeffer, J. 1994. *Competitive Advantage Through People: Unleashing the Power of the Work Force.* Boston: Harvard Business Publishing.

29. Bronson Methodist Hospital. 2006. Malcolm Baldrige National Quality Award Application. [Online information; retrieved 9/20/08.] www.baldrige.nist.gov/ Contacts_Profiles.htm.

30. Fottler, M. D., R. C. Ford, and C. P. Heaton. 2002. *Achieving Service Excellence: Strategies for Healthcare.* Chicago: Health Administration Press.

31. Heskett, J. L., W. E. Sasser, and L. A. Schlesinger. 1997. *The Service Profit Chain: How Leading Companies Link Profit and Growth to Loyalty, Satisfaction, and Value.* New York: Free Press.

32. Griffith, J. R. 2009. "Frontiers of Hospital Management." *Journal of Healthcare Management* 54 (1): 30–44.

33. Bernd, D. L. 2008. *Trustee* 61 (2): 30.

34. Walshe, K., and T. G. Rundall. 2001. "Evidence-Based Management: From Theory to Practice in Health Care." *Milbank Quarterly* 79 (3): 429–57.

35. Kovner, A. R., and T. G. Rundall. 2006. "Evidence-Based Management Reconsidered." *Frontiers of Health Services Management* 22 (3): 3–22.

36. Montori, V. M., and G. H. Guyatt. 2008. "Progress in Evidence-Based Medicine." *JAMA* 300: 1814–16.

37. National Guidelines Clearinghouse. 2008. [Online information; retrieved 9/9/08.] www.guideline.gov.

38. Montori, V. M., and G. H. Guyatt. 2008. "Progress in Evidence-Based Medicine." *JAMA* 300: 1814–16.

39. Swing, S. R. 2007. "The ACGME Outcome Project: Retrospective and Prospective." *Medical Teacher* 29 (7): 648–54.

40. Pfeffer, J., and R. I. Sutton. 2006. *Hard Facts, Dangerous Half-Truths, and Total Nonsense: Profiting from Evidence-Based Management.* Boston: Harvard Business School Press.

41. Kaplan, R. S., and D. P. Norton. 1996. *Balanced Scorecard: Translating Strategy into Action.* Boston: Harvard Business Publishing.

42. Studer, Q. 2008. *Results That Last: Hardwiring Behaviors That Will Take Your Company to the Top.* Hoboken, NJ: J. Wiley & Sons Inc.

43. Deming, W. E. 1986. *Out of the Crisis.* Cambridge, MA: Massachusetts Institute of Technology, Center for Advanced Engineering Study.

44. Griffith, J. R., and K. R. White. 2005. "The Revolution in Hospital Management." *Journal of Healthcare Management* 50 (3): 170–89.

45. Griffith, J. R. 2009. "Frontiers of Hospital Management." *Journal of Healthcare Management* 54 (1): 30–44.

46. Kovner, A. R., D. J. Fine, and R. D'Aquila. 2009. *Evidence-Based Management in Healthcare.* Chicago: Health Administration Press.

47. For a useful summary of the issues, see Fottler, M. D., S. J. O'Connor, and M. J. Gilmartin. 2006. "Motivating People." In *Health Care Management: Organization, Design, and Behavior,* 5th ed., edited by S. M. Shortell and A. D. Kaluzny. Clifton Park, NY: Thomson Delmar Learning.

48. Sarbanes Oxley Act of 2002, P.L.107-204.

49. Franklin, B. 1760. *Some Account of the Pennsylvania Hospital,* 1954 edition, edited by I. B. Cohen. Baltimore, MD: The Johns Hopkins Press.

2 CULTURAL LEADERSHIP

In a Few Words

Excellent healthcare organizations (HCOs) have carefully maintained a culture that deliberately delights both customer and provider stakeholders. Leadership under this culture has five functions:

1. Promote shared values by establishing, disseminating, and modeling attractive mission, vision, and values.

2. Empower associates so that they feel they can change their work environment to improve mission achievement.

3. Listen responsively to associates so that their needs are met and the responses model the organization's values.

4. Support service excellence that helps delighted associates delight patients.

5. Celebrate and reward success.

All leaders are trained to accomplish these functions and are encouraged to work on their own advancement. Processes exist to stimulate the culture and deal with potential problems.

Critical Issues in Cultural Leadership

1. *Creating the best place to give care in order to* be *the best place to get care*. Listen to associates, identify what they need to fulfill the mission, and provide it.

2. *Implementing responsive leadership to build and sustain the culture.* Use training, selection, and modeling to create an environment where the values become real.

3. *Measuring and continuously improving the HCO's culture.* Use associate and customer satisfaction measures to improve relationships and communication.

4. *Establishing a program to respond to resistance and protect against damage.* At the senior management and governance level, handle potentially divisive issues and destructive behavior.

Consider these questions as you read the chapter.

1. Do you agree that managers are responsible for answering work team questions? Are you comfortable with the responses outlined in Exhibit 2.3? What other approaches might real managers take to these questions, and what would be the implications for a transformational culture?

2. To what extent are the following statements true?
   a. Managers do not give orders.
   b. Managers do not make decisions.
   c. Managers spend a lot of time listening.
   d. The governing board's calendar ultimately forces a decision.
   e. Imagination is an important managerial skill.

3. Suppose a colleague at an HCO says, "I don't think our culture is where it should be." Conversely, another colleague says, "I disagree. I think our culture is fine, and we spend too much money on training and rounding." What data would you review to validate or clarify their concerns? How would you reach a consensus on defining "where it should be"? On "too much money," or better yet on "the right amount of money"?

4. What is the best way to answer an associate (physician or senior employee) who says, "We've always done it this way. I don't see why we should change"?

5. You're rounding, and associates say the following things. How do you respond?
   a. "The toilet's broken in a patient's room. I called hours ago, but nobody's shown up."
   b. "We really need some new equipment. How do we get it?"
   c. "[Name of associate] was late today and sick yesterday. Third time this month!"
   d. "[Patient]'s husband walks with a cane. She says he can't come see her because it's so far from the parking lot."

Culture establishes how an organization feels to customer and associate stakeholders. Chapter 1 notes that excellent HCOs build a transformational culture that attracts the respect and support of stakeholders using five major functions that address values, empowerment, communication, service excellence, and rewards. Leadership is critical in forming and sustaining the transformational culture. Leaders align goals with the mission, vision, and values. Leaders listen, empower, and teach. Leaders inspire associates to set higher goals and reward achievement. These activities make the culture real and permanent. The ability to perform these activities is an essential competency for managers and is critical for senior managers.

Purpose

The purpose of cultural leadership is

to effectively implement transformational management of teams from the bedside to the boardroom

and

to sustain an environment where all associates are empowered and motivated to meet their customers' needs.

Many HCOs have 100 or more work teams, including caregiving, clinical support, logistic, and strategic support. All of the teams have customers. Patients are the customers of both caregiving and clinical support teams. Logistic support teams have other teams as customers, or **internal customers**. Clinical support teams and some logistic teams, such as security and patient relations, serve both patient and internal customers. All teams require support.

Internal customers
Associates and teams who work inside the HCO

    Chapter 3, on operational leadership, establishes the core technology that provides effective structure, filling universal team needs for people, information, supplies, and facilities. Excellence requires not only this structure but also an environment that encourages team members to do their best. The functions of cultural leadership create and sustain that environment.

Functions

Excellent HCOs implement six functions to achieve their cultural purpose. As shown in Exhibit 2.1, these six functions are synergistic, and the whole is substantially more than the parts. The core approaches relate across several functions, and the examples given in the exhibit illustrate varied applications of approaches rather than unique events. It is hard to say where one function ends and another begins; for example, saying thank you is a communication function, but it is also a reward. A training session inevitably contains more messages than simply the operation lessons learned.

EXHIBIT 2.1
Functions
of Cultural
Leadership

Function	Intent	Implementation	Examples
Promoting shared values	Establishes a central moral focus Protects individual rights Creates an intrinsic reward	Visioning exercises Display and repetition Training Repetitive modeling Rewards	Mission/vision/values on badges Orientation emphasis Celebration of exceptional effort
Empowering associates	Strengthens associate self-image Encourages continuous improvement Promotes responsiveness to customers	Training Manager training Repetitive modeling Rewards	Demonstrated mastery of work procedures 360-degree manager assessments Associate roles on PITs Encouragement
Communicating with associates	Identifies and responds to concerns Prevents information loss	Manager training Meeting management Display and repetition Repetitive modeling Rewards	Reports on goal achievement Rounding Blogs and e-mails PITs and group meetings
Supporting service excellence	Focuses associates on meeting customer needs	Goal setting Operational management Training Repetitive modeling Rewards	Goal negotiations Reports on goal achievement Customer relations training Service rewards and celebrations
Encouraging, rewarding, and celebrating success	Reinforces appropriate behavior Builds associate loyalty	Performance measurement Celebrations Incentive compensation	Patient satisfaction "Caught in the Act" program Bonuses
Improving the transformational culture	Increases return from culture over time	Review of learning, perceptions, attitudes, and achievements	Better programs to assist new leaders Improvement of incentive system

PIT: process improvement team

The culture depends on sound operations to deliver adequate supplies, staff, and facilities. An associate missing a patient's treatment pack is not likely to contribute to a process improvement team (PIT). When logistic support fails and the bonus cannot be earned, the reward system becomes a source of frustration. Teamwork alone can get exceptional results. A MASH unit, or field hospital, is an example. The unit faces challenging casualties and uses team spirit to overcome battlefield handicaps, but this approach cannot be sustained indefinitely or across hundreds of teams. Too much energy goes into solving operational problems, finding people, and building work-arounds.

Working from a strong operational base, seven approaches can promote the culture:

1. Promoting key messages, including the mission, values, and negotiated goals, by deliberate repetition and multiple displays
2. Listening and responding so that barriers to achievement are promptly identified and removed
3. Modeling the desired behaviors
4. Providing training in job processes so that the associate is not only competent but also confident
5. Training leaders and managers so that their actions consistently reinforce the values and the commitment to the mission (The tools to promote culture are themselves learnable.)
6. Negotiating to reach agreement on realistic limits and points of contention
7. Rewarding desired behavior with celebrations and tangible incentives

These approaches are included in an integrated plan to build and sustain a culture that *delights* customers and associates. ("Delight" is the highest possible satisfaction response.)

Promoting Shared Values

In excellent HCOs, the mission is displayed prominently and repeatedly on printed materials, on websites, and even on associates' badges. For example, the mission of SSM Health Care—"Through our exceptional health care services, we reveal the healing presence of God"—appears at the top of every page of its website (see www.ssmhc.com/internet/home/ssmcorp.nsf). SSM's values—compassion, respect, excellence, stewardship, and community—are given less display but are emphasized in other ways.

Training is a critical component in establishing a mission- and value-driven culture. Applicants are asked to read and accept the mission and values before completing an application. Orientation begins with a strong and clear

Chief executive officer (CEO)
The agent of the governing board who holds the formal accountability for the entire organization

commitment. Many excellent HCOs have the **chief executive officer** (CEO) or a senior manager meet all new associates to explain the mission and values and the HCO's ways of expressing its commitment to the mission and values. Training makes clear that "respect" rules out any form of harassment of customers or associates and that "stewardship" requires maintaining confidentiality of patient records and personal information. Training covers the proper forms of behavior, dress, and address, so that contacts with customers and other associates are carried out consistently to professional standards.

The leader's role is one of reinforcing these messages. All leaders are trained in how to conduct personal interviews and meetings, and how to deal with recurring issues. Leaders promote shared values by asking questions: "How do our decisions reflect our mission?" "What services are our customers seeking?" "How can we best serve patients' health needs?" Leaders "microtize" the vision. In other words, they break down the overall vision to describe how it affects each work unit and individual. They ask, "What's the unit's mission and how does it contribute to the larger HCO mission?" They encourage each associate to think through the answer to that question, building understanding and commitment.[1]

Empowering Associates

An empowered associate understands that she can and should change the work environment when some part of it interferes with mission achievement. Effective healthcare requires the integration and coordination of countless details. For even a moderately complex therapy, identities must be checked, diagnoses verified, treatment planned, explanation and reassurance offered, hands washed, interventions completed correctly at the right time and recorded, and these activities must be performed many times by many associates with vastly different skill levels.

Training provides a foundation; empowerment makes it happen. Empowerment allows all associates, even those in the least-skilled positions, to accept the professional role of agent for the patient or the customer. The leadership role is to reinforce empowerment by listening, responding, reassuring, explaining, encouraging, and rewarding. This role has been termed **servant leadership**,[2,3] which emphasizes the leader's obligation to be sensitive and responsive.

Servant leadership
The leader's obligation to be sensitive and responsive to associate needs

Empowerment and servant leadership are more than specific acts; they are learned traits. They create a culture where questions can be asked, answers sought, and changes implemented. They remove blame. They reassure associates that the HCO's commitment to its mission and values is real. They create a culture that makes teammates comrades and work intrinsically rewarding.

Communicating with Associates

Mercy Health System, 2007 recipient of the Malcolm Baldrige National Quality Award, describes its communication program in its Baldrige application as follows:

> In support of [its culture of excellence], senior leadership adopted a Servant-Leadership Philosophy. This philosophy is based on the belief that when leaders provide excellent service to partners, partners provide excellent service to customers. This approach inverts the traditional, top-down management style; thus, organizational leaders become facilitators whose role is to serve those who provide value to patients and other stakeholders. . . .
>
> Senior leaders' personal demonstration of commitment to the organization's values is a critical element in the servant leadership approach. With this underlying philosophy, [the executive council (EC)] has adopted the following best practices:[4]
>
> - Frequent, open, and honest communication—EC members bring issues to weekly EC meetings for full discussion, supporting integrated system strategies;
> - "Cruising and connecting"—EC members perform weekly administrative rounds, connecting with partners to seek out new ways to better serve their needs;
> - Personal renewal and connections with patients and customers—EC members perform line work alongside staff annually and review patient complaints weekly; and
> - Monthly luncheons—EC members conduct small group sessions [with members of their accountability hierarchy] to promote two-way communication.

The Mercy program is noteworthy for several reasons. First, it is deliberately opposite from the traditional "command and control" perspective that prevailed in many organizations until the late 1990s. That perspective is so deeply rooted in the American workplace that most associates and all leaders must be carefully taught about the new model and how to work effectively within it. Second, the Mercy program mandates frequent, direct contact between the leaders and associates and between workers and customers. Third, it includes systematic review of customer complaints. Fourth, it expects the organization's senior management to roll up their sleeves and pitch in with their teams. Fifth, it expects all managers to model desirable behavior and to reinforce formal training.

Much of communications is about the systematic transfer of facts. It is part of the operational foundation described in Chapter 1 and 3 and expanded in Chapter 10, on knowledge management and information services.

Leaders routinely participate in factual communication and accept accountability for doing it well. Cultural leadership requires more. It requires that the leader consistently reinforce the values by words, attitudes, and actions. The reinforcement is often supplied by two components of communication that have traditionally been overlooked—listening and modeling.

Listening   Transformational management depends heavily on making all communication with associates. The intent is to ensure that every associate's concerns will be heard, be understood, and receive a constructive response. The emphasis on response distinguishes transformational from transactional and older management styles. It is a major factor in associate satisfaction[5] and essential to the overall performance improvement that transformational management achieves.[6]

Listening is what makes communication two-way, and it is a skill that can be taught by example and learned by practice. Listening skill can easily be tested, by rephrasing what has been said and asking for verification: "Let me restate what I heard, and you tell me if it's right." In excellent HCOs, listening opportunities are created by planned one-to-one conversations; *rounding*, where leaders meet workers in their units; informal meetings with small groups of employees; and town-hall meetings. It includes focus groups, where small, relatively homogeneous panels are encouraged to discuss open-ended questions, and nominal group technique, where individuals and small groups pursue subjective estimates and expectations. Listening need not be face to face. It may also be done through random sampling surveys and respondent-initiated comment cards, in both paper and electronic modes. It is a job of not only associates but also other stakeholders.

Modeling   Transformational leadership relies heavily on repetition and consistency. Transformational leaders are expected to act out the HCO's values and to demonstrate how they are applied. Sharp HealthCare clearly describes the attitudes and behaviors it desires and expects from workers and managers:[7]

12 Employee Behavior Standards
1. It's a Private Matter: Maintain Confidentiality
2. To "E" or Not to "E": Use E-mail Manners
3. Vive La Différence!: Celebrate Diversity
4. Get Smart: Increase Skills and Competence
5. Attitude is Everything: Create a Lasting Impression
6. Thank Somebody: Reward and Recognition
7. Make Words Work: Talk, Listen, and Learn
8. All For One, One For All: Teamwork
9. Make It Better: Service Recovery
10. Think Safe, Be Safe: Safety at Work

11. Look Sharp, Be Sharp: Appearance Speaks
12. Keep in Touch: Ease Waiting Times

5 "Must Haves"

1. Greet people with a smile and "hello," using their name.
2. Take people where they are going.
3. Use key words at key times: "Is there anything else I can do for you? I have the time."
4. Foster an attitude of gratitude.
5. Round with reason.

and, for all associates working with patients, an AIDET acronym:

Acknowledge: Acknowledge people with a smile and use their names.

Introduce: Introduce yourself to others politely.

Duration: Keep in touch to ease waiting times.

Explanation: Explain how procedures work and who to contact if they need assistance.

Thank You: Thank people for using Sharp HealthCare.

All managers are expected to model this behavior. "Senior Leaders are expected to exhibit the Core Values, Behavior Standards, and Five 'Must Haves,' and serve as role models for employees, volunteers, physicians, suppliers, and partners."[8]

Supporting Service Excellence

The service excellence model diagrammed in Exhibit 2.2 is the goal of the transformational culture. It expands the concept of agency or stewardship ("I am doing this *for* you") to one of shared commitment ("I am doing this *with* you"). The moral foundation of service excellence is to serve others as one wishes to be served, an important step beyond fulfilling a contract.[9] The trust implicit in agency is raised to a new level of partnership. All associates, specifically managers, become partners in satisfying the patient as the ultimate customer. Service excellence is demonstrated rather than proven (rigorous proof is both intellectually and practically challenging), and all excellent HCOs follow the service excellence model. The model is extremely powerful financially. Small gains in numbers of patients served generate big increases in profits, providing funds for the costs of the operational foundation.

The new level of trust must begin with leadership. Leaders must trust associates and make that trust clear. They must also work to remove the frustrations and conflicts that associates face, freeing the energies they consumed to improve patient care. They do this by promoting shared values, empowering, communicating, and implementing the operational foundation (discussed in Chapter 3). In HCOs that are converting from transactional cultures, leaders work consistently to promote the values, increase empowerment as associates understand and accept it, and identify the most promising opportunities for

EXHIBIT 2.2
The Service
Excellence
Chain in
Healthcare

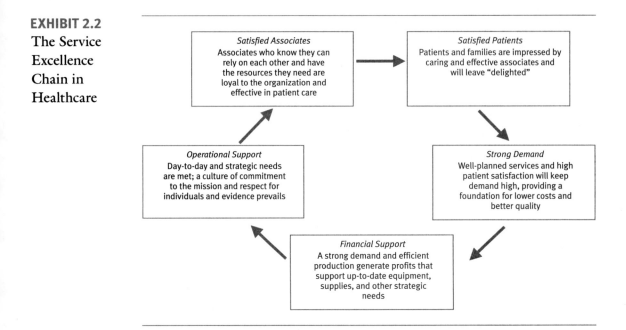

improvement (OFIs). Solving all problems at once is not possible, and people learn new concepts at different rates. By identifying teams that are ready to move forward and supporting them, management demonstrates the transformational potential and gains skill in making the transition. These actions also provide compelling evidence of the strength of the organization's commitment and the power of the transformational approach. The transition snowballs. The bold volunteers, the perceptive follows, and the crowd joins in.

Negotiating   Service excellence and transformational management must deal with the realities of the world. Perfection is rarely possible. Not every problem can be addressed at once. People disagree. Some critical resources—particularly space and money—must be assigned to some and denied to others. Excellent HCOs recognize realities as part of their culture. OFIs are a measure of where realities have fallen short of desires. The leadership must resolve these realities in acceptable ways. Negotiating to find the best solutions is an ongoing process. To sustain the culture, managers must be skilled at the process. Training, mentoring, and counseling create a culture where the following goals are universally understood and accepted and almost universally met:

1. Every position is entitled to an honest hearing.
2. The best answer is driven by two fundamental statements:
   a. Mission achievement is the basic criterion.
   b. Fact and science guide our evaluation of each decision.
3. Each decision is subject to test as it is implemented. The strategy is to measure

the emerging reality, catch OFIs quickly, and correct them. Any process can be improved.

4. This decision process, while not perfect, meets every stakeholder's needs better than any alternative process does.

This set of goals is at the core of the transformational culture. Exhibit 2.3 shows some recurring sources of contention, illustrating the implications of these goals. In all cases the negotiation path is specific, honest, and factual. In most cases, it points to an underlying process, offers to explain the process, and notes how the process itself is subject to continuous improvement.

Although the solution paths in Exhibit 2.3 look like common sense, they are a major departure from traditional management styles. Weak HCOs have difficulty implementing such an approach for several reasons. First, it requires understanding that any associate is free, even encouraged, to raise any issue that concerns him or her. Second, issues like these are recurring, so they are settled by formal processes rather than by individual judgments. Third, leaders must be trained in how to respond to these concerns because they arise frequently. Good answers begin with a reassurance that the concern is legitimate; trained leaders should always assume the associate's good intentions and never place blame. They offer an explanation for how the current situation was reached and how the underlying process can be improved. The approach in itself reduces disagreement. Consistently applying it allows associates to evaluate their situation themselves, reframing concerns to suggestions that will win acceptance.

Some issues are too complex for the responses listed in Exhibit 2.3. They require detailed investigation and extensive effort to resolve. Some leaders become specialists at helping people resolve disagreement. The basic elements of this process are as follows:

1. Help the conflicting parties fully understand all aspects of their position, including the causes, implications, and alternative solutions.
2. Explore carefully for areas of agreement, and build solutions upon these.
3. Conduct the negotiations openly and show respect for all participants and a clear commitment to the fundamentals of mission achievement and scientific evidence.

When these elements are carried out, the participants may leave thinking that they lost or that an error was made, but they concede that their case was fully and fairly heard.

Leaders sustain a culture of continuous improvement. Much of continuous improvement is operational. It requires a strong fact base, training in process analysis, and a formal structure for review of complex proposals. Having these

Continuous Improvement

EXHIBIT 2.3

Frequently Negotiated Issues and Solution Paths for Excellent HCOs

Issue	Negotiation Path	Implications
"This is an unsafe situation."	"Thank you for noticing it. Security will evaluate it and give you a report. When you get the report, let me know if you're satisfied.	Value: Safety is critical for all associates. Unsafe situations are not tolerated. Fact: A trained team evaluates risks and follows through.
"We need new equipment."	"We spend millions each year on new equipment, so we have a careful, competitive review process. Units that show how the investment will improve quality, efficiency, or customer satisfaction usually get their requests."	Value: New equipment is important to fulfilling the mission, but money does not grow on trees. Fact: New equipment is justified based on specific improvements in important operational measures.
"How many nurses (or other staff) do we have?"	"That's a good question. We have a nurse staffing system, and we monitor benchmarks and patient outcomes. If you think your floor staffing should be changed, and your coworkers agree, we'll form a performance improvement team to re-evaluate it."	Value: Providing enough nursing to ensure quality and patient satisfaction is part of our mission, but so is control of costs. Fact: Staffing is set by a specific process that includes measures of effectiveness and process improvement.
"I disagree with the protocol."	"We use caregiver panels to select our protocols, and we try to follow the evidence-based medicine rules. Would you like to meet with the chair of your panel to discuss your concerns?"	Value: Science drives the clinical practice. Fact: Any protocol is a candidate for improvement. Suggestions are welcome and are evaluated carefully.
"This patient does not fit the protocol."	"Caregivers are expected to use their professional judgment to leave the protocol when indicated. We do ask for a note in the chart, so that it reflects what is being done."	Value: Care is patient-centered. Professionals are expected to exercise judgment. Fact: Judgment must be documented for effective communication and for later review.
"My supervisor isn't fair."	"I'm sorry to hear that. Tell me more about your concerns, and we'll see how we can improve things."	Value: Associates are important stakeholders, but there are two sides to every argument. Fact: The HCO has a variety of training and counseling programs to resolve common sources of dissatisfaction, but using them requires a candid and thorough understanding of the cause.
"I want more money."	"Let's talk about that. We set our compensation carefully, and human resources can show you how we arrived at yours. We also offer bonuses, and you get a regular report on yours. One way to get more money is to win a promotion. Let's go over some steps you might take to do that."	Value: Compensation needs to be fair to all stakeholders. Associates are encouraged to improve. Fact: Compensation is based on an objective process. The HCO measures employee contribution, rewards effort, and encourages growth.

in place is important, but the stimulus to innovate and the implementation of improvements must come from the work teams themselves. The culture must encourage innovation. The work teams identify process-related questions. The responses to those questions should follow the initial goals of negotiation (Exhibit 2.3). When they do, their tone encourages the search for improvement. Answers that blame, are evasive, or shut off discussion cause a quick loss of team commitment.

First-line leaders can form PITs as they see fit. In excellent HCOs they are trained to do so often. They can form PITs to identify OFIs, or PITs to plan bigger PITs, or one-person PITs. The PIT is simply a device to identify improvement. As the agendas get more complex, knowledgeable superiors, internal and external consultants, and just-in-time training all support the team's ability to examine and improve its work processes. A key constraint—the PIT must include all who are affected by the change—is easy to learn and, when violated, easy to correct by adding the missing viewpoint to the PIT. In a transformational environment, establishing linkages to negotiate new processes, or gaining approval from the performance improvement council (PIC), is simple. Senior management's commitment is tested often, but is easy to sustain. If dietary tells nursing it cannot deliver late meals, a negotiation process begins. Senior management offers several possible answers, but denying inpatients lunch is not one of them.

Implementation is rarely uneventful, even with the best advance planning. Pilot tests are essential for complex changes. They can present extraordinary challenges for the participants, who will need extra support and encouragement. A successful transformational culture has an underlying bias toward change. This bias is expressed by being encouraging from the start, giving support during the change, and celebrating success throughout the process. Much of this is demonstrated in words, attitudes, and actions such as pitching in and getting help.

Encouraging, Rewarding, and Celebrating Success

On a day-to-day basis, all managers must identify and celebrate particularly positive examples of implementing the values. The most common form of celebration is a simple recognition and encouragement: "Mary, you did a great job with that patient's needs." Many organizations use public reporting to identify positive behavior, sometimes called "Caught in the Act." Any associate or visitor can submit a description of an act he or she thinks is exceptional. The submission identifies the associate and the act and is immediately posted to the associate's record. Weekly or monthly, a panel of associates reviews the submissions and selects the winners, who then receive recognition and prizes.

Improving the Transformational Culture

The culture itself, distinct from the work processes, contributes to mission achievement in several ways:

- It trains, empowers, and rewards associates, making them partners, not agents, in turning the service excellence model into a reality.
- It encourages a blame-free environment that facilitates PITs.
- It creates the "best place to give care" mind-set, which encourages associates to remain with the HCO, thus increasing the return on the ongoing training investment.

As the culture improves over time, an increasingly knowledgeable and committed associate group develops. The measures available to evaluate the culture are discussed in a later section. Generally, the human resources department leads the review of the progress made, but the PIC also pays direct attention to this endeavor. Both systematic and individual OFIs can be identified and improved through the study or use of the other functions.

People

HCOs need significant numbers of managers and leaders, from small patient care teams to CEOs. The total is on the order of 500,000 nationwide, a number similar in magnitude to the number of physicians. More than 10,000 new leaders may be needed each year to accommodate retirements. To sustain excellence, an HCO must develop a program that identifies and develops its leadership cadre.

Sources of Leaders

First-level leaders are commonly promoted from team membership, usually because they have demonstrated exceptional mastery in both the relevant knowledge and interpersonal skills. Managers and division directors are often promoted from first-level leaders, but at higher ranks they may be recruited from other organizations. Executive search firms facilitate finding appropriately qualified people. In many logistic and strategic support areas, experience in other industries is relevant. While clinical managers are often promoted from within or from similar HCOs, accounting and marketing managers may have gained the necessary knowledge and skills in banking or retailing. Consultants often move to executive posts, and vice versa.

Senior executives of HCOs have had 10 to 20 years of experience in management and leadership with increasing accountability. For senior management, an understanding of the clinical and financial structures is essential but not easily grasped. Senior managers usually reach their positions by following one of three routes:

1. Obtaining a graduate degree in healthcare management and moving up the organizational hierarchy from an initial administrative, support position
2. Developing an interest in management and learning its skills from being a patient care or clinical support professional; this interest then grows as the person is given broad exposure and opportunities for executive education
3. Transitioning from a strategic or logistic position into a management role through building a record of excellent performance in large HCOs or consulting companies and then pursuing graduate education in healthcare management

Many excellent senior leaders come from outside healthcare, but most have spent their careers mastering the industry and its details. Leadership development programs must recognize the differences in leaders' background and devise ways to build comprehensive skill.

Qualifications for Leaders

Leaders should be identified and promoted on the basis of their contributions. Exceptional associates may be selected to become first-level leaders, while skilled first-level leaders may become managers, and so on. Prior success alone is not sufficient for success after promotion. The transition is often challenging. A prominent researcher in management development notes:[10]

> [B]ecoming a manager required a profound psychological adjustment—a *transformation of professional identity*. First-time managers had to unlearn the deeply held attitudes and habits they had developed when they were responsible simply for their own performance. Prior to a managerial promotion, their contribution depended primarily on what they did personally, drawing upon their own expertise and actions. As managers, on the other hand, they had to come to see themselves as responsible for setting and implementing an agenda for a whole group. To use an orchestral analogy, new managers had to move from concentrating on one task, as an accomplished violinist does, to coordinating the efforts of many, like a conductor. To set the agenda for a whole group and to motivate and inspire others to accomplish that agenda were much more complicated than most people anticipated.

Each level of leadership presents different kinds of adjustments. Promotion generally means higher levels of abstraction, more diversity of teams, more complex problems of integration, and more challenging conflicts demanding resolution.

Leadership requirements were formerly described by global characteristics such as degrees or years of experience. The concept of **competencies**—profiles of skills, knowledge, and attributes (SKAs) that can be matched to positions and candidates—has expanded the opportunities to describe leadership requirements, evaluate

Competency
Having requisite or adequate ability or quality that results in effective action and/or superior performance in a job

candidates, and develop learning opportunities. While specific certifications remain important, particularly in medicine, nursing, and accounting, leadership position descriptions have tended to a finer-grained approach, looking for evidence of mastery of SKAs known to be associated with high performance. Gilmartin and D'Aunno, in reviewing the research in healthcare management competencies, conclude:[11]

> [A]cross the three disciplines of nursing management, public health, and health-services management, there is agreement on competencies in [seven] areas for effective leadership. These areas are (a) interpersonal relationships, (b) communication, (c) finance and business acumen, (d) clinical knowledge, (e) collaboration and team building, (f) change management, and (g) quality improvement.

Note that three of the seven competencies listed by Gilmartin and D'Aunno are knowledge-based—finance and business acumen, clinical knowledge, and quality improvement—and the other four are primarily skills. Dye and Garman identify 16 competencies that they believe distinguish great leadership from good leadership. Their list is more introspective, identifying personal values and emotional strengths.[12]

It is feasible to identify a specific leadership position—say, manager of primary care offices, or intensive care nurse manager—and describe the requirements in terms of the SKA competencies. Interviews can be conducted, references can be checked, and written documentation can be reviewed to assess each candidate's record and to compare it with the competency requirements. Of course, each candidate's profile will be different. One may have documented excellence in interpersonal skills, team building, and change management, while another may possess exceptional business acumen, clinical knowledge, and clinical quality improvement. It is unlikely that any candidate will exactly match the desired profile. Even with a specific leadership position in view, it is difficult to determine whether excellence in change management is better than excellence in clinical knowledge or whether strength in interpersonal relationships overcomes a weakness in clinical quality improvement. The task of judging is often assigned to a small search committee. Once a leader has been selected, the comparisons between desired and actual competencies are useful in planning a training program. The way the leader is supported by training and coaching may be more important than the fine details of competency or the choice between competing candidates.

Leadership requirements change as leaders advance. The competency requirements expand. Business acumen becomes more important. The breadth of clinical and professional understanding required grows, but the need for mastery of specific areas diminishes. Rather than leading a team, the manager must lead team leaders, and the teams become more diverse. The processes for change management become more complex. Management education programs emphasize preparation for the advanced leadership positions. In a study of the top qualities for hiring an early careerist healthcare manager, employers rank-ordered the most important skills as interpersonal communication, working in teams, planning and managing projects, solving business problems, and professional ethics.[13] As managers approach the senior levels, formal education has a clearer role. The evidence assembled by Gilmartin and D'Aunno suggests that graduate management education contributes to overall competency. Shorter executive programs are less clearly supported, but both are felt by participants to be helpful.[14]

Leadership Development Programs

Leadership development, an internal program to assist all managers in improving leadership skills, is a critical element of excellent HCOs. Leaders from diverse cultural and professional beginnings must collaborate effectively. All levels of leadership must maintain the continuous improvement system, promote and implement the work of PITs, and address the identified needs of associates and customers. For long-run success, they must model the behaviors expected of associates; respond to associate needs; maintain alignment and integration between teams; and effectively use the elements of the cultural, operational, and strategic foundations. A leadership group with these abilities is the product of a development program with the following elements:

1. The cultural foundations are made clear to all associates and are consistently reinforced by leaders at all levels.
2. Promotion to any leadership position is based on demonstrated superiority in relevant subordinate positions and mastery of competencies required in the new position.
3. Promoted leaders receive substantial training in the cultural and operational requirements of their new position. This includes classroom education, coaching, encouragement, and modeling by superiors.
4. Every leader has a program of personal development intended to improve current performance and to prepare them for the next promotion.
5. Just-in-time training and guided experience help leaders overcome the challenges in completing their work, simultaneously broadening their skills and knowledge.
6. The organization's succession plan identifies at least one successor for every position and coordinates with the successor's development plan.
7. For individuals seeking the highest ranks of leadership, the development plan includes deliberate expansion in two directions—a graduate degree in management and experience in leading a relatively autonomous unit.

Historically, leaders have negotiated their own careers. A leadership development program brings organizational resources to help leaders in this regard. Individual skill and ambition remain critical. Management is learned by doing, and this process presents opportunities for intellectual and emotional growth:[15]

> . . . [B]ecoming a manager was largely a process of *learning from experience*. New managers could only appreciate their new role and identity through action, not contemplation. They learned what it meant to be a manager and how to be one by facing real problems with real consequences. They grappled with four transformational tasks: (1) learning what it really means to be a manager; (2) developing interpersonal judgment; (3) gaining self-knowledge; and (4) coping with stress and emotion.
>
> . . . [M]anagers must be prepared to learn about themselves (their identities, strengths, and limitations), be willing to make necessary changes, and be able to cope with the associated stress and emotions. There is no magic or quick fix. Only with self-awareness, empathy, discipline, and practice can new managers master the human competencies.

At the same time, well-planned intervention and support is valuable. Role models, mentors, and counselors can provide material help. A supportive environment can minimize the consequences of beginners' errors. The investment pays off in two ways: (1) Supported managers are more likely to remain with the HCO because they like the environment, and (2) supported managers gain skill and effectiveness that help them successfully address complex issues:[16]

> [O]rganizations taking a very disciplined and rigorous approach to leadership development generally produce more leadership talent.
>
> . . . [What characterizes best practice firms] is the far greater extent to which they measure their efforts. For example, they measure the quantity of leadership talent for specific roles. They measure the attrition rate of their leadership talent. They catalogue jobs, assignments, and bosses that are more developmental in nature. They then make strategic use of this knowledge by moving managers into these roles and under these supervisors to ensure development.

Paths for Beginners

Transformational leadership is learned behavior. For beginners in the healthcare management field, this means the following:

1. *Commitment or the will to succeed outweighs the path to success.* The evidence shows that many different paths lead to successful HCO leadership careers. Technical or professional academic credentials are relatively more important at the lower leadership levels. Even for clinical chiefs, the competency required is in leadership rather than clinical areas. The biggest barriers to advancement

may be the emotional stress and new learning required, rather than any specific knowledge or skill.

2. *Practice is the foundation for mastering competencies.* Leadership is at its root a performance activity like singing, drawing, or playing soccer. As such, it can never be learned solely from printed material or classroom study; it needs to be applied in practice. Many lessons can be learned vicariously; others' experience is a valuable guide.

3. *Guided practice—with training, coaching, and feedback—helps more leaders succeed and do so faster.* Practice without coaching and training lacks the value of history; each lesson must be learned anew through trial and error. The use of quantitative goals and routine performance measurement provides focus and identifies learning opportunities.

4. *Regular review of competencies, identification of personal OFIs, and planned actions are critical to leadership development.* As with any other kind of performance activity, leadership benefits from following a disciplined program that includes a routine review of progress.

5. *Establishing a plan or goals for the future is helpful.* A vision of what might be, a plan for realizing that vision, and a method for marking milestones reached allow leaders to get closer to their desired future.

6. *Formal education has a role in leadership development, particularly for the leader who has built the foundations of commitment and practice.* In an evidence-based environment, knowledge is steadily accumulated and codified. Formal study offers the opportunity to capture the wisdom gained from large numbers of trials.

Measures

The culture, leadership functions, individual leadership skills, and leadership capability are all systematically measured, reported, and benchmarked in high-performing HCOs. Goals are set and achieved for both the organization and the leaders.

The Culture and Leadership Functions

The culture can be measured directly by survey and indirectly by the measures of associate satisfaction. The usual practice is to rely on the latter, assuming that a culture is effective if associate retention and satisfaction are high and other indicators (e.g., recruitment shortage, lost time) are near benchmark. That approach can be refined by measuring the leaders' capability to carry out the cultural functions (see Exhibit 2.1). The basic approach follows a strongly results-oriented model attributed to Kirkpatrick:[17]

1. *Reactions:* The leaders should be satisfied with the development activities they are offered.

2. *Learning:* The leaders should be able to recite what they have been taught.

3. *Transfer:* The leaders should be able to apply the learning.
4. *Results:* The learning should improve mission achievement measured in the unit's operational scorecard.

The Kirkpatrick model assumes that any investment in training must ultimately be justified by mission achievement. The central measure of leadership is the accomplishment of the goals of the six operating dimensions, as shown in Exhibit 2.4. Put simply, leaders are judged by their results. The Kirkpatrick model implies that any culture getting good mission results is a good culture. It also implies that if mission results are unsatisfactory, the culture should always be considered as one possible cause.

The leadership development course or program associated with the measures shown in Exhibit 2.4 requires the administration of ongoing surveys to evaluate participant reaction and learning. Two different surveys of the associate group must be conducted. One scores the satisfaction of associates, separating leaders from team members. The second, called the **360-degree survey** or **multi-rater review**, assesses leaders' skills as seen by subordinates, peers and colleagues (e.g., suppliers), and superiors. The results of the two surveys, shown below, enable evaluation of performance for each leader and the collective leadership team.

360-degree or multi-rater review
Formal evaluation of performance by subordinates, superiors, and peers of the individual or unit

1. *Reactions and learning can be assessed for most of the training and other programs that support each function.* For instance, associates completing orientation can be asked to recite the mission, vision, and values to display their knowledge. Leaders completing training programs can be asked to report their satisfaction and be tested on content. Also, clients can be surveyed to assess the skills of their counselors or mentors.
2. *Transfer, or ability to apply the components of the leadership culture, can be assessed by surveys of associates and by observation.* All associates, including leaders, participate in a satisfaction survey at least annually. The opinions of each leader's subordinates, along with anonymous comments, are a basic rating of leadership skills. Retention, absenteeism, and work-related injury are known to be influenced by leadership skill. Scores below those of peers or benchmarks are OFIs that can be addressed by retraining, counseling, or mentoring.

    The 360-degree or multirater review is a critical part of the transfer assessment. Skilled interpretation is important, but the process provides valuable feedback. The measured performance should be supplemented by counseling.
3. *Mission-related results are assessed through the unit operational measures.* Making an inference from the results must be done with care, but the question "Is this OFI related to weaknesses in our culture and leadership?" is always legitimate to ask. Review of transfer assessments and other OFIs often suggests the answer. The suggestion can be tested by corrective action on a trial-and-error basis.

EXHIBIT 2.4
Measures of
Leadership
Functions

Input Oriented	*Output Oriented*
Demand	*Output and productivity*
Counts of new hires and promotions; goal is 100% new-leader participation	Counts of program attendance and completion are routine
	Direct cost per leader served is a productivity measure that can be benchmarked
Cost and resources	
Direct costs of programs are measured and reported by human resources	*Quality*
	Quality of training programs is assessed by survey, examination, observation, and later job performance
Total cost of leadership development is difficult to estimate because many developmental activities are integrated into other work	360-degree reviews directly measure leader capability
Human resources	*Customer satisfaction*
Leader retention is expected; each leader departure is reviewed and analyzed	Associate satisfaction, retention, absenteeism, and work-related lost time measure the leader's effectiveness
Leader satisfaction is assessed by survey	All measures of unit performance reflect on leadership

Exhibit 2.5 shows how the leadership measures are used in a service excellence context. Several important inferences are made here. Although these are often documented in actual applications, they are not proven causal links. In real life, they may not always work. Step 2 is where careful judgment must be used. For example, an operating unit is below benchmark on quality, productivity, or patient satisfaction, creating a mission-related OFI. A root cause question is, "Can the OFI be achieved by improving the culture?" The answer is indicated by the measures of associate satisfaction, retention, absenteeism, and safety.

If none of these is below the comparable units, the answer is probably negative. Something else is the root cause. If a few are below, a retraining or improvement effort for the unit leader may be in order as a trial-and-error solution. The greatest risk of error lies in the possibility of an overlooked factor: Perhaps both the mission achievement and the associate response are attributable not to leadership but to a poorly designed work process. The professional response is to ask two further questions at step 3: How good is the evidence supporting the assumption that leadership is improvable? What other possible causes might be contributing to the OFI? These questions increase the probability of finding the true root cause.

EXHIBIT 2.5
Relating
Leadership
and Culture
to Mission
Achievement

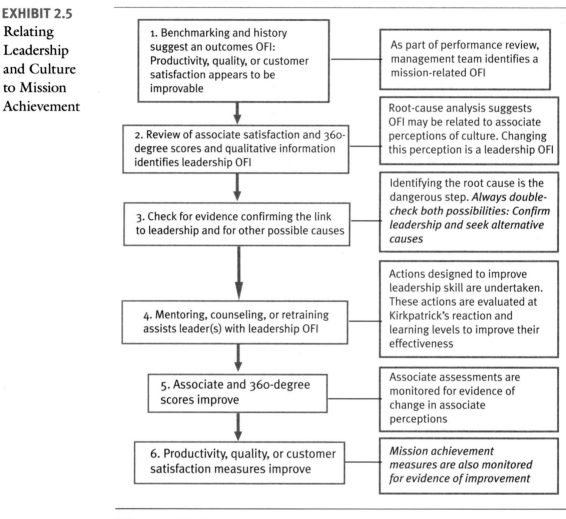

1. Benchmarking and history suggest an outcomes OFI: Productivity, quality, or customer satisfaction appears to be improvable

As part of performance review, management team identifies a mission-related OFI

2. Review of associate satisfaction and 360-degree scores and qualitative information identifies leadership OFI

Root-cause analysis suggests OFI may be related to associate perceptions of culture. Changing this perception is a leadership OFI

3. Check for evidence confirming the link to leadership and for other possible causes

Identifying the root cause is the dangerous step. *Always double-check both possibilities: Confirm leadership and seek alternative causes*

4. Mentoring, counseling, or retraining assists leader(s) with leadership OFI

Actions designed to improve leadership skill are undertaken. These actions are evaluated at Kirkpatrick's reaction and learning levels to improve their effectiveness

5. Associate and 360-degree scores improve

Associate assessments are monitored for evidence of change in associate perceptions

6. Productivity, quality, or customer satisfaction measures improve

Mission achievement measures are also monitored for evidence of improvement

OFI: opportunity for improvement

Assessing Leaders as Individuals

Each leader has an annual 360-degree or multi-rater review—subjective evaluation by his or her superior, peers, and subordinates—to supplement the measures of unit performance. These evaluations may be supplemented with detailed competency self-assessments, such as those developed by the National Center for Healthcare Leadership and the Healthcare Leadership Alliance, which allow individuals to compare their skills with those demonstrated by successful managers.[18]

These results are then reviewed by the leader and his superior to create a professional development plan—a program that uses a mix of mentoring, special assignments, and continuing education to identify and address OFIs. For example, an early-career leader's development plan may include one or more senior mentors, an assignment to a PIT or task force in charge of an issue outside the leader's day-to-day responsibilities, and a course in process analysis such as Six Sigma. A senior leader's plan may involve a coach from outside the organization, membership on the board of a small not-for-profit, and advanced leadership education from a university.

Leaders are held accountable for their professional development plans and for assisting less-experienced leaders in advancing their careers. Many organizations put a premium on diversity, seeking to advance underrepresented groups, including women, to higher management levels. The goal of this effort is to incorporate the demographic characteristics of the community into the organizational hierarchy.

Ensuring Leadership Continuity

Leadership vacancies are created through attrition, retirement, or organizational growth. They can occur suddenly, and they can seriously disrupt organizational performance. A **leadership succession plan** is a systematic process for evaluating the leadership requirements for each position, identifying potential candidates for those positions, and prompting the candidates to develop the skills necessary for being successful in higher-level roles. Its primary purpose is to fill leadership vacancies with available internal talents. The succession plan is periodically updated; at the senior levels, it is reviewed and approved by the governing board. Exhibit 2.6 shows the package of leadership function assessment, individual leadership plans, and succession plans used by high-performing HCOs to maintain and improve their leadership group.

Leadership succession plan
A written plan for replacing people who depart from management positions

The succession plan is relatively easy to create. Each leader identifies and rank-orders two or three candidates among her direct reports whom she deems qualified to be her successor; then, each candidate's personal development plan is reviewed and developed in preparation for the eventual opportunity. However, the process does raise some complex issues:

- The plan implies that the HCO expects its leaders to be promoted, rather than remain at one level. When a vacant position is filled, the internal candidates who are not selected may leave. The HCO will have invested in their development, and they may join competitors.
- Associates not included on the potential candidates list may demand an explanation for why they were not chosen.

General Electric (GE), a company frequently cited for its succession and leadership development strategies, exemplifies these issues. In 2001, GE publicly identified three candidates as successors to the retiring CEO, Jack Welch. When Jeffrey Immelt was selected for the post, the other two candidates left the company. GE invests heavily in leadership development, and its leaders compete for learning opportunities and positions on the succession plans. These leaders are highly attractive to other companies at all levels.[19]

EXHIBIT 2.6 A Comprehensive Leadership Management Program

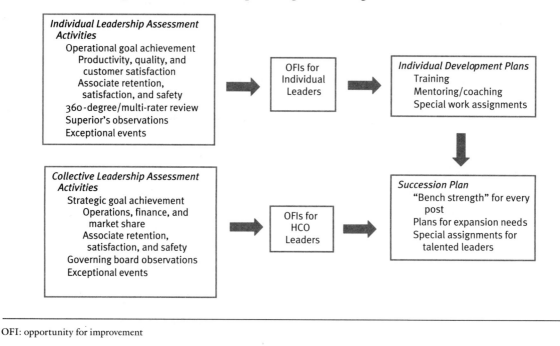

OFI: opportunity for improvement

Despite these concerns, the succession plan is strongly endorsed as good practice. The program has several important features:

- It tends to attract "the best and the brightest."
- It rewards learning and achievement.
- It builds a culture of "a great place to give care" that supports the retention of not only more people but also more capable people than alternative approaches, in spite of these issues.

Managerial Issues

The transformational culture and the leadership functions described in this chapter are universal among HCOs that report high performance. No other model is documented as successful. As best can be judged, as of 2010 transformational culture is not common in American HCOs. Neither is it simple to establish or maintain. It demands a drastic shift in behavior and attitudes of some old-school managers, and a commitment to learning and change.

For HCOs today, the most critical managerial question is, "What's the path from tradition to transformation?" For HCOs that have become transformational, at least three strategies may prevent an erosion of success: maintaining the ethical foundation, resolving disagreements, and protecting against destructive behavior.

Starting the Path to Transformational Culture

Many HCOs are "pretty good." That is, they have no crisis problems, and their associates are hard working and committed to doing a good job. But these HCOs do not measure everything, and without measures, their goal-setting and continuous improvement efforts lag. Benchmarks, when they discover them, are eye-openers. Their culture could be described as "benign." They wouldn't disagree with Sharp's behavior standards and "Must Haves," but unlike Sharp, they don't insist upon them. They think communicating is a great idea, but unlike Bronson, they don't have a neat list of 34 specific things they do, and why they do them (see Exhibit 1.8). That's where most of the known high-performing organizations started, and where most HCOs are likely to start.

How does a "pretty good" HCO move to excellence? The following strategy is a place to start:

1. They restate and re-commit to their mission, vision, and values. They use the visioning process to build broad consensus on purposes. Dozens or hundreds of stakeholders participate in this process. They come to express their opinions, but also come to understand the meaning and support behind the words themselves.[20]
2. The senior management team examines its own attitudes and behaviors and agrees unanimously to the effort.
3. The governing board adopts the concepts of the reinvigorated vision and accepts the challenge to move to excellence, recognizing that the changes will be profound. The board sets milestones and anticipated completion dates.
4. The senior leaders begin to spread the new culture by changing their behavior to reflect servant leadership.
5. As the senior leaders "cruise and connect," they seek ways to demonstrate the power of a transformational culture and look for teams to help with pilots and demonstration sites.
6. The success of pilots and demonstrations is widely celebrated and used to show the nature of the new culture and the HCO's commitment to it.
7. Mentoring, modeling, and training are used to develop managers into leaders.
8. The operational foundation and strategic protections are developed to support continuous improvement and evidence-based management.

The success of this strategy depends on two conditions. The first is that consistent commitment must be made. Many HCOs are afflicted with the flavor-of-the-month approach to improvement: This year, it is Lean, and next year, it will be servant leadership; everyone knows the year after it will be something different. Transformational management is not an annual, it's a perennial. It takes time to grow, but its rewards are continuous. Senior management's examination of its own attitudes and behaviors (step 2 above) must be diligent for at least three years. The transformational commitment must not be abandoned, even when the HCO institutes other programs.

The second condition is the simultaneous move to strengthen the operational foundation and evidence-based management. It is the subject of Chapter 3. Leadership is important. Transformational culture is essential. Results require solid work processes. Even if I think my boss is great and the team is the best I have ever worked with, it is tough to improve if the staff is always short-handed, the laundry is missing, and the record is unreliable. The operational foundation addresses these details.

Maintaining the Ethical Foundation

The mission, vision, and values are inherently moral statements. Patient care is recognized as a virtue by most of the world's religions. The stakeholders' commitment to mission and values is an extension of that virtue. But the day-to-day pursuit of servant leadership, continuous improvement, and stakeholder satisfaction inevitably reaches challenging ethical frontiers, causing troubling and difficult concerns for some stakeholders.

These concerns have no easy solutions: "Should our mission be community health or excellence in care?" (see Exhibit 1.7), "Is it right to pay bonuses?" and "What are patients' end-of-life rights?" Answering them requires a clear understanding of the ethical foundations underpinning not just HCOs, but our culture. Senior management and governance leadership in particular need that understanding.

The ethical foundation of transformational management is rooted in a utilitarian, post-Enlightenment moral philosophy. It drives most policy in the United States and is reflected in the Declaration of Independence:

> that all men are created equal, that they are endowed by their Creator with certain unalienable rights, that among these are life, liberty and the pursuit of happiness. That to secure these rights, governments are instituted among men, deriving their just powers from the consent of the governed.

These bold assertions took centuries to implement, but we have as a nation clearly established that "men" is to be read as "persons," without regard to race or gender. Servant leadership is shorthand for "deriving their just powers from the consent of the governed." As noted in Chapter 1, the rights of life, liberty, and pursuit of happiness lead to obligations of autonomy, non-maleficence, beneficence, and justice that underpin the ethical commitments of the caregiving professions. The Institute of Medicine reaffirmed these commitments when it established the universal goals of healthcare: safe, effective, patient-centered, timely, efficient, and equitable.[21]

The ethical foundations are supported by laws and regulations that reflect formal stakeholder consensus. Various laws and regulations speak to obligations, conflict of interest, and transparency of information (e.g., federal acts covering employment practices, emergency care, confidentiality, compensation, and accounting practices). Professional HCO leaders and managers, like professional caregivers, are expected to adhere to professional codes of conduct, such as the American College of Healthcare Executives *Code of Ethics*.[22] The commitment to empiricism also stems from enlightenment thought. Evidence-based medicine and evidence-based management are simply recent adaptations of the scientific method that arose in the seventeenth century. It means that the search for facts drives all analytic and improvement activity.

Excellent HCO cultures systematically help their associates follow these codes by developing and implementing policies and procedures that promote ethical decision making. Their training programs reflect both the spirit and letter of regulation. Their policies are carefully checked for compliance. Many have compliance officers who are assigned full-time to that task. Their servant leadership structure offers ready assistance when ethical questions arise, as they frequently do in healthcare.

Consistent support of these values is essential. Leaders are required to model ethical behavior. Sharp's insistence on its associates' adherence to standard attitudes and behaviors reflects the importance of consistency. Associates are entitled to wonder if the organization is sincere; if leaders do not follow through consistently, a climate of doubt develops and the culture deteriorates. Reinforcing the desired behavior is also important, and opportunities to do so arise frequently. Team leaders can reassure and comfort caregivers who have faced particularly demanding situations. Extra efforts can be reported by anybody, using "Caught in the Act" cards.

Organizational **ethics committees**, which began as support for clinicians facing difficult issues related to individual patients, have expanded their role to advise on broader ethical issues. In HCOs undertaking research, the ethics committee is complemented by an institutional review board, which monitors ethical issues in research and approves research protocols for involving patients or associates. The ethics committee strives for membership that reflects stakeholder concerns, often drawing on ethicists, managers, clinicians, patient representatives, and local religious leaders. Ethical decision-making tools identify and involve all stakeholders of an ethical conflict in determining root causes and implementing approaches that reduce their occurrence and associated costs. Some evidence suggests that having an ethics committee is highly cost effective because an unresolved ethical concern reduces the effectiveness and efficiency of the treatment process.[23]

Ethics committee

A standing multidisciplinary committee that is concerned with biomedical ethical issues and decision-making processes, formulation of policies, and review and consultation of medical ethical issues

The ethical foundation is especially sensitive to, and must be protected from, unethical behavior. "Everybody does it" is an easy excuse for all kinds of unacceptable activity. It must be countered promptly with "but not around here." Senior management commitment to enforcement is essential. Enforcement of ethical rules is deliberately divorced from training programs and consultation opportunities. Instead, it is carried out as part of the strategic protection audit activities, although compliance officers have dual roles of consultation and enforcement. Excellent HCOs view violations of individual rights and the regulations established to protect them as extremely serious. Deliberate violation is often grounds for immediate discharge.

Resolving Fundamental Disagreements

The transformational culture emphasizes negotiations to allow stakeholders to seek the solutions best for all. The program of negotiation, described earlier, is deliberately designed to identify and resolve differences of opinion as quickly as is consistent with stakeholder rights. Negotiating in this manner is effective; it not only resolves many concerns and disputes but it reassures associates that independent thought is desirable behavior, and if it leads to dispute the path to resolution is reasonable. Many common disagreements are ironed out by *first-response negotiation*. Some issues, however, are deeply imbedded and thus require more attention; these are usually addressed by senior management and governing board members.

What might be called the *appeals process* is driven by the following agreed-upon principles:

1. *Equity, not equality, drives the organization's ultimate position.* Under an equity concept, each stakeholder is treated fairly in terms of his or her contribution. Under an equality concept, each is treated equally.[24] While the definition of contribution is never easy, the concept forces participants to recognize realistic differences in influence.

2. *Evidence drives the decisions.* Objective measurement trumps tradition, status, and opinion. What is best for the patient is what is scientifically determined to be best. What is realistic for the associate is the best the associate can expect elsewhere.

3. *Negotiation is improved by patience, listening, and imagination.* Many apparent conflicts are actually misunderstandings. Careful listening expands understanding and reveals consensus opportunities. Imagination—thinking outside the box—identifies new opportunities to resolve apparently conflicting needs.

4. *Stakeholders and associates are free to terminate their relationship with the organization; conversely, the group can terminate its relationship with any stakeholder.* The usual goal for everyone is to retain and strengthen relationships, but it is occasionally necessary for some people to seek separate paths.

5. *The governing board's calendar ultimately forces a decision.* The calendar itself is set for the good of the whole, and it is always subject to negotiation and amendment. Again, for the good of the whole, the organization must appropriately, as Hamlet says, "take arms against a sea of troubles, and thus opposing, end them."[25]

Perhaps the most important of these is number five. It states that no single stakeholder, or stakeholder group, can hold the majority hostage. Even disassociation, reconfiguration, or closure is at some point superior to continued dispute, and it is the obligation of the governance structure, described in Chapter 4, to identify when that is so. Disputes rarely reach this level, but it is important to the long-run success of the transformational culture that such an outcome is a realistic, if remote, possibility.

Protecting Against Destructive Behavior

The core issue in dispute resolution is to protect the HCO against a minority stakeholder group with seriously divergent goals or against individuals with intentions to impair the organization. Protection begins with a security system (see Chapter 12). It includes strategic protections (see Chapter 1), particularly the multistep corrective action process for associates. An individual whose values or actions are in serious conflict with the organization is warned, offered retraining, warned again, and, if necessary, terminated. As are the final steps of dispute resolution, the final steps of corrective action are rarely necessary.

Suggested Readings

Collins, J. C. 2001. *Good to Great: Why Some Companies Make the Leap...and Others Don't.* New York: HarperBusiness.

Dye, C. F., and A. N. Garman. 2006. *Exceptional Leadership: 16 Critical Competencies for Healthcare Executives.* Chicago: Health Administration Press.

Kouzes, J. M., and B. Z. Posner. 2007. *The Leadership Challenge,* 4th ed. San Francisco: Jossey-Bass.

Lee, B. D., and J. W. Herring. 2008. *Growing Leaders in Healthcare: Lessons from the Corporate World.* Chicago: Health Administration Press.

Pfeffer, J., and R. I. Sutton. 2006. *Hard Facts, Dangerous Half-Truths, and Total Nonsense: Profiting from Evidence-Based Management.* Boston: Harvard Business School Press.

Shortell, S. M., and A. D. Kaluzny. 2006. *Health Care Management: Organizational, Design and Behavior,* 5th ed. Clifton Park, NY: Delmar Cengage Learning.

Notes

1. Kouzes, J. M., and B. Z. Posner. 2007. *The Leadership Challenge,* 4th ed. San Francisco: Jossey-Bass.
2. Greenleaf, R. K. 2002. *Servant Leadership: A Journey into the Nature of Legitimate Power and Greatness,* edited by L. C. Spears. New York: Paulist Press.
3. Washington, R. R. 2007. "Empirical Relationships Between Theories of Servant, Transformational, and Transactional Leadership." *Academy of Management Proceedings,* pp. 1–6.
4. Mercy Health System Malcolm Baldrige National Quality Award application. 2007. [Online information; retrieved 12/16/08.] www.baldrige.nist.gov/Contacts_Profiles.htm.

5. Lowe, K. B., K. G. Kroeck, and N. Sivasubramaniam. 1996. "Effectiveness Correlates of Transformational and Transactional Leadership: A Meta-Analytic Review of the MLQ Literature." *Leadership Quarterly* 7: 385–425.

6. Gilmartin, M. J., and T. A. D'Aunno. 2007. "Leadership Research in Healthcare." *Academy of Management Annals* 2: 394–96.

7. Sharp HealthCare Malcolm Baldrige National Quality Award application. 2007. [Online information, Preface i-ii; retrieved 12/16/08.] www.baldrige.nist.gov/Contacts_Profiles.htm.

8. *Ibid.*, p. 1.

9. The precept is fundamental in most religions, in most moral philosophy (including Immanuel Kant and John Rawls), and in most judicial systems.

10. Hill, L. A. 2004. "New Manager Development for the 21st Century." *Academy of Management Executive* 18 (3): 121–26 [124].

11. Gilmartin, M. J., and T. A. D'Aunno. 2008. "Leadership Research in Healthcare." *Academy of Management Annals* 2: 397.

12. Dye, C. F., and A. N. Garman. 2006. *Exceptional Leadership: 16 Critical Competencies for Healthcare Executives.* Chicago: Health Administration Press.

13. White, K. R., and J. W. Begun. 2006. "Preceptor and Employer Evaluation of Health Administration Student Competencies." *Journal of Health Administration Education* 23 (1): 53–64.

14. Gilmartin, M. J., and T. A. D'Aunno. 2008. "Leadership Research in Healthcare." *Academy of Management Annals* 2: 397.

15. Hill, L. A. 2004. "New Manager Development for the 21st Century." *Academy of Management Executives* 18 (3): 121–26 [122–24].

16. Conger, J. A. 2004. "Developing Leadership Capability: What's Inside the Black Box?" *Academy of Management Executive* 18 (3): 136–41 [138].

17. San Diego State University. *Encyclopedia of Educational Technology.* [Online information; retrieved 6/9/09.] http://coe.sdsu.edu/eet/articles/k4levels/index.htm.

18. National Center for Healthcare Leadership. [Online information; retrieved 3/11/09.] www.nchl.org/ns/programs/LDS_10_25_06.pdf; Healthcare Leadership Alliance. [Online information; retrieved 3/11/09.]. www.healthcareleadershipalliance.org/directory.htm.

19. See the General Electric website (particularly www.ge.com/company/culture/leadership_learning.html) and GE's case studies (e.g., Slater, R. 2000. *The GE Way Fieldbook—Jack Welch's Battle Plan for Corporate Revolution.* New York: McGraw-Hill).

20. Ryan, M. J. 2004. "Achieving and Sustaining Quality in Healthcare." *Frontiers of Health Services Management* 20 (3): 3–11.

21. Institute of Medicine, Committee on Quality Health Care in America. 2001. *Crossing the Quality Chasm: A New Health System for the 21st Century*, p. 39. Washington, DC: National Academies Press.

22. American College of Healthcare Executives. 2009. [Online information; retrieved 6/10/09.] www.ache.org/ABT_ACHE/code.cfm.

23. Nelson, W. A., W. B. Weeks, and J. M. Campfield. 2008. "The Organizational Costs of Ethical Conflicts." *Journal of Healthcare Management* 53 (1): 41–53.

24. Phillips, R. 2003. *Stakeholder Theory and Organizational Ethics*, 85–118. San Francisco: Berret Koehler Publishers.

25. Shakespeare, W. *Hamlet*, Act 3, Scene 1.

3 OPERATIONAL LEADERSHIP

In a Few Words

Evidence-based management requires an effective operational infrastructure whose purpose is to ensure that the healthcare organization's (HCO) array of services is effectively designed, aligned, integrated, and continuously improved. Organizational leaders, particularly senior management, must perform five functions to achieve that purpose:

1. *Boundary spanning.* Monitor all external stakeholder groups to identify changes in their needs and desires. Forecast the need for services, the number of services to be supplied, and the size of these services.

2. *Knowledge management.* Ensure that each individual and team has prompt, complete, and reliable information for achieving their goals.

3. *Accountability and corporate design.* Establish explicit expectations of every team, and assemble an integrated array that optimally meets community needs.

4. *Continuous improvement.* Pursue opportunities for improvement (OFIs), set goals, and implement improvement in a timely and coordinated fashion.

5. *Sustaining and improving.* Ensure that the infrastructure is continuously improved.

The operational infrastructure must be developed in parallel with the transformational culture. It requires a strong system of logistic and strategic support services to meet the needs of the caregiving teams.

Critical Issues in Operational Leadership

1. *Maintaining contact with all stakeholder groups.* Conduct surveys, listen, and hold formal meetings to ensure a balanced, timely flow of information from external to internal stakeholders.

2. *Sizing the organization and its components.* Use the epidemiologic planning model to size clinical and other units to meet clinical needs.

3. *Measuring and reporting performance.* Maintain a system of complete, timely performance measures and benchmarks.

4. *Supporting a learning organization.* Maintain consultation and training services to meet all performance improvement needs.

5. *Resolving issues in a timely manner, and adhering to an annual calendar.* Use the board's authority to limit negotiations and prevent unnecessary delay.

Consider these questions as you read the chapter.

1. How would a first-line leader act to fulfill the purpose and functions of operational leadership in her area? What operational topics would you include in a training program for new leaders? For example, what responsibility does a head nurse have for boundary spanning? For planning the size of her service? How does she discharge these responsibilities?

2. How does the senior leadership team know that it has filled the purpose and functions of operational leadership well? How do individual senior leaders evaluate their own contribution?

3. Exhibit 3.4 and the section on organization design suggest that the traditional organization table, reflecting the accountability hierarchy, has diminished in importance and that the hierarchy now connotes "resources and support." If that is true, how are the activities of multiple teams coordinated? For example, trace the ways an organization coordinates patient meals or the rules an inpatient care unit needs to function effectively. How are those rules negotiated? Why can the inpatient unit rely on these rules, and what if the unit cannot? Does it matter whether food service is provided by employed associates or by a contracting company?

4. Senior management is having a hard time with step 5C of Exhibit 3.7. It is now mid-May, and the operating scorecards do not align with the strategic scorecard. What options do they have? What is the best way to proceed?

5. "Physicians . . . are crucial to . . . overall success" (page 97). Why is this so? If it is so, name some good steps for senior management to take with the medical staff?

Chapter 1 describes the excellent HCO as an array of teams empowered, assisted, and rewarded for seeking excellence in their activity. The teams must be aligned and integrated; the whole must be as effective as the parts. Alignment and integration demand a common culture (Chapter 2), and a common infrastructure of processes, and rules that facilitate the solutions to complex problems. The infrastructure (or operational foundation) is essential to strategic scorecard success. It keeps the HCO and its mission consistent with stakeholder needs. It ensures that every team receives support services. It generates a consistent approach, deployed across many different teams, that allows the teams to learn, improve, and collaborate in producing a superior overall product.[1] The infrastructure is systematically sustained by specific actions of senior management. This chapter describes those actions. Like other components of the HCO, the infrastructure itself is measured and improved.

Purpose

The purpose of operational leadership is

> **to sustain an infrastructure to ensure that the HCO's array of services is effectively designed, aligned, integrated, and continuously improved.**

Effective design emphasizes having all the services the market needs, but not those the organization cannot properly support. Effective alignment rests on a uniform approach to culture, training, and communication. Effective integration requires shared information and collective goal setting. Continuous improvement requires a common mission, capital allocation, and a reward system.

The operational infrastructure implements evidence-based management. It supports a measured, protocol-driven clinical system; stresses continuous improvement; systematically explores the external environment; and implements through organizational units: how they will be sized, located, measured, and coordinated and how they will interact and be improved. Its success is improvement of the strategic measures. It complements and is equally essential with as the purpose of cultural leadership: To sustain an environment where every associate is empowered and motivated to meet his or her customers' needs (see Chapter 2).

The operational infrastructure is a large and expensive component of most HCOs. It includes all the logistic and strategic support activities described in chapters 10 through 15. It is managed by senior management, which establishes the direction, importance, and implementation of these activities. Senior management stimulates the widespread use of these activities; more important, it aggregates the information into an ongoing strategic process fitting the HCO to its environment.

Functions

To implement the operational infrastructure, senior management returns conceptually to the basic contribution of the organization, fulfilling needs that the stakeholders cannot fulfill by themselves, and improves the processes for reaching decisions rather than focusing on the decisions themselves. When these processes are aligned, the chances of correct decisions—those that optimize the long-run contribution to the mission—are maximized. The functions shown in Exhibit 3.1 ensure that alignment is reached between the HCO and its stakeholders.

Boundary Spanning

Long-term survival requires ongoing adaptation to changes in the environment. Surveillance identifies the OFIs that arise from those changes. Planning analyses translate the OFIs to quantitative forecasts and explicit business plans that the governing board can weigh and adopt. Effective boundary spanning means that a specific plan is created for every existing and proposed unit of the HCO and for all critical resources, including funds, caregivers, facilities, and information. These plans must stretch far enough into the future to allow orderly adaptation to change.

Surveillance Stakeholder needs change, and any unmet stakeholder need can ultimately impair excellence. Technology, population changes, attitudes, caregiver shortages, financing mechanisms, and regulations drive change in healthcare. Processes that worked well last year will require a redesign to work next year. HCOs that fail to adapt to changing needs fade and disappear, sometimes with surprising speed. Beyond redesign of internal processes, the HCO is an important citizen in the community and, as such, should participate in community-related discussions about issues such as income, education, health, safety, and needs of the disadvantaged.

HCO customer stakeholders expect progress, but also continuity and stability. More than other service industries, the community HCO is expected to keep pace with changes in the environment rather than to be replaced by a new model. This emphasis on long-term survival is promoted by the not-for-profit corporate structure, which is more difficult to dismantle than stock corporations or partnerships, and by tax exemptions that give not-for-profit HCOs a competitive advantage. HCOs' actual life spans reflect this. Many of America's hospitals have century or more histories, much longer than public stock corporations.

Identifying and rank-ordering the OFIs that arise from external change require an ongoing system of listening to and negotiating with customers. Members of the governing board (see Chapter 4) are selected, in part, to be aware of many stakeholder constituencies. Its members and senior management are expected to keep current on state and national developments

EXHIBIT 3.1

Functions That Sustain Operational Infrastructure

Function	Intent	Implementation	Examples
Boundary spanning	Monitor all external stakeholder groups to identify changes in their needs and desires Forecast patient needs to plan staffing and facilities	Governing board members, senior executives, and other managers solicit stakeholder perspectives and describe HCO opportunities Ongoing market analysis identifies trends in patient and associate needs Epidemiologic planning model sizes all clinical units	Board members selected for prior community service Senior managers participate in community services such as education and housing; monitor state and national developments that could affect the HCO Quantified plans for services, facilities, and personnel reflect trends in community need
Knowledge management	Provide prompt, complete, and reliable information for any associate or team purpose	Strong clinical and business information systems, widespread access, and a culture of communication Training for repetitive tasks Just-in-time training for arising tasks	Automated patient record and access to clinical information E-mail and intranet Readily accessible data warehouse with operational measures, goals, benchmarks, and current achievements
Accountability and corporate design	Establish explicit expectations of every team Provide an integrated array that optimally meets community needs	Expectations and accountability are established and integrated in the annual goal-setting process Corporate structures such as subsidiaries, joint ventures, and strategic partnerships support a broad scope of healthcare activities, including primary, acute, and post-acute care	90-day plans used to reach agreed-on goals HCO includes primary and continuing care services, forms joint ventures with medical staff, and merges with another HCO HCO organizes caregiving teams into service lines and makes effective clinical support services available
Continuous improvement	Improve measured performance Reach decisions in a timely and coordinated fashion	PITs develop improved processes, guided by a PIC, which coordinates and integrates improvements PITs and goal-setting process follow a quarterly and annual calendar	The annual goal-setting and budgeting activities proceed according to a prearranged timetable initiated and finished by governing board action PITs are scheduled to complete their work in time to coordinate with budget deadlines
Sustaining and improving the operational infrastructure	Improve the operational and strategic foundations	Sessions of the governing board and senior management meetings are devoted to review of infrastructure effectiveness measures, identification of OFIs, and development of improvements	Annual goal-setting process improved, additional performance measures installed and benchmarked Expanded strategic protection Expanded analytic and training support for PITs

OFI: opportunities for improvement; PIC: performance improvement council; PIT: process improvement team

that might affect the HCO. Associates are encouraged to participate and assume leadership roles in community activities beyond healthcare. Marketing surveys and customer-listening activities cover a broad spectrum of current and potential customers and target specific groups with unique needs. Senior management meets often with community groups and managers of other services. Much time is spent exploring what stakeholders like and do not like, how serious their concerns are, and which alternatives are attractive. This knowledge allows process improvement teams (PITs) and planning teams to formulate proposals that meet a broader spectrum of stakeholder needs. The inputs from systematic listening often form the difference between a successful proposal and a contentious negotiation.

The program that helps Sharp HealthCare relate to the San Diego community is one example. Sharp, a 2007 recipient of the Malcolm Baldrige National Quality Award (MBNQA), claims its "involvement in San Diego's well-being is comprehensive":

- When key community health issues or new health threats are identified, Sharp collaborates with appropriate public officials for safe, evidence-based, patient-centered, timely, efficient, and equitable resolution.
- Sharp's leaders serve as board members on many community organizations.
- Sharp's comprehensive environmental, health, and safety management program, including emergency/disaster management, ensures a safe and secure environment for customers/partners.
- Staff and leaders present a strong showing of support and participation each year in community fundraisers.
- Sharp hosts many free community preventive health offerings, such as flu shots, lectures, and screenings.
- Sharp offers the Weight Management Health Education program providing health maintenance to employers and employees and free, weekly programs to the community.
- Additionally, managers are encouraged to donate a minimum of 22,000 collective hours annually to community service.[2]

Effective boundary spanning, as shown in Exhibit 3.2, has four requirements:

1. A network of listening activities must be established so that the HCO has entrance into and recognition with specific stakeholder groups.
2. Trust must be established and common values recognized, so that the stakeholders are candid and comfortable with discussing complex topics.
3. Associates must be trained to hear accurately what the stakeholders are saying and to represent the HCO's perspective.
4. The knowledge gained from dozens of individual contacts must be systematically assembled, analyzed, and integrated.

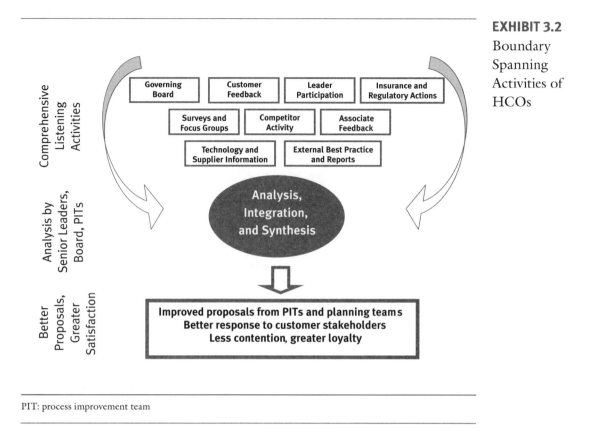

EXHIBIT 3.2
Boundary
Spanning
Activities of
HCOs

PIT: process improvement team

Excellent HCOs achieve these components by consistently pursuing listening opportunities, repeatedly demonstrating their commitment to values, training their associates, and systematically assembling and reviewing notes from contacts. The results serve as a rich source of OFIs and a valuable background for improving all kinds of internal processes.

Planning Services Using Forecasts of Need and Demand

All healthcare services are ultimately delivered by specialized teams and facilities. The success of the HCO depends on the correct sizing of those teams and facilities. Each service offered must be large enough to meet needs and operate effectively, but not larger. The array of services must meet community needs without exceeding the available funds. It must be carefully based on population and market trends, compared to available funds and performance benchmarks, and evaluated relative to alternative investments. Some services are referred to distant HCOs, as the local community does not generate enough demand to support them. Many important decisions must be made months or years in advance. To solve this problem, high-performing HCOs use an **epidemiologic planning model**, a tool that forecasts the number of patients who require a specific service. The elements of the model are shown in Exhibit 3.3.

Epidemiologic planning model
A statistical analysis and forecast of the health needs of the community served

EXHIBIT 3.3
Elements of the
Epidemiologic
Planning
Model

For any specific clinical service

Question	Solution	Example
What population will use the service?	People live in small geographic areas. The population of these areas is measured and forecast by the U.S. Census Bureau.	Births for Ann Arbor, Michigan, and surrounding areas
What part of that population is at risk for needing the service?	The risk of a disease is dependent on age, genetics, income, and lifestyle. These factors are used to forecast demand.	Births are a function of the number of females by age and certain socioeconomic characteristics
What part of the population at risk will select our service?	Historical data and surveys estimate the fraction of those with the disease who seek care from our team (market share).	Women in and around Ann Arbor choose between two obstetrics services. Home deliveries and travel to other services are rare.
How many specialized people will we need to meet this demand?	Protocols and historical and benchmark data show the number of patients an individual provider can successfully treat.	Each of the obstetrics services must establish the numbers of obstetricians, family practitioners, midwives, registered nurses, and other caregivers required.
How big a facility will we need to meet this demand?	History, benchmarks, and simulation models show how many rooms and specialized facilities will be required.	The 2012 University of Michigan obstetrics delivery service will have "50 single room maternity care beds in the Birth Center"*

*Information from the University of Michigan Health System, C. S. Mott Hospital. 2008. [Online information; retrieved 4/21/09.] www.med.umich.edu/mott/touch/new_facts.html.

The epidemiologic planning model draws on five major sources of data to produce forecasts of the proper size and staffing for a specific service:

1. *Population.* Unbiased population forecasts for states are prepared by the U.S. Census Bureau. These forecasts must be translated to small areas, minor civil divisions, or postal codes. Most HCOs draw patients from a few dozen areas and heavily from only a few. Both the counts and the characteristics of the small areas must be forecast at least a decade into the future.

2. *Disease risk.* This is estimated based on population characteristics. Large databases of hospital admissions, specific treatments, drug usage, and other

indicators are used to identify the risk of occurrence of specific medical needs, which are measured by

- Incidence: the number of new cases in the population in a given period;
- Prevalence: the number of cases at a point in time; and
- Demand: the number of cases that actually sought service.

By dividing the population into small, homogeneous groups (e.g., white males, aged 40–65 years, earning between $50,000 and $75,000 per year, with post–high school education) and analyzing patterns of incidence of common diseases for these groups, precise estimates of incidence, prevalence, and demand can be made.

3. *Market share.* This is the fraction of the total demand that will seek care at a specific HCO. Patients have choices for most services, such as selecting a local competitor, traveling to a larger HCO, or deferring care. Surveys and historic usage data are used to estimate market share. Market share is forecast subjectively, on the basis of the HCO's ability to retain or increase its attractiveness to patients.

4. *Staff requirements.* These are estimated on the basis of the capacity of each skill level required. Capacity is measured by history, survey, and benchmark. Requirements for physicians by specialty, registered nurses, other nursing personnel, and total personnel are forecast for each service. These are compared against intentions of current staff to identify recruitment needs.

5. *Facility requirements.* These are estimated on the basis of the numbers of patients expected and the length of time they will require service plus allowances for idle time. Allowances are as small as feasible, given the need to not turn patients away and to meet patient and associate schedules. Allowances differ by service, and they significantly increase the physical capacity required. Some services, such as newborn delivery and emergency cardiac catheterization, cannot be delayed. Allowance must be made to meet the peak, rather than the average, demand. For less pressing care, neither patients nor associates like night or weekend service. Allowances are forecast using protocols, history, and benchmarks. Facility requirements are often calculated by simulation models or by comparison to best practices.

The basic estimating equations are as follows:

$$\{\text{Demand}\} = \left\{\begin{array}{c}\text{Population}\\\text{served}\end{array}\right\} \times \left\{\begin{array}{c}\text{Risk of}\\\text{need of}\\\text{service}\end{array}\right\} \times \left\{\begin{array}{c}\text{Market}\\\text{share}\end{array}\right\}$$

$$\left\{\begin{array}{c}\text{Total}\\\text{personnel}\\\text{required}\end{array}\right\} = \left\{\begin{array}{c}\text{Demand}\\\text{per work}\\\text{period}\end{array}\right\} \div \left\{\begin{array}{c}\text{Service}\\\text{per}\\\text{provider}\end{array}\right\}$$

$$\left\{ \begin{array}{c} \text{Facility} \\ \text{required} \end{array} \right\} = \left\{ \begin{array}{c} \text{Maximum} \\ \text{or average} \\ \text{demand per} \\ \text{work period} \end{array} \right\} \times \left\{ \begin{array}{c} \text{Time} \\ \text{required} \\ \text{per service} \end{array} \right\} \div \left\{ \text{Allowance} \right\} \div \left\{ \begin{array}{c} \text{Time of} \\ \text{facility} \\ \text{availability} \end{array} \right\}$$

Calculations for a scheduled service (e.g., primary care office visit) are relatively straightforward. The epidemiologic planning model examines several characteristics of the population (at least age, sex, income, education, health insurance coverage) to estimate the demand. Market share is established by a planning committee, considering relevant prior experience. If the demand is 300 visits per week, the anticipated market share is one-third, and the office teams (one physician, one registered nurse, and one clerical associate) can see 15 visits per shift for 10 shifts, then:

$$\left\{ \begin{array}{c} \text{Teams} \\ \text{required} \end{array} \right\} = \left\{ \begin{array}{c} 30 \text{ visits} \\ \text{per shift} \end{array} \right\} \div \left\{ \begin{array}{c} 15 \text{ visits} \\ \text{per shift} \end{array} \right\} = 2$$

If each visit requires 30 minutes per examining room, and cleanup sometimes delays room readiness, only 90 percent of capacity can be used:

$$\left\{ \begin{array}{c} \text{Number} \\ \text{of rooms} \end{array} \right\} = \left\{ \begin{array}{c} 30 \text{ visits} \\ \text{per shift} \end{array} \right\} \times \left\{ \begin{array}{c} 30 \text{ minutes} \\ \text{per visit} \end{array} \right\} \div \left\{ 0.9 \text{ allowance} \right\}$$

$$\div \left\{ \begin{array}{c} 240 \text{ minutes} \\ \text{per room} \end{array} \right\} = 4.17 \text{ rooms}$$

The planning committee must address the question of four rooms, with delays and overtime about one day a week, or five rooms. Given customer and caregiver satisfaction issues, the committee will probably decide on five rooms, but this decision will increase project cost.

The epidemiologic planning model is implemented by purchasing access to a sophisticated computerized analysis that combines population forecasts and usage data from a variety of national sources and applies them to local areas. The resulting projections are translated to actual personnel and facility forecasts by internal or external consultants, negotiating the personnel and facilities parameters with local associates. The size of many support services, such as parking and human resources, is driven by the aggregate forecast of clinical services; this process is described further in chapters 14 and 15. The epidemiologic planning model is essential to virtually every service and is referenced in all the following chapters. The governing board has the final decision on the size of clinical services. Senior management is responsible for negotiating a recommendation that is acceptable to the associates involved in the service and the board.

Knowledge Management

Knowledge—evidence—is at the core of high-performing HCOs and the theory of evidence-based management. Poudre Valley Health System (PVHS), the 2008 MBNQA recipient, explains what is involved in knowledge management:[3]

PVHS' ability to meet and exceed the expectations of quality care, prompt service, and friendly staff is dependent upon the timely availability of information for the workforce, suppliers, partners, collaborators, patients, and the community. To optimize the flow of accurate, real-time information, PVHS has established a secure, user-friendly network that is appropriately accessible to all stakeholders, regardless of geography or time of day. In this network, the central repository [has] associated content-specific functions such as:

- Clinical Information. Electronic health records, Picture Archive and Communication System (PACS), lab results, poison control, [automated pharmaceutical dispensing, and medication reconciliation].
- Physician Information Center (Provider LINK). Clinical information (see above); subscription-based online resources, such as MD Consult, CINAHL, and online medical journals.
- Decision Support. "Key Performance Indicator" reports; electronic data interchanges (automatic supply tracking, ordering, and billing with nearly 100 percent of PVHS vendors); Information Center (service utilization, patient demographics, market trends).
- Financial Information. Patient billing, payroll, accounts receivable, revenue cycle management
- Employee Information Center. Patient census (by unit or outpatient department); bed management (number of patients by unit/facility and admission/discharge projections); time clock; due dates for mandatory annual learning test, tuberculosis testing, performance reviews, time clock entries, pay stub, and benefits; performance reviews; balanced scorecard and quality data; patient satisfaction data; Medline; policies/procedures; forms; calendars; job postings; directories.
- Patient Information Center. GetWell Network, educational materials, gift shop, newborn photo gallery, and health resources, such as a diabetes management tool and a database for identifying potential drug interactions.

This array of information is increasingly Web-based and supported by a substantial infrastructure (further described in chapters 10 and 11). The infrastructure implements the following criteria for all knowledge, whether electronically or conventionally distributed:

1. *Access.* The user gets the screens or documents needed, with minimal delay.
2. *Protection.* Access is limited to appropriate users and protected against loss, service interruption, or deliberate distortion.
3. *Accuracy.* The information on the screen is valid and reliable.
4. *Completeness.* The user gets all the information needed.

These criteria are achieved by systematic processes that support the library of work processes, protocols, and measures; training; and communications network.

Library of Work Processes, Protocols, and Measures

The content of the library is conceptually all relevant facts about the HCO and its components, including historical information. The access, protection, and accuracy criteria must be applied to the library because it is the resource for training and the communications network.

High-performing HCOs deliberately pursue a broad access strategy. Personal information about patients and associates must be protected by law. A small set of strategic information, largely relating to work in process, must be protected to allow orderly decision making. Beyond that, the strategy is to make information available. Access is made faster by electronic records and search engines. PVHS notes that it also communicates "through newsletters, reports, bulletin boards, posters, mailings, media, and [other] approaches."[4] Open access enhances empowerment, speeds communication, and reduces errors. Under this strategy, much information becomes public, or nearly so. The dangers cited against broad access (competitors, lawsuits, misinterpretations) have not proven to be significant.

Protection is achieved by providing each user with an identification and password, organizing the users in groups and the knowledge in sets, and allowing groups access to specific sets of information. Protection also requires safeguarding not just the records but also the communications network. (This is handled by specific information services functions described in Chapter 10.)

Accuracy of information is critical. Modern information management uses three approaches to improve the accuracy of information (they are expanded in Chapter 10):

1. *Screens and information input design.* Well-designed screens (and paper forms) discourage errors and encourage completeness. Electronic entry adds edit and audit protections that increase accuracy and completeness. Procedures can follow an outline or template that helps make them complete and easier to comprehend. Tags allow cross-referencing and retrieval.
2. *Standardization of performance measures.* Performance measures have become increasingly complex. Ideally, users should be assured that (a) each measure reflects the process it purports to measure (validity); (b) variation from prior values, goals, or benchmarks is meaningful (reliability); and (c) the cause of the

variation is reasonably under the users' control. High-performing HCOs rely on a measurement review committee to assist in developing and testing measures. The committee emphasizes nationally defined measures as a priority for two reasons: These definitions are rigorously developed and tested and national standardization is essential for benchmarking. When unique measures must be created or national measures adjusted for local conditions, the committee also provides expert guidance.

Many measures are obtained by survey. The design and administration of surveys are a science, and commercial companies provide standardized packages for various purposes. Such a package ensures the consistent application of surveys and provides automatic benchmarking and analysis of statistical sensitivity.

3. *Audits.* High-performing HCOs have extended the internal audit activity to all dimensions of the operational and strategic scorecards.[5] Critical and other measures may be audited routinely to check their accuracy.

The goal of these efforts is to make transparent the measures used to evaluate performance, identify OFIs, and analyze alternative processes. The measures are valid and reliable, and they are accepted as reliable by the participants in PITs and planning sessions.

Completeness as a criterion means that the library is constantly expanding. Processes get extended, additional measures and adjustments get approved, and histories get longer. Modern knowledge management depends on computer technology. High-performing HCOs expect to expand applications, usage, and storage.

Training

High-performing HCOs are distinguished by their commitment to training, providing 80 to more than 100 hours a year per full-time associate, about twice the average HCO investment.[6] Training takes two forms: scheduled and just in time. Scheduled training prepares associates for recurring needs. It is used for orientation, preparation for promotion, standardization of work methods, and implementation of ongoing values such as HIPAA enforcement and harassment prevention. It can be offered in a variety of modes, including online courses and on-site exercises. Just-in-time training is offered when the skill involved is used less frequently. With access to the library, it is often self-training. Looking up clinical evidence and verifying a procedure on the Internet are just-in-time training topics. Coaching a new manager and helping a PIT chairperson manage a meeting are other examples. (*The Well-Managed Healthcare Organization* is used in both scheduled and just-in-time training. Professional managers master the content to construct effective systems. The book is also a reference guide.)

Communications Network

A great deal of the knowledge necessary for HCOs is ephemeral. It is essential in framing short-term responses to patient and other needs and must be communicated quickly and accurately. E-mail, which is documented and does not require simultaneous participation, has proven to be a major step forward, as are electronic records where current observations and requests can be entered. Broad access to communication is encouraged, as in other knowledge management activities. Accuracy and completeness are improved by multiple users; erroneous material is questioned and corrected or abandoned. Protection has not proven to be a serious issue. E-mail and Web access are certainly misused, but the key to control is passive rather than active. Policies are in place that forbid spamming, deliberate distortion, and other improper messaging. They are supported by the recorded identity of senders as desirable and are brought into play when complaints are received.[7]

The culture is an important factor in making communications networks effective. PVHS and other high-performing HCOs make clear that communication must be responsive. Failing to answer completely and constructively is not acceptable.

Accountability and Corporate Design

Accountability   Much has been written about how to design organizations in general[8] and HCOs specifically.[9] The traditional starting point is the **accountability hierarchy**, a reporting path that allows each team to communicate its needs to the larger organization and to ensure the governing board of negotiated acceptance of goals. The hierarchy groups teams with closely related interests into a single division, divisions into departments, and so forth. It establishes managerial rank and titles, with work teams reporting directly to "managers," who report to "division directors" or similar titles, who report in turn to senior management. (Titles differ, but they should be consistent within a single HCO.) The hierarchy is reflected in the traditional pyramid table of organization (see Exhibit 3.4).

Accountability hierarchy
A reporting and communication system that links each operating unit to the governing board, usually by grouping similar centers together under middle management

Excellent HCOs that operate under evidence-based management have moved substantially beyond the hierarchy concepts. They retain an accountability hierarchy, because it is essential in negotiating goals and monitoring performance, but they emphasize multiple lines of communication as shown in the lower section of Exhibit 3.4. Direct communication between teams is encouraged. Support teams are encouraged to think of serving other teams as internal customers. PITs deliberately seek representatives of all affected teams. Management listening activities and surveys are avenues for less-structured discussion. Unlike the classical bureaucratic organization where the hierarchy connoted power and authority, the hierarchy in the modern HCO connotes resources and support. Power accrues from facts, ideas, visions, and goals; authority is a last resort in conflict resolution.

Service lines
Operating units designed around patient-focused care for related disease groups and similar medical specialties

Senior management maintains the hierarchy. Most hierarchies organize patient care around **service lines**, clinical support around groups of related services,

EXHIBIT 3.4
Leadership
Structure,
Communica-
tions, and
Accountability

Leadership Level	Common Names	Goal Setting and Monitoring Function
Governance	Governing board, board of trustees	Set corporate goals, monitor progress and strategic protection, make strategic decisions
Senior leadership	Senior leadership, senior management, or senior vice presidents	Provide fact base for all goal-setting activities, assist all units in goal achievement
Intermediate leadership	Division directors	Translate corporate goals to individual teams, assist teams in coordinating with other teams, assist teams in goal achievement
Team leadership	Managers, head nurses, chiefs	Negotiate team goals, maintain coordination with supporting teams, assist team in goal achievement
Work team	Named by function	Participate in goal setting, monitor team performance, report OFIs, participate in PITs
Associate	Employees, partners, volunteers	Participate in goal setting, monitor personal performance, report OFIs, participate in PITs

Traditional Table of Organization

The traditional pyramidal Table of Organization is created by identifying a line of formal communication from the governing board to the associates such that each associate has a single point of contact to a team leader and each team leader has a single point of contact to a superior:

While the line of formal communication is still important, Tables of Organization themselves seriously understate the communications possibilities and are now infrequently used.

Modern Communications Network

Each team is engaged in multiple ongoing relationships, and the same is true of all its partners.

OFI: opportunity for improvement; PIT: process improvement team

and logistic support around functions such as human resources management and financial management. Specifics will differ with size. HCOs do not have the same levels of hierarchy.

The levels of Exhibit 3.4 identified as "leadership" constitute the HCO's leadership team. The higher levels carry broader and more diffuse responsibilities.

Managers at every level of the hierarchy are expected to do the following:

- Listen continuously to the units, individuals, and patients in their assigned area.
- Achieve agreed-on goals for service, and resolve all issues that threaten goal achievement, either by direct action or by seeking assistance outside their area.
- Initiate requests for assistance from other areas, and respond to requests from other areas.
- Convey the organization's global needs, and negotiate realistic improvement goals in their assigned area.
- Participate in PITs and other continuous improvement activities.

These obligations ensure that each team has a prescribed purpose, a guideline for size, an operating location, a formal contact for communicating unmet needs, and a path for negotiating goals for operational measures. These elements both support the individual teams and coordinate their contribution to the organization as a whole.

At higher levels, the expectations of leaders are more complex. By definition, senior management is accountable not only for large groups of services but also for the support activities (including measurement) that underpin the HCO's performance. To be successful, accountability must pass three tests (shown in Exhibit 3.5):

1. *Control.* Operational scorecard performance should equal or exceed negotiated goals. In units large enough to have strategic scorecards, senior leaders are collectively accountable for strategic performance.
2. *Comparability.* The organization's scorecard values should be less than the values in alternative sources for the product or service, and should be acceptably close to benchmark or best-practice values.
3. *Profitability.* At the level of aggregation at which revenue is received, expenditures should equal the amount paid minus an allowance for funding the long-run strategic goals of the organization. (Very few accountability centers actually receive revenue. With insurance payments increasingly "bundled" around a care episode, only service lines and hospitals receive revenue and can assess profitability. Certain services may be deliberately subsidized; this amounts to a negative allowance.)

Test	Definition
Control	Goals for quality, satisfaction, and cost are met or exceeded.
Comparability	Performance meets or exceeds the performance of competing alternatives (market) and is approaching or equal to benchmark.
Profitability	Unit cost is less than or equal to payment received minus an allowance for HCO strategic needs. (This can be applied only to aggregates of accountability centers that receive payment.)

EXHIBIT 3.5
Tests of Successful Leadership Accountability

Corporate Design

The corporate design of an HCO consists of charters, bylaws, and long-term contracts that establish the HCO's legal entities and link together its major units. The reality is that American healthcare is fragmented into a large number of separate vendors. The traditional provider groups—such as community hospitals, medical practices, and specialty providers—are shown in Exhibit 3.6. All of these are legitimate HCOs, and most provide a small fraction of the care needed to sustain individual or community health. Care is so fragmented, and individual units are so small that healthcare is frequently called a "cottage industry." The fragmentation is believed to be an important opportunity to improve quality, service, and efficiency.[10] A dominant model—the equivalent of Walmart in retailing or the uniformity found in fast foods or hotels—has not emerged.

Healthcare reform is likely to increase pressure for integration and strengthen incentives for improving cost and quality. The weaknesses of the current cottage arrangement have been extensively documented. Private, physician-owned corporations that offer specialty outpatient care have been shown to be less efficient than hospital-oriented HCOs.[11] Physician ownership creates a conflict of interest and the potential for excess use of services.[12] Public for-profit hospital ownership has suffered in recent years from major legal difficulties, principally fraudulent billing. The largest for-profit companies have all settled major Medicare claims.[13] Not-for-profit ownership gives the local community greater control over the size and scope of the healthcare enterprise.[14] Although some religious HCOs have exemplary records of community service, their distinction over similar organizations is minor.[15,16,17]

A substantial amount of horizontal (within group) integration has occurred in recent decades. Most not-for-profit hospitals are now in systems, albeit mostly small, single community systems that retain privilege contracts with independent physicians. National companies dominate for-profit hospital systems. National companies have acquired large market shares in nursing home care, dialysis, and pharmacies. Medical practices have moved toward large groups.[18] Not as much vertical (across groups) integration has occurred.

EXHIBIT 3.6
Traditional
Types of HCOs

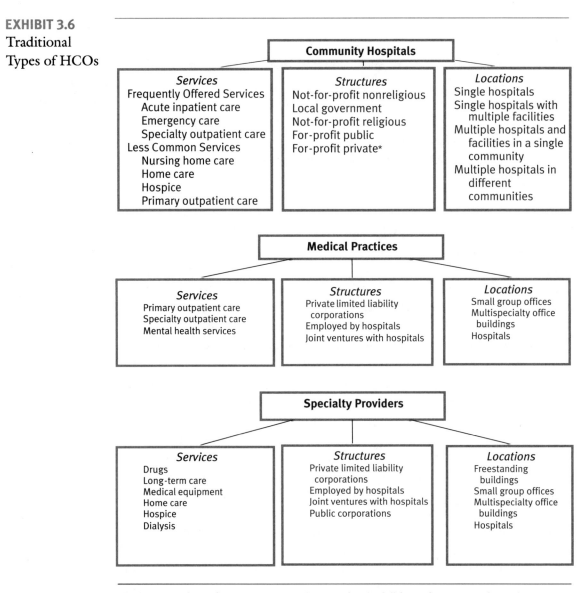

*HCA, a private for-profit corporation, owns about one-fourth of all for-profit community hospitals.
NOTE: This is not a comprehensive list. HCOs are listed in order of prevalence; that is, community hospitals are more common than specialty providers.

However, many acquisitions and formal joint ventures have drawn physicians and hospitals closer.

The high-performing HCOs presented in this book often operate multisite, multipurpose systems. They are acquiring or joint-venturing with medical practices and non-acute services. They have extended their influence through a variety of collaborative efforts, forming consortiums, joint ventures, and partnerships with private, charitable, and government organizations that share components of their overall mission.[19,20,21] Also, many include their own health insurance or healthcare financing mechanisms. The emerging corporate design includes a parent corporation, wholly owned subsidiaries, partially owned joint ventures, and long-term strategic partnership contracts without ownership. It is increasingly both vertically and horizontally integrated.

Senior management and governance must define these structures and revise them as local conditions change. Specific rules in the Internal Revenue Code define permissible relationships between tax-exempt and taxable entities. Parent and subsidiary corporations may file independently for tax exemption under Internal Revenue Service regulations. Tax exemption generally requires community control and pursuit of a purpose consistent with congressional intentions for exemption.[22] The corporate design is based on boundary spanning results and implemented as part of the strategic positioning activities. All corporate design decisions are ultimately made by the governing board (as part of its strategy function; see Chapter 4) based on proposals from senior managers and the associates directly involved in the activity under study.

The best corporate design remains to be developed, and most HCOs will move through stages of affiliation. Centralized corporations must overcome arguments that they are more dangerous, more costly, or less responsive than the cottage industry. Their counter-argument lies in four characteristics of evidence-based medicine and evidence-based management:

1. It strengthens the physician's role as selector of protocol (diagnostician) and monitor of protocol, with the obligation to depart from the usual path when it is failing the patient.
2. It empowers nurses and other caregivers both to provide physician-ordered services and to identify and meet additional patient needs, so that the care supports maximal recovery.
3. It stresses measured, audited, benchmarked performance in all components of care, enabling the results to be shared with the governing board and the stakeholders.
4. It approaches benchmark performance through continuous improvement.

Well-designed corporate systems that use transformational and evidence-based management meet the requirements for success better than other corporate models. The HCOs that have done so and documented their achievement have annual expenses that range from $500 million to several billion dollars and offer a relatively broad scope of services in several geographic locations. They have religious and secular not-for-profit owners. It appears likely that government and for-profit HCOs can also benefit from the evidence-based transformational model, although thus far no such example has been reported. Small corporate structures will continue to be important as joint venture partners and affiliates of large organizations.

Continuous Improvement

The system for continuous improvement must imbed the cycle of identify/ analyze/test/evaluate into the routine of the organization. The search for OFIs must be ongoing, PITs must make steady progress, PIT findings must be implemented, and expected results must be included in next year's goals. The operational foundation for continuous improvement has three major parts: an annual planning calendar, an internal consulting resource, and a process for conflict resolution.

Calendar for Annual Planning

All business organizations must make timely response. Whether the HCO is a 20-bed critical access hospital with three or four physicians and 50 nursing personnel or a healthcare system like Kaiser Permanente with 150,000 associates in eight states, the outside world does not wait for the HCO. Excellent organizations maintain their timeliness with an explicit calendar that tracks the fiscal year (see Exhibit 3.7). Adhering to the calendar is the responsibility of senior leadership. Following are the main steps of the annual planning process followed by Mercy Health System (see Exhibit 3.7):

- *Step 1.* The process starts at the governing board retreat with the board's thorough review of data and information gathered from boundary spanning, responsive communication, and performance measurement. The board refines long-range plans into short-term goals for all dimensions of the strategic performance measures (see Exhibit 1.11). The board's task is to balance customer and associate needs, establishing organization-wide goals that sustain excellence but are still realistic.
- *Steps 2, 3, and 4.* The senior management team begins the translation to operational goals for every unit. With advice from the team, the board's finance committee establishes the amount of funds available for capital replacement and expansion. The team begins dialogue and negotiations with division leaders, who in turn work with unit managers.
- *Step 5A.* All work groups set operational goals using the strategic goals as a guide along with OFIs. The division and senior leadership must integrate the operational goals to meet the strategic goals through negotiation. This is a complex process that occurs at step 5.
- *Step 5B.* Consensus is reached on the goals at all levels and then summarized in dashboards or scorecards.
- *Step 5C.* Negotiations conclude, and explicit operational goals for every group in the accountability hierarchy are established. These operational goals are aggregated to the board's strategic goals.

The process through Step 5C takes six or seven months, leaving five or six months for Step 6.

EXHIBIT 3.7 Mercy Health System's Annual Planning Calendar

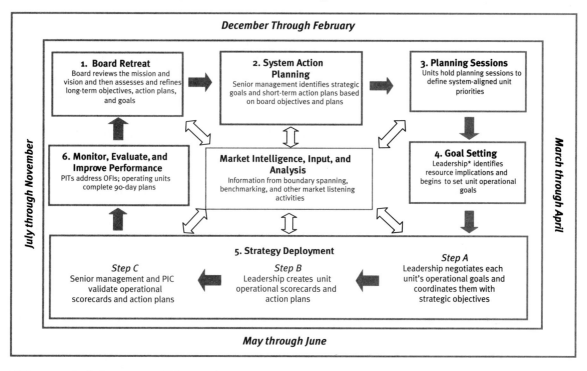

OFI: opportunity for improvement; PIT: process improvement team

*Leadership is composed of all management associates

NOTE: Market intelligence activity occurs throughout the year, but it is emphasized at the board's annual retreat. The activity is described in Chapter 15.

SOURCE: Adapted from Mercy Health's MBNQA application, p. 7.

- *Step 6.* PITs design new processes to address OFIs. These improvements allow the board to raise the strategic goals in the next annual planning round, driving continuous improvement. The improvements anticipated by the PITs must be implemented and included in goal negotiations. Every PIT project managed by the PIC is monitored on an implementation queue, and appropriate changes in unit goals are built into the next budget cycle. The implementation is achieved by 90-day interim goals. The 90-day goals are usually achieved, but a recovery process is in place should plans not work out as expected.

The relentlessly forward-looking characteristic is a major source of strength for an HCO. The boundary spanning, communication, PIT, planning, and 90-day implementation activities seek, find, and celebrate better performance. The negotiated goals are realistic, and the improvements to support them have been tested. Thus, almost all operational goals in high-performing HCOs are achieved. There is little to fix because the planning activities anticipate the problems and prevent them.

Resource for Internal Consulting

The larger PITs and the PIC follow formal processes as well. Each PIT, large or small, has a charge, a specified membership, and a timetable. Larger PITs usually have two kinds of technical assistance—meeting management and systems analysis. Members of the PIT have ongoing responsibilities, and their time must be used efficiently. PIT meetings must be well managed, and information must be prepared in advance, agendas defined, debate appropriately moderated, and minutes kept. The PIT chair is trained to lead meetings and is assisted by a meeting manager who handles the details.

Fact-finding and analyses must be assigned to personnel who have the time, skills, and resources to do them. A number of formal approaches to analysis are popular, including Lean, Six Sigma, and GE Work-Out. These approaches provide rigor, objectivity, and thoroughness, and they require trained leaders. Tasks such as implementing the epidemiologic planning model or designing a staffing system demand experience and skills and take substantial time. To support their continuous improvement efforts, large HCOs rely on in-house consultants, while small HCOs hire external consultants. The roles that consultants must fill are detailed in chapters 14 and 15.

Process for Conflict Resolution

Change frequently requires substantial relearning and (occasionally painful) adjustment. Conflicts, defensiveness, and denial can be anticipated in the PIT process. These are best handled in private sessions where emotions as well as facts can be explored, alternatives investigated, and accommodations made. The process of conflict resolution, discussed in Chapter 2, is a negotiation activity that supports the culture. The annual planning calendar is an essential part of conflict resolution because it establishes a deadline for resolution. Many serious conflicts will test that deadline, and it is the governing board's job to hold to this date judiciously. That action rules out foot dragging, red herrings, and obfuscation as strategies to protect limited interests. The culture reinforces the board's action. Listening has occurred, facts have been gathered and tested, and the opinion of colleagues has been established. The case is won or lost, and continued objection is fruitless.

Sustaining and Improving the Operational Structure

The senior leadership team leads the PIC and assists the work teams and accountability groups in carrying out continuous improvement for all units. It also must apply this process to the cultural and operational infrastructure. This is done by evaluating both quantitative and qualitative evidence about the improvement processes themselves. The quantitative indicators (see Exhibit 3.9) should be improving. Many qualitative indicators arise from various listening activities and unexpected events; examples are shown in Exhibit 3.8.

Systematic listening, suggested several times in Exhibit 3.8, includes generating logs or written reports of noteworthy findings. Logs and reports must be aggregated, summarized, and critically reviewed. Aggregation and summary are assigned to an appropriate internal consulting unit. The OFIs can

Function	Qualitative Indicators	Sources
Boundary spanning	Stated satisfaction of major customer stakeholders Competitor activities Activities of excellent HCOs in other communities Changes in healthcare financing Changes in healthcare technology Changes in local employment, attitudes, or civic commitments	Systematic listening and comments of customer stakeholder leadership Published and suspected actions of competitors Published reports and awards Consultants' reports Government legislation and regulation Reports from literature, trade, and professional associations
Organization design	Requests for service expansion Effectiveness of PITs Customer and associate complaints or service concerns Effective adoption of new technology	Systematic listening and comments of associate stakeholders Logs and reports of unexpected events Consultants' advice and record of other HCOs
Responsive communication	Associate complaints or concerns Unionization efforts Success of new hires and promotions Terminal interview comments	Systematic listening and comments of associate stakeholders Individual interviews and personal evaluations
Continuous improvement	Difficulty in negotiating goals Complaints about PITs or timetable	Minutes and observations of PIT participants

EXHIBIT 3.8
Qualitative Indicators of OFIs for Maintaining the Cultural and Operational Infrastructure

OFI: opportunity for improvement; PIT: process improvement team

then be rank-ordered by importance and feasibility. Members of the PIC can individually identify and rank-order OFIs. Their written reports can be aggregated and consensus can be reached using nominal group technique.[23] Using several perspectives generates a more objective and thorough evaluation.

Many of the questions that arise in evaluating the infrastructure revolve around, "How do we fall short on our values and vision?" Those questions are challenging to answer. Inherent biases cause disabling blindness. Cultural competency is an important example. It is not uncommon to overlook some population sectors, leaving them to feel ignored. The first step toward overcoming these weaknesses is for the senior leadership team to reflect on the question. The second is to form review teams who are sensitive to the issues. These teams can pursue several possibilities to identify OFIs, such as comparing the HCO's boundary spanning with best practices in other communities and reported in the literature or conferring with leaders of cultural groups.

EXHIBIT 3.9
Performance Measures for Infrastructure Functions

Function	Infrastructure Concept	Measures	Sources	Examples
Boundary spanning	Maximizing external stakeholder satisfaction	Trends and variations in satisfaction surveys Counts of unexpected events Financial performance Quality-of-care measures Community health measures	Ongoing patient surveys Ad hoc surveys of other stakeholders Records of complaints and incidents Financial reports Medical records Community health surveys	Surveys of employers and potential patients Profit and funds available for investment Bond rating Global patient satisfaction scores Adverse patient care events Percent of community immunized Percent of community with premature loss of life or function
Corporate design	Uniformity of performance Extent of service Competitor relations	Market share Efficiency of care Per capita cost of care Variation in internal performance improvement Unmet or delayed demand	Surveys of market share Cost per case and length of stay Analysis of trends, variation and percent of benchmark for operational and strategic measures	Patients leaving area for care Case-mix adjusted cost per case Dartmouth Atlas* cost and use per capita Unit(s) not progressing toward benchmark Undersized unit with service delays Oversized unit with excess capacity Competitor growth
Responsive communication	Associate satisfaction, retention, and complaints	Satisfaction surveys Retention, absenteeism, and vacancy measures Number of issues raised	Routine surveys and human resources statistics Summaries of rounding and other listening activities	Tenure of associates Percent of "loyal" associates Percent of RN positions vacant Number of food service complaints
Timekeeping	On-time planning	Delays in annual planning process PITs completing on time	Annual planning activity Minutes and records of PIC	Budget delivered on time Percent of PITs completing charge without time extension
Sustaining and improving	Continuous improvement	Board scores Outside audits	Board self-evaluation Auditor reports	Percent of board stating "complete satisfaction" Joint Commission deficiencies

PIC: performance improvement council; PIT: process improvement team; RN: registered nurse

*Information from The Dartmouth Atlas of Hospital Use, a Web-based small-area reporting system. The site provides estimates of cost per capita and hospital days per capita from Medicare data. See www.dartmouthatlas.org.

People

HCO leadership requires an extensive and challenging set of operational competencies. These competencies are typically supplied to first-line leaders by in-house training and coaching. The program of preparation for senior leadership usually includes formal education, planned experience, and mentoring. (See Chapter 2 for an expanded discussion of these concepts.)

Measures

Evidence-based management assumes that objective measurement is the best source for all judgments and evaluations. The strategic and operational performance measures assess inputs (demand and quantity, cost, and quality of resources) and outputs (production, efficiency, quality, unit cost, and customer satisfaction). This approach does not translate easily to the infrastructure. The infrastructure does not create a tangible product, and much of the resource used to maintain it is blended into other activities. It is still necessary to measure the infrastructure as objectively as possible to keep it sound and identify its OFIs.

The quantitative measures available for assessing the infrastructure are shown in Exhibit 3.9. These measures indicate how well a specific part of each function has been addressed.

They are often difficult to benchmark and complicated to interpret. For example, "board self-evaluation" and "ad hoc surveys of other stakeholders" cannot reasonably be compared across different communities. Community health measures can be compared and benchmarked, but the HCO is only one of many factors that affect the statistics. As a result of these complexities, interpreting these numbers is not as straightforward as it is for operational and strategic measures. Qualitative information is relatively more important. The full array of opportunities must be carefully explored to establish the right goals.

The issues involved in evaluating local market information provide an illustration. Much about the local market can be measured, such as the percentage of patients leaving the community and their reasons, the shares of local competitors and their trends, the number and size of competitors, and the per capita cost of care for the community. For many of these measures, even the proper goal is debatable. The desirable level of patients leaving the community is different for different locations. Two communities—one 40 miles outside Phoenix and the other 40 miles outside Minneapolis, for example—are not likely to accept the same levels as goals. The number of competitors is likely to be a historic accident, and one cannot say that two competitors are better than four or that Community A is better than Community B because it has more HCOs per 100,000 people.

While the per capita cost of care can be benchmarked, community income and education are important contributors. An HCO in a community with high unemployment and low post–high school education should not be directly compared with an HCO in a suburban community filled with professional families.[24] Both HCOs can lower the per capita cost in their communities, but they cannot overcome the social and economic differences.

The process for evaluating OFIs and establishing goals should give primacy to objective measures, but it should never ignore qualitative information. When judging the measures of infrastructure, the balance shifts toward qualitative information. The key questions for evaluation are as follows:

1. Is the HCO moving in the correct long-term direction? Has the overall progress been sufficient?
2. Is progress uniformly deployed across the HCO?
3. What are the most important OFIs and improvement goals?

Because of the complexity and importance of the task, the evaluation is usually carried out by both the governing board and senior leadership. They meet at a retreat to allow time for thorough discussion of carefully analyzed quantitative and qualitative data. The consensus reached establishes the priorities for strategic OFIs and shapes the future position of the HCO.

Managerial Issues

The transformational and evidence-based approach described in chapters 1, 2, and 3 is an unchallenged best practice for managing community-oriented HCOs. The measures and benchmarks that document excellence are themselves a major step toward evidence-based management. The case for transformational management is strongly supported by the general management literature and by its documented HCO applications.

The fact that this model for high performance is relatively rare as of 2009 suggests that the most critical managerial issues are starting and sustaining the transition. The reported cases developed the cultural and operational elements in parallel. It is likely that pursuing the cultural transition creates demands for knowledge that are supported by the evidence-based approach, and efforts to use the knowledge are successful in a culture of empowerment. The Managerial Issues section of Chapter 2 pursues these questions for the transformational culture. This chapter discusses the issues that arise in evidence-based management.

Starting the Path to Evidence-Based Management

Assuming that your HCO is "pretty good," how does it strengthen the operational foundation? The path is clear enough.

1. *Assemble the available strategic measures.* High-performing HCOs use about 30 strategic performance measures (see Chapter 4, Exhibit 4.3), many of which are commonly available and benchmarked. For most HCOs, the news on initial review of these indicators will be grim. On measures covering financial performance, quality, and efficiency available from Medicare reports, median performance is about two-thirds of best; the lowest quartile is about half of best.[25] A similar variation exists in the community cost of care.[26] Recent data on quality of care suggest modest improvement at best.[27] Based on these measures, more than half the community hospitals in the United States have substantial OFIs. The quality improvement potential is measured in tens of thousands of lives and the cost improvement in hundreds of billions of dollars.

2. *Renew the governing board commitment to a community mission.* The board must accept the opportunity to improve and the reality of that task. Although it would seem automatic that members of the governing board of an HCO would be committed to achieving a mission of excellent care or health for their community, it is not. A for-profit HCO must put emphasis on return to shareholders ahead of all other concerns. (An argument can be made that transformational management does pay off for shareholders, as supported by solid evidence in both the healthcare[28] and hospitality industries.[29]) Board members of a not-for-profit HCO may have several personal goals that conflict with the HCO's mission, such as using the membership as a tool for social or business gain or viewing the membership as an honorific role rather than as a community obligation. These are forms of agency or accountability failures—that is, the board members are failing to act as agents for the community as a whole. Defenses against such failures lie in board leadership process and selection (described in Chapter 4). Leadership, selection, and process are particularly powerful. Board officers can focus attention on the mission. They can insist on boundary spanning and order a visioning exercise. They can use the agenda to ensure that OFIs are not forgotten and calendar deadlines are met. They can identify and elect new members from the community who can commit to the HCO's mission and are skilled in transformational and evidence-based management.

3. *The governing board must understand the opportunity to improve and be motivated to pursue improvement.* Board members are selected for their community commitment and demonstrated skill. They arrive with little knowledge of HCO management and often strong emotions remaining from personal and family healthcare. High-performing HCOs educate them specifically about their board roles. New board members in the best HCOs receive several days of initial training,[30] and a portion of each meeting is devoted to continuing education. The education clarifies the commitment to transformational and evidence-based management so that each trustee understands how the OFIs are addressed and what the board's responsibility is. Members learn that the board must complete six functions (listed in Chapter 4) for the HCO to reach excellence. They learn

to expect measured performance and continuous improvement on the strategic scorecard and to work with management and clinical leadership to attain the goals.

4. *Senior leadership must understand the model.* The initiative and the work to achieve excellence must come principally from senior management. While the effort is not overwhelming, it is probably harder than sustaining mediocre performance. The first step—leaving the front office and starting to listen sincerely to associates and patients—is not dangerous, but senior managers must have the skill to solve at least a few of the problems presented, the vision to understand what is being built, and the personal leadership skills to explain and convince. The skills necessary for these tasks are not difficult to acquire (they are discussed in Chapter 2). Developing measures and continuous improvement should be done sequentially, beginning with the strategic scorecard and continuing unit by unit as time and funds permit. A number of consultants offer assistance on both the transformational and evidence-based aspects. The Baldrige process and its state analogues offer an inexpensive method of learning that is strongly endorsed by award recipients.[31,32] Unfortunately, if senior leaders do not understand the opportunity to improve, it is not likely that the governing board will correct them, and no public agency or market device exists that stimulates interest and learning.

These three elements—board commitment, board knowledge, and senior leadership capability—appear to explain why progress is so halting. The lack of a public agency that insists on improvement makes it easy for HCOs to remain "pretty good." Two elements frequently cited as requirements for the transition are, in fact, not.

First, the transition is not capital intensive. The HCO does not need a substantial financial reserve to start or sustain the transition. The underlying dynamic of the approach, that better-supported associates do a better job—suggests that listening and measuring are critical starting points. Both activities are self-sustaining, and a small initial investment in each is likely to identify a number of relatively easy-to-solve OFIs. These generate efficiencies that lead to cash surpluses and quality improvements that improve both patient and caregiver satisfaction. Material improvement can be seen in the second year, and major shifts are possible in three years.[33,34]

Second, although the traditional management model divides the HCO into domains of authority (e.g., "the doctors," "the board," "the nurses"), these groups have good reason to support rather than oppose a convincing plan for an evidence-based approach because they (and other associates) will find the work more satisfying. When incentive compensation is added to the plan, few caregivers will argue for the old ways. For the governing board, improvement in the strategic measures, which reflects mission achievement, is a compelling argument. There are undoubtedly transition failures, although there are no published reports. The cause of failure is more likely related to a breakdown in trust and systematically meeting associates' needs than to resistance to change.

Understanding the Risk Factors of the Model

So far, none of the documented implementations has reported difficulties that caused the HCOs to question the model; in fact, these HCOs are strongly committed to pursuing it further.[35] Therefore, a review of the weak links or risk factors is hypothetical. The following factors deserve careful consideration:

1. *Good physician and nurse relations are crucial to the culture and to overall success.* Physicians and nurses are the people who actually deliver care and relate most closely to patients and families. Any successful improvement program requires their active support. Evidence suggests that many caregivers in traditional settings are less than satisfied.[36] High-performing HCOs have recognized the primacy of these two groups, building extra listening mechanisms, investing in expanded training for supervisors of caregiving teams, working through leaders recognized by their peers, and celebrating gains. Their record shows that the startup interval—when OFIs vastly exceed improvements—is manageable. Obviously, not every OFI can be pursued and fixed in the short run. Evidence that progress can be made and that the support is genuine is sufficient to increase caregiver satisfaction and win caregiver support. The cultural change that results from the initial efforts helps PITs address more complicated problems. Caregiver support, satisfaction, and performance improvement should continue to grow as the transition matures.

2. *Some changes in the payment system could make the model much more important.* The evidence suggests that high-performing HCOs can thrive under prevailing reimbursement schemes. All high-performing HCOs report adequate earnings and cash flow for their operations, usually surpassing comparable institutions. Improvements in clinical and logistic processes eliminate waste. The savings pay for the extra costs associated with the model—chiefly a vastly expanded investment in education, added costs for managing the measurement system, and incentive payments. Note, however, that some HCOs receive substantially less income than others, even though they deliver as much or more care. They are in highly disadvantaged economic areas, with large numbers of uninsured and persons covered under Medicaid. It is not clear that these HCOs can overcome their disadvantages of location and limited finance and sustain the model in the same form as it is described here. Several changes to traditional approaches are in place or under active study:

- The Centers for Medicare & Medicaid Services (CMS) published *Roadmap for Quality Measurement in the Traditional Medicare Fee-for-Service Program* to expand its current quality measurements and incentives.[37]
- In 2008, CMS changed its payment regulations to eliminate payment for hospital-acquired complications.[38] If a patient is injured as a result of a fall while in the hospital, care becomes more complex and expensive.
- Readmissions or repeated hospitalizations that result from failures of follow-up care are "prevalent and costly."[39] There is interest in eliminating or reducing payment for readmissions. Such a change would provide strong incentives to improve follow-up care and other outpatient support.
- *Bundled payment* is a combined payment, rather than multiple individual physician and hospital payments. Its impact is to align physician and hospital incentives to control cost, providing strong motivation for collaboration in managing complications and selecting the most cost-effective treatment. CMS began a demonstration project in 2009, bundling payment for 28 cardiac and 9 orthopedic procedures.[40]

High-performing HCOs are better equipped to respond to all of these changes. Any form of episode-based reimbursement compensates HCOs and physicians for therapeutic interventions more highly than preventive activity, and efforts to support the health of groups of patients are not compensated at all. The result is a reward structure that only partially supports a mission of excellence in care and perversely discourages a mission of community health. Several of the reported high-performing HCOs pursue community health activities in spite of the financial disincentive. To the extent they are successful, they reduce the need for care and the HCO's income. They also reduce specialist physicians' income. Thus, vigorous pursuit of a community health goal reduces the need for specialist care and may make it more difficult for the community to support specialists. It also reduces the community's income from outside healthcare payments.[41]

3. *Unrealistic governing board demands could threaten the model.* To preserve a culture of trust and respect, the negotiations between stakeholders must be perceived as fair. An effort by some stakeholder groups to exploit others is likely to destabilize the model and potentially destroy it. The governing board has sufficient power to do this by demanding more for customer stakeholders than the current processes can support. This situation can occur several ways. First, the board can set unrealistic goals at the outset of the annual budgeting process. Second, the board can insist on substandard wages or benefits, creating shortages of critical personnel. Third, the board can accept unrealistic demands from a specific stakeholder group, leading to imbalances and destroying trust. To avoid all this, the board's membership must reflect the entire community, with a clear customer majority. Board discussions

must not only strive for equal representation but also be conveyed to all stakeholders. In other words, fairness and transparency of board discussions and actions can strengthen the model.

4. *Operations management failure could threaten the model.* Empowerment demands an effective response from the organization. If an associate points out that a process is failing, the HCO must redesign that process to prevent further failures. If a measure is incorrect and misleading, it needs to be fixed. A responsive attitude is important to sustain the culture; a responsive organization is important to sustain the operations. Consequently, certain logistic and strategic components must grow in size and effectiveness. Training expands and recruitment shrinks, diminished by the high retention rate. Counseling and mentoring must grow. In-house consultation must grow. Audit activities must grow. Information processing must grow to support the library and communications network. Marketing must grow to support more refined boundary spanning.

Measuring and benchmarking these services are challenging. It is easy to undersize them because the effects are deferred and widely dispersed. The successful approach is to use demand and customer satisfaction measures as a guide to find the appropriate size. The customers are all internal, and they demand prompt, effective service. Delays can be measured. The quality of service can be assessed by auditing the work product. Training should be measured using Kirkpatrick's level 3—effective transfer or application of the lesson (see Chapter 2 for the discussion of Kirkpatrick's model). Cost and productivity can be benchmarked against other programs of similar capability. Large systems have some advantages. They can centralize some services, standardize others, and analyze details of comparable programs. Small systems, on the other hand, may be well advised to meet customer needs as their dominant goal, only secondarily working to improve cost and productivity.

5. *Lack of sincere commitment could threaten the model.* The model succeeds because it gains greater support and loyalty from stakeholders than competing approaches. The gravest danger is to lose that support, and the greatest threat is the presence of unfair advantage. Free-riders are inherently destructive; they destroy the dynamic of working together for rewards and replace it with self-serving agendas and hypocrisy. The seriousness of this risk is what makes strategic protection and the vigorous correction of agency failure necessary. No high-performing HCOs brag about their protection system, but that system is present as a silent portion of the culture. The continued record of the reported organizations suggests that it is effective.

The evidence-based model, which has led a growing number of HCOs to success, is not simple. With its cultural, operational, and strategic foundations and its leadership functions, the approach demands ongoing effort from a large number of well-trained people. But the training can be easily mastered, and the effort itself is more effective and more rewarding. The overview of the model presented in this chapter sets the stage for the specific actions discussed in the following chapters.

Suggested Readings

Butler, G., and C. Caldwell. 2008. *What Top-Performing Healthcare Organizations Know: 7 Proven Steps for Accelerating and Achieving Change.* Chicago: Health Administration Press.

Collins, J. C. 2001. *Good to Great: Why Some Companies Make the Leap...and Others Don't* New York: HarperBusiness.

———. 2009. *How the Mighty Fall ... and Why Some Companies Never Give In.* New York: HarperCollins.

Malcolm Baldrige National Quality Program. 2009. "Health Care Criteria for Performance Excellence." [Online information; retrieved 3/11/09.] www.baldrige.nist.gov/PDF_files/2009_2010_HealthCare_Criteria.pdf.

Pfeffer, J., and R. I. Sutton. 2006. *Hard Facts, Dangerous Half-Truths, and Total Nonsense: Profiting from Evidence-Based Management.* Boston: Harvard Business School Press.

Notes

1. Malcolm Baldrige National Quality Award Program. 2009–2010. "Healthcare Criteria for Performance Excellence." [Online information, p. 35; retrieved 12/30/09.] www.quality.nist.gov/Criteria.htm.

2. Sharp HealthCare, Baldrige Application. 2007. "Preface." [Online information, p. 6; retrieved 12/16/08.] www.baldrige.nist.gov/Contacts_Profiles.htm.

3. Poudre Valley Health System, Baldrige Application. 2008. "Summary." [Online information, pp. 17–18; retrieved 6/17/09.] www.baldrige.nist.gov/PDF_files/2008_Poudre_Valley_Application_Summary.pdf.

4. *Ibid.*, p. 18.

5. Griffith, J. R., and K. R. White. 2003. *Thinking Forward: Six Strategies for Highly Successful Organizations.* Chicago: Health Administration Press.

6. Griffith, J. R. 2009. "Finding the Frontier of Hospital Management." *Journal of Healthcare Management* 54 (1): 59–72.

7. American Health Lawyers Association. 2003. "Sample E-Mail Usage Policy for Healthcare Organizations." *Journal of Health Law* 36 (2): 365–76.

8. Daft, R. L. 1998. *Organization Theory and Design*, 6th ed. St. Paul, MN: West Publishing.

9. Leatt, P., G. R. Baker, and J. Kimberly. 2006. "Organization Design." In *Health Care Management: Organizational Design and Behavior*, 5th ed., edited by S. M. Shortell and A. D. Kaluzny, 314–55. Clifton Park, NY: Cengage Delmar Learning.

10. Corrigan, J. M., and D. MacNeil. 2009. "Building Organizational Capacity: A Cornerstone of Health System Reform." *Health Affairs* 28 (2): w205–w215.

11. Carey, K., J. F. Burgess, Jr., and G. J. Young. 2008. "Specialty and Full-Service Hospitals: A Comparative Cost Analysis." *Health Services Research* 43 (5, Pt. 2): 1869–87.

12. Kahn, C. N. 2006. "Intolerable Risk, Irreparable Harm: The Legacy of Physician-Owned Specialty Hospitals." *Health Affairs* 25 (1): 130–33.

13. Galloro, V., J. Mantone, and M. Taylor. 2005. "Picking Up the Tab: Healthcare Chains Put the Past Behind Them, Resolving Past Unpleasantries in Order to Make a Clean Start in the New Year." *Modern Healthcare* 35 (1): 6–7.

14. Galloro, V. 2007. "Owners' Manual. With For-Profits, The Great Unknown Is Who the Primary Investors Are." *Modern Healthcare* 37 (14): 36, 38.

15. White, K. R. 2000. "Hospitals Sponsored by the Roman Catholic Church: Separate, Equal, and Distinct?" *Milbank Quarterly* 78 (2): 213–39.

16. White, K. R., C. E. Cochran, and U. B. Patel. 2002. "Hospital Provision of End-of-Life Services: Who, What, and Where?" *Medical Care* 40 (1): 17–25.

17. White, K. R., J. W. Begun, and W. Tian. 2006. "Hospital Service Offerings: Does Catholic Ownership Matter?" *Health Care Management Review* 31 (2): 99–108.

18. Casalino, L. P., E. A. November, R. A. Berenson, and H. H. Pham. 2008. "Hospital-Physician Relations: Two Tracks and the Decline of the Voluntary Medical Staff Model." *Health Affairs* 27 (5): 1305–14.

19. Griffith, J. R., and K. R. White. 2005. "The Revolution in Hospital Management." *Journal of Healthcare Management* 50 (3): 170–89.

20. Robinson, J. C. 2001. "Organizational Economics and Health Care Markets." *Health Services Research* 36 (1, Pt. 2): 177–89.

21. Gurewich, D., J. Prottas, and W. Leutz. 2003. "The Effect of Hospital Ownership Conversions on Nonacute Care Providers." *Milbank Quarterly* 81 (4): 543–65.

22. Internal Revenue Service. *Application for Recognition of Exemption Under Section 501(c)(3) of the Internal Revenue Code, Instructions for Form 1023.* [Online information; retrieved 6/17/09.] www.irs.gov/pub/irs-pdf/i1023.pdf.

23. Tague, N. R. 2004. *The Quality Toolbox*, 2nd ed. [Online information, pp. 364–65; retrieved 6/18/09.] www.asq.org/learn-about-quality/idea-creation-tools/overview/nominal-group.html.

24. McMahon, L. F., Jr., R. A. Wolfe, J. R. Griffith, and D. Cuthbertson. 1993. "Socioeconomic Influence on Small Area Hospital Utilization." *Medical Care* 31 (5 Suppl): YS29–36.

25. Griffith, J. R., J. A. Alexander, and D. A. Foster. 2006. "Is Anybody Managing the Store? National Trends In Hospital Performance." *Journal of Healthcare Management* 51 (6): 392–406.

26. Dartmouth Atlas of Health Care. "All Hospital Discharges per 1,000 Medicare Enrollees Hospital Referral Region Level Rates." [Online information; retrieved 12/30/09.] http://cecsweb.dartmouth.edu/atlas08/datatools/dgraph.php?event=AD_DIS&eventtype=UTIL&geotype=STD_HRR&year=2005.

27. Leapfrog Group. "Leapfrog Hospital Survey Results 2008." [Online information; retrieved 4/27/09.] www.leapfroggroup.org/media/file/leapfrogreportfinal.pdf.

28. Galloro and Mantone (2005).

29. Gunter, H. 2007. "Ritz-Carlton Brand Evolves to Stay Relevant." *Hotel & Motel Management* 222 (7): 18–19; Pitts, R. A., and D. Lei. 2000. *Strategic Management: Building and Sustaining Competitive Advantage,* 380–90. Cincinnati: South-Western College Publishing.

30. Griffith and White (2003), pp. 35–40.

31. Calhoun, G. S., J. R. Griffith, and M. E. Sinioris. 2008. "The Foundation of Leadership in Baldrige Winning Organizations." *Modern Healthcare* (Suppl.): 9–20.

32. Bea, J. 2009. "Practitioner Response." *Journal of Healthcare Management* 54 (1): 45.

33. Griffith and White (2003); North Mississippi Medical Center, Baldrige Application.

34. North Mississippi Medical Center, Baldrige Application.

35. Calhoun, Griffith, and Sinioris (2008).

36. Weinstein, L., and H. M. Wolfe. 2007. "The Downward Spiral of Physician Satisfaction: An Attempt to Avert a Crisis Within the Medical Profession." *Obstetrics & Gynecology* 109 (5): 1181–83; Ruggiero, J. S. 2005. "Health, Work Variables, and Job Satisfaction Among Nurses." *Journal of Nursing Administration* 35 (5): 254–63.

37. Centers for Medicare & Medicaid Services. [Online information; retrieved 6/24/09.] www.cms.hhs.gov/QualityInitiativesGenInfo/downloads/QualityMeasurementRoadmap_OEA1-16_508.pdf.

38. *Ibid.*, www.cms.hhs.gov/HospitalAcqCond.

39. Jencks, S. F., M. V. Williams, and E. A. Coleman. 2009. "Rehospitalizations Among Patients in the Medicare Fee-for-Service Program." *New England Journal of Medicine* 360 (14): 1418–28.

40. Centers for Medicare & Medicaid Services. [Online information; retrieved 6/23/09.] www.cms.hhs.gov/apps/media/press/release.asp.

41. Griffith (2009).

4 STRATEGIC LEADERSHIP: GOVERNANCE

In a Few Words

The governing board must establish a strategic direction for the healthcare organization (HCO) that meets stakeholder needs and resolves conflicting views. The board's critical functions, which in turn implement the strategic direction, are as follows:

1. Maintain management capability.

2. Establish the mission, vision, and values.

3. Approve corporate strategy and annual implementation.

4. Ensure quality of clinical care.

5. Monitor performance against plans and budgets.

6. Improve board performance.

Boards succeed at the critical decisions because they follow carefully designed processes for selecting and educating members, managing their agenda, and improving their own performance. The board's measures of success are a balanced scorecard of the organization's financial, market, operations, and human resources management and a checklist of process control.

Critical Issues in Strategic Leadership

1. *Establishing a culture of respect, honesty, and service:*
   - Work with the chief executive officer (CEO), the medical staff, and senior leadership
   - Maintain honest and service-oriented governance processes

2. *Using realistic forecasts to create a plan for mission achievement:*
   - Listen to stakeholder voices, and fairly balance stakeholder needs
   - Translate the mission to a business plan
   - Use a long-range financial plan
   - Monitor a strategic scorecard of organizational performance

3. *Working with physicians and other caregivers to improve quality and efficiency of care:*
   - Maintain the medical staff organization as a partnership that provides a mutual benefit

4. *Keeping the board as an effective forum for meeting stakeholder needs:*
   - Maintain the board's understanding of stakeholder needs
   - Monitor and improve the board's own performance

Consider these questions as you read the chapter.

1. Should every community have its own HCO with its own mission, or should hospitals be like Walmart, where the mission is universal? If there is a virtue to an individual mission, what is it, and how should a local governing board establish a mission?

2. How would stakeholders' lives change if an HCO created no vision and values statements? If the vision and values were passed by the board but otherwise ignored?

3. Consider common board decisions like the mission, scope of service, corporate structure, and budget. What does the CEO contribute to those discussions? How does the board evaluate the CEO's contribution? What makes the relationship effective, and what erodes the relationship?

4. Would you add or take away any dimensions to the strategic scorecard? What happens if the board ignores a dimension or sets an easy goal? A goal too challenging? How does the CEO respond to a member who says, "We can't have better quality without spending more money"? What should the board do if a dimension is below benchmark and not improving?

5. Why should the governing board evaluate its own performance? How does a board build in evaluation so that it is not overlooked? Should a board use both the balanced scorecard and the "ten measures" (see Exhibit 4.4) to evaluate its work?

An HCO's strategic foundation is defined by ongoing sets of specific decisions—the mission, vision, and values; the kinds and locations of services; the prices and wages offered; the rights and duties of individual customers and associates; the way consensus is obtained and disputes resolved; and the way goals are set and the organization responds to a changing world. The decisions must be a timely response to the stakeholders' changing needs. They must balance the multiplicity of needs and opportunities. A successful decision is measured by the breadth and strength of stakeholder satisfaction. The board succeeds when the enterprise succeeds; the enterprise succeeds when, and to the extent that, it attracts and retains customer, caregiver, and supplier stakeholders. These concepts are measured in the strategic scorecard.

Purpose

The purpose of the governing board of a well-managed HCO is

> **to create and maintain a foundation for relationships among the stakeholders that identifies and implements their wishes as effectively as possible.**

This purpose has become increasingly challenging in this new era of accountability. Customer stakeholders now demand improvements in patient safety, more rigorous cost control, greater scrutiny of community benefit, and the transparency of managerial practices.[1] Provider stakeholders expect strong support and a congenial culture. Stakeholders' decisions to participate are based on their perceptions of the HCO's ability to be a great place to get care, a great place to work, or a cost-effective addition to their insurance plan. Associates and other stakeholders expand and implement the strategic foundation, but the board is by definition the ultimate authority.

This purpose, called the "managerial perspective" or "corporate perspective" of governance, is deceptively complex and not universally understood.[2] It is perverted by failures in the board's agency relationship with stakeholders—for example, when the board becomes captive to the CEO, or when board members gain as individuals at the expense of the stakeholders. It is a contrast to and often confused with two other purposes that have been proposed for not-for-profit governance.

The *resource distribution* perspective views the organization as a source of largesse and the governing board as a body to distribute resources. Such a purpose is sometimes called "political" because the role of legislative bodies and politics, in general, is to distribute resources.[3] The HCO's expenditures are income to various stakeholders and an important economic resource. The HCO is among the largest employers, and a large share of its income comes from outside the community (see Chapter 1). Under this perspective, physicians, suppliers, and employees gain importance, compared to the users of healthcare. Distributional equity is a matter of constant concern, and politics is chiefly devoted to it.[4]

The *resource contribution* perspective views board members as contributors of resources to the organization. In contrast to the resource distribution perspective, the resource contribution model emphasizes the funds or services board members may donate or the influence they can bring to bear on critical external relations. Naming to the board a member of the richest family in town or the mayor is an example, and so is the appointment of a leading lawyer in the hope of reduced legal fees.

The role of the owners complicates the board's purpose. In the for-profit tradition, the focus is on maximizing profit. Stockholders are the dominant stakeholders, and success is measured by profitability. Board members—usually called *directors*—are compensated for their efforts and are usually given strong incentives to achieve financial goals. Board directors select opportunities that maximize profit. In the not-for-profit tradition, the owners are the members of the community served. This community ownership concept arises from legislation and the courts and is less precise than the stockholder concept. The original concept of a charitable organization was to make no profit and disburse assets,[5] but in recent decades HCO boards have accepted the need to ensure continued, and even expanding, mission achievement. That need requires a profit and its reinvestment for the community's benefit.[6] Governing board members may also be called **trustees**, rather than directors, reflecting their acceptance of the assets in trust for the community. Their decisions should be those that best fulfill community needs. Trustees are rarely compensated, except for out-of-pocket expenses. Important legal barriers exist to the board's ability to liquidate or transfer the assets of the HCO outside the owning community. By law, the equity of a not-for-profit HCO cannot be distributed to any individual.

Trustees

Members of the governing board of not-for-profit HCOs who volunteer their time to the organization; their only compensation is the satisfaction they achieve from their work. The title reflects their acceptance of the assets in trust for the community; also may be called *directors*

Most organizations probably use a balance of all three perspectives. Excellent organizations, however, emphasize managerial perspective.[7,8,9] Evidence shows that not-for-profit HCOs that have adopted the managerial perspective have better organizational performance.[10]

Functions

Managerial approaches to governance generate a set of functions or tasks that the board must perform effectively to support the organization.[11] The decisions that HCO boards must make to achieve excellence are described in Exhibit 4.1.[12] These functions describe the governance needs of almost any HCO, from a small home care company or doctor's office to a large integrated system. Small organizations may not have a formally designated board, but their leaders must still accomplish these functions.

EXHIBIT 4.1

Functions of the Governing Board

Function	Intent	Implementation	Examples
Maintaining management capability	Establish a professional capability to • provide the board with timely, thorough, relevant, and accurate information; and • implement the board's decisions	Recruit a CEO and review her/his contribution to the HCO Establish policies for recruiting, developing, and compensating other managers Maintain a plan for management succession	Select a CEO Evaluate executive performance Establish senior management compensation Review compensation and bonus program for all managers
Establishing the mission, vision, and values	Agree on common goals and core values of the organization Articulate the goals as a guiding concept	Undertake a visioning exercise Maintain ongoing communication with stakeholder representatives Conduct an annual review	Revise the mission/ vision/values Meet with medical staff leadership Hold a retreat for annual environmental assessment
Approving the corporate strategy and annual implementation	Establish the scope and organization of services and set strategic annual improvement goals	Balance the vision against current realities Establish plans for expansion and renewal Maintain competitive plant and equipment	Approve plans for implementation Set the annual strategic goals Approve the capital and new programs budget
Ensuring quality of clinical care	Maintain a central commitment to quality medical care Attract and retain the most competent physicians, nurses, and other caregivers	Approve the strategic goals for quality improvement Approve the privileges of attending physicians Approve compensation programs for caregivers	Encourage PITs to address important quality-of-care OFIs Approve medical staff bylaws Approve quality-related incentives
Monitoring performance against plans and budgets	Ensure implementation of annual goals	Review reports of strategic performance Monitor progress of long-term projects	Review quarterly reports of strategic scorecard Review progress reports of search activities and construction
Improving board performance	Ensure that the governance function remains competitive	Annually review individual and collective performance	Conduct confidential survey of member perspective

OFI: opportunities for improvement; PIT: process improvement team

Maintaining Management Capability

Typical trustees have full-time occupations, volunteer their services, and have only limited time for the HCO. They serve only a few years and will be replaced by others. Board decisions are made by committee, whereas implementation requires an individual. All of these factors—the competing obligations, the lack of continuity, and the need to implement the decisions—limit what a board can accomplish on its own. Thus, the first function of governance is to assemble an executive team. Typically, this is done by hiring a CEO, establishing a rewarding relationship with that individual, and assisting that individual in building and supporting an effective team.

CEO Selection and Support

The CEO selects and ensures accountability of all other employees of the organization, coordinates the design and operation of the HCO, and represents the board and the owners internally and externally. CEOs act for the board in all emergencies and in rounding and listening activities, where they must infer and interpret the board's desire. The CEO controls many of the internal facts the board sees and influences what external facts are brought to the board's attention. The CEO is critical to key factors tied to organizational success: the CEO's timely sharing of relevant and accurate information, a board that actively advises and challenges management, and board education.[13]

The CEO and the senior management team are often the only people in the community who are professionally trained in healthcare delivery. That training covers technical questions of need, demand, finance, quality, efficiency, law, and government regulation that are not included in the training of doctors, lawyers, or businesspersons. As such, the executive staff is the sole routine source of information in this complex and rapidly changing area.

Many say that selecting the CEO is the most important decision a board will make because of the impact the CEO has on other board decisions. The decision is also exceptionally difficult. It involves judging the future skills of individuals, always a hazardous undertaking. It is made without the assistance of a CEO, whereas other decisions have the benefit of the CEO's counsel. It is made infrequently, and the people who make it may never have selected a CEO before.

How does a board make such a difficult decision? The best way is to follow with extra thoroughness and care the rules that improve all high-level personnel decisions. A description of duties and responsibilities should be in place. The job description should be translated into selection criteria that identify the desired skills and attributes of the individual. The priority or importance of these criteria and the ways in which these skills will be measured in specific applicants should be specified. A national search for candidates is usually appropriate. For most U.S. organizations, the law requires not only equal opportunity on the basis of race, age, sex, and disability but also affirmative action in seeking candidates who are disadvantaged on those grounds.[14] The backgrounds of qualified individuals must be carefully veri-fied. Executive search firms provide assistance with each of these steps; they contribute by having broad relevant experience and by developing a pool of potential candidates.

The selection process is only the beginning of a relationship. Sustain-ing the CEO–board relationship over time allows both the organization and the executive to grow. Four major elements are the focus of ongoing review, with a formal annual process:

1. *Develop a mutual understanding of the employment contract.* There is usually a contract between the board and the CEO. More formal, written contracts have become popular in recent years, but much of the relationship depends on an underlying relationship of trust and communication.[15] Among not-for-profit hospitals in 2005, 66 percent had formal CEO employment contracts.[16] The contract should specify the general duties of the CEO, the mechanisms for re-view of performance, and the approach to compensation. It should also state the procedures for terminating the relationship, including appropriate protection for both the organization and the CEO. Properly performed, the CEO's job is now and always has been high risk.[17,18] Thus, even handshake agreements should include appropriate protection if the CEO must leave the institution.

2. *Agree on short-term (usually one year) personal goals.* All managers in well-run organizations have explicit, usually quantitative, goals. Those for the CEO are related to the goals of the institution as a whole; they emerge from resource al-location processes described later.

3. *Establish the base compensation.* Compensation includes salary, employment benefits offered to all employees, unique benefits offered to the CEO, terms for bonuses and merit increases, an agreement on the disposition of any inciden-tal income the CEO might earn as a result of related professional activity, and an agreement on both voluntary and involuntary termination compensation. Unique benefits usually exploit the mutual interests of the organization and the CEO and the income tax laws. Hospitals have come under increased scrutiny by the Internal Revenue Service (IRS) and the Government Accountability Office, requiring them to account for excess compensation and benefits. Effective in the 2008 tax year, not-for-profit HCOs must file an IRS Form 990 for an extensive inclusion of executive compensation packages.[19] Legal counsel should be con-sulted before nonsalary compensation and perquisites are offered to be certain that they are not prohibited by laws and regulations.

   The only enduring guideline for designing a compensation package is the marketplace—that is, what the institution pays a specifically prepared person and what that person could earn in a similar employment elsewhere. For all large HCOs, and for increasing numbers of small ones, the market-place is the national market for people trained and experienced in healthcare management. While not-for-profit compensation generally does not equal the levels given in similar-sized for-profit organizations, senior managers earn about ten times the median personal income, and CEOs receive substantially more. The IRS monitors executive salaries and questions those that appear to exceed the market.[20]

4. *Establish incentives for goal achievement.* Incentive compensation is increasingly common.[21] The incentive should be based on the overall achievement of the organization and can be determined either by a prospectively agreed-on formula or by retrospective evaluation against previously agreed-on criteria. The payment can be quite large—on the order of 50 percent of total compensation. Incentive-based compensation both motivates the executive and documents that community needs are being met, and it may be more palatable to the general public than a high salary.

Management Development and Succession

The board is responsible for a management succession plan and a program to develop managers.[22] The plan and the program are designed by the CEO and senior management and approved by the board with at least an annual review. The plan identifies specific internal candidates to replace key executives, including the CEO. The management development program includes a review of management compensation and incentives, evaluation of the competencies of all managers, identification of individual improvement opportunities and plans for enhancing skills, and an assessment of preparation for promotion. Many leading HCOs pay particular attention to issues of diversity in management, seeking not only equal opportunity for women and members of disadvantaged groups but also a diverse managerial workforce that mirrors the characteristics of the population served and the employee workforce.

Establishing the Mission, Vision, and Values

The governing board establishes the mission, vision, and values. It manages the extensive stakeholder discussions that support both the statements and their acceptance throughout the organization (see Chapter 1; examples of missions are shown in Exhibit 1.7). The board's role is to monitor the reality and effectiveness of the mission in light of evolving stakeholder needs. It implements this function through its annual environmental assessment and goal-setting activities. It periodically revisits the mission, vision, and values with a "visioning exercise" (Chapter 2), not so much to change these core commitments as to refresh stakeholder understanding.

Approving the Corporate Strategy and Annual Implementation

As the board and the HCO progress through the annual calendar (see Chapter 3, Exhibit 3.7), the board makes the final decisions in shaping both the short- and long-term performance. These are resource allocation decisions, distinguished from the mission and vision by the commitment to expend resources in certain directions. They progress from corporate strategies to long-term plans, financial plans, and annual goals. In all cases, management proposes the action and its justification. The board reviews the proposal for consistency with stakeholder needs, mission, and prior actions, and in most cases the board approves the management proposal.

The initiative for strategic opportunities comes from the environmental assessment (see chapters 3, 14, and 15). A successful assessment generates dozens, even hundreds, of new business opportunities and ways of meeting old goals. The most realistic of these should be developed and evaluated through scenarios. **Scenarios** often begin with sketches of various outcomes for the community: Several of the common topics for these scenarios are shown in Exhibit 4.2. The initial scenarios can be quite abstract and ambiguous. They evaluate alternative **strategic opportunities** and must eventually be refined into specific **business plans** that shape the HCO's directions. Business plans often involve quantum shifts in facilities, service capabilities, or market share. They can include mergers, acquisitions, joint ventures, and large-scale capital investments. Strategic opportunities are sometimes triggered by external events and require rapid decisions. The governing board of the well-run HCO quietly but thoroughly evaluates the more probable strategic scenarios in advance and is therefore prepared for prompt action when required.

Setting Corporate Strategies

Scenarios
Alternative approaches to improving the profile of opportunities reflected in the environmental assessment

Strategic opportunities
Opportunities that involve quantum shifts in service capabilities or market share, usually by interaction with competitors, large-scale capital investments, and revisions to several line activities

Business plan
A model of a specific strategy or function that guides design, operations, and goal setting

Once the strategies and priorities are established, management develops specific plans for facilities, personnel, marketing, and operations (see chapters 14 and 15). These are often multiyear plans with specific implications for the annual plans. The board reenters the decision process when a final set of plans has been developed and documented. It ratifies or selects among the final proposals. The board's initial role—establishing the strategic direction and outlining the specific goals to be met—is far more important than the final ratification. As the plan is implemented, the board reviews progress as part of its monitoring function.

Long-Term Planning

A crucial test of the strategic and long-range planning activities comes when the financial impact is assessed. This involves realistic assumptions about future market share, prices, and costs that are used to build a **long-range financial plan** (LRFP), which shows earnings, debt, and capitalization for at least the next seven years. The plan is actually a sophisticated financial model that can quickly calculate the implications of major decisions.

Long-Range Financial Plans

Long-range financial plan (LRFP)
An ongoing projection of financial position showing earnings, debt, and capitalization for at least the next seven years

EXHIBIT 4.2
Strategic
Scenario
Questions for
Healthcare
Organizations

Issue	Strategic Response	Questions
Expansion/ closure	Expand existing services Add new services Close or reduce services	Demand trends, financing, Cost and quality of service Ability to support high-tech specialties Impact on other services
Local affiliations	Specific affiliation opportunities	Expansion, closure Existing affiliations Size and strength of competitors Antitrust considerations Regional affiliation opportunities
Regional affiliations	Specific affiliation opportunities	Expansion, closure Impact on local market share Costs and benefits foreseen Local political issues
Relation to insurers	Contract acceptance Cash flow reduction Joint venture	Market response Profit and cash flow implications Variety of plans available to local buyers
Relation to physicians	Contracts Joint ventures	Primary care physician preferences Specialist preferences Existing physician organization
Relation to employees	Shortages Surpluses Workforce skills	Projected supply and demand for workers by specialty Programs for associate development Programs for associate satisfaction, commitment

The plan integrates the strategic business plans and tests their reality. It accepts estimates of the demand, revenue, and cost for various strategic opportunities and shows the impact on profit and debt structure under varying market and price assumptions. The alternatives that generate the most favorable combination of customers served and capital structure can be identified. All the elements are interrelated. A new service affects market share, prices, cost, and profits. It may be redesigned several times to fit the LRFP. The process—generally undertaken by management and reported to the board when a successful fit has been reached—is a critical step in ensuring productive plans.

The LRFP is also used to identify immediate financial needs. The survival of any enterprise, for-profit or not-for-profit, requires ongoing cash flow. Long-term obligations such as construction contracts or bond debts must be met along with current price needs. Equipment and facilities must be replaced. Most HCOs operate in a relatively fixed price environment. Medicare and other government programs establish revenue; the HCO has little chance to negotiate the amounts. The LRFP generates a cash need for each year. Forecasts of costs come from the internal goal-setting process described in Chapter 3 under "Continuous Improvement." The two must be resolved. The governing board initiates this process by setting financial goals from analysis of the LRFP.

Boards of high-performing HCOs set goals for all of the multidimensional strategic measures of performance shown in Exhibit 1.11.[23] The process, originally limited to financial goals, is still called "budgeting" and "goal setting" in many HCOs.

Annual Goals

A mock-up of the summary report for Saint Luke's Hospital, a 2003 winner of the Malcolm Baldrige National Quality Award in Health Care, is shown in Exhibit 4.3. Saint Luke's used five financial goals; seven customer satisfaction goals; five "development" or marketing goals; eight "clinical and administrative quality goals," six of which were indexes reflecting composites of more detailed dimensions; and six "people" goals. In the goal-setting process, the governing board negotiates the performance expected for each measure. Saint Luke's has expanded the concept of goal achievement to "stretch goals"—those that might be achieved with luck and effort. It has also established a "target"—the benchmark for the measure. The color-coded system reports progress toward each goal. (The green, yellow, and red zones are represented in shades of gray in the printed text.)

The specific measures used in the strategic goals can be changed from year to year as part of the goal-setting process. Some, like the financial performance summaries, tend to be permanent. Others are current targets. They are spotlighted in the report for a year or two and then replaced, often because benchmark has been achieved. The measures dropped from the report usually remain in the budget detail but are no longer the focus of board review. The strategic goals are the basis for senior management to negotiate the operational goals used by the smaller units of the organization.

The board participates in goal setting at three critical points—establishing the dimensions to be included, setting budget guidelines, and approving the final budget proposal. In addition to the dimensions shown in exhibits 1.11 and 4.3, the board establishes a target for programmatic capital expenditures each year. The amount sets the stage for competitive review of capital and new program requests. The review process, which involves many parts of the HCO, is described in several of the following chapters.

The board mandates that, wherever possible, four conceptual referents (such as the following) are used to evaluate current performance and the opportunity to improve. (Some referents may be unavailable for specific measures.) The board's emphasis on these referents is an important reinforcement for evidence-based management.

Referents for Goal Setting

EXHIBIT 4.3

Saint Luke's Hospital Strategic Scorecard

Scoring Criteria 2010

	Key Measures	Bench-mark	Adj. Score	+4 / 9	+3 / 8	+2 / 7	+1 / 6	Goal / 5	-1 / 4	-2 / 3	-3 / 2	-4 / 1	Raw Score
PEOPLE	Retention												
	RN Vacancy Rate												
	Employee Satisfaction**												
	Diversity												
CLINICAL & ADMINISTRATIVE QUALITY	Inpatient Clinical Care Index												
	Appropriate Care Measure (ACM) Index												
	Order Set Utilization Index												
	eICU Index												
	Outpatient Clinical Care Index												
	Patient Safety Index												
	Operational Index												
	Infection Control Index												
	Medical Staff Clinical Indicator Index												
CUSTOMER SATISFACTION	Would Recommend (HCAHPS)												
	Patient Loyalty - SLHS "Would Recommend" 5's only												
	Timeliness of Care and Service												
	Responsiveness to Patient Needs												
	Aver ER Wait time - Home Disposition (Tracking BRD)												
	Student Education Index												
GROWTH & DEVELOPMENT	Eligible IP Market Share (Primary/Secondary)												
	Eligible IP Market Share - Strategic Product Lines												
	Profitable Eligible IP Market Share (Primary Only)												
	OP Surgeries - Count												
	Unsuccessful ER to ER Transfers Not Meeting Criteria												
	Days to Budget												
	Research Index												
FINANCIAL	Operating Margin												
	Operating Cash Flow												
	Days Cash on Hand												
	Net Days in Accounts Receivable (IP/OP)												
	Patient Volume (revenue % to budget)												
	Realization Rate vs Budget												

Scores at this level will be flagged blue.
Scores in the green range will be flagged in green.
Scores at this level will be flagged in yellow.
Scores at this level will be flagged in blue.

** Indicates annual measure.

Exceeding Goal
Goal
Moderate
Risk

	2010	1 Qtr	2 Qtr	3 Qtr	4 Qtr		Overall Score
	Overall Score						Goal
							Stretch

For current performance to be scored greater than Level 1, the current performance value must meet or exceed the scoring criteria within a Level.

For FINANCIAL: Scoring ranges based on agency ratings

Note: The scoring criteria was modified in 2006: The scoring range changed from a 10-tier range to a 9-tier range, and the color coding for meeting goal was expanded to accommodate common cause variation.

SOURCE: Reprinted with permission from Saint Luke's Hospital.

1. *Trends.* Last year's value, or a time series of several years, provides an initial baseline and allows judgment on the direction of the measure.
2. *Competitor and industry comparisons.* What other similar organizations are achieving provides crude guidelines, even if the available information is not strictly from competitors.
3. *Benchmarks.* The benchmark value may be from a non-HCO—for example, the standards for financial ratios that are driven by the total bond market, not simply healthcare bonds, or the healthcare cost levels of a country with a different system.
4. *Values.* The benchmark for some measures (e.g., worker injuries, patient safety violations, infant deaths) is not good enough. The proper goal for these measures is zero. Focusing on the zero goal is often a powerful motivator, producing major gains and falling benchmarks.

Approval of Annual Goals

The goal setting is a detailed, complicated construction that involves almost the entire organization and requires several months to complete. (Goal setting is discussed in many chapters in this book: Chapter 10 expands the measurement concepts, and the contributions of management support services are described in chapters 11 through 15.) The final goal set is a book-length document for larger HCOs, containing the expectations for each work group. The financial expectations—the traditional budget—are major works in themselves, with several parts (see Chapter 13). The final capital budget lists the approved projects in priority order and is supported with detailed descriptions and timetables for each project. In general, the final review is a fine-tuning exercise within the original guidelines. Final approval should be anticlimactic; a well-managed goal-setting process uses the referents, conforms to the guidelines, and settles most questions before it is submitted for approval.

Ensuring Quality of Clinical Care

The fourth essential function of the governing board is unique to HCOs. The governing board is legally responsible for ensuring the quality of medical care.[24] The board is responsible for exercising the duty of care on behalf of the patients and the community and on behalf of physicians who desire to participate, and the organization as a whole is liable for damages should they fail. In addition to these legal requirements, The Joint Commission has specified many of the structures by which the board and the hospital medical staff discharge this duty. The growth of quality measurement, service lines, and evidence-based protocols has simplified the issues involved. The Joint Commission requires the measurement and improvement of outcomes of care as specified in its Core Measures.[25] The Centers for Medicare & Medicaid Services is now compensating hospitals directly for achieving quality goals.[26]

In addition to approving explicit annual quality goals, the board has the following five obligations:

1. Approve the **medical staff bylaws**.
2. Appoint medical executives at all levels.
3. Approve the plan for medical staff recruitment and development, a part of the long-range plans.
4. Approve appointments and reappointments of individual physicians, after a review according to the bylaws.
5. Approve contracts with physicians and physician organizations.

Some basic facts heighten the importance of the board's quality-of-care activities. First, the HCO is an expensive capital resource made available to the doctors by the owners in return for either profit or community healthcare. The board has an obligation to see that the owners receive fair value for the use of the resource. The courts have interpreted that obligation to include limiting privileges to the competence and proficiency of each physician or other affiliate of the medical staff (i.e., allied health professionals not employed by the HCO requesting privileges).[27] Second, physicians are a uniquely expensive and critical resource for the community. A shortage of physicians in a community is a serious threat to the quality of care and indirectly limits growth of the workforce. A surplus may encourage marginally necessary treatment that is both costly and dangerous. If community demand is low relative to the supply, costs will mount drastically, and lack of practice may impair quality. Third, most doctors would find their income severely reduced without participation in an HCO. Doctors deserve fair treatment and equitable opportunities to participate. The process of peer review can be subverted for the personal gain of some members;[28] the board's responsibility is to see that this does not occur. In short, the issues involve a sensitive balance of community and professional needs on both quality and economic dimensions.[29]

Most of the activity is carried out by management and the medical staff. The details of the processes involved are addressed in Chapter 6. The core concept is one of **peer review**—the care of all patients is subject to review by a group of similarly trained physicians. Peer physicians work within the bylaws, and the **medical staff organization** and the senior management team provide appeal and mediation opportunities that keep the review process fair. The board's role is usually limited to oversight and final approval. The board also serves as a final arbiter in case of disputes, but these should be rare.

Medical staff bylaws
A formal document of the governance procedures for physicians and others who provide care in the organization; approved by the governing body

Peer review
Any review of professional performance by members of the same profession

Medical staff organization
The organization of an HCO's staff members that provides a structure to carry out policies, expectations for quality of clinical care, and communication from physicians to the governing body

Monitoring Performance Against Plans and Budgets

The hallmark of successful organizations is to be future oriented, set achievable goals, achieve them, and celebrate success. Well-managed organizations work on a no-surprises assumption that carefully developed agreements will meet legal and ethical standards and will generally come to pass. Monitoring is not policing; it is an activity to prevent problems and to find insights for the next round of goal setting. Recent law and social action in the United States have emphasized the duty of governance to control compliance with ethical and legal standards, including such issues as accurate information, protection of assets, protection of confidentiality and other individual rights, and conformance to laws governing contracts. While much of the legal obligation to control is established only for publicly listed for-profit corporations,[30] the trend has widespread support both in society at large[31] and among healthcare influentials.[32] Excellent organizations use board review that is future oriented and preventive. They build a culture where noncompliance is never a reasonable path to follow.

The board performs four monitoring functions that promote both excellence and compliance.

Routine Surveillance of Performance Data

The strategic measures established in the goal-setting process are monitored by the board monthly or quarterly. The concept and the reality are that most values reported on the Saint Luke's template (Exhibit 4.3) will be in the green or blue zones, exceeding the minimum goal and moving toward benchmark. Reports in the yellow zone are a signal to management rather than the board. Reports in the red zone—below the minimum goal—are rare but serious. When they occur, management is expected to be prepared with a 90-day plan for recovery. Board intervention should be extremely rare. Intervention draws the board into details of management that it is not equipped to handle. Worse, intervention draws the board away from the strategy-oriented functions it alone can do.

Acceptance of Reports from Auditors, Accreditors, and Other External Agencies

Good practice now requires that the audit activities needed for strategic protection report directly to the governing board so that the auditors are insulated from threats and conflicting interests. The result of the expansion of audits is not only greater protection against fraud but also greater accuracy in reporting and greater trust in the numbers throughout the organization.

Several outside agencies monitor performance from a public perspective and report directly to the board, usually through an audit committee. The no-surprises assumption applies: Clean reports are expected, and exceptions, though rare, get immediate and unpleasant readjustment.

The **external auditor** is selected by and accountable to the board, usually through an audit committee. The audit attests that the accounting practices followed by the organization are sound and that the financial reports fairly represent the state of the business. A **management letter** points out real or potential problems that might impair either of these

External auditor
A certified public accounting firm that attests that the accounting practices followed by the organization are sound and that the financial reports fairly represent the state of the business

Management letter
Comments of external auditors to the governing board that accompany their audited financial report

two statements in the future. The management letter is, in effect, an audit of the internal auditor and the board's ultimate protection against misrepresentation, fraud, or misappropriation of funds.

Accreditation by The Joint Commission or the American Osteopathic Association (AOA) (through its accrediting agency, Healthcare Facilities Accreditation Program) is accepted as *deemed status* for the Conditions of Participation in Medicare and Medicaid and many health insurance plans.[33] Almost all acute care hospitals are accredited. Excellent hospitals generally exceed Joint Commission or AOA standards; serious or repeated difficulty meeting them suggests major weaknesses in the organization. The Joint Commission's website allows public access to reports on individual hospitals showing quantitative assessments of improvement in clinical performance. The Joint Commission's National Patient Safety Goals and National Quality Improvement Goals address common errors in patient care, such as misidentification of the patient or miscommunication of orders. The quality improvement goals measure outcomes of clinical care, such as heart attack, heart failure, community-acquired pneumonia, and pregnancy and related conditions.

The National Committee for Quality Assurance accredits health insurance plans and physician organizations. It has emphasized measured clinical performance since its founding in 1990.[34] As a result, accredited insurance plans provide many measures of clinical quality, many of which are incorporated into pay-for-performance incentives available to many hospitals and their physicians.[35] The board should review the available information on these measures and should also receive the reports of any accrediting or certifying examinations for its physician organization partners.

Various laws now govern specific activities such as patient record confidentiality, rights of employees and physicians, management of environmental hazards, and compliance with accounting regulations. **Compliance programs** are procedures designed to ensure compliance with specific regulation, such as Civil Rights, HIPAA (Health Insurance Portability and Accountability Act), or Medicare Fraud and Abuse. They are the responsibility of the executive office, but governing board oversight is required. Bond-rating agencies investigate all outstanding judicial or regulatory issues; their reports are a useful summary for the board. In 2002, Congress passed the Sarbanes-Oxley Act to impose numerous requirements on corporations regarding their governance and internal control arrangements.[36] Although Sarbanes-Oxley does not apply to not-for-profit corporations, the legislation has been widely accepted by leading HCOs.[37] If a committee of the board receives and acts on a thorough annual report of compliance, and any interim reports of serious difficulties, the organization is protected from the more severe penalties of these laws.[38,39]

Compliance programs

Programs designed to meet statutory and regulatory requirements; may be based on legislation or voluntary efforts such as accreditation

In addition to approval of physician contracts, the governing board routinely approves real estate transactions, acquisitions, mergers, joint ventures, and contracts involving large sums of money. The review includes compliance with legal requirements, and the existence of the review protects stakeholders against unexpected major changes in direction. In well-managed HCOs, these transactions arise from strategic opportunities that the board has previously discussed.

Approval of Major Contracts and Transactions

Improving Board Performance

An effective board must be thorough in its environmental assessment, imaginative in its search for solutions, and deliberate in its eventual actions. It must also be timely—responding to issues promptly—and efficient—not wasting the time of its members and other participants in the decision process. Well-managed organizations meet these criteria by a triple strategy of disciplined operation that emphasizes scheduling, preparation, focus, and delegation; deliberate educational programs for board members; and the use of systematic board performance review.[40]

The board, like all units of excellent HCOs, is expected to monitor and improve its own performance. It does this through an annual self-assessment that is usually led by a committee of the most senior members, a group that often also serves as the nominations committee. The members are often surveyed to determine their independent opinions of how well the board has completed the five functions and what opportunities for improvement (OFIs) should be pursued. They are often asked to assess their own contribution, an approach that helps identify new leadership and discourage "deadwood." The committee compiles these comments and its own observations and leads a discussion of how board processes can be improved. Surveys of boards in other industries confirm that boards that assess their members and themselves tend to be more effective than those that do not.[41]

The essential question in assessing the board's performance is whether stakeholder wants have been satisfied as well as realistic alternatives would permit. The board's performance is the corporation's performance, as reflected in the balanced scorecard and as compared to competitors and benchmarks.

Assessing Performance

In addition to the balanced scorecard measures, boards can use checklists of recommended practice to assess their performance; Bryant and Jacobson (2005) have proposed the ten measures shown in Exhibit 4.4. This checklist of good practices helps the board carry out its trust obligations. It complements, but does not replace, the balanced scorecard. A successful board should comply with all ten measures, but it should also have a near-benchmark scorecard.

EXHIBIT 4.4

Ten Measures of Board Effectiveness

1. Meeting legal requirements	Bond-rating agencies include a due diligence review of the organization's compliance with all outstanding legal obligations. The board, at a minimum, should always require that one of its committees have access to all such due diligence reports and any responses from senior management.
2. Compliance orientation	Corporate compliance is a process of honest self-scrutiny, often involving objective third-party evaluators. When done properly, it produces an attorney–client privileged report that the board of directors or an appropriate board committee can study in depth and monitor steps taken in response. Boards should insist that senior management develop a corporate compliance mentality, in which legal shortcomings are routinely defined, identified, analyzed, and corrected. A formal compliance program reduces legal risks and constitutes another best practice of good governance.
3. Continuing governance education (CGE)	The board chair, the CEO, and the governance committee chair should together take the lead in ensuring meaningful CGE for the entire board and not just its new members. Every board should have its formal and informal CGE calendar for each year, supplemented by having individual board members lead the discussions after their attendance at CGE events.
4. Use of dashboards	Dashboards (e.g., Exhibit 4.3) help boards realize that policy decisions should result in performance improvements. Appropriate and regular use of dashboards will build governance confidence and will easily distinguish those boards from the ones not using such governance best practices.
5. Agenda practice	Some form of board self-evaluation and executive sessions should occur at *each* board meeting. Good practice encourages questions, seeks balanced presentations, and makes a deliberate effort not to disparage any good-faith question.
6. Conflicts of interest*	Conflicts of interest should be announced at every meeting. "If board members will just remember three simple rules about conflicts of interest, they will generally want to do the right things.

    a. Undisclosed conflicts are, by definition, not 'in good faith,' which has the legal effect of nullifying all the directors' statutory immunities.

    b. Undisclosed conflicts can, since 1996, produce substantial federal excise taxes on affected individuals who are corporate insiders and who obtain excess benefits from their organizations.

    c. An apparent, but not real, conflict can cause almost as much trouble as a real one in terms of public embarrassment for individuals and [not-for-profit] boards."

* *continued*

EXHIBIT 4.4
continued

7. Corporate governance committee	The committee should meet regularly throughout the year; seek and nominate appropriate new members; review all outside reports and board effectiveness materials, plans, and continuing education; propose new measures, procedures, and bylaws as indicated; and investigate violations of confidentiality and conflict-of-interest policies.
8. Voluntary Sarbanes-Oxley compliance	The landmark Sarbanes-Oxley Act does not apply to not-for-profit organizations except to provide whistle-blower protection. But its rationales *do* apply. Governance committees should study the act and recommend such easily identifiable steps as CEO and CFO certification of financial statements and clarification of who should and should not serve on the board and various committees.
9. CEO evaluation	CEO evaluation is best coordinated through a board committee, but all members of the board should be invited expressly to participate. The evaluation should relate to board-established objectives and include an opportunity for open-ended comments as well as ones responsive to specific questions. The evaluation should directly affect a year-end bonus or the next year's base compensation. The board chair should share the evaluation with the CEO in a personal meeting. The process should include both the CEO's self-evaluation and the CEO's reaction to the board's evaluation.
10. Board planning and evaluation	Each of the foregoing nine areas of conduct includes some form of planning for the institution, but no single one of them "asks whether the full board is invested in helping to plan the overall future of the organization. Board self-analysis should include what *all* directors/trustees think about: a. their collective tackling of the foregoing nine measurable elements in the last year, b. the organization's prospects for the future, and c. their individual contributions and/or misgivings about what each has done or not done for the organization."

*Conflicts of interest: real or potential personal financial benefit that may accrue from a given board decision.

SOURCE: Used with permission from The National Center for Healthcare Leadership. Bryant, L. E., Jr., and P. D. Jacobson. 2006. "Practices for Measuring the Effectiveness of Ten Best of Nonprofit Healthcare Boards." *Modern Healthcare* Supplement, December.

A wave of governance failures in the for-profit world around 2002 led to rethinking and strengthening of board practices and authority. One element that has gained popularity is the use of regular executive sessions, where only nonmanagement board members remain. The purpose of the session is to allow outside members complete freedom to discuss the performance of the

Executive Sessions

CEO or other issues in the early stages when they can most effectively be addressed.[42] An executive session can be part of each regularly scheduled board meeting.

People

Board Membership

Society has established, through law and tradition, two minimum criteria for the actions of governing boards. The first is that the yardstick of action is prudence and reasonableness, rather than the looser one of well intentioned or the stronger one of successful. Board members should be careful, thoughtful, and judicious in decision making; they need not always be right. The second is that the board members hold a position of trust for the owners. They must not take unfair advantage of their membership and must, to the best of their ability, direct their actions to the benefit of the whole ownership. Board members must avoid situations that give some owners special advantage, particularly an advantage to themselves. In not-for-profit corporations, the board members must attempt to reflect the needs of all individuals in the community who depend on the institution for care.

Excellent boards seek members who are committed to the criteria of prudence and trust. They select their members through a continuing search, and they support their members with ongoing programs to help them make the biggest possible contribution. This section discusses board selection criteria, processes, compensation, education, and support. It also addresses two special issues of membership: conflicts of interest for board members and roles for physicians and CEOs on boards.

Membership Qualifications

Skill and Character Criteria

Board members should be able to make the challenging and sophisticated decisions required in the five managerial functions. Members should bring to each meeting good judgment based on an acute sense of the best interest of the owners as a whole. For not-for-profit HCOs, board members must recognize the community as owner. What characteristics predict these critical skills?

- *Familiarity with the community.* The raison d'être of community boards is their ability to relate healthcare decisions to local conditions. This means insight into how much money the community should pay for care, how to recruit professionals to the community, how to attract volunteers and donations, how to make community members feel comfortable as patients and associates, and how to influence local opinion and leadership. Different groups in the community will have different views on these questions. The board should have members who represent the diversity of the community but whose understanding transcends their own sex, race, and social group.

- *Familiarity with business decisions.* Most board decisions are multimillion-dollar commitments. They are measured and described in the languages of accounting, business law, finance, and marketing. The HCO boardroom, like other board-rooms, is a place where technical language is frequently used to communicate complex concepts. There is also an emotional component to multimillion-dollar decisions. Although householders can make excellent board members, moving from hundred-dollar decisions to million-dollar decisions takes some practice. Previous experience at decision making is important to gain the necessary famil-iarity with the language and as psychological preparation.
- *Available time.* Board service on even a medium-sized community hospital requires a substantial time commitment—one day per month at a minimum, but more for officers and committee chairs. People who do not have the time to master the information and participate actively in debate are unlikely to guide the organization effectively.
- *A record of success.* The best predictor, more important than general experience or formal education, is how well the person has done on similar assignments. This indicator is important after the individual has joined the board as well. Effective members should be promoted to higher board offices. Reliance on achievement is a way of overcoming biases in selecting board officers. Objective criteria open opportunities for members of disadvantaged groups.
- *Reputation.* The general reputation or character of an individual is important in two senses. First, like the record of success, it is an indication of what the indi-vidual will do in the future. Second, it serves to enhance the credibility of the in-dividual. Persons with reputations for probity frequently gain influence because of that reputation. What they say is received more positively. Boards have a legal obligation for prudence. The appointment of people whose reputation is suspect could be construed as imprudent.

Representation criteria are related to the resource distribution functions of the board. Many people support the political argument that only a member of a certain constituency can understand truly how the organization treats that group. They believe a good board should have representation from women, the poor, ethnic groups, labor, and so forth. The concept of representation can be extended to include employees, physicians, nurses, religious bodies in-volved in ownership, and other groups. Stakeholder constituencies are usually pleased by recognition at the board level. **Representation Criteria**

Several caveats must be attached to representation criteria. First, and most important, representatives who lack the necessary skills and character are unlikely to help either their constituency or the community at large. Sec-ond, excellent boards act by consensus for the community as a whole. The concept of resource distribution tends to foster adversarial positions, compro-mise instead of consensus, and division instead of enhancement of resources. Third is the problem of tokenism. A seat on a board, particularly a single seat, does not necessarily mean influence in the decisions. Finally, the appointment itself changes the individual. The lessons of the boardroom are not available to their constituents, and over a period of time, the board members are co-opted from the view for which they were selected. Tokenism and co-optation can be deliberate adversarial strategies to diminish a group's influence.

Affirmative action to ensure that competent individuals are not excluded from board membership is encouraged under the law and seems likely to make organizations more successful. A balance can be best struck if two points are kept in mind:

1. *Board members are appointed as individuals, not as representatives.* They should be competent to serve in their own right, regardless of their position in the community.
2. *Board members act on behalf of the community as a whole.* This does not rule out special considerations of groups with unusual needs, but it places those considerations in a context—they are appropriate to the extent that they improve the community as a whole.

Board Selection

Selecting board members involves issues of eligibility, terms, offices, committees, and the size of the board as well as the actual choice of individuals. Officers and committee chairs have more power than individual members, so their selection is especially important.

Appointment to Membership and Office

Most HCOs have self-perpetuating boards—the board itself selects new members and successors. Other methods include election by stockholders—the prescribed procedure in stock corporations—and election by members of the corporation who sometimes are simply interested members of the community. Boards of government institutions are frequently appointed by supporting jurisdictions or, rarely, through popular votes. In multicorporate systems the parent corporation appoints subsidiary boards, usually from local nominations. Boards generally elect their own officers. In addition to the officers, a number of committee members and chairs must be appointed, a job usually left to the chair but appropriately subject to discussion or approval.

Role of the Nominating Committee

The nominating committee nominates both members and officers. As Exhibit 4.4 notes, the committee also manages the board's self-evaluation and resolves issues of conflict of interest. It is usually a standing committee with membership determined by the bylaws. It is common to put former officers on the nominating committee; such a strategy emphasizes continuation of the status quo in the organization. Thus, organizations wishing for fresh ideas broaden nominating committee membership and charge the committee with searching more widely for nominees. It is typically in the confidential discussions of the nominating committee that individuals are suggested or overlooked, compared against criteria, and accepted or rejected. This makes the nominating committee one of the most powerful groups in an organization. Sophisticated leaders generally seek membership, or at least a voice, on this committee.

Nominees are usually asked beforehand if they will serve, and the best candidates frequently must be convinced. On most boards and similar social structures, truly contested elections and overt campaigning are rare. Many organizations nominate only one slate for boards and board offices. Formal provisions for write-in candidates and nominations from the floor are a safeguard that is rarely used. In the normal course of events, selection occurs in the nominating committee. The committee often proposes not only board members but also corporate and board officers and chairs of standing committees.

Size, Eligibility, and Length of Terms

The number of nominations to be made each year is a function of the number of board members and the length of their terms. Board sizes range from a handful to a hundred, although between 10 and 20 members are most common. The size of not-for-profit hospital boards has decreased slightly since 2000, with an average board size of 13.3 in 2007.[43] Larger boards tend to be honorific, delegating the actual governance functions to an executive committee.

Terms are generally three or four years, and the number of terms that can be served successively is usually limited. Lengthy terms or unlimited renewal of terms can lead to stagnation; it is difficult for the nominating committee to pass over a faithful member who wants to serve another term unless the rules forbid it. Too-short terms reduce the experience of officers as well as members. (It is possible to allow officers to extend their service beyond the normal limits.) Inexperienced officers rely more heavily on the CEO, thereby increasing the CEO's power at the expense of broader insight.

The size, terms, and limits are related. If there are 15 members, three-year terms, and a two-term limit, there will be five nominations each year, but only two or three new people will be added in most years. The median experience of board members will be about three years. Similarly, 16 members, four-year terms, and a two-term limit will add two new people yearly, and the median experience will be nearly four years.

In addition to length of service, many organizations have eligibility clauses related to the owning corporation. For-profit boards can require stock ownership. Church-sponsored organizations, even when they are operated as secular community institutions, can require that board members be from the religious group. Some government and voluntary not-for-profit institutions require residence in the political jurisdiction for board membership. Other eligibility clauses include phrases like "good moral character," although so much judgment is implied that they are more selection than eligibility criteria.

Compensation

The rewards for serving are complex. They include the satisfaction of a Samaritan need, pride in professional achievement, public recognition, association with community leaders, and sometimes commercial opportunities that relate indirectly to recognition and association. They do not include significant direct financial reward. Board members are compensated in less than 10 percent of hospitals, although monetary compensation is rare in not-for-profit HCOs.[44] The Volunteer Protection Act of 1997 affords greater protection against personal liability for trustees who are not compensated.[45] However, with governance activities becoming more complex and challenging, consuming increasing amounts of time, and exposing board members to enhanced scrutiny and liability, board compensation may emerge as a component of effective governance.[46]

CEO Membership

The CEO is always an active participant in board deliberations. Because their principal livelihood is from employment at the organization, CEOs have fundamental conflicts of interest in serving on the board. The conflict is particularly apparent when possibilities for consolidation or conversion are considered. It also occurs when other employees or doctors present grievances against the CEO. Although less obvious, CEOs can influence the board by controlling the information it receives (including the minutes) and by their role in suggesting the agenda.

Most hospital boards make the CEO an *ex officio* member, although there has been a steady decrease in CEOs with voting privileges in not-for-profit HCOs, suggesting a growing separation of management and governance.[47] CEOs hold offices, such as chair of the executive committee or president of the corporation. The justification lies in the same rule governing other conflicts—that the community's potential benefit exceeds its potential loss. It appears to be correct; evidence shows that organizations that deeply involve the CEO in strategic decisions have better financial performance.[48]

Physician Membership

Physicians who practice at the HCO also have clear conflicts of interest. The national consensus, however, is even clearer for physicians than for CEO board membership; in fact, The Joint Commission recommends physician representation. Empirical evidence indicates that hospitals that have physicians in board roles have better mortality and morbidity performance—that is, their scores on important measures of quality of care are superior[49] and their financial performance improves.[50] However, the results are not automatic and depend on specific implementation.[51] Physician representation improves overall success: The board needs to hear the viewpoint of doctors, and doctors need to know their views are being expressed. Many HCOs set aside seats for doctors and solicit nominations from the medical staff. It is not un-common for the medical staff to elect its representatives to a minority of the board.[52] Physician representation can approach 50 percent, but large fractions in not-for-profit corporations raise questions of inurement, tax exemption, and antitrust. The IRS relies on explicit rules to avoid inurement and to retain tax exemption.[53] Antitrust considerations forbid physicians (or other vendors) from collusion in restraint of trade.

Appointment of a few physicians is not a panacea, however. They are added to the board as community members, not representatives. Conflict-of-interest rules can silence a physician when his or her viewpoint is most critical. HCOs use a variety of other mechanisms to emphasize each physician's partici-pation in the decisions most immediate to his or her practice (see Chapter 6).

Board Organization

Board committees weigh the importance of various issues, evaluate differing political perspectives, identify interrelationships and opportunities to com-bine or separate issues, and resolve issues that do not require full board atten-tion. They analyze facts and educate members. They develop expertise in a given area, such as finance. They often expand representation, including oth-ers beside board members. Finally, they can take on especially sensitive issues, such as compensation, nomination, auditing, and medical staff membership, in a more discreet setting.

Committees

Well-managed boards delegate routinely to **standing committees**—permanent units of the board, established in the bylaws of the corporation. As shown in Exhibit 4.5, finance, compensation, audit, and nominating commit-tees are almost universal. By 2006, more than half of HCO governing boards had in place a quality committee to review processes of care, mortality, dashboard indicators for clinical qual-ity, patient safety, and patient satisfaction.[54] Gover-nance committees that review board performance have been effective in other industries.[55]

Standing committee
A permanent committee established in the bylaws of the corporation or similar basic documents

Each standing committee should have a clear, recurring agenda that cannot be handled well by other structures. The use of an executive com-mittee appears to be diminishing among small boards, where routine use is unnecessary. The overall tendency is toward a small, active board, with a few important standing committees. The counter trend in healthcare systems is toward a large network of such boards, but with a central board that has final authority over reserved powers—those specifically not delegated to subordi-nate boards.

Beyond the few standing committees, well-managed boards of all sizes use **ad hoc committees**, formed as appropri-ate to the issue at hand for a specified time period. An organization often has several ad hoc commit-tees working simultaneously and reporting to the

Ad hoc committee
A committee formed to address a specific purpose, for a specified time period

EXHIBIT 4.5
Typical
Standing
Committees of
the Governing
Board

Committee	Function	Membership
Executive	Act on behalf of full board in emergencies Less commonly, assume governance functions, making the full board advisory or honorific	Officers (chair, vice chair, secretary, treasurer), standing committee chairs, CEO and CFO
Quality	Develop strategic goals for quality improvement and safety Set the quality agenda Receive and recommend approval of quality and safety reports Review physician appointment and reappointment and results of focused quality studies	Board chair, COO, CMO, CNO, chair of the quality improvement council, clinical and nonclinical members
Finance	Establish long-range financial plan, debt structure, and initial budget guidelines Monitor budget performance	Treasurer, CFO, potential future chairs
Compensation	Review executive performance Award increases and bonuses Link senior executives' compensation to quality and patient safety indicators Ensure compliance with IRS, GAO, and Sarbanes-Oxley (if for-profit)	Officers, former officers, legal counsel
Audit	Review financial audit, Joint Commission reports	Officers, former officers
Nominating	Nominate new board members and board officers Review board performance and individual contribution Annually evaluate individual conflicts of interest Suggest improved processes	Senior board officers

CFO: chief financial officer; CMO: chief medical officer; CNO: chief nursing officer; COO: chief operating officer; GAO: Government Accountability Office; IRS: Internal Revenue Service

board or its standing committees. Large numbers of people can be involved. Effective use of ad hoc committees deliberately expands representation and participation, using clear goals, acceptable solution parameters, and timetables to guide and empower larger groups. The committee knows it must produce a solution within the parameters if possible and report back for further instructions if it cannot.[56] The boundaries of an acceptable decision are established in advance, and decisions within the boundaries are usually accepted by the board with limited debate. Scheduling, preparation, focus, and delegation allow diverse opinions to be heard, evaluated, debated, and revised. Ad hoc committees bring the most knowledgeable members into each decision. They open opportunities for conflict resolution and promote understanding and consensus. Even if a minority is opposed to the final outcome, the members understand the logic that determined it and are convinced that the process was appropriate.

The rules for operation of the board are recorded in **governance bylaws**. These specify quorums, requirements for passage of specific items, duties of committees and officers, and procedures for the conduct of business. Matters such as the use of a consent agenda or the board's calendar are usually covered in procedural memoranda that supplement the bylaws.

Governance bylaws

A corporate document that specifies quorum rules of order, duties of standing committees and officers, and other procedures for the conduct of business

Multicorporate Governance Structures

The original concept of a governing board was of the ultimate authority for an independent corporate unit. The managerial functions identified above derive from that concept. They are the set of activities that must be referred to the most central level to be properly coordinated. The nature of hierarchical organizations is such that one can affiliate several corporate units and establish governance functions for the affiliates, setting up boards that report to boards. For example, an HCO that operates two hospitals, a medical group practice, a home care, and a hospice as subsidiaries needs at least one board, but it might have as many as five—one for each entity. (Technically, any separately incorporated unit must have a board, but the requirement can be met by a small group of employed officers. The discussion here is of boards that include other stakeholder representation.)

Subsidiary boards make four contributions that have made them popular in larger HCOs:

1. They expand representation, allowing local leaders to retain a sense of influence over their institution and local preferences to be reflected in operating decisions. This is particularly important when the subsidiaries operate in different markets; as a result, most multistate systems have local subsidiary boards.
2. They allow board specialization. The home care and hospice board would allow input from stakeholders with expertise and interest in these services, for example.
3. They permit joint ventures with other corporations and partnerships with the medical staff. Various service lines can be separately incorporated with different groups of physicians who serve on the boards.
4. They allow identification of taxable endeavors and protect the exemption of activities that qualify under the Internal Revenue Code.

Subsidiary boards operate under the concept of **reserved powers**. Reserved powers are held permanently by the corporate board. Their purpose is to make sure the subsidiary continues to follow the central mission and vision and to resolve conflicts between subsidiaries. (A similar concept, called *super majority,* requires the support of certain stakeholders in votes dealing with certain issues.) Reserved powers usually include the rights to buy or sell other corporations and real estate; issue stock or debt; approve long-range plans, LRFPs, and annual goals; appoint or approve board members and the CEO; and approve bylaws. Within the limits imposed by reserved powers, subsidiary

Reserved powers
Decisions permanently vested in the central corporation of a multicorporate system

boards tend to work as corporate boards do. They carry out the managerial and resource-related functions for their organization, making recommendations to the parent board on the reserved matters.

Exhibit 4.6 shows the board structure of Henry Ford Health System, a $3.4 billion a year HCO that serves about 20 percent of the metropolitan Detroit market of 4.5 million people. The system has 12 subsidiary boards that involve 150 members and report to a system board of 44 members. The 12 boards allow almost 200 people to participate in the activity of the corporation. It is sufficiently flexible to allow the system to run a successful insurance company, participate in a variety of partnership activities with several other large healthcare providers and insurers in the area, and operate HCOs oriented to specific local communities and reflect their histories and preferences. About a dozen other corporate entities exist but are managed by internal directors. With the exception of the 1,000-member Henry Ford Medical Group, which is accountable to the system board through the regional units, these entities are mainly special-purpose organizations that handle insurance and real estate activities.

Joint Venture Boards

Much acute care is now delivered in service lines that focus on a specific clinical area such as women's health. It is common to establish the service line as an explicit collaboration between the HCO and a group of its physicians. It is often desirable to incorporate the service line separately and to share its governance with the participating physicians. The arrangements can either be contractual or by establishing jointly owned corporate subsidiaries, commonly called *joint ventures.*

Joint ventures normally have boards that represent the participating groups. They can be either for-profit or not-for-profit. They are often designed to require approval of parent corporate boards or super majorities on matters such as major expansion, change in direction, or dissolution. The joint venture structure is flexible and convenient to allow physician ownership and shared financial rewards. The actual models in place are not automatically effective, however. A review of literature concludes, "The evidence base for the impact of many models of economic integration is either weak or nonexistent, with only a few models of economic integration having robust effects."[57]

EXHIBIT 4.6 Henry Ford Health System Governance Structure

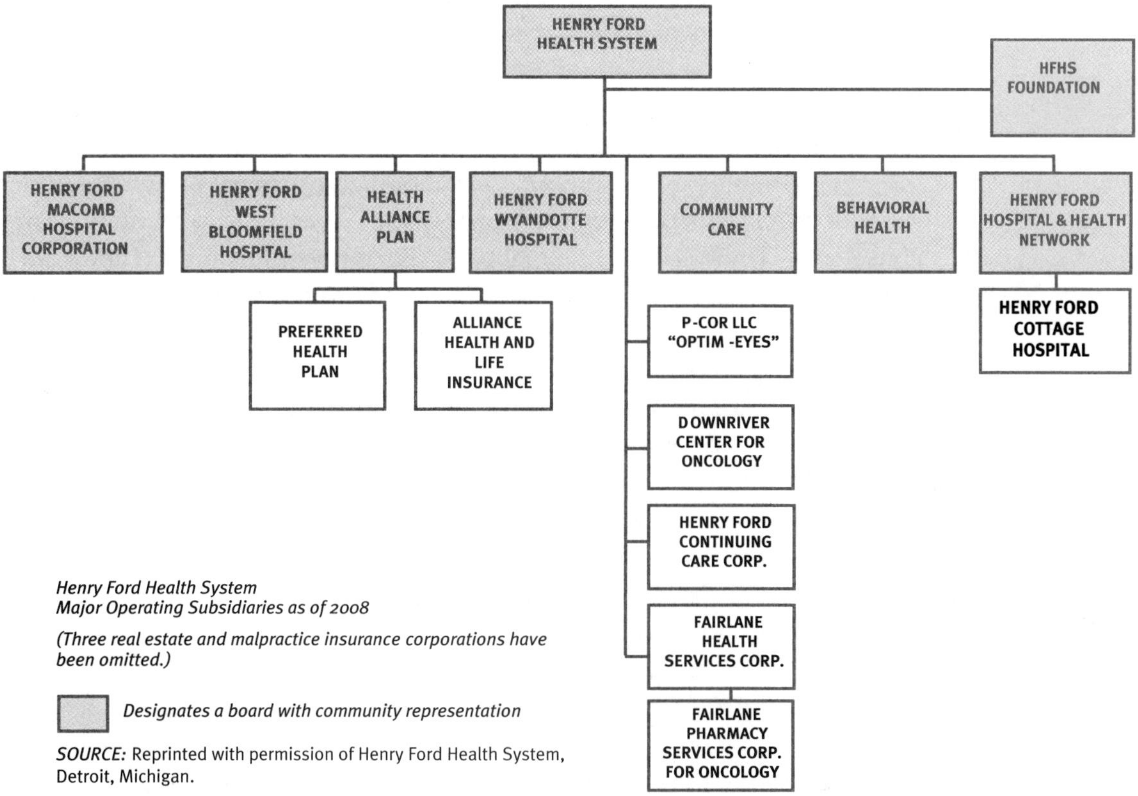

Henry Ford Health System
Major Operating Subsidiaries as of 2008

(Three real estate and malpractice insurance corporations have been omitted.)

Designates a board with community representation

SOURCE: Reprinted with permission of Henry Ford Health System, Detroit, Michigan.

Joint ventures need not be limited to service lines. Understanding the competition, even in hotly contested local markets, is a form of cooperation. For healthcare, competition is regulated by federal and state law, which generally encourages rivalry to win customers under specified conditions such as licensure, fair advertising, and avoidance of collusion or discrimination. The law permits various kinds of collaboration. HCOs are learning to exploit both aspects of regulated markets. Thus, they can and do compete and collaborate with each other simultaneously. In Kansas City, Saint Luke's Health System and the local unit of HCA, a national for-profit hospital system, collaborate to run a cancer center.[58] In Iowa, two Catholic systems collaborate to provide referral care and telemedicine to a larger rural area.[59] Arrangements like these are formed because they offer routes to market advantages that are more practical than other available alternatives.

Education and Information Support for Board Members

Evidence from California voluntary hospital boards shows that educated boards achieve greater financial success.[60] New members need education in several unique aspects of healthcare management. There are also issues unique to the particular institution. While new members should bring fresh perspectives, they should not operate in ignorance of history. New-member orientation programs include tours, introductions to key personnel, conveyance of written documents and texts, and planned conversations and presentations. A typical list of subjects is shown in Exhibit 4.7. Catholic Health Initiatives, a successful HCO system operating in 20 states, mandates a three-day off-site training program for each new trustee in its member HCOs.[61]

Ongoing board education is accomplished by special programs—time set aside from business to explore new ideas and best practices—often using consultants. To be effective, formal programs for board members should follow certain rules. Brevity is essential. Small segments should be scheduled for each specific topic. Most important, members should be active participants. Questions should be encouraged, the style should be conversational, and the discussion should be extended over several sessions. Both orientation and ongoing board education should be evaluated through the Kirkpatrick level 3—effective application (see Chapter 3).

After orientation, most board members' learning is informal and on the job. Well-organized boards make committee appointments carefully, allowing new members to become acquainted with the organization in less demanding assignments. They fill chairs with experienced members; they use chairs and organization executives to help members learn as they serve. The four critical committees—executive, quality, finance, and nominating—should be composed of the more seasoned board members, and their chairs should be members nearing the end of service. The nominating committee is frequently the last service of former officers.

In addition to on-the-job learning, high-performing HCOs now include educational programs in their agenda. These serve to clarify specific situations, keep the board current with national and regional trends, and provide background on complex issues. Many disagreements between stakeholders stem from avoidable misunderstandings and ambiguities of positions. Thus, the "backgrounding" helps the board make clearer, less controversial decisions.

Measures

Board performance is measured primarily by the strategic scorecard. Values on the scorecard should be improving and approaching benchmark. If they are stagnant or declining, the board must negotiate more aggressive goals and explore with management or outside consultants how to achieve them. Specific OFIs for the board arise from the measures proposed by Bryant and Jacobson (see Exhibit 4.4). Many OFIs arise from qualitative comments; the board's nominating committee identifies and prioritizes them in its review processes.

EXHIBIT 4.7
Board Member
Orientation
Subjects

Mission, Role, and History of HCOs

What healthcare organizations give to the community

Difference between for-profit, not-for-profit, and government ownership

How HCOs Are Financed

Operating funds

Private insurance

Government insurance

Uninsured patients

Sources and uses of capital funds

How HCOs Strive for Excellence

Quality and safety agenda

Service lines

Empowerment and transformational management culture

Performance measurement

Continuous improvement

HCO–Physician Relations

Nature of contract between doctors and healthcare organizations

Concept of peer review

Trustee responsibilities for the medical staff

Functions of the Governing Board

Maintain management capability

Establish the mission, vision, and values

Approve the corporate strategy and annual implementation

Ensure quality and appropriate medical care

Monitor organizational performance

Continuously improve board performance

Duties of Trustees

Duty of loyalty (conflict of interest)

Duty of care

Conflict of interest

Fiduciary and compliance duties

Trustee liability

Confidentiality

Managerial Issues

The board's continuous improvement function, structure, and educational program described in this chapter are all designed to increase board effectiveness. They have all been used effectively by high-performing HCOs—that is, those that are near benchmark on strategic performance measures. They help many boards overcome the pitfalls of governance: incomplete information, inability to reach decisions, and unbalanced response to stakeholder needs. Even with them, boards and senior management must be vigilant to help the board make the best decisions.

Operating Discipline

The board can fail by making the wrong decision or by not deciding, and the latter may be the most common failure. Operating discipline keeps track of the agenda so that no item is lost and all items receive a timely decision. The board's six functions are driven by the HCO's annual planning calendar (see Exhibit 3.7). They provide a checklist for what must be done each month. If the board falls behind in its duties, the rest of the organization is stymied.

Maintaining timeliness is often challenging. Most board actions are by consensus—unanimous agreement—rather than by a majority vote. This gives minority positions substantial power. A committed minority can successfully stall a position valuable to the whole. In the worst case, when several stakeholder groups use this possibility, the board becomes a deliberate weapon to avoid change. Operating discipline brings to the board items that can be handled without acrimonious dissent. Preparation, agenda management, use of committees and subcommittees, and deliberate negotiation all have a role. Board leadership and senior management use these tools to identify and resolve differences, building both the proposal details and the consensus in a stepwise progression.

Preparation

CEOs and their staffs are responsible for preparing appropriate factual documentation for every agenda item. They have the responsibility for conducting the environmental surveillance, identifying issues, analyzing and developing proposals, and understanding the needs of the community. Staff is used extensively to gather and disseminate facts and to identify potential conflicts. Establishing the fact base is a major justification for the strategic support activities described in chapters 10 through 15. Not only does it provide the due diligence that foresees and avoids implementation problems, but it also identifies potential conflicts and opens alternatives for negotiated solutions.

The other aspect to preparation is general rather than specific to the issues at hand. Most issues take meaning from context; the better the environment and the decision-making processes are understood, the better the specific decision is likely to be. Thus, board selection and education are important preparation. Well-managed boards begin major issues with backgrounding. They balance the importance of the issue with the team managing it. They frequently pair inexperienced and experienced members to facilitate on-the-job learning.

Focused Agendas

The actual agenda management falls heavily on the board chair, the committee chairs, and the CEO. A discussion may have any of several outcomes in view: general education and backgrounding, exploration of controversial or complex topics, plan to develop a proposal through committees, or action on specific proposals. Both the outcome and time allotment are made clear to the board at the start of the discussion. A major issue may come before the board for each of these outcomes as it evolves, is understood, and is finally resolved.

Successful boards tend to focus on major issues one at a time, attempting to comprehend all aspects of the single issue and reach a consensus understanding of it. Meetings feature a few issues or a single issue in depth, rather than a superficial review of several topics. Ongoing information not related to the priority issues is often consolidated into a **consent agenda**—a group of reports passed without discussion. Members may request to remove a matter from the consent agenda if

Consent agenda
A group of agenda items passed without discussion unless a member requests a review; used to focus attention on priority matters

they have a specific concern. Such requests are rare and are usually granted by the chair or by motion of the board.

Retreats are effective as devices to focus board attention. They can be held in comfortable off-site settings, emphasizing the departure from usual practice. Longer sessions allow fuller presentation of issues and background. Additional representatives of medical staff and management can be invited, facilitating understanding, acceptance, and implementation of the final decision. Consultants and guests from the community can be used to expand knowledge of factual and political issues.

Use of Committees and Subcommittees

The purpose of the focused agenda is not to suppress debate or force inadequately prepared decisions but to ensure that no aspect of the board's functions is neglected at the expense of discussion that can be completed in a less central environment. Thus, issues that arise from board discussion are referred to standing or ad hoc committees, and within these committees to subcommittees or less formal discussion. Moving the issue away from the boardroom allows more voices to be heard, more alternatives to be explored, and more candid expressions of viewpoint.

Senior management plays a critical role in this process. It identifies stakeholders with interests and brings them to the committees. It seeks best practices that demonstrate the ways others have solved the issues. It painstakingly explores positions, developing the understanding that is the first stage of negotiating solutions.

Negotiation

Progress usually involves designing proposals that meet most or all stakeholder needs and do not impair the special needs of any one group. Proposals that might generate powerful resistance are avoided. Compromise is the rule; radical reform is rare. Although this realism slows progress, it is inherent in the culture of respect. The fact that HCOs that use this model succeed shows that there are avenues where material progress can be made. Extensive negotiation is often necessary to find them. Negotiation takes place at all levels, from individual meetings to major committees, but rarely in the board meeting itself. Senior managers often negotiate directly to shape proposals that will gain consensus. Their skill at shaping consensus proposals and then implementing them "as advertised" is a major factor in maintaining stakeholder loyalty.

Legal and Ethical Issues of Board Membership

Three areas of legal and ethical concern are known to create governance difficulties:

1. *Conflict or duality of interest,* where a board member has a personal financial gain or risk in the decision at hand. The duty of loyalty holds that members of governing boards should not serve when their personal financial interests

conflict with those of the owners. Conceptually, this is clear enough. In practice, it is hard to find people who meet the criteria for board membership but who have not also become involved in activities that eventually will conflict. Conflict of interest is inherent in any democratic structure, and it cannot be permanently resolved. Each member annually declares in writing his or her major activities and holdings. Individuals are expected to disqualify themselves from discussion and voting on an issue whenever appropriate, but they may be asked to do so by the chair or another member. Good practice calls for an announcement of conflicts at each board meeting, with attention to the specific agenda. It is generally agreed that the external auditor and the legal counsel should not serve as board members.

2. *Inurement,* where a board member improperly receives financial gain from the assets of a corporation. Inurement rules apply to not-for-profit corporations. Actions by trustees that lead to their personal financial gain can be inurement. Inurement often means compensation in excess of the market value provided. The IRS monitors executive and other high-level salaries and can deny tax-exempt status to an organization that allows inurement.[62]

3. *Conversions,* where the assets of a not-for-profit corporation are transferred to a for-profit corporation at less than their true value. Conversion (when not-for-profit assets are converted to for-profit ownership) and consolidation (when one corporation merges with another, regardless of tax structure) raise important questions of fairness to the owners. Because of this, they place trustees and directors at unusual risk. Boards usually hire special legal counsel skilled in these transactions.[63] Large-scale conversions and consolidations often require regulatory or judicial review.

Lawsuits over these matters serve to reinforce the ethical duties. Board members can be sued as individuals, although such suits are rare. Lawsuits must demonstrate a trustee's failure in one or more of the three duties of loyalty, care, and disclosure, such as failing to take due care, deliberate self-serving, or unnecessarily risky behavior. The board's legal counsel should guard against individual liability as well as guide the board as a whole. Directors' and officers' liability insurance provides legal and financial assistance against suits that might be placed.

Carrying out the management and leadership activities delegated by the board is a demanding professional career (and is the subject of the remaining 11 chapters). The resources that HCOs use to carry them out cost as much as or more than many clinical activities but are arguably more important. Delivering babies is important, but only if the mothers and babies receive safe, effective, patient-centered, timely, efficient, and equitable care. Those goals are met through the processes that the board starts and that management carries out.

Suggested Readings

Alexander, J. A., T. G. Rundall, T. J. Hoff, and L. L. Morlock. 2006. "Power and Politics in Health Services Organizations." In *Health Care Management: Organizational Design and Behavior*, edited by S. M. Shortell and A. D. Kaluzny, 276–310. Clifton Park, NY: Delmar Cengage Learning.

The Alliance for Advancing Nonprofit Health Care. 2009. "Advancing the Public Accountability of Nonprofit Health Care Organizations: Guidelines on Governance Practices." www.nonprofithealthcare.org.

American College of Healthcare Executives. 2010. *Contracts for Healthcare Executives*, 5th ed. Chicago: Health Administration Press.

Conger, J. A. (ed.). 2009. *Boardroom Realities: Building Leaders Across Your Board.* San Francisco: Jossey-Bass.

Joshi, M. S., and B. J. Horak. 2009. *Healthcare Transformation: A Guide for the Hospital Board Member.* Chicago: American Hospital Association.

McGinn, P. 2009. *Partnership of Equals: Practical Strategies for Healthcare CEOs and Their Boards.* Chicago: Health Administration Press.

Notes

1. Orlikoff, J. E. 2005. "Building Better Boards in the New Era of Accountability." *Frontiers of Health Services Management* 21 (3): 3–12.
2. Kane, N. M., J. R. Clark, and H. L. Rivenson. 2009. "The Internal Processes and Behavioral Dynamics of Hospital Boards: An Exploration of Differences Between High- and Low-Performing Hospitals." *Health Care Management Review* 34 (1): 80–91; Conger, J. A., E. E. Lawler III, and D. L. Finegold. 2001. *Corporate Boards: Strategies for Adding Value at the Top.* San Francisco: Jossey-Bass.
3. Alexander, J. A. 1990. "Governance for Whom? The Dilemmas of Change and Effectiveness in Hospital Boards." *Frontiers of Health Services Management* 6 (3): 39.
4. Ehrenreich, B., and J. Ehrenreich. 1970. *The American Health Empire: Power, Profits, and Politics.* New York: Random House.
5. Rosenberg, C. E. 1987. *The Care of Strangers: The Rise of America's Hospital System.* New York: Basic Books.
6. Seay, J. D., and B. C. Vladeck. 1988. "Mission Matters." In *In Sickness and In Health: The Mission of Voluntary Health Care Institutions*, edited by J. D. Seay and B. C. Vladeck, 1–34. New York: McGraw-Hill.
7. Conger, Lawler, and Finegold (2001).
8. Collins, J. 2001. *Good to Great.* New York: HarperBusiness.
9. Griffith, J. R., and K. R. White. 2005. "The Revolution in Hospital Management." *Journal of Healthcare Management* 50 (3): 170–90.
10. Alexander, J. A., and S.-Y. D. Lee. 2006. "Does Governance Matter? Board Configuration and Performance in Not-for-Profit Hospitals." *The Milbank Quarterly* 84 (4): 733–58; Alexander, J. A., Y. Ye, S.-Y. D. Lee, and B. J. Weiner. 2006. "The Effects of Governing Board Configuration on Profound Organizational Change in Hospitals." *Journal of Health and Social Behavior* 47: 291–308.
11. Conger, Lawler, and Finegold (2001).
12. Kovner, A. R. 1985. "Improving the Effectiveness of Hospital Governing Boards."

Frontiers of Health Services Management 2 (1): 4–33. See also commentaries by R. F. Allison, R. M. Cunningham, Jr., and D. S. Peters.

13. Kane, Clark, and Rivenson (2009).

14. U.S. Department of Labor. 2001. [Online information; retrieved 7/16/01.] www.dol.gov/dol/asp/public/programs/handbook/discrim.htm.

15. Alexander, J. A., B. J. Weiner, and R. J. Bogue. 2001. "Changes in the Structure, Composition, and Activity of Hospital Governing Boards, 1989–1997: Evidence from Two National Surveys." *The Milbank Quarterly* 79 (2): 253–79.

16. Alexander, J. A., S.-Y. D. Lee, V. Wang, and F. Margolin. 2008. "Changes in the Monitoring and Oversight Practices of Not-for-Profit Hospital Governing Boards 1989–2005." *Medical Care Research and Review,* 1–16. [Online information; retrieved 1/8/09.]; American Hospital Association and American College of Healthcare Executives. 2008. "Executive Compensation: A Primer for Establishing Reasonable Compensation." [Online information retrieved 1/27/09.] www.ache.org.

17. Kinzer, D. M. 1982. "Turnover of Hospital Chief Executive Officers: A Hospital Association Perspective." *Hospital & Health Services Administration* 27 (3): 11–33.

18. Weil, P. A., S. A. Wesbury, A. H. Williams III, and M. D. Caver. 1991. "Hospital CEO Turnover. Phase II: A Longitudinal Study Comparing Leavers and Stayers (1979–1990)." *Healthcare Executive* 6 (3): 30–31.

19. American Hospital Association and American College of Healthcare Executives (2008).

20. McDermott, W., and L. L. C. Emery. "Non-Profit Executive Compensation Issues." The Governance Institute. [Online information; retrieved 5/5/05.] www.governanceinstitute.com/cd_421.aspx?contentID=.

21. Alexander, Weiner, and Bogue (2001), p. 268.

22. Conger, J. A., and R. M. Fulmer. 2004. "Developing Your Leadership Pipeline." *Harvard Business Review* 81 (12): 76–84.

23. Griffith and White (2005).

24. Marren, J. P., G. L. Feazell, and M. W. Paddock. 2003. "The Hospital Board at Risk and the Need to Restructure the Relationship with the Medical Staff: Bylaws, Peer Review and Related Solutions." *Annals of Health Law* 12 (2): 179–234.

25. The Joint Commission. [Online information; retrieved 2/2/09.] www.joint commission.org/NR/rdonlyres/5DD15D2A-09A0-4353-8290-C3C73A1E763F/0/SIWGVisionpaperfuturegoals.pdf.

26. Centers for Medicare & Medicaid Services. [Online information; retrieved 2/2/09.] www.cms.hhs.gov/HospitalQualityInits/08_HospitalRHQDAPU.asp.

27. Marren, Feazell, and Paddock (2003).

28. *Patrick v. Burget et al.* 1988. 486 U.S. 94, No. 86-1145, Supreme Court of the United States.

29. Greene, J. 2008. "It's a Privilege." *Trustee* 61 (3): 8–11. [Online information; retrieved 8/11/09.] ABI/INFORM Global. (Document ID: 1454011371).

30. Hann, D. P. 2001. "Emerging Issues in U.S. Corporate Governance: Are the Recent Reforms Working?" *Defense Counsel Journal* 68 (2): 191–205.

31. Hamilton, R. W. 2000. "Corporate Governance in America 1950–2000: Major Changes but Uncertain Benefits." *Journal of Corporation Law* 25 (2): 349–70.

32. Institute of Medicine, Committee on Quality of Health Care in America. 2001. *Crossing the Quality Chasm: A New Health System for the 21st Century.* Washington, DC: National Academies Press.

33. The Joint Commission. [Online information; retrieved 1/27/09.] www.joint

commission.org/StateFederal/deemed_status.htm; American Osteopathic Association. [Online information; retrieved 1/27/09.] www.osteopathic.org/index.cfm?PageID=acc_hfapArchive.

34. National Committee for Quality Assurance. [Online information; retrieved 2/2/09.] www.ncqa.org/tabid/675/Default.aspx.

35. *Ibid.*

36. Public Accounting Reform and Investor Protection Act of 2002, P.L. No. 107-204, 116 Stat. 745 [2002]).

37. Alexander, J. A., G. J. Young, B. J. Weiner, and L. R. Hearld. 2008. "Governance and Community Benefit: Are Nonprofit Hospitals Good Candidates for Sarbanes-Oxley Type Reforms? *Journal of Health Politics, Policy and Law* 33 (2).

38. *Ibid.*; Evashwick, C. J., and K. Gautam. 2008. "Governance and Management of Community Benefit: How Can Hospitals Be Positioned to Address New Challenges?" *Health Progress,* pp. 10–15.

39. U.S. Sentencing Commission. 2000. "2000 Federal Sentencing Guideline Manual." [Online information; retrieved 2/2/09.] www.ussc.gov/2000guid/TABCON00.htm.

40. Connelly, M. D. 2004. "The Sea Change in Nonprofit Governance: A New Universe of Opportunities and Responsibilities." *Inquiry* 41 (1): 6–20.

41. Conger, Lawler, and Finegold (2001).

42. Orlikoff (2005).

43. Lockee, C. 2008. "Board Structures and Practices." *Healthcare Executive* 23 (2): 62–63.

44. *Ibid.*, p. 62.

45. Volunteer Protection Act of 1997. (P.L. 105-119).

46. Orlikoff (2005).

47. Alexander, Lee, Wang, and Margolin (2008).

48. Molinari, C., L. Morlock, J. Alexander, and C. A. Lyles. 1993. "Hospital Board Effectiveness: Relationships Between Governing Board Composition and Hospital Financial Viability." *Health Services Research* 28 (3): 358–77.

49. Shortell, S. M., and J. P. LoGerfo. 1981. "Hospital Medical Staff Organization and the Quality of Care." *Medical Care* 19 (10): 1041–52.

50. Goes, J. B., and C. Zhan. 1995. "The Effects of Hospital–Physician Integration Strategies on Hospital Financial Performance." *Health Services Research* 30 (4): 507–30; Molinari, C., M. Hendryx, and J. Goodstein. 1997. "The Effects of CEO–Board Relations on Hospital Performance." *Health Care Management Review* 22 (3): 7–15.

51. Succi, M. J., and J. A. Alexander. 1999. "Physician Involvement in Management and Governance: The Moderating Effects of Staff Structure and Composition." *Health Care Management Review* 24 (1): 33–44.

52. Alexander, J. A. 1986. *Current Issues in Governance,* 15–18. Chicago: Hospital Research and Educational Trust.

53. Whitehead, R., Jr., and B. Humphrey. 1997. "IRS Eases Rules for Physician Representation on Governing Boards." *Healthcare Financial Management* 51 (3): 36, 38–39.

54. Jiang, H. J., C. Lockee, K. Bass, and I. Fraser. 2009. "Board Oversight of Quality: Any Differences in Process of Care and Mortality?" *Journal of Healthcare Management* 54 (1): 15–30; Joshi, M. S., and S. C. Hines. 2006. "Getting the Board on Board: Engaging Hospital Boards in Quality and Patient Safety." *Journal on Quality and Patient Safety* 32(4): 179–87.

55. Conger, Lawler, and Finegold (2001), p. 70.

56. Griffith, J. R. 1994. "Reengineering Health Care: Management Systems for Survivors." *Hospitals & Health Services Administration* 39 (4): 451–70.

57. Burns, L. R., and R. W. Muller. 2008. "Hospital–Physician Collaboration: Landscape of Economic Integration and Impact on Clinical Integration." *Milbank Quarterly* 86 (3): 375–434.

58. Saint Luke's Hospital. 2003. Malcolm Baldrige National Quality Award Application, vii. Kansas City, MO: Saint Luke's Hospital.

59. Griffith, J. R., and K. R. White. 2003. *Thinking Forward: Six Strategies for Highly Successful Organizations*, 87–118. Chicago: Health Administration Press.

60. Molinari, Morlock, Alexander, and Lyles (1993).

61. Griffith and White (2003).

62. U.S. Internal Revenue Service, Ruling 69-383. 1969.

63. Bryant, L. E., Jr. 1998. "Responsibilities of Directors of Not-for-Profit Corporations Faced with Sharing Control with Other Nonprofit Organizations in Health Industry Affiliations: A Commentary on Legal and Practical Realities." *Annals of Health Law* 7: 139–58.

5 FOUNDATIONS OF CLINICAL PERFORMANCE

In a Few Words

Clinical performance is the degree to which clinical professionals and healthcare organizations (HCOs) provide care that meets or exceeds the Institute of Medicine (IOM) aims. Excellence is achieved through the use and continuous improvement of protocols based on the best available clinical evidence. An excellent HCO has both patient management and functional protocols to guide clinical care, training so that its associates are skilled at implementing the protocols, and a clinical improvement plan that measures and benchmarks performance and stays current with science. Many believe it should also have strategies for improving community health. Clinical excellence demands overall excellence—functions for logistics, strategic planning, and conflict resolution must be maintained by the organization's senior leadership.

Critical Issues in Clinical Performance

1. *Using patient management protocols to guide clinical care:*
   - Select and adapt protocols to guide care of similar patients
   - Encourage careful professional guidance and support for individual patients
   - Use individualized and interdisciplinary plans of care and case management for complicated cases

2. *Using functional protocols to ensure safe, reliable, patient-centered care:*
   - Ensure quality and safety by standardizing care processes
   - Coordinate functional protocols across professional boundaries

3. *Continuously improving clinical care:*
   - Ensure qualified caregivers
   - Develop a service line structure to facilitate clinical accountability
   - Measure and report outcomes and effective care processes
   - Use patient care teams to identify opportunities and coordinate changes in care

4. *Supporting a culture of evidence-based medicine and evidence-based management:*
   - Maintain the scientific foundation of medicine
   - Measure and improve operating performance
   - Provide a structure for discussion, adaptation, and conflict resolution

5. *Strengthening prevention and health promotion:*
   - Understand the costs and benefits of prevention
   - Develop coalitions to promote health

Consider these questions as you read the chapter.

1. Why should clinical performance be focused on outcomes? Why are six dimensions (safe, effective, patient-centered, timely, efficient, and equitable) of measurement necessary? Why is it important that medical diagnosis is a heuristic process?

2. What are the contributions of a protocol? How does an HCO improve compliance with protocols? When might compliance be incorrect? Do the answers to these questions differ for patient management and functional protocols?

3. What is the role of individualized patient care plans and case management? When are these important, and how are they integrated with patient management protocols?

4. How could an HCO improve clinical performance without service lines? Should an HCO focus clinical measurement in an office of quality management? How would you develop functional protocols for functions like drug administration, which involves several different accountability units?

5. Is the best mission for a hospital "excellence in patient care" or "healthy community"?

The vision of safe, effective, patient-centered, timely, efficient, and equitable healthcare now guides all excellent caregiving teams. As noted in Chapter 1 (see Exhibit 1.1), the purpose of HCOs is to support caregiving teams as they realize that vision for all kinds of needs, from prevention to acute emergencies to end of life. Patient care teams must use interdisciplinary approaches, communicating across professional boundaries.[1] They must satisfy team members and retain their loyalty.[2] The twenty-first century marketplace will demand no less.[3]

The foundations to achieve the vision are now well established:

- Skilled professional caregivers who can diagnose disease from symptoms and complaints
- Trained support caregivers who can respond to patients' needs
- Patient care protocols that show the most common path to cure or palliation
- Functional protocols that ensure uniform delivery of care
- Ongoing patient listening and flexibility that identify and meet each patient's unique needs
- Community health assessment that allows the HCO to give excellent care and contribute to health promotion

These foundations allow HCOs to aggressively pursue quality across a continuum that incorporates office, home, and inpatient care. They permit HCOs to respond to consumer criteria, increase attention to the prevention and consequences of disease, and collaborate with nonhealthcare organizations to improve community health, reducing the long-term cost of healthcare.

Purpose

The first purpose of clinical care in a community HCO is

excellence in healthcare to identify and meet each patient's healthcare needs.

Implementing this purpose requires an array of teams skilled in diagnosis and treatment, balanced with the community's needs, and supported with effective logistics. Many excellent HCOs also pursue a second purpose of improving community health:

to identify and meet the community's healthcare needs.

Implementing the second purpose requires excellence in care. It goes beyond it to minimize unnecessary use of health services, through collaborative efforts to promote health, prevent disease, and curtail unnecessary treatment.

In the typical community, these purposes are fulfilled in the daily practice of thousands of caregivers led by doctors and nurses working intimately with each patient. The evidence is clear that the task is not uniformly well executed.[4,5,6,7] Quality of care,[8] utilization of services,[9,10] and patient satisfaction[11] vary substantially among communities, organizations, and physician specialties. This chapter establishes the conceptual foundations that are used by excellent HCOs to support their clinical teams. The following chapters will describe the important supporting functions for physicians, nurses, clinical support services, and community health.

Functions

Exhibit 5.1 describes five functions an HCO's clinical organization must perform.

Ensuring Accurate Diagnosis

Diagnosis, the process of determining the nature of disease, drives all of evidence-based medicine. The codification of disease initiated by Sydenham in the seventeenth century and now represented by the International Classification of Disease, version 10,[12] provides the foundation for all treatment. The diagnostic process is not simple. It integrates information from the patient's complaint, history, physical examination, and diagnostic testing. It is **heuristic**—that is, it systematically employs a trial-and-error mechanism that recognizes uncertainty and proceeds cyclically as more information is gathered. It continues even after treatment is begun, until the patient is discharged. Exhibit 5.2 shows the major steps in the diagnostic process.

Exhibit 5.2 is a useful conceptual model, but most real care is substantially more complicated. Several additional considerations are critical to understanding the realities of modern patient care:

Heuristic
Systematically employing a trial-and-error mechanism that recognizes uncertainty and proceeds cyclically as more information is gathered

1. *The process is heuristic throughout.* Although the diagnosis becomes surer as the patient progresses, some possibility of revision to either the plan of care or treatment remains until discharge. Actual care is more dynamically heuristic than the exhibit suggests. The primary caregiver begins constructing the differential diagnosis when the patient walks in and adds or rules out possibilities almost continuously as examination and care progress.
2. *Many patients have multiple complaints and multiple diagnoses.* For many middle-aged and elderly patients, the process goes on for years. In complex cases, multiple caregivers and clinical support services participate in ongoing review. In intensive care units, for example, advanced monitoring techniques, observation, and listening are continuous.
3. *The "differential diagnosis" introduced around the start of the twentieth century is the key to managing the uncertainty.* It establishes a framework for selecting diagnostic testing and treatment.[13]

Function	Description	What the HCO Does
Ensuring accurate diagnosis	Diagnosis is the critical contribution of the caregiver. It is an ongoing heuristic process driven by observation and interaction with the patient.	Selects effective caregivers; monitors their effectiveness Provides training to maintain and improve clinical skills Supports responsive listening to patients' needs Provides diagnostic clinical support services
Ensuring excellent care—safe, effective, patient-centered, timely, efficient, and equitable care	Treatment is responsive to diagnosis. It is driven by patient management and functional protocols, but individual patient response must be closely monitored.	Updates and maintains protocols; trains caregivers in their use Ensures patient safety and minimizes risks Provides informed consent Maintains logistic support Keeps a record of care Coordinates care
Individualizing patient care planning and treatment	Treatment is also heuristic. Patient variability is met by continued monitoring, individualized and interprofessional plans of care, and case management.	Provides specialist consultation Provides nursing care Supports communication among caregivers, patient, family, and subsequent caregivers
Improving community health	Communitywide approaches promote healthy behavior, prevent injury and disease, and promote cost-effective use of services. The HCO builds these collaboratively with other community organizations.	Measures community health with a set of indicators and benchmarks Catalyzes community interest Collaborates with other organizations Promotes effectiveness De-markets unnecessary care
Improving clinical performance	Measurement and benchmarking of clinical outcomes and processes identify OFIs. PITs address them. Training implements improved performance. Success is rewarded.	Supports measurement and benchmarking Supports PITs Uses protocols, training, and incentives to implement improved methods

OFIs: opportunities for improvement; PITs: process improvement teams

EXHIBIT 5.1
Functions of the Clinical Organization

4. *In all but the simplest cases, clinical support services provide diagnostic testing to confirm or rule out each of the differential diagnoses.* Specialists perform and interpret these tests. They and treatment specialists are available as consultants to the primary caregivers.

5. *Definitive treatment for serious disease often involves referral to a treatment specialist.* The treatment specialist typically manages a specific diagnosis and returns care to the primary caregiver when that treatment is complete. Ongoing care of chronic illness is typically managed by the primary caregiver.

For many patients the process becomes a team effort, led by the attending physician. The process meets the IOM goals when

- no treatable diagnosis is overlooked;
- no diagnosis is treated that should have been ruled out;
- the patient is fully informed about the diagnoses and allowed to exercise control over treatment selection;
- all decisions are reached in a timely manner; and
- all diagnostic tests are safe, effective, and efficient.

All failures in the diagnostic heuristic are costly. Some are very costly, and a few shorten life. Diagnostic failure is stressful for caregivers. High-performing HCOs support all aspects of the process, reducing failures and making themselves "a great place to get care" and "a great place to give care." The HCO's clinical, logistic, and strategic support systems contribute in several ways to reducing failures and meeting the goals.[14]

Ensuring Excellent Care

Clinical activities are not random or haphazard but are formalized, often scientific responses to specific patient stimuli. Every time nurses give an injection, they make several specific checks on the site, the patient's name, the drug, skin preparation, and equipment. Every time surgeons start an operation, the anticipated equipment is prepared in advance. Every time patients describe symptoms to their physicians, the physicians' responses are predictable for that symptom, considering other information at their command. This predictability is essential in achieving the IOM vision. It allows the identification of expectations in clinical behavior, which, in turn, leads to the formulation of protocols that guide clinical performance. Protocols are consensus statements on the right act in a given set of circumstances. They are used to integrate the caregiver's diagnoses with the patient's plan-of-care goals (cure or palliation) and the specific actions of treatment.

Protocols are not mechanistic, however. The physician is obligated to monitor the patient's progress and to modify the protocol to fit the patient's needs, as Exhibit 5.2 shows. In some situations, no treatment choice provides a clearly superior result. When this occurs, the IOM aim of patient-centered

EXHIBIT 5.2
Simplified
Diagnostic
Process

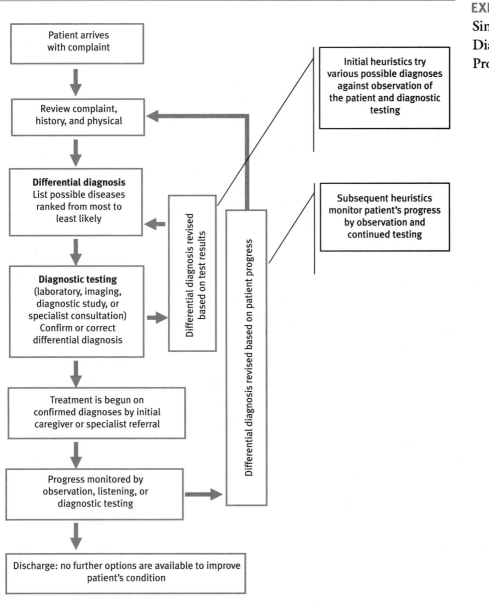

care and the ethical principle of autonomy on which it is based become critical. For example, for the diagnosis of prostate cancer, there is an array of treatment options but a lack of evidence that any of those treatment choices is superior. However, the costs are widely variable, as shown in Exhibit 5.3.[15] The patient will choose. Providing him with comprehensive and accurate advice is clearly critical to achieving both patient-centered care and efficiency.

Equitable care requires that all patients receive the same screening opportunity, the same access to information and advice, and the same access to

EXHIBIT 5.3
Average Cost
for Alternative
Prostate Cancer
Treatments

Treatment	Explanation	Cost
Watchful waiting	Active plan to postpone intervention, usually with exams and testing	$ 2,436
External beam radiation therapy	Multiple doses of radiation over several weeks	$12,224
Radical prostatectomy	Complete removal of prostate gland	$22,921
Brachytherapy	Implantation of radioactive seeds	$28,872
Intensity-modulation radiation therapy	Advanced radiation beam therapy targeted at tumor	$51,069

NOTE: The costs are for two years of care.

SOURCE: Used with permission from Leonhardt, D. 2009. "At What Cost." *New York Times* (July 8): A16. ©New York Times Graphics.

treatment. Over time, comparative effectiveness research will improve our understanding of prostate cancer care. It is essential for providing better information about alternatives for both patient and physician decision making.[16,17] The underlying uncertainty will be diminished, but it will never disappear. There will always be a frontier of scientific knowledge, where patient counseling will make important differences in total cost of care for a community.

Exhibit 5.4 shows the HCO contribution to excellent care—that is, care that fulfills each of the IOM aims. Two major functions are fundamental—protocol-driven activities and appropriate and continuous training and education of caregivers.

Implementing Protocols

Definition and Types of Protocols

Protocols reflect consensus reached in advance regarding the correct professional response to specific, recurring situations in patient care. Clinical protocols present several advantages. First, they make cooperation possible and are necessary to allow any level of sophisticated teamwork. Reflecting this necessity, clinical protocols are developed by the professions themselves. Second, they provide the basis for assessing or monitoring clinical performance. Third, they have become a convenient statement of contracts with patients and insurers.[18] The courts and the marketplace have reinforced the right of consumers to have their care conform to clinical standards developed by professionals. Protocols can be divided into two types—functional and **patient management**—depending on the level of application.

Functional protocols determine how procedural elements of care are carried out. They cover tasks of care accomplished by individuals (such as giving an injection or taking a chest x-ray) and sets of activities for

Patient management protocols
Formally established expectations that define the normal steps or processes in the care of a clinically related group of patients at a specific institution

Functional protocols
Procedures and sets of activities to carry out elements of care

Goal	Purpose	Activity	Examples
Safe	Minimize risk and unanticipated outcomes	Safety practices Engineering controls Safety plans Risk management plans	Functional protocols Training Hand-washing "Huddles" before surgery Patient fall precautions
Effective	Treatment meets desired outcome	Selecting treatment options based on evidence Monitoring for changes in response to treatment Patient management protocols	Guidelines for preventive screening Guidelines for diagnostic testing Watchful waiting for prostate cancer versus radiation or surgery
Patient-centered	Coordinate care that is individualized	Pre-care planning Nursing care Psychosocial considerations Cultural and language competency Patient education in care alternatives	Advance directives Interpreters Discharge follow-up Planning for post-discharge home care with appropriate caregiver education
Timely	Right treatment at the right time at the right place	Accurate and timely diagnosis Decreasing waiting times	Door-to-intervention time Early detection and intervention for patient complications Prompt transfer to a higher level of care
Efficient	Achieving quality with lowest cost	Evaluating lower cost alternatives of treatment, supplies, and pharmaceuticals	Functional protocols and training Standard treatment packs Standardizing drug formularies
Equitable	All persons have equal access to best treatment	Evaluating appropriateness of intervention when resources are scarce, depending on patient's condition and pros and cons	Uncompensated care Community outreach For certain costly cases (i.e., transplant) without scarce resource, refer to ethics committee for assistance in making decisions

EXHIBIT 5.4
HCO Contribution to Excellent Care

team procedures (such as surgical operations, rehabilitation programs, or multi-step diagnostic activities). They are usually written but are often carried out from memory. They are established and maintained by the individual professions and the functional accountability hierarchy of the organization.

Exhibit 5.5 is an example of a functional protocol. The profession most directly involved usually establishes functional protocols, and these protocols are codified in textbooks for the profession. Modification may be necessary to accommodate the equipment and facilities or the patient population of a specific site. In many cases, the profession involved can accomplish this without assistance. Other applications will require review by other professionals or support personnel to ensure coordination. Functional protocols are major contributors to patient safety. Most failures—from falls to infections to wrong-site surgery to drug errors—trace to incomplete, inaccurate, or overlooked functional protocols. These failures cause tens of thousands of undesirable outcomes each year, and the available evidence suggests that little progress has been made toward their correction.[19]

Functional protocols exist in large numbers. They are designed to ensure that the activity will have the desired outcome (e.g., the wound dressing will protect the wound, the laboratory value will be correct). They also provide a basis for teamwork and simplify and standardize the medical record. Good functional protocols have the following components:

- *Authorization*—statement of who may order the procedure
- *Indication*—statement clarifying clinical conditions that support the appropriate use of the protocol
- *Counterindications*—conditions where the procedure must be modified, replaced, or avoided
- *Required supplies, equipment, and conditions*—all special requirements and the sources that meet them
- *Actions*—clear, step-by-step statements of what must be done
- *Recording*—instructions for recording the procedure and observation of the patient's reaction
- *Follow-up*—subsequent actions, including checks on the patient's response, measures of effectiveness, indications for repeating the procedure, and disposal or clean-up of supplies

Functional protocols tend to be stable over time and between patients and institutions, but they can be modified to improve quality and efficiency. An important source of improvement is eliminating unnecessary or inappropriate procedures by making the indications or authorizations more restrictive. For example, elaborate diagnostic tests and expensive drugs can reference failure of simpler approaches as indications. Some very expensive procedures can require prior approval or a formal second opinion. The activities themselves can be modified to be safer or less expensive; changes in equipment and

EXHIBIT 5.5
Example of
a Functional
Protocol for
Medication
Order and
Fulfillment

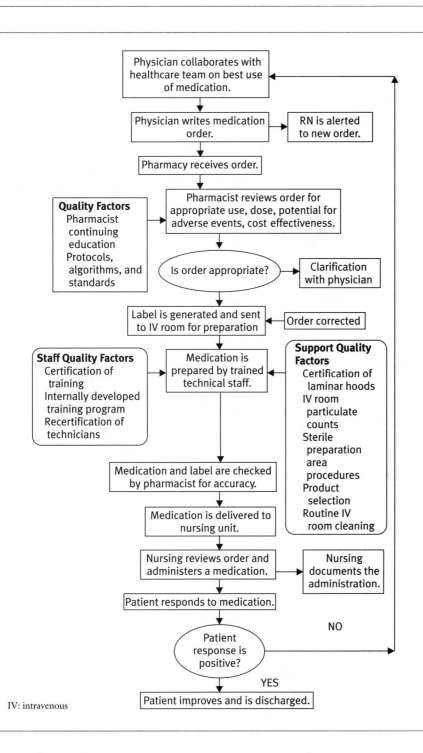

IV: intravenous

supplies often require such adjustments. Follow-up specifications can improve patients' reactions by describing specific signs or symptoms and the appropriate response. Computerized physician order entry and medication reconciliation systems are examples of procedure improvements in the dispensing of unit-dose drug administration used in inpatient care. The new systems have better controls for reminder alerts to guard against prescribing the wrong drug, administering the wrong dose, or recording the dose incorrectly. The result is both lower cost and higher quality.[20,21]

Sets of interrelated functional protocols have become more commonplace. Surgical care provides several examples. Preoperative care includes obtaining informed consent, instructing the patient, obtaining final diagnostic values from lab and x-ray, completing the pre-anesthesia examination, and administering preoperative medications. To perform surgery without delay, each activity must be orchestrated to occur at the earliest possible time and in the proper order. The preoperative care process requires advance agreement on the tasks and their order among several clinical support and medical professions. Many of these agreements are independent of the patient's specific disease. They become components of patient management protocols for several hundred surgical procedures.

Patient management protocols (also called pathways, guidelines, or simply protocols) define the normal steps or processes in the care of a clinically related group of patients at a specific institution. Patient management protocols are organized around episodes of patient care, classified by symptom, disease, or condition such as chest pain, pneumonia, or pregnancy. They specify the functional components of care, outcomes quality goals, and, by implication, the cost. They are developed by cross-functional teams and are written so that they can be easily communicated among the caregiving professionals, thereby increasing efficiency and reducing the chance of error. If the patient's plan of care includes enrollment in a research protocol (i.e., treatment pathways for some cancer diagnoses or other experimental treatment), the informed consent is more detailed and must be in compliance with federal and HCO institutional review boards.

Clinical practice guidelines
Systematically developed statements to assist practitioner and patient decisions about appropriate healthcare for specific clinical circumstances

Protocols are developed from **clinical practice guidelines**—"systematically developed statements to assist practitioner and patient decisions about appropriate health care for specific clinical circumstances."[22] Several hundred conditions now have established nationally promulgated guidelines that serve as a basis for local review and implementation. Many conditions have several published guidelines. The protocol represents selection and implementation of guidelines at a particular institution. Most inpatient institutions have protocols in place for several dozens of their most common conditions.

In 1998, the Agency for Healthcare Research and Quality (AHRQ) established the National Guideline Clearinghouse (NGC) on the Internet. The NGC lists guidelines contributed by other organizations. The guidelines are prepared under the auspices of appropriate organizations with documented literature searches. Key components of the NGC include the following:

- Structured abstracts (summaries) about each guideline and its development
- Links to full-text guidelines, where available, and/or ordering information for print copies
- Palm-based personal digital assistant downloads of the NGC's "Complete Summary" for all guidelines represented in the database
- A Guideline Comparison utility for a side-by-side comparison of attributes of two or more guidelines
- Unique guideline comparisons (including international) called Guideline Syntheses that cover similar topics and highlight areas of similarity and difference
- An electronic forum—NGC-L—for exchanging information on clinical practice guidelines and their development, implementation, and use
- An annotated bibliography database on guideline development methodology, structure, evaluation, and implementation
- An Expert Commentary feature[23]

As of 2009, the NGC has nearly 2,100 guidelines for most common diseases and conditions and a number of prevention activities.

Individual institutions develop protocols by reviewing and revising published guidelines. No guideline should ever be implemented without careful review of the implications of using it in a specific institution. The review should be undertaken by a cross-functional process improvement team (PIT) that can explore all the ramifications of the protocol in advance, including trials as necessary. The development process has at least three advantages. First, it opens the debatable issues and encourages discussion and consensus. Second, it allows the caregivers time to learn new approaches. Third, it checks the proposed guidelines against current practice and pilot tests to identify areas where new supplies, tools, or training will be required.

Sources and Criteria for Patient Management Protocols

There are three important ways to achieve the necessary flexibility and adaptability of guidelines:

1. *Protocols should be reviewed regularly to identify changes in the evidence for specific practices.* The NGC's comparison tool makes it easy to identify the changes in guidelines. The developing team is reassembled periodically to consider these changes.

2. *Protocols emphasize conditional expectations,* a branching logic to allow the guidelines to fit a larger set of real patients. The chest pain protocol shown in Exhibit 5.6, for example, connects at steps 34 and 38 to further protocols that prompt for aneurysm, embolus, pericardial disease, chest wall and pleural disease, and gastrointestinal disease. The notes go on to several rarer possibilities. The fact that the list is specified improves the chance that the right disease will be detected and treated.

3. *Protocols should include provisions for the attending physician to justify exceptions.* Where no scientific consensus on the correct action is available, any evidence that indicates the doctor is aware of the expectation and is departing from it in good faith is acceptable. The general approach can often be expanded by

- specifying the optional or conditional possibilities. For example, selecting the thrombolytic agent has a big impact on the final cost, but the Institute for Clinical Systems Improvement (ICSI) leaves the selection to the treating physician because of lack of evidence of advantages of one thrombolytic agent over another.[24]
- establishing a statistical estimate of the frequency of conditions. For example, the team managing the protocol might measure the relative frequency and the outcomes of percutaneous coronary intervention (PCI) and thrombolysis to compare with national statistics or between different groups of patients.

Example of a Patient Management Protocol

Exhibit 5.6 outlines the guidelines developed by the ICSI for diagnosing and treating chest pain—the most common symptom of acute myocardial infarction (AMI or heart attack)—of a patient presenting to the emergency department (ED).[25] The ICSI guideline is one of several AMI guidelines listed by the NGC. Exhibit 5.6 is part of an integrated set of guidelines that supports cardiac care from primary preventive measures to tertiary prevention or rehabilitation. The guideline is accompanied by 69 pages of references to and discussion of the supporting literature. To maintain an evidence-based approach, the sources are graded from random control trials (the best) to "medical opinion" (the weakest).

The guideline begins with triage, a rapid evaluation to identify chest pains likely to be related to the circulatory system. More than 5 million patients a year appear at EDs with AMI symptoms, averaging about three patients a day for all the EDs in the nation. Others appear at other care sites. Part 1 of the guideline shows the initial management of patients who arrive at other sites or who call with the complaint. Part 2 shows the ED procedures. Those who have an AMI (only about 10 percent) are in a life-threatening situation.[26] The supporting literature reveals an interesting fact: Treatments begun within an hour of arrival save twice as many lives as those that are delayed for several hours.[27] Based on this research finding, the notes for step 25 state that thrombolytic therapy should be instituted as early as possible in the ED, or angiogram/primary PCI (step 26, described in annotation #45; not shown in the exhibit) should be performed within 90 minutes of arrival with a target of less than 60 minutes.[28]

Step 20 of Exhibit 5.6 shows the steps that must follow the triage of a potential AMI in the ED. The actions include administering oxygen, intravenous fluids, electrocardiogram (ECG), medical examination, and an aspirin. If the patient is unstable, advanced cardiac life support adds airway management, defibrillation, and more drugs to the treatment. As these needs

EXHIBIT 5.6 Example of a Patient Management Protocol for Acute Chest Pain, Part 1: Initial Evaluation

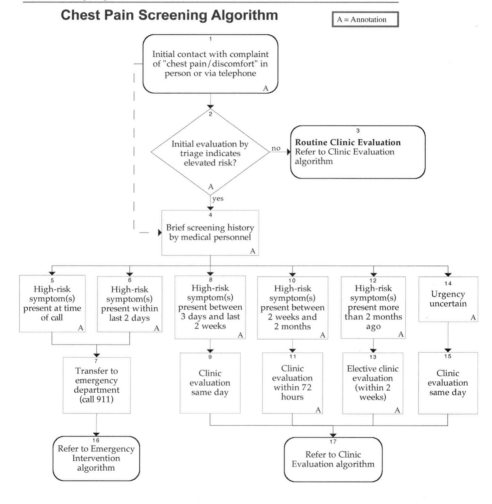

Health Care Guideline:

Diagnosis and Treatment of Chest Pain and Acute Coronary Syndrome (ACS)

Chest Pain Screening Algorithm

cannot be known in advance, all the support necessary for all the steps in the algorithm must be available 24/7. The interpretation of the laboratory and ECG data is critical and requires substantial skill:

Initial errors in ECG interpretation can result in up to 12% of patients being categorized inappropriately (ST elevation versus no elevation), demonstrating

EXHIBIT 5.6 Example of a Patient Management Protocol for Acute Chest Pain, Part 2: Emergency Intervention (*continued*)

Emergency Intervention Algorithm

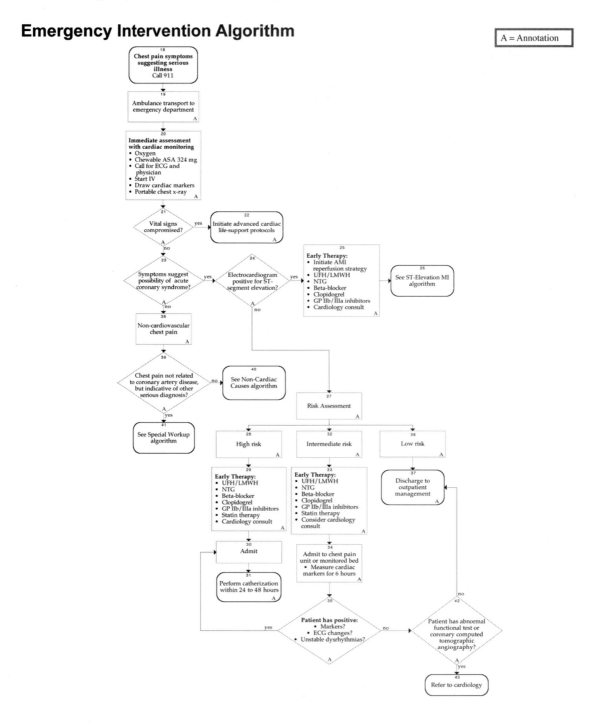

EXHIBIT 5.6 Example of a Patient Management Protocol for Acute Chest Pain, Part 3: Clinic Evaluation (*continued*)

ST-Elevation Myocardial Infarction (STEMI) Algorithm

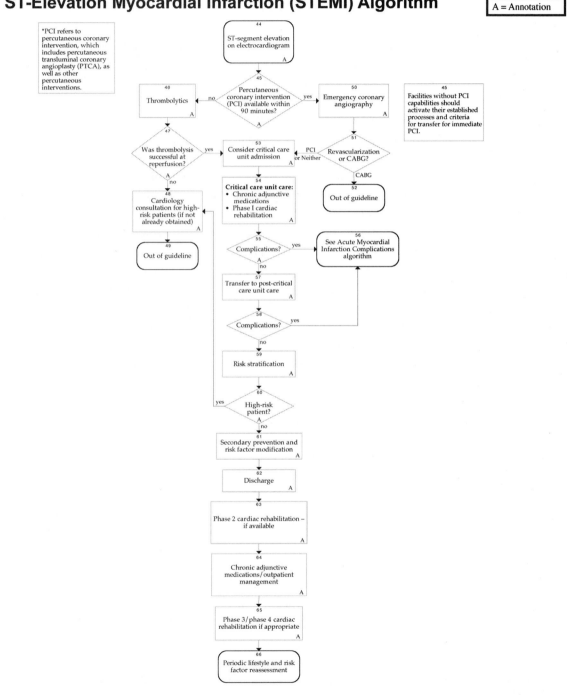

a potential benefit of accurate computer-interpreted electrocardiography and facsimile transmission to an expert.[29]

From a management perspective, this guideline is challenging. Here is what must happen to ensure compliance:

- Emergency physicians, other emergency caregivers, cardiologists, and primary care physicians must reach consensus about accepting or modifying the guideline for local use. This will involve a local review team and a publicized opportunity for those not on the team to comment.
- A triage nurse for each shift must be trained to identify ischemic pain, or a triage physician must be designated. (Potential AMI patients arrive without notice, on any shift.)
- Sufficient ECG equipment must be readily available in the ED. For larger departments, two or three dedicated machines may be needed. Supplies and equipment for advanced life support must also be available.
- Several people on each shift must be trained in administering the 12-lead ECG so that a person is available when needed. "Code teams" to handle cardiac arrest and manage advanced life support must also be trained. For smaller departments, telemedicine coverage for skilled ECG interpretation must be arranged.
- All ED nurses must be trained in the treatment at step 20 so that they start it without a written order when the triage person indicates it.
- A mechanism must be in place to deliver the blood draw to the laboratory. The laboratory must respond with blood chemistry analyses within about 20 minutes.
- Arrangements must be made for skilled ECG interpretation by training emergency physicians, acquiring interpretation software, or arranging for fax to a cardiologist. The laboratory data must also be interpreted by a skilled physician.
- Consensus must be reached in advance on the criteria for selecting among the reperfusion options, which vary substantially in cost, effectiveness, and risk of complications depending on the patient's exact condition.
- Provision must be made for thrombolysis reperfusion and, if available, PCI within 60 minutes. A team outside the ED usually performs these procedures.
- Informed consent for PCI or open-heart surgery must be obtained from the patient or next of kin, if possible.

Taken as a whole, steps on the guideline represented a new level of performance for most EDs when they emerged in the mid-1990s.[30] The guidelines and the evidence are strong enough to suggest a legal standard of care—EDs failing to meet it are at risk for malpractice liability. Several critical elements of the guideline are not about clinical judgment or care plans, but about organization and teamwork. It will take a deliberate effort to get the AMI patient to definitive treatment early. Consensus building, training, advance preparation, and practice are the keys to success. In addition to these mission-critical steps, the patient's family should get explanations and reassurance. After the 30-minute interval, arrangements must be made for completion of the medical record, billing, and transfer to inpatient care.

Part 3 of Exhibit 5.6 shows the initial evaluation for less threatening care. It starts a process for managing ischemic heart disease and hypertension, a common chronic illness that will deteriorate to life-threatening events if not controlled by exercise, diet, and drugs. Several other parts of the algorithm that deal with follow-up care are not shown.

The flow process design of exhibits 5.5 and 5.6 is popular in guidelines and protocols because it shows the sequencing and conditional relationships of each step. It fits the initial AMI treatment particularly well. Other approaches—detailing activity by the calendar or day of stay, for example—are also used. The best form is the one that yields the best outcomes. The flowchart with detailed documentation is the most prevalent.

Good guidelines and protocols contain their own measurements of quality. For the chest pain guideline in Exhibit 5.6, the principal outcome measure is percentage of patients with AMI who survive at discharge or at a specific time after discharge. Readmission is a likely measure for patients believed to be without AMI at step 38. Adjustment of the survival and readmission rates for risk factors such as comorbid conditions, obesity, or smoking is appropriate, but the success rates are likely to be high (around 85 percent), reducing the amount of information that can be obtained.[31] (The ED with 250 admissions per year might have only three deaths per month. The impact of adjustment and the improvements from the protocol would be difficult to detect.) Process measures cover completion of various steps, such as administration of aspirin and oxygen, percentages of patients who meet timelines, delays for patients who do not meet timelines, and other process failures. The expectation is that failures are rare and individual events could be investigated for correctable causes.

Patient management protocols improve individual caregiver performance in four ways:

Using Protocols to Improve the Delivery of Care

1. An evidence-based guideline is supported by training and becomes habitual.
2. Several professions can use it to anticipate and coordinate care events.
3. Caregivers can use it as shorthand or an outline to guide their decisions and their communications to others. The individual care plan becomes the exception to the guideline.
4. The guideline defines the measures of performance and incorporates information collection that can be used for its evaluation and improvement. The individualized plans also contribute information for guideline revision.

Functional protocols improve processes by several different mechanisms:[32]

- Eliminating unnecessary or redundant tasks, which often appear when two functional groups compare their functional protocols or usual practices
- Alerting for tasks previously overlooked or omitted—this often improves quality by ensuring the optimal outcome or by preventing a complication
- Standardizing supplies, with savings through volume discounts, inventory, and training costs.
- Scheduling or resequencing to reduce errors or delays—this frequently has implications for quality, cost, and satisfaction
- Substituting lower-cost personnel for specific activities
- Reengineering the care process—the new process may combine several of the preceding opportunities and require substantial investment, but it delivers a better product overall

Protocols have supported major changes in short inpatient stays and improved survival rates;[33] the use of less expensive sites for care, such as rehabilitation hospitals, same-day surgery programs, and **palliative care** options; and the development of alternatives to expensive and dangerous treatments, such as spinal fusions for back pain.

Palliative care
Treatment to manage and reduce pain, discomfort, and other uncomfortable symptoms of life-limiting diseases or conditions with no known cure; services are provided in a holistic manner to include the patient and her family

Although protocol adoption presented challenges in changing practice patterns, the use of evidence-based medicine has become widely accepted with better information systems, measures, and incentives for payment. Patient management protocols are now the standard of care for most disease.[34] Protocols and evaluation of clinical outcomes are beginning to be included in continuing medical education programs.[35]

Caregiver Training and Selection

Particularly given the importance of the diagnostic process, protocols are not sufficient to guarantee excellent care. (The wrong diagnosis will lead to the wrong protocol.) The HCO must have a process to ensure caregiver competence (knowledge and skill obtained through formal education and experience and regulated by licensure and certification bodies) and proficiency (evidence that the clinician's education and experience are current). For physicians and some other allied health professionals, this process is called **credentialing**, described in more detail in Chapter 6. The HCO credentials other professionals through similar processes by their profession and the human resources management system.

Credentialing
The process of validating a professional's eligibility for medical staff membership and/or privileges to be granted on the basis of academic preparation, licensing, training, certifications, and performance

The credentialing process applies to specific patient populations defined by treatment, diagnosis, or age. For example, a physician would be credentialed for uncomplicated vaginal deliveries or for care of diabetic patients. Credentialing must ensure continued competence and demonstrated proficiency. As protocols change, new treatment modalities are determined, and new technology is developed, the caregiving professionals must receive education on revised and new functional protocols and refresher courses on established protocols. This is typically accomplished with an in-house education training and development function centered on both functional and patient management protocols. For beginning professional caregivers and nonprofessional clinical workers, substantial in-house training programs may be required with a phase-in approach to delivering care independently.

As described in Chapter 2, the HCO's culture must encourage continuous learning and self-improvement. Managers and leaders must be quick to implement new and revised protocols, develop training and development programs for professional and support personnel, and evaluate educational OFIs to tailor training and development plans to each individual.

Record Management

Diagnostic excellence requires two kinds of knowledge: rapid communication of patients' current needs and understanding of the clinically indicated responses. For the first kind, high-performing HCOs are moving rapidly to electronic medical records (EMRs). EMRs make recording faster and more complete, include safeguards to improve accuracy, and speed transmission of patient-related information. Patient management and functional protocols establish the foundation for effective clinical response. Although only a fraction of patients fit the protocols (it is unlikely that *any* patient perfectly fits a protocol), the protocol provides a scientifically justified foundation of shared information. However, strategies, incentives, and techniques are needed to improve the speed of which the best-known scientific practices are disseminated and implemented throughout clinical environments.[36] Departing from evidence-based patient management protocols is usually a matter of changing a few elements, which is far different from starting patient care with a blank sheet of orders.

Clinical Support Services and Specialist Consultation

Excellent care requires an array of specialist consultation and referral, including the clinical support services such as laboratory and imaging. The HCO's credentialing process and operational scorecards support excellent services from all clinical support services and specialties. A large team of qualified specialists is obviously an asset, but rural communities cannot support more than a few specialists. Formal affiliations with larger centers are superior to individual patient referrals. They establish a commitment to practical service, allow sharing of expensive resources such as magnetic resonance imaging machines, support measured performance and annual goal setting, and can include educational services and advice on protocols. Telemedicine and referral linkages are making remote consultation more practical, extending services in rural areas. The anticipated volume of activity can be established using the epidemiologic planning model.

Strategic Support

Behind these elements, high-performing HCOs work strategically with markets and money. Delays are eliminated, quality is improved, and cost is minimized by sizing each service according to its epidemiologic needs. Market share is enhanced because patients are delighted with their service. New equipment is available because funds are on hand to buy it. Credentialing standards can be upheld because the organization not only is "a great place to give care" but also pursues recruitment and individual development aggressively. The underlying reason that it can afford to do this is that care that meets IOM goals is inherently less costly than care that falls short. High-performing HCOs understand both *why* financial success is important and *how* it can be obtained.

Individualizing Patient Care Planning and Treatment

Protocols are useful for most patient diseases and conditions, but **patient care plans** apply the selected protocols to the patient's individual situation, making sure that the protocols meet the patient's needs. All patients have a plan of care. For more complex care needs, the plan of care includes more caregiving team members with a greater opportunity for collaboration on care needs. The **interdisciplinary plan of care** (IPOC) is a process that includes the patient, family, and all clinical disciplines involved in planning and providing care to patients, from system point of entry, throughout the entire acute care episode, and to the next level of care.[37] Many seriously ill patients have several diagnoses that require integration of multiple patient management protocols. IPOC is not replaced by patient management protocols; it integrates them. Every patient's individual needs should be evaluated to make sure the protocol will meet them. IPOCs form the basis for managing clinical uncertainty and complexity, and they are a foundation for case management programs.

Patient care plans
Expectations for the care of individual patients based on an assessment of individual needs

Interdisciplinary plan of care (IPOC)
A process that includes the patient, the family, and all clinical disciplines involved in planning and providing care to patients, from system point of entry, throughout the entire acute care episode, and to the next level of care

An IPOC is generally initiated by a nurse and developed prospectively, with input and collaboration from physicians and other members of the caregiving team. The IPOC considers input from the patient and family and the patient's presenting needs or symptoms. The caregiving team reviews the options, beginning with the patient assessment, and selects the most appropriate patient management protocol in light of the patient's condition. Goals are developed with the patient for the episode of care and across the trajectory of the illness or condition. The patient's plan of care considers psychosocial and spiritual support, educational needs, cultural and linguistic needs, and community resources and post-discharge planning. A critical aspect of patient care planning is listening to the patient, being vigilant to subtle changes in the patient's condition, and communicating with the attending physician and other caregivers about the patient's progress on plan-of-care goals.

The IPOC forms the basis for providing high-quality therapeutic services, such as surgical or other invasive interventions, rehabilitation and therapies (physical, occupational, speech), intensive care, and pharmaceuticals. Communication between and among caregivers is facilitated by interdisciplinary rounds and team meetings and documented in the EMR. Unnecessary or ineffective treatment is discouraged, and the institutional ethics committee is consulted for unresolved treatment decisions.

A good IPOC addresses all of the following elements:

- *Assessment*—comprehensive review of the patient's diagnosis, disabilities, and needs and identification of any unique risks
- *Treatment goals*—statement of clinical goals, such as "eliminate congestive heart failure," and functional goals, such as "restore ability to dress and feed self"
- *Component activities*—a list, often selected from relevant care guidelines and functional protocols, of procedures desired for the patient
- *Recording*—a formal routine for recording what was done and reporting it to others who provide care to the patient
- *Measures of progress and a time schedule for improvement*—where possible, measures of improvement should be used and should parallel the goals developed in the assessment
- *Danger signals and counterindications*—specific events that indicate a need to reconsider the plan

The IPOC supports both the patient management protocol and the case management approach to improvement. Management protocols build on the similarity of patients; case management deals with their uniqueness.

Case Management

Some patients have exceptionally complex care needs that require formalizing a comprehensive clinical strategy. Case management uses expanded IPOCs for complex problems, such as multiple concurrent conditions, and expensive chronic diseases, such as end-stage heart failure and multiple sclerosis. Care for these patients is usually long term and often goes beyond medical assistance. Emotional support is often an issue. Family and community contributions are important, and special equipment and facilities are often necessary. In the most complex cases, the care plan may be a written consensus of professional viewpoints, closely monitored to gain the best possible results while minimizing costs.[38,39] Although costs may be reduced for certain diseases and conditions, evidence does not show that case management reduces overall hospital costs.[40]

Improving Community Health

The clinical management strategy must address not only those who become patients but also the health of citizens in the community. Prevention and health promotion for citizens before they become patients or in parallel to the caregiving relationship are central to developing improved outcomes for chronic disease in a high-performance U.S. health system.[41] Prevention is generally considered to be a direct intervention to avoid or reduce disease or disability. Preventive activities are undertaken by caregivers and by civic agencies for prevention services, such as pure water, criminal justice, and legislation on firearms and dangerous substances. Health promotion includes all activities to change patient or customer behavior. It is undertaken by caregivers and by civic agencies such as public health departments, education systems, and voluntary associations. It has become an important topic for employers.

HCOs provide prevention and health promotion for four reasons:

1. The moral commitment of all caregiving professionals is to health, clearly including prevention.
2. Prevention opportunities arise from the same scientific knowledge as treatment opportunities. More than 1,300 NGC guidelines reference prevention, and that number is increasing.[42]
3. Healthcare professionals are respected authority figures, and their advice is given at times when the patient is receptive.
4. Prevention helps communities that own HCOs. Each episode of illness prevented translates eventually to reductions in cost of care. A healthier community has more workers and lower health insurance costs, making it a better place to build or expand business. (Ironically, disease prevention reduces hospital and physician revenues. Well-managed institutions do it anyway; it is probably essential to avoid bankrupting the major healthcare financing programs.)

Prevention can be categorized as primary, secondary, or tertiary, and health promotion tools can be used to change behavior on all three levels. *Primary prevention* takes place before the disease emerges to eliminate or reduce its occurrence. Immunization, seat belts, condoms, sewage treatment, and restrictions on alcohol sales are examples. *Secondary prevention* reduces the consequences of disease, often by early detection and treatment. Self-examinations for cancer; routine dental inspections; mammographies; colonoscopies; and management of chronic diseases, such as diabetes, hypertension, and asthma, are examples. *Tertiary prevention* is the avoidance of complications or sequelae. Early physical therapy for strokes, retraining in activities of daily living, and respite services to help family caregivers are examples. Secondary and tertiary prevention are done mainly by caregivers and the patients.

Functional and patient management protocols should incorporate all categories of prevention and health promotion. For example, functional protocols for injections, surgical interventions, and other treatments prevent both hospital-acquired infections and injury to caregivers. Home care visit protocols include inspection for hazards and discussion of patient needs and symptoms with family members. Diabetic and cardiovascular care protocols include selection of the optimal pharmacological treatment and guidance to the patient in lifestyle and nutrition. Prenatal, postnatal, and childcare protocols include immunizations; checks for potential developmental disabilities; and education for the mother on child development, nutrition, home safety, and domestic violence.

HCOs differ in the extent to which they pursue prevention and health promotion. Those with an "excellence in care" mission focus on services that occur between the caregiver and the patient. Those with a "community health" mission extend their reach to broader efforts to minimize disease and its impact. Chapter 9 addresses the distinction and its implications as well as strategies for improving community health.

Improving Clinical Performance

As with other elements of organizations, excellence in patient care is the result of continuous improvement. Patient care is a complex system with many heuristic loops. The primary caregiver maintains a heuristic review of the diagnosis and ensuing treatment. The patient management and functional protocols contain heuristic cycles. Nurses and other clinical professionals are explicitly trained to monitor individual patient performance. Professional caregivers are expected to learn and stay current. These are all heuristic loops aimed at the individual patient or provider. The HCO's role is to improve the complex system as a whole. It does this with formal performance measures, benchmarks, negotiated goals, and OFIs for team performance. The process requires aggregating patients with similar disease or condition (now usually called "service lines"), reflecting both similarities in treatment and the specialist structure of both medicine and nursing.

Success requires both a cultural (Chapter 2) and an operational (Chapter 3) foundation. The cultural foundation is an expansion of the values of respect and compassion so that the following become true and are believed by most associates:

- Each associate of the organization understands that his or her work is on behalf of patients and that excellence will be rewarded.
- Individual judgment is expected and encouraged to meet particular patient needs and unusual circumstances. Guidelines for particular instances when protocols should be overridden are widely publicized and included in education programs.
- Each caregiver understands that he or she is privileged to provide optimum care and to represent his or her patients' needs vigorously.
- The expectation-setting process emphasizes scientific sources and is approached as a stimulating intellectual challenge—a rewarding rather than a burdensome event.
- All workers and managers understand the importance of respect for each individual's contribution, open exchange of information, and prompt response to questions.

- Participation in the development of expectations is widespread. An effort is made to ensure that no one is surprised by an unanticipated demand for change.
- The climate encourages change while also reassuring associates of their personal security. The major components of reassurance include consistent procedures and processes; well-understood avenues for comment and prompt, sensitive response; avoidance of imposed consensus; and recognition of the importance of dissent.
- Compliance with expectations for the process of management (e.g., scheduling, documentation, timeliness, courtesy) is accepted as essential. Violations are discouraged with measured sanctions promptly applied. For example, the penalty for incomplete medical records (usually a temporary loss of privileges) is quickly and routinely applied. As a result, well-run organizations have few incomplete records.
- A spirit of fairness and helpfulness characterizes discussion of departures from the expectations about the care itself. The fact that such departures are rare permits extensive investigation. Sanctions are used reluctantly but predictably in the case of repeated unjustifiable practice.
- The values of the organization are advertised. Recruitment emphasizes the philosophy of the organization so that it attracts doctors and employees who are congenial to its orientation.

These values are summarized in the core values of leading HCOs, Exhibit 5.7. AHRQ has developed "Hospital Survey of Patient Safety Culture," which assesses associate perceptions of the clinical culture. The instrument is useful to hospitals for tracking their own performance and establishing benchmarks.[43]

As discussed in Chapter 2, senior leaders establish an organizational culture of quality and safety and focus priorities on clinical performance and

EXHIBIT 5.7
Core Values
of High-
Performing
HCOs

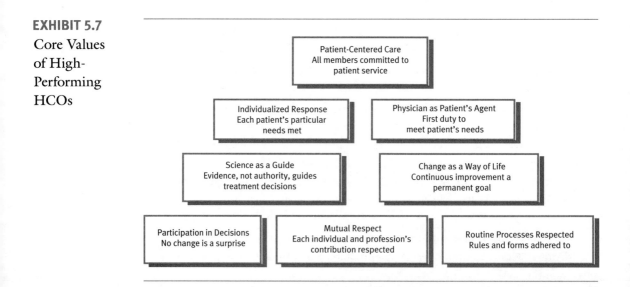

quality outcomes. Clinical managers integrate quality and safety principles into the workplace. They should also serve as examples, modeling quality principles in their interactions with staff and customers.[44]

People

In the daily care of patients, caregiving teams tend to be small and transient. They change composition as the attending physician or hospitalist, nurses, and pharmacy and therapy professionals participating in the patient's IPOC change. Many teams have physician or advanced practice professionals as leaders. Nurses are the most numerous caregivers in total. Nonprofessional caregivers are important contributors and are usually taught by the HCO. The transient teams are drawn from larger and more permanent groups organized in service lines or as clinical support services. They are accountability units of the organization, with formal goal setting, performance measurement, and participation in the reward structure.

Clinical professionals lead caregiving teams. One hallmark of a profession is a formal recognition process usually called certification, licensure, or registration. Several hundred such processes exist in healthcare, and more than 100 in medicine alone. They typically require both classroom and practice education as well as continuing education to maintain competencies. Completion of appropriate requirements is an initial step for credentialing in each profession. Professionalism is commonly justified as protecting the consumer by establishing knowledge and skill requirements. While this may be so, it also creates economic monopolies that increase the profession's income and the customer's cost of care.[45] Thus, the question of professional domain (i.e., what requirements are necessary for a given task?) is one in which customer stakeholders have a profound interest. One role of the HCO is to exercise that interest wisely. As protocols are implemented, many opportunities arise to substitute less expensive nonprofessionals for professionals. Most applicable law makes this acceptable so long as professional supervision is available. Part of the negotiation to translate guidelines to protocols should include establishing the clinically necessary level of training for each task, as opposed to the political position of the professions involved. The evidence-based rules of medicine and management are the correct drivers: Tasks should be completed by the lowest level of skill that can do them safely. When the evidence, either for the individual patient or in general, suggests that a higher skill is necessary, that skill should be supplied.

Organization

In a well-managed HCO, clinical performance is embedded in the fabric of the organization and the healthcare professions, with ultimate accountability to the governing body. Service lines provide most hospital-based care. They are accountability hierarchies that divide up the patient population by clinical need, measuring and benchmarking their performance and negotiating annual goals. The organization of these units is discussed in Chapter 6. Some centralized functional units remain, such as nursing, laboratory, imaging, and pharmacy. As noted in Chapter 2, these units have a customer–server relationship to the service lines. They are described further in chapters 7 and 8.

The complexities of excellent care are such that many HCOs use specialized internal consulting activities to support their work teams and clinically oriented PITs. Internal specialists in quality management have additional education in quality monitoring and reporting. Healthcare quality management professionals may complete special training and pass an examination, sponsored by the National Association for Healthcare Quality, to be designated as a Certified Professional in Healthcare Quality.[46] Infection-control practitioners are generally nurses or other clinicians with advanced education in epidemiology and microbiology. They may be certified by the Association for Professionals in Infection Control and Epidemiology and earn the Certification in Infection Control credential.[47] Physicians are certified by the Infectious Diseases Society of America through the American Board of Internal Medicine. Similarly, risk-management professionals may earn certification in risk management, sponsored by the American Society for Healthcare Risk Management.[48] The specialists and their staffs are truly consultants. They do not have authority over accountability units. Such authority is known to erode the empowerment of the clinical teams.[49]

Exhibit 5.8 shows a possible organization of service lines supported by several centralized functional services and an internal consulting unit. Reality is far more complex than the exhibit; effective HCOs collaborate constantly both in clinical teams around individual patients and in improvement teams to design protocols and work processes. The skeletal framework that supports this collaboration provides a mechanism for setting goals consistent with the mission, achieving the collaboration those goals require, and resolving issues that arise in the implementation.

Measures

Exhibit 5.9 shows the operational scorecard template for any service line. The details differ, particularly in the demand and quality measures. The operational scorecard can be applied to components of service lines, such as specific primary care offices or specific inpatient units for acute care services. In most applications, a few measures are selected in each dimension for goal setting. Those that have achieved benchmark or are not candidates for improvement can be dropped and replaced by others better related to current needs. The dropped measures remain available for analyzing OFIs. When the service line is separately incorporated, a strategic scorecard can be constructed for it as well. Strategic scorecards are required for joint ventures.

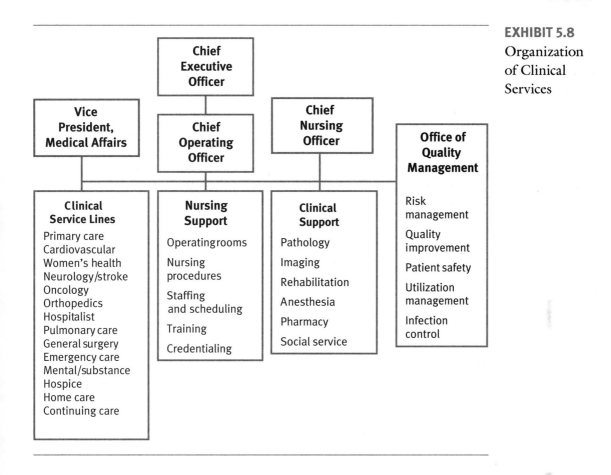

EXHIBIT 5.8
Organization of Clinical Services

Chief Executive Officer

Vice President, Medical Affairs

Chief Operating Officer

Chief Nursing Officer

Office of Quality Management

Clinical Service Lines

Primary care
Cardiovascular
Women's health
Neurology/stroke
Oncology
Orthopedics
Hospitalist
Pulmonary care
General surgery
Emergency care
Mental/substance
Hospice
Home care
Continuing care

Nursing Support

Operating rooms

Nursing procedures

Staffing and scheduling

Training

Credentialing

Clinical Support

Pathology

Imaging

Rehabilitation

Anesthesia

Pharmacy

Social service

Risk management

Quality improvement

Patient safety

Utilization management

Infection control

Demand and Output

Output—the use of services—is captured in accounting systems, which generate detailed data on the kind of service (or occasionally product, such as a drug). Demand for care is often inferred from output, but it can be measured in patient scheduling and intake systems. Direct measurement permits identification of scheduling delays and lost cases, valuable for improving market share.

The epidemiologic planning model constructs demand forecasts from available community information. Forecast demand provides a denominator for market share. It can support detailed analysis of community sectors selecting the HCO for specific services. It is also useful in evaluating effectiveness. The model can construct benchmarks for major clinical events. These can be compared to actual demand to identify overuse or underuse.

Quality Assessment

Both outcomes and process quality measures have expanded substantially in recent years. The new measures often contain sophisticated adjustments to

EXHIBIT 5.9
Profile of
Service Line
Operational
Scorecard

Dimensions	Examples
	Input Measures

Demand

Requests for care	Patient arrivals, appointment requests, consultation and referral requests; often specified by patient age, service, and location
Market share	Percent of total demand from community
Appropriateness of service	Percent of expected or benchmark demand from epidemiologic planning model
Logistics of service	Hours of availability

Cost/Resources

Total costs per patient	Labor, supplies, plant, indirect costs for service line
Resource condition	Occupancy and percent of capacity rates, age of equipment, failure rates of equipment

Human Resources

Supply	Staffing levels, staffing shortfalls, vacancy rates
Training	Average hours of training per associate
Employee satisfaction	Associate loyalty, retention or termination, absenteeism, work loss days from accident or injury

	Output Measures

Output/Productivity

Patients treated	Discharge counts by specified group
Cost per case	Total costs per discharges by specified group
Cost per treatment	Costs for specific activity such as surgical operations or examinations per patients receiving

Quality

Clinical outcomes	Outcomes assess patient condition at discharge
Procedural quality	Procedural measures assess completion of specific tasks or events
Structural quality	Structural measures assess availability and adequacy of service, particularly staffing and facility safety

Customer Satisfaction

Patient satisfaction	Post-discharge surveys, counts of "Caught in the Act," complaints, service recovery and unexpected incidents
Referring physician satisfaction	Survey, rounding, complaints
Other customer satisfaction	Community surveys, boundary spanning activities
Access	Delays for service, unfilled demand

remove factors beyond the service's control. They have become practical as electronic record keeping has expanded.

The National Quality Measures Clearinghouse, a service of AHRQ, provides detailed information on definitions, adjustments, scientific foundation, and rationale for measures and measure sets. Many measures are used by several sites and can be benchmarked. As of August 2009, the Clearinghouse had 1,236 disease-specific measures and 217 measures for the care of mental disorders. A hierarchical array links related measures. Most of the measures are for outcomes, and some measure appropriateness of care or procedural compliance. The Clearinghouse is the starting point for any discussion of clinical performance measurement.[50]

The Joint Commission National Patient Safety Goals promote specific improvements in patient safety. Updated each year since 2003, the goals address

- accuracy of patient identification;
- communication among caregivers;
- medications safety;
- infections;
- medication management;
- patient falls;
- response to changes in a patient's condition; and
- universal protocol for invasive diagnosis or treatment (i.e., conducting a pre-procedure verification process, marking the procedure site, and performing a time-out).

The Leapfrog Group also calculates regional outcomes quality, efficiency, and effectiveness scores on a battery of common inpatient diseases.[51] The National Quality Forum endorses 34 practices that should be universally used in clinical settings to reduce the risk of harm to patients. Fourteen practices can generate patient-specific compliance counts. Achievement scores are easily calculated from EMRs,[52] and they are also procedural quality measures. All of these can generate achievement scores—counts of the patients who received the desired activity, a common form of process measure.

In addition, The Joint Commission looks for evidence that the HCO encourages patients' active involvement in their own care as a safety strategy and explicitly identifies and addresses safety risks.[53] The Leapfrog Group also advocates performance improvement practices and surveys HCOs to assess their compliance. The Leapfrog Group's standards include computerized physician order entry system, intensive care unit physician staffing, and evidence-based hospital referral for certain high-risk procedures. Twenty of National Quality Forum practices are general standards of organization, which are consistent with the transformational and evidence-based foundations. The general standards of The Joint Commission, the Leapfrog Group, and the

National Quality Forum, while useful for process review, do not readily generate ongoing measures.

Structural measures of quality—basically counts of availability of appropriate resources—are now rarely useful for quality assessment.

Quality Measures and Pay for Performance

A growing number of private and public healthcare payers, including Medicare, have embraced pay for performance (P4P) as a means to improve the health of patients and foster new behaviors from physicians.[54] As stated in Chapter 1, P4P initiatives are collaborations with providers and other stakeholders to ensure that valid quality measures are used, that outcomes measures are true indicators of quality of care (for example, a patient classified as having substandard care because of an outcome measure of "poor control" might actually be receiving good quality of care),[55] that providers are not being pulled in conflicting directions, and that providers have support for achieving actual improvement.

P4P is intended to foster new behavior from physicians by providing incentives that improve care for people with chronic illnesses. P4P also enables health plans to treat sicker populations without spending more, although more research is needed to gauge long-term results.[56,57] As a national health policy initiative, P4P is expected to change physician and hospital behaviors, improve healthcare quality, and decrease costs[58,59] without unintended consequences, such as overtreatment or a focus on the incentive to the exclusion of other mitigating factors.[60] This expectation may be more hope than reality. Measures that can identify OFIs often lack the reliability and sensitivity necessary for incentive compensation. Small sample sizes, unusual populations, and simple, random variations plague many proposed applications.[61]

Patient and Associate Satisfaction

Satisfaction data are now collected by survey. HCOs contract with companies that specialize in population surveys. Reliable information requires careful monitoring of the sample, rigorous and standardized question design, deliberate efforts to improve response rates, statistical analysis, and benchmarking. Patient satisfaction data include HCAHPS measures of patient perception of quality of care as a condition of Medicare participation, with specific questions to address the larger functional services such as nursing and rehabilitation therapies. Exhibit 5.10 shows the questions involved; they identify several specific elements of the patient experience that are controlled by the organization, such as pain management and explanation of pharmaceuticals. The questions must be incorporated in commercial patient satisfaction surveys, and public reporting is required and posted on the website of the U.S. Department of Health and Human Services and on other websites.[62] The response to the functional services is often critical to the overall patient satisfaction. Respondents are identified by disease group, allowing easy tallying for the accountable teams.

Unless otherwise indicated, responses are "Never, Sometimes, Usually, Always"

EXHIBIT 5.10
HCAHPS®
Hospital
Patient Survey
Questions

Your Care from Nurses

1. During this hospital stay, how often did nurses treat you with <u>courtesy and respect</u>?

2. During this hospital stay, how often did nurses <u>listen carefully to you</u>?

3. During this hospital stay, how often did nurses <u>explain things </u>in a way you could understand?

4. During this hospital stay, after you pressed the call button, how often did you get help as soon as you wanted it?

Your Care from Doctors

5. During this hospital stay, how often did doctors treat you with courtesy and respect?

6. During this hospital stay, how often did doctors listen carefully to you?

7. During this hospital stay, how often did doctors explain things in a way you could understand?

The Hospital Environment

8. During this hospital stay, how often were your room and bathroom kept clean?

9. During this hospital stay, how often was the area around your room quiet at night?

Your Experiences in the Hospital

10. During this hospital stay, did you need help from nurses or other hospital staff in getting to the bathroom or in using a bedpan? (Yes, No. If no, go to Question 12)

11. How often did you get help in getting to the bathroom or in using a bedpan as soon as you wanted?

12. During this hospital stay, did you need medicine for pain? (Yes, No. If no, go to Question 15)

13. During this hospital stay, how often was your pain well controlled?

14. During this hospital stay, how often did the hospital staff do everything they could to help you with your pain?

15. During this hospital stay, were you given any medicine that you had not taken before? (Yes, No. If no, go to Question 18)

16. Before giving you any new medicine, how often did hospital staff tell you what the medicine was for?

17. Before giving you any new medicine, how often did hospital staff describe possible side effects in a way you could understand?

continued

EXHIBIT 5.10
continued

When You Left the Hospital

18. After you left the hospital, did you go directly to your own home, to someone else's home, or to another health facility? (Own home, Someone else's home, Another health facility. If another, go to Question 21)

19. During this hospital stay, did doctors, nurses or other hospital staff talk with you about whether you would have the help you needed when you left the hospital? (Yes, No)

20. During this hospital stay, did you get information in writing about what symptoms or health problems to look out for after you left the hospital? (Yes, No)

Overall Rating of the Hospital

Please answer the following questions about your stay at the hospital named on the cover. Do not include any other hospital stays in your answer.

21. Using any number from 0 to 10, where 0 is the worst hospital possible and 10 is the best hospital possible, what number would you use to rate this hospital during your stay?

22. Would you recommend this hospital to your friends and family? (Definitely no, Probably no, Probably yes, Definitely yes)

About You

23. In general, how would you rate your overall health? (Excellent, Very good, Good, Fair, Poor)

24. What is the highest grade or level of school that you have completed? (8th grade or less, Some high school but did not graduate, High school graduate or GED, Some college or 2-year degree, 4-year college graduate, More than 4-year college degree)

25. Are you of Spanish, Hispanic or Latino origin or descent? (Yes, Puerto Rican; Yes, Mexican, Mexican-American, Chicano; Yes, Cuban; Yes, Other Spanish, Hispanic, or Latino; No, not Spanish, Hispanic, or Latino)

26. What is your race? Please choose one or more. (White, Black or African American, Asian, Native Hawaiian or other Pacific Islander, American Indian or Alaska Native)

27. What language do you mainly speak at home? (English, Spanish, Some other language. Please print.)

SOURCE: Reprinted from Agency for Healthcare Research and Quality. 2009. [Online information; retrieved 3/11/09.] www.hcahps.org/Files/V4%200%201-20-2009%20Appendix%20A%20-HCAHPS%20Mail%20 Survey%20Materials%20(English).pdf.

Associates are also formally surveyed. Associate satisfaction is closely linked to retention, return on training investments, and patient satisfaction. Specialist physicians are generally associated with specific disease groups; their response is an important source of marketing and quality insight. It is common to supplement surveys with focus groups or discussions with specific physicians to identify opportunities for improvement. Primary or referring physicians can be surveyed, but a direct approach to high-volume referrers and selective discussions with those not referring as frequently can be revealing.

Managerial Issues

The issues that trap hospitals in mediocrity are failures of transformational and evidence-based management. In recent decades, evidence-based management has made substantial gains. Arguments about protocols and measurement have been resolved; a governing board that fails to endorse these approaches and set improvement goals is now at serious risk of financial or legal difficulties. As the measures reveal OFIs, management must successfully address four issues: sustaining a culture of teamwork and respect, managing the occasional failure of credentialing, dealing with adverse events, and resolving interprofessional rivalries.

Sustaining a Culture of Teamwork and Respect

Serious illness requires not just teams but also teams of teams. Many of the caregivers who contribute to the same patient never meet one another; they are in different locations or on different shifts. Team coordination becomes an important issue. Breakdowns are most common not in the activities of a single caregiver but in the handoff from one caregiver to another and one team to another. Critical information is lost, causing something to be done wrong, delayed, or left undone.

Effective team communication is a function of both culture and process. The cultural element establishes a commitment to a common mission and to values of respect, compassion, and continuous improvement. These values encourage communication. The modeling behavior of leadership helps all associates understand that they are expected to listen to and speak on the patient's behalf. Key to this process is the EMR. Structured around patient management and functional protocols, the EMR can clearly and succinctly summarize needs, accomplishments, and next steps. In many cases, it can alert the caregivers to hazards or omissions.

Credentialing and Ensuring Continued Competence

The credentialing mechanisms are rigorous and detailed, but a large majority of applicants are accepted and an even larger percentage pass subsequent reviews. Professional education is designed to prepare qualified people, and it does, in large numbers. The issue is how to deal with the occasional failure of renewal. The best response is careful monitoring of ongoing performance, particularly unanticipated clinical events and deteriorating outcomes and process scores, coupled with personal interviews, counseling, and a step-wise program of correction.

Failure to act on early signals has serious consequences. The individual involved rarely improves; continued problems generate a destructive signal about the HCO's commitment to vision and values. Retraining and supervised activity are often helpful. Although expensive and difficult for the individuals involved, direct supervision can protect patients from serious harm and the HCO from massive costs. Only after these efforts have failed is it necessary to withdraw approval. By that time, the case is usually ironclad.

Minimizing and Responding to Unexpected Clinical Events

Protocols, credentialing, and continuous improvement substantially reduce the chance of error, but unexpected clinical events will still occur. Some of them will have catastrophic consequences for the patient and will be viewed as malpractice. The method for dealing with these events is now clearly established and documented. It calls for rigorous application of the following rules:

1. Every unexpected clinical event with negative consequences for the patient is reported by the caregiving team involved. The **unexpected event report** system is often used.
2. Minor events are candidates for service recovery (see Chapter 11) and OFIs for continuous improvement.
3. Major events are thoroughly and objectively reviewed. The HCO reaches a decision about liability. If it is liable, it offers an appropriate, immediate financial settlement. If it is not liable, it offers its sympathy and appropriate nonfinancial support. If its offers are not acceptable to patients or survivors, the HCO allows the matter to proceed to mediation or trial.
4. The record of major events is systematically studied for OFIs.

Under this approach, there is no malpractice crisis. The HCO should go to court rarely, and only when it expects to win. The cost of settlement is much less than the cost of defense, and the OFIs revealed steadily reduce the incidence of events.[63]

Unexpected event report
Written report of an untoward event that raises the possibility of liability of the organization

A common source of clinical failure is the lack of support and logistic services to carry out the clinical processes that caregiving teams know to be necessary for their patients. Each time a clinical team must improvise, or stop and wait, costs and the chances for error mount. Successful organizations minimize these events. The result is that their outcomes are better, their costs tend to be lower, and their associates are more satisfied.[64]

Resolving Interprofessional Rivalries

As noted, protocols frequently allow less skilled personnel to provide care under supervision by more skilled staff. The well-managed HCO can train people for specific activities and supervise them effectively, providing an important opportunity to reduce costs by substitution—that is, the generalist substitutes for the specialist, the nurse for the physician, and the technician for the nurse. But these substitutions create potential income losses for the practitioners.

Well-managed organizations must be sensitive to these concerns, but they must press forward with sound solutions in spite of them. The criterion must be evidence of safety and effectiveness. The rules under the "Resolving Fundamental Disagreements" section in Chapter 2 must be applied in clinical discussions. The disputants must leave the debate thinking that they were fairly treated. The situation in which one group of stakeholders uses its economic power to stymie progress for all must be avoided.

Suggested Readings

Black, J., with D. Miller. 2008. *The Toyota Way to Healthcare Excellence: Increase Efficiency and Improve Quality with Lean.* Chicago: Health Administration Press.

Carroll, R. (ed.). 2009. *Risk Management Handbook for Health Care Organizations, Student Edition, 5th Edition.* San Francisco: Jossey-Bass.

The Joint Commission. *Accreditation Standards* (published annually). Oakbrook Terrace, IL: The Joint Commission.

Kelly, D. L. 2006. *Applying Quality Management in Healthcare: A Systems Approach,* 2nd ed. Chicago: Health Administration Press.

Lambert, M. J. 2004. *Leading a Patient-Safe Organization.* Chicago: Health Administration Press.

Nelson, E. C., P. B. Batalden, and M. M. Godfrey (eds.). 2007. *Quality by Design: A Clinical Microsystems Approach.* San Francisco: Jossey-Bass.

Spath, P. L. 2005. *Leading Your Healthcare Organization to Excellence: A Guide to Using the Baldrige Criteria.* Chicago: Health Administration Press.

Notes

1. Spear, S. J. 2005. "Fixing Health Care from the Inside, Today." *Harvard Business Review* 83 (9): 78–91.
2. Griffith, J. R., and K. R. White. 2005. "The Revolution in Hospital Management." *Journal of Healthcare Management* 50 (3): 170–90.
3. The Leapfrog Group. 2009. [Online information; retrieved 5/27/09.] www.leapfroggroup.org.
4. Schuster, M. A., E. A. McGlynn, C. R. Pham, M. D. Spar, and R. H. Brook. 2001. "The Quality of Health Care in the United States: A Review of Articles Since 1987." Appendix A of *Crossing the Quality Chasm: A New Health System for the 21st Century.* Washington, DC: National Academies Press.
5. Institute of Medicine, Committee on Quality of Health Care in America. 2000. *To Err Is Human: Building a Safer Health System,* edited by L. T. Kohn, J. M. Corrigan, and M. S. Donaldson, 29–35. Washington, DC: National Academies Press.
6. McGlynn, E. A., S. M. Asch, J. Adam, J. Keesey, J. Hicks, A. DeCristofaro, and E. A. Kerr. 2003. "The Quality of Health Care Delivered to Adults in the United States." *New England Journal of Medicine* 348 (26): 2635–45.
7. Casalino, L., R. R. Gillies, S. M. Shortell, J. A. Schmittdiel, T. Bodenheimer, J. C. Robinson, T. Rundall, N. Oswald, H. Schauffler, and M. C. Wang. 2003. "External Incentives, Information Technology, and Organized Processes to Improve Health Care Quality for Patients with Chronic Diseases." *JAMA* 289 (4): 434–41.

8. O'Kane, M., J. Corrigan, S. M. Foote, S. R. Tunis, G. J. Isham, L. M. Nichols, E. S. Fisher, J. C. Ebeler, J. A. Block, B. E. Bradley, C. K. Cassel, D. L. Ness, and J. Tooker. 2008. "Crossroads in Quality." *Health Affairs* 27 (3): 749–58.

9. Gawande, A. 2009. "The Cost Conundrum." *The New Yorker.* [Online information; retrieved 7/2/09.] www.newyorker.com/reporting/2009/06/01/090601fa_fact_gawande?yrail.

10. *Dartmouth Atlas of Healthcare.* 2009. [Online information; retrieved 5/28/09.] www.dartmouthatlas.org.

11. The Commonwealth Fund. 2009. [Online information; retrieved 5/27/09.] www.whynotthebest.org.

12. World Health Organization. 2007. *International Statistical Classification of Diseases and Related Health Problems,* 10th revision. [Online information; retrieved 7/7/09.]. http://apps.who.int/classifications/apps/icd/icd10online.

13. Cabot, R. C. 1911. *Differential Diagnosis.* Philadelphia: W. B. Saunders Company.

14. Swenson, S. J., J. A. Dilling, D. S. Milliner, R. S. Zimmerman, W. J. Maples, M. E. Lindsay, and G. B. Bartley. 2009. "Quality: The Mayo Clinic Approach." *American Journal of Medical Quality* 24 (5): 428–40.

15. Leonhardt, D. 2009. "In Health Reform: A Cancer Offers an Acid Test." *New York Times,* July 7.

16. Conway, P. H., and C. Clancy. 2009. "Comparative-Effectiveness Research: Implications of the Coordinating Council's Report." *New England Journal of Medicine* 361 (4): 328–30.

17. Conway, P. H., and C. Clancy. 2009. "Transformation of Health Care at the Front Line." *JAMA* 301: 763–65.

18. Peterson, E. D., N. M. Albert, A. Amin, J. H. Patterson, and G. C. Fonarow. 2008. "Implementing Critical Pathways and a Multidisciplinary Team Approach to Cardiovascular Disease Management." *The American Journal of Cardiology* 102 (5A): 47G–55G.

19. Longo, D. R., J. E. Hewett, B. Ge, and S. Schubert. 2005. "The Long Road to Patient Safety: A Status Report on Patient Safety Systems." *JAMA* 294 (22): 2858–65.

20. *Hospitals & Health Networks.* 2001. "Medication Safety Issue Brief. Using Automation to Reduce Errors. Part 2." *Hospitals & Health Networks* 75 (2): 33–34.

21. Agrawal, A., and W. Y. Wu. 2009. "Reducing Medication Errors and Improving Systems Reliability Using an Electronic Medication Reconciliation System." *Joint Commission Journal of Quality and Patient Safety* 35 (2): 106–14.

22. Field, M. J., and K. N. Lohr (eds.). 1990. *Clinical Practice Guidelines: Directions for a New Program,* 38. Washington, DC: National Academies Press.

23. National Guideline Clearinghouse. [Online information; retrieved 5/27/09.] www.guideline.gov/about/about.aspx.

24. Institute for Clinical Systems Improvement. 2008. "Diagnosis and Treatment of Chest Pain and Acute Coronary Syndrome." [Online information on National Guidelines Clearinghouse website; retrieved 5/27/09.] www.guideline.gov/summary/summary.aspx?doc_id=13480&nbr=6889#s23.

25. *Ibid.*

26. Varada, R., S. Manaker, J. Rohrbach, and D. Kolansky. 2005. "Acute Myocardial Infarction Following a Negative Evaluation of Chest Pain." *Journal for Healthcare Quality* 27 (4): 26–31.

27. Ryan, T. J., J. L. Anderson, E. M. Antman, B. A. Braniff, N. H. Brooks, R. M. Califf, L. D. Hillis, L. F. Hiratzka, E. Rapaport, B. J. Riegel, R. O. Russell, E. E.

Smith III, and W. D. Weaver. 1996. "ACC/AHA Guidelines for the Management of Patients with Acute Myocardial Infarction: A Report of the American College of Cardiology/American Heart Association Task Force on Practice Guidelines (Committee on Management of Acute Myocardial Infarction)." *Journal of the American College of Cardiology* 28 (5): 1328–428.

28. Institute for Clinical Systems Improvement (2008).

29. Ryan, T. J., J. L. Anderson, E. M. Antman, B. A. Braniff, N. H. Brooks, R. M. Califf, L. D. Hillis, L. F. Hiratzka, E. Rapaport, B. J. Riegel, R. O. Russell, E. E. Smith III, and W. D. Weaver. 1996. "ACC/AHA Guidelines for the Management of Patients with Acute Myocardial Infarction: A Report of the American College of Cardiology/American Heart Association Task Force on Practice Guidelines (Committee on Management of Acute Myocardial Infarction)." *Journal of the American College of Cardiology* 28 (5): 1340.

30. Katz, D. A. 1999. "Barriers Between Guidelines and Improved Patient Care: An Analysis of AHCPR's Unstable Angina Clinical Practice Guideline, Agency for Health Care Policy and Research." *Health Services Research* 34 (1, Pt. 2): 377–89.

31. Thiemann, D. R., J. Coresh, W. J. Oetgen, and N. R. Powe. 1999. "The Association Between Hospital Volume and Survival After Acute Myocardial Infarction in Elderly Patients." *New England Journal of Medicine* 340 (21): 1640–48.

32. Spath, P. L. (ed.). 1997. *Beyond Clinical Paths: Advanced Tools for Outcomes Management*. Chicago: American Hospital Publishing.

33. Peterson, Albert, Amin, Patterson, and Fonarow (2008).

34. Montori, V. M., and G. H. Guyatt. 2008. "Progress in Evidence-Based Medicine." *JAMA* 300: 1814–16.

35. Mazmanian, P. E., D. A. Davis, and R. Galbraith. 2009. "Continuing Medical Education Effect on Clinical Outcomes: Effectiveness of Continuing Medical Education: American College of Chest Physicians Evidence-Based Education Guidelines." *Chest* 135 (3 Suppl.): 49S–55S.

36. Bloomrosen, M., and D. E. Detmer. 2010. "Informatics, Evidence-Based Care, and Research: Implications for National Policy. A Report of an American Medical Informatics Association Health Policy Conference." *Journal of the American Medical Informatics Association* 17: 115–23.

37. Lewis, C. K., M. L. Hoffmann, A. Gard, J. Coons, P. Bichinich, and J. Euclide. 2005. "Development and Implementation of an Interdisciplinary Plan of Care." *Journal for Healthcare Quality*. [Online information; retrieved 5/27/09.] www.nahq.org/journal/ce/article.html?article_id=223.

38. Christianson, J. B., L. H. Warrick, F. E. Netting, F. G. Williams, W. Read, and J. Murphy. 1991. "Hospital Case Management: Bridging Acute and Long-Term Care." *Health Affairs* 10 (2): 173–84.

39. Williams, F. G., L. H. Warrick, J. B. Christianson, and F. E. Netting. 1993. "Critical Factors for Successful Hospital-Based Case Management." *Health Care Management Review* 18 (1): 63–70.

40. White, K. R., G. J. Bazzoli, S. D. Roggenkamp, and T. Gu. 2005. "Does Case Management Matter as a Hospital Cost-Control Strategy?" *Health Care Management Review* 30 (1): 32–43.

41. Commission on a High Performance Health System. 2009. *The Path to a High Performance U.S. Health System: A 2020 Vision and the Policies to Pave the Way.* New York: The Commonwealth Fund.

42. National Guideline Clearinghouse (2009).

43. Agency for Healthcare Research and Quality. 2009. "Hospital Survey on Patient Safety Culture: 2009 Comparative Database Report." [Online information;

retrieved 5/28/09.] www.ahrq.gov/qual/hospsurvey09/hosp09summ.htm.

44. Proenca, E. J. 2007. "Team Dynamics and Team Empowerment in Health Care Organizations." *Health Care Management Review* 32 (4): 370–78.

45. Starr, P. 1982. *The Social Transformation of American Medicine*, 21–24. New York: Basic Books.

46. National Association for Healthcare Quality. 2009. [Online information; retrieved 5/27/09.] www.cphq.org.

47. Association for Professionals in Infection Control and Epidemiology. 2009. [Online information; retrieved 5/28/09.] www.apic.org.

48. American Society for Healthcare Risk Management. 2009. [Online information; retrieved 5/28/09.] www.ashrm.org.

49. Wardhani, V., A. Utarini, J. P. van Dijk, D. Post, and J. W. Groothoff. 2009. "Determinants of Quality Management Systems Implementation in Hospitals." *Health Policy* 89 (3): 239–51.

50. National Quality Measures Clearinghouse, U.S. Agency for Healthcare Research and Quality. 2009. [Online information; retrieved 8/14/09.] www.qualitymeasures.ahrq.gov.

51. The Leapfrog Group. 2009. "Safety Practices." [Online information; retrieved 5/28/09.] www.leapfroggroup.org.

52. National Quality Forum. 2009. [Online information; retrieved 5/28/09.] www.qualityforum.org.

53. The Joint Commission. 2009. "National Patient Safety Goals." [Online information; retrieved 4/1/09.] www.jointcommission.org/PatientSafety/National PatientSafetyGoals/09_hap_npsgs.htm.

54. Centers for Medicare & Medicaid Services. 2005. "Medicare 'Pay for Performance (P4P)' Initiatives." [Online press release; retrieved 5/28/09.] www.cms.hhs.gov/apps/media/press/release.asp?Counter=1343.

55. Kerr, E. A., D. M. Smith, M. M. Hogan, T. M. Hofer, S. L. Krein, M. Bermann, and R. A. Hayward. 2003. "Building a Better Quality Measure: Are Some Patients with 'Poor Quality' Actually Getting Good Care?" *Medical Care* 41 (10): 1173–82.

56. Jones, R. S., C. Brown, and F. Opelka. 2005. "Surgeon Compensation: 'Pay for Performance.' The American College of Surgeons National Surgical Quality Improvement Program: The Surgical Care Improvement Program, and Other Considerations." *Surgery* 138 (5): 829–36.

57. Rosenthal, M. B., R. G. Frank, Z. Li, and A. M. Epstein. 2005. "Early Experience with Pay-for-Performance: From Concept to Practice." *JAMA* 294 (14): 1821–23.

58. The Commonwealth Fund. 2005. "Early Experience with Pay-for-Performance: From Concept to Practice. In the Literature." [Online article; retrieved 12/12/05.] www.cmwf.org/publications/publications_show.htm?doc_id =307183.

59. Hasselman, D. 2009. "Provider Incentive Programs: An Opportunity for Medicaid to Improve Quality at the Point of Care." Center for Health Care Strategies, Inc. [Online information; retrieved 5/28/09.] www.chcs.org/usr_doc/P4P_Resource_Paper.pdf.

60. Damberg, C. L., K. Raube, K. K. Teleki, and E. Dela Cruz. 2009. "Taking Stock of Pay for Performance: A Candid Assessment from the Front Lines." *Health Affairs* 28 (2): 517–25.

61. Hayward, R. A. 2008. "Access to Clinically Detailed Patient Information: A Fundamental Element for Improving the Efficiency and Quality of Healthcare." *Medical Care* 46 (3): 229–31.

62. Centers for Medicare & Medicaid Services. 2009. "Fact Sheet: Hospital CAHPS® (HCAHPS®)." [Online information, retrieved 3/11/09.] www.cahps.ahrq.gov/

content/cahpsOverview/CAHPS-ProgramBrief.htm; The Commonwealth Fund. 2009. [Online information; retrieved 3/12/09.] www.whynotthebest.org; U.S. Department of Health and Human Services. 2009. [Online information; retrieved 3/12/09.] www.hospitalcompare.hhs.gov.

63. Boothman, R. C., A. C. Blackwell, D. A. Campbell, Jr., E. Commiskey, and S. An-derson. 2009. "A Better Approach to Medical Malpractice Claims? The University of Michigan Experience." *Journal of Health and Life Sciences Law* 2 (2): 125–59.

64. Spear (2005).

6

THE PHYSICIAN ORGANIZATION

In a Few Words

Physicians are the clinical leaders of the healthcare organization (HCO). They are associated with the organization principally by a contract for the privilege to treat patients but also by employment, joint ventures, and volunteer activities. They are accountable for the quality of care through service lines and monitoring of their individual performance, but they are given substantial autonomy to fulfill their role as agents for individual patients. The physician organization implements systems for improving the quality and efficiency of care; approves the credentials and monitors the performance of individual physicians; assists in planning the number and kinds of doctors; conducts continuing education for its members and other caregivers; provides a network of communication among physicians, the organization, and the governing board; and participates in designing compensation and other collective compensation arrangements. The organization is built around service lines, but it also provides a medical staff structure. The performance of physicians is measured directly from patient care; the performance of the physician organization is measured primarily by its effectiveness in recruiting and retaining members. The HCO's goal is to offer each physician a place to practice excellent medicine with similarly committed colleagues and reliable organizational support.

Critical Issues in the Physician Organization

1. *Organizational design:*
   - Build a network of communication so that every doctor is confident of his or her empowermen
   - Develop effective physician leaders
   - Manage multiple compensation approaches

2. *Achieving excellent care:*
   - Meet clinical needs effectively and promptly
   - Implement and improve protocols and interdisciplinary plans of care
   - Use the physician organization to support continuous improvement
   - Establish physician and HCO accountability

3. *Credentialing and recruitment:*
   - Recruit and retain qualified physicians
   - Provide continuing education to physicians and other caregivers
   - Plan medical staff capacity to ensure effective care
   - Monitor and improve individual performance

4. *Compensation:*
   - Ensure physicians a competitive income
   - Reward process and outcomes quality
   - Meet physician demand for flexible commitments and income security

QUESTIONS FOR DISCUSSION

Consider these questions as you read the chapter.

1. The traditional model of hospital privileges and fee-for-service practice can be described as a partnership, a sharing of responsibility between the physicians and the institution. What does each partner contribute, and what do they expect to get from it? How is this changing now?

2. The emergence of service lines tightened the bonds between physicians in similar specialties and their accountability to the governing board. The service line contracts often include employment, risk sharing, and joint capital investment arrangements that go well beyond traditional privileging. Why might this be a positive development? What are some alternatives, and where will the relationships go in the future?

3. Many primary care physicians claim that they no longer need medical staff membership or hospital privileges to take care of their patients. They feel it is an inefficient drain on their time, and it is difficult for them financially. Should the hospital ignore their concerns and let them drift off from the organization? If not, what should the hospital do to make affiliation attractive?

4. What is the relationship between the physician leaders of the service lines and the medical staff organization and the chief medical officer (CMO)? Can the CMO represent the interests of management and the physician organization at the same time?

5. Some flash points in physician relations are recurring and predictable. How would a well-managed organization deal with the following:
   - Interspecialty disputes: orthopedics and imaging, surgery and cardiology, or primary care and specialists
   - Emergency referrals: providing specialist care to emergency patients, who often arrive at inconvenient times and without insurance or financing
   - Multispecialty group versus single specialty groups
   - Impaired physicians

Physicians have been ascribed magical powers, granted extraordinary privileges and confidences, and expected to assume extra moral obligations since the dawn of human existence. The twentieth century saw a revolution in this social contract. The magical powers became reality through scientific advance. The growth of knowledge supported protocols and care management processes,[1] and, with these advances, "evidence" replaced "judgment" as the criterion for quality.[2] Specialization caused the privileges and confidences once vested in a single individual to be divided among many. The physician became a team leader who coordinates the work of a dozen or more caregivers. Medical care became a team event rather than a one-to-one relationship.

The good part of this revolution has been incompletely and unevenly deployed to actual patients. Several studies show that only about half of all patient–physician encounters result in optimal treatment.[3,4] Also, change has created substantial turmoil within medical practice. In the early twenty-first century, about 20 percent of doctors were unhappy with their profession. Satisfaction varies substantially by geographic location.[5,6] The perception of unhappiness may be greater than the reality. The fraction of dissatisfied physicians may be smaller than in some other professions (e.g., nursing) and does not appear to be larger than in law or dentistry.[7]

Purpose

The purpose of the physician organization is

> **to recruit and retain physicians necessary to provide excellent care to the community.**

This purpose implies a negotiated relationship between the community stakeholders and the physicians, deliberately using the HCO as a framework. The community brings substantial dowry to the relationship. It offers access to facilities, equipment, and trained personnel essential to the physician's practice, and it facilitates the physician's compensation through various healthcare financing programs. In return, it asks for the physician's commitment to its mission, compliance with its rules and procedures, and the maintenance of professional competence. Like all relationships, this one is potentially stressful. The framework must be robust enough to withstand the stresses that arise and respond to them in a constructive manner.

Functions

In excellent HCOs, the purpose is fulfilled in six major functions:

1. Achieve excellent care
2. Credential and delineate privileges
3. Plan and implement physician recruitment
4. Provide clinical education for physicians and other professionals
5. Communicate and resolve unmet needs
6. Negotiate and maintain compensation arrangements

These functions are summarized in Exhibit 6.1.

Achieving Excellent Care

Achieving excellent care results from correct application of protocols and interdisciplinary plans of care (IPOCs) combined with ongoing performance measurement, continuous improvement, and rewards. Patient management protocols open the possibility of a formal accountability between the specialist group and other clinicians treating patients and the hospital as a whole. The service line concept creates that accountability, which is effective in improving cost and quality of complex inpatient and outpatient care.[8]

Function	Contribution	Examples	
Achieving excellent care	Provide high-quality, cost-effective healthcare	Continuous improvement of care through clinical protocols Case management Prevention	**EXHIBIT 6.1** Functions of the Physician Organization
Credentialing and delineating privileges for physicians and related professionals	Ensure continued effectiveness of individual staff members	Recruitment and selection of new members Renewal of privileges	
Planning and implementing physician recruitment	Ensure an adequate supply of well-trained physicians	Physician needs planning Recruitment	
Providing clinical education for physicians and other professionals	Ensure a well-trained body of caregivers	Case reviews Protocol development Scientific programs Graduate medical education	
Communicating and resolving unmet needs	Bring a clinical viewpoint to all activities of the organization	Governing board Strategic planning Budgeting participation	
Negotiating and maintaining compensation arrangements	Allow customer access to a full range of healthcare financing opportunities	Negotiation and implementation of risk-sharing contracts with payers and intermediaries	

Clinical protocols are implemented within the clinical services lines. User panels, similar to process improvement teams (PITs), assemble and review guidelines, examine the practicality of each step, modify the guideline or operating practices as necessary, and recommend the final protocol. The opportunity to comment on any protocol is extended to all physicians. Equipment recommendations are specified and subject to the usual competitive review. A new protocol often requires changes in the training for nonphysician caregivers, and these changes must be arranged with the professional group involved and with human resources.

As with PITs, each panel has a charge, membership, and a timetable. The charge is to establish the initial set of care procedures for typical patients with a specific disease or condition. Membership must include all the caregivers directly involved. Each step of the protocol must be achievable by the designated team members—that is, they must have the training, information, supplies, and equipment they need every time the step arises. This is often a complex problem. New equipment must be purchased, new training provided, and scheduling reviewed to ensure that caregivers are available when patients need the care. Both referring and follow-up caregivers must be involved so that those transitions go smoothly. Leadership of the panel is usually assigned to the specialists who treat the largest percentage of patients with the disease or condition.

The result is extended panel membership, incorporating primary care physicians, specialists, hospital-based specialties (pathology, radiology, anesthesiology, and emergency medicine), nurses, and pharmacy and rehabilitation professions. Some conditions, depending on their severity, are treated by different practitioners. For example, midwives, neonatal nurse practitioners, family practice physicians, obstetricians, and pediatricians can successfully manage obstetrics and newborn care. Nurse practitioners, family practice physicians, general internists, cardiologists, and cardiovascular surgeons manage cardiovascular patients depending on their severity. Hospitalists—internists who specialize in caring for patients in hospitals—are widely employed for managing complex inpatient care and for decreasing lengths of stay, readmission rates, in-hospital mortality, and costs.[9] All of these groups must be involved in protocol design. Several versions of the protocol may result, reflecting the needs of patient subsets. The criteria for assigning patients must be clear.

As indicated in Chapter 5, all clinical teams have performance measures and goals that cover the six dimensions of the operational scorecard. Negotiating and monitoring these goals is part of the service line responsibilities. The service line reviews performance against benchmark, competition, trends, and values; establishes opportunities for improvement (OFIs); and develops PITs to translate the opportunities to improvement. Improvement is rewarded; the service line negotiates and distributes the rewards.

Credentialing and Delineating Privileges

The entire structure of care depends on recruiting and retaining professionally qualified caregivers. Physicians, with their broad responsibilities, have the most rigorous mechanism to review qualifications, called *credentialing and privileging*. The credentialing model is also used for dentists, psychologists, and podiatrists. Similar but slightly less formal processes are used for nurses, pharmacists, and other clinical professionals. Excellent care depends at several different levels on the skill and knowledge of individual physicians. Diagnosis, treatment selection and monitoring, and completion of diagnostic and therapeutic interventions are individual professional activities that are only as good as the physician performing them.

Credentialing and privileging are functions to ensure minimum levels of physician competence and proficiency. Following a rigorous procedure (outlined below), each physician's credentials, including any recent performance, are reviewed by several medical staff review bodies that make a recommendation to the governing board. The governing board is responsible for granting privileges to participate in the physician organization and to provide specific treatment within his or her training and experience and the capabilities of the HCO. Each physician is empowered to practice good medicine, including the authority to select, implement, and depart from protocols. Equally important, each physician can rely on other members of the medical staff to have the necessary skills and diligence.

Elements of Privilege

The privilege agreement is nationally standardized by accrediting organizations—National Committee for Quality Assurance and The Joint Commission—and by various court decisions. It is a contract with four critical elements:

1. *Bylaws.* The physicians collectively establish mutually acceptable rules and regulations. These define the physicians' rights to participate in the organization and provide care as part of the organization, the obligation to ensure quality and economy of care to their own patients, and the obligation to participate in educational and quality improvement activities. They may also define rules for compensation. The bylaws also define how the physician organization makes decisions, including its accountability hierarchy, and how the rules may be amended. Given the complexity of most of these issues, the bylaws are supplemented by various procedural statements included by reference. Because the privileges give access to the community-owned resources of the institution and endorse the physician to patients and intermediaries, the bylaws are approved by both its physician members and the governing board. Each physician accepts the bylaws as part of the privilege agreement.

The bylaws are the principal source of due-process protection. They establish all procedural elements, including application requirements, timing, review processes, confidentiality, committees and participants, methods of establishing expectations, sources of data, and appeals procedures. Regular review and updating of the bylaws are important.

2. *Privileges.* The organization extends the privilege of treating patients within the HCO to each physician willing to accept the bylaws and judged competent to participate. The privilege is extended for specific kinds of patient care, matching the physician's training, specialty certification, and demonstrated capability. It is limited to one or two years, and physicians are reappointed based on peer review of actual clinical performance. The review process that leads to privileges is frequently called *credentialing*. Those privileged to practice are traditionally called **attending physicians**.

Attending physicians
Physicians who have the privilege of using the hospital for patient care and who are designated as the physician of record for particular patients

Because each physician accepts responsibility for his or her own patients and the obligation to participate in peer review, only physicians judge other physicians on medical matters. (Reports from other professionals are part of the review, but physicians make the final recommendation to the governing board.) In larger organizations the group of peers is physicians with similar specialization. This concept of peer review is a central element of professional autonomy. It is highly prized by most physicians, and they invest much time and energy in carrying out their obligations.

In addition to physician members of the HCO medical staff, there may also be bylaws provisions for licensed independent allied health professionals to practice. Bylaws specify the level of membership, scope of privileges, and supervising authority. Examples may include podiatrists, clinical psychologists, advanced practice nurses, physician assistants, orthotists, and opththalmic technicians.

3. *Independent physician–patient relationship.* Each physician establishes his or her own relationship to each patient and is expected to pursue diligently the obligations of that relationship; that is, the contract recognizes that the physician has explicit obligations to his or her patients as individuals. This is the concept of agency. The organization recognizes agency independent of the physician's compensation; that is, a salaried physician has the same obligations to patients as one who works under fee-for-service.

4. *Continuous quality improvement and peer review.* Physicians who receive privileges are expected to participate in the ongoing activities of the organization, including developing protocols and providing assistance to other clinical professions. They are also expected to participate in reviewing the quality of care of their peers and be the subject of such review. Privileges will be curtailed should the clinical performance of the physician fail to meet the expectations of peers. Privileges can be withdrawn for failing to participate in other activities as required by the bylaws.

The contractual consideration on the part of the institution is access to its resources, sometimes including health insurance contracts or other monetary compensation; on the part of the physician, it is willingness to practice good medicine and accept the obligations.

Privileges are granted only through a precisely defined process intended to protect the rights of all parties. The major steps are specified in detail in the bylaws and are shown in Exhibit 6.2. The major clinical review is by the specialty department. For the initial credentialing, they rely on references, certifications, and the applicant's portfolio of previous work. For recertification, they rely on measures, reports of unexpected events, and in some cases, direct observation.

Privilege Review Process

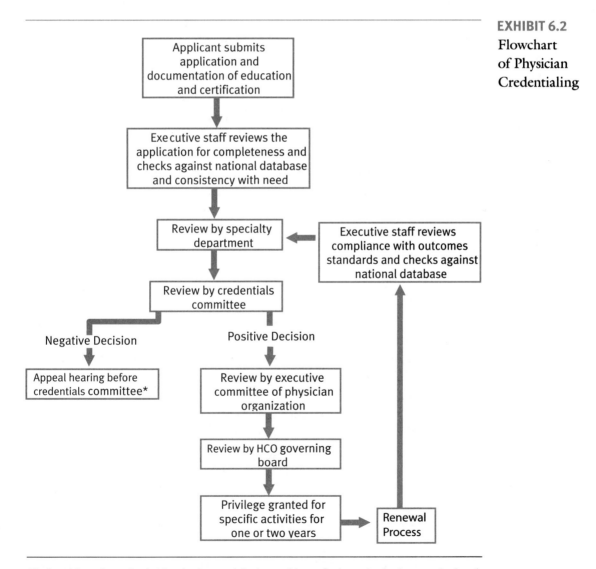

EXHIBIT 6.2
Flowchart of Physician Credentialing

* Both positive and negative decisions by the appeals body are subject to further review by the governing board.

Credentials Committee

The credentials committee review is the first of several steps beyond specialty review to ensure objectivity and equity in the process. The ideal member of the credentials committee possesses the attributes of a good judge: He or she is patient, consistent, thorough, factual, and considerate. Clearly, clinical knowledge and skill are required, but detailed clinical evaluation should occur in specialty review. The opinion of peer specialists must be sought when appropriate. Committee members should be widely respected. Physicians with other important leadership tasks should not serve simultaneously on the credentials committee, and membership should rotate fairly frequently. A management representative, usually the vice president for medical affairs, should staff the committee, both to assist with the workload and to ensure compliance with the bylaws. The committee must follow the bylaws rigorously. Following the bylaws in one case but not in another is potentially discriminatory. General failure to follow the bylaws is capricious.[10] Institutions are liable for failure to provide due process, failure to remove incompetent physicians, and failure to establish appropriate standards of practice. The individuals who participate in the process are liable for arbitrary, capricious, or discriminatory behavior.[11]

The management representative implements all procedures under the bylaws and the direction of the chair. Formal procedures for advance notice, agenda, attendance, minutes, and appeal mechanisms are mandatory. The summary of the individual's activities must be compiled in writing and documented; it may include formal evaluation by peers.[12] Physicians under review must have the opportunity to see the information compiled about them and to comment on it. Because the committee should function at a secondary level, evaluating the sum of the year's activities rather than actual patient care, the need for new direct testimony is minimized. When necessary, the statements must be carefully identified and recorded. Review of procedures by legal counsel is desirable.

Should either party appeal the credentials committee's decision, the grounds must be documented. Both the HCO and the physician should be represented by counsel in the appeals session. Final decision must be made by the governing board, again subject to the rules established in the bylaws. Physicians denied privileges often sue the HCO. The documentation is the defense. Excellent HCOs prevent lawsuits through the careful maintenance of due process and the documentation of sound evidence in support of the committee's decisions. They also protect committee members and others in the credentialing chain with insurance and legal counsel. Properly run, the credentials process will not be negatively viewed by the medical staff.[13] A sound monitoring process at the service line level, combined with a supportive culture, can assist any physician who encounters difficulty. In extreme cases, resignation or leave of absence is an option to avoid loss of privileges.

The Health Care Quality Improvement Act of 1986, Title IV of P.L. 100-177, mandates reporting of loss of credentials or other disciplinary action to a federal information bank. The purpose of the act is to reduce the chance of an incompetent physician moving to a new location and misrepresenting his or her skills. Specifically, the act requires HCOs to

1. notify the National Practitioner Data Bank of
   - any physician's or dentist's loss of credentials for any period greater than 30 days,
   - any voluntary surrender of privileges to avoid investigation,
   - any requirement for medical proctoring or supervision imposed as a result of peer review,
   - any malpractice settlement against any member of the medical staff or "other health practitioner" as defined in the act, and
2. check the information bank prior to initial privileging.

The act, by raising the standard of proof, also protects any person who reports to or works for a professional review body, such as an accredited organization's credentialing committee, from legal action by the individual disciplined.[14] Although the act was well intended, little or no evidence exists that it changed behavior. It appears that many credentialing committees seek alternatives that evade the reporting requirement.[15]

Medical quality and performance improvement are based on the use of prospectively accepted protocols and measured performance, as discussed in Chapter 5. These simplify the credentialing review to five questions:

1. Does the physician comply with general requirements for continuing education, maintaining certification, and meeting minimum levels of activity?
2. Does the physician correctly perform the procedures that are his or her direct responsibility, including appropriate selection of, compliance with, and departure from protocols?
3. Does the physician achieve outcomes consistent with the expectations of the community, with due consideration of differences in the population being treated?
4. Has the physician avoided all activity that directly threatens the rights or safety of patients or colleagues?
5. Does the physician have appropriate interpersonal communication skills, and does he or she abstain from disruptive behavior?[16]

The committee seeks evidence that negative answers to these questions are rare and unlikely to be repeated. It grants or renews privileges whenever that evidence is convincing. In initial reviews, the first and the last questions are verified directly, and references are sought as evidence on the others. In subsequent reviews, emphasis is placed on the physician's recent actual performance. The best credentials process limits its review to only these questions. Other issues of quality, patient satisfaction, and cost effectiveness are handled by the quality improvement activities of the medical departments. The credentialing activity is deliberately separated from protocol setting and monitoring to permit fuller exploration of clinical issues in a scientific rather than a judgmental environment. The use of protocols as a referent ensures that the physician will not be held to a unique standard and makes it possible for the committee to evaluate physicians from all specialties. The vast majority of physicians will pass review without difficulty.

Denial of Privileges

An HCO may deny or discontinue the right of a physician to use its facilities and personnel in the care of patients on either of two grounds. The first is quality—that is, the physician fails to comply with properly established criteria governing quality of care and good character, as discussed earlier. The second is economic—that is, the physician overtaxes the facilities available for the kinds of care he or she expects to give or provides a service that is not supported by the institution as a whole. Thus, a hospital is not obligated to accept a cardiac surgeon if it has no cardiologist, if it has no cardiopulmonary laboratory, or if evidence suggests that it has insufficient demand to support a high-quality practice. Similarly, a physician organization is not obligated to accept a pediatric hematologist if it routinely refers pediatric hematology, has no laboratory facilities for pediatric hematology, or is satisfied that the existing arrangements are in the best interests of its members.

Information and Data Support

The record required by the credentials committee has two major components. Initial reviews require the credentials themselves—documents and references testifying to the education, licensure, certification, experience, and character of applicants. The applicant is often charged with collecting the documents, although these must be scrutinized and verified by the organization. Medical staff reappointments require information on the clinical performance of current staff members. Physician clinical performance assessment systems may be used to quantify physician performance based on the rates at which their patients experience certain outcomes of care and/or the rates at which physicians adhere to evidence-based protocols during their actual practice of medicine.[17]

Two groups—the hierarchy of the physician organization and HCO employees who support the quality review, utilization, and risk-management processes—monitor clinical activity and prepare reports during the year on clinical outcomes. For negative outcomes, processes are in place for the physician to review the cases and justify his or her actions. In complex cases and in accordance with the medical staff bylaws, additional information may be requested using a formal hearing process to protect the rights of the physician.

Specialty Certification

It is increasingly common to insist on full certification in a specialty as a condition of membership or, in the case of young physicians still completing their training, a specific program and timetable for earning certification. Thus, the prototype for specification of privileges is that set of activities normally included in the specialty. Well-run HCOs have several additional requirements regarding privileges:

- Maintenance of specialty certification. Many specialties have continuing education requirements.
- Restrictions based on the capability of the hospital and the supporting medical specialists. (An individual physician may be qualified to receive a certain privilege, but the hospital may lack the necessary equipment, facilities, and complementary staff.)
- Maintenance of a minimum number of cases treated annually to ensure that the skills of both the physician and the hospital support team remain up to date.
- For new or expanded privileges, evidence of relevant education and successful treatment of a number of cases under supervision.

The judgments of national specialty boards cannot be the sole criterion for assigning a specific privilege, for two reasons. First, the issue of quality is not as simple as it looks initially. Family practitioners and general internists argue that they can handle a great many uncomplicated cases without referral, while obstetricians, pediatricians, and medical subspecialists argue that their specialized skills are more likely to promote quality. There are two parts to resolving these arguments. One is to correctly identify the needs of each patient. The identification of the patient's total needs is as important a part of the quality of medical care as the excellence of a specific treatment. It may be wise to sacrifice some elegance in the treatment of a specific disease to improve the patient's total medical condition. The higher the value placed on comprehensive care, the stronger the generalists' argument. Many thoughtful analysts believe that comprehensiveness is undervalued in American healthcare and that the balance has shifted too far toward specialization.

The second problem arising from excessive limitation of privileges is its effect on physicians' incomes. The specialties sometimes conflict with one another or reflect self-interest. A decision to limit obstetrics to obstetricians and newborn care to pediatricians transfers income. It may reduce the income of family practitioners and the availability of physicians throughout the community. It will also increase the fees charged per delivery. The traditional fee structure tends to reward procedures more than diagnosis and specialization more than comprehensiveness and continuity. The result has been relatively low incomes for family practitioners, general internists, and pediatricians. The disparity has generated some sensitivity, and an organization that limits privileges excessively may find itself unable to recruit or retain these specialties. Limitations should be monitored carefully by the executive office, acting on behalf of the governing board, for compliance with the mission and all aspects of its long-range plan.

Physician Impairment

The credentials committee faces certain predictable problems, among them the impaired physician. Physicians, like other human beings, can be disabled by age, physical or mental disease or condition, declining cognitive ability, personal trauma, disruptive behavior, and substance abuse. The prevalence of these difficulties among practicing physicians is hard to estimate, but it is generally conceded to be between 5 percent and 15 percent.[18] Thus, a medium-sized HCO could have a dozen physicians either impaired or in danger of impairment at any given time.

The response of the credentials committee should be tailored to the kind of problem. Aging and uncorrectable physical or mental disability must force reduction of privileges. Alcoholism, abuse of addictive drugs, behavioral instability, and depression may be more common among physicians than among the general public. Treatment for depression and substance abuse is clearly indicated, and programs designed especially for physicians can be reached through state medical societies. Arrangements can be made to assist impaired physicians with their practices during the period of recovery, thus ensuring that patients receive acceptable care without unduly disrupting the physician–patient relationship or the physicians' incomes. Larger organizations often have a committee or group set up specifically to deal with this problem. Although this group usually keeps affected physicians' identities secret, its activities must be coordinated with those of the credentials committee. While every reasonable effort at rehabilitation should be made, the credentials committee is ultimately accountable for recommending the suspension or removal of privileges.

Trends in Credentialing and Privileging

The privilege system has robust flexibility. It can cover care in various settings, be tailored to unique geographic needs or special markets, and adapt to any insurance or physician payment system. It accommodates other professionals who give medical care—for example, dentists, psychologists, podiatrists, nurse specialists, and chiropractors. It permits but does not require tangible compensation as part of the consideration. It differs from the usual employment relationship between an organization and its associates, principally in providing more adequate protection to the physician, primarily to allow the physician to carry out agency obligations. It formally implements empowerment. The CEO and the management staff, in contrast, serve at the pleasure of the governing board and can be discharged at any legally constituted meeting for any grounds not discriminatory or libelous. Only civil service, some union contracts, and the tenure system of professors provide individuals rights similar to credentialing.

Planning and Implementing Physician Recruitment

A successful physician organization should be properly sized to the community it serves. If it is too large, individual physician income and professional satisfaction goals will not be met, skills may be lost through lack of practice, and physicians may face strong temptations to pursue unnecessary treatment.[19] If it is too small, patients will be unable to get timely service and an adequate choice of practitioners. Physicians may be overworked, endangering quality and the satisfaction of both practitioners and patients. One solution is to leave the physician supply to the market, essentially allowing physicians to come and go as they individually evaluate the community's willingness to support their service. A better alternative is to plan the staff size as part of the strategic and long-range planning of the institution.

The HCO lacks the authority or the right to deny a physician the right to open or close a practice. But it can deny access to the hospital, and it can recruit for needed specialists. Well-managed HCOs do this, using the best available planning information to assist physicians in this critical business decision. Because they do it effectively, they help their communities overcome shortages, maintain quality of care, and avoid excess cost.

The HCO's medical staff planning activity is an indirect control over fee-for-service income. In effect, it is based on assumptions that the physicians involved will fulfill demand for effective care and will avoid unnecessary procedures. By putting planned goals and recruitment strategies in place, the HCO makes a clear statement about the kind of medical practice it wants for the community. It also begins to implement the underlying philosophy of compensation that applies to all associates—that is, an associate's income should be the same as he or she could earn for equivalent effort elsewhere.

The conceptual model for planning is an extension of the general epidemiologic planning model discussed in Chapter 3. It is applied to each specialty of the physician organization. In Model 1, the epidemiologic model forecasts equation (1). The services provided per physician year can be estimated from history. The physicians involved are surveyed about their work intentions, such as retirements, leaves, and plans to change their HCO affiliation. The survey can improve the forecast of services provided as well as provide a forecast of physicians available. **Modeling Future Need for Physicians**

Model 1

$$(1)\quad \left\{\begin{array}{c}\text{Number}\\\text{of services}\\\text{needed}\end{array}\right\} = \left\{\begin{array}{c}\text{Population}\\\text{at risk}\end{array}\right\} \times \left\{\begin{array}{c}\text{Average services}\\\text{per patient year}\end{array}\right\} \times \left\{\begin{array}{c}\text{Market}\\\text{share}\end{array}\right\}$$

$$(2)\quad \left\{\begin{array}{c}\text{Number of}\\\text{physicians}\\\text{needed}\end{array}\right\} = \left\{\begin{array}{c}\text{Number}\\\text{of services}\\\text{needed}\end{array}\right\} \div \left\{\begin{array}{c}\text{Services provided}\\\text{per physician year}\end{array}\right\}$$

$$(3)\quad \left\{\begin{array}{c}\text{Physician}\\\text{recruitments}\\\text{needed}\end{array}\right\} = \left\{\begin{array}{c}\text{Number of}\\\text{physicians}\\\text{needed}\end{array}\right\} - \left\{\begin{array}{c}\text{Number of}\\\text{physicians}\\\text{available}\end{array}\right\}$$

While Model 1 works well with major clinical events, like neurosurgery and advanced cancer treatment, it is impractical for primary care and the more general specialties. An alternate model, Model 2, uses standard ratios of physicians per population based on the aggregate service experience of existing health systems and communities.[20]

Model 2

$$(1) \quad \left\{ \begin{array}{c} \text{Number of} \\ \text{physicians} \\ \text{needed} \end{array} \right\} = \left\{ \begin{array}{c} \text{Population} \\ \text{at risk} \end{array} \right\} \times \left\{ \begin{array}{c} \text{Standard} \\ \text{physicians} \\ \text{per population} \end{array} \right\}$$

$$(2) \quad \left\{ \begin{array}{c} \text{Physician} \\ \text{recruitments} \\ \text{needed} \end{array} \right\} = \left\{ \begin{array}{c} \text{Number of} \\ \text{physicians} \\ \text{needed} \end{array} \right\} - \left\{ \begin{array}{c} \text{Number of} \\ \text{physicians} \\ \text{available} \end{array} \right\}$$

Model 2 still requires the survey of physician intentions. Its weakness is the standard, which may or may not be reliable for the future in a specific community.

Both models have difficulty reliably forecasting the appropriate role of the various specialties. While the incidence of disease is relatively predictable, procedures to treat a disease and what specialty uses them change unpredictably. New technology, prevention, and improved protocols change the kind of response and the specialty required. (The use of angioplasty, stents, and coronary artery surgery is one dynamic arena that affects the numbers of cardiovascular surgeons and invasive cardiologists.) Patient acceptance of alternative sources of care is not uniform. (The acceptance of midwives is an example.) A wide variation exists across communities in physician supply levels. Prepaid group practices have witnessed an increased use in specialist physicians while maintaining an overall physician-to-population ratio that is 22 percent to 37 percent below the national rate.[21] Within the usual range of values, it may be difficult to detect any major change in population health.

Developing a Physician Supply Plan

The physician supply plan is a vital contribution to effective physician relationships. It allows the hospital to identify community needs and move to meet them in a timely manner. It also allows the hospital to protect the income of effective practitioners. In primary care, the analysis must be carried to small geographic areas because easy access to primary care physicians appears to be important in patient satisfaction. Nurse practitioners, midwives, family practitioners, internists, psychiatrists, obstetricians, pediatricians, hospitalists, and emergency physicians are all prominent primary care providers.

Good practice calls for a careful analysis of the present situation and anticipated changes using both models to explore a range of possible outcomes and their consequences. A forecast of incidence based on local history is usually obtained through the cross-functional teams and the specialties involved. One based on national data should also be used, with due regard to benchmarks and published scientific opinion. Several referents—such as values for staff model HMOs, benchmarks among similar-sized cities, and means adjusted for anticipated insurance trends—should be considered to evaluate current levels and show the implications for physician supply.

The analysis and the alternative forecasts should be used to stimulate discussion among physicians and the governing board. Widespread understanding of the opportunities improves individual decision making. Discussion may prompt early retirements or deliberate recruitment. The governing board is obligated to address indications of undersupply and severe oversupply.

Few communities have a surplus of primary care providers. A recruitment strategy is essential to remain competitive. It must specify the need by type of provider and location and then consider incentives necessary to attract qualified applicants. A sound approach will promote discussion of the issue among all affected groups, leading to recommendations from the physician organization and final acceptance by the institutional board.

High-volume specialties (cardiology, endocrinology, obstetrics) should be individually forecast. High-cost, low-volume specialties (neurosurgery, neonatology) should be carefully justified before the institution commits capital and personnel. A plan to provide a specific referral specialty service affirms that sufficient local demand will exist to maintain the quality and to justify the cost. In general, highly specialized treatment of disease incurs high fixed costs that must be spread over large populations to be cost effective. The income expectations of the specialists themselves are high, and substantial clinical support is necessary. Unit cost falls rapidly as volume increases. It is also true that treatment teams caring for high volumes of patients will have better-quality results.[22] As Exhibit 6.3 shows, for any given treatment there is an increasing quality structure, a declining cost structure, and increasing specialist incomes as volume increases. There are also competitive standards for all three. If competitive standards are not met, patients and payers will select other sources, after allowing for any inconvenience, such as travel to a remote site. The standards dictate a critical volume—V_q, V_i, V_c. An HCO that operates a specialty below its critical volumes faces poor quality, inefficiency, and often financial losses.

Cardiovascular surgery provides a useful example. The need is dependent on the population of the community, its age, and its health habits. The United States averaged 2,057 operations per million persons in 2003, and the volume of surgery per site was approximately 700 per year.[23] A community of approximately 350,000 persons is necessary to provide average volumes. The institution that cannot attract that much demand faces unit costs higher than the competitive standard. The surgeon who works in that institution faces lower-than-average income. Both face the problem that outcomes may be below achievable levels because the team does not get enough practice.

EXHIBIT 6.3
Critical Volumes for Specialty Services

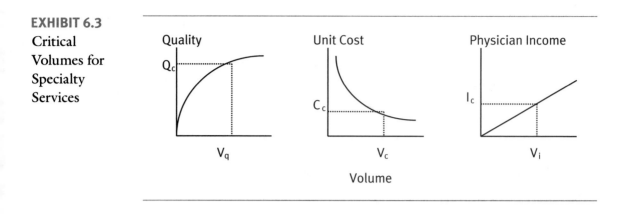

The medical staff plan protects physicians against new competitors, because the HCO will decline privileges to applicants exceeding the planned numbers. If physicians were to do this themselves, it would be collusion in restraint of trade, a violation of antitrust law. Because of this, although medical staff comment should be solicited on the plan, final approval must rest with the governing board.

Integrating the Physician Recruitment Plan with Other HCO Plans

The HCO must make capital investments to support the physician supply. The investment decisions are part of the strategic or long-range plan of the institution discussed in Chapter 14. Decisions are made first on the question of scope of service—"Should we have a cardiovascular surgery program?"—and second on the actual facilities and number of physicians required. As illustrated in Exhibit 6.4, the physician recruitment plan is an extension of these decisions.

The advantages of formal planning are summarized in Exhibit 6.5. These help sell the HCO to physicians and, when backed by an effective plan of service, make the HCO "a great place to give care."

Recruiting Physicians

Most communities must recruit physicians. Population growth, aging, and retirements of the current staff create vacancies that must be filled. Good physicians have their choice of practice locations, and they are actively recruited even in times of relative surplus. A recruitment offer frequently includes arrangements for office facilities and services, income guarantees, health insurance participation contracts, malpractice coverage, membership in a medical partnership or group, and introductions to referring physicians or available specialists. A substantial capital resource is necessary to assemble these elements. At the same time, physicians want to work where their colleagues are capable and friendly; complex offers require early assurance that medical credentials are acceptable; and selecting the right candidate involves assessment of clinical skills.

Planning Step	Example	Result
Environmental assessment; mission and vision	Will service population support advanced inpatient referral services?	Adequate demand for referral services in general
Strategic plans and long-range financial plan	What are priority health needs? Which can be met at a competitive price; which can be served by others?	Cardiovascular surgery is one of several services under consideration
Service line plans and recruitment plans	Forecasts for number of procedures, professional personnel, other personnel, and facilities and equipment	Recruitment of cardiovascular surgeon(s) and team(s)
Implementation and goal setting	Review of actual volumes, outcomes, and costs	Continuation, expansion, or contraction of cardiovascular program

EXHIBIT 6.4
Cardiac Surgery as an Example of Combined Strategic, Service, and Physician Planning

Recruitment has become a relatively well-codified activity, carried out by a search committee of the physician organization. It includes the following:

- Establishment of criteria for the position and the person sought
- Establishment of compensation and incentives
- Advertising and solicitation of candidates
- Initial selection
- Interviews and visits
- Final selection and negotiation

Because access to the institution is important to almost all physicians, because the institution's governing board makes the decision to grant physician privileges, and because the institution often supplies much of the capital required, recruitment is commonly a collaborative activity. The institution's support contributes to success.

EXHIBIT 6.5
Advantages
of Physician
Supply
Planning

Advantage	Physician Benefit	Institution Benefit
Restricted entry of competing physicians	Protection against excessive competition; assurances of "fair" income	Medical staff commitment to effective care
Shared information and cooperative analysis allow more accurate forecasts	See future sooner and more clearly, and have more time to react	Improve safety, return, and market attractiveness of investments
Facility and employee needs integrated with physician needs	Support available when needed	Volumes adequate to keep costs and quality competitive
Better management of physician supply	Facilitate potentially painful transitions	Meet community demand for access Reduce pressure for inappropriate treatment
Better management of insurance contracts	More options for insurance contracts More income stability More market share	Broader array of options for customers More market share

Providing Clinical Education

The physician organization has at least two educational functions; in larger organizations it has three. All staffs are responsible for promoting the continuing education of their own members and for assisting in the clinical education of other associates of the institution. Larger organizations and academic medical centers have responsibilities for postgraduate and, occasionally, for undergraduate (i.e., candidates for the MD or DO degree) medical education.

The interrelation of education with continuous improvement and the development of consensus protocols should not be overlooked. Analysis of past performance, benchmarking, the design of new processes, and the preparation of protocols are educational activities in themselves, affecting the quality improvement, credentialing, planning, and educational functions simultaneously. Increasingly, the educational function is driven by the continuous improvement process.

Continuing Medical Education

Continuing education for physicians is routinely required for licensure and specialty certifications. Many educational programs are offered outside the organization; these do not substitute for the continued study of the organization's own patients. Much education now occurs through the protocol development teams. Education helps ensure that every caregiver fully understands the protocols; develops group pressure to encourage compliance; and, by changing behavior beforehand, eliminates personal confrontations over failures.

Continuing education need not be limited to clinical subjects. Programs to help physicians understand the corporate approach to decision making; to gain skills in organized activities such as team building; and to learn fundamentals of technologies, such as quality control and cost accounting, are also important.

How much to invest in staff education is a difficult judgment. Programs are often expensive to mount, but they are more expensive to attend. The opportunity cost of physicians' time is high, and educational time must be judged in the context of the demands of family and practice and, particularly, other organizational demands on the physicians' time. Education outside the hospital is often useful, but availability differs by community. The Joint Commission and all physician specialty associations agree that all physicians should have access to sufficient educational opportunity to stay current. This requires, and The Joint Commission specifies, at least monthly educational meetings with required attendance. Beyond this minimum, it is probably wise to decentralize decisions about staff education to the lowest feasible unit of the staff and to accommodate the programs they suggest when attendance indicates cost-effective investments. Note that large, successful HCOs, such as Kaiser Permanente, Sentara Healthcare, Henry Ford Health System, and Intermountain Healthcare, invest heavily in education. They use their size to assemble programs that might not be cost effective for smaller institutions.

By tradition, preparation, and law, the physician is the leader of the healthcare team. With this leadership comes an obligation to educate others, not only other clinical professionals but also trustees, executives, and other management personnel. A particularly important part of this education deals with new clinical developments. New approaches to care frequently require retraining for personnel at several levels, and physicians should participate in that education. In addition, trustees and planners rely on the medical staff to identify new opportunities for care and to make clinical implications clear in terms that promote effective decisions. Many of these educational requirements are met through participation on various committees and day-to-day associations.

Education of HCO Associates

Medicine has acknowledged its obligation to train new physicians since Hippocrates. Clinical training of medical students occurs in a limited number of institutions that incorporate such training in their mission. In 2009, more than 400 teaching hospitals and health systems offered postgraduate medical

Postgraduate Medical Education

education programs for **residents** and *fellows*—licensed physicians completing specialty education.[24] (Residents and fellows are also called *house officers*. Beginning residents were formerly called *interns*, but the term is no longer encouraged.) Many of these sites were in vertically integrated HCOs, although 34 percent of postgraduate medical education programs were in academic medical centers.[25]

The content of this education is controlled through certification by individual specialty boards and is coordinated through the Accreditation Council for Graduate Medical Education (ACGME). House officers are paid stipends during their residencies because they provide important direct service, because hospitals feel they are a valuable source of recruits, and because their presence has long been thought to improve overall quality of care. An important benefit to both the community and the attending staff is that house officers are expected to cover patient needs at times when attending physicians are not present. In addition, many of the programs suitable for house officers are appropriate continuing education for attending physicians, and educating house officers is educational in itself.

ACGME has identified six general competencies of physicians and has begun a program to assess residents' mastery of these competencies:[26]

1. *Patient care* that is compassionate, appropriate, and effective for the treatment of health problems and the promotion of health
2. *Medical knowledge* about established and evolving biomedical, clinical, and cognate (e.g., epidemiological and social–behavioral) sciences and the application of this knowledge to patient care
3. *Practice-based learning and improvement* that involves investigation and evaluation of their own patient care, appraisal and assimilation of scientific evidence, and improvements in patient care
4. *Interpersonal and communication skills* that result in effective information exchange and teaming with patients, their families, and other health professionals
5. *Professionalism,* as manifested through a commitment to carrying out professional responsibilities, adherence to ethical principles, and sensitivity to a diverse patient population
6. *Systems-based practice,* as manifested by actions that demonstrate an awareness of and responsiveness to the larger context and system of healthcare and the ability to effectively call on system resources to provide care that is of optimal value

ACGME's action means that all new physicians and most of medical leadership must address the emergence of evidence-based medicine, team-based care, and the need to work within a larger system.

Communicating and Resolving Unmet Needs

The emphasis that transformational management places on communication applies to the medical staff. Excellent HCOs make systematic efforts to build a communicating culture:

1. Physician representatives are included in all discussions of major decisions, as shown in Exhibit 6.6.
2. Senior managers devote significant time to individual and group contact with physicians.
3. Formal surveys are used to measure physician satisfaction, as with other associates.
4. Physician leaders, like all managers, are trained to listen, respond effectively, and report.
5. Physicians are invited to serve on the governing board.
6. A complex accountability structure (Exhibit 6.9) provides two avenues for discussion of most issues.
7. Formal mechanisms for conflict resolution are built into the medical staff bylaws, but they are used as a last resort.

The goal is a structure where all physicians are empowered and confident that their voices will be heard in decisions that affect their practices. This means not only listening but also effective avenues to identify issues, discuss implications, and resolve conflicts.[27] Trust between the parties is a critical factor.[28] Success requires a robust network of communications that identifies issues promptly, solicits and organizes opinion about them, and resolves them fairly.[29] All physicians should be close to someone whom they respect and who can hear their concerns and either resolve them or explain how they can participate in the resolutions. Encouraging comments and resolving them openly create an environment where issues can be aired, discussed, and decided. Ideally, all physicians should be convinced that they have heard the issues, that they have had a fair opportunity to be heard about the issues, and that the final decisions optimize market realities, without having had to waste unnecessary time on either step.

Building a Communicating Culture

The major constraint is physician time. Efforts outside their practice reduce the time they have for patient care. Many prefer the latter, and all generate revenue from it. Some specialties are more constrained than others. Primary care physicians may have offices some distance away and full calendars in their clinics. Specialists are more likely to be nearby and, because they earn more per minute of clinical effort, are more able to devote time to management issues. This creates an imbalance that must be explicitly addressed.

EXHIBIT 6.6
Physician
Representation
on Decision
Processes

Decision Type	Example	Physician Participation
Mission/vision	Visioning exercise	Extensive individual participation Review committees Governing board membership
Resource allocation	Environment assessment Strategic plans	Governing board membership Leaders participate in annual review
	Services plan Financial plan	Membership on board planning and finance committees
	Facilities and human resources plans	Representation on committees and consultation for services directly involved
	Physician recruitment plan	Advice from each specialty unit Opportunity for individual comment
	Budgeting	Participation between line units and services particularly involved
	Capital budgeting	Major voice in ranking all clinical equipment purchases Participate in general ranking of capital equipment
Clinical care issues	Process design	Participation by service line in all patient management protocol development Review of relevant functional protocols Participation or consultation in clinical PITs
Organizational	Personnel selection	Credentialing of all physicians Participation on executive search committees
	Implementation plans	Participation by service line
	Information plan	Participation in plan and relevant pilot programs
	Conflict resolution	Membership in mediation efforts and appeals panels

PITs: process improvement teams

Physician time is saved by training leadership and by preparation and flexibility in committee activities. Meetings and meeting agendas should be designed with a respect for physicians' time. Advance preparation and distribution of relevant background material make a noticeable difference, as does proper preparation by the chair. Teleconferencing and attendance as needed should be encouraged. Special efforts are made to hear the primary care viewpoint.

Most physicians learn the communications culture by experience. Just-in-time training—a review of process at the start of major discussions—is helpful. Where communication and trust are supported by a strong formal system, informal devices can be used to great advantage. If all staff members are confident of their empowerment, much can be accomplished through informal discussions. In well-run HCOs, nonmedical managers make a deliberate effort to maintain informal communications with the medical staff, even going to their offices to meet them. Many successful CEOs and COOs undertake the monitoring function personally. The new CEO of a Philadelphia health system put many miles on his car while employing this strategy, but, as one private practice physician put it, "at least he [was] out of the corporate palace." By visiting physicians in their offices, hospital managers and executives demonstrate their understanding of the value of a physician's time and show a willingness to become acquainted with physicians on a more personal level.[30]

Representing Physicians on the Governing Board

The practice of providing designated positions on the board for the physicians has become almost universal and is an important advantage of community-based HCOs. Exceptions are mainly limited to those institutions whose corporate charters or enabling legislation preclude such participation. Physicians nominate their colleagues in many organizations. To satisfy tax exemption rules, the board majority must remain nonphysicians; rarely do physicians constitute more than a substantial minority. These few individuals, who make up only a fraction of the specialties, ages, and financial arrangements of the staff as a whole, cannot represent the complex needs of all physicians. Like other board members, they are expected to vote for the best interests of the community, rather than for any short-term advantage to themselves or to the physicians. They serve the medical staff more by making sure the physicians' opinions are fully and fairly heard than by any specific representation.

Resolving Conflicts

The intent of the communication network is to identify potential conflicts in advance, analyze and understand them, and respond in a way that is constructive for all parties. The extensive participation in PITs and various committees identifies and resolves many issues, but the process is more contentious than it appears. Conflicts arise between specialties, between clinical support services and attending physicians, between the HCO and specialty groups, and between individual physicians. Painful sacrifices may be involved in settling them. The well-managed HCO attempts to resolve many conflicts through organizational guidelines and processes. The organization's bylaws specify not simply the rights and obligations of each party but also the methods by which communication is encouraged and disagreements are resolved and the roles of each office and standing committee of the physician organization. For disagreements that are particularly serious, the negotiation and conflict resolution approaches described in Chapter 2 are applicable.

Negotiating and Maintaining Compensation Arrangements

An HCO's financial relationship to its medical staff is complex. The early twentieth century tradition of independent physician practice and hospital operation has eroded steadily and seems almost certain to erode further. It too often fails to provide either patients or buyers with safe, effective, patient-centered, and efficient care. As noted earlier, the medical staff plan is an indirect HCO control on fee-for-service income. Various alternative approaches have arisen over the past 50 years; some have had limited success, but none has emerged as the dominant twenty-first century model.

The HCO's goal in all compensation is a "fair" income, one that is equivalent to what would be earned in a similar effort elsewhere. The goal is difficult to measure because a great many variables are involved in "equivalent," "similar effort," and "elsewhere." The concept is clear, however, and intuitively acceptable to most people. The HCO "delights" physicians by providing trained people and good tools and the patients themselves by "delighting" the physicians' customers. The compensation offer is viewed in light of the total package. Confidence that they will have what they need and their patients will get what they need is more important to good doctors than a larger income.

HCO–Physician Contracts

As of 2010, most physicians earn most of their income from modified versions of fee-for-service payment, but they are also compensated directly by the HCO and purchase services from it. The economic interactions of physicians and the HCO are shown in Exhibit 6.7. Five types of contracts underlie the arrangements in Exhibit 6.7:

1. *Salary arrangements.* These permit the physician to be a full- or part-time employee of a corporation, either for patient care or for managerial activity.
2. *Contracts providing office management.* These allow physicians to escape overhead costs and managerial obligations. Almost any office service can be involved, from the facility itself to office employees, supplies, and malpractice insurance. The institution can manage these services in a manner that encourages seamless communication for consultation, referral, and admission of patients. The physician must pay fair market value for the service. Tax, inurement, and fraud issues must be avoided by contract design.

3. *Sale of existing practices.* This allows physicians to seek early retirement or to liquidate a fee-for-service practice in favor of a salaried one. Practices are also sold by the organization to new physicians.

4. *Collective contracts with insurance intermediaries.* These offer physicians increased access to insured populations. Intermediaries can contract directly with physicians or jointly with the institution and the physician, and they can impose terms such as credentialing or incentives for quality and patient satisfaction.

5. *Joint investment ventures.* These offer physicians the opportunity to make an equity investment with the anticipation of return and a saleable asset. These are the most problematic relationships—as they raise tax, inurement, and fraud issues—that must be carefully avoided. They also present some management problems, as when ownership becomes frozen to a limited group of physicians or when the value of the asset falls and the asset becomes illiquid.

The advanced levels of Exhibit 6.7 require ongoing economic relationships with physician groups. The HCO and its physicians become economic partners in pursuit of incentive payments.

Financial contracts between HCOs and physicians are subject to important legal constraints. Explicit payment for increasing the profit of the HCO is illegal under a ruling of the Office of Inspector General of the U.S. Department of Health and Human Services.[31] Specific arrangements that might have the impact of increasing profits to the HCO or earnings to the physician fall under Stark law and fraud and abuse provisions of the Medicare contract.[32] Many states have laws that regulate physician incentive compensation.[33] Excellent HCOs always obtain legal counsel for financial contracts with physician.

Compensation Arrangements with Insurers

The historic fee-for-service physician payment was fee-based, procedure oriented, and paid directly from patient to physician. Under insurance, where the patient no longer pays directly, fee-for-service creates an incentive for physicians to do more procedures and favor the higher-priced activities. Quality is left to the market, the collective judgment of individual patients. Payment systems changed slowly but continuously in the twentieth century, as payment moved from direct to insured fees, negotiated fees, global fees, and capitation.

All recent compensation approaches require *risk pools*—panels of participating physicians who can be paid collectively with incentives for quality, effectiveness, and patient satisfaction. Panels are usually constructed around service lines. Individual physician incentives are generally statistically unsound.[34] The HCO is directly involved because its performance affects incentive achievements, and because incentive achievement affects its revenue. Combined with the changes in medical technology, changes in compensation have moved the economics of practice from solo practice to groups of

EXHIBIT 6.7

Compensation Relationships Between HCOs and Individual Physicians

Relationship	Type	Example
Independence	Traditional	Physician arranges own payments and contracts
Salaried for clinical services	Employment	Physician spends full or part time providing medical care, in return for a salary
Salaried for management services	Employment	Physician spends full or part time providing administrative services for the organization in return for a salary
Purchase of service	Service contract	Physician leases office, personnel services, or information services from the institution
Joint sales agreement	Preferred provider panels	Physician and institution agree to participate for separate patient care fees
Shared risk contract	Capitation or fee-based risk sharing	Physician and institution agree to a payment arrangement and share risk for appropriate patient care
Shared ownership	Joint ownership	Physician and institution hold joint ownership in real property
Shared equity	Joint venture	Physicians and institution hold joint ownership in a patient care business venture

increasing complexity and interaction with the HCO. The major compensation possibilities for medical care are shown in Exhibit 6.8. All but the first three require panels of physicians.

The transition is ongoing; the ultimate solution is not yet in view. Each of these mechanisms establishes a different incentive for the physician, and no incentive perfectly matches all patients' needs. The evidence of improved effectiveness that results from the incentives is mixed.[35] The incentives enhance or detract from other organizational mechanisms, such as the overall culture, the effectiveness of protocol support, and the measurement of critical performance variables.[36] The incentives reward complex treatments far more than prevention. It may be impossible to provide appropriate preventive service and maintain a reasonable income in fee-for-service primary care.[37]

Recent healthcare financing models recommend an integrated set of reforms for changing the way the nation pays for healthcare, to reward high-quality care and prudent stewardship of resources and to encourage reorganization of the healthcare delivery system. The recommended reforms would

EXHIBIT 6.8
Types of
Physician
Compensation
for Patient Care

Type	Description
Fee-Based Compensation	
Unrestricted fees	Physician sets fee for each service; no control of cost or utilization
Limited fees	Physician sets fee for each service within statistical limits; no control of cost or utilization
Negotiated fees	Physician accepts fee schedule; price is controlled but not utilization
Withhold of fees	Percentage of fee is withheld subject to meeting cost goals; limits intermediary risk for both price and utilization
Cash incentives	Cash bonus for attaining specific targets
Combinations	For example: Negotiated + Withhold + Incentive
Capitation-Based Compensation	
Global capitation	Primary care physician accepts full risk for all costs
Shared capitation	Physician organization and institution accept full risk
Primary capitation	Primary care physician accepts risk for nonspecialist, noninstitutional care
Specialist capitation	Specialist accepts a fixed annual payment for each referred patient
Combinations	For example: Primary withhold + Specialist capitation + Institutional negotiated fee
Carve-out	Specific services can be carved out of the general arrangement and paid on a separate basis

- strengthen and reinforce primary care by revising the Medicare fee schedule to enhance payment for primary care services and to ensure annual increases that keep pace with the cost of efficient practice;
- institute new ways of paying for primary care to encourage adoption of the medical home model and promote more accessible, coordinated, patient-centered care, with a focus on health and disease prevention;
- promote more effective, efficient, and integrated healthcare delivery by adopting more bundled payment approaches to paying for care over a period of time or for the duration of an illness, with rewards for quality, outcomes, and efficiency; and
- correct price signals in healthcare markets to better align payments with value.[38]

The **medical home** is a concept or model of care delivery that includes an ongoing relationship between a provider and patient, around-the-clock access to medical consultation, respect for a patient's cultural and religious beliefs, and a comprehensive approach to care and coordination of care through providers and community services.[39] It has been reported as successful in several communities, but it is far from universal. Like other advanced payment concepts, it brings physicians and caregivers into closer relationship. Challenges remain in evaluating and disseminating the medical home model.[40] The bundled-payment concept ties physicians and HCOs under a common payment.

The approaches to cost and quality incentives are varied, but all are consistent with the transformational culture, network of communication to physicians, protocols, and service line accountability with measured performance and continuous improvement used by excellent HCOs.

People

On average, there are two physicians for every 1,000 persons in the United States.[41] They tend to concentrate in urban areas, although most disadvantaged areas have shortages.[42] Larger HCOs have several hundred physicians who represent a wide variety of specialties and a growing number of nonphysician practitioners.[43] Technology and economics have increased the differences among the practitioners. Less than half are in primary care. As the first point of contact for most patients, primary care practitioners work mainly in private offices, clinics, and emergency departments. They have critical roles in referring patients to specialists and hospitals[44] and in continuing care of patients with chronic illnesses.[45] The majority of doctors are in referral or specialty practice. Specialists work mostly in institutional settings and, by definition, see a limited range of conditions in which they are expert.

Physician Leadership

Well-managed HCOs routinely identify and rely on medical leaders. They form the backbone of the physician organization, filling the key positions and forming the communications network. Leaders are not difficult to identify. They emerge naturally in informal discussions, and most physicians will simply state their leadership candidates. There is surprising consensus. A sound program identifies leaders early in their careers and begins assigning activities appropriate to their skills. As the physicians mature, their experience deepens and their assignments become more complex. A set of physicians moves through the ranks, toward the critical committee assignments, executive positions, and board membership. Large-scale organizational changes require strong leaders, and such leaders gain additional leverage if they are physicians and their organization employs its doctors.[46]

Organization of Physicians

Physicians in larger HCOs are now primarily organized by service line. Negotiating goals for physician service lines is possible as long as the volumes of care under discussion support reliable performance measurement. Doing so is in the interests of the customer stakeholders. It allows the HCO and its medical staff to document clinical excellence. It also forms a foundation for both privileging and compensation negotiations, allowing both the HCO and its physicians to earn incentives under the more recent compensation plans.

HCOs also maintain a medical staff organization that serves to approve the credentialing and planning recommendations, and they participate in the capital budget allocation. The resulting structure is almost impossible to diagram because different topics take different paths, but Exhibit 6.9 shows the basic concept. Senior management is more involved than the exhibit suggests, participating in direct negotiations with both joint venture and unincorporated service lines, attending most meetings of the medical staff, and advising the governing board on all matters that reach it. The vice president of medical affairs is almost always credentialed and privileged in his or her specialty and often retains a small active practice.

Measures

Like any other accountable unit of the organization, the physician organization should have measures of performance and formal expectations for the coming year. The various units shown in Exhibit 6.9 should be accountable for multidimensional expectations about their own performance. Incorporated service lines should have strategic scorecards that incorporate market, quality of care, patient satisfaction, associate satisfaction, and financial measures. These are aggregated separately from the measures of clinical performance discussed in Chapter 5 and from corporate financial reports. Except for financial measures, unincorporated service lines can construct similar strategic scorecards. In addition, the various organizational units should assess their own operations. Exhibit 6.10 suggests some approaches that will identify OFIs.

Managerial Issues

Physician–HCO relations are a traditional "hot spot" in HCO management. Much about the physician organization is in flux as of 2010. Major reforms in the insurance structure are likely to lead to increased collaboration between physicians and between physicians and the HCO. At the same time, evidence-

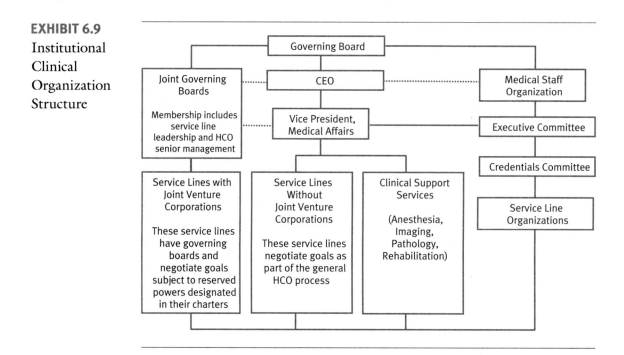

based medicine provides a solid foundation for identifying and resolving issues. Benchmarks and protocols show what is possible and make collaboration more attractive than adversarial relations. Actions by the medical profession, particularly the changes in residency competencies, will help younger physicians adjust to the changes. Transformational cultures will help HCOs identify and correct causes of stress in the relationship. Three areas are likely to need ongoing management attention: (1) managing the potential conflict in values, (2) maintaining a sufficient supply of caregivers, and (3) negotiating compensation agreements.

Managing Conflicting Values

HCOs and physicians have different ways of thinking, arising from the physicians' agency commitment to patients and the turbulent history of HCO–physician relations. Physicians are ethically committed to act as agents for their patients. HCO managers are ethically committed to act as agents for the community or the owners. These commitments are usually synergistic, a commitment to a common goal of excellent care. There are situations where they conflict.

Resolving the conflicts is an important managerial issue. Resolution must recognize the physician's empowerment but must enforce commitment to basic rules and values.[47] It is achieved by encouraging the physician to revise the IPOC and depart from protocol whenever it is in the patient's best interest. This policy supports the physician's ethical commitment and recognized right to manage care, and it establishes an accepted ethical priority:

Dimension	Applicable Measures
Demand	Difficult to measure except by associate satisfaction
Cost	Cost budgets for assigned functions
Associate satisfaction	Surveys of physician satisfaction Meeting attendance Incidents that cause excessive disruption
Outcomes and efficiency	Cost/physician served can be calculated and compared to similar organizations Review by internal or external consultants
Operations	Review by internal or external consultants Items that arise from associate satisfaction
Customer satisfaction	The service lines monitor patient quality and satisfaction The customers of the physician organization components are the associates they serve The customers of clinical support units are both patients and associates

EXHIBIT 6.10
Operational Measures of Physician Organization Performance

Individual patient needs cannot be sacrificed for the good of the whole. At the same time, the departure from protocol is recorded so that the incident can be reviewed as an OFI, and the physician's judgment is recorded for peer review in the rare event that review is indicated.

In a national report on physician perspectives on U.S. hospitals, three of the top five listed physician priorities on what affects the physician–hospital relationship the most dealt with how well the HCO's senior leaders communicate, respond, and collaborate with physicians to meet their practice needs.[48] Engaged physicians demonstrate the following psychological traits:

- *Investment.* Physicians have an emotional relationship with the hospital, share in its mission and values, and have a sense of pride in their association with the HCO.
- *Involvement.* Physicians take an active role in improving hospital performance and join with the HCO in providing excellent care.
- *Advocacy.* Physicians demonstrate behaviors that build the brand of the HCO by recommending the HCO to patients, physician colleagues, and the community at large.[49]

To engage physicians, HCO leaders must listen attentively to the needs and concerns of their physicians, involve them in decision making, make an effort to understand the language of medicine and their physicians' contributions to excellent patient care, and show that they are valued by the organization's senior leaders. HCOs with high levels of physician engagement:

- receive higher revenue and earnings per admission and per patient day,
- increase referrals from engaged physicians,
- reduce physician recruiting costs, and
- sustain significant growth and profitability.[50]

Most important, engaged physicians with high levels of satisfaction contribute to the overall mission of providing excellent patient care.

Maintaining Adequate Physician Supply

Most HCOs likely work in an environment of shortages of physicians and professional nurses. Research by the Association of American Medical Colleges predicts increasing physician supply shortages to keep pace with baseline demand, with an estimated shortfall approaching 20 percent by the year 2025.[51] The aging population, who consume more healthcare services, is the major contributor to this demand.

HCOs that delight their physicians recruit successfully. Delighted physicians stay with the organization. They are more open to the experimentation necessary to meet the future. They also become effective recruiters. The key to physician satisfaction is clear enough; it is a network of communication and effective response to issues that arise. Excellent HCOs achieve this by maintaining the culture and operations described in this text. Physicians are delighted when they are sure that they are empowered, that their patients get what they need, that they can rely on their colleagues, and that income and patient satisfaction goals will be met. In other words, the solution to delighting physicians is to implement the strategies in all 15 chapters of *The Well-Managed Healthcare Organization*.

Negotiating Compensation Arrangements

The issue of physician recruitment must also recognize a changing work ethic. Younger physicians desire more control of their time and part-time work during child-bearing years. They also desire the certainty of employment over the risks of fee-for-service practice.[52] Large HCOs with employment approaches to physician compensation (e.g., Mayo Clinic, Henry Ford Health System, Kaiser Permanente) are thriving. The model for the future is likely to emphasize income guarantees for many physicians. The role of more entrepreneurial structures may decline. These approaches are not easy to manage in themselves, and the challenge is greater when the HCO must operate both employment and fee-for-service models.

The solution for most HCOs is not only to begin experimentation promptly and monitor best practices as they evolve. It is also to continue planned medical staff recruitment and to continue to emphasize that the

HCO and its community want "effective" care and not unnecessary intervention or omission of scientifically valid treatment. When this is implemented, both the medical staff and the HCO give this clear signal to the excessively greedy physician: This is not the community where you want to work.

Suggested Readings

Cohn, K. H. 2005. *Better Communication for Better Care: Mastering Physician–Administrator Collaboration.* Chicago: Health Administration Press.

Delio, S. A. 2005. *The Efficient Physician: 7 Guiding Principles for a Tech-Savvy Practice,* 2nd ed. Englewood, CO: Medical Group Management Association.

Gassiot, C. A., V. L. Searcy, and C. W. Giles. 2007. *The Medical Staff Services Handbook: Fundamentals and Beyond.* Sudburry, MA: Jones and Bartlett.

Hammon, J. L. (ed.). 2000. *Fundamentals of Medical Management: A Guide for the Physician Executive,* 2nd ed. Chicago: American College of Physician Executives.

Holm, C. E. 2004. *Allies or Adversaries: Revitalizing the Medical Staff Organization.* Chicago: Health Administration Press.

The Joint Commission. *Comprehensive Accreditation Manual for Hospitals* (issued annually). Oakbrook Terrace, IL: The Joint Commission.

Starr, P. 1982. *The Social Transformation of American Medicine,* 198–232, 420–49. New York: Basic Books.

Notes

1. Bodenheimer, T., M. C. Wang, R. G. Rundall, S. M. Shortell, R. R. Gillies, N. Oswald, L. Casalino, and J. C. Robinson. 2004. "What Are the Facilitators and Barriers in Physician Organizations' Use of Care Management Processes?" *Joint Commission Journal on Quality and Safety* 30 (9): 505–14.

2. Evidence-Based Working Group. 1992. "Evidence-Based Medicine. A New Approach to Teaching the Practice of Medicine." *JAMA* 268 (17): 2420–25.

3. McGlynn, E. A., S. M. Asch, J. Adams, J. Keesey, J. Hicks, A. DeCristofaro, and E. A. Kerr. 2003. "The Quality of Health Care Delivered to Adults in the United States." *New England Journal of Medicine* 348 (26): 2635–45.

4. Casalino, L., R. R. Gillies, S. M. Shortell, J. A. Schmittdiel, T. Bodenheimer, J. C. Robinson, T. Rundall, N. Oswald, H. Schauffler, and M. C. Wang. 2003. "External Incentives, Information Technology, and Organized Processes to Improve Health Care Quality for Patients with Chronic Diseases." *JAMA* 289 (4): 434–41.

5. Landon, B. E., J. Reschovsky, and D. Blumenthal. 2003. "Changes in Career Satisfaction Among Primary Care and Specialist Physicians, 1997–2001." *JAMA* 289 (4): 442–49.

6. Zuger, A. 2004. "Dissatisfaction with Medical Practice." *New England Journal of Medicine* 350 (1): 69–75.

7. Mechanic, D. 2003. "Physician Discontent: Challenges and Opportunities." *JAMA* 290 (7): 941–46.

8. Griffith, J. R., and K. R. White. 2003. *Thinking Forward: Six Strategies for Highly Successful Organizations,* 57–85. Chicago: Health Administration Press.

9. Gregory, D., E. Baigelman, and I. B. Wilson. 2003. "Hospital Economics of the Hospitalist." *Health Services Research* 38 (3): 905–18.

10. Showalter, J. S. 2004. *The Law of Healthcare Administration,* 4th ed., 439–43, 457. Chicago: Health Administration Press.

11. *Ibid.,* pp. 447–48.

12. Ramsey, P. G., M. D. Wenrich, J. D. Carline, T. S. Inui, E. B. Larson, and J. P. LoGerfo. 1993. "Use of Peer Ratings to Evaluate Physician Performance." *JAMA* 269 (13): 1655–60; Norman, G. R., D. A. Davis, S. Lamb, E. Hanna, P. Caulford, and T. Kaigas. 1993. "Competency Assessment of Primary Care Physicians as Part of a Peer Review Program." *JAMA* 270 (9): 1046–51.

13. Hargraves, J. L., R. H. Palmer, E. J. Orav, and E. A. Wright. 1996. "Are Differences in Practitioners' Acceptance of a Quality Assurance Intervention Related to Their Performance?" *Medical Care* 34 (9, Supplement): SS77–86.

14. Health Care Quality Improvement Act P.L. 99-177. 1986. Rockville, MD: U.S. Department of Health and Human Services, Health Resources and Services Administration, Division of Quality Assurance and Liability Management.

15. *Ibid.,* 2009. "Lack of NPDB Reporting Brings Peer Review Practices into Question." National Practitioner Data Bank Report. *Credentialing and Peer Review Legal Insider* 6 (8): 1542–600.

16. Rosentein, A. H., and M. O'Daniel. 2008. "A Survey of the Impact of Disruptive Behaviors and Communication Defects on Patient Safety." *Joint Commission Journal on Quality and Patient Safety* 34 (8): 464–71.

17. Landon, B. E., S. L. Normand, D. Blumenthal, and J. Daley. 2003. "Physician Clinical Performance Assessment: Prospects and Barriers." *JAMA* 290 (9): 1183–89.

18. Storr, C. L., A. M. Trinkoff, and P. Hughes. 2000. "Similarities of Substance Use Between Medical and Nursing Specialties." *Substance Use & Misuse* 35 (10): 1443–69.

19. Rice, T. H., and R. J. Labelle. 1989. "Do Physicians Induce Demand for Medical Services?" *Journal of Health Politics, Policy and Law* 14 (3): 587–600.

20. Holm, C. E. 2004. "A Guide to Medical Staff Development Planning." In *Allies or Adversaries: Revitalizing the Medical Staff Organization,* 27–52. Chicago: Health Administration Press.

21. Weiner, J. P. 2004. "Prepaid Group Practice Staffing and U.S. Physician Supply: Lessons for Workforce Policy." *Health Affairs* (Web Exclusive): W4-43–59.

22. Luft, H. S., D. W. Garnick, D. H. Mark, and S. J. McPhee. 1990. *Hospital Volume, Physician Volume, and Patient Outcomes: Assessing the Evidence.* Chicago: Health Administration Press.

23. U.S. Census Bureau. 2003. *Statistical Abstract of the U.S., 2004–2005,* no. 164. Washington, DC: U.S. Census Bureau.

24. Association of American Medical Colleges. 2009. "Council of Teaching Hospitals and Health Systems." [Online information; retrieved 7/14/09.] www.aamc.org/members/coth/start.htm.

25. Association of American Medical Colleges. 2005. *AAMC Databook: Statistical Information Related to Medical Education,* Table G7. Washington, DC: AAMC.

26. Accreditation Council for Graduate Medical Education. 2009. [Online information; retrieved 7/14/09.] www.acgme.org/outcome/comp/compMin.asp.

27. Burns, L. R. 1999. "Polarity Management: The Key Challenge for Integrated Health Systems." *Journal of Healthcare Management* 44 (1): 14–31.

28. Zazzali, J. L. 2003. "Trust: An Implicit Force in Health Care Organization

Theory." In *Advances in Health Care Organization Theory*, edited by S. S. Mick and M. E. Wyttenbach, 233–52. San Francisco: Jossey-Bass.

29. Holm, C. E. 2004. "Techniques to Foster Effective Working Relationships." In *Allies or Adversaries: Revitalizing the Medical Staff Organization*, 85–103. Chicago: Health Administration Press.

30. *Ibid.*

31. Wiehl, J. G., and S. L. Murphy. 1999. "Gainsharing: A Call for Guidance." *Journal of Health Law* 32 (4): 515–63.

32. Center for Medicare & Medicaid Services. "Medicare Fraud and Abuse." [Online information; retrieved 10/14/09.] www.cms.hhs.gov/MLNProducts/downloads/110107_Medicare_Fraud_and_Abuse_brochure.pdf.

33. Stauffer, M. 2000. "Finance Issue Brief: Bans on Financial Incentives." *Issue Brief: Health Policy Tracking Service* (June 1): 1–10.

34. Hofer, T. P., R. A. Hayward, S. Greenfield, E. H. Wagner, S. H. Kaplan, and W. G. Manning. 1999. "The Unreliability of Individual Physician 'Report Cards' for Assessing the Costs and Quality of Care of a Chronic Disease." *JAMA* 281 (22): 2098–105.

35. Petersen, L. A., L. D. Woodard, T. Urech, C. Daw, and S. Sookanan. 2006. "Does Pay-for-Performance Improve the Quality of Health Care?" *Annals of Internal Medicine* 145 (4): 265–72.

36. Shortell, S. M., J. L. Zazzali, L. R. Burns, J. A. Alexander, R. R. Gillies, P. P. Budetti, T. M. Waters, and H. S. Zuckerman. 2001. "Implementing Evidence-Based Medicine: The Role of Market Pressures, Compensation Incentives, and Culture in Physician Organizations." *Medical Care* 39 (7, Supplement 1): 162–78.

37. Zuger, A. 2004. "Dissatisfaction with Medical Practice." *New England Journal of Medicine* 350 (1): 69–75.

38. Guterman, S., K. Davis, C. Schoen, and K. Stremikis. 2009. *Reforming Provider Payment: Essential Building Block for Health Reform*. New York: The Commonwealth Fund.

39. Association of American Medical Colleges. 2008. "Medical Home Concept Gains Momentum." [Online information; retrieved 7/14/09.] www.aamc.org/newsroom/reporter/march08/medicalhome.htm.

40. Carrier, E., M. N. Gourevitch, and N. R. Shah. 2009. "Medical Homes: Challenges in Translating Theory Into Practice." *Medical Care* 47 (7): 714–22.

41. U.S. Bureau of Labor Statistics. [Online information; retrieved 8/20/09.] www.bls.gov/oco/ocos074.htm#projections_data.

42. U.S. Department of Health and Human Services, Health Resources and Services Administration. [Online information; retrieved 8/20/09.] http://bhpr.hrsa.gov/shortage/.

43. White, K. R., D. G. Clement, and K. G. Stover. 2008. "Healthcare Professionals." In *Human Resources in Healthcare: Managing for Success*, 3rd ed., edited by B. Fried and M. Fottler. Chicago: Health Administration Press.

44. Drain, M. 2001. "Quality Improvement in Primary Care and the Importance of Patient Perceptions." *Journal of Ambulatory Care Management* 24 (2): 30–46.

45. Casalino, L., R. R. Gillies, S. M. Shortell, J. A. Schmittdiel, T. Bodenheimer, J. C. Robinson, T. Rundall, N. Oswald, H. Schauffler, and M. C. Wang. 2003. "External Incentives, Information Technology, and Organized Processes to Improve Health Care Quality for Patients with Chronic Diseases." *JAMA* 289 (4): 434–41.

46. Lee, T. H. 2010. "Turning Doctors into Leaders." *Harvard Business Review* 88 (4): 50–58.

47. Wachter, R. M., and P. J. Pronovost. 2009. "Balancing 'No Blame' with Account-ability in Patient Safety." *New England Journal of Medicine* 361 (14): 1401–06.

48. Press Ganey Associates, Inc. 2008. *Hospital Check-Up Report: Physician Perspectives on American Hospitals.* South Bend, IN: Press Ganey Associates, Inc.

49. Paller, D. 2009. "Physician Partnership: Creating Powerful Relationships." Press Ganey Associates, Inc. [Online information; retrieved 7/14/09.] www.press ganey.com/galleries/default-file/Physician_Partnership_Creating_Powerful_ Relationships.pdf.

50. Gallup. 2009. "Physician Engagement." [Online information; retrieved 7/14/09.] www.gallup.com/consulting/healthcare/15385/Physician-Engage ment.aspx.

51. Association of American Medical Colleges. 2008. *The Complexities of Physician Supply and Demand: Projections Through 2025.* [Online information; retrieved 7/14/09.] www.aamc.org/workforce.

52. Mechaber, H. F., R. B. Levine, L. B. Manwell, M. P. Mundt, and M. Linzer for the MEMO Investigators. 2008. "Part-Time Physicians…Prevalent, Connected, and Satisfied." *JGIM: Journal of Internal Medicine* 23 (3): 300–03.

7 NURSING

In a Few Words

Nursing is a major player in today's healthcare delivery system. Nurses have a broad role:

- Assessing patients, identifying desired outcomes, and monitoring progress

- Developing an interdisciplinary patient care plan

- Improving quality and ensuring safety

- Educating patients and caregivers

- Designing a professional nursing practice culture

These are nursing's responsibilities not only to patients/clients/residents who need acute care but also for primary care, long-term care, home care, and palliative care settings. Supporting this role requires transformational leadership that ensures optimal numbers of well-prepared staff and makes nurses loyal associates who want to continue to work and will encourage others to work for the organization. The nursing organization maintains infrastructure and processes for recruitment, functional protocols, professional development, and nurse satisfaction that meet those needs.

Critical Issues in Nursing

1. *An adequate supply of nurses at all levels must be recruited and trained.* Nationally, there are shortages not only of nurses at various training levels but also of faculty to prepare them. Healthcare organizations (HCOs) must take steps locally and collaborate nationally to increase the supply.

2. *The transition to service lines has created a dual accountability in nursing—to the service line team and to the nursing organization.* The nursing organization is emerging as the source of standards for common elements of nursing care (functional protocols), staffing and scheduling models, training for nonprofessional nursing personnel, and training for nurse supervisors.

3. *A culture of improvement must replace the silos of professional authority and a culture of blame.* Care must be designed around evidence-based protocols. To improve patient and

associate safety, nurses and others must feel free to report errors and near misses and must work with others to devise processes that eliminate them.

4. *Retention of nursing personnel is essential.* Turnover is costly, both in direct dollars for finding and training new personnel and in hidden costs of errors and team efficiency. HCOs that show their respect for nurses in a culture of empowerment—answering questions, providing adequate support, and encouraging participation in protocol selection and performance improvement—achieve benchmark turnover rates below 10 percent per year.

QUESTIONS FOR DISCUSSION

Consider these questions as you read the chapter.

1. In view of a national nursing shortage and nursing education not keeping pace with workforce demands, how would you ensure an adequate supply of nurses in your organization? What short-term and long-term actions would you propose?

2. Nursing has six levels of professionalization: technician, practical or vocational, registered, baccalaureate, specialist, and advanced practice. Any real care team must be composed of a specific number of nurses at one or more of these levels. That requires decisions in advance about what patient needs will be and a scheduling system that produces the expected number. How does an HCO approach this problem? What are the criteria for an excellent staffing and scheduling system?

3. If all nurses are organized along clinical service lines, what would be the role of the chief nursing officer? What are some potential conflicts that might arise between the traditional nursing organization hierarchy and service line management? How would you resolve these?

4. Advanced practice nurses (APNs) are used in a variety of settings where they replace physicians. The most numerous applications are in outpatient primary care and chronic disease management, but some have been used in intensive care units. Why are these changes occurring? Are they a good idea? How would you ensure appropriate use of APNs in these settings?

5. How would you select and prepare nurses for supervisory roles? What does a nurse supervisor need to know? How does he or she get it?

I n the healthcare field, nurses are as ubiquitous as doctors and are about four times more numerous. There is virtually no place that they have not made a contribution. Nurses are critical to inpatient care; usually relevant to outpatient care; central to palliative, hospice, home, and long-term institutional care; and important to disease prevention. Nurses also make major contributions to the interdisciplinary plan of care (IPOC) and case management, patient care protocols, and health promotion. Organizationally, nursing is by far the largest clinical profession. Its contribution is clearly recognized by patients. In its annual survey on the honesty and ethical standards of various professions, the Gallup Organization reports that Americans rate nurses at the top of the list.[1] Most people, when asked to evaluate their inpatient care, speak first not of the doctor but of the nurse. Furthermore, if they think well of the nursing care, they tend to rate the whole experience, even the bill, more favorably.

Although nursing could be viewed as a major clinical support service (CSS), we treat it separately in this chapter because nursing is large and central to most HCOs. It differs from other CSSs both in scale and in a unique role of coordinating other CSSs. It employs nearly half of the typical HCO workforce, and it schedules and monitors the contributions of all other CSSs.

Purpose

The purposes of nursing are

> **to deliver excellent care to each patient through the management of resources**
> and
> **to maintain a professional work environment that ensures nursing associates' competence and satisfaction.**

Florence Nightingale saw the nursing role as stretching from emotional support to control of hazards in the environment. She articulated the objective of assisting the patient to **homeostasis**—a state of equilibrium with one's environment—when she said in 1859 that nursing consists of those activities that "put the patient in the best condition for nature to act upon him."[2] This concept prevails in most of the more modern definitions, with the added goal of restoring the patient's independence[3] and nursing advocacy for individuals, families, communities, and populations.[4]

Homeostasis
A state of equilibrium with one's environment

Obviously, preventing the loss of equilibrium is better than trying to regain it. Prevention of illness and promotion of health have always been important in nursing. Nurses' work with well individuals and families includes immunization, education, environmental safety, and disease screening. For persons who are ill or injured, the route to homeostasis includes a nursing assessment or diagnosis, the development of an individualized care plan, the implementation of the plan, and the evaluation of the plan by specific nursing care or activities requested of other services. Even for the person who is ill, preventing the spread of disability is as important as correcting losses. Nurses instruct patients and their families in adapting to disease and disability, speeding their recovery, and minimizing the risk of further impairment.

The role of the nursing organization is to see that the purposes are uniformly implemented for all patients, across the HCO's spectrum of outpatient, inpatient, and continuing care.

Functions

As shown in Exhibit 7.1, the nursing organization must perform five functions, beginning with the provision of excellent patient care. Nursing must also coordinate all other care. It provides the bulk of patient and family education and much of community health education. As the day-to-day leaders of most patient care teams, managing nurses must have managerial skills, including the ability to sustain the transformational environment, plan staffing and resource management, and provide staff development. The nursing voice is critical on most planning committees, protocol selection committees, and process improvement teams (PITs), and they are expected to improve their own performance.

Delivering Excellent Care

The widespread practice applications of nursing, and the breadth of the role of nurses, make nursing a critical focal point for high-performing HCOs. In meeting the Institute of Medicine's goals of safe, effective, patient-centered, timely, efficient, and equitable care, nursing contributes to higher levels of performance.[5] The leading institutions are achieving this with a sophisticated program of knowledge management, enhanced education and development, improved protocols, better logistic support, and above all, attention to an organizational culture that promotes nurses' value, their personal and professional needs, and job satisfaction. Exhibit 7.2 summarizes the contributions of nursing in delivering excellent care.

Nursing process
A system of assessing patients, diagnosing individual nursing care needs, planning care, implementing plans, and evaluating care

Implementation of the Nursing Process   Nurses deliver excellent care by implementing the **nursing process**, a system of assessing patients, diagnosing individual nursing care needs, planning care, implementing plans, and evaluating care. Exhibit 7.3 shows the elements of the nursing process with knowledge management resources and examples.

Assessment   Upon the patient's admission, the nurse evaluates the patient, reflecting the nursing process (see Exhibit 7.2), and takes into consideration the patient's total set of diseases and disabilities, general physical and emotional condi-

EXHIBIT 7.1

Nursing Functions

Function	Activities	Results
Delivering excellent care	Implement the nursing process: Identify patients' needs, nursing diagnosis, and care plan Integrate nursing process with IPOC Coordinate IPOC implementation Evaluate patient progress Use case management for complicated cases	Optimal outcomes are achieved for safe, effective, patient-centered, timely, efficient, and equitable care Each patient has a nursing diagnosis and care plan The plan is coordinated with patient management protocols and IPOCs Progress toward maximal function is monitored
Coordinating and monitoring interdisciplinary care	Effective communication and integration with physicians, other CSSs, and other service lines Pursuit and correction of gaps or problems in care management	Interdisciplinary patient rounds and IPOCs used to coordinate care Schedules and coordinates diagnostic testing and therapeutic interventions Patient and family needs for spiritual care, social services, palliative care, and ethics consultation are identified and met
Educating patients, families, and communities	Meet or exceed expectations of patients, other stakeholders Maintain professional nursing model and advancement in knowledge and skill-based competencies	Patient education materials Mentoring programs for new nurses Management and leadership development programs Continuing education program (in-house) Promoting professional certification and advancement
Maintaining the nursing organization	Project future personnel and facility needs; budget; ensure appropriate number and skill of staff complement Recruit, select, retain, and motivate an effective workforce based on participation, HCO decision involvement, and empowerment	Effective skill mix (RN, LPN, unlicensed assistive personnel, contract) and numbers of personnel to match patient needs Facility, equipment, and supply needs met
Improving nursing performance	Continuous improvement of nursing practice Translate nursing research into practice improvements Integrate organizational structures and management processes to plan and deliver nursing care Inspire shared vision, commitment, and creative responses to challenges	Nursing practice councils for improvement, education, research, standards Performance reviews Shared governance Competitive salaries and benefits Positive relationships established within HCO and community Budgets, facilities, equipment plans, emergency preparedness plans and drills, marketing strategies Leadership development plans

CSS: clinical support service; IPOC: interdisciplinary plan of care; LPN: licensed practical nurse; RN: registered nurse

EXHIBIT 7.2
Nursing and
the Goals of
Excellent Care

Goal	Nursing Role	Examples
Safe	Eliminate biological, physical, human, and psychological risks in both the inpatient and home environments Maintain safety of diagnosis and treatment	Any safety hazard that nursing identifies in a patient care setting is corrected by nursing or by the appropriate support unit. Nurses work with patients and families in home settings to promote safety. Nursing administers drugs and monitors all treatments, promotes hand washing, and assesses patient mobility and psychological status.
Effective	Monitor the care process and provide the early warning for any deviation from the plan Evaluate patient progress toward comprehensive recovery; identify and remove barriers	In intensive settings, nurses are in virtually constant contact with patients. As recovery progresses, nurses set recovery goals and milestones, teach, motivate, and celebrate progress.
Patient-centered	Identify each patient's unique characteristics and adapt protocols to accommodate them	Nurses evaluate tastes and preferences as well as allergies and sensitivities. Nursing identifies cultural variations and adapts to provide culturally competent care.
Timely	Minimize the duration of the patient's disability	Nursing schedules and coordinates many treatments and activities. Effective nursing speeds recovery and eliminates complications. It shortens length of stay and prevents relapse.
Efficient	Minimize the total cost of care and disability	Nursing cost is measured by correctable disability as well as its direct cost. Drug errors, falls, adverse events, delays in care, and failures to respond are all partially within nursing's control. These occurrences make inadequate nursing care expensive.
Equitable	Ensure that care is equally available without regard to ethnicity, culture, gender, or sexual orientation Ensure patients' rights, including the right to refuse treatment	Nurses monitor their own and other caregivers' behavior to eliminate prejudice and unjust responses. Nurses explain care options to patients and families, help them reach decisions, and implement those decisions.

EXHIBIT 7.3
Nursing
Process
Example
for Airway
Management

Elements of the Nursing Process	Resources and Guidelines	Example
Assessment	Objective and subjective data	Vital signs, breath sounds, observation of difficulty breathing; laboratory results; physical examination
Nursing diagnosis	North American Nursing Diagnosis Association (NANDA) International	Ineffective airway clearance related to tracheobronchial infection (pneumonia) and excess thick secretions as evidenced by abnormal breath sounds, crackles, wheezes, change in rate and depth of respiration, and effective cough with sputum
Plan of care	Interdisciplinary plan of care (IPOC)	Effective airway clearance as evidenced by normal breath sounds, no crackles or wheezes, respiration rate 14–18 per minute, and no cough by within one week
Implementation of care	Nursing Interventions Classification (NIC)	Instruct and assist patient to TCDB (turn, cough, deep breathe) for assistance in loosening and expectorating mucus every two hours
Evaluation of care	Nursing Outcomes Classification (NOC)	Monitor improvements in breathing, expectorating mucus, and objective measures of oxygen profusion by physical examination and results of diagnostic tests; adjust goals; communicate with physician and CSS for modifications to patient management; provide education on stopping smoking, if applicable.

CSS: clinical support service

tion, family and social history, and the physician's history. Family views are important, and a description of the patient's home environment is frequently required. At this time, the nurse also notes medication allergies and advance directives (e.g., living will, durable power of attorney for healthcare).

The nursing assessment includes objective and subjective information. Objective criteria are based on facts, such as visual inspection, palpation, and vital signs (temperature, pulse, respirations, blood pressure). Subjective information is also obtained based on the experienced and intuitive observations of the nurse and the patient's verbal and nonverbal responses to questions, such as "on a scale of 1 to 10, what is your level of pain now?"

After an assessment is completed, the nurse identifies one or more nursing diagnoses. A **nursing diagnosis** is a standardized statement about the health

Nursing Diagnosis

Nursing diagnosis

A standardized statement about the health of a client for the purpose of providing nursing care; identified from a master list of nursing diagnosis terminology

of a client (who can be an individual, a family, or a community) for the purpose of providing nursing care. Nursing diagnoses are identified from a master list of nursing diagnosis terminology maintained by the North American Nursing Diagnosis Association (now known as NANDA International).[6] Nursing diagnoses provide the basis for a common language in identifying interventions and measuring outcomes, thus a more evidence-based approach to nursing care.

Care plans are also written for "at risk" problems as well as for "wellness." These follow a similar format, only designed to prevent problems from occurring and to continue or promote healthy behavior.

Plan of Care   The nursing care plan establishes nursing procedures and expectations for outcomes. It expands and individualizes the patient management protocol to reflect nursing's more comprehensive assessment. The care plan is more formal in inpatient and extensive outpatient care and is often left unwritten in brief, uncomplicated outpatient encounters. A good care plan does the following:

- adapts the care protocol to the specific needs of the patient;
- anticipates individual variations to prevent complications;
- establishes a plan for nursing interventions (NICs) (Patient-specific nursing treatments are defined and standardized by a Nursing Interventions Classification [NIC] list and may be classified according to 433 interventions.[7]);
- organizes the major events in the hospitalization or disease episode to minimize overall duration;
- establishes realistic clinical outcomes (NOCs) and a timetable for their achievement (Nursing Outcomes Classification [NOC] is a comprehensive, standardized classification of more than 300 patient/client outcomes developed to evaluate the effects of nursing interventions.[8]);
- incorporates a discharge plan; and
- identifies potential barriers to prompt discharge, and plans to investigate and remove them.

Throughout the encounter (episodic care) or over the course of a disease or condition (ambulatory or chronic care), the nurse evaluates the effectiveness of the nursing interventions and adapts or modifies the plan, as needed. With input from the patient, family members, physicians, and other clinical professionals, the nursing care plan is integrated into the IPOC. The timetable and advance planning on potential barriers are effective devices to reduce length of stay and cost per case.

A major role for nurses in planning care is to recognize early signs of a patient's changing or worsening condition and to communicate those changes to the physician or other provider for early intervention and modification of patient care management protocols. If a patient's condition worsens quickly, nurses may contact **rapid response teams** to intervene with pre-approved emergency treatment protocols. Rapid response teams have additional training in critical care management and teamwork and have been shown to be successful when nurses feel safe and supported in deploying the teams.[9]

Rapid response team
Caregivers with training in critical care management and emergency treatment protocols; deployed when a patient's condition suddenly deteriorates

Information technology significantly aids patient care plan development. Models for specific diseases, analogous to the clinical protocols discussed in Chapter 5, may be incorporated. Components of the care plan can be assembled from standard nursing practice protocols. Nurses can develop a plan more quickly and with less risk of oversight by modifying a disease model to individual needs. They can control the specific content of several thousand activities by relying on approved nursing practice protocols.

Implementation and Evaluation

Nursing care, like medical care, is heuristic. Nurses measure the effectiveness of their interventions as to whether they have met the goals for health and wholeness, as determined in conjunction with the patient. The evaluation is made on the goal date set. The evaluation indicates whether the client has met the goal; the evidence of whether or not the goal was met; and if the care plan is to be continued, discontinued, or modified. If the care plan is problem-based and the client has recovered, the plan is discontinued. If the client has not recovered, or if the care plan was written for a chronic illness or ongoing problem, it may be continued. If certain interventions are not helping or other interventions are to be added, the care plan is modified and continued.

Case Management

For patients with multiple diseases or complex conditions that exceed the scope of single patient management protocols, case management is used for managing care across the span of illness and various sites of care. Case management has emerged as an effective device for managing complicated disease processes, for patients who require long courses of convalescence, and for those at risk for costly care. Case management begins with a sophisticated care plan, often developed by a multidisciplinary team of caregivers and often integrating several protocols. The plan identifies specific goals, CSS and medical services to meet them, measures of improvement, and timetables. Nurses often manage the cases once the plan has been agreed on, working to see that the various services are effectively coordinated.

Contribution to Excellent Care

Nursing pursues its own heuristic process of assessment, diagnosis, treatment, and evaluation. It differs from medicine and is complementary and necessary for optimal outcomes. Standardized language developments that classify and measure nursing diagnosis, interventions, and associated outcomes (e.g.,

NANDA, NIC, NOC) have strengthened an evidence-based foundation for nursing.[10] Magnet programs help nursing deliver excellent care by implementing a culture of evidence-based nursing and supporting transformational management.

Coordinating and Monitoring Interdisciplinary Care

Major medical care is a multiteam event. Nurses generally coordinate and monitor the teams throughout the episode of care, whether it is in an inpatient, outpatient, or home setting. The goal is to organize all elements of care in the least costly and most patient-satisfactory elapsed time. Nursing's oversight responsibility includes recording progress against the IPOC, sequencing and scheduling CSS diagnostic and treatment interventions (including transportation), and monitoring for irregularities in logistics and patients' responses to interventions.

Maintaining Progress of the Interdisciplinary Plan of Care

During the patient's episode of inpatient or outpatient care, it is necessary to maintain a comprehensive, current record of the activities contributing to diagnosis and treatment. The patient record, also called the medical record, is increasingly computerized as the electronic medical record (EMR). In electronic form, the patient record is accessible to all caregivers and is constantly up to date. In the increasingly automated intensive care environments, much data are entered from monitoring machines. The shared record includes symptoms and complaints, concurrent disease or complication, working diagnosis, medical orders, and the nursing care plan. These are integrated into an IPOC, which summarizes diagnostic orders and results, treatment to date, and the patient's response. The IPOC must also include safety alerts, such as patient allergies and language barriers. The professional members of the patient care team are responsible for their own entries into the record, although under certain conditions, nurses and clerical personnel under nursing supervision may make entries for physicians.

Nursing has traditionally monitored patient progress, and it continues to do so. Nurses' observations of patient condition are an important part of the record, and nursing is positioned to be the first to notice most failures, delays, or adverse reactions to care processes.[11] Nursing acts to correct or overcome all difficulties that arise. Before the EMR, this activity involved telephoning and negotiating, which occupied up to half of the time for inpatient nursing. So far, few studies have been conducted, with mixed results, on the impact of the EMR.[12]

The nurse is responsible for the following kinds of monitoring activities:

- Ensure that the patient's physician has completed diagnosis, treatment, and appropriate follow-up activities in an appropriate and timely manner.
- Report clinical observations to the physician and other members of the caregiv-

ing team.

- Identify progress of patient goals as identified in the IPOC.
- Assess and report relevant psychosocial and family-related factors.
- Assess effectiveness of nursing interventions.
- Know where patients are, and receive them from the CSS.
- Receive and transmit results of reports from the CSS.
- Prepare and forward unexpected events reports.

Nurses use the information to identify omitted, inconsistent, and incorrect actions and actions that had unintended outcomes.[13]

The nurse as a patient advocate is expected to take appropriate action diplomatically and effectively. Nurses catch omitted, wrong, lost, conflicting, and delayed reports and orders on a daily basis. Organizational cultures that are group oriented, with a greater extent of quality improvement program implementation, tend to promote higher reporting of quality-assessment and risk-management data, such as medication administration errors.[14] They are the first to see unexpected results and unsatisfactory treatments. They remind, persuade, cajole, and convince others to correct these problems quickly so that the problems do not escalate.

Patient Scheduling

Inpatient and outpatient support service scheduling is generally performed via computer scheduling systems that are integrated with other support service functions, such as the laboratory, radiology, and surgery. Nurses or scheduling personnel obtain information directly from patients and coordinate care with support service departments.[15] Scheduling must accommodate limitations in the patient's physical condition and competing demands of various support services. Most of the services require direct physical contact with the patient, and many of the services have sequencing requirements (e.g., perform before meals or before certain other services).

Nursing's responsibility is shifting to active monitoring of the automated process and to more effective preparation of each patient. For improved quality, advanced schedules permit prospective review of compliance with the patient management protocol, even though it may be only a few hours before the events are to take place. A reduction in duplicated and unusable tests and orders can be expected. Prompt fulfillment of scheduled orders also reduces stat (or immediate) requests.

Patient Transportation

Nursing may also be responsible for the safe transport of inpatients. Although many outpatients can follow guidance from facilities wayfinding services to reach the various CSSs, inpatients are frequently impaired by their illness and must be moved by hospital personnel. The task is time consuming but important to patient safety and satisfaction. Employees who do it may be supplied by nursing or a unit of facility and guest services (see Chapter 12). They should be educated both in guest relations and in handling the medical emergencies that may arise while the patient is in transit.

Educating Patients, Families, and Communities

Nursing's constant contact with patients and their visitors contributes to a prime role in educating and communicating. Nursing's prominent role in satisfaction surveys stems from the fact that patients and families see more of nursing than any other CSS and from the supportive design of the nursing role. People expect nurses to be sympathetic and sensitive to human needs, and people are vocally grateful when nurses are sympathetic and sensitive and disappointed when they are not. Managing service and patient satisfaction is a powerful marketing tool, as satisfied customers are less likely to switch provider services and more likely to recommend services to others.[16]

Nursing success in communicating with the family or other significant persons in the patient's life is a critical element of overall patient satisfaction. Reassurance and explanation help families who are unfamiliar with disease and the critical care environment. The broad outline of the care plan is given to the family, including the anticipated dates of key events such as surgery and discharge. This serves a dual function, relieving anxiety and permitting the family to prepare. Life-limiting illness is an important case. Nurses can improve the effectiveness of advance directives and patient advocates, both by encouraging patients and families to address the issues involved and by supporting the advocate in stressful decisions. When death is imminent, or when more costly life-sustaining treatment has been forgone, palliative care focuses on pain management and comfort care interventions designed to make death as peaceful as possible, whether it occurs in the home or an institution.[17] Nursing support for the patient and family during the dying process and afterward is useful to promote healthy grief management.

Nursing has extensive and important educational responsibilities relating to the management of disease. HCO nurses teach individual patients and their families about the role of prevention and risk-factor management. Community health nurses teach prevention and health promotion to groups of citizens for primary prevention and advocate appropriate secondary prevention. If these activities are performed well, future disease is reduced. Patient, professional, and community satisfaction is improved. Thus, expectations for prevention are an essential part of care plans. As a consequence of much shorter hospital stays, the site for health education is shifting to ambulatory care.

General education, offered to the public at large and usually provided to group settings, is another vehicle. Support groups for stressful events other than disease (e.g., divorce, childbirth, caregiving) have become popular following the disease-oriented model (e.g., ostomy care, Alcoholics Anonymous, hemophilia). Nurses provide educational programs and counseling and organize and assist support groups.

Maintaining the Nursing Organization

The nurse manager plays a central role in the unit culture and is accountable for goals in worker satisfaction, retention, and safety. To achieve Magnet-level performance, the nurse manager must be specifically trained in transformational management: how to encourage associates, respond to recurring questions, implement process and protocol changes, and celebrate gains. These skills are taught through programs in human resources.

Sustaining the Transformational Culture

Leading HCOs back up formal education with responsive listening by superiors and senior management. They routinely assign coaches and mentors to new nurse managers, and they use a mentoring system to develop new staff nurses. They use personal development programs for their nurses and nurse managers and carefully monitor the nurse managers' own satisfaction. The result is that these HCOs have low turnover, attractive work sites, and a stable nursing associate group that gains skills from experience and training. Leading HCOs have implemented systems of care that promote nurse empowerment. These systems have substantially increased nurse retention while elevating quality and cost outcomes.[18]

Nurse managers must be skilled in the importance of effective listening and celebration. They are supported and coached by both senior and HCO nursing leaders. They are expected to carry out the practices of servant leadership, as described in Chapter 2. Because the interface often involves interdisciplinary collaboration, nurse managers maintain proficiency in teamwork, mediation, and consensus building.

Well-orchestrated staffing systems are important to delivering excellent nursing care. Systems presuppose structural foundations, such as adequate numbers of well-trained nurses.[19] The American Nurses Association recommends that nurse staffing be tailored to the specific needs of each unit, based on factors including patient acuity, the experience of the nursing staff, the skill mix of the staff, available technology, and the support services available to nurses.[20] Although California has mandated minimum nurse staffing levels since 2004 and other states have attempted to follow suit,[21] there is little evidence that regulatory approaches are effective in improving quality.[22,23] Involving nurses in the decision-making role in the care they provide is the most important consideration in developing staffing approaches.

Staffing

Given that up to 90 percent of nursing costs are labor costs, getting the right number of nurses for the patients' immediate needs is a critical management function. The nursing care functions are time-consuming activities that cannot be properly performed when nurses are in short supply. Staffing decisions establish the number of professional, technical, and clerical nursing associates required for each nursing unit. The results of staffing decisions establish scheduling and daily assignment requirements and set the nursing expense budget. Combined with forecasts of patient demand, they generate long-range human resource plans.

The staffing process establishes expectations for hours of care per patient day, by skill level. It is based on forecasts of demand and patient need (acuity) and generates a forecast of fixed staffing and, in some units, variable staffing. Inpatient nurse staffing decisions are made for each nursing unit and shift. They establish the number and mix of personnel (e.g., RNs [registered nurses] and LPNs [licensed practical nurses], unlicensed assistive personnel, coordinators) required for the expected range of acuity and census. These physical requirements for associates are easily translated into labor costs. The decision about the level of staff is negotiated; increases in staffing must be justified by the marginal improvement in quality, cost per case, or patient and worker satisfaction. The labor expense budget is determined almost automatically once the staffing pattern and the forecasts of demand are selected.

Fixed staffing is used in many settings where demand does not vary (such as outpatient clinics and long-term care) and where demand cannot be predicted (such as in the obstetrics and inpatient care units). Flexible labor budgets use variable staffing models to adjust the actual staff according to patient need, usually on a shift-by-shift schedule.

Patient requirements are radically different in long-term care, critical care, emergency departments, and surgical services such as the operating room and the post-anesthesia care unit. In many of these areas, requirements differ by day of week and by random variation in patient arrivals and acuity. Team approaches are aimed at reducing costs by substituting less skilled personnel under the supervision of professional nurses.[24] The desired staff for a nursing unit and shift is usually expressed in a table, such as in Exhibit 7.4.

The solution in Exhibit 7.4 treats staffing as an integer problem, making no changes smaller than eight hours or one full shift. The exhibit keeps staffing between 3.9 hours and 4.0 hours per patient day and between 40 percent and 45 percent RN level or higher. Staffing for odd numbers of censuses is the same as the preceding even numbers; hours per patient day drop to about 3.9. The shading in the exhibit shows the changes as census varies. At extreme lows—few and not very sick patients—only 20 FTEs [full-time equivalents] are needed; when the floor is full and patients are very sick, 30 FTEs are needed. Given weekends, holidays, and random fluctuation, a typical inpatient unit staffing can be expected to vary widely in the course of a year.

Scheduling   The budgeted staffing plan must be translated to work schedules for specific employees. Predictable absenteeism, educational leaves, holidays, and nonpatient care assignments must be accommodated in the schedule. A well-designed scheduling system has the following characteristics, listed in approximate order of importance:[25]

EXHIBIT 7.4 Example of a Nurse Staffing Model for an Inpatient Unit

Weighted Patient Census	Number of 8-Hour Shifts						Staffing Statistics			
	Nurse Manager	BSN Team Leader	RN	LPN	Technician	Clerk	Total Nursing Staff	Total Hours	Hours/ Weighted Census	Percent RN
40	1	4	4	2	7	2	20	160	4.0	45%
42	1	4	4	2	8	2	21	168	4.0	43%
44	1	4	4	3	8	2	22	176	4.0	41%
46	1	4	5	3	8	2	23	184	4.0	43%
48	1	4	5	3	8	3	24	192	4.0	42%
50	1	5	5	3	8	3	25	200	4.0	44%
52	1	5	5	3	9	3	26	208	4.0	42%
54	1	5	5	4	9	3	27	216	4.0	41%
56	1	5	6	4	9	3	28	224	4.0	43%
58	1	5	6	5	9	3	29	232	4.0	41%
60	1	5	6	5	10	3	30	240	4.0	40%

- Desired staffing mix is ensured for safe patient care; overstaffing and understaffing are minimized.
- Time and effort required to create complex staff schedules are minimized.
- Overtime, float, and agency usage is reduced, and personnel are scheduled according to their designated specialization, professional competence, and agreed-on work commitment (i.e., full-time or part-time).
- Schedules for individuals are maintained four or more weeks in advance, but with the ability to manage staffing on a daily basis.
- Schedules minimize unnecessary transfers between units and shifts.
- Weekends, late shifts, and other less desirable assignments are equitably distributed. ("Equitably" is usually not "equally"; one nurse's preferences are not the same as another's.)
- Personal requests for specific days off are accommodated equally, so long as they are submitted in advance, can be met within cost and quality constraints, and do not exploit other workers.

Assignment

Assignment makes the final adjustment of staff on each unit and shift, based on the best available estimate of immediate need, by changing the number of personnel on a given unit or, in some cases, by changing the number of patients on a unit. Thus, if the nursing unit shown in Exhibit 7.4 had absenteeism or an unpredicted increase in census or acuity, extra personnel would be moved there to help meet the load.

Some variation can be handled by the ability of the nursing staff to adapt to higher workload demands. Although nurses may be expected to increase productivity in dealing with workload peaks, higher nurse-to-patient ratios enhance job satisfaction, thereby contributing to recruitment and retention strategies.[26] The 25 people assigned to the unit in Exhibit 7.4 for the average of 50 patient equivalents can treat 60 patient equivalents acceptably for a day or two; they cannot sustain that level without quality, patient satisfaction, and personnel satisfaction problems.

Census management can also be used to reduce variation in nurse staffing requirements. Many leading HCOs employ sophisticated bed-management systems and specially trained personnel to assign patients to units with adequate nurse staffing levels, appropriate professional competencies of nurses, and proximity of the patient to important CSSs. When possible, patients are scheduled to reduce variation in weighted census. In organizations with several similar treatment units, incoming patients can be placed in units with surplus staff.

Remaining staffing variation is usually met by calling in part-time or back-up nurses, requesting overtime from available workers, and transferring cross-trained workers between units. The use of back-up staff and transfers may be necessary, but it should be minimized. Agency personnel brought in on contract are expensive, and training is outside the HCO's control, although a study in Pennsylvania suggests that agency nurses are well trained and generally effective.[27] Transfer of personnel from one location to another within the hospital presents similar difficulties. Most nurses do not like to be transferred, and the problems of cross-training and unfamiliar work reduce job satisfaction. Quality may deteriorate as a result.

Improving Nursing Performance

All nursing teams are responsible for maintaining the transformational culture and for improving unit performance. They monitor the operating scorecard of their unit, as described below. In addition, the nursing organization must monitor and improve overall nursing performance. It does this by aggregating the individual unit data, comparing data to benchmark, identifying opportunities for improvement (OFIs), and developing PITs to improve practice and negotiate new goals. It also maintains training programs for all levels of nursing personnel.

Improving Unit Performance

Nurses manage most care units. Physicians are also accountable for performance, but their activities often span several units. Their focus is patient and service line; nursing teams are focused on the patient and their unit. Nurse managers are explicitly expected to monitor performance, identify goals that might be in danger, and help team members improve performance. They are actively supported by both the nursing organization and senior management, who are frequent visitors and responsive listeners.

The nursing organization includes clinical specialists who can assist with nursing-process issues. Many excellent HCOs also provide nurse managers with resource specialists—more experienced nurses who are not in the direct accountability hierarchy. Under this system, each team has support for any kind of problem, as shown in Exhibit 7.5. Many problems are non-recurring. Those that recur become OFIs and candidates for PITs. The unit is always represented on the PIT.

Goal setting is usually done through the service line organization and always involves physicians as well as nurses. The nursing organization also pursues OFIs and suggests goals. Hand washing and patient instruction are recent campaigns for many HCOs, led jointly by nursing and medicine.

Improving Protocols

The nursing organization manages the functional or practice protocols that define the nursing activity. Many functional protocols require explicit training for associates. It is usually arranged through human resources but provided by the clinical organizations. Nursing is responsible for the continuous improvement of its own functional protocols. It is so central to most complex

EXHIBIT 7.5
Assistance Available to Nursing Teams

Problem	Support Available
Equipment, supply, or facilities failure	Plant services associates are trained to respond promptly. Their operating scorecards assess both delays and nurse satisfaction as customers.
Personal difficulty of team member	Human resources has counseling and retraining services.
Harassment or inappropriate behavior toward a team member	Harassment is defined by the associates. Human resources, the nursing organization, and senior management are trained in effective responses.
Staffing shortage	The nursing organization runs the staffing model and is committed to an effective solution. The solution may involve a PIT addressing ways to improve staff productivity or reduce variability in patient demand.
Unexpected clinical event	Reporting is mandatory. The unit team is trained to make emergency response. It may participate in service recovery, further analysis, or a PIT addressing risk management.
Unexpected customer or associate event	The unit team is expected to pursue appropriate service recovery, emergency response, and reporting for review of trends. Reporting is mandatory.

NOTE: In all of these examples, an unanswered call can be reported either to the nursing organization or senior management, who are expected to correct the problem and eliminate recurrence.

care that it is a major contributor to patient management protocols. Its central position gets it involved with many CSS functional protocols.

The service lines manage patient management protocols. Adopting a patient management protocol without active participation by nurses is probably impossible. Nurse specialists have a particular role here because their specialization makes them expert on particular diseases and conditions.[28] Management must ensure that appropriate consultation occurs and is constructive.

Implementing Evidence-Based Interventions

The unit's and organization's performance toward optimal outcomes helps determine when and how to improve functional and management patient protocols. Support is provided by HCO knowledge management and diligence in identifying problem areas. When OFIs are identified, nursing's role is to interpret the root cause, revise protocols, and teach associates practices based on the best evidence. Nursing implements evidence-based research that determines which course of action will lead to better outcomes.

Changes in nursing protocols are carried forward in a sophisticated program of training and development of associates, demonstrated proficiency of revised protocols, and inclusion of the required competencies in evaluations of performance.

People

Team Members

Nursing as a profession and as a unit of HCOs is almost as diverse as medicine. Nurses have careers that reach from high-tech in the operating room and ICU [intensive care unit] to high-touch in the home and hospice and that include general and public health services that do not involve individual patient care. In addition, there are significant numbers of managerial jobs. The patterns of education, specializations, and practice sites reflect this diversity.

Educational Levels

Nursing has a broad scope of educational programs, practice boundaries, and licensure restrictions. Within nursing are RNs, LPNs, and certified nursing assistants. RNs have a variety of educational backgrounds—a two-year associate's degree, a three-year hospital diploma, or a four-year baccalaureate preparation, as can be seen in Exhibit 7.6. Many nursing activities are carried out by people with varying educational preparation and professional direction.

This structure has led to a career ladder that accommodates repeated return to formal education, via LPN training; diploma; and associate, baccalaureate, master, and doctoral degrees. The growth of community colleges, which offer both LPN and associate degree programs, has made this career ladder more accessible. Registration—the traditional recognition of professional nursing qualification—is available with as little as two years' study after high school. Hospitals support the academic preparation with practice op-

EXHIBIT 7.6
Educational
Levels of
Nursing
Associates

Title	Degree or Certificate	Education Required
Baccalaureate Degree Not Required		
Nursing assistant or nurse technician	Certificate	Only hospital in-service training is required
Licensed practical nurse	LPN	One-year junior college program, also called "licensed vocational nurse"
Diploma in nursing	RN	Hospital-based program of three years post-high school qualifying for RN, but not the baccalaureate, degree
Associate in nursing	RN, ADN	Two-year community college program qualifying for RN and associate degree. The degree is accepted as partial fulfillment of the baccalaureate
Professional Level, Baccalaureate or Higher Degree Required		
Baccalaureate nursing degree	BSN	Four years beyond high school in an accredited college or university are required
Nurse anesthetist	BSN, CRNA	One year after the baccalaureate degree is required
Nurse practitioner	BSN, MSN, CNP	Master's degree is generally required; specialty certification is required
Nurse midwife	BSN, MSN, CNM	Post-baccalaureate education; master's degree is generally required
Clinical specialist	MSN	One or two years post-baccalaureate study; specialty certification is required
Public health nurse	MPH	Two years post-baccalaureate study
Nurse manager	MSN or MHA	Two years post-baccalaureate study
Nurse doctorate	PhD, DNP	Four or more years post-baccalaureate study

ADN: associate degree in nursing; BSN: bachelor of science in nursing; CNM: certified nurse midwife; CNP: certified nurse practitioner; CRNA: certified registered nurse anesthetist; DNP: doctor of nursing practice; MHA: master in health administration; MPH: master in public health; MSN: master of science in nursing; PhD: doctor of philosophy

portunities. They also teach many specific skills. New graduates are routinely assigned to experienced preceptors for extensive orientation and demonstration of skill proficiency. Diploma programs run by hospitals, once the major source of RNs, have diminished in favor of participation in associate and baccalaureate programs. Well-run HCOs are specifying baccalaureate nursing degrees for many assignments, such as critical care, team leadership, supervision, and primary nursing. In addition, job satisfaction and career retention have been shown to be more positive in bachelor's-level nurses than in associate's-level nurses.[29]

Advanced Practice Nurses

Generally, nurses with post-baccalaureate education and additional specialized certification and experience are called **advanced practice nurses** (APNs).

Nurse practitioners serve as the regular healthcare provider for children and adults during health and illness. Nurse practitioners perform physical examinations; diagnose and treat certain acute and chronic medical conditions; order, perform, and interpret diagnostic studies; prescribe medications and other treatments; provide health maintenance care; and collaborate with physicians as outlined in the rules and regulations of the Nurse Practice Act of the state in which they work.[30] **Nurse midwives** provide uncomplicated obstetric care, including prenatal, delivery, and postnatal services. **Nurse anesthetists** provide anesthetics to patients in collaboration with surgeons, anesthesiologists, and others. Legislation passed by the U.S. Congress in 1986 made nurse anesthetists the first nursing specialty to be accorded direct reimbursement rights under the Medicare program.[31]

Case managers assist care teams in finding the least costly solution in a lengthy and complex treatment.[32] Patients with permanent or long-term illness or disability develop complex medical and social needs. They often require services from several medical specialties, and social services are necessary to allow them to function at the highest possible level. Nurses, particularly those with post-baccalaureate education and considerable clinical experience, are well positioned to become case managers. Certification is available but not required by law.

The *clinical nurse leader* (CNL) and *doctor of nursing practice* are emerging APN roles. The master's-prepared CNL assumes accountability for healthcare outcomes for a specific group of clients within a unit or setting through the assimilation and application of research-based information to design, implement, and evaluate client plans of care. The CNL serves as a lateral integrator for the healthcare team and facilitates, coordinates, and oversees the care provided by the healthcare team.[33] The doctor of nursing practice (DNP) emphasizes the preparation of leaders for clinical practice, health policy, administration, and clinical research. DNP-prepared

Advanced practice nurse

A master's-prepared nurse with specialization and licensure to practice as a nurse practitioner, nurse anesthetist, nurse midwife, clinical nurse specialist, clinical nurse leader, or other advanced specialist role

Nurse practitioner

A registered nurse who has advanced education and certification to carry out expanded healthcare evaluation and decision making regarding patient care; boundaries of independent practice are set by state laws

Nurse midwife

A registered nurse who has advanced education and certification to practice uncomplicated obstetrical care, including normal spontaneous vaginal delivery, without direct physician supervision

Nurse anesthetist

A registered nurse who has advanced education and certification to administer anesthesia without direct physician supervision

Case manager

A health professional who advocates for the patient to receive the most appropriate treatment with acceptable quality in the most effective manner and appropriate setting at the best price

nurses work at the highest level of clinical practice with nurse researchers to provide leadership in nursing in a variety of settings,[34] with complementary roles between the DNP and the more research-oriented PhD degree in nursing.[35] The American Association of Colleges of Nursing (AANC) has proposed the DNP degree as the minimum requirement for advanced practice nursing by 2015.[36,37]

Nurses are represented in senior leadership, and they make up a significant proportion of middle management. Some are general line managers, supervising large staffs and being accountable for a broad range of expectations. Nurse clinicians with graduate education in the problems of certain patient groups are particularly well prepared for this role in service lines. An acute care nursing unit is a substantial managerial challenge that involves 50 or more employees working 24/7; an annual budget in excess of $3 million; and routine contacts with many physicians and most clinical support services as well as finance, human resources, and environment of care management. Nurse administrators must blend management and leadership competencies with the core ideology of nursing,[38] drawing on the model developed by the American Organization of Nurse Executives.[39]

Nurse Administrators

Explicit in the ANCC Magnet-designation model is a style of leadership that listens, supports, empowers, and shares decision making with nurses based on evidence, benchmarks, and best practices. Many organizations ascribe to the shared governance model of nursing, wherein various councils develop and oversee the major dimensions of nursing and interdisciplinary practice.[40]

Nurses practice in the community as well as in HCOs. HCO nursing is far larger, but community nursing is important to improve the health status of communities.

Practice Settings

Most nurses work in HCOs and specialize both by activity and by patient characteristics, as shown in Exhibit 7.7. Some specializations, such as operating room and critical care nursing, emphasize technical skills. Others, such as extended care of the chronically ill, emphasize comfort and palliative care, but most specializations blend both. All facets of nursing require an understanding of physiology, pharmacology, and disease processes. Unlicensed assistive personnel—nursing assistants, technicians, and secretaries—support nurses in most specialties. Nursing assistants and technicians are likely to possess certifications and specialty training for the site and type of patient population being served.

HCO Nursing

Community nursing emphasizes prevention and health promotion for the well population. Contacts are often in groups and outside the healthcare framework, providing group and individual counseling and limited personal care

Community Nursing

EXHIBIT 7.7
Nursing
Practice
Specialties in
HCOs

Site	Nature of Activity	Common Subspecialization*
Acute Hospital		
Operating rooms	Collaborate with surgical team	Pediatric, surgical specialty
Birthing suite	Pre- and post-partum care, assist delivery	High-risk obstetrics, neonatology
Intensive care and post-anesthesia care	Demanding, technically complex bedside care	Surgical, cardiovascular, and neonatal
Intermediate care	Less demanding bedside care, patient instruction, and emotional support	Medical, surgical, and pediatric
Emergency services	Wide variation	Trauma, flight
Ambulatory care	Direct care, patient instruction, and emotional support	Surgery, oncology, and cardiology
Primary Care Office	Screening, case management, patient instruction, and limited direct care	By primary care specialty
Rehabilitation	Direct care, patient instruction, and emotional support	Cardiovascular, stroke, and trauma
Long-Term-Care Facility	Bedside care, emotional support	Skilled and extended care
Home Care	Bedside care, emotional and family support	Palliative care
End-of-Life Care Hospice Palliative care	Bedside care, emotional and family support	Inpatient, home, and palliative care; pain management

* Other specializations, such as pediatric subspecialties, also exist.

in settings where people congregate, such as schools, workplaces, churches, public health departments, and senior-citizen centers. Efforts are made to reach populations at particular risk, and financing often includes elements outside the usual health insurance structures. Unlicensed assistive personnel are used less often in this setting. Nursing is only one of several professions that can supply the activities.

Community nursing's advantages lie in the respect for nurses among the target populations and in the nurses' ability to relate the specific topics to a broader context of health and disease. Well-run HCOs have moved decisively toward preventive services, as a way not only to improve the health status of the communities being served but also to reduce the total cost of care.

Organization

Nurse managers in excellent HCOs lead teams accountable for operating scorecards, as indicated in Chapter 5. They work directly with physician leaders of the service lines, identifying OFIs, participating in PITs, and negotiating improvement goals. They are also supported by a strong nursing organization led by a chief nursing officer (CNO) or nurse executive with an organization to ensure credentialing, manage nurse training and development, recruit and retain a competent and proficient nursing workforce, implement nursing practice standards and functional protocols, and maintain consistent performance of nursing activities. The CNO is a member of senior management and acts as the principal strategic and operational executive to ensure uniform achievement of good nursing practice.

Formal patient care teams with negotiated annual goals usually divide their work among several transient teams assigned to specific patients. In acute inpatient settings, the teams are led by a professional nurse and vary in size and skill levels, depending on patient needs. The leader of the formal team is usually a baccalaureate or higher–educated nurse, called a nurse manager. The nursing organization design can be modified to fit home care, hospices, rehabilitation, and extended care facilities. Specific policies, procedures, and skills differentiate the various services. Clearly, the procedures for operating rooms are different from those for outpatient psychiatry, but the structure of teams and accountability hierarchy is the same. The staff nurse for chronic care may be an RN or an LPN; for acute units, an RN; and for intensive care, an RN with a baccalaureate or master's degree. The skill required for outpatient care depends on the role, which can be filled by an LPN or RN.

The nursing organization in larger HCOs often provides a management structure to support first-line nurse managers, completing the structure described in Exhibit 5.8. The nurse teams have one accountability—to their service line—but two lines of support, from their service line and from the nursing organization, as shown in Exhibit 7.8. This structure is flexible and powerful, and it promotes excellent care. It requires ongoing communication among the professional caregivers; in planning sessions, PITs, and training activities; and when resolving issues.

Measures

The combined developments of evidence-based medicine, electronic information management, and the NOC have made measuring performance of most nursing teams feasible. Formal schemes for measuring nursing care in educational environments[41] and care settings are implemented in excellent

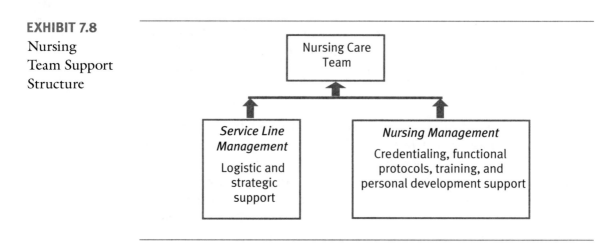

hospitals.[42] The array of data from NIC and NOC, using the NANDA paradigm, will provide increasingly valuable answers to core nursing questions about best practice, staffing levels, and training methods. As EMRs make application of the measures more practical, the ability of nursing to identify outcomes and relate them to nursing practice will create evidence based nursing.

The typical accountability center can measure, set expectations, and achieve improvements on all six dimensions. A nursing management minimum data set (NMMDS) includes uniform standards for the collection of comparable essential patient data.[43] The National Quality Forum has developed 15 standards for nursing-sensitive care for which additional data may need to be collected.[44] Examples are shown in Exhibit 7.9.

The rich measurement set depends heavily on information systems. As the systems are installed, obvious avenues of improvement appear and are explored. Initially, these are at the level of a single process; integrated and service line opportunities appear later. The process of identifying and addressing these opportunities appears to take several years in most organizations. A third, more rewarding and more challenging phase is beginning, where medicine, nursing, and other CSSs collaborate toward a goal of cost-effective care.

Managerial Issues

Given the cyclical shortage of nursing personnel, management has two critical tasks. One is to keep nursing work attractive so that young people are encouraged to enter nursing and for all nurses to stay in nursing. The other is to improve nurses' effectiveness, using the clinical team concept to amplify each professional nurse's contribution to patient care. The CNO and the senior management team have a number of vehicles to complete each task. It is noteworthy that Magnet-designated hospitals and other hospitals that follow similar principles generally do not have nursing shortages. They recruit,

EXHIBIT 7.9
Nursing
Performance
Measures

Dimension	Inpatient Examples	Outpatient Examples (Home Care Program)	Community Nursing Examples
Demand	Number and acuity of patients, % emergencies	Scheduled home visits, delay for visit	Enrollment in programs, % eligible attracted
Costs	Nursing hours per patient day,* medical supplies	Payroll costs, home supplies, travel costs	Faculty cost, facility cost, promotional cost
Human resources	Skills mix, education and certification,** nurse satisfaction,** turnover, vacancies	Skill mix, satisfaction, turnover vacancies	Skill mix, satisfaction, turnover vacancies
Output/ productivity	Discharges, cost/ discharge, cost/member month	Visits, visits/ patient, patients/visiting nurse, costs/patient month	Number of presentations, attendance, cost/ member
Outcomes quality	Falls prevalence, urinary tract infections, ventilator-associated pneumonia, pressure ulcer prevalence*	Daily living scores, hospitalizations, transfers to long-term care	% members smoking, % seeking prenatal care, child trauma
Process quality	% complete care plans, medication errors, % presurgery patient education, pain assessement**	% visits late or missed; errors in equipment, supplies	Member awareness, curriculum evaluation, facility evaluation
Patient satisfaction	% "very satisfied," number of complaints	% "very satisfied," family satisfaction	Audience evaluation, member satisfaction
Physician satisfaction	% of referring physicians and attending physicians "very satisfied," complaints	% of referring physicians "very satisfied," complaints	Physician awareness, satisfaction, complaints

NOTE: Measures marked with an asterisk (*) have been endorsed by the National Quality Forum (NQF) as National Voluntary Standards for Nursing-Sensitive Care (www.qualityforum.org). Measures marked with two asterisks (**) are included in the American Nursing Association National Database of Nursing Quality Indicators (www.nursingquality.org).

develop, support, and reward their nursing personnel at all levels in ways that make nursing satisfying work. They "seek and destroy" work elements that are unnecessarily frustrating. They use every element of each nurse's skills so that scarce resources are efficiently employed.

Recruitment and Retention

Nursing—the nurse manager or charge nurse—usually assumes responsibility for the day-to-day operation of patient care teams. The teams are extensively supported, both by the nursing organization and the logistic and strategic units, but they themselves are important management units. Maintaining them involves sustaining the transformational culture, leading the goal-set-ting negotiations, and handling the staffing and scheduling of team members.

The issues are made more challenging by the shortage of nurses. There continues to be national concern about the shortages of professional nurses[45] because of the aging of the nursing workforce[46] and the lag in nursing educa-tion capacity keeping pace with demand.[47] A medium-sized HCO employs 400 or more individual nurses, most of whom are inpatient nurses—a job that is both physically and emotionally demanding. Compensation is now comparable with that of professional opportunities such as teaching and phar-macy, although neither of those jobs combines the hours, physical demands, and critical responsibilities of a staff nurse. It is not surprising that staff nurse turnover is high, sometimes exceeding 50 percent per year. Excellent HCOs keep turnover below 10 percent.[48]

Efforts to maintain a sufficient cadre of qualified nurses begin with a deliberate effort to reduce turnover and increase work satisfaction.[49,50] Reten-tion is less expensive than recruitment.[51] More important, the satisfaction of current staff is quickly sensed by potential recruits, and a reputation as a good place to work is a powerful asset. Most important, evidence exists that nurse satisfaction is related to outcomes measures of patient care quality. In 2009, about 6 percent of high-performing HCOs[52] were designated by ANCC's Magnet Recognition Program for administering exceptional patient care, for providing good nursing practice environments, and for their ability to attract and retain nurses.[53] Magnet-recognized hospitals have consistently demon-strated three distinct core features that are elements of a professional nursing practice model: (1) professional autonomy over practice; (2) nursing con-trol over the practice environment; and (3) effective communication among nurses, physicians, and administrators.[54]

Improve Nursing's Effectiveness

The tools leading hospitals use to achieve excellent outcomes are consistent with the operating and cultural foundations described in chapters 1 through 3, emphasizing a transformational culture with effective clinical and other support services, service excellence, and continuous improvement. The following is a checklist that a CNO or COO might use to review progress toward the critical tasks.

1. *Culture.* A culture of respect is established by the mission, vision, and values and is supported with training and incentives. Management must "listen" to learn how nurses actually perceive the culture. Listening (see Chapter 15) includes surveying, rounding, forums, open-door policies, and other activities that generate a thorough and timely understanding of nurses' needs.

2. *Staffing.* The organization must ensure that nurses are rarely or never forced into either dangerously low staffing or excessive overtime. It should also offer flexibility in assignments. A sophisticated program of workload analysis, shift-by-shift monitoring of need, scheduling, and a trained pool of additional personnel is necessary to staff clinical teams effectively. Management must install and maintain the program and monitor it with staffing measures. In cases where staffing is inadequate, management must be prepared to divert or defer patients.

3. *Communication.* Much nursing time is wasted in rework associated with lost orders or test results. Computerized order-entry systems substantially reduce this waste. Similarly, pharmaceutical management systems reduce errors and speed drug distribution. More advanced EMRs also increase nurse productivity and patient safety. Management should provide order-entry and pharmacy systems and move with deliberate speed to fully digitalized records.

4. *Ongoing education and credentialing.* Each level of nursing, technician through advanced practice, can improve and expand its contribution through specific clinical education programs and credentialing. Similarly, nurse managers can be trained and coached in the details of their work. Management should invest in more than five days of training per associate per year.

5. *Clinical protocols.* Practice guidelines of all kinds improve quality and promote effective collaboration in clinical teams. They must be kept up to date. Management is responsible for an effective, ongoing process to review and revise protocols. The review process should routinely include nurses and use frontline knowledge in the revision.

6. *General continuous improvement.* Both clinical and nonclinical processes are always improvable. Measures and benchmarks identify opportunities; networking with other organizations reveals best practices. Management must support an ongoing program that improves both the care activities and the activities that support care, such as supplies, amenities, and financial management.

7. *Transforming the patient care environment.* Studies have shown that nurses spend only 31 percent to 44 percent of their time in direct patient care activities.[55] Changes to the nurse work environment could increase the amount of time available for direct patient care by removing obstacles to the efficient performance of routine nursing tasks.[56] Implementation of patient-centered design, systemwide integrated technology, seamless workplace environments,

and vendor partnerships may positively affect care delivery and allow nurses to spend more time caring for patients.[57]

Excellent nurses and excellent patient care are central to the mission and performance of excellent HCOs. Nurses are powerful patient advocates, and their interventions optimize clinical effectiveness. Excellent HCOs recognize, empower, and reward nurses for their major contribution to patient care.

Suggested Readings

American Nurses Association. 2009. *Nursing Administration: Scope and Standards of Practice.* Silver Spring, MD: American Nurses Association.

Dunham-Taylor, J., and J. Z. Pinczuk. 2009. *Financial Management for Nurse Managers: Merging the Heart with the Dollar,* 2nd ed. Boston: Jones and Bartlett.

Hall, L. M. 2005. *Quality Work Environments for Nurse and Patient Safety.* Boston: Jones and Bartlett.

Institute of Medicine. 2004. *Patient Safety: A New Standard of Care.* Washington, DC: National Academies Press.

———. 2004. *Keeping Patients Safe: Transforming the Work Environment of Nurses.* Washington, DC: National Academies Press.

Lindberg, C., S. Nash, and C. Lindberg. 2008. *On the Edge: Nursing in the Age of Complexity.* Bordentown, NJ: Plexus Press.

National Quality Forum. 2004. *National Voluntary Consensus Standards for Nursing-Sensitive Care: An Initial Performance Measure Set.* Washington, DC: NQF.

Powell, S. K., and H. A. Tahan. 2009. *Case Management: A Practical Guide for Education and Practice,* 3rd ed. New York: Lippincott Williams & Wilkins.

Sullivan, E. J. 2008. *Effective Leadership and Management in Nursing,* 7th ed. Upper Saddle River, NJ: Pearson-Prentice Hall.

Notes

1. The Gallup Organization. 2009. "Honesty and Ethics Poll Finds Congress' Image Tarnished." [Online information; retrieved 4/19/10.] www.gallup.com/poll/124625/Honesty-Ethics-Poll-Finds-Congress-Image-Tarnished.aspx.
2. Florence Nightingale, quoted in V. Henderson. 1966. *The Nature of Nursing,* 1. New York: MacMillan.
3. Abrams, S. E. 2007. "Nursing the Community: A Look Back at the 1984 Dialog Between Virginia A. Henderson and Sherry L. Shamansky." *Public Health Nursing* 24 (4): 382–86.
4. American Nurses Association. 2003. *Nursing's Social Policy Statement,* 2nd ed., 6; American Nurses Association. 2004. *Nursing: Scope and Standards of Practice,* 7. Washington, DC: American Nurses Association; International Council of Nurses. 2009. "Definition of Nursing." [Online information; retrieved 8/31/09.] www.icn.ch/abouticn.htm.

5. Institute of Medicine, Committee on Quality of Health Care in America. 2001. *Crossing the Quality Chasm: A New Health System for the 21st Century,* edited by L. T. Kohn, J. M. Corrigan, and M. S. Donaldson. Washington, DC: National Academies Press.

6. North American Nursing Diagnosis Association. 2009. [Online information; retrieved 7/23/09.] www.nanda.org.

7. Bulechek, G. M., H. K. Butcher, and J. M. Dochterman. 2007. *Nursing Interventions Classification,* 5th ed. St. Louis, MO: Mosby.

8. Swanson, E., S. Moorhead, M. Johnson, and M. L. Maas. 2007. *Nursing Outcomes Classification,* 4th ed. St. Louis, MO: Mosby.

9. Donaldson, N., S. Shapiro, M. Scott, M. Foley, and J. Spetz. 2009. "Leading Successful Rapid Response Teams: A Multisite Implementation Evaluation." *Journal of Nursing Administration* 39 (4): 176–81.

10. Muller-Staub, M. 2009. "Evaluation of the Implementation of Nursing Diagnoses, Interventions, and Outcomes." *International Journal of Nursing Terminologies & Classifications* 20 (1): 9–15.

11. Meurier, C. E. 2000. "Understanding the Nature of Errors in Nursing: Using a Model to Analyse Critical Incident Reports of Errors Which Had Resulted in an Adverse or Potentially Adverse Event." *Journal of Advanced Nursing* 32 (1): 202–07.

12. Mador, R. L., and N. T. Shaw. 2009. "The Impact of a Critical Care Information System (CCIS) on Time Spent Charting and in Direct Patient Care by Staff in the ICU: A Review of the Literature." *International Journal of Medical Informatics* 78 (7): 435–45.

13. American Society for Healthcare Risk Management. 2001. "Perspective on Disclosure of Unanticipated Outcome Information." Chicago: American Society for Healthcare Risk Management of the AHA; see also The Joint Commission. 2009. *Comprehensive Accreditation Manual.* Oakbrook Terrace, IL: The Joint Commission.

14. Wakefield, B. J., M. A. Blegen, T. Uden-Holman, T. Vaughn, E. Chrischilles, and D. S. Wakefield. 2001. "Organizational Culture, Continuous Quality Improvement, and Medication Administration Error Reporting." *Journal of Medical Quality* 16 (4): 128–34.

15. Computerized order-entry systems have been adopted by most HCOs for laboratory procedures. However, computerized order entry and scheduling for other ancillary departments is not as widely adopted. See Staggers, N., C. B. Thompson, and R. Snyder-Halpern. 2001. "History and Trends in Clinical Information Systems in the United States." *Journal of Nursing Scholarship* 33 (1): 75–81.

16. Thomas, R. K. 2004. *Marketing Healthcare Services.* Chicago: Health Administration Press.

17. White, K. R., P. J. Coyne, and U. B. Patel. 2001. "Are Nurses Adequately Prepared for End-of-Life Care?" *Journal of Nursing Scholarship* 33 (2): 147–51.

18. Griffith, J. R. 2008. "Finding the Frontier of Hospital Management." *Journal of Healthcare Management* 54 (1): 57–72.

19. Kane, R. L., T. Shamliyan, C. Mueller, S. Duval, and T. J. Wilt. 2007. *Nurse Staffing and Quality of Patient Care.* Rockville, MD: U.S. Department of Health and Human Services, Agency for Healthcare Research and Quality, AHRQ Publication No. 07-E005.

20. American Nurses Association. 2009. [Online information; retrieved 10/6/09.] www.safestaffingsaveslives.org.

21. Nelson, R. 2008. "California's Ratio Law, Four Years Later." *American Journal of Nursing* 108 (3): 25–26.

22. Sochalski, J., R. T. Konetzka, J. Zhu, and K. Volpp. 2008. "Will Mandated Minimum Nurse Staffing Ratios Lead to Better Patient Outcomes?" *Medical Care* 46 (6): 606–13.

23. Chapman, S. A., J. Spetz, J. A. Seago, J. Kaiser, C. Dower, and C. Herrera. 2009. "How Have Mandated Nurse Staffing Ratios Affected Hospitals? Perspectives from California Hospital Leaders." *Journal of Healthcare Management* 54 (5): 321–35.

24. Sullivan, E. J. 2008. *Effective Leadership and Management in Nursing*, 7th ed. Upper Saddle River, NJ: Pearson/Prentice Hall.

25. Cerner Corporation. 2005. [Online information; retrieved 7/5/05.] www.cerner.com.

26. Havens, D. S., and L. H. Aiken. 1999. "Shaping Systems to Promote Desired Outcomes: The Magnet Hospital Model." *Journal of Nursing Administration* 29 (2): 14–20.

27. _____. 2007. "Fears About 'Agency' Nurses Unfounded." *American Journal of Nursing* 107 (11): 21.

28. Oberle, K., and M. Allen. 2001. "The Nature of Advanced Practice Nursing." *Nursing Outlook* 49: 148–53.

29. Rambur, B., B. McIntosh, M. V. Palumbo, and K. Reinier. 2005. "Education as a Determinant of Career Retention and Job Satisfaction Among Registered Nurses." *Journal of Nursing Scholarship* 37 (2): 185–92.

30. American Academy of Nurse Practitioners. 2009. [Online information; retrieved 7/20/09.] www.aanp.org.

31. American Association of Nurse Anesthetists. 2009. [Online information; retrieved 7/20/09.] www.aana.com.

32. Park, E., and D. L. Huber. 2009. "Case Management Workforce in the United States." *Journal of Nursing Scholarship* 41 (2): 175–83.

33. Begun, J. W., J. Tornabeni, and K. R. White. 2006. "Opportunities for Improving Patient Care Through Lateral Integration: The Clinical Nurse Leader." *Journal of Healthcare Management* 51 (1): 19–25.

34. Acorn, S., K. Lamarche, and M. Edwards. 2009. "Practice Doctorates in Nursing: Developing Nursing Leaders." *Nursing Leadership* 22 (2): 85–91.

35. Dracup, K., L. Cronenwett, A. I. Meleis, and P. E. Benner. 2005. "Reflections on the Doctorate of Nursing Practice." *Nursing Outlook* 53 (4): 177–82.

36. Lancaster, J., and G. P. Bednash. 2008. "AACN Commentary on 'Professional Polarities in Nursing' Response to the Article by Elaine S. Scott and Brenda L. Cleary." *Nursing Outlook* 56: 50–51.

37. American Association of Colleges of Nursing. 2004. "AACN Position Statement on the Practice Doctorate in Nursing." [Online information; retrieved 7/23/09.] www.aacn.nche.edu/DNP/DNPPositionStatement.htm; Morton, P. 2009. "The Doctor of Nursing Practice Degree: What Does the Future Hold?" [Online information; retrieved 7/23/09.] www.aacn.org/wd/nti2009/nti_cd/data/papers/main/34137.pdf.

38. Jennings, B. M., C. C. Scalzi, J. D. Rodgers III, and A. Keane. 2007. "Differentiating Nursing Leadership and Management Competencies." *Nursing Outlook* 55: 169–75.

39. American Organization of Nurse Executives. 2005. "AONE Nurse Executive Competencies." *Nurse Leader* (February): 50–56. [Online information; retrieved 7/23/09.] www.aone.org/aone/pdf/February%20Nurse%20Leader—final%20draft—for%20web.pdf.

40. Porter-O'Grady, T. 2008. *Interdisciplinary Shared Governance: Integrating Practice, Transforming Health Care*, 2nd ed. Boston: Jones and Bartlett.

41. Canham, D., C.-L. Mao, M. Yoder, P. Connolly, and E. Dietz. 2008. "The Omaha System and Quality Measurement in Academic Nurse-Managed Centers: Ten Steps for Implementation." *Journal of Nursing Education* 47 (3): 105–11.

42. Hendrix, S. E. 2009. "An Experience with Implementation of NIC and NOC in a Clinical Information System." *CIN: Computers, Informatics, Nursing* 27 (1): 7–11.

43. Huber, D., L. Schumacher, and C. Delaney. 1997. "Nursing Management Minimum Data Set (NMMDS)." *Journal of Nursing Administration* 27 (4): 42–48.

44. National Quality Forum. 2007. "Nursing Performance Measurement and Reporting: A Status Report." Issue Brief No. 5. Washington, DC: NQF.

45. Buerhaus, P. I. 2008. "Current and Future State of the U.S. Nursing Workforce." *JAMA* 300 (20): 2422–24.

46. Buerhaus, P. I., and D. O. Staiger. 2000. "Trouble in the Nurse Labor Market? Recent Trends and Future Outlook." *Health Affairs* 18 (1): 214–22.

47. White, K. R., D. G. Clement, and K. R. Stover. 2008. "Healthcare Professionals." In *Human Resources in Healthcare: Managing for Success*, 3rd ed., edited by B. Fried and M. Fottler. Chicago: Health Administration Press.

48. Griffith (2008), p. 62.

49. Upenieks, V. 2005. "Recruitment and Retention Strategies: A Magnet Hospital Prevention Model." *Medsurg Nursing* (Supplement): 21–27.

50. Needleman, J., P. I. Buerhaus, S. Mattke, M. Stewart, and K. Zelevinsky. 2001. "Nurse Staffing and Patient Outcomes in Hospitals." Final Report, U.S. Department of Health and Human Services, Health Resources and Services Administration, Contract No. 230-99-0021. Boston: Harvard School of Public Health; Stamps, P. L. 1997. *Nurses and Work Satisfaction: An Index for Measurement*, 2nd ed. Chicago: Health Administration Press.

51. PricewaterhouseCoopers Research Institute. 2007. "What Works: Healing the Healthcare Staffing Shortage." [Online information, p.1; retrieved 9/4/09.] www.pwc.com/us/en/healthcare/publications/what-works-healing-the-healthcare-staffing-shortage.jhtml.

52. American Nurses Credentialing Center. 2009. "Growth of the Program." [Online information; retrieved 7/23/09.] www.nursecredentialing.org/Magnet/Program Overview/GrowthoftheProgram.aspx.

53. Scott, J. G., J. Sochalski, and L. Aiken. 1999. "Review of Magnet Hospital Research: Findings and Implications for Professional Nursing Practice." *Journal of Nursing Administration* 29 (1): 9–19.

54. Havens and Aiken (1999); Purnell, M. J., D. Horner, J. Gonzalez, and N. Westman. 2001. "The Nursing Shortage: Revisioning the Future." *Journal of Nursing Administration* 31 (4): 179–86; Mills, A. C., and S. L. Blaesing. 2000. "A Lesson from the Last Nursing Shortage: The Influence of Work Values on Career Satisfaction with Nursing." *Journal of Nursing Administration* 30 (6): 309–15.

55. Tucker, A. L., and S. J. Spear. 2006. "Operational Failures and Interruptions in Hospital Nursing." *Health Services Research* 41: 643–62.

56. Hendrich, A., M. P. Chow, and W. S. Goshert. 2009. "A Proclamation for Change: Transforming the Hospital Patient Care Environment." *Journal of Nursing Administration* 39 (6): 266–75.

57. *Ibid.*, p. 274.

8 CLINICAL SUPPORT SERVICES

In a Few Words

Most seriously ill patients require support well beyond what a physician and a nurse can give alone. This support comes from several services that in many ways are the core contribution of the modern healthcare organization (HCO)—pathology (or laboratory), imaging, operating suites, anesthesiology, pharmacy, rehabilitative and palliative care therapies, social service, and others. Each of these can and does exist independently; the HCO's role is to ensure safe, effective, patient-centered, timely, efficient, and equitable care, providing a comprehensive and integrated one-stop shopping that is superior to service offered by independent providers. To do this, the HCO must first create an environment where qualified professionals and other associates want to work. Then it supports the clinical support service (CSS) to achieve excellence within its domain. The HCO provides a stable market for CSSs and integrates them into overall clinical excellence. It also often provides information management, training and personnel services, physical facilities, and strategic guidance. Measured performance, annual goals, and continuous improvement are required for a successful relationship.

Critical Issues in Clinical Support Services

1. *Achieving evidence-based medicine:*
   - Reach and exceed standards for safety and reliability of CSS activities
   - Eliminate underuse and overuse of CSS
   - Keep up with changing technology

2. *Providing "brag about" comprehensive service:*
   - Coordinate multiple clinical support needs
   - Computerized order entry and results reporting
   - Convenient consultation for physicians and nurses
   - Manage the complex patient with multiple diseases or conditions

3. *Recruiting and retaining qualified CSS professionals:*
   - Make the organization the best place to work
   - Reward performance improvement
   - Provide continuing education

4. *Outsourcing and contracting for CSS:*
   - Keep CSS costs and service comparable to those of the competition
   - Devise relationships that benefit both customer and associate stakeholders
   - Understand and capture benefits of scale in CSS

Consider these questions as you read the chapter.

1. Consider a pharmacy that serves a large HCO and is measured by the six dimensions in Exhibit 8.6. Which measures are the highest priorities? Should an improvement program focus on these measures or a broader set? How would you motivate the pharmacy team to improve?

2. Scheduling and coordinating patients' tests and treatments are often issues that involve several CSSs. Some CSS tests or treatments must be scheduled in specific sequences. Patients sometimes must be moved from place to place. Delays should be minimized, but service times are not always predictable. How does an excellent organization address these problems? What are the roles of the individual CSS?

3. The emergence of service lines has substantially changed the accountability of CSS personnel. Many professionals have dual reporting—to the service line and to the CSS—and some have drifted away from their CSS accountabilities. What is an effective model to integrate CSS training with patient-focused care? (For example, assigning respiratory therapists and ultrasound technologists to a cardiovascular service line.) How should the organization resolve arguments over "rights" of CSS professionals?

4. A small hospital in a well-managed healthcare system can consider three ways to obtain a CSS. It can "stand alone," hiring its own professionals. It can "outsource," buying service from a local provider that would otherwise be a competitor. It can "affiliate," arranging for training, procedures, and supervision through its system or one of its larger affiliates. How should the system decide what to do? Who should be involved in the decision?

5. Technology advances rapidly in many CSSs. To keep up, investments must be made in learning, training, and equipment. What are the roles of the HCO manager, the CSS management, and governance in deciding how much to invest in keeping up? Do the functions of continuous improvement and budgeting provide an adequate framework to decide when specific new technology is appropriate? If not, what improvements would you suggest?

In addition to physicians and nurses, caregiving requires services from dozens of specialized professionals providing important clinical information (diagnostic services) or specific interventions (treatment services). Laboratory testing, imaging, endoscopic procedures, cardiac, and other invasive vein procedures are commonplace diagnostic services. Drug selection and administration, surgery, anesthesia, obstetric delivery, and physical therapy are common treatment services. Many patients also require behavioral, spiritual, and psychological services such as social service, pastoral care, and health education. Challenging ethical dilemmas arise in patient care, and HCOs provide resources to deal with them. These CSSs are provided through centralized support units or by professionals assigned to a service line accountability center. Most, but not all, CSSs are ordered by an attending physician. They are needed at several sites—outpatient offices, the acute care hospital, long-term care facilities, and home. A serious illness may require several hundred diagnostic, therapeutic, and consultative services from the CSSs listed in Exhibit 8.1.

The HCO makes an important contribution to providing and coordinating these services, guaranteeing their quality, making them convenient to both caregivers and patients, and ensuring their optimal contribution to each patient's care. Each CSS has its own technology and procedures discussed extensively in its specific professional literature. The HCO contracts with each CSS, establishing performance goals and helping the CSS achieve them. The HCO's competitive advantage is its ability to integrate the package for each patient's needs, fulfilling in total the goal of safe, effective, patient-centered, timely, efficient, and equitable care.

Purpose

The purpose of any CSS is

> **to provide its specialized services at a level that is clinically excellent and meets patients' and caregivers' needs.**

The purpose of the HCO is to assist each CSS in achieving its purpose and

> **to provide each patient with exactly the set of services needed and integrate those services into an excellent whole.**

These two purposes are different, but they are both possible under a common mission, vision, and values. The differences establish the relationship between the CSS and the HCO, giving each critical functions. When the functions are understood, there are several alternatives for affiliation between the CSS team and the HCO. Employment is the most common, but contracts, joint ventures, and corporate subsidiaries are also possible.

EXHIBIT 8.1
Clinical
Support
Services in a
Large HCO

Diagnostic Services	Therapeutic Services
Audiology	Anesthesia
Cardiopulmonary	Pain management
Electrocardiology	Surgical and obstetric anesthesia
Pulmonary function	Blood bank
Invasive cardiology	Nursing
Clinical laboratory	Birthing suite
Chemistry	Surgery and post-anesthesia care
Hematology	Wound care
Histopathology	Optometry
Bacteriology and virology	Orthotics
Autopsy and morgue	Palliative care
Consultative services	Pharmacy
Ethics committees	Dispensing and advising
Institutional review board	Intravenous admixture
Diagnostic imaging	Radiation therapy
Radiography	Rehabilitation services
Computerized tomography	Physical therapy
Positron emission tomography	Respiratory therapy
Radioisotope studies	Speech pathology
Magnetic resonance imaging	Occupational therapy
Ultrasound	
Electroencephalography	Social and Counseling Services
Electromyography	Community support groups
	Grief counseling
	Pastoral care
	Psychological care
	Social service

An HCO's profile of clinical support services must be consistent with its mission and strategic plan. This means that the size and scope of each CSS must be defined by the HCO, and the annual goals must be negotiated with the CSS and ultimately approved by the HCO governing board. At the same time, each CSS professional has multiple options to pursue his or her career. To make that negotiation attractive to the CSS professionals, the HCO must make itself the preferred place to practice, the "best place to give care."

Functions

It is obvious from Exhibit 8.1 that CSSs have different characteristics, yet similarities emerge at one level of abstraction above these differences. The managers of social service and radiation therapy, for example, share common functions, which are identified in Exhibit 8.2.

EXHIBIT 8.2
Functions
of the CSS,
Showing
Service
and HCO
Contributions

Function	CSS Role	HCO Role
Providing excellent care	Select, use, maintain, and teach functional protocols. Participate in patient management protocol selection and development.	Assist in designing work processes and training programs. Ensure appropriate voice in patient management protocol-selection committees.
Maintaining patient relationships	Schedule patients effectively. Train associates in identifying patient needs and using techniques to improve acceptability of care. Maintain cultural competence. Provide for uninsured patients.	Maintain a central scheduling system. Provide associate sensitivity training. Provide translators and cultural competence training. Recognize burden of nonpaying patients in contract.
Maintaining consultative relationships	Assist caregivers with protocol administration. Consult on questionable cases. Provide training to other professions on advances in their CSSs.	Support CSS involvement in PITs and planning activities. Incorporate consultation and training into contract. Resolve rules for nonprofessional administration of CSS services.
Planning and managing operations	Negotiate appropriate long-term relationship. Negotiate goals for operational scorecard dimensions.	Negotiate appropriate long-term relationship. Establish compensation and contribution from HCO's annual strategic goals.
Promoting continuous improvement	Benchmark, identify OFIs, and establish and participate in PITs.	Negotiate, support, and reward improvement.

CSS: clinical support service; OFI: opportunity for improvement; PIT: process improvement team

Providing Excellent Care

Both diagnostic and treatment CSSs are integral parts of healthcare. They must individually and collectively meet the Institute of Medicine goal of safe, effective, patient-centered, timely, efficient, and equitable care. They do that with the following processes:

1. *Patient management protocols.* These are adopted by protocol-selection committees on which CSS members participate. They control effectiveness because they specify when CSSs are required, optional, or not recommended. As a result, they also control the demand for service, placing the sizing of the CSS as an HCO function.

2. *Functional protocols.* Virtually all CSS activities are scripted, learned processes that are recorded as functional protocols. The protocols must be designed to achieve benchmark safety, effectiveness, and efficiency. Each CSS profession designs, tests, and maintains the processes it uses. It identifies and validates performance measures based on the functional protocols. The HCO includes the measures and continuous improvement in its contract.

3. *Scheduling systems.* It is important not only to provide each patient with timely service but also to maintain an orderly workflow within the CSS. Sophisticated scheduling systems achieve this by managing the demand stream, as shown in Exhibit 8.3. The best scheduling systems integrate all CSSs to minimize the length of the patient care event.

4. *Training.* Each CSS must rely on a mix of professional and nonprofessional associates. Maximizing the contribution of nonprofessionals is important to improve safety, patient-centeredness, and costs. It is achieved by careful training and transformational supervision. The HCO shares the training duties, providing training in supervision and continuous improvement, cultural competence, and other issues shared by several CSSs. The CSS supplies training for its functional protocols, but it often collaborates with human resources management to implement and evaluate the training.

Throughout all the functions, the HCO role can be summarized as providing coordination and support. It maintains the scheduling system (see "Maintain Patient Relationships" below). It uses process improvement teams (PITs) and planning committees to negotiate questions that interface caregivers and CSSs. These questions range from coordination and availability of services (Will Imaging have full service 24/7? What are arrangements for inpatient meals delayed by testing?) to coverage of uninsured patients (Who pays the rehabilitation costs for an uninsured trauma patient?) to privileges for a specific CSS assigned to various associate groups (Will images taken in outpatient offices be included in the medical record, and which will be read by the imagist?).

Maintaining Patient Relationships

All CSSs have both patient and caregiver customers. Caregivers order the services; patients receive them; caregivers receive notice of results. Although the clinical laboratory works principally with specimens and pharmacy supplies many drugs through nursing, most CSSs require intimate patient contact. Given an excellent care function, the issues in satisfying patients are scheduling, amenities, and identifying unusual needs.

The scheduling issues are demanding. The patient needs prompt attention for both safety and efficiency. CSS delays often add to the total length of stay and increase the cost per case. The CSS needs a manageable workflow. Its associates need planned schedules, but they also need to have work to do. Idle time drives up the cost per test and reduces their skills.

Sophisticated scheduling systems allow CSSs to balance workflow to their teams while meeting patient needs, including emergencies. The concept for the scheduling system is shown in Exhibit 8.3. Unless volumes of work are large (the laboratory and pharmacy, for example), a CSS that simply accepts patients as they come will have periodic idle times and overflow demand. The first wastes money, and the second endangers safety and effectiveness. Sophisticated scheduling systems can substantially reduce both problems. The secret is to identify a set of patients who do not have emergency needs and are willing and able to come on call. Nonemergency patients already in the HCO are an example. As Exhibit 8.3 shows, emergency patients get immediate care. On-call patients get a fixed future date, but they also can be called sooner. Scheduled patients get a fixed future date. At a given level of emergency allowance, overall efficiency will increase and overall delays will decrease by calling in patients.

Sophisticated computerized scheduling systems are available for major support services and for admission and occupancy management.[1] These programs keep records, print notices, and provide real-time prompts to caregiving associates. They automatically monitor cancellations, overloads, work levels, and efficiency. They are integrated with ordering and reporting systems so that the entire process of obtaining a CSS is automatic from the point of the doctor's decision to order it. Most scheduling systems can also be operated in a simulation mode to analyze the costs and benefits of alternative strategies. Simulation outputs are useful in both short- and long-term planning to evaluate potential improvements in demand categorization, resource availability, and scheduling rules.

The scheduling system requires each CSS to establish available hours. The hours should be based principally on efficiency considerations. CSSs should be open only when sufficient demand is expected to support efficiency and skill in the minimum team. Arrangements must be made to call in associates for life-threatening emergencies.

The HCO provides logistic services for many CSSs. These include knowledge management, training and other human resources management, environmental services, accounting and financial services, and internal consulting. They also include sensitivity training for cultural competence, translators, and assistance with patients who present unusual circumstances. The CSS is the customer and final monitor of these services. It should alert its HCO management contact about any failure and expect prompt response. The HCO's ability to provide reliable high-quality logistic service should be an attraction for a closer relationship.

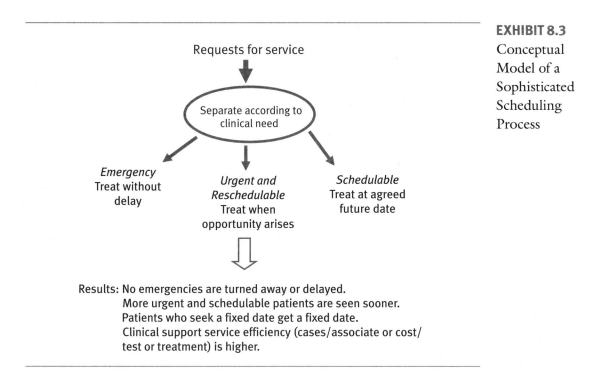

EXHIBIT 8.3
Conceptual
Model of a
Sophisticated
Scheduling
Process

Maintaining Consultative Relationships

CSSs must view caregivers as customers and recognize that caregivers often have competitive alternatives. Although a few can work directly with patients, most CSSs require physician or advanced practice professional orders. To win the orders, CSSs must meet caregiver needs. Caregivers have several different needs:

- *Excellent CSS care.* Overall care cannot possibly reach excellence unless the CSS achieves excellence.
- *Accuracy and effectiveness.* Errors in diagnostic tests create unnecessary costs and dangers for patients. Caregivers need to be confident in CSS results.
- *Prompt service.* Delays in CSS prolong the care process, reducing efficiency. They also erode patient satisfaction.
- *Patient support.* The patients' overall response to the care, both clinically and in terms of satisfaction, is often influenced by the CSS.

These needs are met by the CSS functions. Caregivers need additional assistance, such as the following:

- *Consultative advice.* Each CSS is an expert resource. Caregivers need to rely on CSS expertise when questions arise about individual patients.
- *Protocol development.* Many questions that emerge from adopting guidelines require CSS participation to answer. Most protocols must be agreed to by the CSS involved.

- *Training.* CSS advances can change how care is given. Many procedures originated in CSS but have moved to general usage; caregivers must often be trained to do them. Others have complex implications for other parts of care, and caregivers must be trained to understand those interactions.
- *Assistance with uninsured patients.* The plans must be worked out in advance and specified in the contract with the HCO (see "Plan and Manage Operations" section).

These needs are met by CSS availability to caregivers, participation in PITs and planning committees, and support of training activities. Those items must be negotiated in the CSS–HCO contract.

Behind several of these issues lies an unfortunate consequence of the payment system. The CSSs have various relationships to payment. Some, such as social service and bereavement counseling, are almost never billed separately. Others, such as outpatient radiology and laboratory, have dual physician and hospital payments. The physician portions of these payments are not limited by regulation to CSS professionals. Primary care or specialist physicians who use imaging equipment in their office can bill most insurance plans for each image. The physician can have the image read as a consultation by a radiologist and then order a second image from the HCO. If a second image is ordered, the radiologist and the HCO also get paid. There are three critical questions here:

1. Is the radiologist's consultation necessary?
2. Are two images necessary?
3. If not, which is better—the one at the office or the one at the HCO?

The problem is not limited to radiology. In one form or another it affects any CSS for which there is direct payment, although it has essentially been solved in pharmacy. There are no general answers to the three questions, in part because technology improvements change the answers. A consultation that was important in 2010 may not be in the patient management protocol in 2012.

Bundled payments by insurers will improve solutions to these questions because they will force all three parties—the referring physician, the CSS, and the HCO—to negotiate a more cost-effective approach. In the meantime, the HCO plays a major role, negotiating the specific solutions in each protocol and service line. The key to the negotiations is commitment to a mission of excellent care and evidence-based medicine. The patient management protocol should specify when tests or treatments are appropriate and allow completion by the lowest-cost associate who can do the test or treatment safely. That associate must have adequate training and support in case difficulties arise. The principles—evidence-based medicine and commitment to the mission—and the negotiating process must both be included in the contract between the HCO and CSS. The principles must be scrupulously implemented by the HCO, but at the same time, the HCO must assure the CSS associates of a competitive income opportunity.

Planning and Managing Operations

Almost any CSS can be envisioned as a small retailing business. Many, in fact, are operated exactly that way. The HCO's strategy is to bring these businesses under one organization. It will ask for commitment to mission and to evidence-based medicine and management. It will enforce these requests by asking for explicit measures of performance, benchmarking, and continuous improvement. It will make its offer attractive by offering a large, reliable book of business, a record of capability in meeting operating needs, and a culture that is attractive as a place to work. In addition, the HCO must show that it will offer competitive compensation. This concept is a difficult one, given the healthcare financing. It does not mean "As much as you can earn someplace else," because the HCO will expect care limited to appropriateness standards and assigned to the lowest capable level of worker. It does mean "As much as you could earn someplace else given that you accept our commitment to mission and evidence-based medicine."

Excellent HCOs implement that approach to CSS management using a three-part strategy. First, the CSS must be carefully sized to realistic market needs, and the HCO must control the size. Second, the HCO must implement its transformational culture to make the work attractive to professional and nonprofessional associates. Third, the HCO must implement evidence-based management in all the logistic and strategic services the CSS needs. The contract must be competitive in the CSS associates' eyes.

Planning and Sizing the CSS

CSS planning is based on the community epidemiologic planning approach described in Chapter 3. For CSSs drawing directly from the community, populations are age-specific community censuses, the incidence rate is the occurrence of disease in the general population, and the market share is the institution's anticipated share of the particular market, as shown in Equation 1.

Equation 1

$$\text{Demand for a service} = \left\{ \begin{array}{c} \text{Forecast} \\ \text{population} \\ \text{at risk} \end{array} \right\} \times \left\{ \begin{array}{c} \text{Incidence} \\ \text{rate} \end{array} \right\} \times \left\{ \begin{array}{c} \text{Average} \\ \text{use per} \\ \text{incidence} \end{array} \right\} \times \left\{ \begin{array}{c} \text{Market} \\ \text{share} \end{array} \right\}$$

For example, the demand for postoperative physical therapy (POPT):

$$\text{Demand for POPT} = \left\{ \begin{array}{c} \text{Forecast} \\ \text{procedures} \\ \text{requiring} \\ \text{POPT} \end{array} \right\} \times \left\{ \begin{array}{c} \text{Percent of} \\ \text{patients} \\ \text{referred} \\ \text{for PT} \end{array} \right\} \times \left\{ \begin{array}{c} \text{PT visits} \\ \text{per patient} \\ \text{referred} \end{array} \right\} \times \left\{ \begin{array}{c} \text{HCO's} \\ \text{market} \\ \text{share} \end{array} \right\}$$

or for breast examinations, where average use per incident is one:

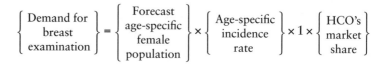

$$\left\{\begin{array}{c} \text{Demand for} \\ \text{breast} \\ \text{examination} \end{array}\right\} = \left\{\begin{array}{c} \text{Forecast} \\ \text{age-specific} \\ \text{female} \\ \text{population} \end{array}\right\} \times \left\{\begin{array}{c} \text{Age-specific} \\ \text{incidence} \\ \text{rate} \end{array}\right\} \times 1 \times \left\{\begin{array}{c} \text{HCO's} \\ \text{market} \\ \text{share} \end{array}\right\}$$

The equation can be specified or aggregated as desired. It might apply to MRI (magnetic resonance imaging) demand by type of procedure, cardiovascular surgeries, births, or any condition for which incidence rates are known.

CSS demand that arises from many different diseases is calculated from general rates of admissions or outpatient visits. Many CSS demands can be estimated from the history of use per patient and forecasts of the number of patients using Equation 2. The equation can be specified or aggregated as needed to obtain reliable results.

Equation 2

$$\text{Demand for widely used CSS} = \left\{\begin{array}{c} \text{Forecast} \\ \text{patient} \\ \text{encounters} \end{array}\right\} \times \left\{\begin{array}{c} \text{Number of} \\ \text{services} \\ \text{per encounter} \end{array}\right\}$$

For example:

$$\left\{\begin{array}{c} \text{Inpatient} \\ \text{pharmacy} \\ \text{demand} \end{array}\right\} = \left\{\begin{array}{c} \text{Forecast} \\ \text{inpatient} \\ \text{admissions} \end{array}\right\} \times \left\{\begin{array}{c} \text{Number of} \\ \text{presciptions} \\ \text{per admission} \end{array}\right\}$$

The equations must be forecast several years into the future and translated into a business plan for the CSS that projects staff requirements by skill level, supply and facility requirements, expected costs, and unit costs. The unit costs can be compared to benchmarks, competitive data, and income forecasts. Annual volumes can be compared to quality minimums. The business plan is presented to both the CSS associates involved and the referring care teams involved for their comments. The plan is presented to the governing board with management's recommendation and both sets of comments. It is adjusted as needed in the annual goal-setting process.

The planning process implements the HCO's mission for quality and cost effectiveness. The service will be started, continued, or expanded when both cost and quality comparisons are favorable. The service should be discontinued, outsourced, or reorganized whenever quality is threatened or cost is not competitive.

Meeting CSS Support Needs

The HCO's offer to the CSS is that it will thrive under closer affiliation. That requires the HCO to provide a full range of logistic and support services and an attractive work environment. Closer affiliation usually means greater capital investment by the HCO.

The CSS associates work side by side with the caregiving teams, and they share the same logistic support and strategic support. The services must be better than the CSS could acquire elsewhere. CSS associates, like all other associates, must feel that the HCO is "a great place to give care." The transformational culture is sustained by three elements:

1. *Responsive listening by senior management.* Rounds should include CSSs, and CSS associates should feel empowered.
2. *Training for CSS managers.* Just as head nurses and logistic support managers are trained to be responsive listeners and to encourage empowerment, CSS managers should be trained. Because of the small size of many CSSs, coaches and mentors come from other CSSs.
3. *Celebration and rewards.* CSSs should participate in celebration of goals that require collaboration as well as in achievements within their CSS. Their compensation should include bonus opportunities that are comparable to those of other associates.

The HCO has a number of alternative contractual arrangements that it can tailor to a specific CSS. Alternative structures, generally ordered in terms of increasing HCO control and increasing HCO capital investment, include the following:

Building an Effective Contractual Relationship

- *Long-term contract with a separately owned corporation.* An independent corporation owns facilities, employs associates, and sells services to the HCO. The contract should specify as clearly as possible the obligations and intentions of both parties. Quality, patient satisfaction, and efficiency standards can be included, with agreement on measures and benchmarks. The HCO can control professional privileges. Hours of coverage, requirements for teaching, and participation on PITs should be specified. It is difficult to incorporate standards for effectiveness or to prevent the contractor from competing as an independent organization.
- *Joint venture corporation.* The HCO gains partial strategic control and can include explicit reserved powers or super majority rules that gain control of size, location, clinical privileges, and management appointments. The corporation can purchase services from the HCO. The principal advantages relate to capital. The joint venture allows CSS professionals to have equity and income compensation. It also permits a for-profit corporation to provide some of the equity capital, relieving the HCO of debt or lease financing.
- *Joint operations.* The HCO owns and operates the facility, including hiring of nonprofessional associates, and can exercise control of privileges, giving it control of size, amenities, and capital investment. Professional guidance is provided by contract with one or several physician corporations.

- *Unified operations.* The HCO owns and operates the facility and employs all professional and nonprofessional associates. This model gives the HCO maximum control, but it must still attract and retain qualified professionals.

Unified operations are the most common solution, particularly among smaller CSSs, and the trend is clearly toward increased HCO control. Revisions to the insurance payment system may encourage even more HCO control. Given the great importance of fixed costs in efficiency, the sizing function is crucial. Services that are missing or too small pose a threat of lost market share to competitors. Those that are too large draw insufficient demand to meet quality and cost standards.

Promoting Continuous Improvement

The evidence-based model of measures, benchmarks, opportunities for improvement (OFIs), improved goals, and rewards fits well within each CSS. It should be routine in all CSSs where the HCO provides operations and should be expected of contract partners and joint venture corporations. For a CSS where the HCO provides some or all capital, there are two interrelated components—setting annual operating goals and identifying and justifying new capital investment. Capital is required for improving and expanding facilities, replacing outmoded equipment, and starting new programs. CSSs are a major user of capital.

Setting Annual Goals

A unit that has been diligent in the preceding year will be able to formulate next year's budget quickly, drawing in large part on work that has already been done in continuous improvement. Quality, costs, patient satisfaction, and associate satisfaction must be based on benchmarks; the management of a CSS that cannot meet benchmarks can usually be replaced by competitors with proven records.

Well-run organizations have clearly defined budget process roles for the CSS, the budget manager (a technical support person or office attached to finance), and the HCO manager. The CSS manager and team are expected to do the following:

- Review the demand forecasts prepared by the budget manager, extending them to the specific levels required in the department and suggesting modifications based on their knowledge of the local situation.
- Identify changes in the scope of services and the operating budget that arise from changes in demand, patient management protocol development, and continuous improvement. Minor changes are incorporated in the operating budget. Major ones are addressed in the capital and new programs budget (discussed below).

- Propose expectations for staffing, labor productivity, and supplies consistent with demand forecasts and constraints.
- Propose goals in the operational scorecard measures for quality and satisfaction, using benchmark and available competitor data.
- Identify OFIs and initiatives that should be developed during the coming year.

The budget manager (see Chapter 13) is expected to do the following:

- Assemble historical data on achievement of last year's budget.
- Prepare forecasts of major CSS demand measures.
- Prepare benchmark and competitor data.
- Promulgate the budget guidelines for changes in total expenditures, profit, and capital investment approved by the finance committee of the board.
- Circulate wage-increase guidelines from human resources and supplies-price guidelines from materials management.
- Assist in calculations and prepare trial budgets until a satisfactory proposal for the board has been reached.

The HCO manager responsible for the CSS is expected to do the following:

- Ensure that the proposed goals do not impair quality or satisfaction in other units.
- Assist the CSS, and encourage steady but realistic improvement.
- Coordinate interdepartmental issues that arise from the budgeting process.
- Meet the budget guidelines set by the governing board or the senior management team.
- Resolve conflicting needs between CSSs.
- Evaluate the progress of the CSS to assist in the distribution of incentives.
- Assist the CSS in pursuing OFIs and implementing them during the coming year.

An important part of the HCO manager's job is facilitating PITs and imple- **Implementing** menting improvements that involve several different CSSs and patient care **Improvements** teams. These improvements are likely to be the most rewarding opportunities. For example, costs of pharmaceuticals have been rising rapidly. A pharmacy might pursue a number of internal initiatives to keep departmental cost increases at a minimum, but control of demand and much of drug safety rests with the medical and nursing staffs. The pharmacy section of Exhibit 8.4 shows some initiatives a pharmacy might support. The strategy for pharmacy addresses four areas: price and inventory, formulary, protocols, and prescribing habits. Three of the four require collaboration with the medical and nursing staffs. Initiatives in each area might continue for several years.

The diagnostic imaging section of Exhibit 8.4 also shows a set of initiatives. Only the first is wholly within the CSS's control. As the exhibit suggests, improvement initiatives take a number of different forms, leading to PITs with different charges, memberships, and timetables.

Negotiating Goals

CSS operational goals must contribute to the HCO's annual strategic goals and maintain competitive excellence. In addition, they must respond to longer term changes. Shifts in patient management, driven by evidence-based medicine and changes in technology, will force many CSSs to make major revisions. Even the well-managed CSS that invests heavily in improvement initiatives may encounter difficulty as medical care changes. The demand for cancer therapies may shift radically if effective new drugs are discovered. The balance between heart surgery and heart catheterization has shifted more than once, as new catheter-oriented stents evolved simultaneously with minimally invasive cardiac surgery. The HCO manager's role includes negotiation of both annual goals and long-term forecasts. The negotiation process has several important characteristics:

- The goal of the negotiations is the optimization of patient needs as a whole, as reflected in competitive needs and external benchmarks. Actions that endanger the HCO's competitive position must be avoided at any cost.
- Competitive financial goals must be met for all parties. HCOs or CSSs that cannot meet those goals must be restructured by consolidation or revision of the mission.
- Each CSS must maximize its own opportunities and defend its own needs, emphasizing quality, patient satisfaction, and associate satisfaction.
- The negotiating team should include physicians and CSS personnel who can implement agreed-on improvements.
- Negotiations:
  - Examine solutions between related CSSs and with outsourcing and external collaboration.
  - Assure the CSS of a fair hearing.
  - Include rewards for CSS managers and associates who contribute to an effective solution.

A strong strategic plan is essential. If the strategic plan and the facilities, information, and recruitment plans derived from that plan are inadequate, it becomes impossible for the CSS to reach competitive levels on all dimensions. Thus, if a CSS falls short of its constraints, the first questions address the effectiveness of CSS operation, and the second questions address the size and scope of the CSS itself, including issues of outsourcing or eliminating the service. Finally, attention turns to the

Issue	Initiative	Measures	Approach
Pharmacy			
Price and inventory management	Purchasing agreement Inventory management system	Unit cost versus wholesale Inventory turns/year	PIT within pharmacy
Formulary management	Generic drug program Automatic stop orders on common drugs Extra controls for very expensive drugs	Ratio of generic to proprietary Drug cost per case Average costs per dose for specific drugs	PITs working with service lines
Patient management protocols	Alternative therapies and prevention Avoid unnecessary drug use and cost	Drug cost per specific treatment episodes	Protocol review committees
Prescribing habits	Protocol compliance Physician education, counseling	Drug costs per capita Drug cost per specific treatment groups	Counseling with service lines
Diagnostic Imaging			
Reduce retakes	Improve functional protocols and associate training	Count of retakes	PIT within imaging
Improve patient scheduling and results reporting delays	Evaluate and install departmental information system	Patient delays for service hours from exam to report	PIT with service lines and other CSSs
Inappropriate exams	Final product protocols, physician education	Disease-specific exams per patient	Protocol review committees and service line counseling

CSS: clinical support service; PIT: process improvement team

EXHIBIT 8.4
Improvement Initiatives in Two CSSs

strategy of the organization as a whole. Repeated and widespread failures in meeting CSS constraints are evidence of an organization or facility that is undersized or underfinanced for market needs. Affiliation with another organization or closure must be considered.

Preparing New Program and Capital Budget Requests

CSS managers are responsible for identifying opportunities and developing **programmatic proposals**—specific proposals for new or replacement capital equipment or major revisions to service—as well as for the annual budget. Technological improvements, aging existing equipment, changing demand, and revisions in the scope of service can require capital equipment or major shifts in the expectations. These must be justified in terms of the HCO's mission. The best investments are those that contribute most to the HCO's core purpose and owners' expectations. All proposals are subject to a competitive review process that places them in rank order and to board action on the basis of the rank order. The review process and board actions are discussed further in Chapter 14.

Programmatic proposals
Proposals for new or replacement capital equipment or major revisions of service

For example, an imaging department may encounter declining demand for inpatient radiographs, increasing demand for convenient ambulatory radiographs and ultrasound, and increasing demand for magnetic and emission tomography. Substantial capital is required to remove equipment no longer needed, purchase new equipment, and recruit and train staff for the expanded operations. The imaging department and the HCO manager prepare detailed business plans for these changes, documenting both the capital and operating cost changes as well as changes in other performance measures, such as process quality and patient and referring physician satisfaction. Internal consulting helps develop the factual basis for the proposal; marketing provides advice on location, hours, and other issues; human resources assists with the training; and finance assists with calculations of cost and return on investment. The benefits—contribution to mission—are identified by imaging, with assistance from the performance improvement council (PIC); clinical customers; internal consulting; and marketing.

The proposal, which might suggest changes that cost several million dollars, advances to competitive review when the imaging department is ready. Competitive review compares the proposal against similar requests from other units, ending with a rank-ordered list submitted to the governing board. The criterion for ranking is long-run mission achievement: What is best for the HCO's owners? The benefits the CSS claims in the proposal are related to its operational performance measures. If the proposal is accepted, imaging is expected to adopt and achieve those goals. Many benefits occur outside the CSS, making the collaborative approach to proposal development essential. The proposal is both strengthened and validated in the process, reducing challenges during competitive review.

All benefits, including quality benefits, must be compared to the treatment alternative that would prevail if the proposal were not adopted.[2] Although many technological advances are described as improvements in outcomes quality, or contribution to patients' health and well-being, the reality is that most proposals involve only convenience and competitive advantage. A service that supplements another one that is available ten minutes away has a quality value equal to ten minutes of travel, even if the service is lifesaving. (It may have a much higher patient satisfaction value.)

Quality-Related Benefits

If, in fact, the proposal changes the number of people in the community who will achieve a more favorable outcome, its contribution can be quantified if disease prevalence rates, population reached, and probabilities of success are known:

$$\text{Contribution} = \left\{ \begin{array}{c} \text{Demand} \\ \text{for a} \\ \text{service} \end{array} \right\} \times \left\{ \begin{array}{c} \text{Probability that} \\ \text{service will} \\ \text{improve outcome} \end{array} \right\} \times \left\{ \begin{array}{c} \text{Value of} \\ \text{improvement} \end{array} \right\}$$

The demand term is estimated by the epidemiologic planning model. The probability of improved outcome comes from clinical literature and is a foundation of evidence-based medicine. Quality benefits can theoretically be scaled by a variety of techniques, including forced-choice surveys and Delphi analysis. Most situations will not be difficult to rank. If a new clinical approach substantially prolongs life, and many competitors are adopting it, it will score well and be adopted. Scales exist for the value of human life, ability to work, ability to care for self, added years of healthy life, and similar major contributions.[3] Review committees should use a consistent scale for valuing clinical contribution and recognize the limitations of the scale.

If a process improvement reduces the need for care, dollar estimates are not challenging. For example, if a new diagnostic process with a demand of 1,000 tests per year will reduce length of stay by one day for one-third of those on whom it is used, and a day of stay is worth a marginal cost of $400, the contribution of the process is about $133,000 per year:

Cost-Related Benefits

$$\text{Contribution} = 1{,}000 \times .333 \times \$400 = \$133{,}200$$

A case can be made for higher values. From an insurer's perspective, the cost per day is the paid price, probably twice the marginal cost. Patients and society might place an even higher price, adding earnings from earlier return to work.

Because of fixed costs and marketing implications, cost and demand are interrelated. First, CSS costs after adoption of the proposal must be competitive with other sources of equivalent services. If they are not, the proposal is inadequate to ensure long-run survival. The CSS must find a way to deliver services competitively. If they are, a benefit is return on investment—the savings a proposal generates expressed as a return on its capital investment over the years of the life of the project or the capital equipment.

Return-on-investment calculations are usually prepared with the assistance of internal consulting and finance. The focus is on changes in cash flows. The contribution can be expressed as return on investment:

$$\left\{ \begin{array}{c} \text{Return on} \\ \text{investment} \end{array} \right\} = \left\{ \text{Contribution} \right\} \div \left\{ \text{Invested capital} \right\}$$

The value of cash in future years is less than the value of immediate cash. Return on investment can be calculated for multiyear cash flow streams, allowing comparison of diverse projects. It is also possible to discount cash flow in future years with an assumed rate of interest, creating a net present value of cash flows. Care must be taken to estimate all costs and demands accurately, including hidden ones, and to be sure the claims for savings can truly be met. The proposed costs will be incorporated as an operating-budget reduction if the project is implemented. Some cost improvements occur outside the CSS, in which case another unit must agree to them. For example, an improved diagnostic test may reduce drug costs or length of stay. In this case, the cost savings must be traced to the unit where they will occur, and that unit must agree to actual budget changes.

Market Share Improvements   Many proposals improve market share or forestall a loss of market share. A claim that a specific capability will attract or protect market share is a justification for capital investment. The value depends on the magnitude of the shift and the fixed cost involved. Replacing equipment that is critical to continued operations is an obvious, high-priority example. If a modern laboratory must have an automated, multichannel blood chemistry analyzer, and the existing one is no longer reliable, the proposal to replace it will not generate much debate. In less obvious cases, the justification is based on the return on investment. Applications are often complicated. Under global and capitation payments, change in cash flow must be calculated at the level of payment involved. The proposal may be a service that has become generally accepted as part of the protocol for a specific disease or procedure.

The justification must be based on service for the care episode, rather than the operation of the CSS. The budget for the patient management protocol or the service line becomes the critical document, rather than that of the CSS. If it reflects competitive cost and quality, the proposal is worth further consideration. For example, a special laboratory for in vitro fertilization is a CSS for a women's service line. It can be justified only as a complete service, including evidence of sufficient actual demand, medical staff recruitment, all costs for couples seeking the service, payments allowed by various insurers, and evidence of competitive rates of successful fertilization. As a result, these kinds of proposals are usually considered strategic, and ad hoc teams are established to evaluate them.

The HCO manager of the CSS and the internal consulting representative are proper advocates of the proposal in the evaluation process. Their job is to prepare the analysis and the justification in the most favorable light. As advocates, they should be prepared to answer questions and make modifications as the proposal progresses. They must also be prepared to accept rejection. By the same token, it is senior management's obligation to see that they do not overstep the bounds of honesty, that others accept their role as advocate, that all projects get a fair and judicious hearing, and that the benefits claimed are translated to actual performance when the project is complete.

Defending Capital Proposals

The feedback to the CSS comes in two ways—through evaluation of its proposals and through participation in the evaluation of others' proposals. Over time, the CSS learns to identify winning proposals earlier, making the process less onerous.

People

Team Members

Many CSS professionals have extensive formal education, licensure, and requirements for continuing education. The education includes mastery of relevant theory and supervised practice so that the student learns the processes, patient indications and contraindications for them, expected outcomes, and the rules governing process design. Although they are in various stages of implementation, the professions of pharmacy,[4] physical therapy,[5] occupational therapy,[6] and nurse anesthesia[7] have adopted practice doctorate degrees as the first professional "entry to practice" credential. To reduce costs, unlicensed aides or technicians perform many of the actual CSS procedures under supervision. The staffing of most CSS units consists of one or two levels of formally educated professionals and one or more levels of technical personnel, allowing each professional to serve a larger volume of patients. Three managerial issues arise:

1. Maintenance of clinical competence and skill for qualified professionals
2. Education and supervision of nonprofessional personnel
3. Resolution of work assignments between professional and nonprofessional personnel

The first is met by a credentialing process that verifies entry and continuing formal education and a continued record of effective practice, as for medicine and nursing. The process is usually assigned to human resources management. The second is addressed in the HCO's educational programs. The training is usually designed and conducted by the CSS professionals and human resources. The third, resolution of interprofessional and intraprofessional work assignments, must bring in advice from customer stakeholders. It is the responsibility of the HCO manager and is discussed in the "Managerial Issues" section later.

CSS Management

The manager of each support service is usually an experienced leader in the healthcare profession associated with the service. Many CSSs—clinical laboratories, radiology and imaging, radiation therapy, anesthesiology, rehabilitation, and cardiopulmonary laboratories—have nonphysician managers along with designated medical directors. Some services—operating rooms and delivery rooms—use specialized nurse managers. These managers collaborate closely with their physician counterparts. Pharmacists, respiratory therapists, and medical social workers have less direct medical involvement, probably because they serve a broad array of specialties.

Beyond their professional training, CSS managers need supervisory skills, including skills in personnel selection, management of committees, continuous improvement concepts, knowledge management, and servant leadership. Managers of the larger CSSs often have master's degrees in healthcare management or in their specialty. Learning effective leadership styles requires more than coursework. Well-managed organizations reinforce good practice with ongoing training, exposure to best practices, coaching, and assistance from internal consulting.

The HCO Manager

Each CSS must be accountable to the HCO governing board. That accountability is through the *HCO manager* (actual titles vary), who is usually a member of the senior management team or someone who reports to a senior manager. The HCO manager has several duties, many of which are described under the CSS functions section above:

1. Responsive listening—rounding frequently, talking with associates in the CSS at all levels, and addressing their needs
2. Communicating—explaining strategic guidelines, other relevant board decisions, OFIs and matters of interest that arise from various surveillance activities, PIC actions, and the work of PITs that potentially affect the CSS
3. Supporting the CSS's PITs with assistance from clinical units and logistic and strategic services
4. Ensuring representation on all PITs that directly affect the CSS
5. Negotiating the annual operational goals—relating the CSS's improvement possibilities to the needs of other units and identifying and resolving issues of coordinating services and improvement activities

6. Supporting and coordinating capital and new program requests with clinical units and other CSSs
7. Maintaining the succession plan for the CSS
8. Arranging the resolution of interprofessional and intraprofessional work requirements
9. Maintaining the agenda for contract renewal or restructuring of the relationship between the CSS and the HCO

The agenda for contract renewal recognizes that there are alternative opportunities to provide many CSSs. Even fully employed CSSs should be reviewed periodically, and contractual relationships should have explicit revision or renewal dates. The HCO manager should monitor both the array of alternatives and the improvement opportunities offered. Although the normal expectation is to continue the relationship, the HCO's stakeholders are entitled to the best available arrangement. Review of alternatives may lead to a new supplier for the CSS; more commonly it identifies OFIs that can and should be addressed under the existing relationship.

Organization

The organization shown in Exhibit 8.5 is built around CSS teams of professional and nonprofessional associates focused by location or function. As the exhibit shows, each CSS team has multiple accountability—to its patients, its customers, and the HCO. Both CSS and service line associates have operational goals. Frequent and open interchange occurs among the CSS team, the patient, and the physician and also between the CSS managers and the service line managers. HCO managers and senior management are accountable for both goal sets. They work to achieve the goals and improvements by responsive listening, monitoring performance, and using PITs to address all issues of integration and coordination.

CSSs vary widely in size and activity. Most CSSs, large and small, provide care in both outpatient and inpatient settings. The smallest have only one or two professionals. In some situations, the CSS may be a single person or a single team. The larger ones, such as the clinical laboratory, imaging, and pharmacy, can have more than 100 associates working in several sites and at several subspecialties and a dozen or more teams. In contract situations, horizontal integration may provide the CSS contractor with a competitive advantage, the ability to meet a superior set of operational goals.

HCO–CSS Relationships

Most small CSSs are employed by the HCO. The larger CSSs with physician leadership often form medical groups and contract with the HCO. At present, horizontally integrated CSS companies are limited. Several moderate-sized companies provide imaging and pathology services. At least one provides extensive pharmacy support. Contracts generally identify the scope of services

EXHIBIT 8.5
Core
Organization
of the CSS

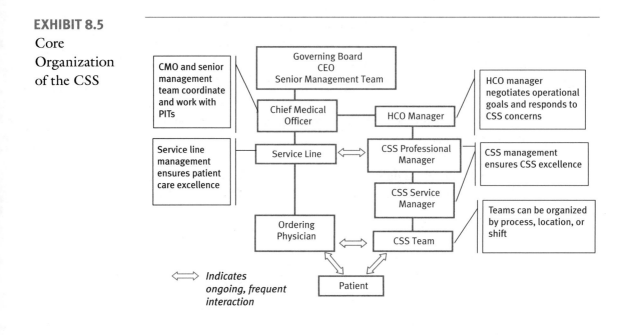

CMO: chief medical officer; CSS: clinical support service; PIT: process improvement team

to be offered, whether those services are exclusive, commitments for space and equipment, and the management of patient-related information. In addition, they should address the operational scorecard measures to be used, the sources of benchmarks, the goal-setting process, the duties for education and continuous improvement, and the incentive arrangements.

Measures

Exhibit 8.6 summarizes the measures for each of the six operational dimensions: demand, cost, human resources, productivity, quality, and customer satisfaction. With rare exceptions, these measures are appropriate for any CSS. Many of the measures are retrievable from ongoing data collection efforts, such as patient and associate surveys, accounting, and electronic medical records. Very small CSSs have sample size problems. Monthly reporting may not be appropriate. Qualitative data—impressions, examples, and evidence from competitors or best practices—assume greater importance. Even the smallest CSS should have measures, benchmarks, OFIs, and annual improvement goals.

Large, complex CSSs have a substantial measurement set, befitting their status as multimillion dollar enterprises. The HCO manager's focus should be on the aggregate performance, which should be routinely compared with benchmark and competitor values. CSS managers normally operate an internal performance improvement program, and they are rewarded financially for

Dimension	Measures	Applications
Demand	Requests for service	Used to forecast staff and other resource needs Specified by time, location, kind of service, and urgency of demand
	Market share	Used to track competitive success Specify by competitor and service, if available
Costs	Fixed/variable, direct and indirect costs Physical units of resources Age and repair records of equipment	Used to analyze and improve work processes Resource use is specified by time, location, and kind of service Equipment records trigger maintenance and replacement
Human resources	Retention, absenteeism, injuries, satisfaction, recruitment, and training statistics	Used to ensure "a great place to give care" Specified by worker
Output and productivity	Units of demand met and not met Cost per unit of output Physical units consumed per unit of output	Used to identify service failures Used to benchmark efficiency Specified by time, location, and kind of service
Quality	Process compliance scores Unexpected event counts	Used to ensure compliance with functional protocols Specified by time, location, and kind of service Unexpected events are investigated 100 percent
Patient satisfaction	Overall satisfaction and specifics of service	Used to ensure favorable patient reaction Specified by time, location, and kind of service
Physician satisfaction	Overall satisfaction and specifics of service	Used to ensure favorable referring physician satisfaction Physician, patient group categories

EXHIBIT 8.6
Performance Measures for the CSS

their success. Part of the HCO's support can include educational programs, PITs to address problems of coordination, and the knowledge management system.

Demand and output measures are increasingly available from electronic order systems and patient records. Cost accounting is supported by the transaction accounting system, which is described in Chapter 13. Equipment records are useful for major items; they typically record uses, load factors (time operated divided by time available), service times, and failures. These records are useful in managing maintenance and determining replacement.

Patient, physician, and associate satisfaction data are determined from HCO-wide surveys. Care must be taken to avoid incorrect inferences from small samples. Internal consulting provides statistical analysis (see Chapter 14).

Patient outcomes quality measures are important but limited. Most CSSs contribute to outcomes successes but cannot be accountable for them because too many other activities are required. For the patient to thrive, all the care activities must be correct. CSS outcomes failures can often be tracked and systematically reduced. Anesthesia, for example, contributes to all successful surgeries but cannot make the surgery a success. It can cause fatalities. Over decades, the anesthesiology profession has studied its failures, improved its processes, and reduced its mortality by several orders of magnitude. In 2005, the national mortality rate was 8.2 per million surgical discharges, one of the lowest among adverse medical events.[8]

Most CSS quality measures are intermediate outcome or process compliance measures. In intermediate outcomes, follow-up inspection or a similar assessment reveals that the CSS activity was or was not correctly performed and yielded the right information for further treatment. In process compliance, the inspection shows that the functional protocol was or was not followed. The two approaches provide in-depth understanding that identifies OFIs and facilitates their correction. Pathology laboratories have pursued these measures successfully, allowing them to ensure the accuracy of their diagnostic reports. The College of American Pathologists maintains libraries of measures, values, and education programs[9] and insists on statistically controlled intermediate outcomes for accreditation.[10]

Managerial Issues

Clinical excellence depends on the caregiving team of physicians, nurses, and their associates and on the information and treatment provided by the CSS. The several dozen CSSs reflect the breadth of patient need. An HCO with an excellence in care mission must ensure that each of these services is effectively delivered. Its senior management team does that by systematically pursuing eight questions:

1. Do we offer the service, or do we refer patients who need it?
2. How big should our service be?
3. What are the standards of performance our service must meet?
4. What is the form of affiliation that best meets our needs?
5. Does the CSS have the coordination it needs?

6. Are CSS activities correctly assigned to professional and nonprofessional associates?
7. What are the continuous improvement goals the affiliates should meet?
8. What are the longer term trends and implications for our affiliates?

These questions view the CSS as a semiautonomous unit. They extend the concepts of evidence-based management and transformational management to support an array of relationships from wholly owned to strategic partnership with the CSS.

Should the HCO Offer the Service?

An HCO is unlikely to offer every possible CSS. Most identify an economically feasible service constellation and then arrange for those CSSs normally required by that constellation. "Normally required" can be assessed by the expected demand inferred from the epidemiologic planning model, the minimum operating sizes of successful CSS examples, and the experience of others that operate a similar constellation. The level where a formal affiliation is preferable is a function of the cost of operating a CSS at acceptable quality and patient satisfaction levels. In general, an HCO would affiliate rather than refer when a CSS meets quality and satisfaction standards and offers an affordable price. The question can be asked at the service line level and aggregated to a larger HCO.

For example, the demand for social services can be assessed by service line—women's services, cardiovascular care, stroke and neurological care, for example—and evaluated both by service line (specialized social service units might be feasible and desirable in high-volume services) and in total. The major possible solutions for services not offered by the HCO are as follows:

- *Not offered.* Patients who need the service are referred elsewhere by their attending physician or seek it on their own.
- *Recommended provider.* The HCO recommends a CSS provider based on evidence of its capability and service.

The choice between the two is a marketing decision. The HCO gives a recommendation when the choice improves overall patient relations.

How Big Should the CSS Be?

The forecast of CSS demand from the epidemiologic planning model indicates the necessary size of the CSS. That forecast must be monitored annually. Shifts in technology, health insurance coverage, and population demographics change the forecast. It is quite possible that a given CSS must be expanded, repositioned, downsized, or closed. The HCO's commitment to excellence in care mandates that it, not the CSS, determines the size and affiliation.

What Are the Standards of Performance?

The standards of performance are determined by benchmarks and minimums for the operational performance measures, particularly those for quality, customer satisfaction, and associate satisfaction. Many CSSs have accreditation standards, either within The Joint Commission standards or through an independent organization. These are minimum standards that should, in general, be fully met. While exceptions may be appropriate, they should receive detailed review and in most cases a plan for correction. (Some accreditation standards may be for the benefit of the service provider, rather than the patient. The clearest challenge to these standards is convincing evidence that patient safety and satisfaction can be met without them.)

Benchmark remains the goal for CSSs, as for all activities. A multiyear plan to reach benchmark may be appropriate. Continued operation below benchmark raises a serious question: If an alternative service is available at benchmark, why should that service be denied the HCO's customer and physician stakeholders? In other words, if this CSS cannot make benchmark, but another one is available that can, is the HCO obligated to transfer to the successful supplier? The ethical principles of beneficence and nonmaleficence suggest a strong obligation. The ethical principle of justice suggests the current supplier deserves a chance to correct the situation. Among other considerations, changing suppliers has a cost in itself, and abruptly terminating a relationship may cause other associates to question the HCO's trustworthiness, eroding a critical component of the transformational culture. (At least one analyst places patient concerns uppermost. Rejecting the more common framework of autonomy, beneficence, nonmaleficence and justice,[11] Davenport substitutes "fidelity" for justice and insists that every patient's right must prevail over associate concerns.[12])

What Form of Affiliation Best Meets the HCO's Needs?

The major possibilities for formal CSS affiliation are described under the contractual relationship section of the operations planning and management function. The best possibility is the one that offers long-term performance closest to benchmark. The criteria are easy to identify but difficult to meet. The preferred solution is probably ownership; the HCO has ultimate control of employment, privileging, capital, protocol selection, training, location, and operating performance measures. Alternatives might be selected to facilitate associate incentives, to reduce capital costs, or to take advantage of skills developed through horizontal integration.

A small number of commercial companies have offered CSS management services. Unlike the record in environmental services, where outsourcing is the rule (see Chapter 12), it appears that few have captured substantial market share. Successful models include pharmacy services, some imaging services, and long-term acute care.

Does the CSS Have the Coordination It Needs?

CSSs are, by definition, *part* of excellent care. Integrating their services into an excellent whole is sometimes a challenge. Patients' needs and various CSSs interact. Certain drugs affect laboratory values; certain procedures require fasting; patient allergies and sensitivities require procedure modification. Changes in a patient management protocol must be incorporated into CSS procedures. CSS performance can be improved with access to parts of the patient record. An affiliation agreement may call for services, such as training, information exchange, and environmental services from the HCO. Failures in meeting these needs impair the CSS's ability to meet its goals and can be catastrophic.

The management role is clear under the ownership model. The HCO manager is expected to round frequently, be available for issues that arise, and provide a constructive response to all requests. The CSS can expect to be invited to any medical committee that is designing a patient management protocol and to any PIT that is addressing an issue of concern. It can rely on its HCO manager to understand and represent its interests. A similar role is appropriate under other affiliation arrangements. These integrating and coordinating activities are essential for the CSS to achieve its goals and thus must be completed regardless of structure.

CSS associates work side by side with other HCO associates. The HCO's culture of empowerment should extend to the CSS associates. If it does not, it may be a source of tension. Thus, part of an affiliated CSS's operating scorecard is its associate satisfaction. The HCO manager should be alert and responsive to potential tensions. CSS managers should be trained in supervision, provided with coaches, and included in multi-rater or 360-degree evaluations to assist them in implementing a transformational culture.

Are CSS Activities Correctly Assigned to Professional and Nonprofessional Associates?

Medical technology tends to begin with specialized professionals; as it ages, it moves to less specialized and nonprofessional caregivers. (Stethoscopes and sphygmomanometers were once the closely guarded tools of physicians, for example.) The transition to broader use is not always smooth, and the payment structure, which sometimes explicitly rewards the use of a specific CSS, complicates the transition. The criteria for the level of skill and training necessary to provide a given test or treatment are straightforward: It should normally be assigned to the lowest-cost associate who is capable of maintaining quality and patient satisfaction standards, and it should be available to all others who can maintain the standard.

Applying the criteria is sometimes challenging. Imaging, anesthesia, and cardiology testing have provided important examples. Should the treating specialists be allowed to read images in their specialty, or must they be validated by a radiologist? With new forms of anesthesia such as conscious sedation, must an anesthesiologist be present? Can a nurse interpret an EKG (electrocardiogram)? Must an echocardiogram (a form of ultrasound imaging) be validated by a radiologist? Definitive studies are rare.[13] Standards of practice, a less rigorous level of evidence, are acceptable. If orthopedists and cardiologists elsewhere are privileged to act on their own interpretation of images, they should be allowed to do that in our HCO. Transfers to non-professionals must be interpreted with care. If a technician can prepare an echocardiogram at the Johns Hopkins Hospital, the task can be assigned to technicians at other HCOs if they are trained and monitored as the Hopkins technician is trained and monitored.

The process to resolve these issues should be assigned to medical staff protocol committees and PITs that can assemble evidence and recommend the safe but cost-effective solution. The committees and PITs must be guided to work from evidence rather than authority. Often, the solution is to permit lower skilled associates to proceed in uncomplicated cases, review the evidence emerging, and broaden their assignment as their record of success grows.

What Are the Continuous Improvement Goals?

One of the contributions of continuous improvement is its ability adjust to changing conditions over time, avoiding a major disruption caused by falling behind the rest of the world. Negotiating annual goals ties each unit to the larger economy and supports a review of the relation of the unit to its environment, including technology, regulation, customers, competitors, and associates. Problems that could become disabling can be identified and corrected well before catastrophe. The annual strategic goals, benchmarks, and deliberate review of best practices and competitor practices stimulate and sustain this process. As a result, the HCO keeps control of CSS activities. It has assurance that the CSS is operating in the best interests of the HCO stakeholders. Even where a CSS operates almost autonomously, the HCO manager maintains comparative performance data, and the contract calls for negotiated goals. Knowing that contract renewal is likely but not automatic makes negotiation realistic.

What Are the Long-Term Trends?

Similarly, the HCO is in control of much of the potential demand for any CSS and is charged with identifying long-term trends. It has the obligation to pursue promptly the implications of these trends. Most problems are easier to solve with advance warning; surprises in the business world are rarely good news.

Many of the most valuable goals require collaboration among several CSSs and service lines. The OFIs are likely to appear in the annual strategic review process or in the deliberations of the PIC, where multiple perspectives can be integrated and overall performance benchmarked. Identifying and pursuing these goals is an important part of the jobs of senior management and the HCO manager. Pursuit usually means extensive discussion with the units likely to be involved, seeking the most effective, least disruptive path to change. In some cases, it can mean extensive revision or termination of relationships with a CSS. The rule for managing those events returns to the ethical balance between rights of patients and rights of associates. Patients must come first, but contractual rights should be upheld. Thus, any contract needs termination clauses, and they set the stage for effective negotiation. Termination should be rare; negotiation should be continual.

Suggested Readings

Brunt, B. A. 2008. *Evidence-Based Competency Management for the Operating Room*, 2nd ed. Marblehead, MA: HCPro, Inc.

Hester, D. M. (ed.). 2008. *Ethics by Committee: A Textbook on Consultation, Organization, and Education for Hospital Ethics Committees*. New York: Rowman & Littlefield Publishers, Inc.

Papp, J. 2010. *Quality Management in the Imaging Sciences*, 4th ed. St. Louis, MO: Mosby.

Reynolds, F. 2005. *Communication and Clinical Effectiveness in Rehabilitation*. Edinburgh, Scotland: Elsevier.

Notes

1. Cerner Corporation. 2009. [Online information; retrieved 7/26/09.] www.cerner.com/public/Cerner_3.asp?id=133.
2. Castaneda-Mendez, K., and L. Bernstein. 1997. "Linking Costs and Quality Improvement to Clinical Outcomes Through Added Value." *Journal for Healthcare Quality* 19 (2): 11–16.
3. Arnold, D., A. Girling, A. Stevens, and R. Lilford. 2009. "Comparison of Direct and Indirect Methods of Estimating Health State Utilities for Resource Allocation: Review and Empirical Analysis." *British Medical Journal* 339 (7717): 385–88.
4. American Association of Colleges of Pharmacy. 2009. [Online information; retrieved 7/26/09.] www.aacp.org/about/Pages/StragegicPlan.aspx.
5. American Physical Therapy Association. 2009. [Online information; retrieved 7/27/09.] www.apta.org.
6. American Occupational Therapy Association. 2009. [Online information; retrieved 7/27/09.] www.aota.org/Students/Prospective/FAQs/FAQDegrees.aspx.
7. American Association of Nurse Anesthetists. 2007. "AANA Announces Support of Doctorate for Entry Into Nurse Anesthesia Practice by 2025." [Online information; retrieved 7/27/09.] www.aana.com/news.aspx?ucNavMenu_TSMenuTargetID=171&ucNavMenu_TSMenuTargetType=4&ucNavMenu_TSMenuID=6&id=9678.
8. Li, G., M. Warner, B. H. Lang, L. Huang, and L. S. Sun. 2009. "Epidemiology of Anesthesia-Related Mortality in the United States, 1999–2005." *Anesthesiology* 110 (4): 759–65.
9. College of American Pathologists. [Online information; retrieved 10/15/09.] www.cap.org/apps/cap.portal?_nfpb=true&_pageLabel=home.

10. College of American Pathologists, Commission on Laboratory Accreditation. "Laboratory Accreditation Program Sample Checklist." [Online information; retrieved 10/15/09.] www.cap.org/apps/docs/laboratory_accreditation/sample_checklist.pdf.

11. Beauchamp, T. L., and J. F. Childress. 1983. *Principles of Biomedical Ethics.* New York: Oxford University Press.

12. Davenport, J. 1997. "Ethical Principles in Clinical Practice." *Permanente Journal* 1 (1). [Online information; retrieved 10/15/09.] http://xnet.kp.org/permanentejournal/sum97pj/principles.html.

13. Schilling, D., A. Rosenbaum, S. Schweizer, H. Richter, and B. Rumstadt. 2009. "Sedation with Propofol for Interventional Endoscopy by Trained Nurses in High-Risk Octogenarians: A Prospective, Randomized, Controlled Study." *Endoscopy* 41 (4): 295–98.

9 BEYOND ACUTE CARE TO COMMUNITY HEALTH

In a Few Words

Community health focuses on sustaining the health and productivity of all citizens. It includes extensive prevention, chronic disease management, all forms of acute and rehabilitative care, continuing care, and palliative care. High-performing healthcare organizations (HCOs) may pursue community health or a narrower mission of excellence in a specific kind of healthcare such as acute hospital care. Community health has many advocates who feel that it is consistent with a not-for-profit structure and long-term healthcare cost control, but current HCO reimbursement does not reward a community health mission. HCOs that pursue it use their management skills to

1. analyze the full array of community health needs, forecasting demand for service, identifying current provider and stakeholder positions, developing opportunities for improvement (OFIs) for all levels of care, and advocating a communitywide response;

2. establish a strategy to address specific needs through direct action, partnerships, or a broad-based community health advocacy group; and

3. operationalize the strategy using the evidence-based and transformational management approaches, with particular attention to supporting a collaborative community approach.

Community health strategies use a unique set of strategic performance measures that emphasize population health and per capita healthcare cost. HCO senior managers must understand and teach concepts of both community health and evidence-based management. They often assist directly in governance roles for affiliated community health services and agencies.

Critical Issues in Community Health Management

- Aligning the mission, vision, and values, and understanding the commitment to community health

- Using effective acute care as a platform for community health

- Assessing the health needs of the community

- Building effective coalitions with other agencies

- Understanding the financial implications of community health

- Improving primary care

Consider these questions as you read the chapter.

1. What are the important differences between a "community health" mission and an "excellence in acute care" mission for a hospital HCO? What would go on a checklist of prerequisites before adopting a community health mission?

2. Your HCO, like many, assists some community groups with health goals rather than support a community coalition with broad goals, such as those shown in exhibits 9.3 and 9.4. What arguments would you prepare to address the governing board:
   a. To support developing a community coalition?
   b. To support continuing the current policy instead of developing a community coalition?

3. The local library holds a monthly town hall meeting attended by more than 100 citizens, recorded for the Web, and covered in several local news media. You are asked to present a program that advocates for improved community health. What would you emphasize?

4. The president of the local not-for-profit hospice wants to have lunch. She is concerned that your hospital HCO is not referring as many patients as it should. Should you invite her to lunch? If so, what should you do to prepare? Whether you meet her or not, what should be in the HCO's next boundary spanning report?

5. Your HCO has purchased a number of primary care practices and developed contractual affiliations with several physician groups so that it now operates a primary care service line. Several of the physician leaders approach you, saying that they would like to move toward implementing the patient-centered medical home concept. Make a checklist of questions you need to think about before you respond.

Community health focuses on sustaining all members at their highest possible level of functioning, for their individual happiness and for the collective benefit. Broadly, community health involves education, jobs, safety, environment, and healthcare.[1] The ideal state, for both the community and individual, is good health and full functioning. The concept shown in Exhibit 9.1 focuses on personal services that support community health, a subset of the full definition. It is still substantially broader than the array of services that most HCOs offer.

Community health

A focus on sustaining all members of a community at their highest possible level of functioning for their individual happiness and their collective benefit

Lower levels of Exhibit 9.1 represent increasingly serious departure from health, where contribution to the community, earning potential, and personal satisfaction decrease and expenditures for healthcare increase. Prevention is superior to treatment, and when illness occurs, the fastest and most complete return to health is the best path. Immunization, exercise, and control of environmental toxins can prevent much serious disease, at much lower cost. Effective primary care prevents many diseases from becoming more serious. Managing chronic illnesses like hypertension, diabetes, bipolar disorder,[2] and lung disease effectively allows many to work and have an active life. Acute care and rehabilitation are critical for some people, but prior prevention and chronic disease management should reduce the need for these expensive services. The last two stages—continuing care and death—are reached by only a few people each year. They are irreversible, but they can be deferred and shortened by focus on more effective management at the earlier stages. Acceptance of death's inevitability can avoid expensive, futile efforts to prolong life.

In broad perspective, the concept of community health has solid empirical support. Substantial income gains arose historically from improving health, first by increase in the food supply and the conquest of infectious disease, particularly through water purification,[3] and later by immunization and improved acute care.[4] Other advanced countries maintain superior health with substantially less expenditure on acute care.[5] In detail, however, moving from the current U.S. system to the ideal is challenging. Prevailing attitudes, organization structures, financing, and employment all must change. Inherent conflicts of interest exist: If I am a cancer treatment specialist, prevention of cancer may reduce my future income. For an HCO, strong programs of community health mean less hospital revenue, starting in places like oncology, cardiovascular care, and the neonatal intensive care unit (NICU). The conflicting missions can be summarized as *community health* versus *excellence in care*. The former explicitly accepts the assumptions in Exhibit 9.1 and the goal of a healthy community. The latter assumes that the HCO's role is limited to the provision of selected parts of the care spectrum, usually those associated with acute treatment and rehabilitation. Examples of both appear in current mission statements of high-performing HCOs (see Exhibit 1.7).

EXHIBIT 9.1
Conceptual
Model of
Personal
Services for
Community
Health

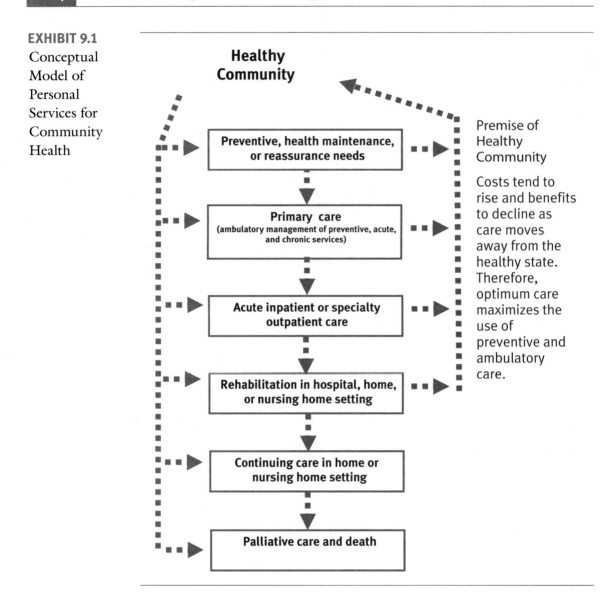

Healthy Community

Preventive, health maintenance, or reassurance needs

Primary care
(ambulatory management of preventive, acute, and chronic services)

Acute inpatient or specialty outpatient care

Rehabilitation in hospital, home, or nursing home setting

Continuing care in home or nursing home setting

Palliative care and death

Premise of Healthy Community

Costs tend to rise and benefits to decline as care moves away from the healthy state. Therefore, optimum care maximizes the use of preventive and ambulatory care.

The national history has not supported the elements of Exhibit 9.1 equally.[6,7] Three interrelated issues have shaped a system that emphasizes acute care, often at the expense of more cost-effective alternatives:

1. *Availability of healthcare financing.* Healthcare reform legislation focuses on acute and chronic care. Hospitalization, the initial focus of health insurance, is still the most widely available and most generously funded.[8] Ambulatory, rehabilitation, hospice, and home care coverage have become more prevalent in the preceding two decades, but payment levels tend to be low and numerous restrictions are in place. In continuing care, Medicaid remains the substantial payer, subject to severe funding problems and restricted to low-income families. Private continuing care insurance, although available, is not widely used.

Many of the patients most in need of the expanded services in Exhibit 9.1 are uninsured. Chronic disease is more prevalent among people with lower income, increasing the chances that those with need will be unable to finance care.

2. *Provider compensation.* The way insurance pays for care and the amount offered affect the income of provider organizations. Hospitals and physicians are compensated separately and are paid on the basis of treatments given rather than health achieved. Payment per treatment creates a dysfunctional reward for additional treatment. It does not reward efforts to sustain the patient's health, and it rewards prolonged, repetitive, and unnecessary care.[9] Primary care and chronic disease management are rewarded at much lower prices than specialty care, to the point where chronic disease management is only about 60 percent effective[10,11] and a serious shortage of primary caregivers has emerged.[12] Public health departments, which might address preventive and health maintenance needs, have been chronically underfunded.[13] Continuing and palliative care has also been less generously funded than acute care.

3. *Organizational responses.* The result of the financing and compensation structure is a vast array of largely unconnected provider organizations. In most communities, doctors' offices, home care programs, and hospices tend to be small, private, for-profit corporations with missions that address single levels of Exhibit 9.1. The nursing homes not affiliated with hospitals are usually owned by multibillion dollar, national, for-profit corporations or small, local, for-profit corporations, but both struggle to provide effective care at available levels of funding.[14] The median size of the 3,000 U.S. hospices was 150 admissions per year in 2007. About half are for-profit.[15] Not-for-profit hospitals pursue their traditional focus on a relatively broad spectrum of acute care, but for-profit specialty hospitals now pursue organ- and disease-specific care. These missions cannot easily be revised. They are understood and accepted by their stakeholders and recognized in law, regulation, and health insurance contracts.

Many healthcare experts feel that the imbalances of the current U.S. system fail to promote community health.[16,17] The critics believe that more attention to health promotion, prevention, and chronic disease management will result in a healthier population with lower healthcare expenditures per capita and a higher earning capacity.[18,19,20]

When an HCO adopts a community health mission, it commits itself to address the imbalances and deal with the structural problems of financing, payment, and existing organizations. This chapter addresses how an HCO can be effective in pursuing a community health mission. The traditional acute care services remain the HCO's core contribution to community health. Achieving high performance in them is an essential part of an expanded mission. Going beyond excellence in acute care to optimize the model in Exhibit 9.1 involves a substantial change in the HCO's role, but it represents a direction that will become increasingly important in the twenty-first century. Among other advantages, resources contributed to community health are included in the IRS Form 990 Schedule H Community Benefit Calculations.[21] In the future, more and more excellent HCOs will adopt the community health mission because doing so creates better communities.

Purpose

The purpose of a community health mission is

to use the HCO as a vehicle to improve community health.

Community health success is ultimately measured by population-based indicators such as immunization rates, rates of preventable disease and premature death, and measures of life expectancy adjusted for ability to lead a normal life.[22] Efforts to implement the community health mission must deal with existing financing and specialized providers. Ideally, they should also address the broader concerns of community income and environment, which are beyond Exhibit 9.1. As a result, many practical solutions are built around collaborations, acquisitions, joint ventures, and other complex corporate and ownership strategies. It is not uncommon for an HCO to adopt part but not all of a community health mission. The expansion of HCOs into the provision of primary care practices is an example. Similarly, many HCOs have added rehabilitation, continuing care, and palliative care services.

Functions

The functions required to implement a community health mission are shown in Exhibit 9.2. They are framed in a way that allows a traditional HCO to move stepwise into community health, expanding via individual services and levels, or by developing a comprehensive response. The functions are applicable to *each* of the levels in Exhibit 9.1 as well as to *all* of those levels. The needs assessment function—understanding and promoting community health—is a contribution to the HCO's strategic planning in itself. Pursued for all levels, it provides a breadth of perspective that protects acute care services from unexpected difficulties. It also identifies an agenda of response opportunities. The remaining functions—identifying, implementing, and improving response strategies—can be applied to single-purpose activities or to a comprehensive community health program.

Understanding and Promoting Community Health

This function is a focused expansion of the HCO's general boundary spanning and forecasting, which measures community need for each component of service. The function (1) provides quantitative forecasts for specific services at each level of Exhibit 9.1, (2) identifies the provider and customer stake-holders who currently provide the service, and (3) provides information on opportunities that can be used to identify and prioritize program revisions.

EXHIBIT 9.2
Functions That
Implement a
Community
Health Mission

Function	Examples
Understanding and promoting community health Forecasting need and demand Identifying intervention opportunities Identifying stakeholder positions Advocating for and promoting health behavior	Working with health department and others to identify important local health issues Forecasting the demand and supply for specific services, such as nursing home care Meeting with community groups to discuss needs and roles Promoting smoking cessation, exercise programs, and reproductive health
Establishing a community health strategy Community advocacy group Mission Performance measures Financing Market, competitive, and collaborative opportunities	Building stakeholder consensus around implications of expanded mission Developing expected outcomes, financial forecasts, and revised physician need forecasts Analyzing alternative ownerships and business models
Operationalizing a community health strategy Service operations: patient recruitment, care planning, staffing, training, budget and finance, continuous improvement Building an integrated network: collaboration with existing units; promotion of community health opportunities	Implementing a strategic measures set and a business plan for a specific service, such as a hospice or a home care program Publicizing community health measures, benchmarks, and best practices Promoting consensus around realistic community health goals
Improving performance Identifying community health OFIs Developing collaborative approaches Building local understanding and contribution Strengthening public commitment	Conducting ongoing review of community health performance Promoting achievements of advocacy group Celebrating goals attained Lobbying for changes in regulation and reimbursement

OFI: Opportunity for improvement

Needs assessment
A process for identifying and quantifying opportunities
for improvement

The three components collectively create a **needs assessment**. The needs assessment is best done comprehensively because the need for specific services is interrelated. Focus on a single level of Exhibit 9.1 can be seriously misleading. For example, the demand for hospital care is interrelated with primary care, home care, and hospice care. Once developed, the needs assessment identifies opportunities in community health in sufficient detail to plan specific responses. It also serves as the foundation for a program to educate stakeholders and promote interest in improvement.

Forecasting Need and Demand

Community health services, like all healthcare services, should be sized to meet expected demand and designed to respond to stakeholder desires, using the epidemiologic planning model introduced in Chapter 2 and the marketing approach and techniques described in Chapter 15. The model can be used to forecast incidence, prevalence, and demand for all the services in Exhibit 9.1. Incidence and prevalence are closely related in acute care, but they are different in chronic care. The prevalence of a disease or condition is an important indicator of need, but it is rarely the same as the demand for services because care can be approached in alternate ways and is influenced by availability of service and the patient's financial resources. All three measures can be benchmarked. There is wide variation across the United States in the incidence and prevalence of disease and in the cost of care.

The model forecasts these measures for a wide variety of diseases and conditions that can be prevented, ameliorated, or managed by community health programs, including many mental illnesses. It can also be used to forecast numbers and characteristics of disease-free people by preventable risk factors, such as obesity or child safety. The full array of community health services is surprisingly large and diverse. Prevention and health maintenance services are available for many different population subgroups. The Centers for Disease Control and Prevention (CDC) Task Force on Community Preventive Services has identified 17 major prevention and health maintenance topics and has listed and evaluated more than 200 interventions.[23]

Specific risks or conditions can be grouped in various ways to facilitate planning decisions. Exhibit 9.3 shows groupings according to the level of prevention, the populations served, and the programs or organizations that provide service. These groupings are important in designing responses.

1. The level of prevention is often key to the cost effectiveness of a specific action and an important factor in prioritizing opportunities. Primary prevention is usually the most cost effective, not only because the interventions (primarily vaccines and behavioral education) are relatively low cost but also because the diseases prevented are often high cost and life-curtailing. Secondary prevention is more problematic. Screening for existing disease has been a popular hospital activity, but its cost effectiveness depends on keeping the cost per case screened

Prevention Level	Examples of Risks	Examples of Prevention Activity
Primary: Maintenance of health	Obesity, smoking, and substance abuse Community control of environmental hazards	Dietary and exercise management "Child proofing" Smoking cessation Lead and asbestos removal Alcohol use laws
Primary: Prevention of specific disease	Infectious diseases Trauma Prematurity and birth defects Ischemic heart disease Stroke	Immunization, infection control Seat belts, helmets, alcohol management, domestic violence Prenatal care Aspirin, anticoagulants
Secondary: Early-stage identification and elimination of disease	Cancer Diabetes Cardiovascular disease Developmental defects	Screening and early treatment Screening and dietary management Drug and lifestyle management Remedial childcare
Tertiary: Reduction of the impact of chronic disease	Post-acute cardiovascular or stroke care, arthritis, trauma	Drug and lifestyle management Rehabilitation Home care and telemedicine

Population at Risk	Examples of Risks	Examples of Prevention Activity
High school students	Safe driving, health maintenance, substance abuse, sexual and reproductive activity	Classroom education, driver training, alcohol law enforcement, counseling services
Young families	Family planning, child safety, domestic abuse, health maintenance, disease screening	Maternal and reproductive health services, counseling, exercise programs, Well-Baby services
Elderly	Functional losses, chronic diseases, terminal illness	Home safety, rehabilitation programs, disease management, palliative care

Service Program	Examples of Risks	Examples of Prevention Site
Primary care	Acute disease, chronic disease, early detection, maternal and child health management	Primary care offices, industrial clinics, school clinics, retail stores
Post-acute recovery	Postoperative rehabilitation	Hospital, rehabilitation center, nursing home
Continuing care	Diminished functional status, terminal illness	Home care program, nursing home, hospice

EXHIBIT 9.3 Grouping of Disease and Prevention Forecasts, by Prevention Level, Population at Risk, and Service Program

low. All positive results must be pursued, but many of these are false, wasting expensive resources. The key to cost effectiveness usually lies in targeting high-risk groups, where false positives are less frequent.[24] Tertiary prevention must focus on a specific disease group, but it can be cost effective when the risks of death and disability are high.[25]

2. The population served is useful in program design—programs can be tailored by age and interest group and promoted through appropriate vehicles, as in high school–based programs for adolescents and primary care office programs for chronic disease populations or women in child-bearing years. The ability to focus both the marketing and care delivery is a major factor in program design. Advertising and care delivered to people who do not need it are a waste.

3. The service program, or kind of intervention, is useful in identifying existing sources of care and potential collaborators. Existing provider organizations can contribute important specialized knowledge and market contacts. Both are useful, making collaboration the strategy of choice in designing responses.

In addition to their role in planning interventions, quantitative forecasts are used to set goals and evaluate results. Success of many primary prevention programs is measured by reduction in incidence. Incidences of early and late detection are used to evaluate secondary prevention. Prevalence of patients by functional status is used to evaluate tertiary prevention. The forecasts are also useful in promoting community awareness and understanding. The Center for Health Care Strategies, a group dedicated to improving health of chronically ill and otherwise disadvantaged people, offers a Web-based return-on-investment model that allows comparison of alternative strategies.[26]

Identifying Intervention Opportunities

The second step in developing the needs assessment is to identify the current providers of various services. Few community health needs are totally ignored. Much more commonly, an existing organization offers some service. Preventive services are offered by HCOs, schools, public health departments, and faith organizations. Primary care is offered by schools, workplaces, retailers, and physicians' offices. Community clinics, many of which are Federally Qualified Health Centers, now serve nearly 20 million Americans. Most of the clinic's clientele are disadvantaged, or as the National Association of Community Health Centers (NACHC) puts it, "medically disenfranchised." The 1,200 NACHC clinics have documented improved quality and effectiveness of care.[27] Rehabilitation is offered through hospitals, rehabilitation centers, home care programs, and nursing homes. Continuing and palliative care is offered through home care, hospice, and nursing home programs. As the examples in Exhibit 9.3 suggest, these services vary greatly by ownership, audience, approach, and resources. They often vary as well in quality and effectiveness. Comparing current services to prevalence and demand identifies unmet needs and opportunities for improved service. The epidemiologic planning model, plus an inventory of current services, generates an OFI list that can be publicized, prioritized, and discussed by various stakeholders.

The inventory must go beyond a simple tally of available services. Deliberate efforts must be made to ensure that programs are meeting community demand and standards for quality, effectiveness, patient satisfaction, and efficiency. Special attention is often necessary for disadvantaged populations.

1. *Unmet demand can be identified from surveys of waiting times for service.* Oversupply can be identified from occupancy information and financial performance. Best practices from similar communities can be used to evaluate both, although a comprehensive approach is necessary. The best practice in many of these activities is neither the most nor the least demand, but it contributes most to a comprehensive measure like mortality or cost per capita.

2. *Safety and quality of patient care apply to all levels.* The Centers for Medicare & Medicaid Services (CMS) now offers quality assessment systems and data for nursing homes, home health agencies, hospitals, and kidney dialysis facilities.[28] Data are drawn from Medicare and Medicaid patients, but these are large proportions of the total patient load for these services. Hospitals expand the CMS data set with additional measures required by The Joint Commission. These values are not made public, but they can be released if the hospitals agree. Hospices are also accredited by The Joint Commission, although no set of specific measures is in place.[29] Various standards for primary prevention activity are available, and the CDC *Community Guide* links to them.[30] In those areas where measurement systems exist, the goal should be to make them public and use them for continuous improvement. In other areas, evidence of commitment to quality, such as maintenance of accreditation standards, should be recognized.

3. *Economy and efficiency are critical.* The nonacute programs in Exhibit 9.1 are generally underfunded. A Walmart business approach—careful program design, selective location, and continuous improvement of cost per case—is essential. This approach goes beyond efficiency. It continuously tests customer satisfaction against economy, seeking to eliminate all costs not essential to sustaining market share. It is substantially different from approaches to acute care, which has much richer financial support.

4. *Effectiveness criteria are also essential.* The community health concept is cost effective only if less costly levels of care substitute for higher cost interventions. Cost effectiveness has been limited principally because the services are provided to persons who did not need them. For example, a home care program can be used to avoid costly days of acute hospital use, but it can also be used to substitute for less costly self-care and family support.[31] To meet cost-effectiveness criteria, the program must encourage the former and strongly discourage the latter. This problem is universal in community care. Even primary prevention, usually the benchmark of cost effectiveness, can be ineffective if the cost of the intervention, including its adverse effects, exceeds the cost of care for the disease. The

vaccine for human papilloma virus has been challenged as not cost effective. The evidence suggests that it is effective only if limited to a carefully defined population.[32]

A substantial consensus on how to implement cost-effective programs is now available on many elements of community health. Prevention criteria are provided by the CDC *Community Guide*. The CDC's Task Force on Community Preventive Services categorizes more than 200 preventive interventions as "Recommended," "Insufficient Evidence," and "Not Recommended." The two categories of recommendation are further divided into "Strong Evidence" and "Sufficient Evidence."[33] The National Guideline Clearinghouse contains criteria for many of the remaining levels of Exhibit 9.1. Primary care guidelines are available for specific risks and age categories. Acute and rehabilitation criteria are offered by disease and condition. Disease-specific guidelines are also offered for home and end-of-life care.[34] The Clearinghouse does not include guidelines for continuing nursing home care, and the demand is known to be dependent on factors such as housing and family support as well as the effectiveness of preceding levels of healthcare. The CMS PACE program OASIS-B measures address issues of effectiveness of continuing care that can identify opportunities to manage continuing care.[35]

Identifying Stakeholder Positions

In most communities, both customer and provider stakeholders have highly focused needs. Many customer stakeholders are seeking a solution to a specific problem that afflicts them or their families. Employers are seeking healthier workers and lower health insurance costs. Many provider HCOs offer a limited service that contributes to a single level of Exhibit 9.1. Building collaboration between these groups is frequently the key to community health success. Collaboration creates three important opportunities. Partners can bring established contacts to important target markets. Partners can bring valuable knowledge and experience in specialized procedures. Partners can share resources for a larger total and more efficient scale of operations. The list of potential collaborators is long. In most communities it includes the following:

- *Government agencies in public health, welfare, education, environment, and justice.* These agencies are frequently in touch with high-risk and disadvantaged populations.
- *Employers.* Many have a financial stake in success through reduced insurance premiums.
- *Faith-based organizations.* These organizations are a source of volunteers and can be effective at marketing community health programs.
- *Civic and cultural organizations,* such as United Way, homeless shelters, and the YMCA.
- *Other HCOs,* including competitors in acute care and potential competitors in other levels of care, under both for-profit and not-for-profit organizations.

Extensive listening is the foundation of collaborative activity. High-performing HCOs pursue an ongoing listening and relationship-building strategy that serves as a foundation for collaborative community health. Their programs have several elements:

1. *Routine surveillance of public information and reports from interested groups and organizations.* Virtually all government information is public. Many nongovernmental organizations involved in health promotion maintain extensive public information in print and on the Web.
2. *Personal contacts* with leadership of important organizations.
3. *Monitoring of consumer interests* through focus groups and surveys.
4. *Creating or supporting communitywide groups sharing health goals.* These may be permanent and official (receiving recognition and financial support from established corporations or government agencies) or ad hoc at varying degrees of formality to address specific topics of interest. HCOs often subsidize these efforts with in-kind support, such as meeting space and computer linkage. They participate in funding recognized entities.
5. *Establishing and maintaining contractual relationships.* Hospitals have ongoing contractual relationships with primary care physicians, nursing homes, rehabilitation services, home care agencies, and hospices. The HCO's acute services are frequently essential to the success of these programs. These relationships can be the foundation for expanded and improved activities and can include substantial HCO capital and operating investment.
6. *Service on other boards and committees by HCO managers and trustees and recognition in HCO board membership or on planning committees and process improvement teams (PITs) with relevant charges.* HCO associates are often willing to volunteer similar services to other community health organizations.

Advocacy and Promotion

An HCO with a community health mission should join and encourage the voices promoting health, assisting in publicizing needs, promoting individual and collective response, and devising solutions. A communications plan for a community includes the following:[36]

1. Clear definitions of services and terminology
2. A summary of the needs assessment, available through the Web and promoted through a collaborative network, including local media
3. Efforts to reach specialized customer stakeholder interests segmented by age, gender, disease risk, and expressed interest:
   • Reports, factual summaries, and reference materials
   • Speaker bureaus and planned communication to customer stakeholder segments
   • Advertising and other promotion to increase customer awareness of individual services
4. Efforts to reach provider stakeholders with reliable information about demand, need, existing programs, and proposed programs

The sites that provide community health activities are all valuable avenues for communication. People who enter them often have specific needs and typically have a receptive bias toward community health concepts. The contact opens an opportunity to expand their understanding. Thus, the promotion strategy, like the implementation strategy, emphasizes collaboration.

The actions of HCOs are important reinforcement for community health concepts. High-performing HCOs do not allow smoking on site. Their emphasis on patient safety is extended to the safety of their associates and guests. They provide and promote cost-effective prevention for patients and families. They provide exercise opportunities, healthy meals, and counseling to their associates. They explicitly recognize patient autonomy, and they encourage the use of advance directives and designated patient advocates. They tailor their benefit programs to promote prevention and meet important health needs. SSM Health Care went beyond Exhibit 9.1 to eliminate bottled water:[37]

> . . . because of the environmental impact of making, transporting and disposing of the bottles. The effort supports the stance of the Franciscan Sisters of Mary, the congregation that sponsors SSM Health Care, to "respect, appreciate and live in harmony with creation and direct our actions to preserve the earth."
>
> . . . "This effort means that more than half a million bottles of water will be eliminated at SSM's facilities each year," says Sister Mary Jean Ryan, FSM, President and CEO of SSM Health Care. One of the biggest problems with bottled water is that it takes fossil fuels to produce the bottles, and then more fossil fuels are used to transport the bottles to their final destination. "Eliminating bottled water is a contribution we can make as a system to protect our fragile environment," says Sister Mary Jean.

Actions like these have both real and symbolic value.

Establishing a Community Health Strategy

As indicated in chapters 2 and 3, any activity of an HCO must have a leadership structure, an explicit purpose contributing to the larger mission, performance measures, financing, and a set of goals. If an HCO establishes a wholly owned patient care venture, these elements are implemented as in other wholly owned care. If it is a collaborative venture, the leadership structure provides a mechanism to monitor the relationship, establish future goals, and resolve difficulties. Strategies in community health are no exception, although they more commonly follow the collaborative approach. In targeted strategies, the elements are established in a two-party contract. These are also common in acute care—for example, in joint venture services lines. At the present time, most HCOs that address community health issues appear to focus on single-issue campaigns rather than a global approach.[38,39] HCOs in a variety of settings have moved to more comprehensive programs, using a variety of collaborative approaches.[40] Successful comprehensive community health strategies use a general community advocacy group to create a leadership structure.

Potential partners exist for most specific community health activities. One could envision a network of two-party contracts, but the list of potential collaborators is long, and effective solutions for many targets require several parties. A more general community-oriented group has three advantages:

Establishing a Community Advocacy Group

1. It brings customer stakeholders into the decisions directly.
2. It brings together provider stakeholders with overlapping interests.
3. It provides a mechanism to identify and prioritize needs across the spectrum of individual opportunities.

The more comprehensive ventures in community health begin early to develop an advocacy group broadly representative of the various interests. The group is designed to bring together diverse interests and viewpoints for the general benefit, building a network of civic engagement on community health. It usually begins with informal visits between individuals, expands to discussion sessions, and in many communities evolves to a formally appointed "commission" or "board" with a regular agenda and established relationships with major stakeholders. The initial discussions of stakeholder positions undertaken as part of the needs assessment provide the starting points. The needs assessment provides the focus.

Many communities already have advocacy groups. Several states have established programs to encourage such groups. The federally sponsored Healthy People Consortium has 350 national membership organizations and 250 state health, mental health, substance abuse, and environmental agencies.[41] Many of the members have local offices or representatives. The National Civic League provides publications, definitions of measures, and other resources to support the development of advocacy groups.[42] The Kansas University Work Group for Community Health and Development offers a multipart "Community Tool Box" of guides, measures, best practices, and examples that it claims is "the largest and most comprehensive resource of its kind in the world."[43]

Once formed, the advocacy group operates as a governing board would to build consensus on strategy. It assumes independent authority and elects its leadership.[44] It also facilitates contracts between various stakeholders to implement the strategy.[45] An HCO that provides high-quality acute care can add materially to an existing community group. Its role in acute care makes it central to many customer markets. New mothers, patients with chronic disease, patients recovering from acute care, and terminal patients are important examples. The HCO also has substantial resources—including strategic planning and needs assessment, facilities, and expertise—that can be contributed to a collective effort.

Exhibit 9.4 describes the goals of a comprehensive community health program (located in Kearney, Nebraska) with 15 years' history. Today, it boasts of "150 organizational stakeholders and over 1,000 volunteers."[46] The

EXHIBIT 9.4

Goals of a Comprehensive Community Health Program

The vision of the Buffalo County Community Partners is that everyone from all corners of Buffalo County work together to improve the quality of life of those who live in and work in this community

BCCP Goals	Description	Results			Target
		2000	*2003*	*2007*	
Youth Who Smoke Regularly	. . . The last ten year focus has been on reducing secondhand smoke. Today they celebrate the new clean indoor air act . . .	24.8%	15.1%	11%	12%
Youth Marijuana Use		14.2%	13.3%	10%	5%
Youth Binge Drinking	. . . county-wide strategic plan to reduce binge drinking, drinking and driving, and underage drinking.	38%	32.6%	23.2%	22.5%
Youth with Thoughts of Suicide	. . . strategy to increase mental health services in rural areas	15.3%	14%	14%	5%
Health and Spirituality	To increase awareness of spirituality's effect on health and healing		79%	86%	Increase
Reducing Obesity (Overweight Adults)	To reduce obesity and overweight by increasing positive health behaviors relative to active living and nutrition	54%	55%	62%	30%
Smoke Free	To increase the percent of smoke free restaurants and businesses to	100%	47%	77%	100%
Access to Health Care	To provide 100% access to health care for residents in Buffalo County	39%*		42.9%**	0%
Safety: Seat Belt Use	To increase seat belt use to 80% of Buffalo County youth actively using their seat belts	76%	79%	81%	80%
Fall Prevention in Older Adults	To reduce falls in older adults (60+ year olds admitted to Good Samaritan Hospital)		42/1,000	31/1,000	Decrease

continued

EXHIBIT 9.4
continued

BCCP Goals	Description	Results			Target
		2000	*2003*	*2007*	
Lead	To decrease the percent of children exposed to lead	6.2%*		5.2%	0%
Affordable Housing	To increase the number of affordable housing units				
Transportation	Expand affordable public transportation services		55,280***	90,440	
Infant Mortality	To reduce infant mortality and post neonatal infant mortality	8.1/1,000	4.6/1,000	2.8/1,000	4.5/1000

* Data for 1997
** Data for 2005
*** Data for 2001

SOURCE: Reprinted with permission from *2008 Report to the Community*. Buffalo County Community Partners, Kearney, NE.

program is notable for its quantitative measurement and deliberate goal setting. Its governing board of 25 people includes individuals from local public health, education, city government, business, and the faith community. Its goals are established by the board. Every goal has measures of achievement. Trends are posted regularly from a variety of sources. The 2010 goals are the second set. The website indicates that only half the 15 goals set in 1996 were fully achieved though some progress was made on almost all.[47,48] The 2010 goal set includes several from the earlier list, but the board has regrouped them into broader market-oriented categories.[49]

Establishing the Purpose of Collaboration

The intent of the collaboration is generally stated as a "purpose" in two-party relationships and as a "mission" in more comprehensive ones. The terminology helps illustrate the independence of the community advocacy group. The most effective groups are independent of the HCO or any other specific member. The purposes they adopt can go well beyond Exhibit 9.1 to more fundamental needs in environment, employment, or education. Health may be important on the list of needs, but far from first. The National Civic League's definition is a prominent example. It emphasizes environment, economy, housing, "people who respect and support each other," cultural heritage, and good government ahead of healthcare.[50] Such a perspective may be necessary to make substantial inroads on many serious health problems.[51]

An HCO's participation in an advocacy group recognizes a concordance between its mission and the group's. Important, sensitive issues are involved in the decision to participate. These relate to the prioritization of resource use between competing elements of a comprehensive community health program and commitments in acute care. The collaborative mission must be carefully implemented to preserve existing relationships. The HCO's mission statement must go beyond excellence in acute care. Wording of mission, like that of North Mississippi Medical Center—"to continuously improve the health of the people of our region"—is an unequivocal commitment that does not interfere with the HCO's ability to deliver quality acute care. Mercy Health System's "provide exceptional healthcare services resulting in healing in the broadest sense" balances traditional with expanded commitment.[52] The goal is to gain understanding and acceptance of the broader mission from all stakeholders and commitment from as many as possible.

Support for a community health mission is obtained through the usual visioning exercise, which deliberately asks hundreds of stakeholders to focus on the group's most basic purposes. The stakeholders are gathered in groups, and the case for community health presented. The case is not complex:

> A healthy community is happier and more productive because the individuals in it are healthier and more productive. There is a lot more to health than simply acute hospital-oriented care. In general, our community needs to be sure we prevent disease whenever possible, treat people with disease as effectively and economically as possible, and help people approaching the end of life do so in comfort, with grace, and if possible in the presence of their loved ones.

This case has broad appeal. It reflects the professional commitment of most healing professions, the values of most faiths, and what most of us instinctively feel. As stakeholders contemplate the mission, several specific and practical questions are likely to arise, and the HCO spokespersons should be prepared to discuss them:

- *Financial implications for current activities.* Implementing a community health mission requires capital that otherwise could be invested in expanding acute services. How will this trade-off be managed?
  1. Capital decisions for the HCO will continue to be made by its governing board in the overall interests of the community, recognizing both the importance of existing relationships and the HCO's unique role in acute care.
  2. The HCO's capital review process is designed to give all stakeholders an opportunity to comment and to identify the most valuable investments in the light of the mission.
  3. The board intends to keep our community competitive with others in all levels of care. The board will support acute care investments that are scientifically sound, efficient in settings like ours, and generally accepted by health insurers.
  4. Our sound financial position allows us to do this, and the board is committed to maintaining that soundness.

The answer places the question in context, clarifies both the authority and the process of decision making, and states the philosophic position of the board. It ensures that, despite the importance of community health, acute care will not be neglected.

- *Income implications for provider stakeholders.* This question is related to the preceding question, but often comes from high-tech specialties, who in the traditional not-for-profit structure receive access to substantial free capital and trained personnel in the HCO. The answer reiterates the first answer, point-ing out the relevant specific opportunities that have been funded recently and noting that the HCO has, in fact, remained competitive with other sites. It also reiterates the HCO's commitment to using its medical staff planning function so that every physician has an opportunity to earn a competitive income. The solu-tion will be successful if the supply of high-tech specialists is kept in balance with clinically justified demand.

- *Justice.* The question is, "Should our HCO serve the needy or the insured, pay-ing customer?" although it is rarely so boldly phrased. The issue is the extent to which the HCO is appropriately a vehicle for overcoming society's more general problems of poverty, income distribution, and disadvantaged populations. The HCO's not-for-profit status is justified in part by its contribution to these problems. The answer for most HCOs is to serve these goals only to the extent external funding permits. That often means a general commitment to offer only services for which payment is generally available and to set a specific limit on the funding to be transferred to uncompensated care.

- *Faith-based restrictions on medical care.* The expanded mission raises several potential areas of ethical conflict in addition to those inherent in acute care. The nonreligious not-for-profit HCO's position emphasizes patient autonomy, the right of each individual to choose his or her care for any reason, including reasons of faith. Religious HCOs operate similarly, but they reserve the right not to provide any treatment or service inconsistent with their faith. Both make an effort to avoid offending those who hold strong convictions. Preventive services, such as reproductive health, are one troublesome area; management of death is another, but less controversial, one. Potentially disturbing positions are imple-mented by carefully targeted promotion, location, corporate separation, and similar devices designed to isolate those who desire the service from those who find it offensive.

To be convincing, the HCO's answers to these questions must be backed by a record of trust and success. The record of the leading hospitals shows that the stakeholder reservations reflected in the questions can be overcome.

Measuring Performance

Community health service teams should be measured like any other health-care team, using the operational dimensions of demand, cost, worker satis-faction, efficiency, quality, and customer satisfaction. Examples are shown in Exhibit 9.5. The teams use history, competition, benchmarks, and values to

EXHIBIT 9.5

Examples of Operational Measures for Community Health Programs

Program	Need/Demand	Productivity	Quality and Effectiveness
Well-Baby care	Incidence from birth data and forecasts Demand from existing programs	Cost/service (e.g., cost of standard vaccine packages) Cost/visit Cost/infant	Percent immunized Incidence of preventable condition reported (e.g., infectious disease, trauma, violence) Incidence of manageable condition reported (e.g., hearing, visual, or functional limitation)
Asthma management	Incidence/prevalence from epidemiologic model or survey Demand from existing programs	Cost/visit Cost/patient-year Cost/capita	Incidence of asthma-related disability from surveys (www.cdc.gov/asthma/questions.htm) Clinical data on asthmatic pulmonary function (outcomes) Clinical data on asthmatic treatment (process)
Home care	Waiting lists or unmet demand Comparison to similar communities Demand from existing programs	Cost/visit Cost/patient-month Cost/capita	Patient, family, and physician satisfaction Adverse events CMS OASIS C measures*
Hospice	Waiting lists or unmet demand Comparison to similar communities Demand from existing programs	Cost/visit Cost/patient-month Cost/capita	Patient, family, and physician satisfaction Hospice referrals as percent of total mortality or disease-specific mortality Hospice-specific quality measures** The *Dartmouth Atlas of Health Care* 2008 Tracking the Care of Patients with Severe Chronic Illness [†]

* www.cms.hhs.gov/HomeHealthQualityInits/06_OASISC.asp#TopOfPage

[†] www.dartmouthatlas.org/atlases/atlas_series.shtm

**Information from Kirby, E. G., M. J. Keeffe, and K. M. Nicols. 2007. "A Study of the Effects of Innovative and Efficient Practices on the Performance of Hospice Care Organizations." *Health Care Management Review* 32(4): 352–59.

NOTE: All programs will measure associate satisfaction and client satisfaction by survey. Program accounting records will measure resource consumption and counts of volumes, scheduling delays, and percent of capacity used.

identify OFIs and set goals. They conduct continuous improvement activities like all other teams. They must be committed to "keep our community competitive," recognizing concerns about impact on the acute care mission.

In addition, individual community health programs are measured strategically in terms of their cost per case and cost per capita. These measures are used in cost/benefit or cost/effectiveness evaluations that provide the scientific evidence supporting the programs. Benefits are usually per capita counts of more serious events avoided (e.g., premature death or disability, preventable disease incidence or treatment incidence like hospitalization, absenteeism and income loss).[53]

Formal evaluation of cost effectiveness is best left to researchers working at a national level. The CDC's Task Force on Community Preventive Services has documented the process it uses to recommend programs.[54,55] Obtaining local outcomes values is sometimes practical. Cost per case and per capita should be monitored and benchmarked as a check on program effectiveness.

As indicated, the HCO's mission in community health must be limited to what can be reasonably financed. Even the largest HCOs cannot ignore the market realities of medical care, including the emphasis on high-tech acute intervention built into both private and government insurance programs. It is arguable that Americans have the healthcare system they want. If they wanted a different emphasis on the levels presented in Exhibit 9.1, there is no shortage of models to copy. On the other hand, many believe that the current emphasis is unstable; the cost cannot be allowed to grow as it has in the past. Community health is a major vehicle to control long-term costs. The balance between these competing visions must be maintained by governing board policies. The policies that have proven effective for HCOs with an acute care tradition are as follows:

Financing

- Every service must be planned and operated in a way that pursues continuous improvement to minimize cost and maximize all revenue consistent with its mission, vision, and values. This means that each service must justify its contribution and that no individual receives care beyond what is effective.
- Capital investments and deficit coverage can be viewed as community dividends or benefits and funded at the discretion of the HCO board using three broad criteria:
  1. All funded activities should have a potential benefit that reasonably exceeds the support required, even though the benefit may be difficult to measure.
  2. The HCO's total investment cannot exceed prudent levels indicated in the long-range financial plan.
  3. Acute care needs that keep the community competitive with others must take priority because they are the HCO's core mission.

These criteria are designed to ensure continued financial performance of the organization as a whole. They force collective consideration of all needs, including community health; provide a cost–benefit criterion for prioritizing opportunities; and protect long-term stability. To protect the acute care activities, many high-performing HCOs set an upper limit to investment in underfunded services. A few, such as SSM Health Care[56] and Catholic Health Initiatives,[57] mandate a minimum as well.

Promoting Community Health Opportunities

The final step in a community health strategy is the systematic use of the existing marketplace to expand the total use of appropriate services. This includes assisting existing organizations to improve and using collaborative opportunities to increase market penetration. Deliberate promotion—*social marketing*[58]—is essential for many community health activities. While people immediately relate "doctor" and "hospital" to "health," none of the rest of the Exhibit 9.1 services has the same level of recall. Some of them, particularly palliative care and some preventive activities, carry negative impressions that education and marketing must overcome. Coalitions with specific interest groups are valuable and completely consistent with social marketing concepts. Many groups with targeted missions have attracted the people most interested in their mission—the core ready-to-buy market. They form an invaluable nucleus for promotion. The acute care services should support these groups, using protocols that limit unnecessary services and encourage appropriate referral.

Competing organizations can also be influenced by a well-designed strategy. They can be drawn into joint ventures, or encouraged by market pressures to expand or improve services. A large HCO controls a substantial market share that it can direct to selected providers on the basis of quality and cooperation. (Potential antitrust implications exist in any action taken directly toward competitors. Although enforcement in comprehensive community care would be unusual, consultation with legal counsel is appropriate.)

Operationalizing a Community Health Strategy

Once established, the strategy must be implemented. Three elements are important. Individual teams must be established, trained, supported, and held accountable, a process no different from acute healthcare. Stakeholder support must be maintained and, if possible, increased. This effort must overcome both ignorance and faulty preconceptions that are more widespread in nonacute services. Finally, coalitions, whether with individual organizations or through an advocacy group, must be maintained and encouraged to be effective.

Supporting Caregiving Teams

The functions that community health units must perform are essentially the same as those required of acute service lines and nursing units. From an organizational perspective, the differences between a hospice, a primary care clinic, a health promotion program for teenagers, and an ICU lie in the clinical details, not the organization. Clinical, logistic, and strategic support must be provided for community health teams as it is for more traditional ones. The organizational foundations for excellence—transformational management, performance measurement, evidence-based management, and evidence-based care—are the same. They must be put in place and supported by education, repetition, and reward.

High-performing HCOs are well equipped to fill these needs, using the same approaches that support acute care teams.

Building Stakeholder Support

Identifying and understanding collective opportunities and building networks of civic engagement are an ongoing challenge. Communities are composed of individuals linked in multiple diverse groups that network their lives. These stakeholder groups are, by nature, advocatory and protectionist, and they are frequently confrontational. Community health is only one area of society where finding the key to collaboration is essential. Education; economic development; and the operating infrastructure of roads, utilities, safety, and justice are others. The solution lies in mechanisms of civic engagement and social connectedness that facilitate coordination and cooperation for mutual benefit.[59] The elements used successfully in many communities are extensions of those used in high-performing traditional healthcare: extensive communication and honest listening, respect for all participants, evidence of the need and the possibility that translates the need to opportunity, continuous improvement, and the willingness to begin with achievable goals and work toward values and benchmarks. These elements are achieved not only by personal leadership but also by identifying and supporting like-thinking partners. Stakeholders become advocates when they are assured that their concerns are met and the benefits are realistic.

For an HCO that is pursuing community health at any level, maintenance of the network of collaborators is an important activity. The advocacy group and individual contracts are the mechanism for identifying, ranking, and pursuing OFIs and for dispute resolution. Each contract should be assigned to an individual manager to monitor, including listening to and negotiating issues that arise. This is no different from monitoring other contracts, such as supplies or joint ventures.

Supporting the Advocacy Group

A successful community advocacy group formalizes the stakeholder participation. It pursues functions that resemble those of the governing board:

1. Establishing the community's health mission, including the scope and roles of contributing groups
2. Maintaining a supportive relationship that allows contributing organizations to identify and achieve specific community health goals
3. Creating an overall strategy, and maintaining financial support
4. Encouraging performance measurement, acceptable quality of care, and comprehensive response to individual patient needs
5. Monitoring general measures of the community health, identifying OFIs, and assisting in response

Community coalitions lack the authority of governing boards, but they can bring stakeholders together, identify collaborative opportunities, encourage contracts between agencies, and draw attention to global measures of community health.

The advocacy group will have an HCO representative who assumes a leadership role with regard to community health. The high-performing HCO has several resources to contribute toward these functions. In addition to a cash contribution, it can offer seasoned governing board members and provide staff support to prepare agendas and manage meetings. It can share the rules and culture that make its own board successful. It can offer its training programs for coalition staff, and it can contribute the time of its senior executives.

Improving Performance

All elements of high-performing HCOs must be subject to continuous improvement. Community health activities are no exception. The cycle of OFI identification, goal setting, process improvement, and celebration of achievement must be built into the model of community health. All the operating units conduct quarterly assessments of progress, identifying and addressing OFIs and preparing for enhanced goals in the coming year. If a community-wide advocacy group exists, the group engages in annual self-assessment and improvement just as the governing board does. The individuals responsible for maintaining the HCO's relationship and the continued success of collaborative ventures also review achievement quarterly, make sure goals are achieved, and work with their partners to identify new goals. A useful guide (Community Health Care's O-Process for Evaluation) to applying the continuous improvement process in community health has been developed.[60]

People

Community health services' caregiving teams must be recruited, trained, and supported like acute care teams. Because of the limited financing, nonacute services of all kinds have operated at lower wage levels than acute care has. The individuals on the teams have been given greater freedom from licensure restrictions. Particularly in continuing care and palliative care, individuals with less professional training tend to have greater autonomy. Volunteers and family members play an important role.

Providing safe, effective, patient-centered, timely, efficient, and equitable care that uses less skilled individuals requires systematic and careful organizational support. High-performing community health sites implement the following elements:[61]

1. Clear, frequently communicated mission and vision
2. Carefully designed work processes and protocols, providing specific advice on when assistance should be sought and how it can be obtained
3. Training for specific duties in a limited situation, such as a dialysis unit or a

nursing home, including indicators of complications and resources to assist when complications occur

4. Measured performance, retraining, celebration, and rewards

5. Frequent and transformational contact, with emphasis on encouragement

This approach is little different from that used in high-performing acute care organizations. Applied with care and diligence, it allows patients, lower-wage employees, volunteers, and family members to support effective care and reduce costs. It has been applied in a variety of community health settings. For example:

- Schoolteachers can be trained to provide instruction on healthy lifestyles, including classroom instruction, individual counseling, and personal modeling of good health habits.[62]
- Volunteers in the faith community can make important contributions. "Parish nurses" promote healthy behavior and undertake screening.[63] "Stephen Ministries" and similar activities can support individuals and families in times of stress.[64]
- Volunteers deliver Meals on Wheels,[65] provide transportation, and assist in all levels of care delivery through palliative care and bereavement support.[66]
- Low-wage workers can be trained to undertake important clinical responsibilities in primary and continuing care settings.[67]
- Family members can be trained to manage patients with severe disabilities.[68]

Measures

Operational

Each community health activity should be measured using the operating dimensions for performance measurement. Exhibit 9.5 shows examples for typical specific activities. A number of approaches adapt the dimensions to the needs of preventive and chronic care teams:

1. *Both need and demand should be measured.* Need should be estimated by population subgroup so that unmet needs can be identified as OFIs. For example, need and demand for primary and secondary prevention services are appropriately measured by age group, geographic area, and cultural characteristics. This allows not only identification of unmet need but also a starting point for correction— through the schools for teenagers and through culturally targeted media and civic organizations for cultural groups at higher risk.

Need is measured by the incidence or prevalence of a specific condition, such as overweight, arrests for driving under influence, pregnancy, and asthma. Statistics for these conditions are drawn from national or regional surveys and databases and are used in the epidemiologic planning model to infer and forecast local values. Effective ambulatory care includes a wide range of needs. Those related to pregnancy, childrearing, and statistically important chronic diseases can be individually forecast. A separate forecast can address other miscellaneous primary care. Home care, hospice, and nursing home care need estimates present unusual problems. The need for these services is influenced not only by disease incidence but also by income, cultural attitudes, and availability of family support. Models for estimating need are available in the literature, but they require household or acute care patient surveys that are expensive to implement.[69,70,71] Occupancy levels, waiting times, and comparisons to similar communities are used as substitutes.

Waiting times are accepted as indicators of unmet demand for all healthcare services. Specific definitions, such as "the third available routine visit date" are used to reduce random variation. Waiting lists or counts are generally less reliable. They frequently accumulate patients who are not actually demanding service, because their condition has changed or their initial entry was opportunistic.[72]

2. *Resource consumption—quantities and cost of resources used—is handled as for any other team.* Resource conditions often emphasize capacity and occupancy. Facilities for these services must sustain high occupancies to minimize costs.

3. *Human resource status is measured by surveys, turnover rates, absenteeism rates, vacancy rates, and safety, as with other healthcare teams.*

4. *Output is measured, as usual, in numbers of clients served and counts of services delivered.* The target population also must be measured. Counts of clients served per 1,000 members of the target population are an important indicator of market penetration. For example, a health behavior program for teenagers would track the number of teenagers participating as a fraction of the number in the community. A hospice program would monitor the number of referrals as a fraction of the number of deaths.

   Productivity is measured as cost per service, cost per case or patient, and cost per capita. Cost per service is a useful test of team efficiency. Cost per case is the product of cost per service times the number of services per client. The number of services introduces an element of effectiveness. Cost per capita is the total cost of the activity divided by the population served. Judgments of program effectiveness or benefit are made at the per capita level. All of these can be benchmarked and used to evaluate OFIs. Quality measurement should include outcomes measures and process measures linked by evidence to those outcomes. The link is often less than fully proven, but the best available indicators should be used.

5. *Customer satisfaction is usually obtained by survey, as it is in acute services.* Client or patient satisfaction is supplemented by family satisfaction and referring physician satisfaction, where appropriate.

The operation of community health activities should include benchmarking, goal setting, and continuous improvement. Each activity should produce a list of OFIs and their needs to address them. These lists can be compiled by the advocacy group and used to guide future efforts. They can be summarized as indicators of overall progress as part of the strategic community health measures.

Strategic

Strategic measures should monitor the overall contribution of community health programs. A "healthy community" is one where people lead long, healthy, productive lives. The concept is commonly implemented by measuring the opposites—death, disease, and activity limitation. The model for the strategic evaluation is provided by *Healthy People 2010,*[73] implemented nationally by the CDC in DATA2010.[74] Unfortunately, DATA2010 is only available at the state level. Community data must be constructed from CDC health statistics, CMS Medicare hospitalization statistics, data from local sources, and ad hoc surveys.

Some states augment the federal data with all hospital admissions and various other health indicators, such as school vaccination records. A uniform crime-reporting system provides data on domestic violence, drug usage, and alcohol-related accidents. Epidemiologic planning models use the public data, often supplementing it with private sources, such as insurance claims, to infer community-level values. The *Dartmouth Atlas* provides data on hospitalizations and per capita expenditures based on Medicare reports for hospital service areas and referral areas. It is updated annually, with a three-year lag.[75] Its measure of Medicare expenditures in the last two years of life is particularly useful as an indicator of chronic disease care effectiveness. Exhibit 9.6 provides a template for available strategic measures. The "Strategic Measures of Community Health" can all be calculated for small civil divisions, such as census tract, postal code area, or township, and aggregated to typical HCO market communities. They can all be benchmarked and trended over time, providing a foundation for a community health needs assessment and an annual review.

In addition to these data, strategic measures of community health should summarize the effort of all the various agencies and organizations involved. If these organizations follow continuous improvement management, they will have operational measures, benchmarks, and OFIs. They will also have conventional financial reports and stakeholder satisfaction data that can support summary statements and OFIs. This data set provides community leaders, including the advocacy group, with a platform of information to set strategy.

Managerial Issues

HCO managers have two roles in community health. First and most important, their professional training gives them a knowledge foundation in the

EXHIBIT 9.6
Community
Health
Scorecard

Dimension	Community Health Examples
Strategic measures of community health	*Measures from government health statistics:* Mortality, by cause, with emphasis on preventable death Natality, with emphasis on neonatal mortality, prematurity, and limitation Infectious disease rates *Measures from Medicare and Medicaid:* Per capita hospitalizations by diagnostic group Incidence of chronic disease Cost of hospitalization Cost of medical care in last two years of life *Measures from government agencies:* Domestic violence Alcohol-related events Heath and immunization of school children *Measures from community surveys:* Health insurance premiums Health insurance coverage Preventable emergency care Pre-morbid and treatable conditions: Obesity, hypertension, depression Unfilled demand for health services
Financial performance	*Financial structure of advocacy group:* Grants and gifts for community health received by advocacy group and member organizations Financial performance of independent, affiliated, and wholly owned organizations supporting community health
Operations of caregiving units	Summary of OFIs from operations at each level of community health, drawn from their operational measures
Market performance and stakeholder satisfaction	Measures of access for disadvantaged groups Measures of cultural competence in healthcare Customer and provider stakeholder satisfaction

scope and value of community health that few others share. HCO managers have unique insight into the interplay of acute care and other community health services. Second, the managerial skills that have led to high performance in acute care are clearly applicable in other health settings. HCO managers know how to implement transformational evidence-based management. That approach is the documented best practice for acute care, and it appears to be equally powerful across the spectrum of community care. The two roles suggest four recurring issues that managers must address: (1) promoting and teaching the issues and opportunities, (2) extending the transformational culture and evidence-based management in community health activities, (3) expanding and improving primary care, and (4) maintaining the network of civic engagement.

Promoting and Teaching Community Health

Several core issues reflected in Exhibit 9.1 are not well understood by Americans at large:

1. *Prevention is in itself a multicomponent activity.* Primary prevention involves environmental management, immunization, and behavioral elements. It has the highest payoff. Even though environmental management (i.e., air, water, and food supply; contaminants such as lead and mold) requires expensive collaborative action, it eliminates disease for a lot of people. Thus, primary prevention generally gives the best return on investment.
2. *Many Americans suffer from chronic diseases such as diabetes, high blood pressure, asthma, and mental illness.* While these diseases cannot be cured, they can be managed. Primary care provides ongoing support to minimize the costs of chronic disease. The support, which can be carried out in large part by nonphysicians, is a major contribution to community health.
3. *Twenty-first century acute care is astonishingly expensive.* Emergency visits are measured in hundreds of dollars, and outpatient treatments often in thousands. A single hospitalization approaches one-half of an individual's annual income. Health insurance hides these costs from the users, as it is designed to do. They cannot be escaped from a community perspective. Although acute care HCOs provide substantial benefits to the community—health to individuals and income through their associates—the cost of those benefits must ultimately be weighed against other social opportunities and the cost of health insurance. The keys to controlling unnecessary use of acute care are evidence-based medicine, evidence-based management, and community health.
4. *The proper goal of the healthcare system at the end of life is to maximize comfort for both patient and family.* This is a different goal from prolonging life, although it is not automatically inconsistent. Americans generally need to be aware of this to understand the difference. Community health programs need to help them implement their understanding.

The first task of HCO managers is to understand these issues. They are not simple. They are not self-evident, and they are not widely demonstrated in the United States today. Once grasped, they force a change in perspective about community health and a new vision of what HCOs can do. As more Americans understand them, major gains can be made. The spread of these ideas will be from professionals—the concepts are entirely consistent with the ethical goals of the healing professions—to other influentials in American communities. Employers, trustees, public officials, elected representatives, religious leaders, and teachers can and should master these concepts. HCO managers must teach them.

Extending Management Concepts to Community Healthcare Teams

The activities of community health teams in prevention, primary care, rehabilitation, continuing care, and palliative care are all different, and so are the activities of labor and delivery teams, emergency teams, surgery teams, and ICU teams. These differences in clinical content do not support any fundamental differences in organization and management.

The keys to high performance are the same across all healthcare. Transformational management approaches that actively support worker needs are one key. Continuous improvement, with its requisite measurement, benchmarking, OFI identification, and goal setting, is the second. Evidence-based medicine is the third key. The science that identifies and develops high technology also provides the facts to support its appropriate use. The combination of the three can be a definition of "evidence-based healthcare management." These keys are being used in all high-performing acute care applications. The same keys likely promote effective community health.

The HCO can create primary care, home care, palliative and hospice, and continuing care service lines by service contracts, joint ventures, or acquisition. It can offer training services to affiliated organizations. It can encourage its leadership to serve on boards of these organizations.

Expanding and Integrating Primary Care

Primary care is a diverse set of clinical events, including critical primary, secondary, and tertiary preventive care as well as more routine support for minor illness and trauma. It is the most frequent contact that people have with healthcare by an order of magnitude. (Five out of six Americans visit a doctor, clinic, or emergency department each year; only one in 16 stays overnight in a hospital.[76]) It is, as noted, not done well. Too many patients fail to get the treatment they need when they need it, leading to more serious illness, work loss, and more expensive care. Part of the problem is patient oriented. Lack of financial resources, lack of transportation, cultural and language difficulties, and the barriers imposed by disease itself make it difficult for some patients to get the care they need. Part of the problem is the diversity and independence of providers. Primary care is provided by private practice offices of physicians, psychologists, advanced practice nurses, podiatrists, and chiropractors; by organized clinics, including community, public health, school, work site, and medical group practices such as Kaiser Permanente's; and by urgent care centers and emergency departments.

The concept of the medical home is an important step toward rationalizing primary care. The concept, which has been around for several decades and has had different labels, is that every patient has a single care team that coordinates his or her ongoing care. Under the leadership of the Commonwealth Fund and the National Center for Quality Assurance, the professional organizations for family practice, internal medicine, pediatrics, and osteopathy adopted standards and guidelines for the *patient-centered medical home* in 2008. The standards identify the following key characteristics:[77]

- Ongoing relation with a personal physician trained in comprehensive care
- Physician-led care team
- "Whole person orientation" emphasizing "care for all stages of life"
- Coordination of care "across all elements of the complex health system"
- Emphasizing quality, safety, and evidence-based medicine
- Using the electronic medical record and knowledge management systems for care, performance improvement, patient education, and enhanced communication

The community health centers are also committed to the patient-centered medical home. It does not solve all problems. It is a complex vision to implement.[78] It has not yet been adopted by several important provider groups, most noticeably obstetricians and emergency physicians.

Any HCO committed to the community health mission should work to implement the patient-centered medical home concept. Community health centers for persons who face difficulties finding care are a proven success.

Maintaining the Infrastructure for Community Health

Community health is not solely the responsibility of traditional not-for-profit HCOs; indeed, those HCOs that select an "excellent care" mission are explicitly limiting their responsibility. For HCOs that accept the obligation, the critical organizational issue is bringing together, coordinating, and if possible expanding a communitywide effort. It is a problem that America has not solved well.

The prevailing theory, simply stated, is that government agencies should be responsible for all of those activities best approached in common: environmental control, safety and legal compliance, public health, and public education. The market should handle all activities best left to individual decision. The not-for-profit, or "non-governmental organization," introduces a third vehicle, more flexible than the first and more committed to the common good than the market, to address unresolved concerns.[79] A theoretical case can be made that local government should address community health; convene the advocacy group; compile strategic measures; and lead in identifying, prioritizing, and achieving OFIs. The reality is that local government is undermanned for challenges in its more central responsibilities. Similarly, the market, although deeply invested in health, deals poorly with its externalities. The not-for-profit might be the best vehicle to approach this complex problem.

When the traditional HCO steps into a role in community health, it is usually the largest and best-funded organization. That gives it substantial leverage. When it has achieved high performance in its traditional areas, it has built an organizational mechanism that increases its leverage and that can be copied successfully by other service organizations. The core problem that it faces is expanding the community's collective effort to identify and address health problems. One way to do that is to acquire and operate service lines for community health needs. Many HCOs have used this path, acquiring or building primary care, rehabilitation, and continuing and palliative care organizations. A second approach is to build coalitions for these services, strengthening other organizations as providers by supporting contracts or developing joint ventures. The best combination remains to be seen. It is likely to include these approaches: support activities for governmental units, joint ventures with primary caregivers, operating contracts with specialty providers in chronic disease, and guidance by an advocacy group with quasi-governance responsibilities.

The management issue is identifying, maintaining, and improving a coordinated approach to community health. The key to its successful completion lies in the diligent pursuit of the four functions, particularly measuring need and performance, maintaining effective interpersonal relationships, rigorously using performance measures to identify OFIs, and pursuing continuous improvement. Introducing the measurement and improvement activities that have been proven successful in acute care substantially improves community health as a whole.

Suggested Readings

Association for Community Health Improvement; see www.communityhlth.org/ communityhlth_app/index.jsp.

Commonwealth Fund. 2008. *The Path to a High Performance U.S. Health System: A 2020 Vision and the Policies to Pave the Way.* www.commonwealthfund.org/ Content/Publications/Fund-Reports/2009/Feb/The-Path-to-a-High-Performance-US-Health-System.aspx.

The Community Tool Box, a service of the Work Group for Community Health and Development at the University of Kansas; see http://ctb.ku.edu/en.

Fonseca-Becker, F., and A. L. Boore. 2008. *Community Health Care's O-Process for Evaluation.* New York: Springer.

National Center for Quality Assurance. 2008. *Standards and Guidelines for Physician Practice Connections—Patient-Centered Medical Home (PPC-PCMH).* Washington, DC: NCQA.

National Civic League; see www.ncl.org/cs/services/healthycommunities.html.

Office of Disease Prevention and Health Promotion, U.S. Department of Health and Human Services. *Healthy People 2020.* [Online information; retrieved 4/20/09.] www.healthypeople.gov/HP2020.

Notes

1. Commission to Build a Healthier America. [Online information; retrieved 4/23/09.] www.commissiononhealth.org.

2. Soreca, I., and F. E. Kupfer. 2009. "The Phenomenology of Bipolar Disorder: What Drives the High Rate of Medical Burden and Determines Long-Term Prognosis?" *Depression & Anxiety* 26 (1): 73–82.

3. Fogel, R. W. 2004. *The Escape From Hunger and Premature Death, 1700–2100.* Cambridge, UK: Cambridge University Press.

4. Murphy, K. M., and R. H. Topel. 2006. "The Value of Health and Longevity." *Journal of Political Economy* 114 (5): 871–904.

5. American College of Physicians. 2008. "Position Paper: Achieving a High-Performance Health Care System with Universal Access: What the United States Can Learn from Other Countries." *Annals of Internal Medicine* 148 (1): 55–75.

6. Starr, P. 1982. *The Social Transformation of American Medicine.* New York: Basic Books.

7. Fuchs, V. R. 2008. "Three 'Inconvenient Truths' About Health Care." *New England Journal of Medicine* 359 (17): 1749–51.

8. Catlin, A., C. Cowan, M. Hartman, and S. Heffler. 2008. "National Health Spending in 2006: A Year of Change for Prescription Drugs." *Health Affairs* 27: 1–29, Exhibit 7.

9. Jencks, S. F., M. V. Williams, and E. A. Coleman. 2009. "Rehospitalizations Among Patients in the Medicare Fee-for-Service Program." *New England Journal of Medicine* 360: 1418–28.

10. McGlynn, E. A., S. M. Asch. J. Adams, J. Keesey, J. Hicks, A. DeCristofaro, and E. A. Kerr. 2003. "The Quality of Health Care Delivered to Adults in the United States." *New England Journal of Medicine* 348 (26): 2635–45.

11. Mangione-Smith, R., A. H. DeCristofaro, C. M. Setodji, J. Keesey, D. J. Klein, J. L. Adams, M. A. Schuster, and E. A. McGlynn. 2007. "The Quality of Ambulatory Care Delivered to Children in the United States." *New England Journal of Medicine* 357 (15): 1515–23.

12. Hackbarth, G. M. 2009. "Reforming the Health Care Delivery System." Testimony by the Medicare Payment Advisory Commission.

13. Public health activity has not exceeded 3.3 percent of national health expenditures in 50 years and has fallen to 2.9 percent since 2002. [Online information; retrieved 4/9/09.] www.cms.hhs.gov/NationalHealthExpendData/02_NationalHealth AccountsHistorical.asp.

14. Levinson, D. "Memorandum Report: Trends in Nursing Home Deficiencies and Complaints," OEI-02-08-00140. Office of Inspector General, U.S. Department of Health and Human Services. [Online information; retrieved 4/14/09.] www.oig. hhs.gov/oei/reports/oei-02-08-00140.pdf.

15. National Hospice and Palliative Care Organization. 2008. "Hospice Care in America." [Online information, p. 9; retrieved 4/23/09.] www.nhpco.org/files/ public/Statistics_Research/NHPCO_facts-and-figures_2008.pdf.

16. Commonwealth Fund. 2008. *The Path to a High Performance U.S. Health System: A 2020 Vision and the Policies to Pave the Way.* [Online information; retrieved 4/15/09.] www.commonwealthfund.org/Content/Publications/Fund-Reports/ 2009/Feb/The-Path-to-a-High-Performance-US-Health-System.aspx.

17. Miller, M. E. 2008. "Report to the Congress: Reforming the Delivery System." Medicare Payment Advisory Commission. [Online information; retrieved 4/8/09.] www.medpac.gov/documents/20080916_Sen%20Fin_testimony%20 final.pdf.

18. Examining Community-Institutional Partnerships for Prevention Research Group. 2006. "Building and Sustaining Community-Institutional Partnerships for Prevention Research: Findings from a National Collaborative." *Journal of Urban Health* 83 (6): 989–1003.

19. Kindig, D. A., Y. Asada, and B. Booske. 2008. "A Population Health Framework for Setting National and State Health Goals." *JAMA* 299 (17): 2081–83.

20. Schroeder, S. A. 2007. "Shattuck Lecture: We Can Do Better—Improving the Health of the American People." *New England Journal of Medicine* 357 (12): 1221–28.

21. U.S. Internal Revenue Service, Schedule H, Form 990. 2009. [Online information; retrieved 5/6/09.] www.irs.gov/pub/irs-tege/f990rschh.pdf.

22. Kindig, D. A. 2007. "Understanding Population Health Terminology." *Milbank Quarterly* 85 (1): 139–61.

23. Task Force on Community Preventive Services. 2005. *The Community Guide: What Works to Promote Health.* [Online information; retrieved 3/11/09.] www.thecommunityguide.org/index.html.

24. Rabin, R. C. 2009. "Benefits of Mammogram Under Debate in Britain." *New York Times.* [Online information; retrieved 4/15/09.] www.nytimes.com/2009/03/31/health/31mamm.html?_r=1&scp=5&sq=breast%20cancer&st=cse.

25. Raikou, M., and A. McGuire. 2003. "The Economics of Screening and Treatment in Type 2 Diabetes Mellitus." *Pharmacoeconomics* 21 (8): 543–64.

26. Center for Health Care Strategies. ROI Forecasting Calculator. [Online information; retrieved 4/16/09.] www.chcsroi.org/Welcome.aspx.

27. National Association of Community Health Centers. 2009. "Chart Book." [Online information; retrieved 8/25/09.] www.nachc.com/client/documents/Chartbook_Update_20091.pdf.

28. Centers for Medicare & Medicaid Services. "Overview of Quality Initiatives." [Online information; retrieved 8/25/09.] www.cms.hhs.gov/QualityInitiativesGenInfo/01_Overview.asp#TopOfPage.

29. Casarett, D. J., J. Teno, and J. Higginson. 2006. "How Should Nations Measure the Quality of End-of-Life Care for Older Adults? Recommendations for an International Minimum Data Set." *Journal of the American Geriatrics Society* 54 (11): 1765–71.

30. Task Force on Community Preventive Services (2005).

31. Weissert, W., M. Chernew, and R. Hirth. 2003. "Titrating Versus Targeting Home Care Services to Frail Elderly Clients: An Application of Agency Theory and Cost-Benefit Analysis to Home Care Policy." *Journal of Aging & Health* 15 (1): 99–123.

32. Kim, J. J., and S. J. Goldie. 2008. "Health and Economic Implications of HPV Vaccination in the United States." *New England Journal of Medicine* 359: 821–32.

33. Task Force on Community Preventive Services (2005).

34. Agency for Healthcare Research and Quality. *National Guideline Clearinghouse.* [Online information; retrieved 4/16/09.] www.guidelines.gov.

35. Centers for Medicare & Medicaid Services. "Minimum Data Set 3.0 for Nursing Homes." [Online information; retrieved 3/17/09.] www.cms.hhs.gov/NursingHomeQualityInits/25_NHQIMDS30.asp#TopOfPage.

36. Butterfoss, F. D. 2007. *Coalitions and Partnerships in Community Health,* 259–61. San Francisco: Jossey-Bass.

37. SSM Health Care. 2005. News release, March 28. [Online information; retrieved 3/13/09.] www.ssmhc.com/internet/home/ssmcorp.nsf/Documents/B85F28E32066A3B786257457005E3775?OpenDocument.

38. American Hospital Association. 2009. "Nova Awards." [Online information; retrieved 3/18/09.] www.aha.org/aha/news-center/awards/NOVA.html.

39. *Ibid.*, "Community Connections, Ideas and Innovations for Hospital Leaders." Chicago: American Hospital Association.

40. *Ibid.*, "Foster McGaw Prize." [Online information; retrieved 3/18/09.] www .aha.org/aha/news-center/awards/foster/index.html.

41. U.S. Department of Health and Human Services. "Healthy People 2010 Midcourse Review: Executive Summary." [Online information; retrieved 3/24/09.] www.healthypeople.gov/Data/midcourse/pdf/ExecutiveSummary.pdf.

42. National Civic League. [Online information; retrieved 3/18/09.] www.ncl.org/ cs/services/healthycommunities.html.

43. The Kansas University Work Group for Community Health and Development. [Online information; retrieved 3/18/09.] http://communityhealth.ku.edu/ctb/ about_the_ctb.shtml.

44. Griffith, J. R., and K. R. White. 2003. *Thinking Forward: Six Strategies for Highly Successful Organizations*, Chapter 4. Chicago: Health Administration Press.

45. Butterfoss (2007).

46. Buffalo County Community Partners. *2008 Report to the Community.* [Online information; retrieved 5/10/10.] www.bcchp.org/node/28.

47. *Ibid.* [Online information; retrieved 5/10/10.] www.bcchp.org/node/28# history.

48. *Ibid.* [Online information; retrieved 4/2/09.] www.bcchp.org/node/30# ImmunizationInfants.

49. *Ibid.* [Online information; retrieved 3/20/09.] www.bcchp.org/html/ grants/2010actionplan.pdf.

50. National Civic League. [Online information; retrieved 3/18/09.] www.ncl.org/ cs/services/healthycommunities.html.

51. Lantz, P. M., R. L. Lichtenstein, and H. A. Pollack. 2007. "Health Policy Approaches to Population Health: The Limits of Medicalization." *Health Affairs* 26 (5): 1253–57.

52. Quoted in Griffith, J. R. 2009. "Finding the Frontier of Hospital Management." *Journal of Healthcare Management* 54 (1): 57–73, p. 64.

53. Kindig (2007).

54. Briss, P. A., S. Zaza, M. Pappaioanou, et al. 2000. "Developing an Evidence-Based Guide to Community Preventive Services—Methods." *American Journal of Preventive Medicine* 18 (1S): 35-43.

55. Zaza, S., L. Wright-de Aguero, P. A. Briss, et al. 2000. "Data Collection Instrument and Procedure for Systematic Reviews in the Guide to Community Preventive Services." *American Journal of Preventive Medicine* 18 (1S): 44–74.

56. SSM Health Care. [Online information; retrieved 4/7/09.] www.ssmhc.com/ internet/home/ssmcorp.nsf/Documents/8E96E101C5A0E122862573CC005 A9C58?OpenDocument.

57. Griffith and White (2003).

58. Kotler, P. K., and N. R. Lee. 2008. *Social Marketing: Influencing Behaviors for Good,* 3rd ed. Los Angeles: Sage Publications.

59. Putnam, R. D. 1995. "Bowling Alone: America's Declining Social Capital." *Journal of Democracy* 6 (1): 65–78.

60. Fonseca-Becker and Boore (2008).

61. Pfeffer, J. 2006. "Kent Thiry and DaVita: Leadership Challenges in Building and Growing a Great Company." Stanford University Graduate School of Business Case OB-54.

62. Nicklas, T. A., C. C. Johnson, L. S. Webber, and G. S. Berenson. 1997. "School-Based Programs for Health-Risk Reduction." *Annals of the New York Academy of Sciences* 817: 208–24.

63. McGinnis, S. L., and F. M. Zoske. 2008. "The Emerging Role of Faith Community Nurses in Prevention and Management of Chronic Disease." *Policy, Politics, & Nursing Practice* 9 (3): 173–80.

64. Introduction to Stephen Ministry. [Online information; retrieved 4/15/09.] www.stephenministries.org/stephenministry/default.cfm/928.

65. Meals on Wheels Association of America. [Online information; retrieved 4/15/09.] www.mowaa.org/Page.aspx?pid=183.

66. Hospice Foundation of America. [Online information; retrieved 4/15/09.] www.hospicefoundation.org/hospiceInfo/volunteer.asp.

67. Proser, M. 2005. "Deserving the Spotlight: Health Centers Provide High-Quality and Cost-Effective Care." *Journal of Ambulatory Care Management* 28 (4): 321–30.

68. Munck, B., B. Fridlund, and J. Martensson. 2008. "Next-of-Kin Caregivers in Palliative Home Care—from Control to Loss of Control." *Journal of Advanced Nursing* 64 (6): 578–86.

69. Lafortune, L., F. Beland, H. Bergman, and J. Ankri. 2009. "Health State Profiles and Service Utilization in Community-Living Elderly." *Medical Care* 47 (3): 286–94.

70. Kadushin, G. 2004. "Home Health Care Utilization: A Review of the Research for Social Work." *Health & Social Work* 29 (3): 219–44.

71. Mara, C. M., and L. K. Olson (eds.). 2008. *Handbook of Long-Term Care Administration and Policy*. Boca Raton, FL: CRC Press.

72. Armstrong, P. W. 2009. "What Do We Know? Limitations of the Two Methods Most Commonly Used to Estimate the Length of the Prospective Wait." *Health Services Management Research* 22 (1): 8–16.

73. Centers for Disease Control and Prevention. *Healthy People 2010*. [Online information; retrieved 4/15/09.] www.healthypeople.gov/Document.

74. *Ibid*. "DATA2010." [Online information; retrieved 3/24/09.] www.healthypeople.gov/Data/data2010.htm.

75. *The Dartmouth Atlas of Health Care*. [Online information; retrieved 3/30/09.] www.dartmouthatlas.org/index.shtm.

76. Centers for Disease Control and Prevention. CDC/National Center for Health Statistics. [Online information; retrieved 8/29/09.] www.cdc.gov/nchs.

77. National Center for Quality Assurance. 2008. "Standards and Guidelines for Physician Practice Connections®—Patient-Centered Medical Home (PPC-PCMH™)." [Online information; retrieved 8/25/09.] www.ncqa.org.

78. Carrier, E., M. N. Gourevitch, and N. R. Shah. 2009. "Medical Homes: Challenges in Translating Theory into Practice." *Medical Care* 47 (7): 714–22.

79. Gray, B. H., and W. J. McNerney. 1986. "For-Profit Enterprise in Health Care: The Institute of Medicine Study." *New England Journal of Medicine* 314 (23): 1523–28.

10 KNOWLEDGE MANAGEMENT

In a Few Words

Knowledge management (KM) has become a core logistic support activity, providing the communication essential for care; defining, acquiring, and maintaining performance measures; and supporting learning activities. KM includes all forms of communication; the networks of voice, computer, and Internet used daily by associates and patients; the data warehouse, an accessible archive of local data; and organized Internet access to useful external sources.

KM protects data and the systems themselves and continuously improves its services. The benefits of KM come only through its customers—the clinical and other service units of the healthcare organization (HCO). KM's continuous improvement is a planned ongoing expansion of service that must be justified by and integrated with changes in patient care and other work processes. Many KM functions can be centralized in multihospital systems or provided by outside contractors. Managerial issues emphasize using the planning activity so that it generates revenue for its own expansion, helping associates understand and deal with variability in measures, and managing outside contractors.

Critical Issues in Knowledge Management

1. *Maintaining the reliability of information:*
   - Define and standardize measures
   - Deal with external causes of variation
   - Deal with random variation

2. *Promoting effective communication of data:*
   - Expand the electronic medical record (EMR)
   - Ensure prompt access to reports and records

3. *Translating knowledge to strategic performance improvement:*
   - Support an evidence-based culture
   - Relate knowledge improvement to clinical service improvement
   - Use centralized and contract knowledge management services

4. *Protecting individual privacy, the archive, and the information systems:*
   - Protect patient and associate privacy rights
   - Guard against failure, misuse, theft, or destruction

5. *Planning improvement and growth:*
   - Develop a plan for knowledge management
   - Continuously improve knowledge management services
   - Capture the benefit of improved knowledge management in the strategic scorecard

QUESTIONS FOR DISCUSSION

Consider these questions as you read the chapter.

1. A clinical service wants to add a new measure that deals with service delay—the number of minutes after arrival that a given event occurs. (A number of these are in existence, such as door-to-needle time, from arrival to catheterization of an AMI [acute myocardial infarction] patient.) Should the service take its proposed measure to the definitions and standards committee? What questions would the committee ask?

2. Your HCO is opening a new clinic using the same EMR and information systems in place at its other clinics. Clerks, nurses, and physicians will all input information to the EMR and several management systems. What should the KM training program for new associates include? How would you accomplish that training economically?

3. When you visit the intensive care unit, the head nurse asks you to explain to the clerical associates (most of whom have a high school equivalency degree) what the risk-adjusted mortality report means. A check on the intranet reveals that the measure is adjusted for the patient's age, sex, provisional diagnosis, and an APACHE (Acute Physiologic and Chronic Health Evaluation) score at the time of admission, based on a systemwide database. The monthly mortality rate is reported as adjusted, with a 3 standard deviation confidence limit. What do you say to the clerks?

4. One clinical service line wants to invest in wireless laptops to make record keeping easier, faster, and more accurate. The staff say they know they must submit to KM planning review. They would like advice on how to prepare a successful proposal. What do you tell them?

5. The HCO's finance committee has set a limit of $100 million per year on new capital investment. Conversion to the EMR will be expensive—at least $40 million per year for three years. The chief information officer has asked you to help develop a case for the investment. What are the next steps?

Computers, the Web, and wireless communication have transformed twenty-first century life, perhaps even more in HCOs than in other venues. Knowledge—the content of communication—has become one of any organization's valuable resources. Knowledge management (KM) has become a major logistic support service that rivals human resources management and boundary spanning activities as a critical factor in strategic success.

Purpose

The purpose of KM is

to translate the HCO's complete knowledge resource to improvement of its strategic performance.

The complete knowledge resource has four essential parts:

1. The learning from many sources that is in each associate's head
2. The current communications that drive each associate's agenda of tasks and record their accomplishment
3. The *data warehouse* of protocols, processes, performance information, proposals, and forecasts that guides the completion of tasks and the continuous improvement processes
4. The library, once represented by books and journals, now increasingly on the World Wide Web

The improvement of strategic performance is a matter of integrating these components in ways that deliver to each associate everything she needs to know, on time and without error. Like teammates, supplies, and equipment, knowledge becomes a foundation of the associate's success. In the continuous improvement world, knowledge means both how to do the job and how and why to improve the job. It must be fulfilled, subject to two constraints:

1. The privacy rights of individuals must be protected at all times.
2. The knowledge resource and the KM system must be protected against failure, loss, or misuse.

The purpose is inescapably tied to the EMR. The federal American Recovery and Reinvestment Act offers $19 billion in subsidies to stimulate adoption of the EMR. The Health Information Technologies unit of the U.S. Department of Health and Human Services posits a vision for the EMR:[1]

The ultimate vision is one in which all patients are fully engaged in their health-care, providers have real-time access to all medical information and tools to help ensure the quality and safety of the care provided while also affording improved access and elimination of health care disparities.

It also offers a timetable through 2015 for achieving the vision.

The EMR is an enhanced communication device with many features that support excellent care. It is only part of the HCO's KM activities, which embrace the full scope of evidence-based management—measurement, benchmarking, process improvement, goal setting, and rewards—and which apply to all HCO units, not simply the clinical ones.

Functions

The purpose is implemented through the five functions shown in Exhibit 10.1. KM can be considered in two parts: "data"—the up-to-the-minute flow of specifics, such as orders, conditions, and performance, that guide the job to conclusion—and "information"—refined and aggregated data that support continuous improvement. The two parts are not truly unique—hardly any data are completely unrefined, and refinement proceeds through several levels—but they support two major sets of KM activity. Both were important before automation. Automation has revolutionized the scope, manner, frequency, and speed with which data and information are generated. The functions will remain, and be better achieved, as the technology continues to improve.

Ensuring the Reliability and Validity of Data

Inaccurate data are misleading and potentially dangerous. Effective use of data requires both maximizing accuracy and understanding the level of accuracy achieved. For example, most applications involve comparing two data sets—this record versus this patient's identification, drug ordered versus drug in hand, actual versus goal, this year versus last year, Team A versus Team B. Two errors are always possible—deciding that the two are different when they are the same, or accepting the two as the same when they are different.

In modern HCOs, with thousands of associates using hundreds of thousands of pieces of information, minimizing both types of error is essential. Four steps are necessary to minimize these errors: (1) Standard definitions must be established, (2) the definitions must be consistently applied as data are captured, (3) statistical specification and adjustment must be included when necessary, and (4) random variation and confidence limits must be estimated. Part of KM is a structure of expert committees, rules, and software to fulfill these steps. The goal is to produce measures that are fully understood and accepted by their users so that the debate can be about the opportunities for improvement (OFIs), not the measures themselves. (Like much of evidence-based management, this is a heuristic process; measures acceptable last year may need redesign.) Sharp HealthCare, a 2007 recipient of the Malcolm Baldrige National Quality Award (MBNQA), identifies the following criteria:

Function	Content
Ensuring the reliability and validity of data	Defines measures and terminology; supports accurate, complete data input; applies appropriate specification and adjustment; estimates reliability of data
Maintaining communications for daily operations	Operates a 24/7 electronic and voice communication utility; supports software used in clinical and business functions; integrates data from multiple sources
Supporting information retrieval for continuous improvement	Retrieves and integrates historical data; supports Web access for research and comparative data for management and clinical decisions Provides protocols, processes, training videos, and other materials that support training programs Provides training in the use of automated systems and consulting service in interpretation and information availability
Ensuring the appropriate use and security of data	Guards against loss, theft, and inappropriate application
Improving knowledge management services continuously	Establishes a prioritized agenda for progress; incorporates user views; commits a block of capital funds for several years; supports an annual review of specific projects

EXHIBIT 10.1
Functions of Knowledge Management Services

- Reference in evidence-based literature
- Use by regulatory and public reports
- Availability of competitor data
- Use by other MBNQA recipients
- Availability of benchmarks in healthcare and beyond

Sharp evaluates potential benchmarks for comparability and statistical validity, reliability, and specification.[2]

Defining Measures and Terminology

Any term that is used in a quantitative system must have a precise definition standardized across all users. Terms like "admission," "patient day," and "unit price" appear straightforward, but in reality they require specific, written definitions to avoid inconsistencies. For example, is a patient kept overnight in the emergency department an admission? How many hours must a patient stay to be counted as one patient day? Is the price what is billed or what is collected?

Many complex terms are used on a national or international basis and must be standardized accordingly. Clinical diagnoses, accounting definitions, and hospital statistics are examples. Diagnoses are standardized as the International Classification of Diseases (ICD), maintained by the World Health Organization.[3] By 2013, the ICD-9 will be replaced by ICD-10. The Centers for Medicare & Medicaid Services (CMS) will no longer accept ICD-9-based claims for payment. Effort is underway to replace ICD-10 with SNOMED CT (Systematized Nomenclature of Medicine–Clinical Terms), a comprehensive set of standard terms for clinical information for use in electronic health records.[4] Similarly, accounting and financial terms are standardized by a national panel—the Financial Accounting Standards Board. The American Hospital Association maintains a set of common definitions and statistics for national reporting.[5] The Joint Commission and CMS have agreed on a set of commonly defined quality measures.[6] HIPAA (Health Insurance Portability and Accountability Act) mandates the use of standard definitions for common patient transactions.[7, 8]

With the advent of computers, it became necessary to standardize not only definitions but also interfacing hardware, software, and data specifications. Much standardization is accomplished through voluntary trade associations, like the American National Standards Institute. The U.S. Department of Health and Human Services supports the National eHealth Collaborative, "a public-private partnership driving the grassroots development of a secure, interoperable, nationwide health information system,"[9] and Healthcare Information Technology Standards Panel (HITSP), a public–private partnership, "to enable and support widespread interoperability among healthcare software applications."[10] HITSP has several hundred specifications, such as implementation of quality measures from the National Quality Measures Clearinghouse and protocols for transferring x-rays and other images.

In HCOs, a committee oversees the definitions of measures used to ensure appropriate standardization. National standards are used wherever possible because they facilitate all forms of outside communication and benchmarking. Failing to follow diagnosis or accounting rules can lead to criminal charges. Measures that have no national standard can be standardized by consensus among the users. Finally, new measures can be used in a single or small set of pilot applications, and they are standardized when necessary to expand their use. The committee can audit use of standard definitions on its own or through internal audit mechanisms. The definition includes statistical specification and adjustment. The committee's decisions are incorporated into educational programs and software to ensure consistent application.

Data Capture   Standard definitions must be rigorously applied to each transaction. Common problem areas are completeness and accuracy. Missing information can be as destructive as errors. The following steps ensure that the information entered into the database is as accurate as possible:

1. *Automated entry is preferable to human entry.* Scanners and devices to retrieve information from electronic archives are superior to their human counterparts. Entry forms, with selections from drop-down lists, are superior to free text.

2. *All important information is edited and audited electronically at entry to ensure accuracy.* Edits are based on a single field of information; the field must contain a certain kind of data, such as certain numbers or letters, or selection from a certain list; these eliminate omissions and keystroke errors. Audits compare two or more fields and flag inconsistency; cross-checks of age, gender, and diagnosis are common examples. Manual audits—reentries by different personnel—can be conducted periodically to assess and maintain the desired accuracy level.

3. *Retrieval is preferable to reentry.* Information should be captured for electronic processing only once. Subsequent references require reentry of a few fields of identifying information before the complete entry can be recovered.

4. *Training and consultation are used to improve accuracy.* Judgment is often required for entries such as account codes or ICDs. Users must be trained to achieve consistency. Managers, accountants, and internal auditors provide advice on difficult questions. Most institutions have nosologists—specialists trained in medical definitions and codes—available to help their clinical teams.

Commercial software is now available for most clinical information-capture operations. It is designed for accurate entry and user convenience, includes extensive edits and audits, and facilitates prompt retrieval and linkage across multiple data sources.

Specification and Adjustment

Accurate definitions and careful data capture substantially reduce noise in data sets. But with human patients being treated by human caregivers, cases are never truly identical; some random variation always remains. As the data are aggregated over time and work sites, questions of comparability arise: How can Population A be made more comparable to Population B? These questions are answered by **specification**, identifying subsets of the data that show less variation, and **adjustment**, using specification subsets to estimate comparable total populations. Specification and adjustment allow apples-to-apples comparison; they are important in many clinical measures. The following example shows the statistical processes involved and the outcome in terms of comparing death rates in two populations.

Specification
A statistical analysis that identifies values for a measure by defined subsets of a population, to measure the extent to which the values change across the sets

Adjustment
A statistical technique using specification to remove variation caused by differences in the relative size of subset populations

Specification

Specification defines more homogeneous subpopulations within a larger, more heterogeneous population. It is necessary whenever parts of the total population have different responses to the measure in question, and the parts vary for reasons outside the organization's control. An example would be infant birth weight, which is affected by socioeconomic characteristics. A month-to-month comparison of low-birth-weight-baby counts is more reliable if it is specified for low-income and higher-income mothers.

Specification is common in clinical measures of cost and quality. Hip-replacement recovery rates can be specified by age and the degree of loss of function before surgery. To forecast births, one specifies the female population by age and marital status, recognizing that young married women are more likely to become pregnant than older or unmarried women. To find homogeneous groups for survival after AMI, one specifies populations by age, gender, education, clinical conditions such as initial blood pressure, and treatment conditions such as use of beta-blockers. For example, a specific subpopulation would be women, over age 50 years, college graduates, with previous history of diastolic blood pressure over 90 mm mercury, and receiving beta-blockers. Common taxonomies for specifying patient care performance are shown in Exhibit 10.2. (The process of specification is analogous to "segmentation" in marketing and is discussed further in Chapter 15.)

Adjustment   Adjusted rates recalculate the whole population rate from the specific rates, standardizing to the characteristics of a single population. They are useful to eliminate differences between populations. For example, mortality rates are adjusted to the age and sex of the U.S. population as a whole. The age-adjusted rate for each state is the mortality rate it would have if its population had the same age distribution as the nation's. The 50 states can then be compared and ranked.

Exhibit 10.3 shows the impact of specification and adjustment. It reports the crude, specific, and age-adjusted death rates for Utah and Florida. The crude rates suggest that Floridians are more likely to die than Utahans. The age-specific rates reveal that is true if they are under 65, but not if they are older. Overall, an age-adjusted comparison shows the Florida rate to be 10 percent lower than that for Utah, not 73 percent higher as the crude rates

EXHIBIT 10.2
Common
Patient
Specification
Taxonomies

Category	Classifications	Category	Classifications
Demographic	Age Sex Race Education	Healthcare finance	Managed vs. traditional insurance Private vs. government insurance
Economic	Income Employment Social class	Diagnosis	Disease classification Procedure Diagnosis-related group Ambulatory visit group
Geographic	Zip code of residence Census tract Political subdivision	Risk	Health behavior attribute Preexisting condition Chronic or high-cost disease

EXHIBIT 10.3

Age-Specific, Crude, and Adjusted Rates: Utah Versus Florida

	Utah			Florida		
	Crude death rate = (10,218 deaths/1,724,000 population) = 5.9 deaths/1,000 population			Crude death rate = (132,717 deaths/12,983,000 population) = 10.2 deaths/1,000 population		
	Age-Specific Death Rates			Age-Specific Death Rates		
Age Category	Deaths	Population (000)	Age-Specific Death Rate	Deaths	Population (000)	Age-Specific Death Rate
0–14	450	538	0.836	2,742	2,412	1.137
15–44	804	789	1.019	11,822	5,595	2.113
45–64	1,446	245	5.902	19,367	2,548	7.601
65–75	2,894	90	32.156	30,618	1,369	22.365
⋯>75	4,624	62	74.581	68,168	1,059	64.370
All ages	10,218	1,724	5.927	132,717	12,983	10.222

Adjusted Death Rate: Utah death rate standardized to Florida population

	Utah Death Rate	Florida Population	Expected Deaths
0–14	0.836	2,412	2,016
15–44	1.019	5,595	5,701
45–64	5.902	2,548	15,038
65–75	32.156	1,369	44,022
⋯>75	74.581	1,059	78,981
All ages	5.927	12,983	145,758

Utah death rate adjusted to Florida population
= Expected deaths/Florida pop. 145,758/12,983 = 11.23

indicate. Many nationally defined clinical measures are adjusted for multiple factors to remove characteristics beyond the caregivers' control and allow fair comparison to trend or benchmark. The possibility of an omitted variable remains, however. It should be raised as part of a root cause analysis: "Are there other characteristics, any other factors outside the unit's control that we should consider?"

Diagnosis is an important basis for specification and adjustment. Diagnosis-related groups (DRGs) and ambulatory patient classifications (APCs) group

Severity Adjustment

patients with similar ICD-9-CM diseases into homogeneous populations and are used for the Medicare prospective payment system.[11] CMS calculates a severity index for each DRG patient group from its entire database. If there are $i = 1, \ldots n$ DRGs, each HCO can calculate its severity-weighted discharges:

$$\left\{ \begin{array}{l} \text{Severity-} \\ \text{weighted} \\ \text{discharges} \end{array} \right\} = \sum_{i=1}^{n} \left(\text{Discharges}_i \times \text{Severity index}_i \right)$$

And its average severity:

$$\left\{ \begin{array}{l} \text{Average} \\ \text{severity} \end{array} \right\} = \left\{ \begin{array}{l} \text{Severity-} \\ \text{weighted} \\ \text{discharges} \end{array} \right\} \div \left\{ \text{Total discharges} \right\}$$

And a severity-weighted cost or length of stay (LOS) for each DRG i (or any set of DRGs of interest):

$$\left\{ \begin{array}{l} \text{Severity-adjusted} \\ \text{average cost/case} \end{array} \right\} = \left\{ \begin{array}{l} \text{Average cost per} \\ \text{discharge DRG}_i \end{array} \right\} \div \left\{ \begin{array}{l} \text{Severity} \\ \text{index DRG}_i \end{array} \right\}$$

$$\left\{ \begin{array}{l} \text{Severity-adjusted} \\ \text{LOS/discharge} \end{array} \right\} = \left\{ \begin{array}{l} \text{Average LOS per} \\ \text{discharge DRG}_i \end{array} \right\} \div \left\{ \begin{array}{l} \text{Severity} \\ \text{index DRG}_i \end{array} \right\}$$

Outcomes other than cost or LOS, such as mortality or recovery rates, can be similarly adjusted. Similar calculations are possible for outpatient care using the APC. Severity adjustment allows at least a crude comparison of costs between HCOs, service lines, or other groupings. It is only a beginning, however; there are many possibilities for omitted variables beyond the caregiving teams' control.

Reporting Variability and Reliability of Estimates

Few performance measures are exact. In healthcare, the list is limited to simple counts and some accounting information. Commonly used measures like laboratory test values, cost per case, length of stay, percent of patients "loyal," and percent of patients surviving are all subject to random variation that can mislead users. Adjustment reduces, but never removes, random variation. Statistical analysis assigns confidence limits around reported values and estimates of the probability that a specific difference is worth investigating. Investigating noise (Deming's *special causes*—meaning factors that are unique and may not recur) is a waste of time; when a variation is significant (Deming's *common causes*), an investigating team is likely to be able to find a cause for the difference. The "level of significance" is in fact the probability that a cause can be found. "Significant at 95 percent" is a forecast that 19 times out of 20 a diligent team will find a potentially correctable cause.

The variability of a measure is as important as the value, and both should be reported. The usual variability indicators are the standard deviation (used to compare two individual values) and the standard error (used to compare two samples with several individual values in each). Modern **statistical process control** software calculates both measures, shows trends and significance graphically, and automatically flags significant differences.

Statistical process control
A method of identifying significant changes in measures subject to random variation

Maintaining Communications for Daily Operations

The communications level of KM maintains the ongoing activities of patient care, clinical support, and logistic and strategic support. Many thousands of individual communications, like a patient admission, a supplies order, an invoice, a paycheck, an e-mail, or a voice conversation, occur each day. With the growth of telemedicine—to support home and office care at distant sites and to provide instant support in intensive care units—the communications network now includes streaming video and live two-way communication.[12,13]

These communications use various hardware and software platforms. Many require integration across platforms. Operating communications must support all of these transactions, and record most of them. As hardware and software have matured, this function has reached very high standards of reliability. It is taken for granted until the rare service disruption occurs. The major components of the function are maintaining the networks, managing the software, and arranging storage and access.

Maintaining the Networks

A local utility for all kinds of electronic communications must be available 24/7/365, achieving reliability near 100 percent. Service must be convenient and prompt. Achieving standards of reliability, promptness, and convenience requires a substantial investment in equipment and support personnel, but like ensuring data reliability, it is the essential foundation for all other KM activities.

The communication utility usually consists of broadband cable that supports computer access, Web access, and conventional telephones, plus wireless capability for computers, handheld devices, pagers, cell phones, clinical telemetry equipment, and two-way radio. The utility is now usually operated as an intranet, allowing access from multiple sites through the Internet and integrating smoothly with outside software. The network achieves reliability with redundancy. Not only are there multiple servers and paths for each kind of activity, but some parts—conventional telephones and two-way radios are examples—are also now principal backup for newer technology.

Managing General- and Special-Purpose Software

General-purpose software—usually Microsoft Office and a number of utilities such as a Web browser, a page designer, a document reader, and a statistical package—now requires little technical support, but information systems (IS) must negotiate the licenses and monitor their use as indicated. Training programs are necessary for most of these applications; many are supplied by the vendor.

HCOs require many special-purpose software sets. The EMR requires a battery of special-purpose software that supports data entry and retrieval from multiple geographic sites; recovers historical data; and generates reports for patient use, performance measurement, and accounting. Each of the clinical, logistic, and strategic support systems now has special-purpose software. Accounting has one of the largest. A typical accounting software system accomplishes the following:

- Billing and collection
- Payroll management
- Supplies management
- Cash and investment management
- Financial accounting and financial reporting
- Cost finding and cost reporting
- Budget development
- Long-range financial plan
- Business analysis

Human resources, facilities management, internal consulting, marketing, and strategic planning have special-purpose software that supports their functions. Clinical support systems have patient, associate, and facility scheduling systems. Many integrate data from specialized hardware, such as imaging or blood-chemistry analyzers. Data are captured directly from these systems and fed to other special or general systems, as when a digital radiographic image is placed in the EMR and forwarded to the imagist for a report. Performance and accounting statistics are generated automatically. The systems are increasingly integrated and sold as "enterprise" systems—comprehensive automated data processing for the activity.

The communications function must ensure that these software packages are supported by network hardware, that they are consistent with the definitions and standards, that their data can be integrated, and that they offer appropriate security. These issues are usually managed by KM associates, working with ad hoc task forces or committees. The software is licensed, and KM manages the licenses, including negotiating prices.

Integrating Data from Multiple Sources

Integrating the wide range of hardware and software platforms has historically been a substantial challenge. Most of the special-purpose software must draw data from several different sources. For example, a caregiver's drug-ordering decision requires data from the patient's record; from a protocol suggesting alternatives; and from a pharmacy system that will audit dosage, contraindications, and drug interactions and update the inventory. It will trigger alerts for the nurse to administer it and record administration. Beyond these communication activities, the data will be integrated to support a variety of analytic applications, such as drug error rates, studies of pharmacy workloads, audits of diagnostic coding, and epidemiologic planning applications.

The modern solution is an intranet, essentially a local version of the Web that accommodates almost any kind of file or platform, and special-purpose software to integrate the information for specific purposes, such as drug management or performance reporting. Historically, many of the information-handling systems developed independently. These systems—called **legacy systems**—were not designed to integrate with others. Over time, the problem of legacy systems will diminish, but the core issue of meeting both the needs of the within-system user and the external user will remain.

Legacy system
Outdated computer software that lacks the features found in more current versions

Supporting Information Retrieval for Continuous Improvement

KM calls for a second level of exchange, where data are aggregated, refined, and turned into information. Information—the evidence in evidence-based management—is used often in several different ways that support the continuous improvement processes, as shown in Exhibit 10.4.

The Data Warehouse and the Web

The data warehouse and Web access facilitate information retrieval. Internal data come from the support service IS and the EMR, as shown in Exhibit 10.4. Examples of important uses of information are shown in Exhibit 10.5. The final assembly of the reports is facilitated by the use of **database management systems** and data-modeling techniques. Database management allows access to individual fields of data within a record so that different sets of records can be accessed and analyzed quickly. For example, discharges can be specified by age, sex, and diagnosis; a set of orders for a specific service can be attached to each diagnosis; and cost information can be added from accounting records to begin an investigation of changing a protocol. Data-modeling techniques allow KM workers to map the sources of the data they need and the calculations that must be made prior to writing a macro or program to generate a report. The archive of performance data is used routinely by the strategic support units to forecast trends, analyze relationships, and model alternative approaches.

Database management system
A system for retrieving shared electronic data designed to facilitate the recovery and use of data

The Web is used to verify the latest published work and consensus positions on complex issues.[14] The National Library of Medicine's PubMed has more than 19 million articles from 5,200 journals indexed in its Medline section. Most have abstracts. Commercial vendors provide direct access to the journals themselves.[15] Alliances and not-for-profit groups, such as the Institute for Healthcare Improvement and the National Center for Healthcare Leadership, maintain websites for supporting organizations. Government organizations, such as the Agency for Healthcare Research and Quality

EXHIBIT 10.4
Examples
of Internal
Data Feeding
the Data
Warehouse

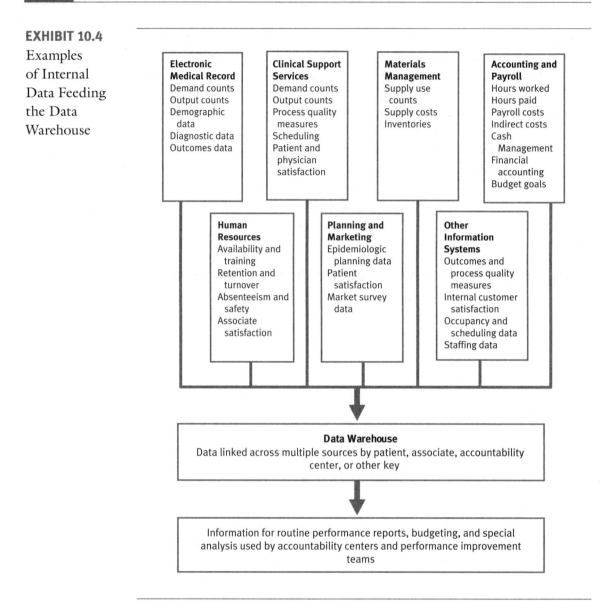

EXHIBIT 10.4
Examples of Internal Data Feeding the Data Warehouse

and the National Library of Medicine, maintain extensive, free access. All of these external sources become important when processes are studied for improvement. The insights gained by these studies help process improvement teams identify new alternatives.

Training and Supporting Users

Success for KM means that the organization as a whole effectively uses information, a more demanding standard than simply providing and explaining the information. Effective use requires a sophisticated user training and support program. Training and support are generally provided in segments, beginning with use of the hardware and software, progressing through common applications, and continuing to interpretation and sources of ongoing support.

Application	Data Warehouse Information	World Wide Web Information
Reporting performance	Recent data relative to goals Graphs, statistical process control	—
Identifying OFIs	"Drill down" to identify potential causes Local benchmarks and comparative performance	Journal articles, collaboratives, and comparative information
Setting goals	Local trends, benchmarks, and forecasts	External benchmarks and best practices
Supporting PITs	Analytic models, simulations, and forecasts	Books and journal articles, regulatory standards, and recommended practices
Reviewing protocols	Reported variances from protocol "Drill down" of outcomes to show patient-specific groups Analytic models and simulations	National clearinghouses, commission reports, journal articles, and books
Managing individual patients	—	Journal articles, guidelines, and diagnostic software

OFI: opportunity for improvement; PIT: process improvement team

EXHIBIT 10.5
Common Uses of Information in High-Performing HCOs

KM often works with other units to provide a comprehensive training experience. Much of the training is delivered just-in-time, in response to issues encountered by PITs. For example, a new associate involved in patient registration (where the identifying information for the medical and billing records is captured) needs training in approaching patients and families, understanding confidentiality and elementary rules about guardianship, using the input screens, and learning the appropriate definitions. Most important, the associate has to know when she needs help and where to get it. (Simple questions become complicated quite easily. What is the correct address for a minor with divorced parents? Who signs the admission form? What do you do if the parents disagree or if one is missing?) Human resources and the associate's manager provide most of this training, but KM is involved at several steps:

1. A video describes the HCO's mission, vision, and values. A second might expand the HCO's policies regarding relations with patients and associates, dress, compensation, and benefits. Mastery of key rules can be tested.
2. A training module teaches completion of electronic forms for data entry. The module can include multiple scenarios that test the associate's understanding.

3. Guardianship, HIPAA, and advance directive materials can be summarized and backed with specific procedures. The associate has access at her computer. Mastery of this material can also be tested.
4. A set of frequently asked questions can be supplemented by the associate's own notes.

The electronic training resources provide a foundation that documents mastery at Kirkpatrick level 3 (application; see Chapter 3 for this discussion), both confirming learning and building the associate's confidence. It does this relatively inexpensively so that it can be complemented by proxy patients, role playing, supervised trial, and mentoring. The combination achieves the goal, which is to create an associate who "delights" the customer, is "loyal" to the organization, and enters the data completely and correctly.

Training for more complex tasks is accomplished similarly, by breaking the process down into components. Thus, sophisticated systems can be built. For example, patient diagnosis is made in standardized words by physicians, translated to ICD codes by clerical employees, and coded to DRGs or APCs by programmed algorithms. Most cases are not difficult to code, but the handling of multiple diagnoses is challenging, important, and commonplace among older patients. The ICD coders have access to code lists with definitions and examples, interpretation of terminology, training in reviewing the record to catch diagnoses omitted by the physician (a review that can be automated in the EMR), and a knowledgeable nosologist or supervisor trained in clinical coding. They can specialize in a limited set of diseases. They also have the option of returning to the physician for further clarification. Finally, a blind test can be run to check inter-coder consistency, and audits can be focused on the codes where errors are more likely.

Ensuring the Appropriate Use and Security of Data

The communication and information systems and archives of KM are resources of incalculable value. They are subject to several perils. Physical destruction or loss can result from mislabeling, theft, fire, electrical power disturbances, floods, magnetic interference, and deterioration.[16] Communications can be interrupted by power or equipment failure. Data, software, and hardware can be stolen or sabotaged by outsiders or associates. Clinical and other personal information owned by the individual patient or associate can be stolen or inadvertently exposed. KM is responsible for managing these risks.

Protecting Against Loss, Destruction, or System Failure

The normal protections against loss, destruction, or system failure are physical protection of sites, duplication of both records and systems, separate geographic locations of originals and duplicates, selection of personnel, and antivirus software. Thus, central processing and archiving sites are safely located and physically protected. Processing hardware is deliberately redundant. Shadow systems maintain duplicate records available within a few seconds. Routine backups are kept in separate, ultra-secure sites. Personnel working in KM are subject to careful selection, bonding, surveillance, and auditing. Outsiders are kept out by passwords and security devices and detected by activity monitors.

The entire KM operation depends on an electricity supply, and some parts have narrow tolerances for voltage and frequency variation. HCOs normally have two separate feeds from the national electric power grid, local generators, and specifically designed "uninterruptible" power supplies for servers that meet the voltage and frequency tolerances.

A well-managed HCO has a formal plan for maintaining protection and confidentiality and a recovery plan for each of the perils. KM is responsible for maintaining this plan, including monitoring effectiveness and conducting periodic drills for specific disasters.

KM is responsible for designing and maintaining systems to protect information against unauthorized use. Most data about individual patients and employees are confidential, and the organization is liable for misuse. HIPAA mandates rigorous privacy and confidentiality protocols that protect patient data from unauthorized use.[17,18] KM must identify the confidentiality requirements and incorporate controls in operations to ensure that they are met.[19] These usually take the form of verifying patient authorization, requiring user identification, and restricting access to qualified users. Identification cards, passwords, and voice readers are currently used to protect access; biometric identification appears possible in the future.

Maintaining Confidentiality of Information

Confidentiality is also important in archiving and retrieval. The archive must be protected from inappropriate use, and reporting must be constructed in ways that prevent inference about individuals from aggregate data. Centralized archiving and monitoring of data uses and users protect against these dangers. Restrictions on access to small sets of data or certain combinations of data can be built into the archive or the data retrieval system.

The issue of confidentiality is important, but relative. Many healthcare confidentiality problems are similar to other information sources that are now automated, such as driving records, credit records, and income tax files. The real question is one of the benefits of convenient access versus the risk of damage.[20] Reasonable steps to reduce the risk are required, backed by ongoing programs to ensure compliance. Manual systems of handling patient and personnel information were far from foolproof. Properly designed, electronic systems can reduce the chance of misuse or inappropriate access and can also improve appropriate use.

Improving Knowledge Management Services Continuously

KM is a rapidly changing activity. It identifies OFIs from its own measurement and benchmarking system, from regulation, from new technology in the marketplace, and from user requests for expanded service. It requires a steady stream of funds for new capital equipment, expanded services, and expanded training and support. Demand for improvement will exceed supply, creating a waiting list that tends to be longer in better-managed organizations. KM improvements are complex. They must be integrated with changes in work processes in other units to yield benefits. Important projects can require several years to complete.[21] As a result, KM requires a sophisticated planning process for continuous improvement,[22] such as the one shown in Exhibit 10.6, managed by a KM planning committee or steering committee. Successful planning processes have several important characteristics:

- *They are built around explicit collaboration with application units, because KM cannot itself control the results.* Most proposals have four parts:
    1. A KM change (new hardware, software, or information capability) will be installed in some HCO activity other than KM.
    2. The installation will support improved work processes.
    3. The improved work processes will improve operational measures.
    4. Improved operations will create improvements in HCO strategic measures. For example, software to improve patient scheduling in outpatient offices will increase the number of patients who can be seen. If marketing and other parts of the primary care service line are effective, outpatients seen and correctly treated will increase. As outpatient visits increase, HCO revenue and profit will increase.
- *They establish project teams with detailed goals, analogous to facility construction projects.*[23] For the outpatient enhancement project, the process improvement team (PIT) must include primary care, nursing, marketing, and KM. It is likely to work through a battery of subteams establishing the software vendor, pilot tests, an installation timetable, revised patient management protocols, and an associate training plan. The PIT will have associates or contractors accountable for progress and operational improvement.
- *The project teams are monitored by the KM planning committee.*[24] Larger HCOs will have several project teams operating at once and will need the planning committee as a managing body.
- *Funding is established on a multiyear basis, usually by allocating a portion of the total funds available for new programs and capital to KM projects.* For the foreseeable future, most HCOs will spend a significant fraction of their available funds on KM improvement. The amounts, the benefits, and the timetables will be built into the long-range financial plan and other planning activities.
- *The governing board's review focuses on two questions, "What are the strategic improvements that justify the investment?" and "How closely do the documented successes from installed projects track the benefits expected?"* These questions put a premium on IS performance and enforce continuous improvement of internal operations.

The process makes KM a supplier to the other units of the organization. It is analogous to the process that an independent vendor of IS uses

EXHIBIT 10.6
Knowledge
Management
Planning Proess

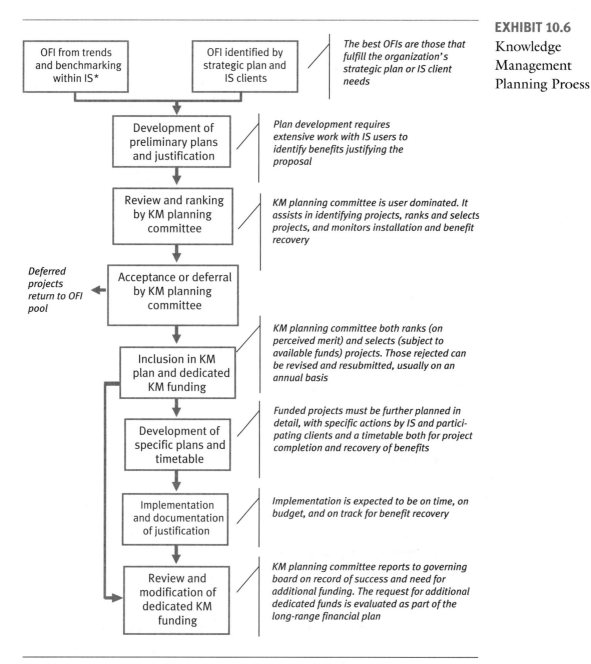

IS: information systems; KM: knowledge management; OFI: opportunity for improvement

to develop its long-range plan. It demands that the KM staff both listen to and work closely with their internal customers. An opportunity that arises internally must be thoroughly studied to develop justifications; that study requires review of its implications for customer work processes.[25] Review by a customer-dominated KM planning committee keeps the department plan and the KM plan focused appropriately on service.

People

KM staff include numerous professionals in programming, hardware maintenance, nosology, statistics, user support, and training. They are led by the chief information officer (CIO) and the KM planning committee and are organized by function.

Chief Information Officer

The role of a CIO has emerged with the growth of KM and has grown with the centrality of KM itself. CIOs report either to the CEO or chief operating officer and are part of the senior management team. The CIO role requires mastery of information technology in healthcare and managerial skills. First and foremost, the CIO must see that the KM unit effectively supports the organization. The role also requires leadership and negotiating skills. In many situations, the CIO's role is to convince others of the power of information and encourage them to use it effectively.[26] Like other senior management, the CIO should have a succession plan for the critical personnel in KM and individual development plans for all managers to help them achieve their potential. Many high-performing HCOs are increasing clinical skills in KM units. Medical information officers have assumed prominent roles on the KM team.[27,28]

Education for the CIO can follow several routes. Training in computer operations, management engineering, or medical records administration provides a useful beginning,[29,30] but an advanced degree in management engineering, business, or health administration is valuable. Many CIOs in larger facilities have doctoral-level preparation. Experience in healthcare information systems is clearly essential. Consulting experience is also common in CIO backgrounds. A professional organization—the Health Information and Management Systems Society—provides continuing education and professional certification.[31]

KM Planning Committee

KM planning and oversight transcends all HCO functional boundaries. As it carries out the steps of Exhibit 10.6, the KM planning committee must deal with issues similar to those faced by the governing board.[32] The charge to the team or committee includes the following:

- Participating in the development of the KM plan, resolving the strategic priorities, and recommending the plan to the governing board
- Ranking KM investment opportunities and recommending a rank-ordered list of proposals to the governing board
- Assisting KM clients in identifying and meeting KM opportunities
- Supporting the definitions and standards committee
- Monitoring performance of the division, and suggesting possible improvements

The KM planning committee routinely comprises key personnel from major departments, particularly finance, internal consulting, medicine, nursing, and clinical support services. The CIO is always a member and may chair the committee. Members of the governing board may serve on the committee. The team uses a variety of task forces and subcommittees, expanding participation in component activities but using its authority to coordinate.[33]

Organization

KM organization must establish accountability for each of its five functions. The data communications function is the largest unit and is often called *operations*. Glandon, Smaltz, and Slovensky suggest that it divides into subsections as indicated in Exhibit 10.7; they also note that many KM units have close ties to other parts of the HCO. Specialists in operations for various support services and service lines are common.[34]

Measures

Performance measures for KM should cover the full set of six dimensions shown in Exhibit 10.8. Benchmarks, customer needs, competitive outsourcing alternatives, and the experience of consultants are used to guide negotiations over annual goals. Most of the measures in Exhibit 10.8 are derived from standard cost accounts, automated operating logs, activities of the KM units, and the details of the improvement portfolio. Many can be automated and obtained at low cost. Some require special surveys of line managers. Consultant evaluations can be used to identify goals. A large number of specific activity measures can be devised to supplement the list in Exhibit 10.8. The KM planning committee has an important role in the goal-setting negotiations.

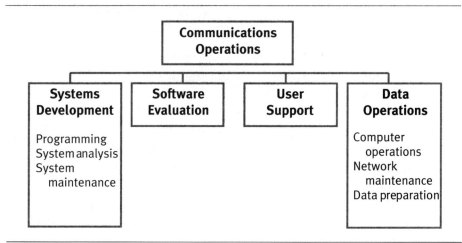

EXHIBIT 10.7
Accountability
Structure for the
Communications
Function

SOURCE: Information from Glandon, G. L., D. H. Smaltz, and D. J. Slovensky. 2008. *Austin and Boxerman's Information Systems for Healthcare Management,* 7th ed., p. 36. Chicago: AUPHA/Health Administration Press.

EXHIBIT 10.8
Measures of
Knowledge
Management
Performance

Dimension	KM Function	Measure
Demand	Reliability and validity of data	New measure requests, response time "Hits" on data warehouse materials Counts of measures in place
	Data communications	System users System peak users
	Information retrieval	Counts of measures, benchmarks in use Counts of service requests Counts of trainees
	Appropriate use and security	Passwords issued Protection systems enabled
	KM planning and improvement	Projects managed
Costs and resources	All	Units and costs of resources Capital expenditure Machine capacity
Human resources	All	Associate satisfaction, retention, absenteeism, and work loss days
Output and productivity	All	Counts of services completed Productivity measures divide cost incurred by counts of service completed
Quality	Reliability and validity of data	Counts of measures benchmarked Statistical tests of reliability, sensitivity Audit scores
	Data communications	Response delay Systems uptime Audit scores Unexpected events
	Information retrieval	Trainee mastery scores
	Appropriate use and security	Audit scores System attacks Consultant ratings
	KM planning and improvement	Projects on time Projects on budget Projects meeting original performance goals
Customer satisfaction	All	Customer surveys, interviews, complaints, and unexpected events

Managerial Issues

Properly implemented KM has become a central component of any excellent HCO's strategy, and an essential foundation for every HCO clinical or support team. Capable associates in all fields now expect KM services; recruitment and retention will be difficult if they are lacking. The KM product—information and knowledge—implements the concept of evidence-based decision making and a learning culture. The mission-critical issues, where hands-on monitoring and support by the senior management team and the KM leadership are essential, are as follows:

- Ensure effective day-to-day communications, and expand implementation of the EMR.
- Promote the integration of information from multiple sources to guide operations improvement.
- Maintain progress of the KM plan components toward excellence in care and improvement of the strategic scorecard.

The keys to achieving these lie in the KM planning committee, the effective delivery and coordination of KM services, and the appropriate use of consultants.

Exploiting the KM Planning Committee

KM is a dynamic activity, a moving target where no HCO can say, "It's finished." That makes the portfolio of projects under the KM planning committee the key to future success. As with the governing board, the committee membership needs to be broad and talented. Education programs and retreats to understand complex issues are useful. Overlapping committee membership with marketing and strategic planning and with the governing board planning committee is essential. The committee should be part of the HCO's "brain trust," along with board leadership, senior management, the medical executive committee, and the performance improvement council.

The committee should make liberal use of subcommittees and task forces, with a goal of identifying and resolving many issues close to their point of origin. The projects in the portfolio should be adequately staffed; full-time managers and implementation staffs are required to move the larger projects. Senior management's listening activity should identify and pursue both opportunities and issues with a goal of increasing the on-time, on-budget, and on-performance outcomes.

There are at least three critical points in the planning committee strategy, beginning with the relationship between the organization's strategic plan and its KM plan. The strategic plan (Chapter 15) is developed as a stakeholder consensus on the direction of improvement. It will identify the organization's most pressing needs. Senior management must align the KM plan with the strategic plan. The path to that is through extensive dialogue with customer units, helping them design their requests, and using subcommittees and task forces to resolve concerns.

The second point is to provide sufficient staff, including KM associates and time contributed by customer units, to ensure that the projects are implemented on time, on budget, and on performance. That requires effective management both inside and outside KM. Inside, KM must meet its goals with customer-responsive services and staff project teams. Outside, the KM projects are mirrored by PITs working to change work processes and generate the planned benefits. All of these steps—capital for the strategic and KM plans, planning project implementation teams, subcommittees and task forces removing roadblocks—take time and money.

The third point is to make sure that funding is adequate for implementation. Many HCOs struggle to find it. The question is the perennial "How can I drain the swamp when I'm surrounded by alligators?" The record of excellent HCOs shows that it has a two-part answer. Part one is the deliberate search for easy gains or "low-hanging fruit." The documented experience has shown that most HCOs have readily available improvements that pay off simultaneously in reduced wasted staff time, better quality, and lower costs. An important part of this dynamic is reducing clinical error. Under DRG payment, errors erode profit; fewer of them mean shorter stays, lower cost per case, and higher margins. If the initial projects are well selected and well implemented, they will generate cash flow. The role of the brain trust is to keep the cash coming.

Part two is to assess cost budgets with great care. While resource consumption is important, the central management questions for KM are not "How much are we spending?" but "What are we getting for the money?" and "How much should we spend?" It is possible to operate KM at an insufficient scale and not recognize it. The customers of KM may be satisfied with service. The cost may be below reported benchmarks. The critical test, which must be explored by the board finance committee, senior management, and the KM planning committee, is not whether current performance is acceptable but whether an additional investment would gain important returns. One way to approach this is a periodic audit by an outside expert, who can compare service as well as cost and identify the technological opportunities. In addition, the audit team can evaluate all the KM activities in light of others' achievements.

Promoting the Use of Knowledge

In addition to sustaining a strong forward motion through the KM planning committee, the information retrieval function and some aspects of the data reliability function are likely to need ongoing management support. The data communication functions of KM now work at or near six sigma levels (three failures per million operations). An HCO with recurring data communications difficulties should seek a thorough review by a skilled consultant organization. Similarly, the security function should be audited periodically by an independent consultant and should offer protection equivalent to similar organizations.

The definition of measures has moved to national or international levels and is incorporated in much special-purpose software. Specification and adjustment have also been automated. Modern data-capture software also approaches six sigma error rates. The issue of residual statistical variability requires continuing managerial attention. Many people have a bias toward accepting a variation as an OFI, without considering the inherent noise in the signal. When the variation is not statistically significant, time will be wasted if it is pursued as an OFI. Worse, some individuals or teams may be identified incorrectly as contributors. This is particularly likely and particularly dangerous when measures are applied to individual physician performance. Physicians' practices are filters; one doctor can easily accumulate a disproportionate fraction of difficult cases and find it hard to deal with that statistically.

The solution is threefold:

1. *Incorporate residual variation (i.e., sigma) in the reported data.* This helps associates learn the underlying principles and their implications. It is increasingly easy to do using statistical process control software.
2. *Pursue as OFIs only those cases that are different from the goal by three sigma or that have a nonstatistical justification.* If there is a "special cause" that can be corrected, the opportunity will arise again in the next period. The delay is cheaper than the cost of error.
3. *Provide local statistical consultation to managers and PITs.* The consultant needs only basic competence in statistics. Complex questions will be answered via the Web or consultation with topical experts. The purpose of local consultation is to guard against pursuing the impossible and to make sure that all associates are protected against incorrect criticism.

Using Outside Contractors and Vendors

KM, like most units of HCOs, can be provided by employees of the organization, by outside contractors, or by almost any combination of the two. The fact that measures are available for all important performance dimensions makes a flexible approach to the ownership possible. A well-managed organization seeks the best performance profile, whether it means internal ownership or contracting. Larger organizations tend to own KM, although every organization relies heavily on commercial vendors for both hardware and software. Smaller organizations tend to contract for comprehensive service.[35]

KM is a highly technical area, where the expertise of an outside vendor may be of great value. It pays to understand the opportunities and hazards of outside contracting and to evaluate the opportunities specifically, in terms of the documented record. At least one organization surveys and ranks major KM vendors.[36]

Several kinds of assistance from outside contractors are available for IS:

1. *Integrated software support.* Commercial companies develop *enterprise systems*—integrated comprehensive software that serves well-managed HCO activities such as a clinical support service or a logistic function (e.g., supply management). The companies that provide the software also maintain it, incorporating changes imposed by outside agencies and technological advances. These vendors sometimes offer customization services as well.
2. *Finance.* Leases and mortgages on hardware are generally available from a variety of outside sources. Software is usually available for purchase or lease from the software vendor. However, transaction costs are associated with dealing with several different companies and using general institutional debt for information systems. An outside contractor can consolidate the financing and offer a comprehensive system on a single lease.
3. *Consultation and planning.* Assistance in analyzing current capabilities, benchmarking, developing an IS plan, and selecting hardware and software is available from consultants. Larger organizations frequently rely on independent consultants to assist them in identifying all information opportunities and selecting a coordinated package.
4. *Facilities management.* A few companies that specialize in HCO needs operate on-site data-processing services under contract. These companies also arrange for financing for the facilities and can be hired for consultation and planning.
5. *Joint developmental ventures.* For those HCOs in a position to develop new or improved applications, collaboration with an established vendor is highly desirable. The vendor brings experience, extra personnel, capital, and a marketing capability if the development succeeds.

In a complex, rapidly moving technical field, the use of a consultant is often prudent. Consultants can assist materially with the IS plan. Few HCOs have the expertise to forecast developments in hardware, software, and applications. Both management consulting firms and IS specialists offer consulting services. There are advantages to each type of company, but the key criteria should be a record of successful engagements and a willingness to match competition or benchmark values on actual performance.

Facilities management of KM—contracting or outsourcing the entire operation—has appealed to both large and small organizations. As with other departments, internal KM should be compared to outsourcing alternatives in terms of specific performance measures. The desired arrangement is based on the best value for the organization as a whole. In the short run, that value is measured by the operating measures in Exhibit 10.8. In the long run, it is reflected in the HCO's strategic scorecard, but the KM planning committee and the brain trust contribute more to the gains than the KM contractor. The contracting firm is expected to name an on-site leadership team with technical skills and knowledge comparable or superior to those the organization could employ. The on-site managers are supported by the broader experience and specialized knowledge of the contractor's other employees. In concept, the model provides a much richer resource than most organizations could provide on their own. Lower-level employees may work either for the contractor or the HCO.

A role remains for internal leadership. The KM planning committee remains in place. It has a major role in selecting and working with contractors. It negotiates the annual performance goals. Contractors have no incentive to limit the hospital's costs and usually will profit from an excessive program for improvement. Thus, even with a facilities management contract, the KM planning committee and hospital governance have the responsibility to require justification, select improvements, and pace the evolution of the information system.

Healthcare systems generally centralize much of KM. They standardize definitions to provide comparative and benchmarking data. They require complete standardization of accounting and internal auditing, which virtually mandates standard software. They can frequently negotiate volume discounts on hardware and software. Training, local planning, and some user support for clinical and other systems must remain decentralized, although teaching aids can be standardized and modern communication allows expert backup that was formerly obtainable only from consultants. The performance measures are critical, as they are in selecting outside vendors. Each hospital in the system is entitled to service and price as good as or better than it could achieve on its own. But each hospital is obligated to produce and implement a plan of KM improvement.

Suggested Readings

Glandon, G. L., D. H Smaltz, and D. J. Slovensky. 2008. *Austin and Boxerman's Information Systems for Healthcare Management,* 7th ed. Chicago: AUPHA/ Health Administration Press.

Green, M. A., and M. J. Bowie. 2007. *Essentials of Health Information Management: Principles and Practices.* Delmar Cengage Learning.

McWay, D. C. 2003. *Legal Aspects of Health Information Management.* Clifton Park, NY: Thomson/Delmar Learning.

Senge, P. M. 1995. *The Fifth Discipline: The Art and Practice of the Learning Organization.* New York: Doubleday/Currency.

Wager, K. A., F. W. Lee, and J. P. Glaser. 2009. *Health Care Information Systems: A Practical Approach for Health Care Management,* 2nd ed. San Francisco: Jossey-Bass.

Notes

1. U.S. Department of Health and Human Services, Health Information Technologies. [Online information; retrieved 9/1/09.] http://healthit.hhs.gov/portal/server .pt?open=512&objID=1233&parentname=CommunityPage&parentid=0&mode=2 &in_hi_userid=10741&cached=true.

2. Sharp HealthCare. 2007. Malcolm Baldrige National Quality Award Application, p. 17.

3. ICD-10, World Health Organization. 2009. [Online information; retrieved 7/29/09.] www.who.int/classifications/icd/en/.

4. National Library of Medicine, Unified Medical Language System. [Online information; retrieved 9/1/09.] www.nlm.nih.gov/research/umls/Snomed/snomed_ main.html.

5. American Hospital Association. 2009. *Hospital Statistics 2010 Edition*. Chicago: Health Forum LLC, an affiliate of the American Hospital Association.

6. The Joint Commission. 2004. "The Joint Commission and CMS Align to Make Common Performance Measures Identical." *Joint Commission Perspectives* 24 (11): 1.

7. Rode, D. 2001. "Understanding HIPAA Transactions and Code Sets." *Journal of AHIMA* 72 (1): 26–32.

8. Roach, M. C. 2001. "HIPAA Compliance Questions for Business Partner Agreements." *Journal of AHIMA* 72 (2): 45–51.

9. National eHealth Collaborative. [Online information; retrieved 8/25/09.] www .nationalehealth.org/AboutUs.

10. Healthcare Information Technology Standards Panel. [Online information; retrieved 8/25/09.] www.hitsp.org/about_hitsp.aspx.

11. Centers for Medicare & Medicaid Services. [Online information; retrieved 6/17/05.] www.cms.hhs.gov/providers/hipps/ippsover.asp.

12. Ries, M. 2009. "Tele-ICU: A New Paradigm in Critical Care." *International Anesthesiology Clinics* 47 (1): 153–70.

13. Kobb, R., N. R. Chumbler, D. M. Brennan, and T. Rabinowitz. 2008. "Home Telehealth: Mainstreaming What We Do Well." *Telemedicine Journal & E-Health* 14 (9): 977–81.

14. Stefanelli, M. 2002. "Knowledge Management to Support Performance-Based Medicine." *Methods of Information in Medicine* 41 (1): 36–43.

15. U.S. National Center for Biotechnology Information, National Library of Medicine. [Online information; retrieved 9/8/09.] www.ncbi.nlm.nih.gov/pubmed.

16. Brown, S. M. 2001. "Information Technologies and Risk Management." In *Risk Management Handbook for Health Care Organizations*, 3rd ed., edited by R. Carroll, 380–405. San Francisco: Jossey-Bass.

17. Office for Civil Rights. "HIPAA Medical Privacy—National Standards to Protect the Privacy of Personal Health Information." [Online information; retrieved 6/21/05.] www.hhs.gov/ocr/hipaa/privacy.html.

18. Gostin, L. O. 2001. "National Health Information Privacy: Regulations Under the Health Insurance Portability and Accountability Act." *JAMA* 285 (3): 3015–21.

19. Glitz, R., and C. Stanton. 2003. "The Health Insurance Portability and Accountability Act (HIPAA) of 1996." In *Risk Management Handbook for Health Care Organizations*, 4th ed., edited by R. Carroll. San Francisco: Jossey-Bass.

20. See R. P. Solomon, "Information Technologies and Risk Management"; P. J. Para, "Evolving Risk in Cyberspace and Telemedicine"; and K. S. Davis, J. C. McConnell, and E. D. Shaw, "Data Management." 2003. In *Risk Management Hand-

book for Health Care Organizations, 4th ed., edited by R. Carroll. San Francisco: Jossey-Bass.

21. Brigl, B., E. Ammenwerth, C. Dujat, S. Graber, A. Grosse, A. Haber, C. Jostes, and A. Winter. 2005. "Preparing Strategic Information Management Plans for Hospitals: A Practical Guideline SIM Plans for Hospitals: A Guideline." *International Journal of Medical Informatics* 74 (1): 51–65.

22. Anderson, J. G. 2003. "A Framework for Considering Business Models." *Studies in Health Technology & Informatics* 92: 3–11.

23. Glaser, J. 2004. "Back to Basics Managing IT Projects." *Healthcare Financial Management* 58 (7): 34–38.

24. Ross, J. W., and P. Weil. 2002. "Six IT Decisions Your IT People Shouldn't Make." *Harvard Business Review* 80 (11): 84–91.

25. Lenz, R., and K. A. Kuhn. 2004. "Towards a Continuous Evolution and Adaptation of Information Systems in Healthcare." *International Journal of Medical Informatics* 73 (1): 75–89.

26. Griffin, J. 1997. "The Modern CIO: Forging a New Role in the Managed Care Era." *Journal of Healthcare Resource Management* 15 (4): 16–17, 20–21.

27. Leviss, J., R. Kremsdorf, and M. F. Mohaideen. 2006. "The CMIO: A New Leader for Health Systems." *Journal of the American Medical Informatics Association* 13 (5): 573–78.

28. Runy, L. A. 2008. "The Changing Role of the CMIO." *Hospitals & Health Networks* 82 (2): 37–42.

29. Moore, R. A., and E. S. Berner. 2004. "Assessing Graduate Programs for Healthcare Information Management/Technology (HIM/T) Executives." *International Journal of Medical Informatics* 73 (2): 195–203.

30. Brettle, A. 2003. "Information Skills Training: A Systematic Review of the Literature." *Health Information & Libraries Journal* 20 (S1): 3–9.

31. Health Information and Management Systems Society. [Online information; retrieved 7/29/09.] www.himss.org.

32. Glandon, G. L., D. H. Smaltz, and D. J. Slovensky. 2008. *Austin and Boxerman's Information Systems for Healthcare Management*, 7th ed., 53–57. Chicago: AUPHA/Health Administration Press.

33. Sjoberg, C., and T. Timpka. 1998. "Participatory Design of Information Systems in Health Care." *Journal of the American Medical Informatics Association* 5 (2): 177–83.

34. Glandon, Smaltz, and Slovensky (2008), 34–37.

35. Menachemi, N., D. Burke, M. Diana, and R. Brooks. 2005. "Characteristics of Hospitals That Outsource Information System Functions." *Journal of Healthcare Information Management* 19 (1): 63–69.

36. KLAS. [Online information; retrieved 9/3/09.] www.klasresearch.com.

11 HUMAN RESOURCES MANAGEMENT

In a Few Words

A healthcare organization's (HCO) associates—its human resource—constitute its most valuable and improvable asset. Their *loyalty* (willingness to continue working and willingness to recommend to others) and *learning* (ability to identify, design, and implement improvements) measure their worth. To implement the service excellence concept, high-performing HCOs have substantially expanded human resources management in recent years. The expansions have come in training programs for individuals and managers, in incentive compensation, and in increased services designed to recruit and retain the human resource that reflects the culture of its community. The expansions must be justified by improvement in strategic measures. They must be reinforced by senior management actions, fairness as perceived by the associates, and an achievable strategic plan.

Critical Issues in Human Resources Management

1. *Treating the human resource as an investment:*
   - Understand the value added by skilled associates
   - Use the transformational culture to build retention
   - Identify and respond to associate developmental needs

2. *Measuring and improving associate loyalty:*
   - Ensure safety and comfort in the workplace
   - Identify and address opportunities for improvement (OFIs) from surveys and collective assessments
   - Listen and respond to OFIs from individual comments

3. *Building a competent workforce and an attractive workplace environment:*
   - Train associates for teamwork
   - Stop overt discrimination and harassment
   - Implement a value of respect
   - Develop rewards and incentives for excellent performance

4. *Promoting service excellence:*
   - Train workers in meeting customer needs
   - Train managers in responding to worker needs
   - Provide rewards for exceptional effort in customer responsiveness

5. *Building workforce diversity and bench strength:*
   - Encourage individual leadership-development plans
   - Identify and assist high-potential associates for advancement
   - Plan for workforce diversity and cultural sensitivity
   - Maintain succession plans for key positions

QUESTIONS FOR DISCUSSION

Consider these questions as you read the chapter.

1. Why have many organizations found that worker loyalty promotes customer loyalty? Are there situations where that might not be true?

2. Why is workforce diversity important in HCOs? Why are some ethnic groups and women underrepresented in higher-paying positions? What are the steps that can improve diversity?

3. The well-run HCO strives for compensation that treats similar positions equitably and that is competitive with similar employment elsewhere. Why? Are there important counter arguments? What are the alternative compensation criteria?

4. Suppose you found yourself in management of an organization that was in trouble on all the strategic scorecard measures in Exhibit 1.11. How would you start recovery, with operations, finance, workforce loyalty, or customer loyalty? What might a successful recovery strategy look like?

5. The chapter argues not that the human resource be treated fairly but that the individual associates must perceive that they are treated fairly. Is that really an important distinction? Why? It notes that perceived fairness requires that senior leadership "go beyond the letter of the law." What happens if they do not meet that standard?

Human resources management (HRM) provides the logistic and strategic support to sustain and improve the human resource. The human resource of an HCO—its associates—includes several dozen licensed or certified job classifications and clinical specialties. Most are employed, but physicians are often affiliated through a privilege contract and others work under long- and short-term service contracts. A not insignificant number are volunteers. In total, a medium-sized HCO requires more than 1,500 associates working at about 1,000 full-time jobs in about 100 different skills.[1]

Each associate joins the organization in a voluntary exchange transaction, seeking some combination of income, rewarding activity, society, and recognition. Some aspects of the exchange relationship with associates deserve emphasis:

1. *The associates are absolutely essential to continued operation.* Evidence from other fields suggests that employee loyalty is important to sustain customer loyalty.[2] Unusually high motivation can provide a margin of excellence, while only a few highly dissatisfied associates can disrupt operations.[3]
2. *Becoming an associate is a free choice for most people.* Success in attracting and keeping associates tends to be self-sustaining; the organization with a satisfied, well-qualified associate group attracts more capable and enthusiastic people.
3. *Almost any patient draws, directly or indirectly, on the services of many associates.* Effective care demands that associates are coordinated. In fact, a great many failures occur at the hand-offs—where the care is transferred from one activity or individual to another.
4. *The associates represent only about 3 percent of the community served, but because of their close affiliation and their frequent contact with patients, they are unusually influential.* They promote the HCO to potential patients. They are an important economic force in the community. When aroused, they are potent politically.

The elements of the organization that establish and sustain an effective workforce have been extensively studied and are well understood.[4] The four characteristics that emerge from the literature as promoting productivity are as follows:

1. Group cohesiveness and effective teamwork, particularly the role of a responsive supervisor[5,6]
2. Guaranteed individual rights[7]
3. Some form of profit sharing or gain sharing
4. Job security and long-term employment

Purpose

The purpose of human resources management (HRM) is

to increase the contribution of the human resource to the HCO's mission by designing and implementing appropriate policies and programs.

In fulfilling its purposes, HRM becomes a central force that shapes and sustains the culture of empowerment and transformation, a major contributor to improvement goals and a critical component of strategy development.

Functions

The functions of HRM are shown in Exhibit 11.1. Modern HRM emphasizes the retention, training, and development of the associate resource. It treats the workforce as a resource that can be preserved and enriched. In excellent HCOs, HRM emphasizes training for virtually all associates, supports the transformational culture by training all managers and supporting their development, and advises on all human resource issues. Traditional HRM functions of recruitment, compensation, benefits management, and collective bargaining continue. They remain a critical but relatively less demanding part of HRM's activities.

Workforce Planning

Workforce planning allows the organization adequate time to respond to changes in the exchange environment with replacement, increases, or decreases in the numbers of associates. The workforce plan is a subsection of the organization's strategic plan (discussed in Chapter 15). It develops forecasts of the number of persons required in each skill by year for three to five years in the future. It also projects available human resources, including additions and attrition, and even specifies the planned retirement of key individuals. It includes a succession plan for key managerial positions.

Developing the Workforce Plan

The workforce plan should be developed using forecasts of activity from the services plan. The services plan is developed from the epidemiologic needs of the community and the long-range financial plans (see chapters 13 and 15). The medical staff plan (see Chapter 6) is a component. Exhibit 11.2 shows a small section of the plan, covering two of several registered nurse groups. As shown in Exhibit 11.2, the plan should include the following:

- Anticipated size of the associate and employee groups by skill category, major site, and department

EXHIBIT 11.1

Functions of Human Resources Management

Function	Description	Example
Workforce planning	Development of employment needs by job category Strategic responses in recruitment, downsizing, training, and compensation	Forecast of RNs required and available by year Strategy for recruitment, retention, and workforce adjustment
Workforce development	Recruitment Selection Orientation Training Diversity and cultural competence	Advertising and school visits Credentials review and interviewing Review mission/vision/values and key workplace policies Specific skill training and continuous improvement courses Special programs for women and minorities
Workforce maintenance	Services Safety records Reduction	Health promotion, childcare, and social activities Counseling, grievance, and collective bargaining management Accident reduction programs, OSHA reports Personnel records, including special competencies Satisfaction survey and analysis Attrition management, retirement incentives, and downsizing
Empowerment, transformation, and service excellence	Management education Service recovery	Programs of human relations skills, continuous improvement skills, and meeting management Programs in service standards Training for service recovery
Compensation and benefits management	Market surveys of compensation Payroll management Benefits design and administration	RN pay scales, RN benefit selection, and benefit cost Compensation, incentives, absenteeism, and benefits use records Health insurance, retirement, and vacation benefit
Collective bargaining	Response to organizing drives, contract negotiation, and contract administration	Management of union collective bargaining contracts
Continuous improvement	Ongoing review of performance of the associate force Ongoing review of HRM activities Identification of OFIs and establishment of improvement goals	Identification of potential shortage situations, recruitment or retention difficulties Continued improvement of workforce satisfaction, retention, and safety Human resources department operational scorecard improvements

RN: registered nurse; OFIs: opportunities for improvement; OSHA: Occupational Safety and Health Administration

- Schedule of adjustments through recruitment, retraining, attrition, and termination
- Wage and benefit cost forecasts from national projections tailored to local conditions
- Summary of strategic activities, such as the development of incentive payments or the increased use of temporary or part-time employees, that will allow the plan to become reality

Because job classifications are recruited in different markets, strategic activities must be identified at the classification level.

A task force that includes representatives from human resources, planning, finance, nursing, and medicine guides the planning effort. The major medical staff specialties and employer departments must individually review the plan components, and their concerns must be resolved. The revised plan is coordinated with the facilities plan because the number and location of employees determine the requirements for many plant and guest services. The final package must be consistent with the long-range financial plan. It is recommended to the governing board through its planning committee.

Using the Workforce Plan

The workforce plan must be updated annually as part of the environmental assessment, along with other parts of the organization-wide strategic plan. The amended plan and the annual budget guidelines direct the development of specific projects for the coming year. The human resources department works closely with the employing departments to translate the plan to workforce adjustments and plans for individuals, including promotions, training, separations, and compensation changes. The financial implications of these actions are incorporated into the employing department budgets.

The workforce plan also guides human resources policies. Data and expectations from the employing departments guide human resources department strategies and immediate actions to manage training, motivation, lost time, and turnover. Improvements in these areas increase the value of the human resource and can be translated into direct gains in productivity and quality by line managers. Recruitment campaigns; guidelines for the use of temporary labor such as overtime, part-time, and contract labor; and compensation, incentive, and benefit design arise from the workforce plan. The plan may be useful in making decisions about new programs and capital because it provides detailed information on the cost of personnel. Even such strategic decisions as mergers or vertical integration can be affected by human resource shortages and surpluses. All of these applications of the plan call for close collaboration with other executives and clinical departments.

The penalty for inadequate workforce planning is loss of the time and flexibility needed to adjust to environmental changes. Many management difficulties are simpler if adequate time is available to deal with them. Inadequate warning causes hasty and disruptive action. Layoffs may be required.

EXHIBIT 11.2

Illustration of Workforce Plan Content

Category	Current Supply (2010)	Need (FTE) 2011	2012	2013	Attrition 2011	2012	2013	Recruitment (Reduction) 2011	2012	2013
RN, inpatient	250 FTE, 300 persons	230	210	200	25	20	20	5	0	10
RN, out-patient	45 FTE, 60 persons	55	60	60	5	5	5	10	10	5

RN (registered nurse) strategy: Recruit from three local nursing schools. Advertise in national and state journals. Offer training to facilitate transfer from inpatient to outpatient. Maintain starting salary 10 percent below given at nearby metropolitan area. Emphasize health, childcare, education, and retirement benefits. Encourage LPNs (licensed practical nurses) to seek further training with scholarship and flexible scheduling opportunities.

Nurse Magnet program: Work with nursing administration to increase nurse loyalty and job satisfaction by training, measured performance, protocols, increased autonomy, and improved supervision. Enhance nursing voice on process improvement teams, senior management, and governance. The Magnet program is expected to reduce nurse attrition to 10 percent or less.

Activity	Cost per Year (in $)	Cost per Employed FTE** (in $)	% of Annual Earnings***
Recruitment/orientation	$ 83,505	$ 293	0.5%
Personnel records, benefits management, and counseling	200,355	703	1.2
Health benefits	817,665	2,869	4.9
Childcare benefits*	133,380	468	0.8
Social Security and Medicare	1,168,215	4,099	7.0
Retirement benefits	534,090	1,874	3.2
Vacation and absenteeism replacements	400,425	1,405	2.4
Human resources training programs	500,745	1,757	3.0
Nurse Magnet program	150,195	527	0.9
Total	$3,988,575	$13,995	23.9%

* Subsidy to Child Care Center. The Center is used by 30 percent of the nurses.
** 285 FTEs
*** Average annual salary is $58,550 in 2006.

RN: registered nurse; LPN: licensed practical nurse; FTE: full-time equivalent

Recruitment is hurried and poor selections may be made. Retraining may be incomplete. Each of these actions takes its toll on workers' morale and often directly affects quality and efficiency. Although the effect of each individual case may be modest, it is long lasting and cumulative. The organization that fails to plan can fall into a cascade of hasty and expedient decisions that erode its fundamental capabilities.

Workforce Development

Under the best conditions, about 10 percent of the workforce will depart and be replaced each year. HRM will be involved in all issues that affect the associates' work life. Building and maintaining the best possible workforce require recruitment, selection, training, and managing diversity. Most of these functions are provided in close collaboration with the associates' work units. These functions provide the foundation of a service excellence program. Return on investment from these programs is high.

Retention of proven associates is generally preferable to recruitment because the cost of recruiting new personnel is surprisingly high—usually 20 to 30 percent of the annual compensation[8]—and the risk of an unsatisfactory outcome is lower for both the organization and the associate. However, expansions, changes in services, and associate life cycles result in continuing recruitment needs at all skill levels.

Recruitment, Selection, and Orientation

A uniform protocol for recruitment and selection establishes policies for the following activities:

1. *Position control.* Documentation of the number of approved employment positions, the identity and hours of persons hired for them, and the number of vacancies control the size of the associate force and protect against improper employment.

2. *Job description.* Each position must be described in enough detail to identify education and training, licensure, and experience requirements to determine compensation and to permit equitable evaluation of applicants. Descriptions are developed by the operating managers and approved and recorded by human resources.

3. *Classification and compensation.* Wage, incentive, and benefit levels must be assigned to each recruited position. These must be kept consistent with the external market, similar job descriptions, collective bargaining contracts, and regulations. HRM maintains the classification. Each class has an associated pay scale, benefit entitlement, and incentive program.

4. *Applicant pool priorities and advertising.* Policies cover affirmative action and priority consideration of current and former employees and employees' relatives for job openings. Policies also cover the design, placement, and frequency of media advertising, including use of the organization's own website and publications. HRM develops and administers the policies.

5. *Initial screening.* "Self-screening," exposing applicants to the mission, vision, and values of the organization and the detailed job description, is used by leading organizations.[9] HRM screening normally includes verifying licenses, verifying data on the application, contacting references, and checking criminal records and listings in the National Practitioner Data Bank.[10] Appli-

cants may also undergo background checks for credit and driving records.[11] Structured interviews are increasingly popular and are believed to be effective.[12] Screening includes a brief physical examination and may include drug testing.[13]

6. *Final selection.* Applicants who pass the initial screening are subjected to more intensive review, usually involving the immediate supervisor of the position and future teammates. Human resources monitors compliance with state and federal equal opportunity and affirmative action regulations and with the job description and requirements.

7. *Orientation.* New associates should learn the organization's mission and values, its policies to encourage their contribution, and its associate support services. They need assistance in a variety of areas, ranging from maps that show their workplace to counseling on selecting their benefit options. Human resources offers a basic orientation program. The new associates' supervisor arranges a unit- and job-specific orientation and should assign more experienced colleagues to help them fit into their work group.

8. *Probationary review.* Employees begin work with a probationary period, which concludes with a review of performance and usually an offer to join the organization on a long-term basis. Often, increased benefits and other incentives are included in the long-term offer. Line supervisors conduct the probationary review, with advice from HRM.

For the medical staff leaders and higher supervisory levels, search committees are frequently formed to establish the job description and requirements, encourage qualified applicants, carry out screening and selection, and assist in convincing desirable candidates to accept employment. The human resources department acts as staff for the search committee and ensures that the intent of organization policies has been met. Internal promotion is often desirable for these positions. A succession plan identifies the candidates for promotion.

Regulatory Compliance   Federal regulations regarding equal opportunity require that no discrimination occurs on the basis of sex, age, race, creed, national origin, or disabilities that do not incapacitate the individual for the specific job. Laws that cover affirmative action require special recruitment efforts and priority for equally qualified women, African Americans, and Hispanics. (Religious organizations may give priority to associates of their faith under certain circumstances.) The regulations include wage and hour laws, the Family and Medical Leave Act, Title VII of the Civil Rights Act of 1964, and the Americans with Disabilities Act. HCOs are required to be able to document compliance with these rules and may be subject to civil suits by applicants who are dissatisfied. HRM monitors and documents compliance.

Many associates are contract workers rather than employees. They work in the HCO for companies that provide services, such as food service and supplies management. HRM is responsible for verifying that the employing company has followed procedures consistent with the HCO's values and the law.

Training is a major component of HRM activity, and an important aspect of associates' work life. It averages about ten days per year for full-time employees. The array of offerings in a large HCO includes the following:

Training

- *Orientation.* This is a review of the organization's mission, history, vision, values, major assets, and marketing claims as well as policies and benefits of employment.
- *Technical skills.* Modern protocols and work processes require precise completion of highly technical activities. Although appropriate professional education provides a foundation, it cannot provide the detail and currency. HRM operates an ongoing educational activity for all associates. Content is developed by the profession or activity involved. HRM assists with learning tools and facilities.
- *Continuous improvement and performance measurement.* This is basic education in continuous improvement and safety practices, including the reason for, meaning of, and application of concepts; how to use several basic tools; and how improvement teams work. Advanced training includes project management skills and more sophisticated analytic tools.
- *Guest relations programs.* This involves role-playing, games, and group discussion techniques that demonstrate ways to carry out service standards and that reinforce responses that show caring behaviors to patients and visitors.
- *Work policy changes.* This reviews the objectives and implications of major changes in compensation, benefits, and work rules.
- *Retirement planning.* This is offered to older workers to help them understand their retirement benefits and plan for retirement transitions.
- *Outplacement assistance.* This is for persons who are being involuntarily terminated through reductions in workforce.
- *Benefits management.* This is guidance on options and procedures for using benefits, including efforts to minimize misuse.[14]
- *Major organizational changes.* This explains permanent or temporary actions, such as new facilities and programs, that affect habits and lifestyles of current workers.
- *Formal continuing education.* Opportunities to advance professionally through study in accredited outside programs are supported by flexible hours and scholarships. Both continuing education and degree programs are supported.

As noted in Chapter 2, all of these programs should be routinely evaluated at three Kirkpatrick levels. (Level 1 is recipient satisfaction; level 2 is content mastery; level 3 is application.) It is difficult to attribute actual performance improvement (Kirkpatrick level 4) to specific activities, but surveys and observations can confirm that the training helps in a continuous improvement program.

Workforce Diversity

Most leading HCOs strive to promote diversity in their workforce, but limited evidence suggests that implementation is not widely successful.[15] Surveys show that women and minorities are still underrepresented in management.[16] The more successful HCOs make a deliberate and vigorous effort to represent the ethnic and gender makeup of their community in their medical staff, management group, and workforce.[17] They adapt job requirements to family needs and work to promote women in management.[18] While this may be driven in part by a belief in social justice, it is also supported by sound marketing theories. Many people seek healthcare from caregivers who resemble them in gender, language, or culture. Increasing attention to the needs of female workers has clearly influenced the structure of employment benefits and the rules of the workplace.[19] Human resources monitors workforce diversity, guards against discriminatory activity, and designs programs that assist all associates to reach their full potential.

Cultural and Linguistic Competence

Sensitivity to the cultural and linguistic perspectives of patients and their families cannot be assumed. Leading HCOs measure cultural diversity, establish goals for service, and evaluate effectiveness of cultural and linguistic services.[20,21]

   Cultural competence is a set of complementary behaviors, practices, and policies that enables a system, an agency, or individuals to work and effectively serve pluralistic, multiethnic, and linguistically diverse communities.[22] The Joint Commission standards address food preferences, translation services, equal standard of care provision, patient assessment and education (literacy and language appropriate), appropriateness of environment, and ongoing staff education.[23] The Joint Commission plans more specific cultural and linguistic standards in 2011.[24] Research findings indicate that although HCOs have begun programs to address cultural and linguistic competence, they fall short of meeting nationally mandated standards.[25,26] Language barriers, religious beliefs, unconventional views of illness and alternative remedies (from birth to death), and diseases or conditions that may emanate from the patient's country of origin[27] reduce patient satisfaction but also impair outcomes.[28] Cultural competence needs are met by training, coaches, ethics committees, and counselors. Linguistic services include bilingual/bicultural staff, trained medical interpreters, and qualified translators.[29]

Cultural competence

A set of complementary behaviors, practices, and policies that enables a system, an agency, or individuals to work and effectively serve pluralistic, multiethnic, and linguistically diverse communities

Workforce Maintenance

The retention strategy of excellent HCOs requires providing competitive services and a safe, comfortable environment, counseling and mediating grievances, and maintaining a personal work record for every associate that includes training, evaluation, and development information.

Most HCOs provide personal services to their employees through their **Employee** human resources department on the theory that such services improve loyalty **Services** and morale and, therefore, efficiency and quality. Evidence to support the theory is limited, but the services are often required if competing employers provide them. Specific offerings are often tailored to the employees' needs. Popular programs are allowed to grow, while others are curtailed. Charges are sometimes imposed to defray the costs, but some subsidization is usual. Commonly found programs include the following:

- *Workplace wellness*—health-risk screening, smoking cessation, nutritional advice, and exercise programs
- *Employee assistance*—counseling and therapy sessions to assist with substance abuse, stress management, and mental health–related services[30]
- *Infant and child care*
- *Social events*—major corporate events and recognition of employee contributions
- *Recreational sports*—sponsored teams and events
- *Credit unions*
- *Voluntary payroll deduction*—for various purposes such as retirement, tax benefits, and charitable donations to organizations such as United Way

Workplace wellness and employee assistance programs have been shown to reduce absenteeism and health insurance costs. Childcare also reduces absenteeism.

HRM is responsible for meeting the requirements and submitting statistics **Associate** for the Occupational Safety and Health Act, which mandates workers' com- **Safety and** pensation for injury, establishes safe practices, and collects worker-safety sta- **Comfort** tistics.[31] It is also responsible for "clearly and regularly" communicating and "effectively" enforcing policies forbidding sexual harassment.[32] The regulations in these areas recognize and reward careful efforts to prevent problems. More important for excellent HCOs, safety and satisfaction are important in retaining associates.

Harassment is both illegal and a serious infraction of the value of respect. In addition to interpersonal activities, a hostile environment can be a violation. It is one in which the employee has specifically complained about practices that "unreasonably interfere with an individual's work performance" or create "an intimidating, hostile, or offensive working environment," and the employer has taken no steps to correct them.[33]

In 2003, hospitals had 3.2 work loss or work limitation cases per 100 FTEs (full-time equivalents); the healthcare industry overall had 2.7, and all private industries had 2.3. Illness and injury from hospital work can be kept at low levels by constant attention to safety. Other industries improved during the 1990s, but healthcare and hospitals have had slower improvement.[34]

Back injuries, needle sticks, and associate infections are preventable. Hazards such as repeated exposure to low levels of radioactivity or small quantities of anesthesia gases can be reduced. The Occupational Safety and Health Act identifies standards for safety in the workplace and supports inspections.[35] Fines are levied for noncompliance.

Much of the direct control of hazards is the responsibility of the clinical engineering and facilities maintenance departments. Infection control, for example, is an important collaborative effort of housekeeping, plant engineering, nursing, and medicine to protect the patient and the associate. Employee protection in well-run organizations stems from procedures developed for patient safety. Oversight responsibility for the environment of care is required by The Joint Commission and is useful in coordinating efforts and monitoring overall achievement. HRM is usually assigned the following functions:

- Monitoring and analyzing safety and complaint measures, benchmarks, federal and state regulations, and professional literature for organization-wide OFIs
- Maintaining or coordinating the completion of material safety data sheets—profiles of hazardous substances with information on safe handling that must be filed with the Occupational Safety and Health Administration and systematically distributed to associates who are exposed to the substance
- Providing or assisting with training in and promotion of safe procedures
- Negotiating contracts for workers' compensation insurance or managing settlements where the organization self-insures

Workforce Reduction

Changes in population, technology, competition, payment for care, and the economy can force any HCO to make substantial involuntary reductions in its workforce. Because job security is an important recruitment-and-retention incentive, such reductions must be handled well.[36,37] Good practice pursues the following rules:

- Workforce planning is used to foresee reductions as far in advance as possible, allowing natural turnover and retraining to provide much of the reduction.
- Temporary and part-time workers are reduced first.
- Personnel in at-risk jobs are offered priority for retraining programs and positions in needed areas.
- Early retirement programs are used to encourage older (and often more highly compensated) employees to leave voluntarily.
- Terminations are based on seniority or well-understood rules, judiciously applied.

Using this approach has allowed many HCOs to limit involuntary terminations to a level that does not seriously impair the attractiveness of the organization to others.

Well-managed HCOs provide an authority independent of the normal accountability for employees who feel, for whatever reason, that a complaint or question has not been fully and fairly answered. Human resources departments often offer ombudsman-type programs that provide an unbiased counselor for concerns of any kind. Personnel in these units are equipped to handle a variety of problems, from health-related issues that are referred to employee assistance programs or occupational health services, to complaints about supervision or work conditions, to sexual harassment and discrimination.

Grievance Administration

Many issues are concerns, rather than grievances, when they are first presented. The function of the ombudsman office is to settle them fairly and quickly and, if possible, to identify corrections that will prevent recurrence. The office's success depends on its ability to meet worker needs before they develop into confrontations or serious dissatisfaction.

A few of the matters presented to ombudsman offices and line officers become formal grievances or complaints. The traditional collective bargaining contract includes a formal grievance process that often becomes adversarial in nature, assuming a dispute has to be resolved between worker and management. Good grievance management minimizes adversarial situations. It begins with development and communication of sound employment policies, effective education for workers and supervisors, and systems that emphasize rewards over sanctions. Its strength is responsive listening. Effective management training produces supervisors who respond promptly to associates' questions and problems and who have substantially fewer grievances.

When disagreements arise, good grievance administration stimulates the following reactions:

- Documentation of issue, location, and positions of the two parties that provides a guide to preventive or corrective action
- Credible, unbiased, and informal review that identifies constructive solutions
- Informal negotiations that encourage flexibility and innovation in seeking a mutually satisfactory solution
- Counseling for the supervisor involved aimed at improving future human relations
- Settlement without formal review whenever possible, either by mutual agreement or by concession on the part of the organization
- Implementation of changes designed to prevent recurrences

These processes are appropriate in both union and nonunion environments. They should make the formal review process typically found in union contracts, leading to resolution by an outside arbitrator, unnecessary in the vast majority of cases. Grievances that go to formal review encourage an adversarial environment. Even if the concession appears relatively expensive, the organization is better off avoiding review and making an appropriate investment in preventing future difficulties.

**Leadership
Development**

Extensive learning opportunities and formal annual performance evaluations provide a foundation for classifying associates. Organizations now think in terms of promotable, capable, and improving workers. (A fourth class—incompetent—is usually warned, retrained, and either reclassified or dismissed.) "Improving" workers are given extra training, mentoring, or counseling to move them to "capable." The promotable associates are offered extra learning opportunities through special assignments, advanced training, expanded mentoring or coaching, committee responsibilities, and activities outside the organization. Their potential is made clear to them, and their favored position is soon grasped by their peers.

Supervisors have explicit goals for developing their subordinates. These often include extra efforts to identify promotable members of under-represented groups. Incentive compensation is awarded for fulfilling these goals in some organizations. New entrants to management are evaluated closely. A *resident* or *fellow* (new associate) is given enhanced training, and a healthcare professional entering management is matched with a mentor and given a planned learning program. New entrants are promoted, and a career development plan of learning goals and a program to achieve them is jointly developed. The process is repeated as they mature, with increasingly challenging goals, building a reserve for higher management positions. (Some, of course, will leave for opportunities elsewhere.)

HRM designs the associate evaluation programs, training for managers, and the policies for identifying candidates. Working with service units, HRM ensures that all policies are administered uniformly and that a clear route of appeal exists against actions the employee views as arbitrary.

**Succession
Planning**

The loss of managers in critical roles through impairment, death, or departure can seriously hamper performance. The CEO and senior leadership are obvious examples, but others (such as the operating room manager and key medical specialists) have similar impact over narrower domains. The loss of any first-line supervisor can impair that unit. Excellent HRM responds with a replacement plan. The plan will identify the competencies required for the post, candidates currently prepared, and candidates who could be prepared through their individual development plans. Should the need arise, the organization may choose to seek a replacement from outside, but internal promotion rewards loyalty and generally reduces the risks that the new person will fail, particularly if careful effort has gone into his or her leadership development.

**Assessment
of Workforce
Development
and
Satisfaction**

The strategy for workforce loyalty manages the full work environment to identify personal development opportunities, to increase associates' skills by meeting development needs, and to retain effective associates.[38] HRM manages associate evaluation and satisfaction assessment and uses its development programs systematically to improve associate skills and capability.

Excellent HCOs generate formal performance evaluations at least annually. These records are used for promotion decisions, pay increases, and training needs. They also form the basis for leadership development. The organization has an ethical and legal responsibility for honesty and fairness. HRM administers competency-based surveys to guide the assessments. It analyzes results and provides benchmarks. It protects associate anonymity. It trains managers in interpreting and presenting results and offers counseling on request. It also maintains the records. The surveys must be carefully worded and administered to ensure comparable and unbiased results. Multirater or 360-degree reviews have become popular; these surveys combine elements of satisfaction and evaluation. They allow evaluation by superiors, subordinates, and internal and external customers.

Associates who leave the HCO are interviewed. Their candid comments can be useful to correct negative factors in the work environment. HRM administers the interviews and presents findings to appropriate managers.

Knowledge Management

HRM maintains a large and sensitive information base about the workforce. This record is computerized, with the content organized around eight core files of information, as shown in Exhibit 11.3. These files contain individual records, including specific competency assessments and development plans. They support the workforce measures and many of HRM's operational measures.

Human resources files, like patient records, must be protected against unauthorized access and misuse. Persons with access to the files must be trained in proper use. More serious questions arise after these basic concerns have been met. Reduction of dissatisfaction, turnover, absenteeism, grievances, accidents, and illness is a socially useful goal of HRM. It is clearly proper, even desirable, to study variations, such as measures of supervisory effectiveness, that can be improved by systems redesign, counseling, and education. Actions based on worker characteristics (e.g., age, sex, race) or records (e.g., illness, grievances) can be illegal (if discriminatory) and are often ethically questionable. Some facts, such as drug-test data, are potentially destructive and libelous if false. Some companies have attempted to deny employment opportunities in situations that present a high risk of occupational injury. For example, female nurses in their childbearing years have been denied employment in operating rooms because of the known pregnancy risks related to exposure to some anesthetics. When questions involving inferences about such matters arise, a review by the HCO's ethics committee or institutional review board is wise.

A sound policy must balance the advantages of investigation against its dangers. These guidelines help:

- *Information access must be limited to a necessary minimum group.* Those with access are taught the importance of confidentiality and the organization's expectation that individuals' rights will be protected.

EXHIBIT 11.3
Core Files
of HRM
Knowledge
Management

File	Uses
Position control List of approved full- and part-time positions by location, classification	Provides a basic check on number and kinds of people employed
Personnel record Personal data, training, development plan, employment record, hearings record, benefits use	Provides tax and employment data aggregated for descriptions
Workforce plan Record of future positions and expected personnel	Shows changes needed in workforce
Succession plan Specific replacement candidates for managerial and other critical posts	Plans internal promotion possibilities for all key positions
Payroll Current work hours or status, wage, or salary level	Generates paychecks Provides labor-cost accounting
Employee satisfaction Results of surveys by location, class	Assesses employee satisfaction
Training schedules and participation Record of training programs and attendance	Generates training output statistics and individual records
Benefits selection and utilization Record of employee selection and use of services	Benefits management and cost control

- *Formal approval must be sought for studies of individual characteristics that affect personnel performance.* Often a specific committee, including associates of the organization's ethics committee, reviews each study. Criteria for approval include protection of individual rights, scientific reliability, and evidence of potential benefit.
- *Actions taken to improve performance should avoid sanctions.* Considerable effort is made to find nonrestrictive solutions. In the operating room example, avoiding the more dangerous gases or implementing special safety practices should be considered before a restrictive employment policy is established.
- *When used, sanctions or restrictions must offer the individual the greatest possible freedom of choice.* The right of the individual to take an informed risk should be respected, and it may reduce the organization's ultimate liability. Material safety data sheets are designed to promote intelligent choices. Such a sheet is required in the operating room example. Its purpose is to promote safety and informed choice. A nurse may accept employment, weighing the risks in light of her lifestyle.

Empowerment, Transformation, and Service Excellence

A culture of empowered and committed associates depends heavily on its managers, who must be not only responsive listeners and motivators but also effective operators—people who meet goals, resolve issues, and "get the job done." Empowerment is meaningless when support systems fail. HRM trains managers and measures Kirkpatrick level 4 (performance results) from that training. It also operates the service recovery program that allows associates to respond on-site to unexpected events.

Supporting Transformational Management

To achieve service excellence, employees at all levels must think of themselves and the organization as empowered and continuously learning.[39] Managers have a critical role; they must exhibit the behaviors required and provide much of the just-in-time education. Non-healthcare companies report substantial investments in managerial training—up to 80 hours per manager per year.[40] A growing number of leading healthcare systems are making similar investments.[41] The training topics include human relations and supervisory skills, facts about policies and procedures, management of process improvement teams (PITs) and collaborative activities, and mastery of tools for continuous improvement.

Skills in Human Relations and Supervision

As discussed in Chapter 1, the concepts of empowerment, process improvement, and service excellence characterize "transformational" as opposed to "transactional" management. Transformational management began to spread widely in American culture only after 1980. It represents a profound change in managerial behavior, essentially from order giving to listening, responding, and encouraging.

Many associates need substantial assistance in learning transformational management skills. Much of the folklore of American industry runs counter to the realities of transformational supervision.[42] Thus, even promising personnel need repeated reinforcement of the proper role and style. Promising workers are identified well before they are promoted and are trained with multiple presentations, using a variety of approaches and media to establish and reinforce basic notions: the use of rewards rather than sanctions, the importance of fairness and candor, the role of the supervisor in responding to workers' questions, and the importance of clear instructions and appropriate work environments.[43]

Typical topics covered include skills in orienting new people, training new processes, motivating workers, answering worker questions, engaging in difficult conversations, and identifying problem workers. Cases, role-playing, recordings, films, and individual counseling are helpful in maintaining a supervisor's performance. Results of supervisory training are systematically evaluated. Content mastery (Kirkpatrick level 2) is tested as part of the programs. Leadership evaluation can assess application (Kirkpatrick level 3). Unit performance improvement reflects Kirkpatrick level 4.

Facts About Policies and Procedures

Effective line supervisors are expected to answer a wide variety of questions from their workers. They are a critical link in applying the organization's policies on the protection of confidentiality, the promotion of diversity, and the elimination of sexual harassment and workplace hostility. They are the first persons most workers turn to for information about compensation and benefits, incentive programs, and policies on leaves. They must master the content important to their area.

HRM manages the communication of policy. They provide in-service courses in major policies, important changes, and procedures for handling recurring situations. They maintain the intranet as an easily accessible, electronically searchable reference. Supervisors can guide associates to these statements. When they are insufficient, HRM counselors assist.

Meeting-Management Skills

Managing meetings and committees, such as those with PITs, is a teachable skill. Meetings should start on time, end on time, have an agenda with appropriate supporting materials and minutes, and accomplish the agenda. Chairs are responsible for keeping to the topic and schedule, making sure all participants are heard, and promoting consensus.

HRM provides training, mentoring, and uniform content when indicated. Committee chairs can learn from formal programs or from a mentor. Larger committees can be assigned support staff. Consultation and assistance are available from HRM at the supervisor's request. HRM's grievance and dispute-resolution skills can contribute in serious disagreements. The Baldrige-winning system SSM Health Care has "Meeting in a Box" programs that include video presentations and discussion guides.[44] The meeting-management package is a major contribution to HCO success. It makes collective activities efficient and effective.

Tools for Goal Setting and Continuous Improvement

Supervisors need a variety of skills to identify improvement opportunities, evaluate them, motivate their personnel, and implement the improvement cycle. These tools are usually taught in several courses of a day or two each. Goal setting and capital budgets have now become complex enough that sessions on how the guidelines are generated, what sorts of improvements and proposals are appropriate, and how to handle the mechanics of preparation and submission are useful. Supervisory personnel are frequently taught advanced performance improvement skills, such as Six Sigma or Toyota Production System. The human resources department often organizes these programs using faculty from planning, marketing, finance, and information services.

Service Recovery

Service recovery is a program that empowers workers to recover from patient service mistakes.[45] Its primary purpose is to retain customer loyalty in situations in which the organization has failed. Its secondary purpose is to create a record of unexpected events that can be used to identify and address

OFIs. When an associate feels that a customer has been treated in a substantially substandard manner, he or she corrects the problem as fully as possible and is authorized to compensate the customer appropriately as well. Patients and families may be given flowers, free meals, free parking, and even waiver of hospital charges, as indicated by the seriousness of the shortfall. All such transactions are reported in depth; these records identify process weaknesses and generate OFIs.

Service recovery is believed to improve customer satisfaction and reduce subsequent claims against the hospital. It has been proven cost effective in other industries.[46] It is an extension of a long-standing procedure of completing written records of unexpected events. Because many of the events are clinical, service recovery is a foundation for a more elaborate program of potential malpractice claims management, described in Chapter 5.[47] The direct cost of the program can be managed with expenditure limits and required documentation. Its contribution is difficult to measure but almost certainly exceeds its cost. The program's success obviously depends on the organization's performance level. A hospital must have sound processes in place and a reasonable record of performance to make service recovery feasible.

Compensation and Benefits Management

Employee compensation includes direct wages and salaries, shift differentials and premiums, bonuses, retirement funds, and a substantial number of specific benefits supported by payroll deduction or supplement. Federal law defines employment status and requires withholding of Social Security and income taxes from the employee and contributions by the employer. Other employment benefits are automatically purchased on behalf of the employee via the payroll mechanism. Compensation constitutes more than half the expenditures of most HCOs. From the organization's perspective, such a large sum of money must be protected against both fraud and waste. From the employee's perspective, accuracy regarding amount, timing, and benefit coverage should be perfect.

The growing complexity of compensation has been supported by highly sophisticated computer software, with each advance in computer capability soon translated into expanded flexibility of the compensation package. The latest developments in payroll have been increased use of bonuses and incentive compensation as well as "cafeteria" benefits, which allow more employee choice. Well-run organizations now use payroll programs that process both pay and benefit data for three purposes: payment, monitoring and reporting, and cost accounting. This software permits HRM to manage compensation issues in the human resources department through position control, wage and salary administration, benefit administration, and retirement fund administration.

Position Control

The HCO must protect itself against accidental or fraudulent violation of employment procedures and standards and must ensure that only duly employed persons or retirees receive compensation. This is done through a central review of the number of positions created, called **position control**. Creation of a position generally requires multiple approvals, ending near the level of the chief operating officer. Positions created are monitored by human resources to ensure compliance with recruitment, promotion, and compensation procedures and to ensure that each individual employed is assigned to a unique position.

Position control

A system of payroll control that identifies specific positions created and filled

The limitation of this activity is important to understand, because it controls the number of people employed rather than the total hours worked. The number of hours worked outside position-control accountability is significant. Position control protects only against paying the wrong person, hiring in violation of established policies, and issuing fraudulent checks. It does not protect against overspending the labor budget.

Wage and Salary Administration

Most HCOs operate at least two payrolls and a pension disbursement system. One payroll covers personnel hired on an hourly basis, requiring reporting of actual compensable hours for each pay period—usually two weeks. The other covers salaried, usually supervisory, personnel paid a fixed amount per period—often monthly. Contract workers are often compensated through nonpayroll systems. Tracking these payments is important to measuring the full cost of the workforce.

Wage and salary administration covers all of these disbursements for personnel costs and includes the following activities:

- *Verification of compensable hours and compensation due.* This is applicable only to hourly personnel. The operating unit is accountable for the accuracy of hours reported and for keeping hours within budget agreements. HRM verifies authorization, applies the appropriate pay rate, and applies policies establishing differentials. Modern systems also identify other elements, such as the worker's location or activity, to support cost-finding activities. The data become an important resource for further analysis.
- *Compensation scales.* Each position is classified and assigned a compensation grade. Human resources conducts or purchases periodic salary and wage surveys to establish competitive pay scales for representative grades. At supervisory and professional levels, these surveys cover national and regional markets. For most hourly grades, the local market is surveyed.
- *Seniority, merit, and cost-of-living adjustments.* Compensation is sometimes adjusted for seniority, merit, or cost of living. Seniority and cost-of-living raises are not directly related either to the market for employment or the success of the organization. Merit raises—increases in the base pay reflecting the individual employee's skill improvements—are difficult to administer objectively and tend

to become automatic. Leading organizations are moving to replace all three adjustments with improved compensation scaling and performance-oriented incentive payments.

Fair compensation should meet three general criteria:

1. *Compensation should equal long-run economic opportunities for similar positions elsewhere.* The test of compensation is the market. Compensation consistently below market rates creates difficulty in recruiting and retaining professionals. Compensation consistently above market rates impairs the competitive position of the organization.
2. *Compensation should reflect actual contribution to the HCO's strategic goals.* This is usually implemented through incentive programs that recognize achievement of operational and strategic goals.
3. *Compensation should encourage professional growth and fulfillment consistent with organizational needs.* Incentives to learn and grow are part of a good compensation program.

Incentive Compensation

The market demand for competitive performance has made tangible reward for individual achievement desirable, and improving information systems have made it possible.[48] An organization built on rewards and the search for continued improvement is strengthened by a system of compensation that supplements personal satisfaction and professional recognition.[49] HCOs have advanced significantly toward this goal.[50]

Certain constraints must be recognized in designing an incentive compensation system:

- The resources available will depend more on the organization's overall performance than on any individual's contribution. They may be severely limited through factors outside the organization's control. The incentives must recognize this reality, emphasizing overall performance (the strategic scorecard) over unit performance (the operational scorecard).
- Equity and objectivity are expected in the distribution of the rewards.
- The individual's contribution is difficult to measure.
- Group rewards attenuate the incentives to individuals. The larger the group, the greater the attenuation.
- The incentive program must avoid becoming a routine or expected part of compensation.

These constraints suggest a *gain-sharing incentive system* based on both strategic and unit performance, with negotiated unit goals, and applied to the individual's work team. Gain-sharing approaches suggest that primary worker groups can effectively set expectations consistent with the needs of the larger organization and that the effort to do so leads to measurable improvement in achievement. Such systems have a growing record of success in HCOs.[51] Under a gain-sharing compensation system, annual longevity increases disappear as incentive pay increases, and incentives provide a substantial portion of compensation, particularly for senior management.

Benefits Administration

Many of the social programs of Western nations are related directly or indirectly to employment, through programs of payroll taxes, deductions, and entitlements. These programs are fixed in place by a combination of market forces, direct legal obligation, and tax-related incentives. HCOs and other employers in the United States support extensive programs of nonwage benefits, which add as much as 30 percent beyond salaries and wages to the costs of employment and are generally exempt from income and Social Security taxes. The exact participation of each employee differs, with major differences depending on full-time or part-time status, grade, and seniority. In general, five major classes of employee benefits and employer obligations exist beyond wage compensation:

1. *Payroll taxes and deductions.* The employer is legally obligated to contribute premium taxes to Social Security for pension and Medicare benefits and to collect a portion of the employee's pay for Social Security and withholding on various income taxes. Certain funds, such as uninsured healthcare expenses and child-care expenses, can be exempt from income taxes by the use of pretax accounts. In unionized companies, dues are usually deducted from hourly workers' pay. While the deductions represent only a small handling cost to the employer, they are an important convenience to the employee.

2. *Mandatory insurance.* Employers are obligated to provide workers' compensation for injuries received at work, including both full healthcare and compensation for lost wages. They are also obligated to provide unemployment insurance, covering a portion of wages for several months following involuntary termination.

3. *Vacations, holidays, and sick leaves.* Employers commonly pay full-time and permanent employees for legal holidays, additional holidays, vacations, and sick leaves. Some also compensate certain other non-worked time such as educational leaves, jury duty, and military reserves duty. They grant unpaid leaves for family needs, in accordance with the Family and Medical Leave Act of 1993,[52] and for other purposes as they see fit. As a result, only about 85 percent of the 2,080 hours per year that nominally constitute full-time employment is actually worked by hourly workers. The non-worked time becomes an extra cost to the organization when the employee must be replaced by part-time workers or by overtime premiums. It is also an important factor in the cost of full-time versus part-time employees. Part-time positions often share in employment benefits only on a drastically reduced basis.

4. *Voluntary insurance programs.* Health insurance is a widespread and popular entitlement of full-time employment. Retirement programs must be funded according to rules similar to those for insurance. Life insurance and travel and accident insurance are also common. Various tax advantages are available for these protections. Both employee and employer contributions are used to fund the programs. The employed group obtains a rate that is much lower than that offered to individuals. Many employers self-insure for these programs. They are generally subject to state laws or the federal Employee Retirement Income Security Act.

5. *Other perquisites.* A wide variety of other benefits of employment can be offered, particularly for higher professional and supervisory grades. Perquisites, generally, are shaped by a combination of tax and job-performance considerations. Educational programs, professional society dues, and journal subscriptions are commonly included. The Internal Revenue Service (IRS) requires mandatory Form 990 reporting of community benefit and executive compensation/perquisites for tax-exempt organizations (nonprofits). Benefits—such as cars, club memberships, and expense accounts—that assist executives in participating in the social life of their community have come under increased scrutiny by the IRS. Public reporting of executive compensation packages to promote transparency has also contributed in reductions of nonwage benefits for executives.[53] Added retirement benefits—actually income deferred for tax purposes—and termination settlements are used to defray the risks of leadership positions. All of the perquisites must meet tests of reasonableness to avoid inurement concerns, and the total compensation for senior management should be approved by the compensation committee of the governing board.

In managing employment benefits, HRM strives to maximize the ratio of gains to expenditure. Four courses of action to achieve this are characteristic of well-run departments; three of them relate to program design and one to program administration:

1. *Program design for competitive impact.* The value of a given benefit is in the eye of the employee, and demographics affect perceived value. A married mother might prefer childcare to health insurance because her husband's employer already provides health insurance. A single person whose children are grown might prefer retirement benefits to life insurance. Young employees often (perhaps unwisely) prefer cash to deferred or insured benefits. Employee surveys help predict the most attractive design of the benefit package. Flexibility is becoming more desirable as workers' needs become more diverse. Recent trends have emphasized cafeteria-style benefit plans, where each employee can select preset combinations.

2. *Program design for cost effectiveness.* Several benefits have an insurance characteristic such that actual cost is determined by exposure to claims. Health insurance,

accident insurance, and sick benefits are particularly susceptible to cost reduction by benefit design. Health insurance, by far the largest of these costs, is minimized by the use of defined contribution approaches, including copayments, premium sharing, and selected provider arrangements. It may also be reduced by health promotion activities.[54] Accident insurance premiums are reduced by limiting benefits to larger, more catastrophic events. Duplicate coverage—where the employee and the spouse who is employed elsewhere are both covered by insurance—can be eliminated to reduce cost. Costs of sick benefits can be reduced by eliminating coverage for short illnesses and by requiring certification from a physician early in the episode of coverage.

3. *Program design for tax implications.* Income tax advantages are a major factor in program design. Many advantages, such as the exemption of health insurance premiums, are deliberate legislative policy, while others appear almost accidental. Details are subject to constant adjustment through both legislation and administrative interpretations. As a result, it is necessary to review the benefit program periodically for changing tax implications, in terms of both current offerings and the desirability of additions or substitutions.

4. *Program administration.* Almost all of the benefits can be administered in ways that minimize their costs. Strict interpretation of benefits can be received well by employees if it is fair, courteously administered, and accompanied by documentation in the benefit literature initially given employees.

Preventing insured claims is important. Absenteeism and on-the-job injuries are reduced by effective supervision. Health promotion, counseling, and employee risk management are effective. Unemployment liability is reduced by better planning and use of attrition for workforce reduction. HRM affects all these activities through employee services, supervisory training, workforce planning, and occupational safety programs.

Retirement Plans

Retirement plan benefits pose different management problems from other benefits because they are used only after the employee retires. Retirement contracts are not fulfilled for many years and represent an unknown, possibly multidecade commitment when use begins. Retirement benefit–related issues include the plan's motivational impact on actual retirements.

Traditional retirement plans and retirees' anticipated health insurance premiums are shown as a liability on the organization's balance sheet. Funds must be committed to meet these liabilities. As a result, traditional plans also include management of invested funds. The employer commitment is fixed (*defined benefit*). The newer 401(k)-type plans allow direct associate contribution and vesting by employers, limiting the HCO's liability to any committed but unvested funds (*defined contribution*). Management of the funds becomes an employee obligation. Both types of funds have tax advantages for the employee; national policy encourages planning for old-age needs. It appears that defined contribution plans will be the rule for younger employees. Defined benefit contracts will diminish as older employees die. The HCO can encourage deductions and suggest management companies for employees' funds.

Retirement benefits affect workforce planning. HCOs use retirement bonuses as a method of workforce reduction. However, it may pay to retain older workers. In general, they are more amenable to reduced hours, have reliable work habits, and are less likely to have unpredictable absences.

Collective Bargaining

HCOs are subject to both state and federal legislation that governs the right of workers to organize a union for their collective representation on economic and other work-related matters. Federal legislation generally supports the existence of unions; state laws vary. Collective bargaining is a declining element in the United States. By 2008, union associates were only 12.4 percent of the U.S. workforce, down from 26 percent shortly after World War II. All-industry outlooks for unionization suggest a continuing decline.[55]

Less than 15 percent of all hospital employees are unionized.[56] The number has been stable or declining for many years. The likelihood of unionization differs significantly by state, with the northeastern states and California most likely. Unionization is far more common in urban areas. In hospitals, unskilled workers and building trades are the most likely to be organized. Nurses are next most likely; other clinical professionals are rarely organized. Periodic efforts to organize attending physicians and resident physicians have gained little headway.[57]

The National Labor Relations Board (NLRB) regulates unions and organization efforts. It requires unions to organize within specific job classes: physicians, registered nurses, all professional personnel other than doctors and nurses, technical personnel (including practical nurses and internally trained assistants and technicians), skilled maintenance employees, business office clerical employees, guards, and all other employees. Any organizing vote must gain support of a majority of all the associates of a given class.[58] An NLRB ruling in 1999 redefined residents as employees (rather than students) and permitted them to organize as a separate group.[59] The NLRB maintains that physicians in private practice are independent contractors and thus are not eligible to organize. Well-managed HCOs respond to organizing drives by hiring competent counsel to guide them in fulfilling their NLRB rights and obligations.

Unions are likely to continue to be important in specific institutions and job classes but are unlikely to expand dramatically. Well-run HCOs will seek to discourage unionization or diminish the influence of existing unions. Such a strategy is actualized through transformational management, which explicitly recognizes employee needs without the need for union representation.

Collective bargaining is usually an adversarial procedure, although HCO management should seek collaboration and avoid confrontation. Well-run organizations use experienced bargainers, have legal counsel available, and promote union participation in ongoing PITs and planning activities. They will accept a strike on issues that depart significantly from the current exchange environment for workers or patients, but as a strategy they avoid strikes whenever possible. Considerable supervisory education is necessary to implement this policy. Supervisors should know the contract and abide by it, but whenever possible their actions should be governed by the goals of transformational management. Any distinction between unionized and nonunionized groups should be minimized.

Continuous Improvement

HRM supports continuous improvement in its own unit and throughout the organization. Its customers are both associates and employing units. The department also prepares its own OFIs and goals and implements its own improvements. HRM will measure its own performance using multidimensional measures. Most of the functions can be benchmarked on cost and quality against competitors and non-healthcare service organizations. Exhibit 11.4 shows typical OFIs and likely outcomes for HRM improvement.

People

Human Resources Professionals

Human resources management emerged as a profession after World War II, in response to the complexities created by union contracts, wage and hour laws, and benefits management. HCOs were sheltered from these developments for several years, but as the need arose, HCOs moved to establish an identifiable human resources system and to hire specially trained leadership for it. Human resources professionals have an identifiable curriculum of formal education and a recognizable pattern of professional experience, and they may be voluntarily credentialed as a Professional in Human Resources (PHR).[60] Healthcare practitioners have an association—the American Society for Healthcare Human Resources Administration, an affiliate of the American Hospital Association.[61] Well-run organizations now recruit persons with experience in the profession generally and preferably in healthcare to fill their human resources director or vice president positions. Professional training and experience contribute to mastery of the several areas in which laws, precedents, or specialized skills define appropriate actions.

Organization of the Human Resources Department

HRM is organized by function, to take advantage of specialized skills and processes. Exhibit 11.5 shows a typical accountability hierarchy for a large HCO with labor union contracts. Small organizations often use consulting organizations for support. (Collective bargaining is less common in small institutions.)

EXHIBIT 11.4
Typical
Improvements
for Human
Resources
Management

Indicator	Opportunity	Example
Potential RN shortage	Expand RN recruitment program	Install expanded part-time RN program, emphasizing retraining, childcare, and flexible hours
High health insurance costs	Promote more cost-effective program	Revise health insurance benefits Install managed care Promote healthy lifestyles
Low incentive payments	Redesign incentive pay program	Expand eligibility for incentives, improve measurement of contribution
Employee satisfaction variance	Identify common causes and address individually	Improve employee amenities Special training for supervisors with low employee satisfaction
Inadequate operational performance improvement	Support line review of causes	Focus groups on motivation Seek evidence of worker dissatisfaction Review incentive programs
Labor costs over benchmark	Support orderly employment reduction	Curtail hiring in surplus categories Design and offer early retirement program Start cross-training and retraining programs

RN: registered nurse

In multistate healthcare systems, human resources tends to be decentralized by work site. While some activities, such as information processing, can be centrally managed, most require frequent contact with employees and supervisors, demanding a local presence. A central office can monitor planning, support more elaborate educational programs, operate a uniform information system, and promote consistency of many policies. Some policies are driven by state laws, which vary. Decentralized representatives available in each site concentrate on implementation of these programs and issues of workforce maintenance and continuous improvement. Similarly, human resources services can be contracted from outside vendors. The use of multidimensional performance measures makes contracting useful, and contracts can be arranged for specific functions or the entire human resources unit. Contracting for all or part of human resources services is probably a viable solution for small organizations.[62]

EXHIBIT 11.5

Organization of a Large Human Resources Department

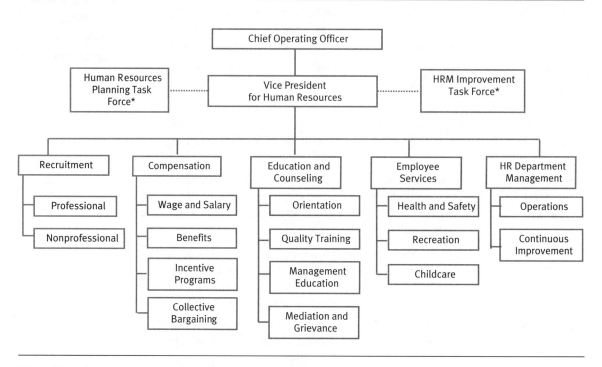

* Dotted lines show advisory relationships. The two task forces draw broadly from within and outside the human resources department.

Measures

HRM requires two measurement systems. One measures the workforce itself; supports planning; and identifies OFIs for recruitment, training, or compensation. The other measures the unit's own performance, using the standard operational measures template. Exhibit 11.6 lists many of the commonly used measures for describing and assessing the workforce.

Measures of the human resource are an important part of the annual environmental assessment. The values for most demand, cost, efficiency, quality, and satisfaction measures can be compared with benchmarks, with competitors, and with the organization's own history. OFIs can be identified and pursued. They are often in specific units of the HCO or job classes. For example, satisfaction or efficiency may be lower in one or two service lines, allowing a focused PIT to identify improvements. The workforce itself changes only slowly. Improvement goals are possible, but they sometimes take several years to achieve.

An additional set of measures is important in assessing the department itself, as shown in Exhibit 11.7. More than 250 metrics exist for various details of department operation, and consulting companies provide benchmarks

Dimension	Measure
Workforce characteristics	Age, sex, ethnic origin, language skills, profession or job, training, certifications, etc.
Demand	New hires per year Unfilled positions Positions filled with short-term contract labor
Costs and efficiency	Labor costs/unit of output Overtime, differential, and incentive payments Benefits costs/associate, by benefit Human resources department costs/associate
Quality	Skill levels and cross-training Recruitment of chosen candidates Kirkpatrick scores Analysis of voluntary terminations
Satisfaction	Employee satisfaction Turnover and absenteeism Grievances

EXHIBIT 11.6
Measures of the Human Resource

and consultation services.[63] The quality of HRM services includes the measures of the workforce as shown in Exhibit 11.6. Specific goals can be set and achieved by HRM. Many require collaboration with operating units, but the improvements should be reflected in their measures as well.

The use of both workforce and effectiveness metrics helps keep the contribution of the department in mind. Concerns are sometimes raised about the cost of human resources activity, such as the cost of employee time spent in training or participating in task forces with a direct human resources goal. These concerns assume that time spent on these activities results in lost production elsewhere. In fact, the premise may be false; the morale or skills improvement resulting from participation may cause production increases rather than decreases.

Managerial Issues

HRM has grown rapidly in recent years because leading HCOs have discovered its potential contribution. Several issues—adequate funding, senior management support, perceived fairness, and strategic alignment—can jeopardize the HRM program.

Adequate Funding

Modern HRM is an expensive support activity. Two weeks of training, substantial bonuses, extensive benefits, and strong associate services increase costs per employee by 50 percent or more. The actual cost of operating HRM

EXHIBIT 11.7
Measures
of Human
Resource
Management

Dimension	Concept	Representative Measures
Demand	Requests for human resources department service	Requests for training and counseling services Requests for recruitment Number of employees*
Cost	Resources consumed in department operation	Department costs Physical resources used by department Benefits costs, by benefit
Human resources	The workforce in the department	Satisfaction, turnover, absenteeism, grievances within the department
Output/ efficiency	Cost/unit of service	New hires per year Hours of training provided per employee Cost per hire, employee, training hour, etc.
Quality	Quality of department services	Goals from measures of the workforce Time to fill open positions Results of training Audit of services Service-error rates
Customer satisfaction	Services as viewed by employees and supervisors	Surveys of other units' satisfaction with human resources Employee satisfaction with benefits, training programs, etc.

* Employees automatically receive many services from human resources and thus are a good indicator of overall demand for service.

is only a small part of this total. High-performing HCOs have viewed these costs as an investment. Exhibit 11.8 shows the core dynamic, which applies as well to other logistic and strategic services. The investment generates a human resource that is adequately sized, appropriately qualified and trained, empowered, motivated, and rewarded. The records of these HCOs show that it will provide care that is safer, more effective, more efficient, better received by patients, and more profitable.

The implication of Exhibit 11.8 is that strategic opportunities drive HRM goals and OFIs. While benchmarks on HRM operational measures are useful, the right cost of HRM is the minimum necessary to achieve the strategic goals, which might be different from another HCO with a different history.

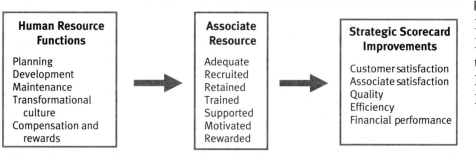

EXHIBIT 11.8
Human
Resources and
the Service
Excellence
Dynamic

Consistent Senior Leadership

As discussed in Chapter 2, the organization's culture is supported through leadership actions and reinforced through consistent messages to associates and other key stakeholders. Senior leadership controls this consistency with two major themes:

1. *Making the mission, vision, and values real.* Service excellence organizations use their mission, vision, and values constantly. The mission, vision, and values are always public, widely disseminated, and referenced in debate. Management must promote them, respect them, and live by them.

2. *"Walking the talk" with the associates.* The messages to the associates are
   - we are truly and deeply committed to our mission (otherwise, we would not be offering incentive pay for mission achievement, providing all this training, and introducing service recovery),
   - we value not only your effort but also your opinion (otherwise, we would not spend so much time doing surveys and inviting you to meetings), and
   - we want to help you grow and be promoted (otherwise, we would not talk about a personal and professional development plan).

As with any communications campaign, these messages must be repeated thousands of times, with high consistency, to be credible. Senior leadership must make a visible presence throughout the organization, and it must respond to associates in ways that convince the associates that they have been heard. That means simple problems are fixed, complicated problems are explained, progress toward solutions is publicized, and roadblocks to progress are removed. The test of success is the associates' belief that management has been fair and aggressive in attacking the improvement agenda. It is measured by survey, face-to-face meetings, incidents, and retention statistics.

Perceived Fairness

An associate's rewards—compensation, learning opportunities, recognition, and work conditions—are perceived to be fair when the associate believes a similar effort elsewhere would receive similar returns. The human resources processes that set compensation, evaluate individual performance, distribute incentives, resolve conflicts, and open learning and promotion opportunities must all pass intense scrutiny. Evaluations must be unbiased. Pay must be systematically matched to competitive opportunities. Bonuses and promotions must be distributed on the basis of individual contribution, and learning opportunities must be distributed on the basis of organizational need. The test is stronger than the absence of a hostile environment; it must be the presence of a comfortable and supportive environment. The actual record must show that gender and ethnic origin do not affect these decisions.[64]

HRM and senior leadership must see that fair processes are in place, enforced, and respected. That, of course, means that leaders must go beyond the letter of the law themselves.

Strategic Achievement

The human resource is the most critical component of strategic achievement. It is strong enough to overcome substantial weaknesses. The human resource itself invents solutions to shortages of information, supplies, facilities, protocols, and processes. It is not the only source of strategic achievement, however. Judicious mission setting, careful analysis of actual market needs and opportunities, and realistic selection of goals are all critical to strategic achievement. These are governance, marketing, and strategic analysis activities. If they are performed well, the model in Exhibit 11.8 will work. If they fail, the human resource, like the financial resource, will disappear and, ultimately, the HCO itself will fail.

Suggested Readings

Dell, D. J. 2004. *HR Outsourcing: Benefits, Challenges, and Trends.* New York: Conference Board.

Fitz-enz, J. 2009. *The ROI of Human Capital: Measuring the Economic Value of Employee Performance,* 2nd ed. New York: AMACOM Books.

Fried, B., and M. D. Fottler. 2008. *Human Resources in Healthcare: Managing for Success,* 3rd ed. Chicago: Health Administration Press.

Huselid, M. A., B. E. Becker, and R. W. Beatty. 2005. *The Workforce Scorecard: Managing Human Capital to Execute Strategy.* Boston: Harvard Business School Press.

The Joint Commission. 2006. *Providing Culturally and Linguistically Competent Health Care.* Oakbrook Terrace, IL: The Joint Commission.

Ulrich, D., and W. Brockbank. 2005. *The HR Value Proposition.* Boston: Harvard Business School Press.

Notes

1. White, K. R., D. G. Clement, and K. G. Stover. 2008. "Healthcare Professionals." In *Human Resources in Healthcare: Managing for Success,* 3rd ed., edited by B. J. Fried and M. D. Fottler, 74–83. Chicago: Health Administration Press.

2. Heskett, J. L., W. E. Sasser, Jr., and L. A. Schlesinger. 1997. *The Service Profit Chain: How Leading Companies Link Profit and Growth to Loyalty, Satisfaction, and Values,* 3–38. New York: Free Press.

3. Pfeffer, J. 1994. *Competitive Advantage Through People: Unleashing the Power of the Workforce,* 27–65. Boston: Harvard Business School Press.

4. Fottler, M. D. 2008. "Strategic Human Resources Management." In Fried and Fottler (2008), 12.

5. Tai, T. W., and C. D. Robinson. 1998. "Reducing Staff Turnover: A Case Study of Dialysis Facilities." *Health Care Management Review* 23 (4): 21–42.

6. Baker, D. P., R. Day, and E. Salas. 2006. "Teamwork as a Component of High-Reliability Organizations." *Health Services Research* 41 (4, Part II): 1576–98.

7. Levine, D. I., and L. D. Tyson. 1990. "Participation, Productivity, and the Firm's Environment." In *Paying for Productivity,* edited by A. S. Blinder, 183–243, 205. Washington, DC: The Brookings Institution.

8. Kocakulah, M. C., and D. Harris. 2002. "Measuring Human Capital Cost Through Benchmarking in Health Care Environment." *Journal of Health Care Finance* 29 (2): 27–37.

9. Liberman, A. 2000. "Pre-Employment Decision Trees: Jobs Applicant Self-Election." *The Health Care Manager* 18 (4): 48.

10. National Practitioner Data Bank. [Online information; retrieved 6/3/09.] www.npdb-hipdb.com/queryrpt.html.

11. Fried, B. J., and M. Gates. 2008. "Recruitment, Selection, and Retention." In Fried and Fottler (2008), 184.

12. Foster, C., and L. Godkin. 1998. "Employment Selection in Health Care: The Case for Structured Interviewing." *Health Care Management Review* 23 (1): 46–51.

13. *Ibid.*

14. Clement, D. G., M. A. Curran, and S. L. Jahn. 2008. "Employee Benefits." In Fried and Fottler (2008), 343.

15. Weech-Maldonado, R., J. L. Dreachslin, K. H. Dansky, G. De Souza, and M. Gatto. 2002. "Racial/Ethnic Diversity Management and Cultural Competency: The Case of Pennsylvania Hospitals." *Journal of Healthcare Management* 47 (2): 111–24.

16. Foundation of the American College of Healthcare Executives. "A Race/Ethnic Comparison of Career Attainments in Healthcare Management: 2008." [Online information; retrieved 6/3/09.] www.ache.org/PUBS/research/Report_Tables.pdf; Foundation of the American College of Healthcare Executives. "A Comparison of the Career Attainments of Men and Women Healthcare Executives: 2006." [Online information; retrieved 6/3/09.] www.ache.org/pubs/research/gender study_execsummary.cfm.

17. Dreachslin, J. L. 2007. "The Role of Leadership in Creating a Diversity-Sensitive Organization." *Journal of Healthcare Management* 52 (3): 151–55.

18. Myers, V. L., and J. L. Dreachslin. 2007. "Recruitment and Retention of a Diverse Workforce: Challenges and Opportunities." *Journal of Healthcare Management* 52 (5): 290–98.

19. McCracken, D. M. 2000. "Winning the Talent War for Women. Sometimes It Takes a Revolution." *Harvard Business Review* 78 (6): 159–67.

20. Dreachslin, J. L., and V. L. Myers. 2007. "A Systems Approach to Culturally and Linguistically Competent Care." *Journal of Healthcare Management* 52 (4): 220–26.

21. Lewis, M. G. 2007. "A Cultural Diversity Assessment and the Path to Magnet Status." *Journal of Healthcare Management* 52 (1): 64–70.

22. Evans, Sr., R. M. 2008. "Workforce Diversity." In Fried and Fottler (2008), 332–33.

23. The Joint Commission. 2006. *Providing Culturally and Linguistically Competent Health Care.* Oakbrook Terrace, IL: The Joint Commission.

24. DerGurahian, J. 2009. "Culturally Aware." *Modern Healthcare* 39 (11): 9.

25. Whitman, M. V., and J. A. Davis. 2008. "Cultural and Linguistic Competence in Healthcare: The Case of Alabama General Hospitals." *Journal of Healthcare Management* 53 (1): 26–40.

26. U.S. Department of Health and Human Services, Office of Minority Health (HHS-OMH). 2001. *National Standards for Culturally and Linguistically Appropriate Services in Health Care: Final Report.* [Online information; retrieved 6/5/09.] www.omhrc.gov/assets/pdf/checked/executive.pdf.

27. Grady, D. 2009. "Foreign Ways and War Scars Test Hospital." *New York Times.* [Online information; retrieved 6/5/09.] www.nytimes.com/2009/03/29/health/29immig.html?_r=1&emc=eta.

28. Cohen, J., B. Gabriel, and C. Terrell. 2002. "The Case for Diversity in the Health Care Workforce." *Health Affairs* 21 (5): 90–102.

29. Agency for Healthcare Research and Quality. 2009. "What Is Cultural and Linguistic Competence?" [Online information; retrieved 6/5/09.] www.ahrq.gov/About/cods/cultcompdef.htm.

30. Clement, Curran, and Jahn (2008).

31. U.S. Department of Labor, Occupational Safety & Health Administration. 2009. [Online information; retrieved 6/3/09.] www.osha.gov.

32. U.S. Equal Employment Opportunity Commission. 1990. Notice N-915-050. "Policy Guidance on Current Issues of Sexual Harassment." [Online information; retrieved 9/14/09.] www.eeoc.gov/policy/docs/currentissues.html.

33. Ibid.

34. Bureau of Labor Statistics. 2006. "Occupation Injury and Illness Data." [Online information; retrieved 6/3/09.] www.bls.gov/iif/oshwc/osh/os/ostb1765.pdf.

35. Wilson, T. H. 2009. *OSHA Guide for Health Care Facilities.* Washington, DC: Thompson Publishing Group.

36. Woodward, C. A., H. S. Shannon. C. Cunningham, J. McIntosh, B. Lendrum, D. Rosenbloom, and J. Brown. 1999. "The Impact of Re-Engineering and Other Cost Reduction Strategies on the Staff of a Large Teaching Hospital: A Longitudinal Study." *Medical Care* 37 (6): 556–69.

37. Burke, R. J., and E. R. Greenglass. 2001. "Hospital Restructuring and Nursing Staff Well-Being: The Role of Personal Resources." *Journal of Health & Human Services Administration* 24 (1): 3–26.

38. Huber, T. P., M. M. Godfrey, E. C. Nelson, J. J. Mohr, C. Campbell, and P. B. Batalden. 2003. "Microsystems in Health Care: Part 8. Developing People and Improving Work Life: What Front-Line Staff Told Us." *Joint Commission Journal of Quality and Safety* 29 (10): 512–22.

39. Garvin, D. A. 1993. "Building a Learning Organization." *Harvard Business Review* 71 (4): 78–91.

40. McColgan, E. A. 1997. "How Fidelity Invests in Service Professionals." *Harvard Business Review* 75 (1): 137–43.

41. Griffith, J. R., and K. R. White. 2005. "The Revolution in Hospital Management." *Journal of Healthcare Management* 50 (3): 170–90.

42. Jansen, E., D. Eccles, and G. N. Chandler. 1994. "Innovation and Restrictive Conformity Among Hospital Employees: Individual Outcomes and Organizational Considerations." *Hospital & Health Services Administration* 39 (1): 63–80.

43. Manzoni, J. F., and J. L. Barsoux. 1998. "The Set-up-to-Fail Syndrome." *Harvard Business Review* 76 (2): 101–13.

44. SSM Health Care. 2005. "Meeting in a Box." [Online information; retrieved 8/15/05.] www.ssmhc.com/internet/home/ssmcorp.nsf/0/8066903 a2b861da b86256c760051d9d5?OpenDocument.

45. Osborne, L. A. 2004. *Resolving Patient Complaints: A Step-by-Step Guide to Effective Service Recovery,* 2nd ed. Sudbury, MA: Jones & Bartlett.

46. Bendall-Lyon, D., and T. L. Powers. 2001. "The Role of Complaint Management in the Service Recovery Process." *Joint Commission Journal on Quality Improvement* 27 (5): 278–86.

47. Boothman, R. C., A. C. Blackwell, D. A. Campbell, Jr., E. Commiskey, and S. Anderson. 2009. "A Better Approach to Medical Malpractice Claims? The University of Michigan Experience." *Journal of Health and Life Sciences Law* 2 (2): 125–59.

48. Milkovich, G., and J. Newman. 2007. *Compensation,* 9th ed. New York: McGraw-Hill/Irwin.

49. Levine and Tyson (1990).

50. Griffith, J. R., and K. R. White. 2003. *Thinking Forward: Six Strategies for Highly Successful Organizations.* Chicago: Health Administration Press.

51. Barbusca, A., and M. Cleek. 1994. "Measuring Gain-Sharing Dividends in Acute Care Hospitals." *Health Care Management Review* 19 (1): 28–33.

52. United States Department of Labor. 2009. "Family and Medical Leave Act." [Online information; retrieved 6/4/09.] www.dol.gov/esa/whd/fmla.

53. GuideStar. 2009. [Online information; retrieved 6/4/09.] www2.guidestar.org/Home.aspx.

54. Aldana, S. G. 2001. "Financial Impact of Health Promotion Programs: A Comprehensive Review of the Literature." *American Journal of Health Promotion* 15 (5): 296–320.

55. Malvey, D. 2008. "Managing with Organized Labor." In Fried and Fottler (2008), 362.

56. U.S. Bureau of Labor Statistics. [Online information; retrieved 9/16/09.] www.bls.gov/news.release/union2.t03.htm.

57. Hoff, T. J. 2000. "Physician Unionization in the United States: Fad or Phenomenon?" *Journal of Health & Human Services Administration* 23 (1): 5–23.

58. Gullett, C. R., and M. J. Kroll. 1990. "Rule Making and the National Labor Relations Board: Implications for the Health Care Industry." *Health Care Management Review* 15 (2): 61–65.

59. Hein, J. G., Jr. 2000. "Employment: NLRB Empowers Residents to Unionize." *Journal of Law, Medicine & Ethics* 28 (3): 307–09.

60. HR Certification Institute. 2010. [Online information; retrieved 4/27/10.] www.hrci.org/certification/ov.

61. American Society for Healthcare Human Resources Administration. 2009. [Online information; retrieved 6/4/09.] www.ashhra.org.

62. Dell, D. J. 2004. *HR Outsourcing: Benefits, Challenges and Trends.* New York: The Conference Board.

63. PricewaterhouseCoopers. 2009. "Saratoga: Human Capital Measurement." [Online information; retrieved 6/4/09.] www.pwc.com/extweb/service.nsf/docid/de40ffb0d40981d385256f17005397cd.

64. Dansky, K. H., R. Weech-Maldonado, G. De Souza, and J. L. Dreachslin. 2003. "Organizational Strategy and Diversity Management: Diversity-Sensitive Orientation as a Moderating Influence." *Health Care Management Review* 28 (3): 243–53.

12 ENVIRONMENT-OF-CARE MANAGEMENT

In a Few Words

The appearance of the facility often generates a patient's or an associate's first impression. Its convenience and functionality influence ultimate satisfaction. The healthcare organization (HCO) should be a perfect example of form following function. Every aspect of the environment of care must be designed and planned with the users in mind. Signage should be abundant and unambiguous, grounds maintained and comforting, guest services friendly and helpful, and security present and effective. Well-designed and well-maintained physical facilities improve overall efficiency and quality. Appropriate facility design promotes patient safety and quicker recovery time. Smoothly operating food service, sanitation, maintenance, and materials management reduce waste and increase effectiveness. Excellent environment of care supports improved financial performance. The HCO is a point of refuge in time of trouble; it must be prepared to handle natural disasters, large-scale accidents, and terrorist attacks. Environment-of-care management achieves these goals with a transformational culture and continuous improvement, often contracting with outside vendors.

Critical Issues in Environment-of-Care Management

1. *Designing space for improved patient outcomes:*
   - Architecture and equipment that emphasize safe design and materials
   - Deliberate attention to a visually welcoming atmosphere
   - Investment in preventive maintenance

2. *Carefully planning the best use of existing space:*
   - Space allocation assigned to one central office
   - Formal, open process for review of requests for expansion
   - Periodic review of space use to determine continuing need

3. *Maintaining excellent security, sanitation, maintenance, and materials management services:*
   - Measurement of benchmarks and goals for service and internal customer satisfaction

- Standards for availability; cost; and quality of plant, plant services, and supplies
- Maintenance of supplier relationships
- Training, support, and rewards for service employees and supervisors

4. *Using contract services to improve performance:*
   - Specification of service requirements in cost, quality, and satisfaction dimensions
   - Benchmarking and comparison of service
   - Contracting with outside suppliers to ensure near-benchmark performance

5. *Developing evacuation and emergency plans capable of handling natural disasters, large-scale accidents, and the possibility of terrorism:*
   - Internal plans for response
   - Drills and testing
   - Coordination with other community agencies

QUESTIONS FOR DISCUSSION

Consider these questions as you read the chapter.

1. To accommodate a rapidly growing and aging community, it is necessary to expand capacity for long-term care by constructing a new wing. How would you determine the primary health concerns for this population, and how would your plan and design meet their medical needs and improve their satisfaction?

2. Your organization will contract with an orthopedic implant supplier. What steps would you take in comparing vendors and selecting and administering a contract of this nature?

3. Patient satisfaction surveys criticize overall appearances and attitudes of employees. What lessons in hospitality might you learn from the hotel industry that would be applicable to improving your organization?

4. Your community HCO is in a large coastal city and in hurricane territory. What issues should your disaster plan address, and how does the HCO create one?

5. You have an offer from a vendor to outsource your entire supplies function. How would you evaluate that offer?

A safe and attractive environment of care determines in large part impressions and attitudes people form about an organization. It is a central component of the HCO's culture and important in promotional activity, not only to patients but also to associates. An excellent environment-of-care system is safe, reliable, convenient, attractive, and economical. It includes facilities, supplies, equipment, security, sanitation, food service, and maintenance services. It is a large system; housekeeping and food service alone often rank just behind the largest clinical departments in number of employees and costs. In HCOs with hospitals, it includes preparation for large-scale disasters, whether natural or manmade.

Exhibit 12.1 shows several HCO environments, non-health organizations with which they are commonly compared, and their special needs. All of these environments must provide safety, comfort, sanitation, and, except for the smallest, food service. All of them have needs unique to healthcare. At the extreme, the acute care hospital provides complete environmental support not only for patients but also for staff and visitors. It must have extra supplies of power and water to allow it to operate through disruptions of those services. It requires narrower tolerances on temperature, humidity, air quality, cleanliness, and wastes. It has high volumes of human traffic and, as a result, has high risks of personal and property safety, including a risk of direct terrorist attacks. Several hazards, including fire, chemicals, radiation, infection, and criminal violence, can be life threatening to employees, visitors, and patients. The well-run organization uses carefully designed, conscientiously maintained programs to make these services transparent, reliable, and risk free.

Purpose

The purpose of environment-of-care management (ECM) is

- **to provide the complete physical environment required for the mission, including all buildings, equipment, and supplies;**
- **to protect organization members and visitors against all hazards that arise in the healthcare environment; and**
- **to maintain reliable guest services at satisfactory levels of economy, attractiveness, and convenience.**

Functions

ECM functions can be grouped into six major categories, as shown in Exhibit 12.2. It is noteworthy that the functions include the management of all the plant, equipment, supplies, and many nonclinical services for guests and associates. The functions range from lawn mowing and snow removal to security guards, signage, and meals to the life-support environments of

EXHIBIT 12.1
Environment-
of-Care
Management
Requirements

Activity	Facility	Non-Health Counterpart	Special Needs
Primary care	Small office	Small retail store	X-ray machine Drugs and clinical supplies Clinical waste removal
Outpatient specialty care	Medical office building	Shopping mall	Special electrical and radiologic requirements Drugs and clinical supplies Clinical waste removal Disaster preparation
Long-term care	Nursing home	Motel	Extra fire safety and disability assistance Drugs and clinical supplies Clinical waste removal Pathogenic organisms Special air handling 24-hour security
Acute and intensive care	Hospital	Hotel	Extra fire safety and disability assistance Drugs and clinical supplies 24-hour security Disaster and terrorism preparation Dangerous chemicals High-voltage radiology Radioactive products Clinical waste removal Pathogenic organisms Special air handling Emergency utilities preparation

surgery and intensive care. Everything must be done well, from sweeping the entranceway to maintaining intensive care unit equipment. A substantial library is available on the components of facilities management systems. Some of the more general works are cited at the end of this chapter.

Facilities Design, Planning, and Space Allocation

The HCO's physical facility—often an array of buildings of multiple ages and several locations—is a resource that must be planned to accommodate future technology and market changes, designed or redesigned to fit user needs, acquired, and uniquely allocated to meet the needs of specific activities in the context of environmental responsibility. The planning and design function is centralized to ensure consistency across the HCO.

Function	Activities	Examples	
Facilities design, planning, and space allocation	Using design to improve performance Planning, building, acquiring, and divesting facilities	Patient-, associate-, and environment-friendly designs Facilities management plan Construction and renovation management Facilities leasing and purchase Space allocation	**EXHIBIT 12.2** Functions of Environment-of-Care Services
Facilities maintenance	Housekeeping and groundskeeping Utilities supply Waste removal Hazardous materials Plant and equipment maintenance	Cleaning, decorating Snow removal, landscaping Heating, lighting, water, and sewage service and protection against service failure Recycling Chemical and radiation hazard management Routine upkeep and repairs	
Guest services	Security Support for associates, patients, and visitors	24/7 personal and facility security Parking Food service Signage and wayfinding	
Materials management services	Purchasing, receiving, storing, and distributing supplies	Clinical supplies Foodstuff Drugs Office supplies Medical gases	
Enhanced environmental management	Risk management Emergency preparedness Life-safety and fire protection Clinical engineering Utility protection	Identifying and eliminating hazards Preparing for large-volume disasters Responding to internal fire or safety problem Maintaining high-tech medical equipment Utility backup and failure prevention	
Performance improvement and budgeting	Customer-focused identification of OFIs Contracting with service vendors Coordinating multiyear plans	Ensuring that internal and external customer needs are met Developing a long-range vision Maintaining competitive services	

OFI: opportunity for improvement

Planning Facility Requirements

ECM begins with planning for space and fixed equipment. Healthcare facilities are built for their users; thus, plans begin with identifying specific needs and architectural specifications. Plans continue through the management of construction contracts and the lifecycle of maintenance, renovation, and eventual replacement.

As shown in Exhibit 12.3, the **facilities master plan** begins with an estimate of the space needs of each service or activity proposed in the services plan. Space needs must be described by location, special requirements, and size. Need is compared to available space, and deficits are met at the lowest cost. *Conversion*—the simple reassignment of space from one activity to another—is the least expensive, but so many healthcare needs require specific locations and requirements that renovation, acquisition, or construction are frequently necessary. The final facilities master plan shows the future location of all services and documents the renovation, acquisition, or construction necessary in terms of specific actions, timetables, and costs.

Facilities master plan
A document that begins with an estimate of the space needs of each service or activity proposed in the services plan

Given a forecast of demand for a service, space requirements are forecast from one of two simple models. Demand can be scheduled or delayed until service is available:

$$1. \quad \left\{ \begin{array}{c} \text{Number of} \\ \text{treatment} \\ \text{facilities} \end{array} \right\} = \left\{ \begin{array}{c} \text{Average numbers} \\ \text{of treatments} \\ \text{per time period} \end{array} \right\} \times \left\{ \begin{array}{c} \text{Hours per} \\ \text{treatment} \end{array} \right\} \div \left\{ \begin{array}{c} \text{Available hours} \\ \text{per facility} \end{array} \right\}$$

Space required per unit of demand is often measured in specific time and facility dimensions, as machine hours/treatment or bed days/patient. For example, for schedulable activities, such as routine outpatient visits, if 320 visits are expected and each use is 15 minutes, and the rooms are available for four-hour sessions, the number of treatment facilities required is:

$$\left\{ \begin{array}{c} \text{Number} \\ \text{of exam} \\ \text{rooms} \end{array} \right\} = \left\{ 320 \text{ visits} \right\} \times \left\{ 0.25 \text{ hours/visit} \right\} \div \left\{ 4 \text{ hours/room} \right\} = 20 \text{ rooms}$$

It is often necessary to add an allowance for various kinds of losses that prevent full use of the space. If, historically, exam rooms can be used only 90 percent of the time, the expected load is 0.90, and the number of rooms required would be:

$$\left\{ \begin{array}{c} \text{Number} \\ \text{of exam} \\ \text{rooms} \end{array} \right\} = \left\{ 320 \right\} \times \left\{ 0.25 \right\} \div \left\{ 4 \text{ hours/room} \times 0.9 \right\} = 22.2 \text{ rooms}$$

The extra 0.2 rooms becomes an opportunity for improvement (OFI): If we can reduce the downtime, we will reduce the project cost and increase the likelihood of funding.

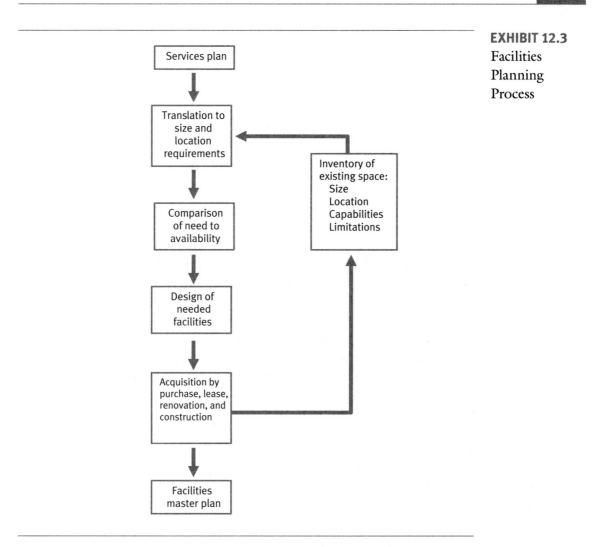

EXHIBIT 12.3
Facilities
Planning
Process

For services that must be met without delay and that vary unpredictably in the number arriving, the maximum number of arrivals expected must be used to plan space.

$$
2. \quad \left\{ \begin{array}{c} \text{Facility} \\ \text{required} \end{array} \right\} = \left\{ \begin{array}{c} \text{Maximum} \\ \text{units of demand} \\ \text{in single period} \end{array} \right\} \times \left\{ \begin{array}{c} \text{Space required} \\ \text{per unit of demand} \end{array} \right\}
$$

For example, in obstetrics services:

$$
\left\{ \begin{array}{c} \text{Number of} \\ \text{delivery rooms} \end{array} \right\} = \left\{ \begin{array}{c} \text{Maximum number} \\ \text{of mothers delivering} \\ \text{in one hour} \end{array} \right\} \times \left\{ \begin{array}{c} \text{One room} \\ \text{per mother} \end{array} \right\}
$$

If a facility is built for maximum demand, it will serve only average demand and be idle the rest of the time. Its expected load will be:

$$\left\{ \begin{array}{c} \text{Expected} \\ \text{load} \end{array} \right\} = \left\{ \begin{array}{c} \text{Average} \\ \text{units of demand} \\ \text{in a single period} \end{array} \right\} \div \left\{ \begin{array}{c} \text{Maximum} \\ \text{units of demand} \\ \text{in a single period} \end{array} \right\}$$

Facilities where emergency demand is often encountered, such as obstetrics and coronary care, will operate with low expected load, sometimes approaching 50 percent. These allowances cannot be changed by internal performance improvement, but they can be changed by centralizing to larger facilities. As a rule of thumb, the allowance is reduced by the square root of the change in demand; four times larger demand reduces the allowance by one-half.

Two other issues can require an allowance: (1) time not acceptable to customers or associates, such as holidays and weekends, and (2) time required for maintenance. Part of performance improvement is minimizing the allowance. For example, it is usually possible to schedule maintenance in times of low demand. Unattractive times can be filled by using incentives—discounts, faster service to customers, or extra pay to associates.

Methods for the actual calculation will get quite complex. Often several methods of forecasting are used to improve confidence in the forecast. For example, surgeries will be categorized by type of room and square feet required. Each type of room will have several sources of demand that are forecast separately. Duration of operations (the "space required per unit") will be studied carefully. Trade-offs will be required; a room designed for a certain specialty might be highly inefficient for other demand. Trade-offs must also be evaluated between the efficiency of high load factors and the increased associate satisfaction from specialization. A simulation model might be constructed to evaluate trade-offs between alternative designs and load factors.

Using Design to Improve Performance

Poor hospital design is among the leading causes of preventable hospital errors, infections, and work-related stress. For example, poor ventilation with two or more patients per room can lead to nosocomial infections, while inadequate or inappropriate lighting is linked to suboptimal patient outcomes and medication errors by hospital staff. Better, safer, and evidence-based design environments promote healing and satisfy healthcare staff.[1] Expert estimates suggest annual hospital construction expenditures to be about 10 percent of total operating costs.[2]

Several design elements are recognized to be important: private rooms, sound control, air quality, ecological impact, signage, and information stations. New design must address wireless communication, delivery robots, and appearance. Bronson Methodist Hospital's new (2007) facility in Kalamazoo, Michigan, introduced many improvements, including art, light, nature elements (such as a central garden courtyard), and information technology (such as touch-screen kiosks).[3] Bon Secours St. Francis Medical Center, a hospital that opened in 2005 in Richmond, Virginia, uses natural elements such as fountains, meditative gardens, and a chapel that opens to walking paths[4] not only for patients, families, and associates but for the surrounding community, ascribing to the urban planning principles of New Urbanism.[5]

Money spent on design innovations and upgrades can be recovered through operational savings and increased revenue. In a study of 19 replacement hospitals, 75 percent experienced overall average increases of 15 percent in admissions, 33 percent in outpatient visits, and 2.5 percent in operating margins in the first year.[6] Investing in better hospitals requires that leadership recognize the need for and plan strategically to promote an environment to minimize stress. Good design is an evolution, rather than an adoption of radical changes.[7] Improved design is clearly an important component of a successful continuous improvement program. Hospitals have begun to follow performance-based building practices, such as LEED (Leadership in Energy and Environmental Design) certification, to maximize ecological sustainability.[8,9]

Renovation, Construction, and Acquisition

Implementing the facilities master plan requires a comprehensive program of real estate and building management that indicates the way the requirements will be met. The unfilled needs, including renovations, must be expanded into specifications and drawings for both space and fixed equipment and translated to reality. Real estate must sometimes be acquired, contracts let, progress maintained, and results inspected and approved before the facility can be occupied. In large projects, several years elapse between approval of the facilities plan and opening day. Plans have specific, carefully developed time schedules.

Real estate is acquired through purchase or lease. It is possible to lease all or part of a facility, including a single lease for a building and equipment designed and constructed specifically for the HCO. Major equipment can also be leased. Real estate transactions generally require governing board approval, and the finance department is always involved (see Chapter 13).

Major construction and renovation usually call for extensive outside contracting. The traditional approach is to retain an architect, a construction management firm, and a general contractor. Construction financed directly by public funds, such as that of public hospitals, usually must be contracted via formal competitive bids. Private organizations frequently prefer more flexible arrangements, negotiating contracts with selected vendors. Recent innovations have simplified the contracts by combining various elements; turnkey construction involves a single contract to deliver the finished facility. Advantages of speed and flexibility are cited, and costs likely can be reduced if the HCO is well prepared and supervises the process carefully. Small renovation projects are often handled by internal staff. As an interim step, the organization can provide design and construction management, preparing the plans and contracting with specific subcontractors.

Regardless of the size or complexity of the project, any project to change the use of space should be carefully planned in advance and closely managed as it evolves. A sound program includes the following:

1. Review of the space and equipment needs forecast
2. Identification of special needs
3. Trial of alternative layouts, designs, and equipment configurations
4. Development of a written plan and specifications
5. Review of code requirements and plans for compliance
6. Approval of plan and specifications by the operating unit
7. Development of a timetable identifying critical elements of the construction
8. Contracting or formal designation of work crew and accountability
9. Ongoing review of work against specifications and timetable
10. Final review, acceptance, and approval of occupancy

Involvement of end users, especially caregiving associates and physicians, in planning and specifying the space requirements from idea conception to completion maximizes space functionality and stakeholder satisfaction and minimizes costly change orders.

Space Allocation

The criterion for allocating existing space is conceptually simple. Each space should be used or disposed of in the way that optimizes achievement of the organizational mission. In reality, this criterion is difficult to apply. Activities tend to expand to fill the available space. As a result, there are always complaints of shortages of space and an agenda of possible reallocations or expansions. When activities shrink, the space is often difficult to recover and reuse. Space is highly valuable and unique: The third floor is not identical to the first. Space also confers prestige and symbolic rewards. Space next to the doctors' lounge, for example, is more prestigious than space adjacent to the employment office. As a result, space allocation decisions tend to be strenuously contested.

Each unit that seeks substantial additional space or renovation must prepare a formal request and gain approval from the space office before submitting a new program or capital proposal. The following guidelines assist in space management:

- Space management is assigned to a single office that permits occupancy and controls access to space. The office participates in new programs and capital budget review activities (see chapters 8 and 13), where most changes originate, and designs appropriate ad hoc review for other requests.
- A key function of the space management office is the preparation of the facilities master plan. Internal consulting and marketing staff assist in the preparation. The draft plan is derived from the services plan, and the final version becomes part of the planning package. The facilities master plan includes forecasts of

specific commitments for existing and approved space; plans for acquisition of land, buildings, and equipment; plans for renovation and refurbishing requirements for existing space; and plans for new construction.

- The facilities master plan is incorporated into the long-range financial plan and annual review and approval processes.
- The plant services department implements acquisition, construction, and renovation. Details of interior design are reviewed and approved by units that will use the space. Financing is managed by the finance department.

Facilities Maintenance

Facility maintenance includes decorating; maintaining lighting, heating, and air conditioning; supplying power; and cleaning and repair for all buildings and grounds. The components are shown in Exhibit 12.4. These activities are required for any facility, even a single family home. They are more complex in HCOs because the facilities are large and multistory, have large traffic volumes, and must operate 24/7/365. Special needs arise from many clinical activities. Facilities maintenance must respond to local conditions, including weather, and be performed in compliance with a variety of federal regulations established by the Occupational Safety and Health Administration (OSHA) and the Environmental Protection Agency (EPA).

Housekeeping and groundskeeping must maintain campuses (of millions of square feet) efficiently and at standards to ensure visual attractiveness and control microbial and other hazards. Some services, such as snow removal and exterior lighting, must be available around the clock. In well-run HCOs these activities are conducted to explicit standards of quality and are monitored by inspectors using formal survey methods. These activities also interact with important programs for environmental safety. Continuous improvement, training, and carefully specified equipment and supplies are used to attain high levels of cleanliness and safety.

Housekeeping and Groundskeeping

Cleaning and landscape services are frequently subcontracted. The most common contracts are for management-level services. The outside firm supplies procedures, training, and supervision; the workers are hourly employees. Large organizations with access to central services for training and developing methods may be able to justify their own management.

Decorating and landscaping are performed with an understanding of public taste and the cost of specific materials. Colors, fabrics, and designs are selected for comfort, durability, and the conformity with applicable life-safety code (rating for fire retardancy and prevention). The best decor creates an attractive ambiance but consists of materials that do not show wear and are durable, fire-rated, and easy to clean. Careful initial design leads to higher capital costs, lower operating costs, and greater user satisfaction. Evidence-based design environments have been shown to contribute to improved patient outcomes.[10]

EXHIBIT 12.4
Facilities
Maintenance
Services

Housekeeping
Interior design
Routine cleaning
  General patient areas
  High-risk patient areas
  Non-patient areas
  Special problem areas
Odor control
Sound control

Groundskeeping
Landscaping
Grounds maintenance
Recycling

Hazardous waste management
Safeguarding hazardous materials
Material safety data sheets
Clinical waste removal

Utilities management
Electrical power
Heating, ventilation, and air conditioning
Lighting
Communications support
Gases supply

Maintenance and repair services
Building and utility maintenance
Equipment maintenance

Utilities Management

Most HCOs need highly reliable supplies of all utilities. Electricity, methane, clinical gases, water, and sewage supplies are generally supported by redundant sources. Heating, ventilating, and air conditioning are usually internally operated and built to meet extreme conditions. Operating rooms and some laboratories have special air-handling requirements. Plant services support the communications systems described in Chapter 10. These are also critical and are protected by redundancy.

Waste Management

In addition to sewage, HCOs have solid wastes to dispose of. The basic strategy is to select supplies that minimize waste, to recycle whenever possible, and to meet special handling needs. *Sharps*—used needles and blades, for example—represent a special problem and are handled through a special collection system from point of use to ultimate destruction. Some chemicals also present unique disposal hazards.

Hazardous Materials and Waste

Environmental needs and biological and chemical hazards in clinical wastes have complicated the problem of waste management. Waste disposal must meet increasingly stringent EPA standards and state and local laws that protect the safety of landfills, water supplies, and air. Many cities require segregation of nonclinical wastes to permit recycling. Federal and state laws govern burning and shipment of wastes. A federal law governs handling and disposal of medical waste[11] and other potentially hazardous materials.[12] Emergency response plans must include requirements for personal protective equipment and clear assignment of tasks, locations, and training to prevent healthcare workers from exposures.

Within the HCO, wastes must be handled correctly and efficiently. Additionally, procedures should outline the steps to be taken for decontaminating patients who seek emergency medical care after being exposed to hazardous materials. Clinical wastes are known to transmit contagious diseases, such as hepatitis and HIV. Specially designed systems for decontamination and waste management must be carefully planned. Personnel who are most likely to come into contact with hazardous materials or waste contamination (e.g., emergency department, housekeeping, and nursing staffs) must be trained. Drills must be conducted for unusual threats.

Following are four basic approaches to managing hazardous materials:

1. *Restricting exposure at the source.* Good design and good procedures for use reduce bacteriological and chemical contamination. Air- and water- handling systems can be made almost completely safe. Special handling is necessary for contaminated wastes. Human vectors in the spread of infection are harder to control, and they include both caregivers and plant personnel. Development of comprehensive control systems and monitoring of actual infection rates are a clinical function usually assigned to an infection control committee, which includes persons from facilities maintenance, housekeeping, and central supply services.

2. *Cleaning and removal.* The housekeeping department is usually responsible for cleaning and removing hazardous substances. Techniques are adjusted to the level of risk. Special cleaning materials and associate protection are necessary for spills of hazardous material.

3. *Attention to exposed patients, visitors, and associates.* Trauma or infection from contaminants can occur either during patient treatment or in cleaning and disposing of equipment. In 2001, OSHA, in response to the Needlestick Safety and Prevention Act, revised the Bloodborne Pathogens Standard to protect workers from exposure to bloodborne pathogens such as hepatitis B, hepatitis C, or HIV.[13] The revised standard requires employers to select safer needle devices, to involve employees in choosing these devices, and to maintain a log of injuries. The office of employee health, which reports to the infection control committee, examines any person believed to be injured or exposed to a bloodborne pathogen and provides care following prophylaxis protocols recommended by the Centers for Disease Control and Prevention.[14] Workers' compensation is available for any employee injury that results from exposure. Visitors and patients are protected from exposure by well-designed clinical waste-removal systems.

4. *Epidemiologic analysis of failures.* Epidemiologic studies are an important part of an infection control program. Studies of the incidence of specific illnesses can identify process improvements and detect impending epidemics. The work requires special training in epidemiology. It is often assigned to a member of the infection control committee.

HCOs usually contract for waste and hazardous materials removal. The contractor team is deeply integrated into the HCO to coordinate these activities. They work side by side with employees on the job and on numerous process improvement teams (PITs).

Maintenance and Repair Services

The objective of maintenance and repair services is to keep the facility and its equipment like new so that patients, visitors, and staff perceive the environment positively or neutrally. The goal is achieved by emphasizing preventive maintenance; fixing or replacing equipment before it is broken is preferable. Well-managed plant systems schedule preventive maintenance for all the mechanical services and specific building areas. They regularly inspect general-use equipment (such as elevators and air handling) and plant conditions (such as floor and wall coverings, plumbing, roofs, and structural members). They perform repairs and routine maintenance as needed, and their logs are used to assess replacement needs. A significant fraction of mechanics' time is devoted to preventive maintenance, and adherence to the schedule is one of the measures of the quality of the department's work.

Outside vendors are used to maintain many specialized equipment items. Well-run organizations tend to place the responsibility for managing the contract on the unit that uses the equipment, if only one unit is involved. The plant department is responsible for equipment in general use, such as elevators, heating, and air conditioning. Actual contracting for all equipment maintenance is centralized through materials management, which must consult with the responsible units.

Equipment repair is frequently an issue in replacement decisions. The unit that uses the equipment initiates requests for replacement, which must be justified and competitively judged. The opinion of repair personnel, both about future needs of existing equipment and issues raised by replacement, should be solicited routinely.

Guest Services

Large numbers of patients, visitors, and staff become the guests of HCOs and require a variety of services. People expect to come to a facility; park; find what they want; get certain amenities such as waiting areas, lounges, or the cafeteria; and leave without even recognizing that they have received service. They expect, and are fully entitled to, strenuous efforts by the HCO to maintain a safe environment. Those who access the organization by telephone or electronic communication expect a similarly complete, prompt, and unobtrusive response. The organization's attractiveness is diminished if the services listed in Exhibit 12.5 are either inadequate or intrusive. The personnel who deliver guest services have an effect on customer and associate satisfaction almost as great as that of nursing.

Guest services frequently involve multiple locations and small work groups, but they require coordinated management and a significant investment in centrally operated support systems. For example, receptionists and security personnel need current knowledge of the location of each inpatient and each special event or activity. Coordinated management of guest services stresses the importance of a satisfactory overall impression. It may also contribute to efficiency by allowing overlapping functions to be eliminated. Relations with housekeeping, security, and facility operations also require coordination.

Security services are necessary in most settings to protect associates, visitors, patients, and property. There are recognized hazards of theft, property destruction, and personal injury to associates and visitors. Both associates and visitors can commit violent acts.[15] The hazard is particularly high in urban areas.[16] High-quality security services are preventive. Security involves controlling access to the hospital, monitoring traffic flow, providing employee identification, and installing lighting to create an environment that is reassuring to guests and discouraging to persons with destructive intentions. Digital cameras and emergency call systems amplify the scope of surveillance. Employee education is helpful in promoting safe behavior and prompt reporting of questionable events. Special attention must be given to high-risk areas, such as the emergency department and parking areas. Uniformed guards serve to be a visible symbol of authority, to respond to questions and concerns, and to provide emergency assistance in those infrequent events that exceed the capability of reception personnel.

Security

    Security is frequently a contract service. It must be coordinated with local police and fire service. Municipal units sometimes provide the contract service, particularly in government hospitals. Not-for-profit HCOs usually do not pay local taxes in support of local fire and police service; as a result, the extent to which taxpayer services should be provided is often questioned. Some states have imposed fees on not-for-profit organizations to reflect the public services provided.

		EXHIBIT 12.5
Security Services	*Communication and Transportation Services*	Guest Services: Workforce, Patient, and Visitor Support
Guards		
Employee identification	Telephone and television	
Traffic control	Messenger	
Facility inspection and monitoring	Tube transport systems	
	Reception and guidance	
Parking Services	Signage	
	Parking	
Food Service	Internet access	
Cafeteria and vending service	Public website design and maintenance	
Patient food service	Intranet design and maintenance	
Routine patient service	Telephone reception	
Therapeutic diets		

Reception and Messenger Services

In a large HCO, several dozen people have reception jobs that involve meeting and guiding the organization's guests. Signs, telephone numbers, and maps aid efficient routing. Web interfaces, both public and intranet, are also reception points. All of these are measured by their effectiveness and user satisfaction.

Patients and large physical items must be moved around the organization, and training in guest relations, emergency medical needs, and hospital geography are necessary to do the job well. Large organizations have circulating vans that connect patients to various sites. Because requests for transportation are often unpredictable and because supervising transporters, couriers, and drivers in the field is difficult, pooling transportation needs presents important efficiencies. Large organizations may have more than one pool, but smaller ones usually combine all messenger and reception activities under one supervisor.

Food Service

The preparation of food for patients, staff, and guests has become a service similar to the food services of hotels, airlines, and resorts rather than a clinical service. Food service should provide inexpensive, nutritious, appealing, and tasty meals that encourage good eating habits. HCOs typically offer a choice of entrees, appetizers, and desserts to each patient on census. "On demand" feeding is popular. Patient meals must also be provided to a variety of clinical specifications. Soft, low-sodium, and sodium-free diets account for up to half of all patient meals; however, bulk foods that meet these specifications can be prepared by personnel without clinical training. Patients are often susceptible to food bacteria, so food service must be conducted to high standards of quality, beginning with control of bacterial hazards and safety in preparation and distribution. Safe food-handling procedures are important to avoid bacterial contamination.

In addition to patient meals, about an equal number of meals are provided to associates and guests, usually in cafeterias. Visitors and employees expect greater variety, a range of prices, and service at odd hours. A snack bar, a coffee shop, and a variety of vending machines with food and drinks are among common offerings. Food service also supports home care and meals-on-wheels distribution.

These concerns are relatively easy to meet through sound general procedures. Food service is frequently contracted. Contract food suppliers meet the quality and cost constraints through centralized menu planning, well-developed training programs for workers and managers, and careful attention to work methods. Nutritional education and consultation and the preparation of special diets to meet medical needs are available through the therapeutic dietetics service. Clinical dietitians have limited contact with the mass-feeding operation, although they are important members of the patient care team; their focus is on diet therapy in post-discharge care.

Materials Management Services

HCOs typically spend 25 to 30 percent of their budget on supplies. Like other industries, they use office supplies, foodstuffs, linens and uniforms, fuels, paints, hardware, and cleaning supplies. They also use surgical implants, whole blood, specialized dressings, x-ray film, single-purpose medical tools, and a large variety of drugs. Most supply costs are represented in the following inventory groups, which are either large volumes of inexpensive items (such as foodstuffs) or relatively small volumes of expensive items (such as implants):

- Surgical supplies and implants
- Pharmaceuticals, intravenous solutions, and medical gases
- Foodstuffs
- Linens
- Dressings, kits, film, and supplies for patient care

Materials management concentrates most supply purchases under a single unit of the organization that is responsible for meeting standards of quality and service at a minimum total cost. The materials management function includes the supply chain activities shown in Exhibit 12.6.

Critics of HCOs argue that the organizations are far below industrial standards.[17] Materials managers work with users, including clinical users like the pharmacy and therapeutics committee, to identify the most economical supplies consistent with patient needs. Many of the costliest supplies are physician-preference items. Their use is standardized through the protocol-setting process. Buyers then negotiate prices, manage inventories, and maintain accounting records of use.

Improvement of materials management lies in systems that achieve the lowest overall costs, rather than those that simply purchase at the cheapest price.[18,19] Specification of supplies is a critical component. Working with PITs and supplies users, materials management personnel strive to standardize items, reduce the number of different items purchased, establish criteria for appropriate quality, and eliminate unnecessary purchases. They examine alternative processes and identify improved methods and new supply specifications. For example, disposables may be compared to reusable alternatives.

Most important, the large volumes of standardized materials can be controlled more carefully for quality, and the high quantity can be leveraged to negotiate lower prices. The purchasing process itself uses long-term contracting and competitive bidding to reduce prices. Most well-managed organizations now use **group purchasing**—cooperatives that use the collective buying power of several organizations to leverage

Group purchasing
Alliances that use the collective buying power of several organizations to leverage prices downward

EXHIBIT 12.6
Functions
of Materials
Management

Material selection and control
Specifications for cost-effective
　supplies
Standardization of items
Reduction in the number of items

Purchasing
Standardized purchasing procedures
Competitive bid
Annual or periodic contracts
Group purchasing contracts

Receipt, storage, and protection
Reduction of inventory size
Control of shipment size and frequency
Reduction of handling
Reduction of damage or theft
Economical warehousing

Processing
Elimination of processing by purchase
　or contract
Improved processing methods
Reduced reprocessing or turnaround
　time

Distribution
Elimination or automation of ordering
Improved delivery methods
Reduced end-user inventories
Reduced wastage and unauthorized
　usage

*Revenue enhancement and cost
　accounting*
Uniform records of supplies usage
Integration of clinical ordering and
　patient billing systems

prices downward. Some large vendors offer comprehensive materials management, providing a complete service at competitive costs.

Vendors can reduce the cost of the materials-handling system. Automation of inventories, ordering, and billing reduces handling costs. Most major vendors supply just-in-time service, effectively bearing the cost of inventory management as part of their activities. Vendors guarantee specific quality levels and are certified to comply with standards of the International Standards Organization. Compliance eliminates the need for routine sampling of received goods. Centralized storage protects against theft and damage. Careful accounting and division of duties guard against theft and embezzlement. Some bulk supplies are delivered by robots to reduce costs. Finally, automated records of used supplies provide data for cost analysis and, in cases where individual payments are made for the supplies, for posting of accounts receivable.

Enhanced Environmental Management

HCOs must meet enhanced environmental requirements in several areas. The programs shown in Exhibit 12.7 are deliberate efforts to ensure operations under exceptionally stressful circumstances (e.g., natural and manmade disasters) or to systematically improve outcomes of environmental management. The Joint Commission standards include these (and more) general standards for environmental programs.[20]

**Risk
Management**   A comprehensive risk-management program keeps a record of adverse or unexpected events from all sources: patient care, associate reports, security

reports, incidents involving guests, notes made during rounds, and responsive listening. That record reflects evidence of the HCO's total exposure and measures the current level of safety. It is subject to reporting variation. As associates become comfortable with reporting and are convinced that the reports will be used to correct risks rather than punish the reporters, the number of reports is likely to increase. The reports can be studied for commonalities, such as locations, hours, or activities of unusual risks. The findings are OFIs.

A risk manager, sometimes called a safety officer, is charged with responsibility to develop, implement, and monitor the risk program. A safety or other committee, which includes representatives of senior management, legal counsel, clinical services, and support services, can monitor the risk-management process, protecting the culture and evaluating OFIs. OFIs are pursued in process-oriented PITs to preserve the blame-free culture. Corrections include process or protocol revision, equipment and facilities redesign, and expanded training for associates. Environmental safety is a part of the larger risk management program. The approach has been repeatedly documented, most dramatically in commercial air traffic, where casualties have become extremely rare. It is highly cost effective, reducing malpractice litigation, associate lost time, and patient complications.

Emergency Preparedness

Emergency preparation for unplanned and unexpected mass casualty events—such as natural disasters, pandemics, large-scale accidents, civil disturbance, or terrorist attacks—is an important and expected function of community HCOs. "Disaster" is defined as any event that suddenly increases demand substantially beyond the HCO's normal capacity. Advance warning, medical

EXHIBIT 12.7
Enhanced Environmental Management Requirements

Programs	Examples
Risk management	Designated risk-management officer Coordinated program that monitors unexpected events, including clinical misadventures, service recovery, and associate work loss or complaint Hazard inspection and correction
Emergency preparedness	Disaster plan Disaster training and routine drills Disaster utilities and communications management
Life-safety and fire protection	Evacuation plans and routes Preparation for radioactive or chemical contamination Life-safety training and drills
Clinical engineering	Inventory of potentially dangerous equipment Preventive maintenance of safety features Reporting of incidents under the Safe Medical Device Act

needs, and the number and severity of injuries differ greatly depending on the disaster. Terrorist attacks have drawn the nation's attention, but the most common disasters are storms and large-scale accidents such as fires and mass-transport crashes.[21]

When disaster strikes, people turn instinctively to the hospital. Victims are brought by rescue vehicles, in private cars, or other means. Even a large emergency service can face 20 times its normal peak load with little warning. Word of disaster spreads quickly through local radio, television, cell phones, and social media (e.g., Twitter, Facebook). The hospital may be inundated with visitors, families, and well-meaning volunteers in addition to the sick and injured. Communication with other community agencies is essential, and normal channels are often overwhelmed or inoperable.

The clinical response to mass casualties begins with **triage**, a method for sorting patients according to needs for various levels of resources. Although specific events vary, generally only a small fraction of victims require hospitalization. A great many more require ambulatory treatment. Temporary stabilization is often important. The Centers for Disease Control and Prevention (CDC) maintains a website of clinical information for both professionals and the public. It provides advice on treatment responses and mass casualty management.[22]

Triage
A method for sorting patients according to needs for various levels of resources

An effective HCO response requires a detailed plan; normal operations must be suspended to the extent possible so that personnel, space, equipment, and supplies can be reallocated to the "surge."[23] The design of the plan is a major project that requires the coordinated efforts of virtually all management. The elements of the response include

- rapid assembly of clinical and other personnel;
- reassignment of tasks, space, and equipment;
- establishment of supplementary telephone and radio communication;
- triage of arriving injured;
- temporary shelter for the homeless;
- continued care of patients already in the hospital;
- housing and food for hospital associates; and
- provision of information to the media, volunteers, and families.

The American Hospital Association (AHA) maintains a disaster-preparedness website[24] and prepared an analysis of needs in the first 48 hours following an attack. AHA identified additional areas that must be addressed to respond to terrorist activity:

- Communication and notification
- Disease surveillance, disease reporting, and laboratory identification

- Personal protective equipment
- Dedicated decontamination facilities
- Medical/surgical and pharmaceutical supplies
- Mental health resources

Others have noted that extended disasters, such as September 11, 2001 and Hurricane Katrina, severely stress associates, and provision for relief and rehabilitation for associates is important.[25]

Training for disaster is difficult, and results are uncertain.[26] The plan must be tested as realistically as possible, and the test often uncovers substantial weaknesses. Once tested, the plan must be rehearsed periodically and include drills with mock casualties and post-drill evaluation.[27,28]

The hospital's response must be coordinated with other community resources. Police, fire, and public health organizations are immediately involved, and schools, churches, and businesses can be converted for emergency needs. Coordination requires careful collaboration on roles, alternative plans, public messages, communications, and central leadership.[29] A military-type command structure is necessary to reduce confusion and address rapidly changing situations. Government public safety personnel generally assume this role, under emergency powers.

The disaster response requires broad involvement from all associates. The need to convert spaces, enhance communication, expand supply distribution, and arrange utilities gives the facilities management department a central role.

Life-Safety and Fire Protection

A life-safety program protects persons and property from fire hazards. The life-safety management plan must include provisions for staff orientation and education on life-safety issues, program-performance monitoring provisions, and periodic plan review. In addition, the plan must establish emergency procedures that address facilitywide and area-specific fire-response needs, fire evacuation routes, and specific roles and responsibilities of personnel at and away from a fire's point of origin and in preparing for building evacuation. A written policy must be developed, implemented, and enforced for the use of interim life-safety measures to address hazards created, deficiencies, or construction projects.[30] State licensure, Joint Commission accreditation,[31] and Medicare certification requirements enforce compliance.

The National Fire Protection Association Life Safety Code requires routine inspection and maintenance of facilities and often dictates specifications of new construction. The length of time before changes in the code become mandatory for an existing building to comply with current codes is variable, depending on the severity of the hazard. When a renovation is made to an area, all violations of current code must be corrected. The degree of departure from current code is an important factor in renovation and remodeling plans. An old building may contain many violations and be costly to renovate.

Clinical Engineering

HCOs require a wide variety of specialized medical equipment that must be maintained near optimum operating condition and repaired or replaced as necessary. Apparatus-like ventilators, magnetic resonance imaging machines, ultrasounds, multichannel chemical analyzers, electronic monitoring equipment, heart and lung pumps, and surgical lasers and robots have become commonplace. The acquisition, maintenance, and replacement of this equipment require specially trained personnel (usually called biomedical or clinical engineers) who can be either employees or contractors. Their understanding of purposes, mechanics, hazards, and requirements allows them to increase the reliability of the machinery and reduce operating costs.

The role of clinical engineering includes the following:

- Assisting the user department or group to develop specifications, review competing sources, and select medical equipment
- Verifying that power, weight, size, and safety requirements are met
- Contracting for preventive and routine maintenance, or arranging training for internal maintenance personnel
- Periodically inspecting equipment for safety and effectiveness
- Developing plans for replacement when necessary

Utility Systems

Utilities for most outpatient offices are no different from those for other commercial buildings, but inpatient hospitals operate sophisticated utility systems that provide air, steam, and water at several temperatures and pressures and filter some air to reduce bacterial contamination.[32] They also provide extra safeguards against failure. For example, hospitals supply high-pressure steam for sterilizing and laundry equipment. The use of higher pressures requires continuous surveillance by a licensed boiler operator. Operating rooms use specially filtered air, and several sites have unique temperature-control requirements.

Electrical systems are particularly complex. Feeds from two or more substations are desirable, approaching the hospital from different directions. In addition, the hospital must have on-site generating capability to sustain emergency surgery, ventilators, safety lights, and communications. Several areas must be able to switch to the emergency supply automatically, requiring them to be separable from other, less critical uses.

Several utilities are unique to hospitals. Most hospitals pipe oxygen and suction to all patient care areas. Many also pipe nitrous oxide to surgical areas. Many hospitals use pneumatic tubes to transport small items such as paper records, drugs, and specimens. A few use robot cart systems to transport large supplies.

Performance Improvement and Budgeting

Performance improvement for environment-of-care services must deal with three realities:

1. The services must view themselves as competing for customer approval. Satisfaction of customer requirements, including both price and quality, must be the consuming objective.
2. Many environment services are delivered by long-term contract with outside vendors, often called "strategic partners." The contracts must meet terms that include continuous improvement. No vendor, nor any employed service team, can consider itself independent of benchmarks and competing suppliers.
3. As a result of strategic partnerships and of the capital requirements for environmental services, improvement planning must adopt a multiyear horizon.

Environment-of-care services must continuously improve quality and efficiency. A housekeeping service, for example, should compare its performance to hotels. Food service must draw its benchmarks from commercial restaurants. At the same time, environment-of-care services must meet the special needs of sick patients and integrate their services with the other systems of the HCO. Improvement opportunities often include process revisions, cross-training, revised scheduling, and special needs that must be coordinated with other units.

Most environment-of-care services are supplied by contract vendors. HCOs can solicit offers from competing companies and compare outside competition to their internal capability. The selected provider should be able to document near-benchmark performance on the operational scorecard, and the contract should explicitly reference continued benchmarking, annual goals, and improvement.

Major change in environmental services, such as changing the vendor, requires long time windows and multiyear forecasting. For example, consider an organization that has operated its own laundry for many years. Its existing equipment is still useful but is aging and already less efficient than current models. As long as the equipment is still serviceable, contract laundry services may not be price competitive, but when the organization faces a major investment to replace that equipment, contract services are suddenly more attractive. Similarly, an opportunity to use the existing laundry space for more productive activities may make contract service more attractive. These needs must be anticipated months or years in advance to gain maximum advantage.

People

Managers and Professional Personnel

ECM has a few widely recognized educational programs. Contract management firms that have extensive on-the-job training programs may be the best source for management talent. A bachelor's degree in engineering is generally considered necessary for facility operation managers, particularly if construction responsibilities are included. Some large organizations also employ architects, a profession with both formal education and licensure.

The American Society for Healthcare Engineering is a professional association that offers publications and educational opportunities.[33] There are licensure requirements for professional engineers and architects in a consulting practice, but they do not apply to employment situations. The AHA offers five certificates in facilities services: certified healthcare environmental services professional, certified healthcare facility manager, certified materials and resource professional, certified professional in healthcare risk management, and added in 2010, certified healthcare constructor.[34] These certifications stress experience and practical training, and they are open to high school graduates.[35] Members of the American Society for Healthcare Engineering of the AHA who hold certifications increased from about 700 in 2005 to nearly 4,500 in 2009, showing an increased commitment to education. The risk-management certificate appears to be in direct competition with the professional certification in healthcare quality offered by the National Association for Healthcare Quality.[36]

Clinical engineers have baccalaureate degrees in engineering and a sequence of professional recognition.[37] Maintenance services on clinical equipment are provided by biomedical equipment technicians. Materials managers should acquire purchasing and supply chain management knowledge, including general business education and relevant experience. Much of the needed knowledge can also be acquired through a well-supervised work experience, which need not be in healthcare. A professional association—Association for Healthcare Resource & Materials Management—provides educational materials and services to supply chain professionals.[38] Security managers frequently have active police experience and at least a bachelor's degree in their field. Food service managers have a bachelor's degree and extensive experience in bulk food preparation.

Several professions are involved in environmental safety. Infection control is within the purview of an infection control practitioner—a nurse or other clinician with special education and training in infectious diseases and epidemiology or certification by the Association for Professionals in Infection Control and Epidemiology—and generally an infectious disease physician consultant. Organizations with high-voltage radiation therapy services usually employ a radiation physicist who can also assist with radiation safety standards and compliance with the Nuclear Regulatory Commission. Large organizations employ toxicologists to assist with control of chemical contamination. There is an engineering specialty known as safety engineering. Consultative services are available in many of these areas. The CDC and local public health departments may also have useful resources.

Outside Contractors

Many components of plant services are routinely outsourced. The plant functions and their components differ little from hospital to hospital, allowing contractors to develop significant advantages in specialized knowledge. Facilities construction, facility operation, maintenance and guest services, and clinical engineering are often provided by outside vendors. Some supply companies provide complete management of the supply function. All plant services, except planning, can be provided by contract with outside vendors. Two forms of contracting arrangements are used. In one, all the associates of the service work for the contractor. In the other, probably more common, management personnel work for the contractor, while hourly workers are the HCO's employees. The contractor supplies processes, training, performance measures, and supervision in both models.

The HCO should specify the operational performance measures. It should negotiate annual improvement goals with the contractors as it does with internal suppliers. It should monitor performance against the goals and independently audit and benchmark as many of the measures as possible. The contract should be periodically reopened, allowing change of vendor if necessary. The vendor competes against similar vendors and against the possibility of internal operations and wins the competition because it does as good a job overall as any alternative.

Training Needs

As environmental control methods and equipment become more sophisticated, workers require orientation, process training, and continuing education on an ongoing basis. In addition to job content, purpose, and method, employee training for several environment-of-care areas must include guest relations. As participation on improvement teams increases, associates must be trained in performance improvement fundamentals. Much technical training is assigned to the contractor, but elements such as orientation and supervision must be integrated with the HCO's training.

Supervisors need all these skills, including mastery of the work methods and explicit training in supervision. In many settings, the folklore of the transactional boss who gives orders and has special privileges must be replaced with an understanding of the supportive, transformational leader who is obligated to find answers to employee questions. Formal education, including case studies and role-playing, establishes the desired model. Constant reinforcement is necessary to keep it in place. Supervisors also need advanced training in performance improvement, budgeting, and regulatory compliance.

These training programs must be carried out at a high school level, and in many communities they must be available in several languages. The emphasis is on action, practice, graphics, and only lastly words. All training programs present important opportunities to build the employee's pride in craftsmanship and loyalty to the organization.

Incentives and Rewards

The most important incentives are nonmonetary. Pride of achievement is probably the most important. It is supported by prompt reporting of formal measures, well-designed methods, appropriate training, and responsive supervision. Recognition of achievement includes both encouragement from the supervisor and celebration of team achievements. The amount of recognition should be tailored to the level of achievement: Any positive response should be recognized by the supervisor, above-average results by coworkers, and extraordinary achievement by the organization at large.

Explicit monetary incentives are most powerful as supplements to nonmonetary incentives; even a small payment serves to show the seriousness of management intent. The gain-sharing approach, with negotiated goals and ongoing measures of progress, is effective. The incentive program can be managed by outside contractors, but if employees work for the HCO, the incentive must be comparable to opportunities in similar job classes. The vendor (outside contractor) can earn incentives similar to those offered in an equivalent internal unit.

Organization

Traditionally, larger HCOs had chief engineers, purchasing agents, housekeepers, security officers, food service directors, and central supply supervisors, each of whom reported directly to senior administrative officers. Comprehensive plant accountability that concentrates these functions under one manager who reports to the chief operating officer has replaced that approach.

Exhibit 12.8 shows a general model for plant systems organization in a large HCO. Any element in Exhibit 12.8 can be contracted to an outside firm. A contract manager employed by the institution must be designated at the level of the contract. (For example, if food service is contracted, the guest services manager is designated as contract manager.) Facility planning and space allocation are the most problematic to contract and the most likely to be retained internally. These services are often supported by a planning committee made up of various space users. The committee helps communicate space issues and may help reduce concerns over space allocation decisions.

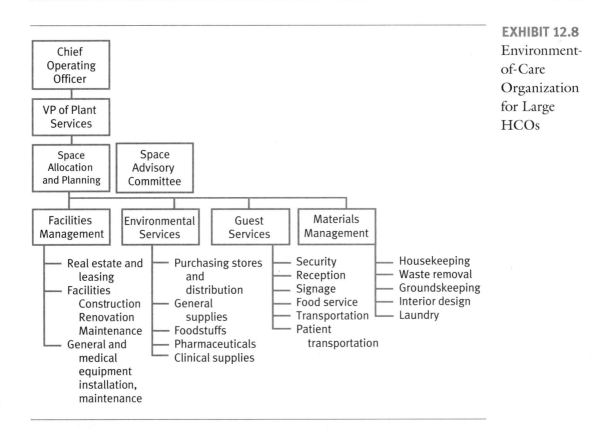

EXHIBIT 12.8
Environment-of-Care Organization for Large HCOs

Measures

All environmental services must first be reliable and safe, then satisfactory to associates and guests, and finally efficient. Measures for the six dimensions of the operational scorecard are well developed and can usually be benchmarked from industrial sites or between hospitals. Human resources measures are similar to those in clinical and other support systems. Customer satisfaction measures recognize that all the other units of the organization are internal customers. Many services also have external customers: patients, families, and other guests.

Output and Demand

Output and demand for plant system services are usually measured identically. Output is simply that portion of demand that is filled, usually 100 percent. Demand is measured differently for each of the functions of the plant system, using various combinations of patient or service requests, specific facility requirement, and duration, as reflected in the examples shown in Exhibit 12.9.

Demand is usually forecast by analysis of historical data on the incidence and duration of demand for each identified physical resource. Peak loads are frequently important. Analysis of cyclical fluctuation and frequency distributions or ranges is frequently required to set sound resource expectations.

EXHIBIT 12.9
Examples
of Demand
Measures for
Environment-
of-Care
Functions

Service Request	Incidence Measure	Duration Measure
Surgery cleanup	Number of cases	Minutes/case
Heating/air conditioning	Degree-days	N/A
General housekeeping	Square footage	Minutes/square foot
Specialized housekeeping	Square footage by type	Minutes/square foot by type
Safety inspection	Specific type	Hours/inspection
Meal service	Meals/day by type	N/A
Security and reception	Personnel by location	Hours/day
Supplies	Units by type	N/A

Many activities of the plant system require short-term forecasts, with horizons ranging from hours to months. Efficiency in supply and service processes, such as housekeeping, heating, and food service, depends on careful adjustment to variation in demand. Well-run organizations supply current estimates of demand for such services from order-entry and nursing-scheduling systems. (Several kinds of service are related to patient acuity.) In the future, patient-scheduling systems will likely be used to forecast demand for these services.

Inventory management calls for slightly longer-term forecasts. The key to efficiency and quality of service is accurate forecasts of demand at the most detailed level possible. These forecasts can be used to operate exchange cart deliveries, which minimizes out-of-stock items and emergency trips, and to maintain optimum inventory levels and ordering cycles. The preparation of these forecasts is normally the obligation of the materials management unit, with guidance from finance and planning. Experienced materials managers can often make useful subjective refinements to statistically prepared forecasts.

Resource Consumption and Effectiveness

Environment-of-care services and products are used by all units of any HCO. Some products and services are sold to patients or customers, but most are consumed by HCO units. Managing the efficiency and effectiveness of these services requires careful accounting, as shown in Exhibit 12.10. Establishing a **transfer price** based on the unit cost allows an in-house "sale" that emulates a market purchase and substantially clarifies accountability. Modern cost accounting (Chapter 13) has allowed accurate estimates of unit cost for most of the goods and services provided by environmental care. The alternative to transfer pricing is cost allocation,

Transfer price
Imputed cost revenue for a good or service transferred between two units of the same organization, such as housekeeping services provided to nursing units

EXHIBIT 12.10
Implications
of Cost
Accounting on
Environmental
Services

Costing Method	Impact on Producing Activity	Impact on Consuming Activity
Transfer pricing	Total cost per unit of service (TC/U) is calculated using activity-based costing TC/U can be benchmarked TC/U can be compared to that of the competition	"Buys" service and controls units consumed Units/patient or customer can be benchmarked, established by protocol, or established by evaluating customer needs and satisfaction
Cost allocation	Total direct cost (TDC) for producing activity TDC can rarely be benchmarked	Receives an allocated "indirect cost" charge for service Indirect cost cannot be benchmarked Consumer has no incentive to control use

which distributes environmental services on an approximation, such as using a department's patient volume or square feet of space.

Transfer pricing has three important advantages:

1. The unit cost of producing the service can be benchmarked, improving the producing unit's goal setting.
2. The unit cost can be compared to competing alternatives, such as purchasing instead of making the service or centralizing producers for efficiency.
3. The consuming unit can benchmark the volume of service used and establish OFIs to optimize the quantity of service. (Note that the "optimum" service is the one that best fulfills the user's mission, but it is not necessarily the least expensive.)

Quality

Exhibit 12.11 shows important measures of quality that are available to almost any HCO. Compliance of product or service with technical specification can be measured. Many processes can be inspected by unbiased experts, who score the result. The Joint Commission standards include a thorough review of structural measures of safety and have moved to emphasize environment-of-care planning, education, performance monitoring, corrective action, and evaluation.[39] Many services have automated records of failure or delay. Others can be estimated from user or inspector surveys.

Inspections are critical to laundry service, food service, supplies, maintenance, and housekeeping. Subjective judgment is usually required, but it is reliable when inspectors are trained and follow clear standards for cleanliness, temperature, taste, appearance, and so on. The frequency of inspection

EXHIBIT 12.11
Measures of
Quality for
Environment-
of-Care
Services

Type	Approaches	Examples
Outcomes	Technical standards	Many environmental services have explicit technical standards developed by organizations such as the National Institute of Science and Technology or the American Society for Quality
	Incident counts	Guest and associate accidents Delay and failure rates Service interruption rates
	Surveys	Guest and associate satisfaction
	User complaints	Service complaints
Process	Raw materials	Technical standards Compliance to purchase specification Failures and returns
	Service/product inspections	Food preparation Cleanliness Job completion
	Contract compliance	Return rates On-time supplies delivery
	Supply failures	Back-ordered items
	Inventory wastage	Losses of supplies
	Automated monitoring	Atmospheric control Power and utility failure
Structure	Facility	Life-safety compliance
	Equipment	Elevator inspections
	Worker qualifications	Stationary engineer coverage

is adjusted to the level of performance, and performance is improved by training and methods rather than by negative feedback. Work reports—brief notes that identify specific events or issues—reveal correctable problem areas in plant maintenance and materials management.

Benchmarks and scientific standards for these values are widely available. Numerous consultants offer information on labor standards for laundries, kitchens, and the like and on cost standards for energy use, construction, renovation, and security. The AHA publishes a manual of materials management supply-cost benchmarks.[40] Constraints on costs are derived from two sources—the competitive prices of outside vendors and the internal needs developed from the budget guidelines. The former are preferable wherever they can be obtained.

Managerial Issues

The focal points for senior leadership attention in ECM are facilities planning and space allocation, the selection and management of outsourcing contracts, and the integration of facilities operations with other activities. The first two of these often generate expensive and difficult decisions. The third is an important source of failures in efficiency, safety, and associate satisfaction.

Facilities Planning and Space Allocation

Facilities planning and space allocation presents unique management problems. It has important symbolic and cultural implications (like "the corner office") as well as major practical implications. It is immutable and unique. Each square foot is exactly that, but because of location, it is different from every other square foot. The decisions have profound implications for individual stakeholders. Conflict is normal and must be systematically managed. Management and governance focus all decisions on the mission.

Facilities planners use the best available objective data to forecast future needs, make their work as transparent as possible, draw all affected parties into the discussion at an early stage, establish and live by the rules for making the decisions, and allow appeals. The strategy for preventing and resolving conflict is to make sure that facts, rather than influence, determine the outcome and to aim for financial success necessary to remain competitive.

Selection and Management of Outsourcing Contracts

The questions of what to outsource, with whom to outsource, and how to ensure the effectiveness of outsourced services are all challenging. Like the facilities planning questions, they have an extensive impact. Ignoring an opportunity to improve regarding outsourcing is as easy as making an error in selecting the improvement. Managers have a duty to see that objective measures and benchmarks are in place for all the environment-of-care functions and that each unit makes steady progress toward its benchmarks.

With these measures in place, the opportunities for improvement are clear to all. The questions, "Should we outsource?" or "Should we change suppliers?" convert to "What improvements must we make to reach benchmark, and how do we achieve them?" In this format, the current supplier is usually given a chance to improve, and it usually does. Supplier change is not necessary because the current supplier in place changes to do the job better. Service managers make it clear that the benchmarks are realistic goals and provide the support to learn and change so that progress can be made. They establish a culture in which ignoring the opportunity is unacceptable. The contract manager reinforces this, recognizing that service alternatives do exist but retaining the current supplier is often the best choice.

Integration of Facilities Operations with Other Activities

Vendors and their associates cannot be viewed as outsiders. "Strategic partner" means "part of our team." Many issues arise from the coordination between clinical services and plant services. New food service systems must coordinate with nursing; patient transportation must adapt to new facility layouts and service needs; and new patient care protocols require new supplies and new delivery methods. PITs must incorporate all the involved services, regardless of contract status.

PIT participation is valuable in three senses. First, the exchange of information leads to a better result, particularly with a skilled vendor that has experience at many HCOs. Second, participants gain insight into the underlying customer needs. They come away from the process understanding why the improvement was necessary and more committed to making it work. Third, participation is a reward. PIT assignments empower associates and provide an opportunity to reward effort.

Suggested Readings

American Hospital Association. 2005. *2005 Performance Indicators Study on Healthcare Supply Cost Management*. Chicago: AHA Publishing.

Guenther, G., and R. Vittori. 2007. *Sustainable Healthcare Architecture*. New York: Wiley.

Hayward, C. 2005. *Healthcare Facility Planning: Thinking Strategically*. Chicago: Health Administration Press.

The Joint Commission. 2009. *Environment of Care Essentials for Health Care*, 9th ed. Oakbrook Terrace, IL: The Joint Commission.

———. 2009. *Planning, Design, and Construction of Health Care Facilities*, 2nd ed. Oakbrook Terrace, IL: The Joint Commission.

Ledlow, G. R., A. P. Corry, and M. A. Cwiek. 2007. *Optimize Your Healthcare Supply Chain Performance: A Strategic Approach*. Chicago: Health Administration Press.

Marberry, S. O. (ed.). 2006. *Improving Healthcare with Better Building Design*. Chicago: Health Administration Press.

McGlown, K. J. 2004. *Terrorism and Disaster Management: Preparing Healthcare Leaders for the New Reality*. Chicago: Health Administration Press.

Puckett, R. P. 2004. *Food Service Manual for Health Care Institutions*, 3rd ed. Chicago: American Society for Healthcare Food Service Administrators.

Reid, P. P., W. D. Compton, J. H. Grossman, and G. Fanjiang (eds.). 2005. *Building a Better Delivery System: A New Engineering/Health Care Partnership*. Washington, DC: National Academies Press.

Schneller, E. S., and L. R. Smeltzer. 2006. *Strategic Management of the Health Care Supply Chain*. San Francisco: Jossey-Bass.

Notes

1. Ulrich, R., C. Zimring, X. Zhu, J. DuBose, H.-B. Seo, Y.-S. Choi, X. Quan, and A. Joseph. 2008. "A Review of the Research Literature on Evidence-Based Healthcare Design." [Online information; retrieved 6/18/09.] www.healthdesign.org/hcleader/HCLeader_5_LitReviewWP.pdf.

2. Robeznieks, A. 2008. "Built to Last: Healthcare Construction Spending Holding Up Well." *Modern Healthcare* 38 (34): 68.

3. Bronson Methodist Hospital. 2005. Malcolm Baldrige National Quality Award Application. [Online information; retrieved 9/17/09.] www.baldrige.nist.gov/Contacts_Profiles.htm.

4. Hewitt, D. H. 2010. "Models from Past Mold the Future in Evidence-Based Health Care Design." *Health Progress* 91 (2): 9–13.

5. Bernard, P. J. 2010. "New Urbanism Drives Hospital Site Plan." *Health Progress* 91 (2): 21–25.

6. Hosking, J. E., and R. J. Jarvis. 2003. "Developing a Replacement Facility Strategy: Lessons from the Healthcare Sector." *Journal of Facilities Management* 2 (2): 214–28.

7. Hosking, J. E. 2004. "What Really Drives Better Outcomes?" *Frontiers of Health Services Management* 21 (1): 35–39.

8. Green Guide for Health Care. 2010. [Online information; retrieved 5/5/10.] www.gghc.org/about.cfm.

9. Zimring, C. M., G. L. Augenbroe, E. B. Malone, and B. L. Sadler. 2008. "Implementing Healthcare Excellence: The Vital Role of the CEO in Evidence-Based Design." *Healthcare Leadership: White Paper Series, 3 of 5.* Atlanta, GA: The Center for Health Design, Georgia Institute of Technology.

10. Ulrich et al. (2008).

11. Environmental Protection Agency. [Online information; retrieved 6/18/09.] www.epa.gov/osw/nonhaz/industrial/medical.

12. Georgopoulos, P. G., P. Fedele, P. Shade, P. J. Lioy, M. Hodgson, A. Longmire, M. Sands, and M. A. Brown. 2004. "Hospital Response to Chemical Terrorism: Personal Protective Equipment, Training, and Operations Planning." *American Journal of Industrial Medicine* 46: 432–45.

13. Occupational Safety and Health Administration. "Bloodborne Pathogens Standard," 29 CFR 1910.1030. [Online information; retrieved 9/22/09.] www.osha.gov/pls/oshaweb/owadisp.show_document?p_table=STANDARDS&p_id=10051.

14. Centers for Disease Control and Prevention. 2001. "Updated U.S. Public Health Service Guidelines for the Management of Occupational Exposures to HBV, HCV, and HIV and Recommendations for Postexposure Prophylaxis." *Morbidity and Mortality Weekly Report* 50 (RR11): 1–42.

15. Smith, M. H. 2002. "Vigilance Ensures a Safer Work Environment." *Nursing Management* 33 (11): 18–19.

16. Smith, M. H. 2002. "Condition Critical: Study Shows Many Hospitals Located in High-Crime Areas." *Health Facilities Management Magazine.* [Online article; retrieved 3/15/06.] www.hfmmagazine.com/hfmmagazine/index.jsp.

17. Langabeer, J. 2005. "The Evolving Role of Supply Chain Management Technology in Healthcare." *Journal of Healthcare Information Management* 19 (2): 27–33.

18. Long, G. 2005. "Pursuing Supply Chain Gains." *Healthcare Financial Management* 59 (9): 118–22.

19. Beth, S., D. N. Burt, W. Copacino, C. Gopal, H. L. Lee, R. P. Lynch, and S. Morris. 2003. "Supply Chain Challenges: Building Relationships." *Harvard Business Review* 81 (7): 64–73, 117.

20. American Society for Healthcare Engineering. 2009. "Joint Commission Environment of Care Standards." [Online information; retrieved 6/18/09.] www.ashe.org/ashe/codes/jcaho/ec.

21. McGlown, K. J. 2004. *Terrorism and Disaster Management: Preparing Healthcare Leaders for the New Reality.* Chicago: Health Administration Press.

22. Centers for Disease Control and Prevention. "Mass Casualty Event Preparedness and Response." [Online information; retrieved 6/18/09.] www.bt.cdc.gov/masscasualties.

23. Ginter, P. M., W. J. Duncan, and M. Abdolrasulnia. 2007. "Hospital Strategic Preparedness Planning: The New Imperative." *Prehospital & Disaster Medicine* 22 (6): 529–36.

24. American Hospital Association. 2009. "Emergency Readiness." [Online information; retrieved 6/18/09.] www.aha.org/aha_app/issues/Emergency-Readiness/index.jsp.

25. Reissman, D. B., and J. Howard. 2008. "Responder Safety and Health: Preparing for Future Disasters." *Mount Sinai Journal of Medicine* 75 (2): 135–41.

26. Williams, J., M. Nocera, and C. Casteel. 2008. "The Effectiveness of Disaster Training for Health Care Workers: A Systematic Review." *Annals of Emergency Medicine* 52 (3): 211–22.

27. Agency for Healthcare Research and Quality. 2008. "Tool for Evaluating Core Elements of Hospital Disaster Drills." [Online information; retrieved 6/18/09.] www.ahrq.gov/prep/drillelements.

28. Jenckes, M. W., C. L. Catlett, E. B. Hsu, K. Kohri, G. B. Green, K. A. Robinson, E. B. Bass, and S. E. Cosgrove. 2007. "Development of Evaluation Modules for Use in Hospital Disaster Drills." *American Journal of Disaster Medicine* 2 (2): 87–95.

29. The Joint Commission. 2006. "Surge Hospitals: Providing Safe Care in Emergencies." [Online information; retrieved 6/18/09.] www.jointcommission.org/NR/rdonlyres/802E9DA4-AE80-4584-A205-48989C5BD684/0/surge_hospital.pdf.

30. National Fire Protection Association. 2009. *Fire Code Handbook, 2009 Edition.* [Online information; retrieved 6/18/09.] www.nfpa.org/catalog.

31. The Joint Commission. 2009. "Environment of Care." In *Comprehensive Accreditation Manual for Hospitals.* Oakbrook Terrace, IL: The Joint Commission.

32. Sehulster, L., and R. Y. Chinn. 2003. "Guidelines for Environmental Infection Control in Health-Care Facilities. Recommendations of CDC and the Healthcare Infection Control Practices Advisory Committee (HICPAC)." *Morbidity and Mortality Weekly Report, Recommendations and Reports* 52 (RR-10): 1–42.

33. American Society of Healthcare Engineers. 2009. [Online information; retrieved 6/18/09.] www.ashe.org.

34. American Hospital Association. 2010. [Online information; retrieved 5/5/10.] www.aha.org/aha/Certification-Center/files/100203pressrel.pdf.

35. American Hospital Association. 2009. [Online information; retrieved 6/18/09.] www.aha.org.

36. National Association for Healthcare Quality. 2009. [Online information; retrieved 6/18/09.] www.nahq.org/certify.

37. American College of Clinical Engineering. 2009. [Online information; retrieved 6/18/09.] www.accenet.org.

38. Association for Healthcare Resource & Materials Management. 2009. [Online information; retrieved 6/18/09.] www.ahrmm.org.

39. American Society for Healthcare Engineering. 2009. "Joint Commission Environment of Care Standards." [Online information; retrieved 6/18/09.] www.ashe.org/ashe/codes/jcaho/ec.

40. Association for Healthcare Resource & Materials Management. 2005. *2005 Performance Indicators Study on Healthcare Supply Cost Management.* Chicago: AHA Publishing.

13 FINANCIAL MANAGEMENT

In a Few Words

The healthcare organization's (HCO) finance and accounting activities record and evaluate its operation for internal and external use. They provide data to understand the sources of revenue, the cost of all activities, and models to analyze alternative future scenarios. They obtain and manage cash for daily operation and long-term growth. They protect the information from distortion and the assets against misuse and loss. The activities are organized around controllership, which handles all the functions related to recording and analyzing costs and revenue; financial management, which manages the organization's capital; and auditing, which ensures accuracy of information and protection of assets. Senior management and governance have a critical role, ensuring that the accounting and finance functions are thoroughly and accurately carried out and that the results are effectively used throughout the organization.

Critical Issues in Financial Management

1. *Supporting an evidence-based culture:*

   How accounting
   - Identifies and reports costs
   - Supports the annual goal-setting process
   - Provides analysis and forecasts for performance improvement teams

2. *Providing adequate financial resources:*

   How finance
   - Identifies long-term financial needs
   - Manages debt and liquid assets to meet needs
   - Negotiates contracts with health insurers to maximize revenue
   - Develops ownership structures that facilitate strategic partnerships

3. *Promoting integrity:*

   How internal and external auditing
   - Ensure accuracy of numbers, even those involving complex calculations
   - Support a culture where honesty is expected
   - Protect the organization's assets

Consider these questions as you read the chapter.

1. Why are performance measures so complicated? Concepts like *cost per case* or *percent postoperative infections* seem simple enough. Why must we use Financial Accounting Standards Board (FASB) rules, do statistical analyses and adjustments, and maintain internal and external audits? What would happen if we didn't do these things?

2. Suppose you are on a process improvement team (PIT) to evaluate an HCO's goal-setting processes. What kinds of measures could evaluate the goal-setting process itself? How hard would it be to benchmark them? Beyond the measures, what else would you do to identify opportunities for improvement in the process?

3. A hard-working associate says to a senior manager, "Our unit just got the bill for human resources. It was huge! We had to pay for the mandatory training for our new supervisor, plus the annual HIPAA, harassment, and disaster management training. Why do we have to pay for this? How do we know we're getting a fair price?" How does the senior manager respond?

4. How much should the audit functions cost? The system described is expensive; many organizations complain that it is excessive. What exactly are the benefits the organization gains from those expenditures, and how are they measured? How will the organization judge whether the investment is wise?

5. How does the organization evaluate its capital and liquid asset management program? What questions would you ask, and what numbers would you ask for, if you were exploring this question with the chief financial officer and her financial management team?

Financial management of the modern healthcare organization (HCO) controls all the assets; posts and collects all the revenue; settles all the financial obligations; arranges all the funding; and makes major contributions to strategic planning, performance measurement, and cost control. It deals directly with all the units of the organization, from the governing board to the primary accountability centers. Its role in HCOs is not substantially different from its role in other industries, although some of the approaches are modified to accommodate not-for-profit structures, health insurance contracts, and the complexity of care delivery.

This chapter describes the contribution that finance makes to other systems (i.e., those tasks that it must do to make the whole succeed). Finance and accounting are subject to much study, regulation, and standardization. Comprehensive texts describe its overall operation. (Several are listed in the Suggested Reading section.) Laws, regulations, contracts, and standard practices control what is done in countless specific situations. This chapter emphasizes the activities that distinguish the most successful HCOs—principally, budgeting, cost reporting and analysis, strategic financial planning and provision of capital, and expanded use of the audits.

Purpose

The purposes of the finance system are to support the enterprise by:

1. **recording and reporting transactions that change the value of the firm;**
2. **assisting operations in setting and achieving performance improvements;**
3. **performing a financial analysis of new business opportunities, new programs, and asset acquisitions to assist governance in strategic planning;**
4. **arranging capital and operating funds to implement governance decisions; and**
5. **guarding assets and resources against theft, waste, or loss, and guarding the information against distortion.**

These five purposes are accomplished through three general functions—(1) controllership, incorporating the first three; (2) financial management, incorporating the third and fourth; and (3) auditing, addressing the last. The finance activity is expected to maintain its own continuous improvement function and support the rest of the HCO. The activities that support these functions are shown in Exhibit 13.1.

Controllership Functions

Transaction Accounting

The transaction accounting function records and reports all transactions that affect the value of the firm and its subsidiaries. Transactions form the basis of all analysis and reporting. Most transactions are either *revenue transactions—*

EXHIBIT 13.1
Functions of
the Finance
System

Function	Activity	Purpose
Controllership		
Transaction accounting	Capture data on all operational transactions	Record and control resources and sales
Financial accounting	Capture nonoperational transactions Create financial reports	Establish value of organization Report to owners and external stakeholders
Managerial accounting	Prepare cost and revenue data for monitoring and performance improvement Prepare special studies for planning and evaluation of improvements	Support all work teams with resource and output data Support PITs with forecasts and models
Goal setting and budgeting	Promulgate budget guidelines and budget packages Forecast major demand measures Compile operating, financial, and capital budgets	Support line management in setting performance goals Coordinate organization-wide activities Support strategic decisions
Financial Management		
Financial planning	Establish the long-range financial plan Conduct financial analysis of new business opportunities, new programs, and large asset acquisitions	Forecast the future viability of the organization Support analysis of alternative strategic opportunities Establish budget guidelines for profit, cost, and capital investment
Pricing clinical services	Develop pricing strategy and support specific price negotiations	Support maximum revenue to the institution and its physicians
Financial structures	Manage multiple corporate structures	Flexibility of financing and operating arrangements Containment of business risks
Securing and managing liquid assets	Manage debt, joint ventures, and stock and equity accounts	Minimize cost of capital Maximize return on assets
Managing multicorporate accounting	Manage working capital Maintain collections and payments	Minimize cost of working capital Settle the organization's accounts with patients, suppliers, and employees

continued

Function	Activity	Purpose	
			EXHIBIT 13.1 *continued*
Auditing			
Internal audits	Verify accounting transactions	Ensuring accuracy of performance management reports Guarding against loss and diversion of property	
Compliance review	Review health insurance contracts, physician compensation, and pricing policies	Ensuring compliance with law and regulation	
External audits	Review accounting systems and decisions affecting financial reports	Attesting to accuracy of financial reports	
Continuous Improvement of the Accounting and Finance Functions			
Stakeholder satisfaction	Monitor and benchmark satisfaction with accounting and financial performance	Ensure compliance with external requirements and satisfaction of customer and associate stakeholders	
Improve performance	Identify, pursue, and implement OFIs	Implement more effective methods and results	

OFI: opportunity for improvement; PIT: process improvement team

those that provide elements of care to patients or other services such as meals to families—or *expense transactions*—those that acquire resources such as personnel, supplies, and equipment. The physical transactions—such as patient days of care, hours worked, and drugs used—are generally captured by the information system described in Chapter 10. Accounting attaches a dollar value and assigns each transaction to a mission-related category. Once captured, valued, and assigned, the transactions support three different analyses—financial accounting, performance reporting, and managerial accounting studies. Transaction accounting keeps finance personnel involved in most areas of the organization.

Revenue transactions record virtually all the HCO's routine cash acquisition, except gifts, loans, and sales of assets. Computerization permits recording extensive detail: the patient, service, quantity, time, and unit or associate supplying the service. The record must meet HIPAA (Health Insurance Portability and Accountability Act) confidentiality requirements.[1] When organized by individual patient, revenue transactions create the **patient ledger**—a detailed record of the individual services or supplies rendered to each patient. The ledger is a financial reflection of the electronic medical record described in Chapter 10.

Patient ledger

Account of the charges rendered to an individual patient

Expense transactions describe all commitments to pay cash. Data captured include the ordering or using person and unit, quantities, allocation, time, and prices of the resource purchased or disbursed. Cost ledgers are organized by type of resource (e.g., labor, supplies). The payroll system records hours worked by employee, generates paychecks, and produces data on labor costs. The supply system provides count and cost data on supplies, issues checks for purchased goods and services, and maintains inventories. Some expense transactions are internal rather than external exchanges; these are called **general ledger** transactions. General ledger entries assign capital costs through depreciation of long-term assets, adjust inventory values, and allocate expenses of central services. They tend to reflect resources that are shared by the organization as a whole rather than by individual accountability centers, and they tend to deal with resources that last considerably longer than one budget or financial cycle.

General ledger
Technically, the record of all the firm's transactions; the term often refers to the fixed and collective assets, such as depreciation, that must be allocated to operational units

The value of most transactions is set by market (i.e., the price of either a purchase or a sale), but because of general ledger transactions and the complexity of healthcare finance, external prices are not available for all transactions or all levels of aggregation. As a simple example, depreciation is an estimate of the loss in value of buildings and equipment based on an arbitrary assumption about the future life; the true change in value is unknown. It is priced according to widely accepted and audited rules so that the estimates are uniform and reliable, although not necessarily valid. More complicated issues arise from "bundled" revenue. Inpatient care is priced as a package, based on diagnosis-related groups (DRGs). Several patient care teams treat most patients; the revenue for each team is not available. Although the pharmacy sells many prescriptions to outpatients for established market prices, it sells many to inpatients where payment is bundled and no pharmacy price is available. Exhibit 13.2 shows the availability of price information by level of aggregate. Estimates must be used when the transaction information is used in the shaded areas. They are prepared as a managerial accounting function.

Financial Accounting

Financial accounting fulfills a direct obligation to the owners, creditors, and the public. It assembles the transactions to state as accurately as possible the position of the institution as a whole in terms of the value of its assets, the equity residual to its owners, and the change in value occurring in each accounting period.

Reporting Financial Information

Four reports have become standard for HCOs and most other nongovernmental enterprises:

1. Balance sheet
2. Income or profit-and-loss statement

EXHIBIT 13.2
Availability of
External Price
Information,
by Type of
Transaction
and Level of
Aggregate

		Expense Transactions			
Aggregate Level	Revenue Transactions	Labor	Supplies	Equipment	General Ledger
Item of care	Partial[1]	Partial	Yes[2]	No	No
Patient	Partial[2]	Partial	Yes	No	No
Responsibility center	Partial	Yes	Yes	Yes	No
Disease group	Partial	Partial[3]	Yes	No	No
Payer group	Yes	Partial[4]	Yes	No	No
Institution	Yes	Yes	Yes	Yes	Yes

NOTES:

1. Certain expensive services, such as physician visits or operating room use, are priced at the transaction level in fee-for-service payment systems but not in case-based or capitation payment systems. An estimate of the direct labor cost is generally available when fee transactions exist.

2. The price paid by the patient or third-party intermediary is available under fee-for-service and case-based payment but not under capitation.

3. The cost of labor to serve patients is directly priced for the more expensive components, where the time expended is captured in the record. Some services (e.g., security) are provided on an aggregate, rather than on an individual basis. Bedside nursing, an expensive component of inpatient care, is accounted at the nursing unit level.

4. Disease-group and payer-group transactions are aggregated from individual patients and are subject to the same limitations, except that the totals paid by each payer are captured directly.

3.   Statement of sources and uses of funds

4.   Statement of changes in fund balances

These summarize the financial activities and situation of the organization in a form now almost universal in the business world. The entries are defined by the FASB.

Financial statements are usually issued monthly to the associates and annually to outside stakeholders. They are a critical report to the governing board, which is obligated to monitor performance and protect assets on behalf of the owners. They constitute the record of the board's discharge of its obligation to exercise fiscal prudence.

The annual statements are audited by the external auditor—a public accounting firm that attests that the statements follow the FASB rules, fairly represent the financial position of the organization, and are free of material distortion. Audited statements are the basis for most of the organization's financial communication with the outside world. Financial intermediaries often demand access to HCO finances as a condition of payment. Audited income statements and balance sheets must be reported to the federal government as a condition of participation in Medicare. Once filed, the reports are accessible to the public under the Freedom of Information Act. Several states now require public release of financial reports as well. HCOs that issue bonds on public markets are also required to reveal standard financial information, plus pro formas that forecast their performance in future years.

As of 2009, not-for-profit HCOs have substantial obligations to report their financial activities through the Internal Revenue Service (IRS) Form 990. The form becomes public information. It is intended to monitor the public's return for the privilege of tax exemption. It requires reporting of income, profit, executive compensation, and community benefit for parent corporations, major subsidiaries, and joint ventures. Community benefit is identified as charitable care, bad debts, Medicaid losses, community health activities, formal education, and research. The reporting schedule requires estimation of the actual cost of each benefit. The values reported on Form 990 are subject to a "reasonableness" test.[2] The IRS may eliminate an HCO's tax exemption in whole or in part on the basis of the values reported.

Well-managed HCOs deliberately publish their financial reports as part of their program of community relations. Subsidiaries of integrated systems, both for-profit and not-for-profit, are not automatically required to disclose their financial information, but many multihospital organizations make them public as basic community relations.

Revenue Accounting

Individual charges are associated with each transaction to calculate **gross revenue**, but the charges have become meaningless under aggregate payment contracts. The actual amount paid—**net revenue**—has become the meaningful value. Patient ledger transactions are summed to generate net operating revenue generated from patient care reported in the income statement.

Under Form 990 requirements, net revenue also establishes charity care—care given to the needy without expectation of payment—and **bad debts**—costs for patients who were expected to pay but did not do so. Patient ledger data are also used in many case-based payment schemes to identify catastrophically expensive cases, called *outliers,* that qualify for special additional payments.

Gross revenue
An entry to the patient ledger of the charge for a specific healthcare service; no longer a meaningful measure

Net revenue
Income actually received as opposed to that initially posted; equal to gross revenue minus adjustments for bad debts, charity, and discounts to third parties

Bad debt
Cost for patients who are unable to pay for care

Nonoperational Transactions

Nonoperating revenue—income generated from non-patient-care activities, including gifts, investments in securities, and earnings from unrelated businesses—is also accounted on the income statement. It is an important contribution to overall profit for many HCOs. The funds flow statement and balance sheet include a number of nonoperational transactions. The sale of assets and the incurrence of debt (and the sale of equity in for-profit companies) generate cash for the firm. The purchase of capital goods, the retirement of debt (dividends and repurchase of stock in for-profit companies), and charges for restructurings consume cash.

Nonoperating revenue
Income generated from non-patient-care activities, including investments in securities and earnings from unrelated businesses

These are recorded with the cash transactions of operations in a statement of sources and uses of funds or funds flow. Subsidiary corporations can be used to handle major ongoing operations, such as donations, unrelated businesses, or joint ventures. Their summary results are included in the owning corporation's balance sheet.

Managerial Accounting

Managerial accounting restructures transaction data to support monitoring, planning, setting expectations, and improving performance. Opposite to financial accounting, it is oriented to produce information for internal organization uses, allowing management decisions about revision, continuation, and discontinuation of services and monitoring operational measures of cost, efficiency, and demand. It is organized around an internal chart of accounts that identifies every accountable unit. It records quantities and costs of resources consumed by the unit, such as labor and supplies (direct costs), and allocated to the unit, such

> **Managerial accounting**
> A process of restructuring transaction data to support monitoring, planning, setting expectations, and improving performance of accountability centers

as depreciation and shared central services (indirect costs or overhead). Traditional allocated costs were often crude approximations; activity-based costing improves the estimates and allows more resources to be treated as direct costs.

Managerial Accounting Reports

Managerial accounting reports identify the quantities and cost of resources consumed, the pricing mechanism (market priced, transfer priced, or allocated), and the assigned transfer and allocated costs. Unit management can classify these costs as fixed, variable, or semi-variable. These reports are now usually electronic. They are available in summary or in detail for each accountable unit and larger aggregates and provide drill-down to individual transactions.

Managerial reports are useful as an ongoing audit of management performance, as a source of detail when an unexpected event occurs, and as a data source for managerial analyses and construction of the following year's goals. The cost reports allow any level of management to say, "Our costs are equal to or better than goals" and to identify the opportunities for improvement (OFIs) for next year's goals.

Managerial Accounting Analyses

The data in the reports can be accumulated and aggregated to support analyses of variation and what-if projections that allow management to identify and evaluate alternatives. Common uses of managerial accounting analyses include the following:

- Preparing and analyzing transfer prices and cost allocation estimates
- Analyzing and forecasting trends in demand, cost, output, and efficiency
- Developing new budget expectations, particularly for new or expanded services when the operating conditions have changed

- Understanding seasonal and day-of-week variation
- Comparing local production with outside purchase, often called make-or-buy decisions
- Comparing alternative protocols or work processes, particularly those substituting capital for labor
- Ranking cost-saving opportunities to identify promising areas in which to eliminate or reduce use
- Preparing forecasts for expanding or closing units

Managerial accounting analysis requires a cost-data archive (a system to retrieve relevant information), the ability to develop simulations and forecasts of future situations, and consultation on the limitations and applications of the data. Specific proposals often call for extrapolation to new work processes. Ideally, finance personnel work directly with accountability centers and internal consulting teams, helping them identify fruitful avenues of investigation, develop useful proposals, and translate operational changes to accounting and financial implications.

Activity-Based Costing

Historically, the precision and reliability of managerial accounting was limited by the difficulties of data collection and analysis. Large blocks of cost were allocated, rather than transfer-priced, using formulas based on assumed proxies such as facility space, number of employees, total direct costs, or gross revenues.[3] Electronic databases permit a significantly more accurate process called activity-based costing (ABC).[4,5,6] ABC activities are work processes that can be defined as needed. They are often work processes under study by PITs.

ABC has three objectives:[7]

1. Show the resource elements of cost so that the producing unit or a performance improvement team can compare to benchmark and evaluate changes in the activity.
2. Provide a transfer price for internal transactions. The transfer price can be compared to prices offered by external vendors. It also encourages the using unit to identify and control consumption.
3. Encourage the producing unit to think of the purchasing units as customers whose needs must be met.

ABC promotes control of services, the use of make-or-buy decisions, and improvement of processes that cross several accountability centers. Entire systems, including information services, finance, executive management, and human resources management, can be evaluated. Alternatives such as mergers, acquisitions, preferred partnerships, and alliances can be modeled. These large-scale reorganizations can change patterns of demand, introduce work processes that were previously impractical, and create other returns to scale. For example:

- A small clinic that fails to generate demand and has excessive fixed costs per case may become viable by a merger or partnership with an outside organization. (The market share served will increase, generating enough demand to cover the fixed costs.)
- The scope of clinical support services may be increased and transfer prices may be reduced by a merger. (The fixed costs will be spread over a larger base. Along with reduced costs, increased volume may improve quality.)
- The costs of governance and executive management may be reduced by merger. (Two senior management teams reduced to one, and the market share increased.)
- A major service, such as imaging, human resources management, financial management, or information services, can be purchased from a vendor. (The vendor has returns to scale and superior experience and is better positioned to keep up to date.)
- The capabilities of smaller units can expand while simultaneously lowering the cost of larger ones. Telemedicine programs for intensive care patients in small hospitals, which provide access to the advice of experienced intensivist physicians and allow centralized specialist monitoring of rural patients, are striking examples.[8]

Goal Setting and Budgeting

The controller's office supports the annual goal-setting process. A section—the budget office—coordinates budget development and accounting reports, working closely with internal consulting and managing the extensive flows of information necessary to support the negotiations. The process takes several months, involves virtually everyone in the organization, and is the stimulus for continuous improvement and operational excellence. As shown in Exhibit 13.3, the environmental assessment and strategic analysis (chapters 4 and 15) lead to goals for the strategic scorecard. Each operating unit uses these and its own OFIs to identify improvements for the coming year. Goals are negotiated for all dimensions of the operational scorecards. Capital requests are separated from the operating goals and are subject to competitive review. The budget process establishes, and the budget documents, a quantitative consensus on expected operations, capital investment, and financing for the next fiscal year. Progress against the budget is monitored by operating managers and overseen by the budget office. The expectation is that all goals will be attained.

The budget describes expected financial transactions and other operational goals for each operating unit, by accounting period, for at least an entire year. Because it takes time to develop, the forecast must cover about 18 months into the future. Well-run institutions budget a second or even a third year in preliminary terms as part of their yearly budget cycle. Multiyear expectations encourage progress toward improvement goals.

Budget Components

Operating budget
The aggregate of accountability-center expenditure budgets and the corporate revenue budget

The final budget has several components, as shown in Exhibit 13.4. The **operating budget** includes the following:

EXHIBIT 13.3
Integrating
Strategic and
Operational
Goal Setting

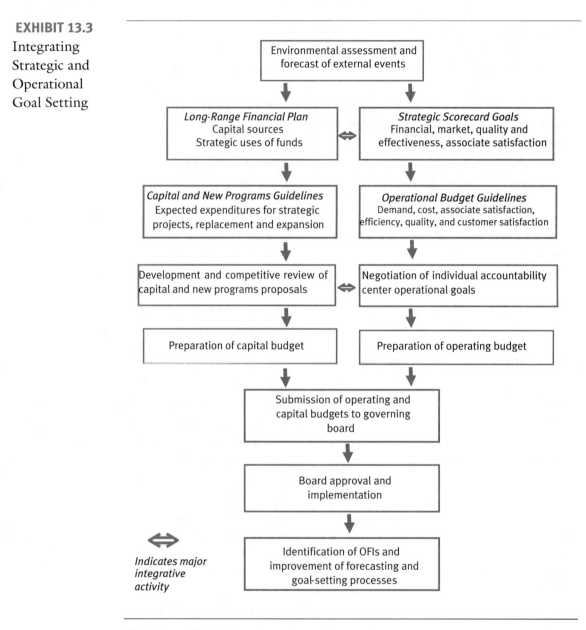

OFIs: opportunities for improvement

- *Accountability-unit budgets by reporting period and kind of resource.* Costs are negotiated with the other five dimensions of operational scorecards. The six dimensions comprise the unit goals for the coming year.
- *Aggregate expenditures budgets, or "roll ups," that summarize larger sections of the organization that parallel the accountability hierarchy.* Similar aggregates are made of the goals for the other operational dimensions.
- *Revenue budgets that show expected income and profits for DRGs at organizational levels that parallel the payment aggregates.* Leading institutions report revenues only at aggregates that can be held accountable, now usually the service line.[9]

Budget	Contents	Use
Operating budget: Accountability centers	Accountability-center-level expectations for demand, costs, human resources, productivity, quality, and customer satisfaction	One- or two-year plan of accountability-center goals
Operating budget: Aggregate	Service line and other aggregate expectations for operational and financial measures	Monitor groups of accountability centers
New programs and capital budget	Approved capital expenditures by strategic category and funding sources	Manage investments in capital equipment and facilities
Financial budgets	Detailed pro forma of corporate income, expense, funds flow, and balance sheet	Verify capital management strategies and confirmation of the long-range financial plan
Cash budget	Projection of monthly cash flows	Manage working capital

EXHIBIT 13.4
Major Budgets and Their Relation to Strategic Goals

The **financial budgets** parallel the required financial reports. Three are more relevant to operations:

1. *The income and expense budget:* expected net income and expenses incurred by the organization as a whole by period

2. *The funds flow budget:* estimates of cash income and outgo by period, used by finance in cash and debt management

3. *The capital and new programs budget:* capital expenditures and new programs accepted by the governing board, with their implications for the operating and cash budgets by period and accountability center

Financial budget
Expectation of future financial performance; composed of income and expense budget, budgeted financial statements, cash flow budget, and capital and new programs budget

The budget development process follows an annual cycle shown in Exhibit 13.5. Completing the cycle takes about six months and demands substantial effort by every manager and executive as well as members of the governing board. During the remainder of the year, managers can focus on the analysis of operations and development of improved methods so that these are ready for implementation with the next cycle.

The Budget Cycle

The operations budget process is managed by *packages*—specific bundles of information that are transferred from one unit or level to another—

EXHIBIT 13.5
Annual
Goal-Setting
Cycle

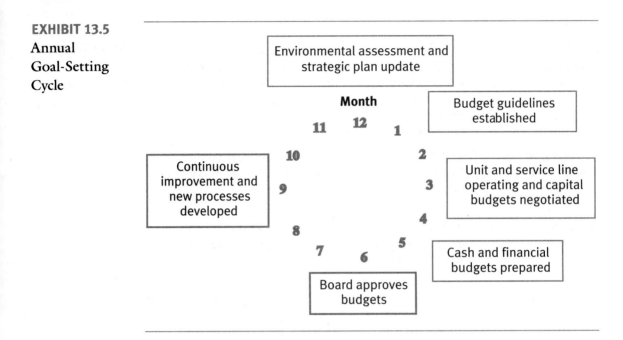

and timetables for package transfers.[10] The package concept allows the budget office to route information to the correct location, permitting many different teams in the HCO to work at once. Exhibit 13.6 shows the major steps, although the process is usually more complex than the figure indicates. As a general rule, a specific information package is available for each accountability center or unit at each step, although later rounds of revision tend to focus on only a few unresolved areas.

The actual calculation is now computerized. Units have direct access to their own electronic files and can change resource requirements and some demand elements at-will up to the package deadlines. At that time, they must submit the packages to central control, where aggregates are calculated and values are checked against historic records for errors or potential difficulties.

Negotiating the Operating Goals

The budget office initiates the process with forecasts of prices and unit activity; trends, benchmarks, and competitor data; and overall strategic goals.

- *Demand for major activity groups, such as primary care contacts, emergency visits, hospitalizations, births, and surgeries, are forecast using statistical analysis of market trends, combined with judgments of executive personnel.*[11] Forecasts for more detailed activities are derived from the major groups. They are developed first by the budget office and then refined for each unit by unit personnel.
- *Resource prices are forecast by type of resource from history and external references.* The purchasing unit usually prepares the price forecasts for supplies, human resources for personnel, and finance for transfer-priced resources. The unit forecasts the quantities of resources to be used. Budget software calculates cost implications.

Month	Finance Activity	Operations Activity	Intent
1 Budget guidelines	Forecast strategic scorecard values for governing board	Distribute instructions, forms, and timetables	Provide targets and information for line managers' guidance
2–4 Operating goals and budget	Provide forecasts, historical, and comparative information to accountability centers and service lines Answer questions and requests for advice Tally proposed operating budgets, check against guidelines, suggest revisions	Negotiate operating goals using guidelines, competition, benchmarks, history, and values	Specify realistic operational expectations for coming year Improve competitive position and mission achievement
5 Cash and financial budget	Develop complete budget for board review Double-check financial implications		Prepare integrated package for board action
6 Board approval of budgets	Recommend final budget to board		Final review
7–11 Process improvement	Report on performance against budget Provide activity-based cost analysis and guidance on improvement opportunities Assist in evaluating new processes	Develop improved processes	Exploit opportunities to improve competitive position and mission achievement
12 Environmental assessment and strategic plan review	Present review of current performance, long-range forecasts, market analysis, and evaluation of current mission and vision	Review and understand competitive environment	Develop consensus on strategic OFIs, environmental conditions Reiterate relevant policy on quality, human resources, and operations

EXHIBIT 13.6
Major Steps in Developing Operations Budgets

OFIs: opportunities for improvement

- *Productivity forecasts are calculated mechanically as the ratio of forecast cost to forecast output.* Both physical and dollar values are important.
- *Quality, human resources, and customer satisfaction values are taken from historical data.* Trend analysis can be used if necessary. Benchmarks are obtained from a variety of sources.

The initial forecasts are *ceteris paribus,* continuation of past conditions. The unit managers and their supervisors respond with plans for the coming year. The forecasts, guidelines from the governing board, and benchmarks discipline the process. Each unit and each measure should move toward benchmark, and the aggregate expectation must match the guidelines. The results of PITs are incorporated into the coming year's goals. The unmet benchmarks or values suggest the OFIs and PITs for study during the coming year.

Negotiating this result is often a substantial effort. It is important to keep the goals realistic. Achieving them allows unit teams to focus on future improvements, preparing for the following year's goals rather than fixing failures. Some organizations use two guidelines—one for minimally acceptable performance and a second stretch guideline for exceptional achievement. Incentives are established for exceptional effort. The unit's supervisors, including senior management, must assist the team in identifying and testing the goals and supporting PITs to develop better work processes. Senior management leads by pointing out benchmarks, making best practices available, encouraging innovation, and rewarding effective results. These actions are a central part of transformational management. They are radically different from the top-down, authoritarian approaches of earlier management systems.

Capital and New Programs Budget

Finance manages capital funds and is deeply involved in evaluating individual capital investment opportunities. Opportunities are evaluated in terms of contribution to mission. The evaluation process is described in detail in Chapter 14. It always includes the operating units involved and internal consulting. Projects can easily expand to include information and human resources management. The evaluation must be able to communicate across many elements of the HCO, including the governing board. It can be managed either by finance or by internal consulting. Finance's responsibilities include validating the forecasts for project costs, including capital and projected operating costs, and for benefits when they involve costs, efficiency, or revenues. Finance also manages the actual expenditures of capital as accepted projects are implemented.

Finance prepares the capital budget, which shows expected expenditures for new plant and equipment by accounting period and tracks the funds available to the enterprise. It manages the sources of capital funds, provides data for the long-range financial plan and the board's annual goal for investments, and prevents distortion of costs or benefits in proposals.

The following are guidelines for a well-run goal-setting process:

1. *The budget and operating goals must constitute an integral whole.* At every level of the organization, the planned activities and goals must be consistent with each other. At higher levels, they must be consistent with the strategic plan, long-range financial plan, and annual environmental survey.

2. *Annual goals or guidelines from the governing board are a major force in gaining consistency and timely progress.* These are established at the outset of the process and include
    - realistic forecasts of net revenue;
    - a minimum acceptable return from operations;
    - a target amount for capital expenditure; and
    - corporate goals for customer satisfaction, quality, and associate satisfaction.

3. *The budget for capital expenses and new programs is separately developed and approved in a process that*
    - establishes quantitative forecasts of improvement in operational or strategic scorecards,
    - permits comparison of the value of programs,
    - allows the approval of new programs and even replacement capital to be adjusted quickly as conditions change, and
    - encourages deletion proposals for obsolete or uneconomical programs.

4. *Line managers are convinced of the realism of the goals, both in terms of organizational need and practical achievability.*[12] Senior managers are effective at negotiating goals and supporting lower managers in achieving them. Budget expectations are almost always achieved. Stretch goals may be used for higher risk or where extra effort is required. They are normally supported by increased incentives.

5. *Continuous improvement is the norm.* Goals move closer to benchmark or value over time. Improvements and benchmark performance are rewarded.

6. *The quality of data and the preparation of information by the budget office, as measured by time to completion, reliability, and ease of use, should improve from year to year, building on past work.*

7. *The budget process itself is subject to continuous improvement, becoming more rigorous over time.* An organization that is having difficulty establishing or meeting its budget must limit its attention to elementary concepts, concentrating on getting guidelines, forecasts, and improvement processes developed and accepted. A well-run organization with many years of budgeting experience will do extensive activity-based costing and stretch scenarios. It also will extend the detail of its reporting, both by type of resource and by number of accountability centers. Similar growth in sophistication would occur in the capital and new programs budget.

Accountability centers and cross-functional team members should fully understand the market forces and planning processes that lead to the budget guidelines, participate in budget development, and be able to anticipate the general direction of the guidelines for at least two years in the future. When an effective dialogue exists, quality and sophistication often improve as a result. Without effective dialogue, there is a constant danger of having the accountability centers adopt an adversarial or destructive approach to the budget.[13]

Monitoring Budget Achievement

Goals negotiated in the budgeting process are normally achieved. Operating units are expected to have used the continuous improvement process to develop, and if necessary test, new methods. Plans for necessary changes in equipment, supplies, and training will have been completed. (Stretch goals will be less certain, but the underlying preparation is still important.)

Any failure represents a serious management issue. It creates a direct problem (resources must be used to correct the specific failure) and an indirect one (those resources are drawn from the effort to identify and achieve next year's goals). In the rare cases where failure occurs, excellent HCOs respond with 90-day plans—specific reevaluations and corrective efforts to return to goal achievement. These plans are administered by the operating teams and their direct managers. The role of the budget office is to produce the reports that monitor progress, provide drill-down detail when needed, and alert senior management to potential failure. Assigning correction responsibility to the operating managers moves away from the blame culture and reinforces empowerment.

Financial Management Functions

The financial management function projects future financial needs, arranges to meet them, and manages the organization's assets and liabilities in ways that increase its profitability. Financial management in this sense is relatively recent, arising from the increased revenue base created by Medicare, Medicaid, and widespread private health insurance and from the opportunities for obtaining credit and equity. Before 1970, hospitals had two sources of funds—retained earnings and gifts. The growth of reliable income streams opened a broad spectrum of financing opportunities. The growth of multiple corporations, bonded indebtedness issued and reissued to minimize interest costs, and deliberate investment in joint ventures for profit is as telling a story of the healthcare industry as is the development of heart transplants. The five functions—financial planning, pricing, management of long-term capital, management of short-term assets and liabilities, and multicorporate accounting—are now essential to survival.

Financial Planning

Financial management is a forward-looking activity with a long time horizon. It begins with the generation of a long-range financial plan (LRFP), continues with the translation of plan values to annual guidelines, and results in establishing the institution's ability to acquire capital funds through debt or equity.

The LRFP incorporates the expected future income and expense for every element of the strategic plan, specifying the amount and the time of its occurrence. It models the financial outcomes for various scenarios, reflecting possible future operating conditions. It is now commonly prepared with specialized software and counsel from a respected accounting firm. The software generates **pro forma** annual statements of income, asset and liability position, and cash flow for many years into the future, allowing senior management and the finance committee of the governing board to assess how well the HCO is prepared to fulfill its mission.

Developing the LRFP

Pro forma
A forecast of financial statements, establishing the future financial position of the organization for a given set of operating conditions or decisions

Activities such as bond repayments and major facility replacement require 30-year financial planning horizons. Although the accuracy of the estimates deteriorates in distant years, large financial requirements must be accommodated even though they are many years away. Most of the attention is focused on the first three to five years, when the irreversible decisions will be made. Topics of interest include the following:

- Cost of borrowing from various sources
- Cash flow required to support debt payments
- Efficiency improvements required to meet market constraints on revenue
- Financial prospects of specific service lines
- Identity and magnitude of various financial risks
- Overall prudence of the financial management

The LRFP process should include evaluation of the widest possible variety of alternative scenarios (what-ifs) that address future uncertainties, such as the following:

- The impact of inflation and the business cycle
- Changes in demand as a result of population shifts, technology, or competition
- Proposed federal and state legislation
- Trends in health insurance coverage and benefits
- Donations, grants, and subsidized funding sources
- Alternative debt structures and timing
- Opportunities for joint ventures and equity capitalization

The HCO might respond by changing profit-margin goals, revising debt structure, acquiring new equity investors, revising expansion strategies, acquiring or divesting units, or even merging or closing. The objective is to identify the optimum operating condition consistent with the mission and to evaluate that condition in terms of its acceptability. Unacceptable LRFP results can force a complete reevaluation of the strategic position, including the continued existence of the institution.

As indicated in Chapter 4, the financial plan is a critical reality check for the organization. The decision about the final plan—selecting the strategies that are best for the stakeholders as a whole—is made by the governing board. Financial management is responsible for generating information about the alternatives. Exhibit 13.7 shows the tests and the kinds of rethinking necessary to make the strategic plan fit financial realities. The financial ratios provide a way to benchmark financial performance. Bond-rating agencies use the ratios and other financial statement data to issue public ratings of the risk associated with long-term debt. Lower ratings (higher risks) bring higher interest costs on debt. A similar but less formal process operates with equity capital and, to some extent, with gifts. Thus, the institution's ability to acquire capital is directly dependent on its ability to construct a competitive LRFP.

The ideal LRFP generates operating costs substantially below expected revenues, creating a steady stream of profits. The organization can invest the funds in growth, community health, or service improvement and can amplify the investment with borrowed, donated, or invested capital. The ideal is not often achieved. High-performing HCOs use the plan to recognize danger signals in advance and makes the necessary adjustments. Several principles guide their actions and are weighed as the plan is considered and adopted:

- *The necessary profit is the amount required to sustain the mission, replacing worn-out and outmoded facilities and equipment and expanding as community need grows.* Well-run not-for-profit HCOs have tended to seek returns in the range of 5 percent of total costs. Large for-profit organizations seek before-tax returns two to three times that high.
- *The criteria for investment decisions are biased toward liquidity and away from risk.* The bias toward liquidity means that most projects must justify themselves in terms of cash flow as well as community benefit. There are four basic causes of increased risk:
  1. Poor prior management has reduced financial capacity.
  2. Management systems lack the control required to meet stated goals.
  3. Individual proposals are inherently risky because they involve speculative goals outside conservative expectations.
  4. The rate of expansion exceeds what the organization can support.

  Well-run organizations guard against the first and second by building and sustaining effective management teams. They meet the third through the programmatic planning process, competitive review, and retention of skilled managers, and they meet the fourth by adhering to the capital investment limits suggested by the LRFP.

Test	External Source	Adjustment Required
Debt ratios	Bond market	Keep debt within bond-rating limits
Price	Buyers and intermediaries	Keep price competitive
Earnings	Bond and equity investment markets	Keep cash flow within bond-rating limits
Demand and market share	Competitor analysis	Keep demand forecast consistent with competitor and market conditions
Cost	Benchmarks, competition	Keep cost at or below (Expected revenue – Needed profit)

EXHIBIT 13.7
Tests and Adjustments in Financial Planning

- *Portions of the available investment funds can be earmarked for strategic purposes, such as development of new markets, replacement of facilities, or technology strategies like information systems.* Earmarking establishes a multiyear level for the category as a whole and forces evaluation of proposals within the category, rather than between category members and other categories.
- *Investment timing and capital management is frequently important.* Well-run organizations invest liquid assets wisely, avoid borrowing at peak interest rates, and refinance to take advantage of low rates.

The LRFP is used by the governing board to establish the annual strategic guidelines for revenue, profit, costs, and capital expenditures. The senior management team develops forecasts of market share, costs, and revenue and prepares a recommendation that translates the cash and profit requirements of the LRFP to the guidelines for the coming year or two. The finance committee of the governing board discusses the recommendation and alternatives and recommends the guidelines to the board as a whole. As noted, the board's action initiates the annual goal-setting process and is a more critical step than the final budget approval, which is often a formality because the negotiated goals meet the guidelines.

Setting the Financial Budget Guidelines

Pricing Clinical Services

The issues in pricing relate to three concerns: the unit of payment, the HCO mission, and the HCO's market strength. The traditional units of payment were fees for specific physician services and charges for hospital services and supplies. Insurance payment systems have moved to progressively broader aggregates in an effort to emphasize outcomes of care rather than inputs. Exhibit 13.8 shows the major options for pricing structures as sequential levels of risk taking and requirements for integration of the institution and its medical staff. All but level 1 require increased collaboration. Caregiving associates must coordinate with each other, and the HCO must support and encourage that coordination.

An HCO with a community health mission, as opposed to an excellence-in-care mission, has a relatively straightforward pricing strategy. Its mission calls for maximizing health, reducing unnecessary use of services, and maintaining high efficiency for all services offered. Its strategic performance measures address the needs of community health as well as those of individual patients and associates. At least in theory and usually in reality, the community health mission minimizes the community's healthcare cost per capita, aligning the mission of the HCO with that of the insurer and insurance buyers. The HCO will accept all levels of Exhibit 13.8, with preference for the higher levels because they reward it and its caregivers for achieving the mission. Prices can then be evaluated based on the LRFP.

For HCOs that pursue an excellence-in-care mission, pricing is considerably more complex. The relation between buyer and seller is adversarial and depends in part on the relative market power. The extent to which the seller has the ability to set the sales price measures monopoly-pricing power. The HCO is frequently in a monopoly situation with regard to uninsured purchasers, and the management of charges to these individuals is a matter of substantial board and societal concern.[14] Although many healthcare systems have acquired some monopoly power over private health insurance contracts,[15] major buyers—such as Medicare, Medicaid, and large commercial insurers—have the balance of market power. Medicare prices are set annually in a national political process.

The Medicare Payment Advisory Commission (MedPAC) conducts research and holds hearings to develop market price recommendations. Medicaid payments are established by the states but are generally less than Medicare. The terms are not negotiable for the individual HCO. For example, between 2000 and 2002, traditional Medicare moved most outpatient, rehabilitation, home, hospice, and mental health care from charges-based to episode-based payments. In 2009, the discussion was around reaching levels 4 and 5 in Exhibit 13.8—bundled payment for episodes of care offered jointly to institution and physicians and incentives that reward the hospital and physician for more effective overall care, which minimize readmissions of chronically ill patients.[16,17]

All HCOs must have a systematic pricing response that recognizes the reality of purchaser pricing power and the broad array of pricing structures. The impact of an offered price must be evaluated using the LRFP. All HCOs have high fixed costs, and as a result, profits are dependent on volume. To retain market share, they must meet most market demands in both price and service. As a practical matter, they cannot walk away from major insurers like Medicare. Pricing strategy cannot be set alone; it must be integrated with a strategy to manage the risks involved.[18]

Structure	Example	Risk for Provider	Integration
1. Fee-for-service/charges	Cash payments, catastrophic and traditional health insurance	None beyond normal business risks	Traditional physician–HCO relationship
2. Negotiated fees and charges	PPO contracts, some traditional insurance contracts	Normal business risks, plus constraints imposed by contract limits	Traditional physician–HCO relationship
3. Fees for episodes of care negotiated separately between HCO and physicians	Medicare DRGs, APCs, some insurance contracts	HCO is at risk for the costs of and quantities of services ordered by physicians within the episode. Physician has no additional risk	HCO must gain physician cooperation to meet its risk
4. Fees for episodes of care offered jointly to HCO and physicians	Single-price contracts for discrete episodes of care, such as cardiovascular surgery or chemotherapy	Both physician and HCO at risk for the cost of the episode	Requires physician–HCO collaboration on cost per episode
5. Fees subject to a group incentive	Contracts with penalties or bonuses for meeting utilization or quality targets, such as readmission penalties	Physician and HCO share limited risk for the cost, quality, and appropriateness of care	Requires physician–HCO collaboration on process improvements to meet specific targets
6. Capitation	Payment contracts independent of disease incidence or actual costs of treatment	Physician and HCO at unlimited risk for the cost of the episode and appropriateness of care	Requires physician–HCO collaboration on cost per episode, utilization, and disease incidence

EXHIBIT 13.8
Pricing Structures for Healthcare Contracts

PPO: preferred provider organization; DRG: diagnosis-related group; APC: ambulatory patient classification

Advanced levels of Exhibit 13.8 force more integration not only between each physician and the HCO but also between physicians. The pricing/risk-management strategy must integrate a broad range of knowledge, from practicing physicians, service line managers, clinical support services managers, and financial analysts. The time frame for strategy implementation must allow for individual learning and the development of effective teams.

The basic HCO response to the risk-sharing approaches in Exhibit 13.8 is an effective program of evidence-based medicine and evidence-based management, as described throughout this text. This holds costs per case to levels that are acceptable to insurers and generally ensures some profit under Medicare. Offers from private insurers will tend to move to the Medicare level. They must be evaluated against the financial needs reflected in the LRFP and the HCO's bargaining strength. Pricing and charging policies must also be established for uninsured patients. Pricing must include guidelines for charity care, arrangements for deferred payment, and management of delinquent accounts.

Securing and Managing Liquid Assets

Finance is responsible for managing all loans, bonds, and liquid assets. It evaluates alternative sources of funds and recommends the best solution to the governing board as part of the funds flow budget. It arranges borrowing; prepares supporting financial information; and manages repayment schedules, mandatory reserves, and other elements of debt obligation. It monitors the financial markets for opportunities to restructure financing. It manages liquid assets (cash and readily saleable investments). It manages endowments of not-for-profit HCOs.

Debt and Equity Capitalization

Successful not-for-profit HCOs have accumulated substantial equity, and their liquidity was increasing up to the recession of 2009.[19] Equity of not-for-profit organizations can increase only from donations and retained earnings. Any HCO must establish a core of equity finance. Equity is also useful in joint ventures, allowing the partners to be rewarded for successful risk taking. For-profit equity investors generally expect returns commensurate with their risk, often several times the return expected by lenders. Tax laws are important in equity finance, from both the point of view of the corporation and that of the investor. They permit not-for-profit organizations to retain tax exemption for their share of the earnings if they hold certain levels of control.

Well-managed not-for-profit HCOs exercise extreme prudence in deploying equity. The bulk of the HCO's investments should be in low-risk debt securities. The HCO can pursue some higher risk investments limited to amounts that the organization could lose without seriously impairing its mission. The rewards for successful use of equity financing through joint ventures are appealing, and this model will probably grow in popularity.

Borrowing, principally long-term tax-exempt bonds, will remain an important form of capital finance. The borrowing capacity of an organization depends on the overall level of risk to the lenders. Elements of the business that have tangible independent value, such as real estate and accounts receivable, are attractive to lenders. The typical community hospital holds long-term debt that is about 50 percent of its equity.[20] Well-managed HCOs deliberately manage their debt and investments to attract lenders at advantageous rates.[21] Effective investment of borrowed funds, maintenance of cash reserves, and profitable operations are all important. In the long run, the organization can maintain a favored position only by investing prudently to enhance its own customer base. Unwise borrowing, excess borrowing, or insufficient investment will diminish the chance of success.

Exhibit 13.9 shows a simplified example to clarify the complex financial and operational issues involved in capital funds acquisition. A certain HCO might plan to spend $50 million over the next three years to expand primary care and outpatient services. It anticipates a handsome increase in net income of $10 million per year from the new service, with relatively small risk that the income will fall below that level. It has several sources for the $50 million. It could use cash reserved from prior earnings. It could seek tax-exempt bonds, which are likely to have the lowest cost of capital. It could create a for-profit joint venture with its physicians or with another corporation and raise part of the money from equity investment. Finally, it could combine any or all of these approaches.

The use of debt finance can substantially increase the project attractiveness, and the use of a joint venture partner can reduce the capital requirement. The combination of the two allows the institution to start the project

EXHIBIT 13.9
Implications of Alternative Funding Sources for an Ambulatory Care Project

Scenario ($ in millions)	HCO Equity Investment	Earnings from Project	Bond Interest Paid*	Net HCO Income/ Year**	Return on Equity***
100% from equity	$50	$10	$0	$10	20%
50% bonds, 50% equity	$25	$10	$2	$8	32%
50% bonds, 25% equity, 25% joint venture equity	$12.5	$10	$2	$4	32%

* Bond interest 8%
** (Project earnings − Bond interest) × (HCO equity share)
*** Net HCO income as percent of HCO equity

with a minimum investment of its own capital and an appealing return on the capital, if earnings match expectations. If earnings fall short, the bond interest is fixed and the entire drop is borne by the equity investors. The partnership with a physician organization commits the physicians to the project's success and reduces the risk of failure.

The number of questions and assumptions required even in this simple example indicates the complexity and challenge. Obviously, accurate forecasts of volume, costs, revenues, and effects on other services are essential, even though opening is several years away. These matters must be addressed in the proposal for the venture. In addition, assumptions must be made about the following:

- *Price and volume interactions for the new service.* Careful understanding of the market tolerance for prices and the risks involved if demand does not meet expectations is essential to evaluate the project and the financing mechanisms.
- *Costs of alternative sources of capital.* Each of the sources has different costs and obligations built into it. The use of retained earnings may impair the organization's ability to meet other needs, such as the replacement of equipment or increase in market share by the acquisition of competitors. Bonds will have an interest rate dependent on the market at the time of sale, the organization's overall financial position, and federal tax policy. Organizations that have been prudently managed in the past will have advantages for all kinds of capital. They will have more retained earnings, lower bond interest, and more debt capacity and thus will be more attractive to outside investors.
- *Impact of the financing on other strategic goals.* The financing may affect competitors or partners in ways advantageous to the organization. A joint venture with primary care physicians may provide an avenue to affiliate them more closely with the organization and may improve the ability to recruit. The result may be higher market share and an increased overall profitability. A joint venture with a potential competitor may reduce risk and expand resources simultaneously.
- *Tax implications.* If ordinary income taxes apply, they will be enough to make substantial differences in the results. (Corporate tax rates were about 35 percent of earnings in 2009.) A tax adviser may be able to find precedents that establish the tax obligations of the various structures, or it may be necessary to seek a letter from the IRS.

The LRFP financial model will be employed to test outcomes not only for the expected conditions but for a range of possible futures. Each major funding avenue will be explored several times, under varying assumptions. Consultants will advise on approaches, assumptions, and implications. The financial results will be evaluated against the marketing and operational considerations. The final solution can be recommended to the board with widespread support from the participants.

Most not-for-profit HCOs have acquired endowments or funds they expect to hold for long periods of time. These funds can be invested for growth or income. The assistance of professional investment managers is advisable. Larger organizations use several different managers. The organization must evaluate its overall investment strategy, weighing its risk against potential earnings. In general, permanently endowed funds return about 5 percent per year, after protecting the corpus against inflation. The return is often dedicated to specific charitable purposes such as research, education, and charity care.

Managing Endowments

Any operation requires **working capital**—funds that are used to cover expenditures made in advance of payment for services. The finance system manages these transactions to maximum advantage for the organization. A healthcare system with a nine-week average billing cycle, a biweekly payroll, and a four-week inventory cycle requires about $25 million in working capital for $100 million of annual expenses. The cost of this capital—about $1 million per year in interest paid or forgone from investments—is the equivalent of 10 or 15 full-time employees.

Managing Short-Term Assets and Liabilities

Working capital
The amount of cash required to support operations for the period of delay in collecting revenue

Working capital management deals in terms of days. Income can be obtained by moving assets rapidly. Cash and other liquid assets are placed where they will obtain the highest return consistent with risk and the length of time available. (Large sums of money can be invested for small interest returns on an overnight basis.) Accounts receivable and inventories are minimized because they earn no return. Accounts payable, payroll, and other short-term debts are settled exactly when due (or when discounts can be applied), allowing the organization to use the funds involved as long as possible.

Cash Management

   Short-term borrowing is available to HCOs. Bank loans and factoring of receivables are common sources. Short-term borrowing is minimized because it costs money. At the same time, however, costs of borrowing need to be compared to opportunity costs of liquidating assets or failing to meet liabilities in a timely fashion. The objective is to reduce total costs of working capital, rather than to avoid borrowing per se. HCOs can reduce capital needs by leasing equipment, paying extra (an effective interest rate) for the privilege of deferring payment.

HCOs are paid for their services once they have submitted an invoice—the patient ledger—to the responsible party. Health insurers insist on substantial documentation of the invoice. Most now require a specific diagnosis following the International Classification of Diseases, and an attestation by the physician who affirms the diagnosis. Because complex diagnoses are more highly paid, entering the correct diagnosis is important to both parties. The HCO should identify all disease but is obviously forbidden to enter nonexistent

Revenue Management

disease. It is also important to prepare the invoice in a timely fashion. Each day of delay—best practice gains payment in less than 50 days—adds to the working capital need. Large HCOs establish a substantial mechanism to prepare invoices promptly, assist the physician to identify all diseases, and audit to avoid violating the law.

Managing Multicorporate Accounting

Many HCOs are now multicorporate structures or healthcare systems. Both for-profit and not-for-profit legal entities are permitted to create or acquire subsidiaries by forming new corporations, purchasing or leasing existing organizations, and investing in other corporations. They can reverse these actions by sale, liquidation, or transfer. The only restrictions on these actions are those established by antitrust laws and regulations that govern tax-exempt status. Investment in a given subsidiary can range from negligible to wholly owned, although to qualify for tax exemption it must be controlled by a not-for-profit board. Any combination of for-profit and not-for-profit entities is possible. The tax obligations of each corporation are considered individually as the structures develop.

Two major types of systems have emerged. First, individual hospitals in the same market have merged, formed joint ventures, or established subsidiaries. These tend to be relatively small—$500 million a year or less. They are essentially the same as individual hospitals. Second, about 100 multimarket systems have become important suppliers of healthcare. Many now exceed $1 billion per year in revenue. Many are religious, and many are for-profit. Kaiser-Permanente, by far the largest system, is a nonreligious not-for-profit healthcare system that includes its own insurance operation. These systems have the opportunity to centralize important components and generate returns to scale; finance, for example, can perform many functions in one office and serve dozens of hospitals. The system's member HCOs can also form multicorporate structures.

The major financial benefits of multiple corporate structures are as follows:

- *Capital opportunities.* Subsidiary corporations of either single-market or large systems offer opportunities to dedicate capital and to raise new capital through borrowing, gifts, or equity. Activities attractive to equity capital can be pursued only through a for-profit structure, but a not-for-profit parent corporation can form a for-profit subsidiary. Large systems offer scale and diversification attractive to bond buyers. As a result, they can obtain lower interest rates.
- *Reward.* Separate for-profit corporations allow various groups to invest in activities of interest to them and to receive financial reward for the success of those activities. Joint subsidiaries can reward physicians for loyalty and quality.
- *Risk.* The liabilities and obligations of the owned or subsidiary corporation cannot generally be transferred to the parent. (There are certain exceptions, and

the law in this area is changing.) Thus, the parent risks only those assets actually invested in the subsidiary.

- *Taxation*. Not-for-profit corporations can be taxed on certain activities, and for-profit corporations can respond to incentives built into the tax law. Separate corporations can frequently be designed with a view toward minimizing the overall tax obligation.

The finance system has the obligation to identify, evaluate, and recommend these opportunities. They must work within the limits established by accepted accounting practice, Medicare fraud and abuse provisions, and IRS regulations.

A relatively common example is an HCO that is exempt from taxes under Section 501(c)(3) of the Internal Revenue Code forming a for-profit corporation with outside investors and then contracting with that corporation to carry out certain activities. The HCO reduces its capital requirement, retains control of the cost and quality of services, and expects to earn profits from its ownership position. The transactions must be priced at fair market value. Joint ventures and equity arrangements with physicians, like other physician contracts, may not offer financial incentives to refer or admit patients to the parent HCO, except in certain types of managed care insurance. They also may not extend tax exemption to physicians in private practice, and they cannot reward physicians for improvement of the profitability of the parent corporation.

Auditing Functions

Any corporate entity is required to maintain control of all its properties for its owners. The governing board and members of management are individually and collectively responsible for prudent protection of assets. They act as agents for owners, and must avoid inurement in not-for-profit organizations. The assets include property, cash, and intangibles such as reputation and established market recognition. In hospital organizations, information is one of the most valuable and at-risk assets. The agency obligation extends through the organization. Asset protection is every associate's responsibility, and specific protection functions are assigned to various units. Assets are further protected by a combination of an internal audit function and a hired external auditor.

Internal Audits

Internal auditing provides an ongoing review of the accuracy of data, the safety of assets, and the systems to protect against misfeasance and malfeasance. The internal auditing function can be outsourced. Many Catholic healthcare systems use the Catholic Healthcare Audit Network, an organization they founded that provides extensive, uniform, and independent auditing.

Information Assets

The organization's data warehouse—the *source of truth*—is protected physically by information services, which is also responsible for the definition and accurate capture of information. The internal audit function monitors actual compliance to definition, whether the reported measure is calculated and recorded exactly. The split responsibilities are deliberate; division and some duplication of functions is a widely accepted pattern for protection. The accounting information in the warehouse is routinely audited, including cash balances and accounts receivables, supplies, and the accurate posting of payroll and other expenses. Basic statistics, such as discharges by DRG or APG (ambulatory patient group), must be audited to assure third-party payers of the validity of charges. In the process of auditing the medical record information, internal auditing can validate the statistics used in specification and adjustment and in many measures of quality.

Physical Assets

Generally, the protection of the physical assets is considered part of the function of the plant system, assigned to security, maintenance, and materials management. Prudent purchasing practices are included in the responsibilities of materials management. The controller is responsible for the physical protection of cash, securities, and receivables. The risk of misappropriation of assets is probably greater than the risks of theft or destruction by outside sources. Internal audit is responsible for estimating the actual loss of physical property and for reviewing processes that protect against loss. The major risks it guards against are as follows:

- Inurement
- Unjustified free or unbilled service to patients
- Embezzlement of cash in the collections and supply processes
- Bribes and kickbacks in purchasing arrangements
- Diversion or theft of supplies and equipment
- Falsified employment and hours
- Purchase of supplies or equipment without appropriate authorization
- Supervision of financial conflicts of interest among governing board members and officers

All organizations face continuing losses of physical assets, and acceptable performance requires continuing diligence. A sound and well-understood program has been developed for this purpose. It has six parts:

1. Detailed, written procedures govern the handling of the various assets and transactions. These procedures primarily rely on the division of functions between two or more individuals and the routine reporting of checks and balances to protect assets. It is common to assign the responsibility for authorizing the

transaction (a payment or a charge) to operating managers and the responsibility for collecting or disbursing funds to accounting personnel.

2. Adequate written records and accounting systems document the actual use of assets. The software used in automated systems must conform to FASB accounting rules.

3. Special attention is paid to collections and cashiering. Significant efforts must be made to ensure that third parties and individuals pay promptly and fully. Payment in cash and checks must be protected against embezzlement. Carefully designed systems to ensure prompt collection and protect receivables and cash rely heavily on the principle of division of functions and on calculations designed to verify completion of transactions.

4. Adherence to risk-control procedures and documentation requirements is monitored through internal auditors.

5. The independence of the internal auditor can be ensured by arranging reporting directly to the chair of the board audit committee.

6. Annual outside audits verify adherence to procedure and validity of reported outcome.

Inurement, Fraud, and Abuse

Not-for-profit structure requires no individual benefit from service to the corporation beyond any stipulated salary or compensation. Inurement is the diversion of funds to persons in governance or management as a result of their position of trust. Under these rules, directors, officers, or trustees are prohibited from engaging in business that allows them to derive financial advantage from their governing board role. The corporation is not enjoined from doing business with a board member, if such business and board membership are in the owners' interests. Thus, the key word is "advantage."

To protect against inurement, the institution must establish, and the internal auditor must enforce, policies that reduce financial conflict of interest. These policies have two parts. First, every governing board member and officer is required to file an annual disclosure statement that identifies all their financial interests and potentially conflicting commitments, including membership on other voluntary boards. Second, members are expected to divorce themselves from any specific decision or action that involves their interests or conflicting affiliations. Well-run organizations achieve this by making the point well in advance of any specific application and by selecting members who understand both the law and the ethics.

The rule applies as well to physicians, but its application is more complex. Physicians cannot benefit beyond specified benefits of privilege to avoid inurement and specific prohibitions (called *fraud and abuse*). All physician contracts must be reviewed for compliance (Chapter 6). Many organizations have an independent compliance officer who is assigned responsibility for the review. The compliance officer should also report independently to the governing board, and his or her activity should be subject to internal audit.

External Audits

Outside auditors certify the financial statements to be correct, usually on a fiscal-year basis. The federal government requires an audit as a condition of participation for Medicare, and many intermediaries have similar requirements. Lenders require annual audits before and during the period of any loan. The external audit is less extensive than the internal, although it now typically includes an assessment of the internal audit. It emphasizes areas of known high risk.

Sampling techniques are commonly used in auditing, with attention focused in proportion to the risk involved. Auditors are expected to maintain a deliberate distance from internal employees being audited, including the internal auditors, and to use objective methods to ascertain the accuracy of reported values for balance sheet items. They are also expected to review accounting processes and to suggest changes that will improve accounting accuracy.

The governing board selects the outside auditors, receives their report and reviews it carefully, and takes action to correct any deficiencies noted. Considerable care in selecting and instructing the auditor is justified.[22] The auditor should be accountable directly to the board's finance committee. The firm should be free of any other financial relationship to the organization. This means that consultants should not be hired from the same firm handling the audit. It is unacceptable to use a firm that is represented on the governing board.

The audit committee of the governing board includes the independent trustees who serve as chair, finance chair, treasurer, or secretary of the board. It may consult with, but should not include, employed associates. The committee formulates instructions to the auditor, revising them annually. The revisions can bring different aspects of the asset-protection system under scrutiny each year. The instructions should be based in part on advice from management but should be confidential between the finance committee and the auditor.

The auditor's report goes directly to the audit committee. Thus, the auditors are free to comment on all levels of management. The auditors' comments on both problems with the accounts and weaknesses identified in the asset-protection policies are included in a document called the management letter, which accompanies the audited financial reports. The audit committee should hear an oral summary and discussion of the management letter. The full board should formally accept both the reports and the letter. The expectation for the management letter is "no deficiencies," and it is usually achieved. Well-run HCOs have little trouble with this system. The success of this system assures all stakeholders of truth and equity, removing those concerns from negotiations.

Continuous Improvement of the Accounting and Finance Functions

In addition to its role managing the financial resources of the HCO, the finance activity is a critical component of evidence-based management, constantly supplying routine and special reports and managing the goal-setting process. It must pursue continuous improvement of all its activities, using its operational performance measures (discussion below) and listening responsively to its many clients.

People

Various professional and skilled personnel work in the finance system of even a small HCO. Many of these people perform tasks that are indistinguishable from those in any other corporation, while others perform tasks that require extensive familiarity with healthcare. On-the-job training is often practical at lower levels, but supervisory people now usually have advanced degrees in accounting or finance.

Professional personnel with healthcare experience are often in short supply. There is a chronic shortage of chief financial officers (CFOs). Recruitment should always be national, health-specific knowledge should be highly prized, and the governing board should be directly involved in the CFO selection. Job specifications for a CFO tend not to depend on the size of the organization. Sustaining qualified, professional financial management in small organizations is a severe problem, one that may underlie more mergers and contract management than is recognized. Contract financial management is available through firms that provide general management.

Chief Financial Officer

The CFO is accountable for the operation of the finance systems, including the financial management functions, and advises the CEO and the governing board on finance issues. The CFO or a deputy also assumes the duties of an employed treasurer in commercial corporations, collections, disbursement, asset control, and management of debt and equity. The HCO treasurer is frequently a trustee who serves principally as chair of the finance committee.

The CFO of a well-run HCO should have substantial experience that includes exposure to the finance systems of several organizations, familiarity with all functions of the finance system, experience with debt management, and demonstrated ability to assist operating management. Evidence of technical skill is important and can be supported both by specimens of work and by references. Evidence of interpersonal skills—particularly the ability to work with people outside the finance department—is also important and can be supported by references. The credentials for a CFO usually include a master's degree in management or business and may include certification as a public accountant. The larger public accounting firms often assist in finding CFOs and, not surprisingly, are also a major source of supply. The recruitment team should include senior management, senior physician management, and governing board representation.

Other Professional Personnel

The functions of finance and accounting require substantial technical knowledge. The leaders of the activity should have experience in the areas where they are accountable. Specialty certification is available. The Healthcare Financial Management Association provides a professional examination. The Certified Public Accountant examination is required for external auditors, and popular among HCO financial managers;[23] the examination includes mastery of FASB requirements. Certification is also available for managerial accounting.[24] The Institute of Internal Auditors offers training programs.[25]

Organization of the Finance System

Within the Finance Unit The organization of the finance system is dictated by its functions and has been thoroughly codified, in part because of the use of separation of activities to protect assets. Budgeting, cost accounting, financial management, and auditing require relatively small numbers of people, with the largest numbers of personnel being in various aspects of patient accounting and collections. Exhibit 13.10 shows a typical organization pattern.

Relation of Finance to Operations Almost every part of the organization shown in Exhibit 13.10 is in direct daily contact with the rest of the HCO, often over sensitive matters. The key to success is maintaining a professional, productive level of exchange. Clear, convenient systems and forms make routine information gathering as efficient as possible. Orientation and training sessions for finance personnel at all levels help them understand clinical procedures and participate in continuous improvement projects. Well-designed processes and training in consensus building make the interactions effective. It should be universally understood that operating management is responsible for setting, achieving, and departing from expectations. Finance personnel provide data and interpret them; they do not enforce budget discipline.

Relation of Finance to the Governing Board The finance system relates directly to the governing board through the finance committee, and the CFO often represents the senior management team on the committee. Provision must be made for executive session of the committee, meeting without members employed by the HCO. Reports from the internal and external auditors should first be received in executive session.

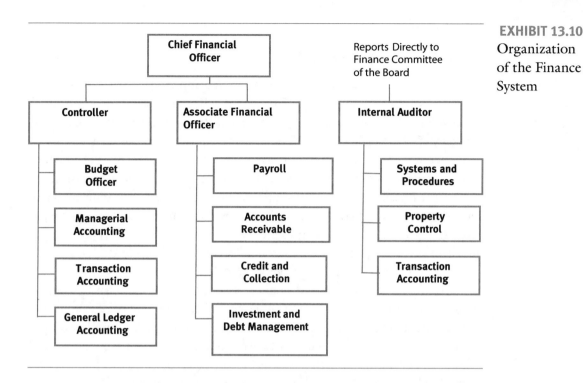

EXHIBIT 13.10
Organization
of the Finance
System

In this and preceding chapters, several tasks have been specifically identified for the finance committee of the board:

- Assist in selecting the CFO
- Annually review the LRFP and recommend the final version to the full board
- Recommend the budget guidelines to the full board
- Recommend pricing policies to the full board
- Review the proposed annual budget, and recommend it to the full board
- Set the final priorities, and recommend the capital and new programs budget to the board
- Receive the monthly or quarterly report that compares operations to expectations
- Support the audit committee, supervising both the internal and external audits
- Review major capital expenditure and financing proposals

This list explains why membership on the finance committee is time consuming and intellectually demanding. Members are important at meetings of the full board as well, and overlapping appointments or joint meetings with the planning committee occur. In addition, the finance committee has routine obligations to approve the HCO's banks and financial contracts, real estate transactions, and contracts over predetermined amounts. The list can easily fill 10 or 12 fast-paced meetings each year. Virtually the entire staff work for the finance committee is prepared by finance personnel.

Measures

Quantitative Performance Measures

The finance activity must be measured using appropriate parts of the operational scorecard, with negotiated goals, benchmarks, and continuous improvement. These measures are entirely different from measuring the organization's financial position. The organization as a whole, not just its finance activity, must be accountable for the financial performance. The finance team is accountable for its operational goals. As for all support activities, the goals must be carefully set, with emphasis on the level of service necessary to support finance's customers. Effectiveness is more important than efficiency. Overemphasizing efficiency presents serious dangers; underperformance in the finance and accounting functions is often difficult to detect and can mount to millions of lost dollars before it is detected.

Costs of accounting and finance, associate satisfaction, and customer satisfaction are measured as in all other activities. The quality of accounting and finance services requires a thorough understanding, but a number of useful measures can be collected and benchmarked. Many of them are derived from financial ratios—relative measures constructed from the financial reports. Measures of demand and output are often problematic. Unlike patient ledger accounting, where the numbers of postings and accounts maintained allow a productivity calculation that can be benchmarked, financial reporting, auditing, and managerial accounting have no readily accessible unit cost. Exhibit 13.11 shows the array of operational measures that can be used to identify OFIs, negotiate goals, and achieve continuous improvement.

Subjective Quality Assessment

As with the governing board, additional insights into OFIs can be gained by systematic collection of opinions. Opinions from associates in the finance committee, internal and external auditors, and customers can be revealing and constructive. Outside consultants can also review performance. The LRFP, other financial analyses, and the budgeting process are particularly likely to benefit from these subjective assessments.

The following are subjectively evaluated criteria met by successful organizations:

- The LRFP, analytic report, or budget package is clear, concise, internally consistent, and consistent with external realities.
- Assumptions and their implications are specified.
- Prudent and reasonable sources have been used to develop external trends, and a variety of opinion has been reviewed whenever possible.
- The plan or report develops contingencies on major, unpredictable future events.

Area and Examples		Goal	Benchmark
Demand Only a few functions—most notably patient ledger accounting—have usable measures of demand		Timely completion of transactions	Rarely available
Cost Number of personnel and labor costs for functions or accountability units		Fully meet customer needs without excess cost	Rarely available
Associate satisfaction Satisfaction, absenteeism, and retention		Retention of all qualified associates	Provided by survey companies
Output and productivity		See *Demand*	Rarely available
Quality			
Current assets and liabilities	Financial ratios for cash and receivables Earnings from short-term liquid assets Days in receivables Short-term borrowing amounts and cost	Minimize cost of current assets and current liabilities, subject to contractual obligations	Ratios, earnings, days, and short-term debt costs can be benchmarked
Long-term assets and liabilities	Endowment earnings Debt service cost, age of plant, and investments in replacement and new technology	Maintain competitive services for patients and associates	Ratios can be benchmarked
Financial and managerial reports	Internal and external audit reports	Zero defect	Not applicable
Analytic and consultative services	User complaints and corrections Post hoc accuracy of forecasts Service delays Comparison to external consultants	Events must be individually evaluated	Not applicable
Customer satisfaction Surveys of user satisfaction		Develop loyal internal customers	User satisfaction can be benchmarked

EXHIBIT 13.11
Operational Measures of Finance and Accounting

- Unexpected events that require modification are unforeseen by competitors and other external sources.
- The plan or report is well received by knowledgeable board members and outsiders such as consultants, bond rating agencies, and investment bankers.

Similar subjective criteria for all finance and accounting functions are available in textbooks and from consultants.

Managerial Issues

Supporting Integrity in All Financial Areas

The preeminent managerial role is the discipline to ensure that all the financial functions are fully achieved, creating an atmosphere of honesty and transparency. These functions are unusually susceptible to human failings—denial, avoidance, neglect, deliberate subversion or falsification, and greed. There is a constant risk that the organization will let some matters slide, particularly when addressing them is likely to be unpleasant. The governing board and its audit committee are the first line of defense against this tendency. They must provide full and visible support for the internal and external audit functions, including support for their independence and unique reporting relationship to governance. Senior management must accept the challenge as well. The culture must support effective action on identified issues, avoid blame for honest error, and reward individuals who raise hard questions. Any threat to the integrity of the assets or the information must be promptly and forcefully addressed. This level of discipline is essential not simply to ensure integrity but also to reassure all associates and suppliers that their own actions will not be undercut by fraud, distortion, or even carelessness. Contracts will be fulfilled. The data will be reliable. Gaming will not be tolerated.

Maintaining a Collegial, Blame-Free Culture

The functions of finance and accounting are so widespread that interaction between finance and other managers is almost constant. If the finance activity is well managed, those interchanges must be perceived by other managers as constructive. Finance personnel must be seen as contributors and colleagues. They have traditionally been viewed too often as adversaries or enforcers. In large part, building constructive relationships is a matter of training and modeling. Finance personnel can be trained to fulfill Sharp HealthCare's 12 behavioral standards and five "Must Haves" (Chapter 2) as well as any associate. The CFO and the finance leadership must understand, implement, and model those behaviors.

Managing Areas at Risk for Conflict

In a disciplined and collegial culture, many of the potential conflicts arise from differences in perspective. Finance has done its job as it sees it; operations managers either do not understand or see it differently. Prompt resolution is essential. The usual tools—listening, further data gathering and analysis, negotiation, counseling, process revision, and retraining—are appropriate. It is rarely necessary to go beyond them to disciplinary action. Potential conflicts are commonplace in the following areas. Experienced managers become familiar with applying these solutions and can teach them by mentoring and example.

Revenue accounting is a common source of conflict. Service line managers want the largest possible income from each case, and much income is controlled by the diagnostic codes assigned. Assigning incorrect codes to increase severity (*upcoding*) is illegal and should be monitored by both internal and external audit. Assigning too few codes or understating the severity of disease is wrong as well, but the fact that the treating physician must attest to the codes under threat of criminal charge causes many physicians to understate severity. The solution is in diagnostic coding assistance, including analysis of diagnostic and treatment orders to ensure capture of all treated diseases. The solution also includes reassurance to the treating physicians. If the audit mechanisms and the criteria for adding diagnoses are understood and reliable, if specific queries are thoroughly discussed and evaluated, physicians will be confident and satisfied. Management's job is to see that both conditions are fully met.

Financial Accounting

Certain elements of the financial reports—such as allowances for bad debts, reserves for changes in payment from large third parties, reserves for financial restructuring, and reserves for employee pensions—must be estimated. The estimates are subjective and can be deliberately varied within FASB limits to affect net income. In intercorporate accounting, allocations for indirect costs are also subjective. Deliberate distortion beyond FASB limits or for individual gain (such as the distortion of profits to ensure incentive payments to management) is illegal. Well-managed organizations use consistent rules for these transactions. They include these rules in contracts with subsidiaries, and audit the contracts to ensure compliance.

The elements of the cost data routinely reported from general ledger transactions, like depreciation costs, charges for central services, and allocated costs, are always a source of contention. Operations managers deserve assurance that the charges are given the same level of scrutiny and rigorous control that their direct costs receive. Senior management should show:

Managerial Accounting

1. Costs of generating these services are accurately accounted and benchmarked.
2. Wherever practical, the best possible source of service is selected. This means that outside vendors are used where appropriate.
3. Transfer prices are used whenever feasible. Transfer prices give using managers control over quantity and can be compared easily to outside vendors.

4. Allocated costs are used only when necessary and are based on fair, reasonable, and consistent allocations.

5. Specific complaints are addressed promptly and thoroughly, and indicated changes are implemented.

Managerial accounting is also used extensively in performance improvement, to model alternative solutions. These applications are often complex technical exercises. The managerial role is to see that all members of the performance improvement team are comfortable with the assumptions and analyses and understand the implications of the findings. This is usually a matter of clear reporting by the analysts, adequate discussion, and thoughtful response to questions. The operations managers' perspective can lead to important improvements in the modeling. Sensitive response to their questions increases their confidence in the results. (Note that the goal is less ambitious than "understand the analysis." People today comfortably use complex technology that they do not fully understand.)

Goal Setting   Setting the annual goals is never easy. The exercise is designed to force the organization to consider the demands of customer stakeholders, and it is inevitably stressful. Three major activities distinguish excellence:

1. *The budget technology is carefully established.* The packages are fully described and understood by operations managers. Calculations are computerized, allowing managers to focus on the decisions rather than on paperwork. The best organizations train managers in how to use the software to explore the implications of various answers. Hands-on training, support from superiors, and mentoring from experienced peers help first-line managers master their roles.[26]

2. *The board's guidelines are clearly explained.* Each manager understands why the guidelines are important, how they were established, and how they are extrapolated from the organization as a whole to his or her unit. Because all members of the team should understand the guidelines, the manager should be able to explain them to others.

3. *The negotiations to reach the budget should be considerate, fair, and realistic.* This inevitably means that some units that are doing well will be challenged to excel, while others that are struggling are given extra support.

Financial Planning   The assumptions are the critical element of financial planning. Results from the LRFP models are often sensitive to small changes in forecasts for demand and prices of patient services and for costs of purchased items. Because they are forecasts, there is no "right" answer. Management should insist on three specific protections:

1. Forecasts are obtained from respected and unbiased sources if available.

2. An effort is made to obtain alternate forecasts.

3. Sensitivity analysis is used in the model to test the impact of alternative forecasts, and the implications of the results are fully discussed.

The implication of these protections is that *ceteris paribus* extrapolations are not enough; critical variables must be thoroughly understood and carefully forecast.

Suggested Readings

Cleverley, W. O., and A. E. Cameron. 2007. *Essentials of Health Care Finance*, 6th ed. Sudbury, MA: Jones & Bartlett Publishers.

Finkler, S. A., D. M. Ward, and J. J. Baker. 2007. *Essentials of Cost Accounting for Health Care Organizations*, 3rd ed. Sudbury MA: Jones & Bartlett Publishers.

Gapenski, L. C. 2009. *Fundamentals of Healthcare Finance*. Chicago: Health Administration Press.

Nowicki, M. 2007. *The Financial Management of Hospitals and Healthcare Organizations*, 4th ed. Chicago: Health Administration Press.

Young, D. W. 2008. *Management Accounting in Health Care Organizations*, 2nd ed. San Francisco: Jossey-Bass.

Notes

1. Centers for Medicare & Medicaid Services. 2009. [Online information; retrieved 5/5/09.] www.hhs.gov/ocr/privacy/index.html.
2. U.S. Internal Revenue Service. [Online information; retrieved 5/22/09.] www.irs.gov/pub/irs-pdf/i990sh.pdf.
3. Prince, T. R. 1992. *Financial Reporting and Cost Control for Health Care Entities*, 89–378. Chicago: Health Administration Press.
4. Cooper, R., and R. S. Kaplan. 1988. "Measure Costs Right: Make the Right Decisions." *Harvard Business Review* 66 (4): 98–106.
5. Player, S. 1998. "Activity-Based Analyses Lead to Better Decision Making." *Healthcare Financial Management* 52 (8): 66–70.
6. Baker, J. J. 1995. "Activity-Based Costing for Integrated Delivery Systems." *Journal of Health Care Finance* 22 (2): 57–61.
7. Finkler, S. A., D. M. Ward, and J. J. Baker. 2007. *Essentials of Cost Accounting for Health Care Organizations*, 3rd ed., 83–97. Sudbury, MA: Jones & Bartlett.
8. Griffith, J. R., and K. R. White. 2003. *Thinking Forward: Six Strategies for Highly Successful Organizations*, 87–117, 153–55.Chicago: Health Administration Press.
9. Voss, G. B., P. G. Limpens, L. J. Brans-Brabant, and A. van Ooij. 1997. "Cost-Variance Analysis by DRGs: A Technique for Clinical Budget Analysis." *Health Policy* 39 (2): 153–66.
10. Berman, H. J., and L. E. Weeks. 1993. *The Financial Management of Hospitals*, 8th ed., 385–585. Chicago: Health Administration Press.
11. Cote, M. J., and S. L. Tucker. 2001. "Four Methodologies to Improve Healthcare Demand Forecasting." *Healthcare Financial Management* 55 (5): 54–58.
12. Abernethy, M. A., and J. U. Stoelwinder. 1991. "Budget Use, Task Uncertainty, System Goal Orientation and Sub-Unit Performance: A Test of the 'Fit'

Hypothesis in Not-for-Profit Hospitals." *Accounting Organizations and Society* 16 (2): 105–20.

13. Swieringa, R. J., and R. H. Moncur. 1975. *Some Effects of Participative Budgeting on Managerial Behavior.* New York: National Association of Accountants.

14. Clarke, R. L. 2007. "Price Transparency: Building Community Trust." *Frontiers of Health Services Management* 23 (3): 3–12.

15. Lindrooth, R. C. 2008. "Research on the Hospital Market: Recent Advances and Continuing Data Needs." *Inquiry* 45 (1): 19–29.

16. Jencks, S. F., M. V. Williams, and E. A. Coleman. 2009. "Rehospitalizations Among Patients in the Medicare Fee-for-Service Program." *New England Journal of Medicine* 360 (14): 1418–28.

17. Davis, K., and S. Guterman. 2007. "Rewarding Excellence and Efficiency in Medicare Payments." *Milbank Quarterly* 85 (3): 449–68.

18. Cleverley, W. O., and J. O. Cleverley. 2008. "10 Myths of Strategic Pricing." *Healthcare Financial Management* 62 (5): 82–87.

19. Carlson, J. 2008. "It's All Downhill from Here: What Started as a Year of Optimism Has Turned into What Some Describe as a Supertough Economic Situation Despite Contrary Reports." *Modern Healthcare* 38 (46): 6–7, 14.

20. Reiter, K. L., J. R. C. Wheeler, and D. G. Smith. 2008. "Liquidity Constraints on Hospital Investment When Credit Markets Are Tight." *Journal of Health Care Finance* 35 (1): 24–33, 29.

21. Wheeler, J. R., D. G. Smith, H. L. Rivenson, and K. L. Reiter. 2000. "Capital Structure Strategy in Health Care Systems." *Journal of Health Care Finance* 26 (4): 42–52.

22. Reinstein, A., and R. W. Luecke. 2001. "AICPA Standard Can Help Improve Audit Committee Performance." *Healthcare Financial Management* 55 (8): 56–60.

23. The Uniform CPA Examination. [Online information; retrieved 5/22/09.] www.cpa-exam.org.

24. The Certified Management Accountant Program. [Online information; retrieved 5/22/09.] www.netexpress.net/~ima/cma.htm.

25. The Institute of Internal Auditors. [Online information; retrieved 5/22/09.] www.theiia.org.

26. Griffith and White (2003), 164–65.

14 INTERNAL CONSULTING

In a Few Words

The internal consulting activity supplies essential knowledge for evidence-based management. It is a clearinghouse for any factual need of the healthcare organization (HCO). It completes an annual environmental assessment and maintains ongoing epidemiologic planning, benchmarking, and statistical analysis. It facilitates legal, regulatory, and ethical review. It responds to all requests by the process improvement team (PIT). It trains PIT members; conducts specific analyses and forecasts; and assists in evaluating alternatives, capital requests, and strategic proposals. It manages change implementation and works to ensure capture of expected benefits.

The internal consulting activity must have accountable senior management leadership, operational performance measures, and its own improvement function. Internal consulting should adequately support HCO-wide improvement. It must earn its costs by the value of performance improvements. An increase in expenditures must be justified by increased value of improvements. Internal consulting must maintain objectivity and empower the PITs and planning teams to make final decisions.

Critical Issues in Internal Consulting

1. *Maintaining and interpreting factual information that describes the community served:*
   - Identify population, economic, healthcare, and competitor trends
   - Plan for service and workforce requirements

2. *Obtaining useful benchmarks and best practices:*
   - Interpret statistical data
   - Help operators identify improvable variation

3. *Providing PITs, planning teams, senior management, and governance with timely and effective knowledge-based support*

4. *Identifying, evaluating, selecting, and implementing new programs and capital investments that yield returns in improved performance*

Consider these questions as you read the chapter.

1. Identify a specific community with at least one moderate-sized HCO. Consider the events important to the HCO in the last few years. What were they? How far in advance could they have been foreseen by the governing board? When and how might they have been introduced in the annual environmental assessment? How can you use this knowledge to specify what is important to look for in the future?

2. The operating room supervisor asks internal consulting what to do about demand he is not able to meet. What should internal consulting offer as a plan for developing a solution?

3. If you were planning an initial discussion about goal setting and capital budgeting for newly appointed first-line supervisors, what topics would you include?

4. Review the control chart on caesarian sections (Exhibit 14.6). The obstetrics service notes that they successfully reduced the mean rate 21 months ago and that the remaining variation is well within the usual definition of a controlled process, which is that no report exceeds 3 sigma control limits. Therefore, they say, no opportunity for improvement (OFI) can be found on caesarian sections. The chief medical officer wants to know what further investigation is appropriate before she accepts this as a valid conclusion.

5. An economic recession has increased charity care and bad debts from 4 percent to 6 percent of net revenues. The board asks for "all possible" cost reductions, and one board member notes that the internal consulting activity "consumes more than $1 million a year. Surely we could defer that." What arguments and data would you assemble to support continuing this activity?

Under evidence-based management, the governing board, senior management, performance improvement teams, and planning task forces all need technical support to improve the quality of complex decisions. This support comes from all of the logistic and strategic activities. Internal consulting coordinates support for these clients, drawing on its own and other resources and focusing on its clients' need to understand future environments.

Purpose

The purpose of the internal consulting operation is

> **to provide information, forecasts, tools, and analyses in support of evidence-based management.**

Under evidence-based management, the most critical operating decisions are analyzed by PITs and planning teams, who are charged with systematic investigation of opportunities, issues, and alternatives. Strategic decisions—fundamental questions about the future of the enterprise—are analyzed by the senior management team for the governing board. The ideal is to make these operating and strategic decisions in such a way that even with complete hindsight, none would be changed. All real organizations fall short, but well-managed organizations come closer than others. They thrive because they collect information exhaustively, forecast carefully, apply tools appropriately, and conduct analyses that allow them to identify the best alternatives. Those are the skills of internal consulting. PITs, planning teams, senior management, and the governing board are internal consulting's clients.

Functions

The questions raised by internal consulting clients arise from the dynamic relationship of the HCO to its stakeholders and from specific proposals for the future. The answers can require input from any logistic or strategic support activity and, in some situations, specific medical and nursing advice. All answers require forecasting—extrapolation to future environments. Internal consulting must coordinate its own resources, those from other units, and external resources to answer those questions as accurately as possible.

The internal consulting functions shown in Exhibit 14.1 emphasize information assembly, analysis, and integration. They divide the work of internal consulting somewhat arbitrarily into projects for the HCO as a whole, for PITs, and for capital investment proposals. The "any other factual concern" function establishes both the unit's universal breadth and its critical limitation to fact-finding rather than decision making. Internal consulting establishes the facts. Its clients decide the HCO's future.

EXHIBIT 14.1
Functions
of Internal
Consulting

Function	Description	Examples
Supporting the organization as a whole		
Environmental assessment	Annual review of changes and trends that affect future performance	Trends in population size, age, and health insurance coverage
Community-based epidemiologic planning	Forecast of community demographics and disease incidence	Trends in births and high-cost diseases Forecasting physician supply
Benchmarking and identifying best practice	Search for external expertise on clinical or other technical topics	Clinical protocols Collaboratives Environmental control
Statistical analysis	Refinement of data to remove extraneous variation; forecasting; statistical process control	Rates adjusted for patient characteristics Correlation Statistical significance
Legal, regulatory, and ethical review	Compliance with guidelines, regulations, court decisions, and the HCO's own values	Federal and state regulatory requirements Cultural competence
Supporting improvement projects		
Increasing effectiveness of process improvement teams	Training in process analysis Direct consultation Outside consultants	Lean and Six Sigma analyses Assistance in process redesign Assistance in pilot trials
Process modeling	Identifying implications of proposed work processes	Cost–benefit analyses Simulations Staffing models
Evaluating and testing alternative solutions	Design of pilots and sensitivity analyses	Reliability tests Worst-case scenarios
Supporting governance	Identifying and evaluating major new services and forms of organization	Mergers and acquisitions New service lines Revised corporate structures
Supporting the capital investment review		
Assisting operating units to identify and prioritize capital opportunities	Identifying competitive proposals and improvements in operating scorecards	Replacing equipment Expanding clinic locations Adding diagnostic services
Developing formal capital requests	Specifying changes in equipment, facilities, and work processes	Documenting renovation needs Forecasting new cost and quality performance
Implementing and integrating		
Implementing and integrating new programs	Coordinating multi-unit changes in facilities, equipment, or work processes	Monitoring new equipment installation Managing new construction Achieving proposal goals
Responding to any other factual concern relevant to the HCO's continued success		
Improving internal consulting and the continuous improvement process		

As shown in Exhibit 14.2, internal consulting has five major vehicles for helping its clients:

1. *Immediate reply.* Many questions require only a short answer, brief discussion, or short follow-up message.
2. *Just-in-time support.* Internal consulting can arrange training or a specific service, including calling on other logistic and support services. For example, the HCO's electrical power manager can consult on new equipment needs.
3. *Designated team member.* Internal consulting can assign one of its staff to participate with the PIT, identifying, clarifying, and arranging fulfillment of PIT needs.
4. *Internal consulting project team.* For complex questions, a team of internal experts can be assembled. Members can come from any part of the HCO. The project team for a proposed clinical service line might include expertise in medicine, nursing, epidemiology, accounting, finance, law, and marketing. The team differs from the initial PIT in the nature of the charge. It is fact-finding; the PIT is charged with a recommendation.
5. *External consultants.* Even a large HCO does not have specialists in every field, and small ones can afford only the most limited internal consulting. Internal and external resources can be combined as well. The internal consulting manager can help select, instruct, and coordinate outside consultants.

The approach outlined in Exhibit 14.2 has four important advantages:

1. It provides every client with a point of contact for technical support.
2. It clearly establishes the client's customer position and gives the client final say over the adequacy of the advice and the process.
3. It has two important feedback loops to ensure timely but thorough service.
4. It allows the internal consulting manager to minimize cost and delay by judicious use of the initial conversation, just-in-time opportunities, and coordination of resources.

It also has three important consequences:

1. *Any clinical, logistic, or strategic support activity that can contribute to the client's issue must respond to the internal consulting call.* Knowledge management, human resources, environment services, accounting, and marketing can expect to contribute frequently to PITs. Internal consulting serves to coordinate and integrate these contributions.
2. *Internal consulting controls all outside consulting contracts.* This allows careful selection of vendor, effective management of the engagement, and full use of less expensive internal resources.
3. *Decision making is assigned to the client.* Internal consulting does not decide. It focuses on the factual foundation needed for evidence-based decisions.

EXHIBIT 14.2

Internal
Consulting as a
Clearinghouse

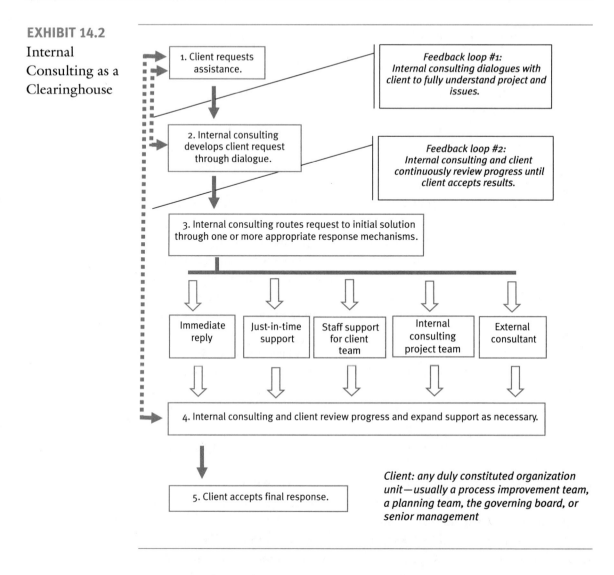

Supporting the Organization as a Whole

In high-performing HCOs, internal consulting provides or coordinates services that support the ongoing activities of governance and management. The major applications are in environmental assessment, the epidemiologic planning model, benchmarking and best practices, statistical analysis, and various legal and ethical reviews, but the commitment to meeting client needs often aggregates these processes and calls on additional sources.

Environmental Assessment

Healthcare organizations reduce risk and uncertainty through scanning activities to forecast expected environmental conditions and design responsive futures.[1] Internal consulting assembles an annual environmental assessment, supporting a detailed quantitative analysis with a written summary highlighting critical changes and opportunities. In addition to the quantitative analysis—and just as important—is the analysis of qualitative information from boundary spanning activities. The report is widely circulated among the HCO leadership and provides background information for many PITs and planning activities.

Good environmental assessment takes into account the following:

- *Community demography, epidemiology, and economy.* A thorough quantitative description of the market being served, identification of all major trends in demographics and disease incidence, and forecasts to the future are essential to the environmental assessment.
- *Patient and community attitudes.* Trends in total purchases of healthcare, sites of care, sources of payment, satisfaction with care, and market share should be reported with material changes highlighted. Patient surveys, complaints, and household surveys are trended and benchmarked. Many important topics must be reported qualitatively. Results from listening, focus groups, direct interviews, and related sources should be summarized in a brief report.
- *Health insurance buyer intentions and health insurance trends.* Trends, prices, and market share of the various insurance products must be examined and forecast to develop a complete perspective. The willingness of employers, unions, and governments to pay for care, and the terms they expect to use for payment generally cannot be quantified, but realistic estimates and a detailed understanding of buyer interests are critical. While state and national trends are important, the view of local groups on key matters such as services, debt, price, and amenities is often the final determinant of planning and financial strategy.
- *Trends in clinical practice.* Technology and the attitudes of practitioners and patients interact to create demands for new services and new modes of delivery. In the 1980s, for example, patients began to prefer outpatient over inpatient care. At the same time, technology supported rapid growth in complex procedures like cardiac catheterization, *in vitro* fertilization, and orthopedic joint replacements. The growth of many changes like these can be forecast using the epidemiologic planning model. Even describing those that cannot be quantitatively forecast improves decision making.
- *Associate attitudes and capabilities.* Trends in the skills and attitudes of current employees, physicians, and volunteers are important background to planning decisions. Formal surveys are now routinely administered. Compensation levels for major groups should be forecast. Most organizations gain additional insights through focus groups and listening activities.
- *Trends in physician supply and organization.* The number of physicians in practice in the community, by specialty and other characteristics, is a critical indicator of both cost and quality of care. The number and level of affiliation with the HCO determines market share. A database is maintained to support physician-organization planning functions (described in Chapter 6).
- *Trends in other health worker supply.* Well-managed institutions forecast their need for professional associates of all kinds. The lead time allows them to adapt

to shortages and surpluses, using advance warning to plan workforce recruitment or reduction.

The planning unit is accountable for a thorough and current database of all of these elements and a written annual review that highlights important trends and developments. It should also be accountable for reporting and, where possible, integrating insights or beliefs regarding future trends offered by members of governance and senior management.

Community-Based Epidemiologic Planning

Internal consulting is the *source of truth* for demographic, disease incidence, and market demand data. It maintains the databases that support epidemiologic planning (see Chapter 3 and applications in many subsequent chapters). It works with clients to prepare multiyear forecasts of demand for clinical and other services. It produces short- and long-run forecasts for a number of measures derived from clinical demand, such as employment, traffic, and supplies. The forecasts are used in strategic positioning (Chapter 15), the development of facility and service plans, and the construction of expectations for the next budget year.

The reliability of the forecasts and the interpretive advice available are critical elements in long-term success of the organization. Important forecasts should be offered with **sensitivity analysis**, exploration of the implications of alternative assumptions about the future. Competent interpretation includes ranges for estimates of incidence rates, advice on specification alternatives, and translation to resource requirements that help operators understand the dynamics of productivity and the uncertainty of forecasts. The epidemiologic planning model is available from national consulting services. The input data requirements are difficult to replicate, even for a large healthcare system. The calculation and presentation software make construction of forecasts, sensitivity analysis, and exploration of alternative scenarios quick and easy. An in-house capability is necessary to retrieve and trend internal data. It also becomes an important resource of expertise on the local situation.

Sensitivity analysis
Analysis of the impact of alternative forecasts, usually developing most favorable, expected, and least favorable scenarios to show the robustness of a proposal and to indicate the degree of risk involved

Benchmarking and Identifying Best Practice

A high-performing HCO needs thousands of benchmarks, and they are not easy to find. Internal consulting provides an expert who knows criteria for evidence and common sources, and who can help clients select benchmarks and improve them. Benchmarking requires standard definitions of the measure being benchmarked. Benchmarking should include finding the best practice for a process. The benchmark data identify the best practice; the organization achieving benchmark is often willing to share its procedures and insights in return for reciprocity. Benchmarks are frequently hierarchical—"best in HCO," "best in system," "best in nation," and "world class." Ranking allows celebration of gains as they occur, but the opportunities for improvement are still clear.

Multihospital systems develop benchmarks for their members. The Centers for Medicare & Medicaid Services (CMS) now provides Hospital Compare data. Commercial companies and consultants offer a variety of cost and quality data sets. National satisfaction surveys include comparative data with their reports. Some comparison sources are voluntary networks that also share best practices. Several successful systems promote direct relationships between associates with similar assignments, forming networks of nurses, purchasing agents, and so forth.[2] Clinical collaboratives, such as those run by the Institute for Healthcare Improvement, offer a way to learn by sharing experiences.[3] Internal consulting assists by collecting the available alternatives and helping the client understand the differences between current and best practice.

Statistical Analysis

Data from the data warehouse and external sources support performance monitoring; the annual environmental assessment; and forecasts that evaluate process improvement proposals, investment opportunities, and make-or-buy decisions. Statistical analysis is essential for all of these applications to identify and deal with sources of variation. A good performance measure removes as much as possible the variation caused by factors outside the associates' control. A good forecast identifies underlying sources of change and incorporates them.

Operating team members and PIT members should be confident of the data in their reports. The question, "How do I know these numbers are realistic?" deserves an honest, reassuring, and technically correct answer. The statistical techniques used to get those answers are increasingly sophisticated and should be carried out or reviewed by a professionally trained statistician. The analysis identifies external causes of variation, specifies their impact, adjusts measures to allow for them, and includes them in forecasts.

Identifying External Causes of Variation

Many elements of both clinical and logistic processes are beyond the control of HCOs and their teams. When measures of these processes are used in evidence-based management, the goals should reflect only factors within the team members' control. When measures are forecast, changes in external factors must be included. External causes are identified from the literature or by statistical test and accommodated by specification, adjustment, and carefully designed forecasting models.

Specification

The process of specification identifies external groups whose performance differs. In marketing, specification is called "segmentation" (Chapter 15). It examines whether specific groups differ in performance characteristics. Specification usually follows established taxonomies, or ways of subdividing populations. Exhibits 14.3, 14.4, and 14.5 show common taxonomies for specifying patients, payers, and providers.

Statistical analysis evaluates the need for specification and designs specifications for individual measures. For example, the frequency of heart

EXHIBIT 14.3
Patient-
Oriented
Specification
Taxonomies

Category	Classifications
Demographic	Age Sex Race Education
Economic	Income Employment Social class
Geographic	Zip code of residence Census tract Political subdivision
Healthcare finance	Managed versus traditional insurance Private versus government insurance
Diagnosis	Disease classification Procedure Diagnosis-related group Ambulatory patient group
Risk	Health behavlor attrlbute Pre-existing condition Chronic or high-cost disease

EXHIBIT 14.3 Patient-Oriented Specification Taxonomies

EXHIBIT 14.4 Insurance Intermediary and Employer Specification Taxonomies

Category	Classifications
Employers	Size Geographic location Industry Ownership Income level Union organization Health insurance benefit Health insurance type
Intermediary	Health insurance type Ownership or corporate structure Size Number of health insurance subscribers Employer groups covered

attacks differs by a number in the Exhibit 14.3 characteristics. The epidemiologic planning model uses most of these characteristics to forecast incidence. The population is broken down by its demographic, economic, and health behavior subgroups, and a forecast is prepared for each segment. The disease category is already specified, and the disease is so serious that insurance status might be ignored. The analyst can test whether

Category	Classification
Individual providers	Training, certification, or licensure
	Specialization
	Organizational affiliation
	Location
	Age
Donors	Interest
	Level of contribution
Organized providers	Scope of service
	Geographic location
	Ownership
	Size
	Market share
	Financial strength
	Competitive position

EXHIBIT 14.5
Healthcare
Provider
Specification
Taxonomies

using a specific category improves the forecast and then develop individual values for each category.

The individual forecasts from specification can be aggregated to generate a single adjusted forecast by assuming a specific mix of categories. In a simplified example, specific cardiovascular mortality rates for an HCO might be calculated in several different age groups and for men and women. Then, the specific rate for each age and gender group is multiplied by the fraction of the comparison population in that group, and the adjusted rate is the sum of those products. The comparison population is usually the national population or a state population. The adjusted rate holds the population structure constant so that the aggregate performance can be compared over time or across several sites.

Adjustment

Forecasts identify trends in data and forecast them to future situations. Several different statistical methods are available to prepare forecasts, and many important measures can be forecast subjectively. Forecasts of important variables, such as demand for a certain service, are usually composites of several methods. Good forecasts also identify most likely, highest, and lowest values so that the implications of forecast error can be evaluated using sensitivity analysis.

Forecasting

Statistical process control
A method of identifying significant changes in measures subject to random variation

Statistical analysis identifies variations that are significant or likely to be correctable, allowing the process manager to avoid futile efforts to correct performance. **Statistical process control** is a method of monitoring performance and identifying promising OFIs. Any measure reported over time can be graphed as

Statistical Process Control

a run chart—a simple line graph of reported values. Exhibit 14.6 shows a run chart and the same data in a control chart, with statistical control limits. The control chart shows that there was a statistically significant change in the underlying process at month 21, resulting in both a lower mean and less variation.

Study of a measure that is in control is not likely to reveal correctable process failures; a process in control is not a good OFI unless a benchmark can be found that is significantly better than the current mean. Exhibit 14.6 also shows that no subsequent month is statistically different from the current mean; the process is "in control." Several different kinds of measures can be handled with process control, identifying the OFIs most susceptible to study and improvement.

Legal, Regulatory, and Ethical Review

Many performance improvement or planning projects raise complex questions of law and ethics. These questions must be resolved by careful study and authoritative information. Well-managed HCOs organize their response around an ethics committee, a compliance office, and experts in environmental management and human resources management. Many larger HCOs also have an institutional review board (IRB) that addresses questions related to research. Operating teams and individuals are encouraged to use these services as well.

Ethics Committee and IRB

An advisory ethics committee is used in most HCOs to assist caregivers, patients, and families with difficult ethical decisions (Chapter 8). The committee's functions should also include "formulating institutional policies to guide the professional staff in making ethical decisions and educating hospital personnel about healthcare ethics in general."[4] Responding to inquiries is a fruitful way to implement all three functions. It improves the consistency and comprehensiveness of protocols and work processes. It catches team members at a teachable moment.

Similarly, questions important to the rights of patients in research situations are addressed by the IRB, or if necessary by the Office for Human Research Protections (OHRP) of the U.S. Department of Health and Human Services. IRB approval is mandatory for any research that directly involves human subjects. Concerns sometimes arise regarding whether quality improvement activities are subject to IRB review. OHRP has made clear that

.... HHS regulations for the protection of human subjects do not apply to ... quality improvement activities, and there is no requirement under these regulations for such activities to undergo review by an IRB, or for these activities to be conducted with provider or patient informed consent.

The OHRP definition of quality improvement activities is quite broad:

... activities conducted by one or more institutions whose purposes are limited to: (a) implementing a practice to improve the quality of patient care, and

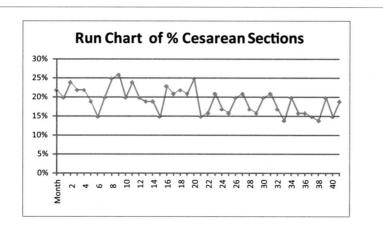

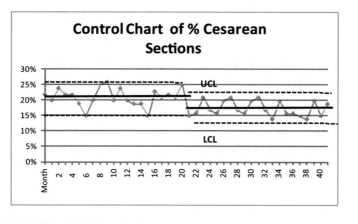

EXHIBIT 14.6
Run Charts
and Control
Charts

(b) collecting patient or provider data regarding the implementation of the practice for clinical, practical, or administrative purposes.[5]

Compliance Officer and Legal Consultation

Many proposals for new services or revised processes involve various regulatory and legal constraints. Real estate transactions, construction, compensation agreements, billing practices, and supervision of nonprofessional caregivers are all areas where legal review is advisable. As a result, many PITs and planning committees need advice. Internal consulting coordinates it with other design and fact-finding activities.

HCOs have created a *compliance officer* position to coordinate and integrate responses on these and other topics that present legal implications. The compliance officer is responsible for issuing guidelines to prevent illegal, improper, or unethical conduct, conducting independent reviews of their operations, and responding to all questions of potential or actual violations.[6] In the absence of a designated compliance officer, the questions must be answered by the HCO's general counsel, an attorney appointed to represent the organization on legal matters.

Environmental and Human Resources Management

HCOs must deal with both general and specific environmental management issues, such as high voltage radiation and hazardous waste. They must also comply with laws and regulations governing worker safety, wages and hours, and collective bargaining. Where collective bargaining contracts are in place, they must be reviewed to identify compliance or amendment. Consultation on such questions is arranged through the environmental management and human resources management activities.

Certificate of Need

Many states require a certificate of need (CON) for new services and construction or renovation. CONs are a form of franchise, a government-issued permission to proceed with capital investment. These laws are enforced with varying degrees of rigor, and their importance is diminishing. In states where they remain, CON success depends on timing, well-designed and attractive services, technically well-prepared proposals, and the support of influential persons in the community. Strategies for dealing with CONs vary. The influence of these laws is arguable.[7] The U.S. Department of Justice has opposed the use of CONs.[8] Most well-run organizations have developed strategies and tactics for gaining the approval of all or nearly all their important options and proposals. Obtaining these approvals is usually the responsibility of the compliance officer or the general counsel, but documentation comes from the project itself, prepared by internal consulting.

Supporting Improvement Projects

Internal consulting has several resources to expand the analytic capabilities of PITs and planning teams. These include helping PITs operate more effectively, conducting advanced process analysis, coordinating skills of other logistic services, modeling of alternative processes, managing outside consultants, and designing pilots and trials of proposals. In addition, internal consulting often works on strategic initiatives for which its client is the governing board or senior management.

Increasing the Effectiveness of PITs

PITs and planning teams bring specialists together from different areas to focus on a shared OFI. They can easily become ineffective and frustrating for their members. Internal consulting has several devices to help the PITs become more effective, including training for PIT members, direct consultation, and outside consultants.

High-performing HCOs provide basic continuous improvement training to all members of the leadership group. New managers and promotable associates are offered short courses (usually one or two days each) in goal setting, capital budgeting, and process analysis. These courses are generally offered by human resources but are staffed by planning personnel. They supplement programs in supervision and meeting management (Chapter 11). They emphasize "how to" and actual examples, working simultaneously on analytic skills, interpersonal skills, and self-confidence.

- Goal-setting courses include a full description of the goal-setting process, emphasizing the governing board role in setting strategic guidelines, the use of benchmarks, the identification of OFIs, the use of PITs to change work processes, and the negotiation processes. Hands-on practice with exercises and cases familiarizes people to computerized budgeting tools. Newcomers are often assigned an experienced mentor for their first round.[9]

- Capital budgeting courses describe how expansions and new equipment are planned, explaining the process to prepare a competitive request, the criteria used in judging requests, and the competitive process of capital allocation.

- Basic process-analysis courses review the philosophy of continuous improvement and its elementary applications. The advantages of measures and an elementary review of measurement use, reliability, and validity are demonstrated, along with simple concepts of variability. Basic tools for analyzing processes are taught with examples and applications. These include flow process charting; bar, scatter, frequency, and Pareto graphs; fishbone diagrams; and run and control charts.[10] The role and functioning of PITs are described. In *action learning* approaches, teams are formed and address real problems with continuous guidance. The approach develops both analytic and team-building skills.

  The basic course allows analysis of simple issues, but its biggest benefit may be in demonstrating what is meant by evidence-based management. It shows that objective study of work processes leads to new and useful insights; performance really is driven by process.

- Advanced training opportunities in process improvement emphasize process control (Six Sigma),[11] elimination of waste (Lean Manufacturing),[12,13] and integration of internal customers (Toyota).[14] The differences between these approaches may be more apparent than real, and no evidence shows that any approach is superior.[15]

This training produces a cadre of managers familiar with the basic approaches of process improvement so that most important PITs have several knowledgeable members.

Advanced Process Analysis

Many important OFIs are too complicated to solve with just the basic tools. Direct consultation can be provided by industrial engineers, accountants, and others with professional training and experience in healthcare applications. Specific needs can be met as they arise, with just-in-time solutions. PITs that address complex problems can have a trained leader assigned to monitor group discussions and coordinate consultation as the issues are raised and understood by the group. The leader can be assisted by a team from internal consulting and other support services. Internal assistance is often preferable to outside consultants. It brings a comprehensive knowledge of the organization that outsider consultants lack, and it is more directly invested in the results.

Coordinating Other Logistic Support

Internal consulting becomes a clearinghouse for coordinating improvement efforts, helping the performance improvement council (PIC) to avoid overlapping or missed opportunities among several PITs. It can help other logistic support units codify frequently needed information and establish processes to answer recurring questions. It can design effective contracts and monitor performance of external consultants, improving timeliness, completeness, and cost effectiveness of service.

Process Modeling

Process modeling allows a much clearer and more detailed picture of proposed improvements. Activity-based cost analysis provides the basis for make-or-buy decisions. Econometric models can indicate price trends. Simulation models allow exploration of hourly operation, testing performance against uncontrollable variation. Markov approaches allow study of complex chains of demand—for example, from the emergency department to the cath lab to the operating room. Optimization models allow examination of trade-offs between resources and outputs and help identify critical constraints.

These models expand understanding of the process under study, identify useful solutions, allow sensitivity analysis, and establish realistic performance goals for the ultimate solution. Although they are substantially cheaper than real-world trials, they are costly to develop, often requiring dozens of hours from highly skilled professionals. Even when a basic model has been developed and tested elsewhere, it must be applied using local data. Data needs are usually extensive, requiring either special studies or sophisticated search of patient record and financial accounting information. Internal modeling capability can be supplemented by consortiums or outside consultants.

Outside Consultants

Outside consultants have the advantage of drawing on similar problems elsewhere, and often they have developed specialized tools and solutions that have a demonstrated record of success. They offer the strength of concentrated effort on a single issue. They bring additional resources on a short-term basis. If they are routinely hired through the internal consulting activity, standardized evaluation criteria and contract approaches will increase the value of their services.

Evaluating and Testing Solutions

The improvement cycle calls for a pilot test of any proposed process revision. Simple changes may require only a week or two of experience and a team meeting to review results. Large process redesigns can involve substantial field trials. The trials are usually less rigorous than random controlled trials—the gold standard used in clinical processes—but making them as rigorous and objective as possible is important. The planning unit is usually responsible for consulting on the experimental design, measures, and criteria. The unit is often used to analyze the data and make a recommendation because it brings improved objectivity.

Important improvement opportunities arise from the governing board and senior management. These often involve relationships with competitors and external stakeholders and have consequences that go beyond the usual PIT. Examples include merger and acquisition opportunities, responses to competitor activity, and corporate restructuring. These opportunities are strategic-level OFIs. They often present special needs for confidentiality and careful development of sensitive information. Although external consultants are usually advisable for such projects, internal consulting can frequently help assemble necessary facts, develop forecasts, and identify implications.

Supporting
Governance
and Senior
Management
Projects

Supporting the Capital Investment Review

Capital investments, such as new programs, facilities, or equipment, represent multiyear commitments to operational processes and programs as well as commitments of limited capital funds. Correct selection of investments is critical to mission achievement.[16] Excellent HCOs have highly developed investment review systems to improve their investment decisions. The review process must promote innovation, making sure that no reasonable opportunity goes unexamined, and select wisely, making sure that the best opportunities are implemented. Reviews must also be efficient, making the right decisions with little delay and minimal demands on associates' time. Scale and equity are also important. Large HCOs commit tens of millions of dollars annually to capital requests and need a process that is perceived as reliable and equitable.

Any investment concept or opportunity needs to be reviewed against several conditions:

Checklist
for Project
Planning

1. *The expected contribution to mission achievement.* This is usually measured by changes in operational goals and, for large projects, changes in the strategic scorecard. The contribution, or return, must exceed the investment required.
2. *Physical constraints.* Changes in facilities involve architectural issues like floor loads, radiation safety, and Life Safety Code requirements. Equipment must fit space and utility constraints and must meet safety requirements.
3. *Asset control and cost minimization.* Purchases must be carefully specified and, if possible, competitively bid. The delivered goods must match the specifications.
4. *Implementation.* Even relatively small projects can involve several steps of equipment changes, renovation, process redesign, and retraining. Installation must be scheduled and coordinated with ongoing activities. Large projects require months or years of management.
5. *The actual contribution to mission achievement.* The expected contribution must be built into the appropriate unit's operational goals, and support must be provided to achieve the improved targets.

Using a formal checklist of questions, such as the one in Exhibit 14.7, increases fairness, helps identify impractical projects quickly, and establishes a rough estimate of potential return. Experienced managers soon learn the level of return necessary to gain funding. They drop or modify projects that fall short, reducing the set of proposals to a manageable group. Advice from internal consulting and finance is available to help apply the checklist and verify the return.

Opportunities are identified as "programmatic" if they focus on a single or small group of accountability units, or "strategic" if they affect several activities. Both can be reviewed using the checklist in Exhibit 14.7. Strategic opportunities are large in size and few in number. They usually have direct board involvement. The issue in applying the checklist is prudent evaluation—that is, diligence in understanding the options and their implications. The strategic process is described in Chapter 15.

Programmatic opportunities are small in size and scope and are numerous. They are reviewed by management. Applying the checklist for programmatic opportunities ensures an effective, efficient, and fair process.

Isolating programmatic capital-related proposals facilitates the following:

- Negotiation of a status quo operating budget, clarifying the current progress of the unit
- More rigorous evaluation of proposed revisions and a competitive review of capital opportunities
- Empowerment of associates; the process not only must identify the best proposals but also must be perceived as predictable and equitable to associates[17]
- Specific implementation of goal changes related to accepted capital proposals

Examples of programmatic opportunities are shown in Exhibit 14.8. Well-managed organizations encourage programmatic proposals because they reflect an alert, flexible work attitude and because they provide OFIs. An abundant supply of programmatic proposals minimizes the danger that the best solution will be overlooked. Hundreds of programmatic concepts originate each year in large HCOs. Dozens survive initial review within the accountability center and are formally documented as proposals.

Programmatic Capital Review The review process for programmatic capital requests, shown in Exhibit 14.9, rank-orders these requests in broadening pools into a single list for the HCO. The final list is presented to the governing board, who identifies how far down the list to fund on the basis of the HCO's annual goals. Board review of individual programmatic requests is rare and generally unwise. The board may amend its capital investment guideline, voting either to reduce the investment because the last accepted proposal can safely be deferred until next

EXHIBIT 14.7
Checklist for
Evaluating
Improvement
Proposals

Mission, Vision, and Plan

What is the relationship of this proposal to the mission and vision?

Is this proposal essential to implement a strategic goal in the long-range plan?

If the proposal arises outside the current strategic goals, can it be designed to enhance or improve the current plan?

Benefit

In the most specific terms possible, what does this project contribute to healthcare? If possible, state the nature of the contribution, the probability of success, and the associated risk for each individual benefiting and the kinds and numbers of persons benefiting.

If the organization were unable to adopt the proposal, what would be the implication? Are there alternative sources of care? What costs are associated with using these sources?

If the proposal contributes to some additional or secondary objectives, what are these contributions, and what is their value?

Market and Demand

What size and segment of the community will this proposal serve? What fraction of this group is likely to seek care at this organization?

What is the trend in the size of this group and its tendency to seek care here? How will the proposal affect this trend?

To what extent is the demand dependent on insurance or finance incentives? What is the likely trend for these provisions?

What are the consequences of this proposal for competing hospitals or healthcare organizations?

What impact will the proposal have on the organization's general market share or on other specific services?

What implications does the project have for the recruitment of physicians and other key healthcare personnel?

What are the promotional requirements of the proposal?

Costs and Resources

What are the marginal operating and capital costs of the proposal, including startup costs and possible revenue losses from other services?

Are there cost implications for other services or overhead activities?

Are there special or critical resource requirements?

Are there identifiable opportunity costs associated with the proposal or other proposals or opportunities that are facilitated by this proposal?

Are there other intangible elements (positive or negative) associated with this proposal?

Finance

What are the capital requirements, project life, and finance costs associated with the proposal?

What is the competitive price and anticipated net revenue?

What is the demand elasticity and profit sensitivity?

What are the insurance or finance sources of revenue, and what implications do these sources raise?

What is the net cash flow associated with the proposal over its life, and what is the discounted value of that flow?

continued

EXHIBIT 14.7
continued

Other Factors

What are the opportunities to enhance this proposal or others by combination?

Are there customers or stakeholders with an unusual commitment for or against the proposal?

Are there any specific risks or benefits associated with the proposal not identified elsewhere?

Does the proposal suggest a strategic opportunity, such as a joint venture or the purchase or sale of a major service?

Timing, Implementation, and Evaluation

What are the critical path components of the installation process, and how long will they take?

What are the problems or advantages associated with deferring or speeding up the implementation?

What are the anticipated changes in the operating budget of the units accountable for the proposal? What changes are required in supporting units?

EXHIBIT 14.8
Examples of
Programmatic
Proposals

Proposal	Description	Approximate Cost	Possible Justification
Renovate operating rooms	Enlarge operating suite into adjacent inpatient unit, modernize	$10,000,000	Increase attractiveness to ambulatory surgery patients
Replace flatwork ironer	Replace old ironer with faster machine less likely to break down	$ 50,000	More reliable service, lower unit-cost laundry operation
Purchase laser surgery equipment	Buy specially designed laser for gynecologic surgery	$ 50,000	Match competitor's investment, improve patient comfort
Expand parking lot	Add 50 spaces for visitors	$ 1,000,000	Relieve crowding for ambulatory patient visits

year or to increase the investment because the benefits of the next rejected proposal are compelling.

Well-run organizations emphasize these elements:

- The operating unit is clearly responsible for identifying opportunities.
- The unit's senior managers act as advocates for the opportunities and coordinate

EXHIBIT 14.9
Programmatic
Capital Review
Process

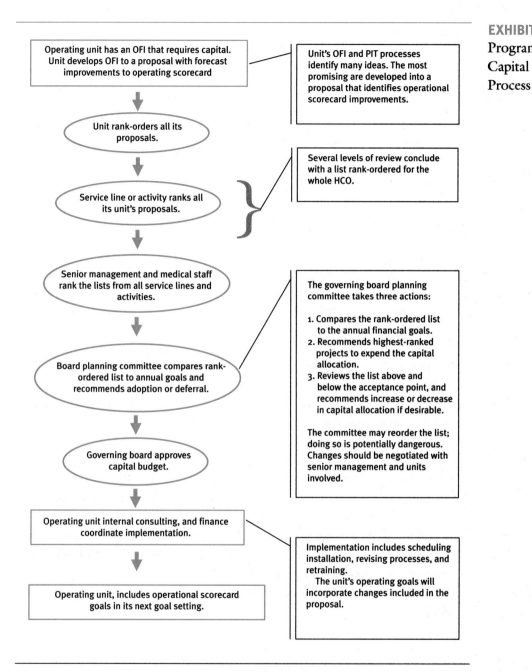

OFI: opportunity for improvement; PIT: process improvement team

support from units, including internal consulting and clinical internal customers.

- Internal consulting assistance is readily available to develop proposals. It, in turn, calls on other logistic and strategic support. Information technology, human resources, environmental services, finance, and marketing are routinely involved.
- Costs and benefits are quantitatively documented in the proposal, and the unit agrees to the benefits as future operational scorecard goals.

- The HCO's mission statement and its commitment to evidence-based medicine and evidence-based management are used as the guide to rank new opportunities.
- There is medical and nursing review and ranking of all projects with clinical implications.
- Clinical and nonclinical proposals are judged competitively against one another, in a common review process that includes medical and clinical support service representation.

Consistency of both process and judgment is the hallmark of success. In most organizations, there is always somebody claiming an urgent need to make exceptions to the review process. A wealthy donor, an unexpected breakdown, and a unique technological breakthrough are frequent rationalizations for exceptions. Organizations that yield often to these pleas discover that there are soon enough exceptions to engulf the process. At that point, political influence and persuasive rhetoric become the criteria that guide investments.

The role of internal consulting is to encourage a broad search for promising ideas, assist proposal development teams in preparing proposals for competitive review, ensure accuracy in forecasts and claims, and support fair review. The following procedures encourage managers to seek intuitive ideas and evaluate them:

- The continuous improvement culture encourages units to seek imaginative ideas. Ideas are respected even when they are unusual.
- Internal consulting staff are readily available to discuss concepts informally, describing the evaluation process and the evaluation issues.
- Internal consulting is a source of knowledge about the plans in existence and the discussion that surrounded related proposals. Partnerships with other units often succeed where freestanding proposals fail.
- Internal consulting helps managers identify and evaluate the benefits that justify the project.

Over time and with internal consulting's help, managers learn to recognize the kinds of proposals that will be successful. Many projects are reshaped, sometimes to entirely new and much more complex ideas. A replacement flatwork ironer in the hospital laundry looks simple, but it should prompt a review of the laundry's future demand, the price of competitive laundry services, the desirability of closing the laundry and purchasing the service elsewhere, and the possibility of actually expanding laundry volume by selling the service to others. If the laundry were to close, valuable space would be open to new uses. The project moves from programmatic to strategic as it raises important issues beyond the original unit. Internal consulting plays an important role in understanding the opportunities and communicating them to senior management.

Note that the planning staff never judge the proposals themselves. They provide facts and concepts to managers and let the managers decide. They protect the process of review itself, discouraging attempts to subvert or avoid it and making the preparation as efficient and fair as possible.

Implementing and Integrating

Once new processes or capital investments are recommended for adoption, two further steps are required:

1. *Implementation.* Many projects require months or years of preparation. Contracts must be let, construction or moving scheduled, installation completed, final reviews passed, and associates trained in new methods before the project is ready for routine use. The benefits of the project are delayed until this work is finished and are impaired if the work is inefficiently managed. Project management is a service in itself. It can substantially reduce both costs and delays. The use of PERT software to coordinate multiple contributions can save millions in large projects.[18]
2. *Integration.* Proposals are accepted because they promise specific performance improvements. Those promises must be built into the operating goals of the units involved. Progress toward them must be monitored, and assistance must be arranged if difficulties are encountered. Internal consulting should continue to monitor progress until the initial goals have been reached or are no longer applicable.

The implementation of projects that require construction or extensive renovation is commonly assigned to environment-of-care management (Chapter 12). Small projects are often monitored by internal consulting. In any case, internal consulting monitors the goal-setting processes to ensure that the claimed benefits are achieved.

Responding to Any Other Factual Concern

Internal consulting is a knowledge management resource for the HCO. Its purpose requires it to pursue any question or issue where understanding or resolution of the issue will be improved by a stronger grasp of the factual situation. Under the ongoing guidance of internal consulting, the HCO as a whole develops an ability to identify, understand, and react to opportunity that becomes a major competitive advantage. The "clearinghouse" role of internal consulting is central here. The availability of a consulting resource is a strong bulwark for evidence-based management. Internal consulting's response to inquiries should routinely exceed expectations.

Improving Internal Consulting

As a major supporter of the HCO's continuous improvement effort, internal consulting must itself model the effort. It maintains an operational scorecard (see the "Measures" section below). It makes a systematic effort to benchmark itself and identify best practices. It identifies, pursues, and implements OFIs within its own operations as it assists others in similar tasks. It sets and achieves improvement goals. In the process, it reviews and improves the role of the PIC and the HCO's overall continuous improvement effort.

People

Team Members

Internal consulting requires trained professionals in several fields. The functions of internal consulting require expertise in statistics, operations analysis, and forecasting plus all the logistic support activities, information, human resources, environmental services, finance, legal counsel, marketing, and strategic analysis. Clinical knowledge is also important. Large HCOs hire statisticians and industrial engineers as the core of the internal consulting team and rely on collaboration with the other logistic units. Small HCOs have a team of quantitatively oriented people and must rely heavily on consultants. Most of these skills can be supplied by outside consultants, and even the largest HCOs can effectively use outside consultants with mastery of specific processes.

The most critical role of internal consulting is as a clearinghouse. In a small HCO, a single person might be the internal consulting resource. Her success would depend less on her knowledge (she could not conceivably master all the skills required) than on her ingenuity in finding knowledge resources, linking seekers to them, and encouraging exploration. In a large organization, professionals with a foundation in any of the areas or in general management can succeed as much by helping their clients reach a successful conclusion as by having a mastery of their technical field.

Organization

The first three functions of internal consulting—support the HCO, support improvement projects, and support capital investment review—have become so important that it is difficult to imagine an HCO succeeding without these functions. The effectiveness with which they are done is a major driver of strategic success. Small HCOs—such as clinics, doctors' offices, hospices, and critical access hospitals—have only two choices. One is to affiliate with a larger HCO, pursuing either vertical or horizontal integration. The other is to purchase service from an external consultant.

Large HCOs must fulfill these functions in a way that makes them a distinctive competency. That requires establishing explicit accountability for each function, with operational measures and goals. One successful structure identifies a senior management team member as the vice president of planning or internal consulting. This individual leads a team responsible for the organization-wide functions and supplies process analysis and statistical capability to improvement and capital investment projects. The team has understood authority to call on all other logistic and strategic support units to assist its projects or to meet general organizational needs. Another common structure assigns the team to the marketing and strategy vice president. No evidence suggests that the label makes any difference.

Most HCOs use external consultants. Assigning contracting authority to the internal consulting group encourages the appropriate use of existing knowledge and the maximum benefit from the consulting engagement. The keys to successful use of external consultants are as follows: **Outside Consultants**

1. *The assignment should be clearly specified in terms of process, timing, and goal.* The clearer the assignment and the more details of the work specified in advance, the better the chances for success. It is sometimes wise to use consultants for general education and to gain fresh insights into vague, ill-defined problems, but such use should be limited to short-term assignments.
2. *Internal skills and knowledge should be fully used before external consultants are engaged, and internal experts should work directly with external ones.* This minimizes cost and maximizes retention of the external advice.
3. *Consultant firms should be selected on the basis of relevant prior experience.* In the absence of direct experience with a consultant, opinions of other clients should be solicited before any major engagement.
4. *Consultant activities should be carefully monitored against the specifications throughout the project.* A timetable and monthly interim achievement checkpoints should be used to monitor progress.
5. *Each consultant must have an explicitly assigned internal supervisor.* Failure to identify a point of contact slows the consultants, adds to their costs, and defeats the possibility of continuous monitoring during the contract period.

Healthcare systems that operate in several locations frequently centralize some aspects of internal consulting to improve the technical skills of personnel, provide economies of scale, and ensure transfer of best practices. Much of the functions that support the organization as a whole can be centralized. With Internet connectivity, it does not matter where the calculations are done, and consistent application across a system provides comparative information. Important aspects of the environmental assessment require an established local presence. Small local staffs provide direct support to the line managers, identify important local variations, and rely on the central staff as a consultant resource. On project assistance, the central resource behaves as a favored external consultant. **Internal Consulting in Multihospital Systems**

Measures

The internal consulting activity, as every other part of the well-run organization, has established performance measures, short-term goals, and regular reporting of achievement against these. A set of measures for a planning unit is shown in Exhibit 14.10. These measures follow the usual operations scorecard dimensions. Many of the measures can be benchmarked, although care is necessary in benchmarking and comparison.

Internal consulting may also be evaluated on technical proficiency, such as the completeness of data, the availability of analytic software, and the use of correct analytic techniques. Periodic evaluation by outside consultants is useful.

Internal consulting, as other logistic services, can be evaluated as a purchasable commodity, by comparing its performance on measures in Exhibit 14.10 to alternative sources, such as a retainer arrangement with outside suppliers. Perhaps more fruitful is to view it as an independent subsidiary, operating as though it were an outside consulting company. That approach leads to an "engagement" mentality on the part of the team members. They must keep logs of activities, and individual effort must be transfer-priced to show costs. Once this is done, the project-specific consulting costs, proposal decisions, projected improvements, realized improvements, and client satisfaction can be tracked. Although some measurements are estimates, even approximations show the unit's success at several different levels:

- Proposal approval rates reflect the ability of the unit to steer clients toward effective projects.
- Cost per project compared to projected performance improvement shows the effectiveness of project-specific services.
- Cost per implemented project compared to average value of implemented projects is an indicator of internal consulting's contribution to mission achievement.
- Total consulting costs compared to the value of all projects implemented also indicates the unit's contribution.

The ultimate judgment that the organization is or is not positioned where it should be in the community is based on the environmental surveillance itself and is inevitably bound up with the judgment of the chief executive officer and the governing board.

Managerial Issues

Three managerial issues are known to be troublesome for internal consulting:

Dimension	Measures	Examples
Demand for services	Count of user requests Projects initiated or assigned Unfilled or delayed requests	Log of requests and assignments Delays to respond to service requests
Cost	Total direct costs Hours on assigned projects External consultant costs Data and information acquisition costs	Full- and part-time personnel assigned to projects External consultant fees Costs of comparative or benchmark information
Human resources	Satisfaction scores of internal consulting personnel Vacancy rates and turnover	Surveys, personal and group discussions of work environment
Productivity	Total cost as percent of HCO operating cost Cost per support request Cost per project completed Total cost as percent of improvements implemented	Contribution, actual improvements in operational measures from completed projects compared to annual costs
Outcomes quality	Forecast accuracy: variation from actual Timeliness: projects completed on schedule Achieved improvements	Variation of annual forecasts from actual Accuracy of epidemiologic planning model forecasts Counts of projects completed on time Counts of projects achieving expected goals
Client satisfaction	User satisfaction surveys Overall planning service Project-specific service – Recognition and resolution of problems – Supportive attitude	Users' responses to services: "Would you rehire?" "Would you recommend?"

EXHIBIT 14.10
Operational
Performance
Measures
for Internal
Consulting

1. What is adequate quality?
2. How big should the unit be?
3. How does the HCO protect the empowerment of PITs and operating teams?

Ensuring Quality of Work

Careless or incomplete work by internal consulting can fatally disable an HCO. Successful planning units excel in four areas: (1) they take extra pains to guard against oversights, (2) they use the best comparative data and the most objective forecasts they can obtain, (3) they are rigorous in their evaluation of costs and benefits, and (4) they work consistently to "delight" their internal customers.

The outcomes quality and customer satisfaction measures on the operational scorecard are important indicators of the success of these values; any deterioration is an immediate OFI. An outside review team can be helpful in identifying specific areas that need improvement. Internal reviews, where a work product by one analyst is critiqued by a second, are also important and should be routine on all large-scale projects. Attendance at technical training programs allows analysts to keep and expand their skills. The visible commitment of the senior management leader is important. Individual performance reviews are also useful and can be tied to incentive compensation.

Sizing Internal Consulting

Many small HCOs exist without any internal consulting capability beyond their owner's wisdom. To compete, a large HCO that invests in internal consulting must cover the cost of the investment with operating improvements. For example, a small privately owned clinic typically operates without internal consulting. A competing clinic affiliated with an HCO bears an indirect cost burden for the internal consulting service but operates in the same market at the same prices. To succeed, it must increase net income compared to its independent competitor, using some combination of increased revenue and decreased costs. In 2009, the case began to be made, and the trend was increasingly clear. The high-performing HCO makes a substantial investment in its information, human resources, environmental services, financial, internal consulting, and marketing capabilities. It uses the total investment to attract both patients and caregivers away from the independent. The underlying business model is as follows:

- Operate in a patient-friendly manner, with better hours, night coverage, responsive caregivers, prompt service, amenities, and quality of care.
- Operate in a caregiver-friendly manner, with empowerment, rewarding values, reliable logistics, and performance incentives.

- Operate efficiently, using improved processes to eliminate waste and higher volumes to reduce unit costs.
- Operate effectively, avoiding unnecessary treatment and promoting overall health so that insurers are willing to pay more for each unit of treatment.

The correct size for internal consulting is the one that maximizes those advantages. The conditions that occur at that optimum are indicated by the operational scorecard:

1. Client needs are met without excessive delay.
2. Clients are satisfied with the service received. (Governance and senior management clients have a special interest in the activities that support the organization as a whole.)
3. Value of individual proposals is substantially higher than the cost of project support.
4. Implementation and integration translate improved processes into improved performance.

And, on the strategic scorecard,

5. The HCO continues to improve and move toward benchmark.

Failure to meet any of these conditions is an OFI, subject to investigation and improvement by the PIC and the internal consulting unit. The opportunity may lie in either size or quality, but an investigating PIT can establish the details.

Note that no benchmark exists for the operating cost of internal consulting. As is true of all logistic services, the optimum cost is not what some other HCO pays but is the minimum expenditure that yields maximum return on strategic performance.

Protecting Associates' Empowerment

The transformational model explicitly empowers the associates with the privilege of changing their work situation to improve mission achievement. Empowerment removes one of the major frustrations of working in a large organization. An empowered worker is entitled to the tools and supplies she needs, knows that she has that entitlement, and uses it effectively to improve her performance. That dynamic is a major component of building "a great place to give care." Internal consulting can endanger empowerment through either of two dynamics:

1. *Information asymmetry.* The knowledge base used by internal consulting can easily appear as arcane, mysterious, and forbidding to associates. With their superior command of the facts, internal consulting associates must guard

against usurping the operating associates' right and obligation to make the final decision.

2. *Loss of control of the PIT or planning process.* Team review of OFIs is inherently expensive, and it can be used as a political device, a graveyard for OFIs that someone in a position of power finds unattractive or inconvenient.

Making Information Transparent

The key to the information asymmetry problem is careful explanation of the what, why, and how of the knowledge management functions of internal consulting. Any PIT or operating team member has the right to understand

- What: definition, provenance, and limitations of all the measures that are used in an analysis
- Why: the implications of alternative measures
- How: the limitations of the analytic process and the implications of alternative processes

Making these elements clear to the associates involved in each project is a professional responsibility analogous to the similar obligation of physicians and lawyers. The client is entitled to the fullest possible understanding to support his or her final decision about the course of action. Fulfilling the responsibility is an important assurance of empowerment. The consultant team must be trained to do that. A question on the client survey, "How often did [internal consulting] explain things in a way you could understand?" will monitor performance. (This wording and the emphasis are taken directly from the HCAHPS patient survey.) The understanding is that results are essential to empowerment and critical in gaining consensus and effective implementation.

Controlling the Planning Process

"We'll study that" is a common response in all kinds of negotiations. It is often the correct response, but empowerment requires that the study be conducted fairly and expeditiously. Using the study as a way to avoid the decision or forward a special interest is destructive. This imposes three duties on the PIC, which internal consulting shares. First, it must scrupulously maintain its commitment to the evidence, making sure that it neither conceals nor distorts any alternative fact, analysis, or proposal. Second, it must ensure appropriate representation on each PIT or planning committee (no unit with a stake in the outcome can be omitted) and a level playing field among members. Third, it must enforce the timetable so that the PIT proceeds in a timely manner. These are matters addressed by the charge, membership, and timetable that the PIC establishes for each PIT. Internal consulting associates assist in implementing them.

Suggested Readings

Alemi, F., and D. H. Gustafson. 2009. *Decision Analysis for Healthcare Managers.* Chicago: Health Administration Press.

Chalice, R. 2007. *Improving Healthcare Using Toyota Lean Production Methods.* Milwaukee: American Society for Quality.

Iezzoni, L. I. (ed.). 2003. *Risk Adjustment for Measuring Health Care Outcomes,* 3rd ed. Chicago: Health Administration Press.

Ozcan, Y. A. 2009. *Quantitative Methods in Health Care Management,* 2nd ed. San Francisco: Jossey-Bass/Wiley.

Porter, M. E. 2008. *On Competition.* Boston: Harvard Business School Press.

Sproull, R. 2009. *The Ultimate Improvement Cycle: Maximizing Profits Through the Integration of Lean, Six Sigma, and the Theory of Constraints.* New York: Productivity Press.

Zuckerman, A. M. 2005. *Healthcare Strategic Planning,* 2nd ed. Chicago: Health Administration Press.

Notes

1. Begun, J. W., J. A. Hamilton, and A. A. Kaissi. 2005. "An Exploratory Study of Healthcare Strategic Planning in Two Metropolitan Areas." *Journal of Healthcare Management* 50 (4): 264–75.
2. Griffith, J. R., and K. R. White. 2003. *Thinking Forward: Six Strategies for Highly Successful Organizations,* 241. Chicago: Health Administration Press; Griffith, J. R., and K. R. White. 2005. "The Revolution in Hospital Management." *Journal of Healthcare Management* 50 (3): 170–90.
3. Institute for Healthcare Improvement. "Collaboratives." [Online information; retrieved 7/8/09.] www.ihi.org/IHI/Programs/Collaboratives.
4. Hester, D. M. (ed.). 2008. *Ethics by Committee: A Textbook on Consultation, Organization, and Education for Hospital Ethics Committees,* 6. New York: Rowman & Littlefield.
5. U.S. Department of Health and Human Services, Office of Human Research Protection. "Quality Improvement Activities Frequently Asked Questions." [Online information; retrieved 6/13/12.] http://www.hhs.gov/ohrp/policy/qualityfaqs mar2011.pdf
6. American College of Healthcare Executives. 2009. "Position Description, Chief Compliance Officer." [Online information; retrieved 7/8/09.] www.ache.org/ newclub/career/comp.
7. U.S. General Accounting Office. 1981. "Health Systems Plans: A Poor Framework for Promoting Health Care Improvements." *Report to the Congress by the Controller General of the United States.* Washington, DC: GAO.
8. Miller, J. M. 2008. "Competition in Healthcare and Certificates of Need." Statement of the Antitrust Division, U.S. Department of Justice. [Online information; retrieved 7/15/09.] www.usdoj.gov/atr/public/comments/233821.htm.
9. Griffith and White (2003), 174–79.
10. Institute for Healthcare Improvement. "IHI Open School Courses." [Online information; retrieved 7/8/09.] www.ihi.org/IHI/Programs/IHIOpenSchool/ IHIOpenSchoolforHealthProfessions.htm?TabId=4.
11. iSixSigma LLC. [Online information; retrieved 10/13/05.] www.isixsigma.com.
12. Lean Enterprise Institute. [Online information; retrieved 10/13/05.] www.lean .org.
13. Sproull, R. 2009. *The Ultimate Improvement Cycle: Maximizing Profits Through the Integration of Lean, Six Sigma, and the Theory of Constraints.* New York: Productivity Press.

14. Minoura, T. 2003. "The 'Thinking' Production System: TPS as a Winning Strategy for Developing People in the Global Manufacturing Environment." [Online article; retrieved 10/13/05.] www.toyota.co.jp/en/special/tps/tps.html.

15. Vest, J. R., and L. D. Gamm. 2009. "A Critical Review of the Research Literature on Six Sigma, Lean and Studer Group's Hardwiring Excellence in the United States: The Need to Demonstrate and Communicate the Effectiveness of Transformation Strategies in Healthcare." *Implementation Science* 4 (1): 35.

16. Prince, T. R., and J. A. Sullivan. 2000. "Financial Viability, Medical Technology, and Hospital Closures." *Journal of Health Care Finance* 26 (4): 1–18.

17. Sorensen D., and D. Sullivan. 2005. "Managing Trade-offs Makes Budgeting Processes Pay Off." *Healthcare Financial Management* 59 (11): 54–8, 60.

18. Internet Center for Management and Business Administration, Inc. PERT. [Online information; retrieved 7/14/09.] www.netmba.com/operations/project/pert.

15 MARKETING AND STRATEGY

In a Few Words

Marketing and strategy are intertwined activities that relate the healthcare organization (HCO) to all its stakeholders, including competitors. Marketing includes identification and segmentation of exchange partners, extensive listening, branding, promotion to customers and associates, and management of relations with competitors and other community agencies. In strategy, the governing board selects the organization's direction and relationships, positioning the HCO through its mission, values, services, and partnerships. Extensive discussion processes—including outreach to stakeholders—identify, prioritize, and implement strategic opportunities.

The managerial role emphasizes the leadership necessary to keep large groups of people with inherently conflicting agendas aligned toward the mission. Alignment is achieved through the tools for continuous improvement, the processes for building consensus, and continuing rewards. Success builds on itself.

Critical Issues in Marketing and Strategy

1. *Marketing is a broad approach to building exchange relationships:*
   - Not limited to patients, it applies to all relationships
   - Not simply promotion, it includes all aspects of the organization's interfaces to the world

2. *Markets are "segmented":*
   - Segments are subgroups with similar needs
   - Both strategy and marketing are usually targeted to specific segments

3. *Listening is fundamental:*
   - Goal is to understand the perspectives of customers, associates, and suppliers
   - Both qualitative (verbal exchange) and quantitative (survey) approaches are used
   - Approaches are often designed ad hoc

4. *Strategies are framed using the tools of evidence-based management:*
   - Strategies integrate the results of listening and the environmental assessment
   - Extensive discussions allow stakeholders to gain understanding and agreement

5. *Senior management and governance manage strategic discussion and implementation:*
   - Commitment to long-term benefit for all, rather than expedient gains for a few, is central to success
   - Large healthcare systems can strengthen both the commitment and the evidence-based tools more readily than small ones can

QUESTIONS FOR DISCUSSION

Consider these questions as you read the chapter.

1. Why are the four Ps ordered as product, place, price, promotion? What sorts of questions would the four Ps prompt for implementing the new Well-Baby programs suggested in the Exhibit 15.2 analysis? How would you answer those questions in a real HCO?

2. Consider a planning team designing a major renovation or expansion of a patient service. Focus groups and surveys will cost nearly $100,000. How might that expenditure pay off? What is your backup plan if you think that's too much money?

3. Successful efforts in health promotion and palliative care could mean less income for the hospital and its doctors and even reduced employment. How would you justify a hospital's investment? Identify the stakeholder segments that must be sold on the concept, and propose the best arguments for each.

4. The "Managerial Issues" section in this chapter suggests that the logistic support functions described in the preceding chapters are vital assets that create a critical competitive advantage for large-scale HCOs. It argues for vertical integration, that multihospital systems should acquire and integrate small HCOs that provide specialized care of various kinds. What are the arguments for vertical acquisition? For retaining the status quo?

5. The second paragraph of the "Managerial Issues" section is an indictment of American healthcare that concludes, "the typical hospital is not strategically managed; it is simply drifting." How could this be true? If it's false, how do you prove that? If it's true, what should be done about it?

The HCO described in the preceding chapters is complex, formal, long lived, and dynamic. It is capable of identifying and meeting the health needs of its community with the latest technology and the most appropriate care. It thrives only because it fulfills the changing needs of stakeholders, as the stakeholders perceive them. The most sophisticated functions of the organization are those that identify, evaluate, and respond to long-term changes in stakeholder needs.

Marketing is the deliberate effort to establish fruitful relationships with exchange partners and stakeholders. **Strategy** is the selection of the profile of stakeholder needs to be met. In successful HCOs, as in other industries, the marketing and strategy are intertwined, creating a seamless, continuous activity that monitors the basic direction of the enterprise; modifies the direction as conditions change; and, in some cases, redirects the enterprise through merger, acquisition, or closure.

Marketing
The deliberate effort to establish fruitful relationships with exchange partners and stakeholders

Strategy
A systematic response to a specific stakeholder need

This chapter describes how excellent HCOs identify a profile of stakeholder needs and position themselves in response. It begins with marketing, reflecting the centrality of the listening function, and continues to the issues of identifying, developing, and selecting strategic alternatives.

Purpose

The purpose of marketing and strategy is

to identify, evaluate, and respond to changes in stakeholder needs.

In a free-market society, both customer and associate stakeholders "vote with their feet," selecting organizations that meet their needs often without fully expressing what those needs are. An organization thrives because it attracts and retains stakeholders better than competing alternatives do.

Success is not strictly the sum of its parts; sustainable relationships tend to be mutually reinforcing. A successful strategy produces stronger relationships and supports further improvement. Ineffective strategies weaken the organization and start a cycle that leads to collapse or reorganization. The issues quickly become complex. A successful strategy must meet several different and interrelated criteria:

- The services offered use processes that are competitive on cost, amenities, and quality.
- Demand is adequate to cover the fixed costs and meet quality standards.
- The work environment attracts and retains associates who are committed to implementing the strategy.

- The services identify and capitalize on a competitive advantage, a reason customers select them over alternatives.
- The constellation of services is one that attracts and builds patient and associate loyalty and that fulfills what patients and associates can realistically expect.

Each of these criteria presents a risk of failure. Only the first criterion is attacked solely by improving the processes within the organization itself. All the rest require attention to the whole environment. The set of solutions is the organization's strategy—sometimes called the *business model.*

The functions of marketing and strategy are summarized in Exhibit 15.1.

Marketing Functions

The term "marketing" has a professional definition that is substantially broader than its common use. Here is one favored by Philip Kotler, a noted professor of marketing:

> the analysis, planning, implementation, and control of carefully formulated programs designed to bring about voluntary exchanges of values with target markets for the purpose of achieving organizational objectives.[1]

Others use a "four Ps" mnemonic to capture the breadth of the concept:

1. *Product.* What exactly is the product or service offered in the exchange? (Includes benchmarks and competitive operational standards)
2. *Place.* Where and how does the exchange take place? (Includes hours of service, geographic locations, and relations between services)
3. *Price.* What is the total economic value of the exchange? (Not only the price paid the vendor but also collateral costs such as transportation and lost income)
4. *Promotion.* What activities are necessary to bring the opportunity to the attention of the stakeholders likely to accept it? (Includes publicity, advertising, incentives)

The order of the four Ps is important. The consequences of bad product design or placement cannot generally be overcome by low prices or extensive promotion. By either definition, marketing applies not just to customers but also to all exchanges, including those with competitors, employees, and other community agencies. Marketing is about relationships. Healthcare marketing must overcome several complexities that affect relationships:

Function	Processes	Purpose
Marketing		
Identifying and segmenting customer and associate markets	Surveillance, data analysis, segmentation of market	Understand stakeholder needs and identify participants whose needs are consistent with the HCO mission
Listening to exchange partners' needs	Surveys, focus groups, monitors, personal contact	Gain a clear and complete understanding of what the HCO must do to attract exchange partners in sufficient number
Developing brand and media relations	Communication to establish awareness of HCO and its scope of services	Make the HCO as a whole attractive to the community by emphasizing widely shared goals in a variety of communication methods
Convincing potential customers to select the HCO's services	Communication to patient populations with specific needs	Make potential patients aware of the services and persuade them to select the organization over its competitors
Attracting and motivating capable associates	Communication to target associate populations, advertising, incentives	Ensure a steady stream of qualified applicants, even in areas of personnel shortages
Managing other stakeholder relationships	Surveillance, senior management listening, partnerships to align other stakeholders	Establish constructive relationships with other organizations such as insurance intermediaries, employers, and providers of competing or complementary services
Improving the organization's marketing activity	Marketing plans, goal setting, evaluating marketing effectiveness	Set goals that move toward benchmarks and values for market share
Strategy		
Maintaining the mission, vision, and values	Visioning exercise	Allow multiple stakeholders to consider and comment on mission, vision, and values
Defining the strategic position	Evaluating and selecting alternative approaches to maximizing mission achievement	Position an array of clinical services geographically to achieve a competitive advantage with an identified population
Documenting the strategic position	Maintaining and coordinating strategic plans	Integrate multiple strategic and programmatic responses
Implementing the strategic position	Managing investments and processes that will achieve the strategic goals	Ensure that the HCO responds to opportunities and threats from external events
Improving the strategic process	Establish goals and opportunities for improvement strategy processes	Continuously improve strategy and strategy formulation

EXHIBIT 15.1

Functions of Marketing and Strategy

- Intimate, life-shaping services about which people have strong and sometimes irrational feelings
- Delivery mechanisms that have high fixed costs (This requires careful adjustment of supply and demand and opens the possibility of differential pricing.)
- Providers who are divided into a large number of professions, who often compete between and within their specialties
- Unpredictable customer expenses that fall disproportionately on a few people (These must be financed by health insurance, bringing a third party into the transaction. The insurance mechanism raises the need for agreement about what is appropriate.)
- Health insurance that is financed largely through taxes and employer contributions, bringing a fourth and a fifth party into the transaction
- Differences of opinion among patients, buyers, providers, and society at large about what is appropriate (Even with protocols, optimum treatment is only imprecisely known; evidence-based conclusions may not be satisfactory to customers; serious disagreements exist about what is necessary or even acceptable.)

In such a complex environment it would be disastrous to think of marketing as a simple or limited activity. Exhibit 15.2 tracks the major functions of marketing as they apply to a single project—Well-Baby care—and to the entire program of a large, established HCO.

Identifying and Segmenting Markets

As Kotler implies, specific targets are the key to marketing. Market **segmentation** differentiates exchange partners into particular subgroups on the basis of groups' exchange need and the message to which they will respond. It is closely analogous to the statistical process of specification (described in Chapter 14) and, in fact, often starts with the same taxonomies. Like listening and branding, it underlies the other marketing functions.

Segmentation
The deliberate effort to separate markets by customer need and the message to which the markets will respond

Market segmentation makes listening and promotion more efficient. People of different ages and genders have unique healthcare needs and may also carry certain insurance, want certain schedules and amenities, and listen to certain media. To attract a given demographic, the organization should work with that insurance plan, provide those schedules and amenities, and advertise in those media. Efforts that are not targeted are inherently inefficient. Segmentation usually goes well beyond demographics and into economic, cultural, and lifestyle issues as the organization attempts to build demand for specific services.

In the Well-Baby example, it is immediately obvious that all mothers are not alike. They and, more important, their approach to childcare differ by education, income, culture, employment, and health insurance coverage. The segments have different needs. Several already have their needs met. Others need specific product and placement—locations, hours, and culturally competent responses. Several are financially constrained, probably by the Medicaid

Function	Well-Baby Illustration	HCO Illustration
Identifying and segment customer and associate markets	Forecast numbers of babies Identify OFI for mission achievement Segment Well-Baby market	Identify and segment local population Forecast size, age, and disease by segment
Listen to stakeholder needs	Use surveys, focus groups, and other listening activities to identify segment-specific needs	Monitor market share, satisfaction, and qualitative concerns by segment Identify OFIs in market-share growth
Develop brand and media relations	Raise mothers' awareness of Well-Baby services with articles, advertisements, and collaboration with community agencies	Make community aware of HCO's services Maintain relations with community agencies Maintain media relations Manage negative media events
Influence potential customers	Design product, place, price, and promotion to attract and retain mothers in specific market segments	Maintain multiple campaigns for specific HCO services and market segments
Attract and motivate associates	Design product, place, price, and promotion to attract and retain pediatricians, nurses, and other caregivers	Maintain multiple campaigns for specific HCO associate needs
Manage other stakeholder relationships	Identify competitors and collaborators Pursue partnerships to enhance Well-Baby goal	Monitor competitor performance Identify collaboration opportunities Pursue partnerships to enhance mission achievement

EXHIBIT 15.2
Illustration of Marketing Functions

OFI: opportunity for improvement

price. Different segments require different promotions, in their language and through their community networks and preferred radio stations, newspapers, and websites. Similarly, the HCO needs to view its total market by segment. Gains in market share come by identifying segments that have unmet needs and designing responses that meet those needs.

Listening to Stakeholder Needs

Marketing requires listening activities to understand exchange partners' perspectives. This understanding promotes dialogue, identifies and prioritizes needs, suggests paths to improved relationships, and reveals opportunities for improved work processes. Excellent HCOs make listening a major part of their activities. They use formal surveys, focus groups, monitors, and a wide variety of personal-contact devices that involve dozens or hundreds of managers. Many of these yield qualitative rather than quantitative information. The marketing unit or department plays a critical role in assembling and interpreting these data.

The major listening approaches are summarized in Exhibit 15.3.

Formal Surveys

Surveys provide the most reliable quantitative information about relationships and attitudes and are widely used in marketing, journalism, and politics. Sampling techniques allow inference from a relatively small number of contacts, and samples can be stratified to reflect specific population segments. Patients and associates are 100 percent sampled, providing regular reports on both summary attitudes toward the organization and its services and insight into perceptions about specific processes. As discussed in Chapter 5, the Centers for Medicare & Medicaid Services (CMS) mandates and publishes results[2] of HCAHPS, a 27-item survey of communication with doctors, communication with nurses, responsiveness, pain control follow-up care, cleanliness, and noise.[3] A similar set—the ambulatory CAHPS—is available from the Agency for Healthcare Research and Quality (AHRQ).[4] Household surveys are also commonly used; they provide data on community attitudes and conditions as opposed to populations of people affiliated with the organization.

Surveys have become highly sophisticated instruments. The questions, timing, method of contact, response rate, and specification of the population can all affect the results so that professional statistical analysis is almost always necessary. Surveys for patients and associates are now provided by commercial companies, which handle these statistical issues and also provide trend, comparative, and benchmarking data.

Monitors

HCOs use a variety of reports generated by the associates, patients, and family directly involved to identify situations where results fall short of expectations or exceed expectations. Leading HCOs now use incident reports and service recovery generated by associates, various complaint vehicles, and cards to recognize exceptional effort by associates. The "trigger" in each of these is the subjective sense that a reportable event has occurred. Underreporting is a serious issue. Associates are trained to report service-recovery situations and clinical errors whenever they occur. Follow-up rewards reporting, avoids blame, and focuses on prevention. The events can be coded by type, location, and severity to indicate trends and processes or units that need attention.

Statistical monitors can be constructed around standardized events like CMS's quality measures, AHRQ's patient safety indicators,[5] and Thomson Reuter's Complications Index.[6] They are derived from the diagnostic codes

EXHIBIT 15.3
Major Listening
Activities

Activity	Description	Application
Formal Surveys		
Patient satisfaction	Telephone, Web, or mail survey	Offered to inpatients and various categories of outpatient care; assesses satisfaction with both amenities and perceived quality of care; usually provided by a national survey firm, which supplies comparative data and evaluates reliability; forms the basis for the "loyal" patient estimates
Associate satisfaction	Telephone, Web, or mail survey	Offered to various categories of associates; usually provided by a national survey firm, which supplies comparative data and evaluates reliability; forms the basis for the "loyal" associate estimates
Community	Telephone or mail survey	Estimates market share, prevalence of insurance, travel patterns, and other characteristics not in the decennial census; can be used to update census data; can be focused on specific population segments
Monitors		
Unexpected event reports	Associate-generated written reports	Associates are encouraged to report any event that represents a serious failure, such as a fall, a clinical error, or an unacceptable delay; gifts to patients under service-recovery programs require reporting
Service recovery	Written reports of actions to correct failures	Associates are authorized to offer gifts or benefits in cases where processes have egregiously failed; the incident and the recovery must be reported in writing
Complaints	Written, oral, or electronic reports from patients or associates	Patients are offered bounce-back cards, and both patients and associates are encouraged to communicate directly with organizational authorities
"Caught in the Act"	Written reports of exceptional behavior by associates	Cards for "Caught in the Act" are publicly available; the events reported are judged by a panel, and prizes are awarded
Statistical process control	Counts of untoward events documented in the patient record	The electronic record can be surveyed for evidence, such as diagnoses; specific drug orders; progress notes; or treatments that reflect adverse events such as infections, falls, treatment errors, and complications; these can be tracked and monitored either as sentinel events—all cases investigated—or using statistical process control (Chapter 14).

continued

EXHIBIT 15.3
continued

Activity	Description	Application
Personal Contact		
Focus groups	Small groups of current or potential customers meeting face to face	Focus groups are encouraged to speak candidly about existing services and explore what is important about proposed services; they provide insight to specific process opportunities that are not revealed in surveys
On-call managers	24/7 designated contact official	A senior manager is always accessible to patients or associates for prompt attention to complaints or difficulties that arise; allows direct intervention and service recovery in complex situations
Walking rounds	Regularly scheduled senior management visits	Personal contact and visits to actual work sites by front-office managers; visits encourage questions, explain positions, reward efforts, validate public pronouncements, and humanize managers
Shadowing and walk-throughs	Observation of a single patient through a complex process	Shadowing allows associates to understand both the process and its impact on patients; walk-throughs actually duplicate patient activity
Mystery shopping	Observation of a competitor's process	Mystery shoppers were initially used to discover competitors' prices; in healthcare, they reveal competitors' processes and competitive advantages

mandated on Medicare hospitalization insurance claims and are required by most insurers. They cover a limited set of events, but one that is relatively free of reporting bias and can be benchmarked and trended. Their most important use is to validate the subjective reporting processes.

Personal Contact

Leading HCOs supplement survey and event data with deliberate personal contact. They encourage senior management to be highly visible in the organization by rounds and on-call responses. They encourage process improvement teams (PITs) to observe and walk through the processes they are studying. They sometimes hire agents to observe and report on competitors' processes. They assemble focus groups—small groups of actual or potential customers who are encouraged to discuss factors in product, placement, and price that are important to them. These personal-contact activities yield only qualitative and highly subjective information, but they accomplish three important goals:

1. They show management's commitment to continuous improvement and put a human face on policies and work requirements.
2. They improve managers' empathy with the work environment.
3. They provide detailed information that is often valuable in solving specific situations.

Personal-contact programs have some important limitations. Managers must be trained to avoid blame in their responses and to stress process analysis and improvement. Personal contact works best when the organization has developed competitive work processes and uses the contact to supplement measurement, process analysis, and goal setting. It cannot be effective in situations where the basic work processes are inadequate. Too many requests to solve specific problems is evidence that issues must be addressed systematically rather than episodically.

Developing Brand and Media Relations

The **branding** function maintains the overall reputation or image of the organization so that it remains attractive to most members of the community at large. Branding usually begins as a communitywide communications effort to convey the mission and the competitive advantages of the organization. Branding activities include public and community relations, image advertising and promotion, maintenance of an attractive website, and media relations. A deliberate program includes descriptive information for various media, relationships with other influential community agencies such as schools and the faith community, and sponsorship of community events such as health fairs and athletic teams. It also includes personal appearances by management and caregivers, deliberate contacts with influentials and opinion leaders, and damage control for negative media events.

Image Building

Branding
A communitywide communication effort to convey the mission and the competitive advantage of the organization

Obviously, success begins with having a good story to tell. An increasing number of HCOs release specific information about finances, service, and quality to the public. National standards for the release and accuracy of public reporting focus on quality and satisfaction performance indicators and are compared to benchmarks and peer organizations.[7]

Image promotion is far from a panacea. It takes a large number of exposures to increase name recognition, and changing the HCO's attractiveness is hard, although increases in quality may be linked to improved branding.[8] Community surveys allow the organization to monitor two dimensions of branding. Familiarity is measured by consumers' ability to recall the name without prompting or recognize it in a list. Attractiveness uses survey questions to assess how the HCO compares to competitors and which attributes are most attractive. The implication is that an established reputation—being among the first two or three names people independently recall for healthcare—is a valuable asset, hard to replace, and well worth protecting.

Media Relations

Most organizations are acutely aware of what is said about them in the media, but the evidence suggests that the public at large is quite resistive to media statements. Nonetheless, the media can portray the organization favorably or unfavorably, and the result often depends on the quality of information supplied by the organization. Media communication is either HCO or media initiated. HCO-initiated communication is the planned release of information as part of branding. Attractive and thorough press releases, strong visual elements (e.g., photos, videos), knowledgeable and articulate spokespersons, and newsworthy information all assist in improving the coverage. A deliberate program of regular information releases and efforts to draw media attention to favorable events promote a positive image. The more information released, the more likely the community's familiarity with and attraction to the HCO would increase.

Media-initiated communication is often related to major news events, such as healthcare to prominent individuals or a healthcare crisis. A crisis is anything that suddenly or unexpectedly has adverse effects on an HCO or its patients, associates, or community. In the worst case, media-initiated communication arises from unfavorable events, such as lowered bond ratings, civil lawsuits, or criminal behavior by associates. Journalists can be hostile when they sense something is wrong. Investigative journalism is an aggressive effort to dig out all the public might want to know, with emphasis on what the HCO might want to hide. Effective handling of media initiatives begins with preventing events that will draw investigation. It is supported by a strong branding program that releases newsworthy, positive information about the HCO. When unfortunate issues arise, the HCO should anticipate reporters' questions and prepare detailed, candid responses. Spokespersons should be identified and equipped with thorough, convincing replies to questions. The organization should have a plan in place for communicating when a healthcare crisis occurs.[9]

Convincing Potential Customers

HCOs are a respected source of information on health matters, and they communicate often with patients and others in their community. Leading organizations work hard to retain respect, tying their branding activities to specific communications about three principal goals:

1. Convince patients to select this provider and services
2. Encourage wellness and disease prevention
3. Adjust patient expectations about care

Reaching the public effectively is challenging. Healthcare messages are often on topics people would rather avoid. Commercial retailers spend far larger sums than not-for-profit organizations are comfortable with.

"Clutter"—the sheer volume of consumer messages—makes registering the HCO on the customers' minds difficult. Despite this, communications programs can reinforce branding and build demand for effective healthcare.

Influence Patient Selection of Providers and Services

The key to attracting and retaining patients is service, more than promotion. Loyal or delighted patients—those who will return when necessary and refer others—are obtained by maintaining service and quality. The most effective way to manage patient satisfaction is to identify service weaknesses and meet them through continuous improvement. Service recovery can supplement but not replace continuous improvement. Beyond performance and recovery, explicit promotion activities play a small role. An HCO may explicitly promote a new or expanded service or a service where a portion of the market could realistically be shifted to or from a competitor. Such a campaign would include websites, press releases, advertising, and incentives such as giveaways and performance events. Customer reactions would be carefully monitored.

Influence Healthy Behavior

HCOs with a community health mission join in the wellness promotion movement to encourage healthy lifestyles and cost-effective prevention behaviors. General promotional campaigns to the well members of the population are an important branding opportunity. They use all media, including print and video material in schools and work sites. More important, the healthcare experience often becomes a *teachable moment*—a window of increased receptivity when messages from healthcare professionals are well received. Messages must overcome complex motivations to pursue the unhealthy behavior. Campaigns repeat the message over and over and use a variety of vehicles to convey and reinforce it. Wellness promotion becomes an ongoing activity that consumes a specific budget and is constantly studied for opportunities to improve cost effectiveness.

Manage Patient Expectations

One aspect of patient satisfaction relates to initial expectations about care. These can be unrealistic. Media reports frequently emphasize dramatic, curative medical intervention and may overstate the power and value of high-tech care. Drug companies overtly hype branded prescriptions of dubious worth.[10] Countering these and restoring realistic expectations are important. In reality, self-treatment and family care are effective in many conditions. In the case of self-limiting disease and terminal disease, there is often nothing healthcare professionals can add.

Similarly, the appropriate use of substitute professionals, such as nurse practitioners in place of physicians or primary physicians in place of specialists, offers advantages in quality, cost, and effectiveness. The marketing approach begins with the attractive provision of the lower-cost service. Promotion helps build awareness of alternatives and provides reassurance to make people comfortable with them, such as reassurance about the availability of technologically advanced care when needed. HCOs promote the use of less skilled professionals; the use of walk-in clinics in place of emergency departments, ambulatory instead of inpatient care, generic instead of brand name drugs, and equally effective substitutes for high-cost intervention; and improved management at the end of life. All of these can reduce the cost of care while sustaining or improving the quality.

Sophisticated targeting can focus directly on specific patient expectations. In advertising, customers tend to perceive what they have been conditioned to expect.[11] For example, advance description of elective surgical procedures can identify many common complications or variations in the recovery pattern and provide instructions or reassurance about them. It can prepare the patient to accept the usual outcomes and, in some cases, convince patients that the rewards of the procedure are not worth the pain, risks, and cost. Clinical problems associated with a high level of dissatisfaction can be identified and studied to devise more satisfactory treatment patterns. These may deliberately emphasize activities that are designed to provide symptomatic relief, such as the deliberate use of chiropractors in place of back surgery in certain cases of low-back pain.[12]

Improve Patient Communication

Successful patient communication is a sophisticated combination of advertising, persuasion, and education. Three approaches improve its effectiveness:

1. *Messages should be carefully targeted to specific population segments where change is desired.* The logic used in prevention and diagnostic testing applies to promotion as well—funds spent communicating to populations who are not involved or are nonresponsive are wasted. While branding usually aims to reach a broad spectrum of the community, promotion should almost always be targeted to specific groups.

2. *Advance plans for promotional campaigns should specify **reach** (the focal audience for the campaign), **frequency** (how often individuals in the focal audience are contacted), media, cost, and measures of expected outcome.* Quantifying the campaign in advance establishes explicit goals and encourages careful review of alternatives.

3. *Campaigns should explicitly involve community partnerships and coalitions.* Building networks to improve health and healthcare offers several advantages. The costs can be shared. Collaboration also builds on the respect these organizations have, bringing familiar faces to the target audiences. The use of sites and agencies other than healthcare allows more complete and candid discussion of the complex issues. For example, on issues of prevention and end-of-life care, churches, congregate-living centers, and senior recreational facilities can hold educational discussions. On other issues, schools and employers can strengthen communication. The collaboration has listening aspects as well. Specific needs can be identified and addressed. The HCO's own associates can participate as partners. Promotion that reaches both patients and staff will improve staff understanding and acceptance as well.

Attracting and Motivating Associates

Although much of the communication to associates is managed by the accountability structure and the human resources unit, many promotional activities also reach the associates. Websites and signage are seen more by associates than customers. Publicity and advertising attract associate attention. The service excellence program (Chapter 11) can be described as a collaboration with associates to realize the mission and vision of the HCO.

Reach
In advertising, an estimate of the number of people who will see or hear a specific advertisement

Frequency
In advertising, the average number of times each person is reached by a specific advertisement

Most large HCOs promote themselves directly to clinical professionals in short supply.[13] Programs to attract physicians who seek locations to practice primary care medicine are commonplace; considerable care and expense is justified in light of the importance of the decision on both sides.[14] Many organizations advertise routinely in nursing, physical therapy, and pharmacy journals to attract new professionals.

Strategic affiliations to recruit personnel are also common.[15] Affiliation with teaching programs enhances recruitment and retention of graduating students. Programs to assist students with summer and part-time work affect not only the students directly involved but also their classmates, who learn by word of mouth. Some institutions reach several years below graduation. Working with inner-city high schools to encourage young people to enter healing professions is popular. Like many promotional activities, it reaches two audiences—the students and the community at large. North Mississippi Medical Center operates a program beginning with "Let's Pretend Hospital, a tool to educate first graders in health care careers."[16] Current nonprofessional associates are also an important source for more skilled opportunities. Scholarships and scheduling assistance to permit further education are common.

Managing Other Stakeholder Relationships

One aspect of marketing is the deliberate management of relationships with other organizations. To understand the issues, it is useful to consider healthcare as a large set of component functions and services. These include inpatient and outpatient service lines, primary care sites, and long-term care facilities. They also include support activities, such as pharmacies and Meals on Wheels, and preventive activities, such as exercise programs, health education, vaccination, and screening. A *cottage model* of healthcare has all of these activities operating as independent units that deal directly with the patient and relate to each other as competitors or independents, with occasional brief contracts. Several vendors compete in each function. Much of U.S. healthcare follows the cottage model—individually owned and operated units providing one or a small set of services to one community. Alternatively, one HCO can include a comprehensive array of all services

Seek Collaborative Opportunities

under a single corporate umbrella. Some large healthcare systems, such as Kaiser-Permanente, Intermountain Healthcare, Catholic Health Initiatives, and the New York City Health and Hospitals Corporation, have incorporated large parts of the array.

An HCO must consider both horizontal (other organizations provide competing or similar services) and vertical integration (other organizations in its market provide complementary services). With which does it collaborate, with which does it compete, and on what terms? The optimum arrangement provides the community with safe, efficient, patient-centered, timely, efficient, and equitable care, but finding that arrangement can be a substantial challenge.

Many contract suppliers, such as emergency physicians, information services, and housekeeping companies, are effective horizontal collaboration examples. The hospital system movement is largely horizontal. Almost two-thirds of acute hospitals are in multihospital systems, often involving formerly competing organizations in the same community. Typical operation of these systems is still far below benchmark.[17] Significant and largely untapped opportunities also lie in vertical integration. Most primary and acute physician care is delivered by small group practices that are independent private corporations. Efforts to vertically integrate medical practices failed spectacularly in the 1990s.[18] A decade later, acute care HCOs were acquiring practices again.[19] Although many systems operate nursing homes, hospices, and home care, most long-term care is delivered by horizontally integrated or independent organizations.

Manage Collaborative Opportunities

Exhibit 15.4 shows some important healthcare components. It suggests that the question about each is "Would this service be improved if it were

1. moved to a tighter ownership/management relationship? or
2. moved to a more independent relationship in direct exposure to market forces?"

The improvement must lie in mission achievement. Closer affiliations may offer an opportunity. The HCO's logistic and strategic support services, its culture as "the best place to give care," and its ability to coordinate care across a spectrum of patient need are valuable resources that can be efficiently shared. But **transaction costs**—loss of flexibility, reduced incentives, and conflicting values among participants—differ with each structure and must be carefully evaluated as well.

Transaction costs
The costs of maintaining a relationship, including the costs of communication, negotiation, and so forth

Large organizations succeed because they invent collaborative mechanisms that are more effective than market forces.[20] The length, goal setting and performance terms, agreements for sharing information, sharing of capital investment, and market exclusivity define the collaboration. One implication

EXHIBIT 15.4

Examples of
Alternative
Collaborative
Structures for
HCO Services

Service or Function	Common Current Arrangement	Possible Alternative Structure
Primary care	Independent physician groups	Joint venture with physician owners Acquire and own practices
Ambulatory services (e.g., oncology, specialty surgery, urgent care)	Independent or horizontally integrated provider	Own or joint venture with physicians Joint venture with competing provider Contract or strategic partnership with horizontally integrated provider
Integrated service line	Owned	Joint venture
Logistic/strategic support (e.g., finance, human resources, knowledge management)	Owned	Contract with strategic partners Centralize in multihospital healthcare organization
Clinical support services	Owned	Strategic partnership with horizontally integrated provider
Health promotion and preventive activity	Independent or not offered	Strategic partnership with community agencies
Long-term services (e.g., home, hospice, nursing home care)	Independent or horizontally integrated providers	Own Joint venture with competing acute care provider Strategic partnership with specialty provider
Low-volume specialty care (e.g., mental, long-term acute care)	Independent or horizontally integrated providers	Joint venture with competing acute care provider Contract or joint venture with current provider

of the pair of questions is that any component of the existing organization can be sold to or merged with another organization or replaced by a contract relationship. Conceptually, an HCO could be a governing board that manages a large set of relationships with independent companies just as easily as it could be a corporation that owns the full array of services. At some point, the transaction costs exceed the benefit of collaboration; independence will be more successful.

Most modern HCOs now collaborate on several major services, of which physician organizations may be the most important. The networks they have created require constant relationship management. Exhibit 15.5 suggests several common levels of collaborative activity:

EXHIBIT 15.5
Spectrum
of Potential
Relationships
with
Organizations

Potential Relationship to HCO
None: arms-length negotiation of each
     encounter
Agreement to collaborate: expression of
     shared elements of mission
Contracts: Prearranged processes for
     patients with certain needs
Strategic partnership: longer term and
     broader commitment, usually including
     negotiation of issues that arise
Joint venture: strategic partnership plus
     shared capital investment
Wholly owned subsidiary: separate
     corporation with defined mission
Unit of parent corporation participates in
     annual goal setting and all appropriate
     programs

Health promotion
or care unit
(e.g., service line, primary
care office, health
promotion program,
hospice, hospital)

- *Short-term, market-driven contracts include patient referrals, purchases, temporary worker contracts, or consulting engagements.* The need for repeat business is the principal force for performance. Standards are set by the market and are often implicit rather than explicit.
- *Strategic partnerships include health insurance participation agreements, physician-hospital privileging, supplier contracts, or outsourcing contracts.*[21] The contract attempts to specify performance characteristics, including incentives, and is written for a year or more. The standards are explicit and are managed like internal organization expectations—that is, they are negotiated regularly. The standards improve over time, and the intent is to keep the partnership in place. The arrangement can be abrogated, however, if desired by either partner.
- *Joint ventures involve capital investment by both partners, such as ambulatory treatment centers or shared high-cost, low-volume equipment.* Joint ventures usually have joint governance or management teams. The capital investment makes them more difficult to abrogate, and they are usually expected to be permanent.
- *Mergers are where the capital, governance, and management of prior corporate entities are replaced by a new combined entity.* Mergers are generally irreversible.
- *Acquisitions are where one existing entity totally acquires another.* The acquiring company owns the capital and continues governance and management. Acquisitions are generally irreversible.

Improving the Marketing Activity

Marketing functions are difficult to evaluate, but annual review, identification of opportunities for improvement (OFIs), and deliberate improvement plans are still critical. Specific promotional campaigns for branding, influencing patient behavior, or specific communication to associates can be quantitatively assessed (see the "Measures" section). More general activities, such as external relations and ongoing associate relations, must be measured by the strategic scorecard. Market share and satisfaction data measure performance. The epidemiologic planning model is useful to compare an HCO's market share with competitor HCOs to analyze the effectiveness of the marketing strategy and to revise the strategy, as needed. Qualitative indicators from listening are important.

Strategic Functions

Strategy—the placement of the organization in its environment—can be said to pick up where marketing leaves off, but more accurately, the two are seamlessly connected. If marketing is about relationships, strategy is the selection and prioritization of relationships. The organization identifies its strategy through its governance processes (Chapter 4) and implements it through its operations. The strategic functions (Exhibit 15.1) are the specific activities that help the organization maintain an effective strategy in a dynamic environment.

Maintaining the Mission, Vision, and Values

The mission, vision, and values represent the most central desires of the owners and stakeholders and, as such, become the cornerstone for all subsequent planning decisions.[22] To fulfill that function, they should be as permanent as possible, but even the most carefully set mission may lose its relevance in a dynamic environment. Even though major change is infrequent in the mission and even rarer in the vision, well-run organizations review the need for change annually. Periodically, the organization should undertake a broad-scale review—sometimes called *visioning*. Actual revisions are developed by extensive listening and discussion among large numbers of stakeholders. Several task forces (often involving hundreds of people) are established to attract representation from most of the organization's stakeholders in the debate about possible revisions. The review process not only develops consensus positions, but it also increases stakeholder understanding of others' viewpoints and the reasons for specific wording. Marketing must manage the task forces, keep track of proposed changes, and arrange for the resolution of serious disagreements. The final changes require formal governing board adoption.

Defining the Strategic Position

As discussed in Chapter 1, the mission, vision, ownership, scope of services, location, and partners of the organization define its **strategic position**. Strategic positioning establishes broad understanding so that the leadership team can implement effectively and respond to external challenges and opportunities. Successful strategic positions are constructed by identifying alternatives (what-ifs),

Strategic position
The set of decisions about mission, ownership, scope of activity, location, and partners that defines the organization and relates it to stakeholder needs

testing the alternatives extensively with simulations and pilots, and evaluating the tests in task forces or committees of the most knowledgeable stakeholders.

Identify Strategic Opportunities

The strategic positioning process is shown in Exhibit 1.14. Strategic alternatives are identified through an ongoing review directed by the senior management team and presented to the governing board for discussion, amendment, and approval. The governing board reviews strategy whenever necessary, but always at the time of the annual environmental review. The fact-finding and analysis are done by marketing, internal consulting, and finance associates, often with assistance from other units.

The review begins by assessing performance on each of the four dimensions of the strategic balanced scorecard—financial, operational, customer, and learning (exhibits 1.11 and 3.4).[23] Achievements are compared to the prior year's expectations, competitor achievements, and benchmarks. Changes in external conditions are noted in the environmental assessment and often flagged as "threats" or "opportunities." Specific areas of each dimension are often categorized as strengths or OFIs, creating a profile that tests both the organization's goals and its performance. The resulting display (called a SWOT [strength, weakness, opportunity, threat] analysis) is checked against the mission and vision and used to identify what the organization could be.

A key part of the review is the study of overall patterns and identification of the interrelationship between the performance dimensions. Study of high-performing organizations is helpful. Innovative thinking that transcends traditional boundaries helps identify truly creative opportunities.[24] Porter's framework for evaluating strategy is useful, both to improve the balanced scorecard measures and to identify important questions. The framework suggests that strategy must address questions from "five forces" or external domains:[25]

1. *Buyers and customers.* What are buyers', patients', and the community's needs? What opportunities for measured improvement are revealed by benchmarking quality, cost, access, and amenities? What unique economic or epidemiologic characteristics should be incorporated into specific strategies?
2. *New technology and substitutes.* What are the implications of new diagnostic and treatment technology? What opportunities exist to reduce the cost of technology, such as by substituting less expensive protocols or changing processes to use less skilled personnel? What opportunities for improvement are presented by new operational technology, such as the electronic medical record and the Internet?
3. *Resource availability.* What funds are available for investment in expansion or renovation? What human resources are required, and how will they be acquired? What opportunities exist to improve retention and service excellence? What land is required? How effectively is the organization using its information resources?

4. *Competitor activity.* What actions are competitors taking, and what are the implications of those actions for our strategy? What opportunities exist to forward stakeholder goals by collaboration with competitors?

5. *Potential competitors and regulatory impact.* What new models of healthcare delivery are being developed elsewhere? Which stakeholder groups might start competing organizations, and why? What regulatory protections does the existing organization have? What incentives are offered to encourage competitors? What actions might the organization take to forestall competition?

The review helps a large number of associates understand the organization's profile of needs and achievements and the possible improvements. The result is that the strategic position is not secret. In the words of the Intermountain Healthcare planner Greg Poulsen, "It's in our competitors' portfolio tomorrow morning."[26] The Intermountain approach is to win not on secrecy but on sound selection and effective implementation. Speed and thoroughness are both important.

Evaluate Strategic Opportunities

The opportunities determined by the review are identified and roughly prioritized. Various ways to improve the institution's position—usually called **scenarios**—are proposed and evaluated against the agenda of opportunities. Some die quickly, as major flaws appear. Others receive detailed and quantitative review, and models of their implications are constructed. Models—also called **business plans**—consist of a narrative that describes the alternative as clearly as possible and identifies how it differs from current practice; they also include a quantitative simulation that forecasts the changes in key strategic scorecard measures. The models and their results are evaluated by teams of associates and stakeholders to test the proposal for contribution to mission, synergy with existing programs, risk of failure, fit with the environment, and fit with accessible resources.

Scenarios
Alternative approaches to improving the profile of opportunities reflected in the environmental assessment

Business plan
A model of a specific strategy or function that guides design, operations, and goal setting

Various devices can be used to stimulate discussion and understanding of alternatives. A matrix that allows two dimensions of desirability to be considered is sometimes useful. There are several alternatives for defining the axes. The versions by the Boston Consulting Group[27] or General Electric[28] are popular. Both lead to a display such as that illustrated in Exhibit 15.6, where the axes are market attractiveness (opportunities for growth or profit) and organizational advantage (internal resources, sometimes called "competencies"). Expanding an existing competency is generally easier than developing new competencies, but ignoring the market is perilous. The display is useful to focus attention on these trade-offs. For example, a small rural hospital, noting a high demand for home care and respite care in its community and its skills for providing such services (Situation A), would

EXHIBIT 15.6
Matrix of
Market
Attractiveness
and Advantage

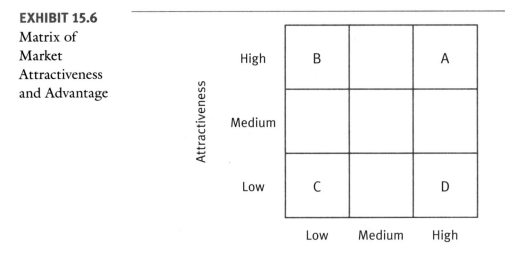

Situation A, where the market is attractive and the hospital has a strong advantage, is one that would be selected for further investment.

Situation B, where the market is attractive, but the hospital faces a large or difficult investment, would be judged on its importance to overall market share.

Situation C, where both market and advantage are low, would be phased out or avoided.

Situation D, where the attractiveness is low, but the hospital has an advantage, would be supported but expanded only to the extent market support could be foreseen.

include them in its plans. Obstetrics, important to the customers but expensive for the hospital (Situation B), would be retained. A high-tech service, only infrequently needed and requiring specialists who are difficult to recruit (Situation C), would be avoided. A service already in place, with specialists who attract market share from elsewhere (Situation D), would be retained or expanded. The resource barrier that exists in C has been met in D, and the investment gives the hospital an advantage.

Strategic Theories

Theories for corporate strategy are common, but they do not transfer easily to the complexities of healthcare. Eastaugh[29] has modified four corporate archetypes designed by Miles and Snow[30]—prospector, analyzer, reactor, and defender—to fit hospitals. The differences between the archetypes are two dimensional, as shown in Exhibit 15.7. One dimension—willingness to seek innovation outside the traditional parameters—is external and tends to higher risk. The other dimension—concentration on meeting quality and cost standards in the core business—is internal, analytic, and risk averse. The evidence suggests that prospectors and defenders do badly; too much risk and too little action are both dangerous. Analyzers do better than defenders; carefully selected innovation is better than sticking too closely to established models. Reactors do worst.

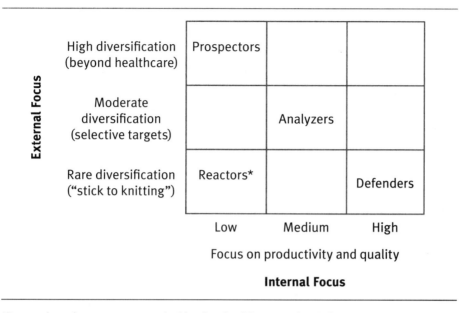

EXHIBIT 15.7
Miles and Snow
Typology of
Strategic Types

*Reactors do not have a strong strategy in either direction. They respond passively to competitors.

Other strategic philosophies have been built around the concept of distinctive competencies—market success depends on excelling in some characteristic that is attractive to customers.[31] They reflect various approaches to defining the competency. Porter's "cost leadership versus [quality] differentiation,"[32] is blunted in healthcare by the insurance mechanism, which protects both patients and physicians from cost differences, but quality and service are important differentiators. Miller and Friesen's "adaptive, dominant, giant, conglomerate, and niche innovator" describes different approaches to strategic opportunities as well as different corporate cultures.[33] Niche strategies deliberately seek highly specialized services that include factors that are difficult for competitors to copy. Specialty hospitals that serve children, the mentally ill, cancer patients, and the like are following niche strategies. Small, rural HCOs that offer primary care and limited hospitalization are also niche strategists, and so are independent home care and hospice organizations.

The specialty hospital movement—independent, usually for-profit doctor-owned facilities that provide a single service line—is a niche strategy.[34,35] Actual experience suggests that specialty hospitals may introduce serious problems for patients who do not clearly fit the niche, have emergency needs, lack funding, or have multiple conditions.[36] Specialty hospitals per se encountered political resistance beginning in 2003.[37,38] In 2006, CMS implemented revised procedures for enrolling specialty hospitals with an emphasis on the provision of emergency care, transparency in hospital investment, and an enforcement of Stark and antikickback rules regarding improper investment (physician self-referral).[39]

The excellent HCOs used as models by *The Well-Managed Healthcare Organization* have pursued comprehensive rather than niche strategies. They have used transformational management, evidence-based management, and the service excellence model to build communitywide customer and provider brand loyalty. They have countered niche competition with service lines and joint ventures that offer niche services in integrated settings. Their strategic thought roughly matches "conglomerate"; they seek comprehensive coverage of market needs and are willing to explore multiple corporate and collaborative structures.

Document the Strategy

Many strategy elements take several years to implement. Implementation processes and new strategies must be coordinated with those in preparation as well as those in place. The decisions that result from the strategic analysis process are incorporated in a set of documents sometimes called the *long-range* or *strategic plans*. The documentation includes the following parts:

- *Environmental forecasts*. These are derived from the environmental assessment, cover about five years, and identify potential directions of change for a second five years. They are updated annually but serve as a central resource and database for the planning activities of all units.
- *Services plan*. This specifies the clinical services and other major activities in which the institution will engage, with annual forecasts of the expected volume and achievement of goals for cost, quality, worker satisfaction, and customer satisfaction.
- *Long-range financial plan*. This summarizes the expected financial impact on income statements, cash flow, long-term debt, and balance sheets (Chapter 13).
- *Information services plan*. This describes the future capability and hardware array of information service, including plans for collection, standardization, communication, and archiving of data (Chapter 10).
- *Human resources plan*. This shows the expected personnel needs, terminations, and recruitment requirements (Chapter 11).
- *Medical staff plan*. This is a part of the human resources plan that focuses on physician replacement and recruitment (Chapter 6).
- *Facilities master plan*. This details the construction and renovation activities (Chapter 12).

Although the plans may be separate documents, the processes that generate the decisions must be integrated. In general, mission and vision drive services and finances, and these, in turn, drive facilities, human resources, and information needs. Thus, the plans have a hierarchical relationship. Internal consulting is responsible for coordinating the strategic plans. The other technical and logistic support services are responsible for their components.

Implementing the Strategic Position

The consensus that emerges from the review of scenarios and the governing board's actions is a set of approved projects to be implemented, with timetables and specific strategic scorecard goals for the next several years. Implementation involves many activities that must be coordinated. The changing environment may open important opportunities or threats. Thus, a critical part of implementation is rechecking the basic strategy against the environment and making adjustments. Implementation is managed by senior management, internal consulting, and the operating teams involved. Most projects have management teams that meet regularly to monitor progress and adapt to occurring changes. Major projects have direct senior management participation, and progress is reported to the board.

People

Associates

Marketing processes are increasingly sophisticated. A master's degree in business or health administration is a useful beginning, but neither degree emphasizes the details of advertising or public relations. Experience with a commercial agency or a successful healthcare marketing team is highly desirable for the senior marketing team.

Consultants are available for most marketing functions. Advertising is purchased from agencies with experience in design, campaign development, and media contracts. Market studies and customer surveys are often contracted to consultants. The consultant should be able to achieve better results and lower costs than if the HCO did the surveys itself. The database that results from continuing study of a market is a valuable proprietary resource. Even if much of the data collection is delegated to consultants, the organization should make an effort to retain the data in their entirety. Consultants can assist in strategic marketing by providing data collection and by undertaking sensitive inquiries. Negotiation is often retained as an activity of the chief executive officer (CEO) or senior staff, but consultants and trustees may be as effective as negotiators, intermediaries, or mediators.

Strategy is learned by practice. A business or health master's degree is a sound beginning. Experience in marketing, finance, or internal consulting is helpful to improve judgment. Several years' participation with an excellent team is important.

Organization

Exhibit 15.8 suggests the formal marketing accountability hierarchy for a large organization. In smaller organizations, most of the specific accountability centers disappear and consultants are used extensively. The dividing lines between marketing, planning, and internal consulting are flexible; the activities can be combined in various ways, including a single unit. In multihospital systems, a central marketing unit can offer in-house consultant service, at least theoretically providing a competitive advantage.

Strategic support is an activity of the entire senior leadership team. Planning, marketing, and internal consulting units generally provide technical assistance, and outside consultants are frequently used. A voice in senior management is essential; in Exhibit 15.8 it is provided by the senior vice president. The role includes monitoring progress on the various marketing and strategic planning activities and keeping the issues of the environmental assessment before the team.

The senior manager who leads marketing and strategy must also defend investment in these activities. The cost of strategic positioning and much of marketing is an overhead item, not easily approached through transfer pricing. (The clients of strategic positioning are the stakeholders, not the units of the organization.) Transfer payments can be established for some marketing services, such as promotional campaigns. The judgment of "enough" investment in strategy and marketing is challenging. The best answer is probably based more on meeting internal judgment than on external benchmarking. Senior management and governance should be convinced that an adequate environmental assessment is being performed and that progress on major strategic agendas is appropriate to long-term market needs. An HCO that cannot meet these conditions is a candidate for merger, acquisition, or closure.

Measures

Measurement of marketing and strategy is challenging but useful. Strategic strength itself can be assessed inferentially from the strategic scorecard. Operational goals can be established for marketing teams and strategic teams. Specific promotions can be measured and compared to goals. Audits by outsiders can often identify specific OFIs. Operational success does not guarantee strategic success, although it certainly contributes to it.

Strategic Activity

Strategic success is measured by the strategic scorecard. The strategic activity itself is diffuse and continuous, making goal setting and accountability difficult. Declines or repeated failure to meet goals are serious negative signals that should never be ignored. Some key indicators apply to the HCO as a whole and to individual service lines:

- *Market share.* Although growth is desirable in many competitive situations, it should not be a universal goal. Many HCOs have high shares of local markets and cannot appropriately increase them. Some competitive situations reflect stable HCOs, where each performs near benchmark on cost, quality,

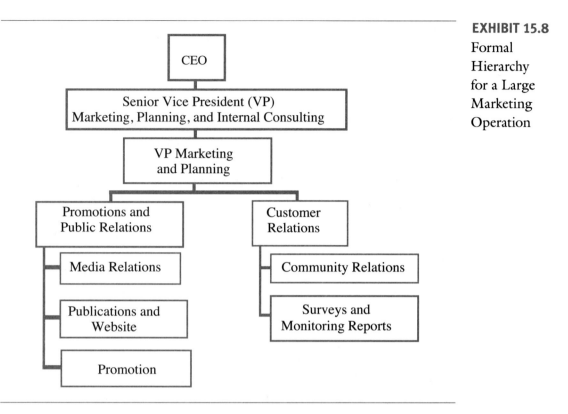

EXHIBIT 15.8
Formal
Hierarchy
for a Large
Marketing
Operation

and patient satisfaction. Growth cannot reasonably improve communitywide performance. Declining market share is a critical signal; if it is not reversed, it suggests that the HCO should be closed, merged, or substantially restructured.

- *Costs.* Excellent HCOs operate profitably most of the time. The business cycle or other unusual situation may temporarily impair profits. Safety-net HCOs and others that operate in impaired economies may have chronic difficulty. The long-term expectation must be for sufficient cash flow (profits plus depreciation) to manage debt and meet replacement needs. An HCO that cannot meet that expectation needs substantial restructuring. Review of other operating measures, particularly patient satisfaction, quality of care, and unit costs of specific services, usually suggests a strong agenda of OFIs.

- *Associate satisfaction.* Failure to attract and retain qualified associates is a signal that requires prompt correction.

- *Overall HCO goal achievement.* A medium-sized HCO sets several thousand specific goals each year and expects to achieve a high percentage of them. A failure rate of more than 5 percent is an important signal, and one that is more than 10 percent is probably disabling. The solution may lie in better performance improvement, an improved and more responsive culture, enhanced training, or more realistic goal setting. It may also involve strategic repositioning.

- *Surprises.* One perspective of strategy is to protect the organization by foreseeing external change in time to adapt to it. Thus, a goal of the strategic activity should be "no surprises"—no unforeseen foreseeable events. Certainly, each major surprise is a sentinel event that is worthy of critical review to understand if it could have been prevented and how.

While interpreting these measures is not as straightforward as many other performance evaluations, the senior management team is properly accountable. The member of senior management charged with marketing and strategic services is obligated to monitor performance and report routinely, keeping the strategic scorecard prominent in all discussions.

Operational Measures

Strategic and marketing services have operational scorecards as well. Total expenditures, although difficult to benchmark, are certainly a focus for goal setting. Client satisfaction, error rates, unfinished assignments, and service delays are useful measures.

Marketing Activity

Promotional campaigns for branding or for specific services should have built-in pre- and post-campaign evaluations. Campaigns identify specific goals, such as market share or behavior change in population segments. Their costs can be estimated, expectations established about outcomes, and actual results compared to expectations. Expectations can be set about exposures (reach times frequency), response rates (demand), costs, costs per exposure and per response, process quality, timeliness, and changes in customer satisfaction and target market share.

Surveys and statistical analysis of behaviors can evaluate the impact of the promotion. For example, an organization might identify several strategies to expand market share, using several service lines; centers of excellence in certain referral specialties; and an expanded availability of primary care physicians. Each of these has specific measures that can be evaluated by surveying the community to gauge recognition of the promotional material and responses and by analyzing trends in new registrants for the various services. Expectations for improvement in these measures can be established and performance evaluated, as shown in Exhibit 15.9. Campaigns may take several years, but interim progress can be evaluated annually.

Audits

Auditing—systematic review by an outside observer team—can supplement these measures, both with increased understanding of accountabilities and evaluation of more subjective marketing activities. An audit performed by an outside consultant might review quantitative results, pointing out comparable values from other organizations. (True benchmarking is unlikely because other communities are not strictly comparable.) A consultant can conduct or validate surveys or analyses that show results. A consultant can review practices, goals, and organization structures and can suggest opportunities for improvement. Even without a consultant, an internal 360-review process

EXHIBIT 15.9
Measures
for Specific
Campaigns

Campaign	Actions	Measures
Centers of excellence in orthopedics, cardiology	Preparation of data on cost per case and quality of results Publication of original research in peer-reviewed journals, distribution of reprints Direct sales to managers of local HMOs, PPOs Competitive bid for Medicare, Medicaid contracts Presentations to primary care physicians Feature stories in local media Media promotion	Increase in listings or contracts with intermediaries Change in total demand, market share Change in cost per case Change in profit per case Cost of campaign per new case Number of public relations appearances, audience size Number of exposures, exposures/target audience member, cost/exposure by medium Survey of awareness and attractiveness Number of subscribers, percent of total market, cost per subscriber Surveys of patient satisfaction
Increased primary care access	Direct mailing to physicians in primary care fellowships Coordination with presently affiliated physicians Meetings with local physicians affiliated with competitors Program of practice acquisition, expansion Introduction of nurse practitioners Media advertising and public relations Program of office support	Number of new responses Number of new physicians recruited Number of nurse practitioners placed, demand for nurse practitioner services Patient visits/physician Delay for emergency, routine, and preventive office visits Patient satisfaction Program cost per new physician, per new visit

HMO: health maintenance organization; PPO: preferred provider organization

can accomplish many of the same objectives by systematically surveying associates in the unit and users of the service. Periodic supplementation by an independent outsider improves the reliability of internal review.

Managerial Issues

Successful organizations succeed because they face strategic issues systematically. Success in strategy is an ability to identify and implement the right changes. It requires technical and cultural skills and effective senior leadership. Success feeds on itself. Because it meets needs, it attracts support, and the support provides resources for further expansion.[40] On the other hand, studies of the failures of HCOs usually reveal that strategic errors were made several years before the ultimate crisis, and often repeatedly.[41] Unfortunately, excellence is extremely rare.[42]

Hospitals and their associated physicians fall alarmingly short on safety,[43] quality,[44] effectiveness,[45,46] patient satisfaction,[47] and cost.[48,49] Studies of trends in available national measures of performance suggest that the typical hospital is not strategically managed; it is simply drifting.[50]

Skills for Successful Strategy

Successful strategic positioning depends on two factors: (1) the ability to identify promising strategies quickly and accurately from a broad range of alternatives and (2) the ability to implement the selected strategies effectively. Hamel and Prahalad point out that corporations that thrive in competitive markets have greater ambition and follow a rigorous program of focused, complementary innovation.[51] In healthcare, provider logic, rather than customer logic, has traditionally driven innovation—that is, new products and services are often driven from the perspective of a technological challenge, rather than the perspective of what the customer might want given a full understanding of the options. (Cesarean sections, circumcisions, prostatectomies, and executive physicals are among the more glaring examples.) Missing, so far, are creativity, role-playing, and break-through innovation oriented around customer realities. There are methods and styles of delivering healthcare we have not yet dreamed.

The hospitals that are now well managed speak of "a journey."[52] They have made a series of changes that, over a period of a few years, has moved them from drift to excellence. Governance and senior management commitment are essential to start the journey and to sustain it. Excellence requires breaking old habits, learning new skills, and building a new culture. Strategic issues require weighing core values. The rewards and penalties are deferred, and the decisions are difficult and sometimes painful. Denial is always tempting, particularly when things are going at least tolerably well. Governance and senior management must support, encourage, teach, and reassure for the change to succeed. The journey is completed by building a strong technical foundation. What begins as commitment is translated to a way of life by tools that make addressing the issues easy and denying them hard.

Strategic Leadership Requirements

In the future, senior management will spend most of their time negotiating relationships. The evidence-based approach and the commitment to mission will provide the foundation for dialogue. A sound tradition of consensus building will make the negotiations fruitful. The governing board will have a role in negotiations and will establish and control the general direction of the organization through its function of selecting the executive, the mission, the strategic position, and the annual goals.

Evidence that the HCO contributes to the whole community is a powerful negotiating tool. Individuals seek their personal betterment, but evidence that the organization meets broader needs suggests both fairness and long-term stability, strengthening the case for a constructive relationship. It is not an accident that associates want to work at excellent organizations or that success feeds on itself. Excellent HCOs are rewards based rather than adversarial. The foundation of their posture toward associates, competitors, and the community at large is collaboration to achieve mutual goals. Potential associates and partners can approach the negotiations, recognizing that the organization fulfills healthcare, employment, and financial goals well and that strengthening the organization benefits the community and its citizens.

Evidence of Commitment to Community Needs

A strong consensus-building process must underpin the negotiations. The evidence from the leading organizations suggests that consensus building has three parts: (1) acceptance of the mission and the evidence-based approach, (2) careful and sensitive listening, and (3) due process. The first preselects, so those who do not accept the validity of the mission and the evidence-based approach need not open discussions. The second provides flexibility and room for innovation. It promotes dialogue to identify innovations and prevents disputes by promptly addressing potentially threatening issues. The third protects the rights of the parties and shows respect. Appeal processes, rules to balance power asymmetries, and mediation and techniques for conflict resolution are available, although the evidence suggests they will not often be needed.

A Consensus-Building Process

In leading HCOs, the trustees are focused on the core strategic decisions that determine the organization's future. The board's governance processes make evading their responsibility difficult. The strategic scorecard and benchmarks help them understand objectively the needs of the organization and the community. Calendars, careful preparation of alternatives, prior work by task forces and committees, and consent agendas structure the decision processes. Guidance from more experienced colleagues helps new members learn responsibilities. The evidence-based approach helps them understand the choices they must make. Strict adherence to conflict-of-interest rules helps them make decisions in the owners' best interest. The best boards now use both individual self-assessment and annual review of the board's decisions and processes to improve their performance.

Trustee Education and Continuous Improvement of Governance

Multihospital System Contribution

The technical and leadership requirements for strategic excellence suggest a powerful advantage for large, multisite healthcare systems. Catholic Health Initiatives,[53] SSM Health Care,[54] and Intermountain Healthcare[55] have exploited this possibility and can document their superiority on the strategic scorecard. Effective healthcare systems can develop expertise in the tools and, in fact, promote learning across their member organizations.

The successful large healthcare system provides four critical contributions:

1. *Shaping the mission, vision, and values to a comprehensive stakeholder perspective and emphasizing those commitments in day-to-day decisions.*[56] The discipline to recognize that long-run success must be mutual success should be the first commitment of the central organization. Catholic Health Initiatives and SSM Health Care show clearly that the discipline can be effectively and productively enforced.
2. *Insisting that the performance of centralized processes be benchmarked.* Moving from purely local healthcare to centralized models is progress only if the measured performance improves. Decisions to centralize are a variant of the make-or-buy decision; they should be made on objective criteria, and implementation should achieve the initial goals. The healthcare system can ensure that this happens.
3. *Maintaining a listening and collaborative environment.* Authoritarian behavior on the part of central managers is profoundly destructive. Sensitive listening, using all the marketing tools to identify both patient and associate needs at the local sites and responding to those needs, makes centralization viable. Senior management also supports a culture of empowerment and transformational management in the local sites.
4. *Maintaining a learning environment.* Systems can and should focus on ongoing education for HCO leaders and trustees. They can reduce the cost of training with centralized learning tools. They can implement succession planning and management development, based on competency assessment tools and plans for addressing deficiencies. They can and do promote mentoring and peer learning across their organization, based on what high-performing HCOs have proven to be successful.

The models for the twenty-first century are with us today. They are too little recognized, too seldom copied, and too often ignored in favor of short-term single stakeholder advantage.

Suggested Readings

Berkowitz, E. N. 2006. *Essentials of Health Care Marketing,* 2nd ed. Boston: Jones and Bartlett Publishers.

Fortenberry, Jr., J. L. 2009. *Health Care Marketing: Tools and Techniques,* 3rd ed. Boston: Jones and Bartlett Publishers.

Kotler, P., and G. Armstrong. 2007. *Principles of Marketing,* 12th ed. Englewood Cliffs, NJ: Prentice-Hall.

Kotler, P., J. Shalowitz, and R. J. Stevens. 2008. *Strategic Marketing for Health Care Organizations: Building a Customer-Driven Health System.* San Francisco: Jossey-Bass.

Swayne, L. E., J. Duncan, and P. M. Ginter. 2009. *Strategic Management of Health Care Organizations,* 6th ed. San Francisco: Jossey-Bass.

Notes

1. Kotler, P., and R. N. Clarke. 1987. *Marketing for Health Care Organizations,* 5. Englewood Cliffs, NJ: Prentice-Hall.
2. Centers for Medicare & Medicaid Services. 2001. [Online information; retrieved 9/29/09.] www.hospitalcompare.hhs.gov.
3. *Ibid.,* 2009. [Online information; retrieved 7/7/09.] www.cms.hhs.gov/Hospital QualityInits/30_HospitalHCAHPS.asp.
4. Agency for Healthcare Research and Quality. 2009. [Online information; retrieved 9/8/05.] www.cahps.ahrq.gov/content/products/PROD_AmbCareSurveys .asp?p=102&s=21.
5. McDonald, K. M., P. Romano, J. Geppert, et al. 2002. "Measures of Patient Safety Based on Hospital Administrative Data—The Patient Safety Indicators." Technical Review 5. Prepared by the University of California San Francisco-Stanford Evidence-Based Practice Center, Contract No. 290-97-0023. AHRQ Publication No. 02-0038. Rockville, MD: Agency for Healthcare Research and Quality. [Online information; retrieved 7/8/09.] www.ahrq.gov/downloads/pub/evidence/pdf/ psi/psi.pdf.
6. Thomson Reuters. 2009. *100 Top Hospitals, 2009.* Evanston, IL: Thomson Reuters.
7. Commonwealth Fund. 2009. [Online information; retrieved 7/7/09.] www .whynotthebest.org.
8. Snihurowych, R. R., F. Cornelius, and V. E. Amelung. 2009. "Can Branding by Health Care Provider Organizations Drive the Delivery of Higher Technical and Service Quality? *Quality Management in Health Care* 18 (2): 126–34.
9. Society for Healthcare Strategy and Market Development. 2002. *Crisis Communications in Healthcare: Managing Difficult Times Effectively,* 7. Chicago: SHSMD.
10. Conrad, P., and V. Leiter. 2004. "Medicalization, Markets and Consumers." *Journal of Health and Social Behavior* 45 (Suppl.): 158–76.
11. MacStravic, R. S. 1989. "Use Marketing to Reduce Malpractice Costs in Health Care." *Health Care Management Review* 14 (4): 54.
12. Curtis, P., and G. Bove. 1992. "Family Physicians, Chiropractors, and Back Pain." *Journal of Family Practice* 35 (5): 551–55.
13. Buerhaus, P. I., K. Donelan, L. Norman, and R. Dittus. 2005. "Nursing Students' Perceptions of a Career in Nursing and Impact of a National Campaign Designed to Attract People Into the Nursing Profession." *Journal of Professional Nursing* 21 (2): 75–83.
14. Pathman, D. E., D. H. Taylor, Jr., T. R. Konrad, T. S. King, T. Harris, T. M. Henderson, J. D. Bernstein, T. Tucker, K. D. Crook, C. Spaulding, and G. C. Koch. 2000. "State Scholarship, Loan Forgiveness, and Related Programs: The Unheralded Safety Net." *JAMA* 284 (16): 2084–92.
15. Cleary, B., R. Rice, M. L. Brunell, G. Dickson, E. Gloor, D. Jones, and W. Jones. 2005. "Strategic State-Level Nursing Workforce Initiatives: Taking the Long View." *Nursing Administration Quarterly* 29 (2): 162–70.
16. North Mississippi Medical Center, 2006. Malcolm Baldrige National Quality Aware Application. [Online information; retrieved 9/30/09.] www.baldrige.nist .gov/Contacts_Profiles.htm.

17. Griffith, J. R., J. A. Alexander, and D. A. Foster. 2006. "Is Anybody Managing the Store? National Trends in Hospital Performance." *Journal of Healthcare Management* 51 (6): 392–405.

18. Jackson, C. 2001. "After Sell-Off, Phycor May Be Heading Toward Extinction." *American Medical News.* [Online information; retrieved 10/31/01.] www.ama-assn.org/sci-pubs/amnews.

19. Casalino, L. P., E. A. November, R. A., Berenson, and H. H. Pham. 2008. "Hospital–Physician Relations: Two Tracks and the Decline of the Voluntary Medical Staff Model." *Health Affairs* 27 (5): 1305–14.

20. Chandler, A. D. 1977. *The Visible Hand: The Managerial Revolution in American Business.* Cambridge, MA: Belknap Press.

21. Roberts, V. 2001. "Managing Strategic Outsourcing in the Healthcare Industry." *Journal of Healthcare Management* 46 (4): 239–49.

22. Zuckerman, A. M. 2000. "Creating a Vision for the Twenty-First Century Healthcare Organization." *Journal of Healthcare Management* 45 (5): 294–305.

23. Kaplan, R. S., and D. P. Norton. 2000. "Having Trouble with Your Strategy? Then Map It." *Harvard Business Review* 78 (5): 167–76, 202.

24. Stacey, R. D. 1992. *Managing the Unknowable: Strategic Boundaries Between Order and Chaos in Organizations*, 80–100. San Francisco: Jossey-Bass.

25. Porter, M. E. 1980. *Competitive Strategy: Techniques for Analyzing Industries and Competitors*, 4. New York: Free Press.

26. Griffith, J. R., V. Sahney, and R. Mohr. 1995. *Reengineering Healthcare*, Chapter 4. Chicago: Health Administration Press.

27. Abell, D. F., and J. S. Hammond. 1979. *Strategic Market Planning: Problems and Analytic Approaches.* Englewood Cliffs, NJ: Prentice Hall.

28. Thomas, H., and D. Gardner. 1985. *Strategic Marketing and Management.* New York: Wiley.

29. Eastaugh, S. R. 1992. "Hospital Strategy and Financial Performance." *Health Care Management Review* 17 (3): 19–31.

30. Miles, R. E., and C. C. Snow. 1978. *Organizational Strategy, Structure and Process.* New York: McGraw-Hill.

31. Mintzberg, H., and J. B. Quinn. 1995. *The Strategy Process: Concepts, Contexts, and Cases,* 3rd ed. Paramus, NJ: Prentice Hall.

32. Porter, M. E. 1980. *Competitive Strategy: Techniques for Analyzing Industries and Competitors.* New York: Free Press.

33. Miller, D., and P. H. Friesen. 1984. *Organizations: A Quantum View.* Englewood Cliffs, NJ: Prentice Hall.

34. Herzlinger, R. 2004. *Consumer-Driven Health Care:Implications for Providers, Payers, and Policy-Makers.* San Francisco: Jossey-Bass.

35. Porter, M. E., and E. O. Teisburg. 2004. "Redefining Competition in Health Care." *Harvard Business Review* 82 (6): 64–76, 136.

36. Schneider, J. E., T. R. Miller, R. L. Ohsfeldt, M. A. Morrisey, B. A. Zelner, and L. Pengxiang. 2008. "The Economics of Specialty Hospitals." *Medical Care Research and Review* 65 (5): 531–53; discussion 554–63.

37. U.S. General Accounting Office. 2003. "Specialty Hospitals: Information on National Market Share, Physician Ownership, and Patients Served." GAO-03-683R. Washington, DC: U.S. General Accounting Office; U.S. GAO. 2003. "Geographic Location, Services Provided, and Financial Performance." GAO-04-167. Washington, DC: U.S. GAO.

38. Devers, K., L. R. Brewster, and P. B. Ginsburg. 2003. "Specialty Hospitals:

Focused Factories or Cream Skimmers?" Issue Brief No. 62. Center for Health System Change. [Online information; retrieved 11/22/05.] www.hschange.org/CONTENT/552.

39. Centers for Medicare & Medicaid Services. 2006. "Final Report to Congress Implementing the DRA Provision Affecting Specialty Hospitals." [Online information; retrieved 7/8/09.] www.cms.hhs.gov/apps/media/press/release.asp?Counter=1941.

40. Griffith, J. R., and K. R. White. 2005. "The Revolution in Hospital Management." *Journal of Healthcare Management* 50 (3): 170.

41. See, for example, Burns, L. R., J. Cacciamani, J. Clement, and W. Aquino. 2000. "The Fall of the House of AHERF." *Health Affairs* 19 (1): 7–41; Walshe, K., and S. M. Shortell. 2004. "When Things Go Wrong: How Health Care Organizations Deal with Major Failures." *Health Affairs* 23 (3): 101–11; Weber, T., C. Ornstein, M. Landsberg, and S. Hymon. 2004. "The Troubles at King/Drew—5-Part Series." *The Los Angeles Times*. [Online information; retrieved 10/21/05.] www.latimes.com/news/local/la-kingdrew-gallery,1,6594064.storygallery.

42. Griffith, J. R., and J. A. Alexander. 2002. "Measuring Comparative Hospital Performance." *Journal of Healthcare Management* 47 (1): 41–57.

43. Leape, L. L., and D. M. Berwick. 2005. "Five Years After 'To Err Is Human': What Have We Learned?" *JAMA* 293 (19): 2384.

44. Jha, A. K., Z. Li, E. J. Orav, and A. M. Epstein. 2005. "Care in U.S. Hospitals—The Hospital Quality Alliance Program." *New England Journal of Medicine* 353: 265–74.

45. Casalino, L., R. R. Gillies, S. M. Shortell, J. A. Schmittdiel, T. Bodenheimer, J. C. Robinson, T. Rundall, N. Oswald, H. Schauffler, and M. C. Wang. 2003. "External Incentives, Information Technology, and Organized Processes to Improve Health Care Quality for Patients with Chronic Diseases." *JAMA* 289 (4): 434–41.

46. McGlynn, E. A., S. M. Asch, J. Adams, J. Keesey, J. Hicks, A. DeCristofaro, and E. A. Kerr. 2003. "The Quality of Health Care Delivered to Adults in the United States." *New England Journal of Medicine* 348 (26): 2635–45.

47. Sofaer, S., and K. Firminger. 2005. "Patient Perceptions of the Quality of Health Services." *Annual Review of Public Health* 26: 513–59.

48. Reid, P. P., W. D. Compton, J. H. Grossman, and G. Fanjiang (eds.). 2005. *Building a Better Delivery System: A New Engineering/Health Care Partnership.* Washington, DC: National Academies Press.

49. Jha, A. K., E. J. Orav, A. Dobson, R. A. Book, and A. M. Epstein. 2009. "Measuring Efficiency: The Association of Hospital Costs and Quality of Care." *Health Affairs* 28 (3): 897–906.

50. Griffith, Alexander, and Foster (2006).

51. Hamel, G., and C. K. Prahalad. 1993. "Strategy as Stretch and Leverage." *Harvard Business Review* 71 (2): 75–84.

52. Ryan, M. J. 2004. "Achieving and Sustaining Quality in Healthcare." *Frontiers of Health Services Management* 20 (3): 3–11.

53. Griffith, J. R., and K. R. White. 2003. *Thinking Forward: Six Strategies for Highly Successful Organizations.* Chicago: Health Administration Press.

54. Griffith and White (2005); Ryan, Sr. M. J. 2004. "Achieving and Sustaining Quality in Healthcare." *Frontiers of Health Services Management* 20 (3): 3–11; SSM Health Care. 2005. [Online information.] www.ssmhc.com/internet/home/ssmcorp.nsf.

55. Bohmer, R., A. C. Edmondson, and L. R. Feldman. 2002. *Intermountain Health Care*, Case 9-603-066. Boston: Harvard Business Publishing; Intermountain Health Care. 2005. Intermountain Health Care Annual Report. [Online information; retrieved 9/17/05.] www.ihc.com.

56. Young, D. W., D. Barrett, J. W. Kenagy, D. C. Pinakiewicz, and S. M. McCarthy. 2001. "Value-Based Partnering in Healthcare: A Framework for Analysis." *Journal of Healthcare Management* 46 (2): 112–32.

GLOSSARY

360-degree or multi-rater review. Formal evaluation of performance by subordinates, superiors, and peers of the individual or unit

Accountability hierarchy. A reporting and communication system that links each operating unit to the governing board, usually by grouping similar centers together under middle management

Ad hoc committee. A committee formed to address a specific purpose, for a specified time period

Adjustment. A statistical technique using specification to remove variation caused by differences in the relative size of subset populations

Advanced practice nurse. A master's-prepared nurse with specialization and licensure to practice as a nurse practitioner, nurse anesthetist, nurse midwife, clinical nurse specialist, clinical nurse leader, or other advanced specialist role

Agency or accountability. The notion that the organization can rely on an individual or team to fulfill a specific, prearranged expectation

Associates. People (employees, trustees and other volunteers, and medical staff members) who give their time and energy to the HCO

Attending physicians. Physicians who have the privilege of using the hospital for patient care and who are designated as the physician of record for particular patients

Bad debt. Cost for patients who are unable to pay for care

Benchmark. The best-known value for a specific measure, from any source

Branding. A communitywide communication effort to convey the mission and the competitive advantage of the organization

Business plan. A model of a specific strategy or function that guides design, operations, and goal setting

Case manager. A health professional who advocates for the patient to receive the most appropriate treatment with acceptable quality in the most effective manner and appropriate setting at the best price

Certificate of need (CON). Certificates or approvals for new services and construction or renovation of hospitals or related facilities; issued by many states

Chief executive officer (CEO). The agent of the governing board who holds the formal accountability for the entire organization

Clinical practice guidelines. Systematically developed statements to assist practitioner and patient decisions about appropriate healthcare for specific clinical circumstances

Community health. A focus on sustaining all members of the community at their highest possible level of functioning for their individual happiness and their collective benefit

Community hospital. A short-stay general or specialty (e.g., women's, children's, eye, orthopedic) hospital, excluding those owned by the federal government

Competency. Having requisite or adequate ability or quality that results in effective action and/or superior performance in a job

Compliance programs. Programs designed to meet statutory and regulatory requirements; may be based on legislation or voluntary efforts such as accreditation

Consent agenda. A group of agenda items passed without discussion, unless a member requests a review; used to focus attention on priority matters

Credentialing. The process of validating a professional's eligibility for medical staff membership and/or privileges to be granted on the basis of academic preparation, licensing, training, certifications, and performance

Cultural competence. A set of complementary behaviors, practices, and policies that enables a system, an agency, or individuals to work and effectively serve pluralistic, multiethnic, and linguistically diverse communities

Customers. Patients and others who use the services of the organization and generally compensate the organization for those services; also, by extension, other units within the HCO that rely on a particular unit for service

Database management system. A system for retrieving shared electronic data; designed to facilitate the recovery and use of data

Empowerment. The ability of an associate to control his or her work situation in ways consistent with the mission

Epidemiologic planning model. A process to rigorously define, measure, and forecast the community served and its needs

Equal employment opportunity agencies. Government agencies that monitor the rights of associate groups; these are among those entitled access to the HCO and its records

Ethics committee. A standing multidisciplinary committee that is concerned with biomedical ethical issues and decision-making processes, formulation of policies, and review and consultation of medical ethical issues

Evidence-based management. Relies heavily on formal process specification and performance measurement

External auditor. A certified public accounting firm that attests that the accounting practices followed by the organization are sound and that the financial reports fairly represent the state of the business

Facilities master plan. A document that begins with an estimate of the space needs of each service or activity proposed in the services plan

Financial budget. Expectation of future financial performance composed of income and expense budget, budgeted financial statements, cash flow budget, and capital and new programs budget

Frequency. In advertising, the average number of times each person is reached by a specific advertisement

Functional protocols. Procedures and sets of activities to carry out elements of care

General ledger. Technically, the record of all the firm's transactions; the term often refers to the fixed and collective assets, such as depreciation, that must be allocated to operational units

Governance bylaws. A corporate document that specifies quorum rules of order, duties of standing committees and officers, and other procedures for the conduct of business

Government regulatory agencies. Agencies with established authority over healthcare activities; licensing agencies and rate-regulating commissions are examples

Gross revenue. An entry to the patient ledger of the charge for a specific healthcare service; no longer a meaningful measure

Group purchasing. Alliances that use the collective buying power of several organizations to leverage prices downward

Healthcare organization (HCO). A formal legal entity that reaches across the panorama of medicine, other clinical disciplines, and business to identify and deliver care to its community

Healthcare system. Healthcare organizations that operate multiple service units under a single ownership

Health Insurance Portability and Accountability Act (HIPAA). A 1996 federal act that establishes standards of privacy for patient information

Heuristic. Systematically employing a trial-and-error mechanism that recognizes uncertainty and proceeds cyclically as more information is gathered

Homeostasis. A state of equilibrium with one's environment

Horizontal integration. Integration of organizations that provide the same kind of service, such as two hospitals or two clinics

Hospice. A model of caregiving that assists with physical, emotional, spiritual, psychological, social, financial, and legal needs of the dying patient and his family; the service may be provided in the patient's home or in an HCO

Hospitalists. Physicians who manage broad categories of hospitalized patients

Incident report. See *unexpected event report*

Interdisciplinary plan of care (IPOC). A process that includes the patient, the family, and all clinical disciplines involved in planning and providing care to patients, from system point of entry, throughout the entire acute care episode and to the next level of care

Intermediary. A payment or management agent for healthcare insurance (e.g., Medicare intermediaries that pay providers as agents for CMS)

Internal customers. Associates and teams who work inside the HCO

Joint ventures. Formal, long-term collaborative contracts usually involving equity investment

Leadership succession plan. A written plan for replacing people who depart from management positions

Legacy system. Outdated computer software that lacks the features found in more current versions

Licensure. Government approval to perform specified activities

Long-range financial plan (LRFP). An ongoing projection of financial position showing earnings, debt, and capitalization for at least the next seven years

Loyal/secure customers. Customers whose opinions of the organization are so positive that they will return for further interaction and will recommend or refer the organization to others

Management letter. Comments of external auditors to the governing board that accompany their audited financial report

Managerial accounting. A process of restructuring transaction data to support monitoring, planning, setting expectations, and improving performance of accountability centers

Marketing. The deliberate effort to establish fruitful relationships with exchange partners and stakeholders

Medicaid agency. The state agency handling claims and payments for Medicaid

Medical home. A concept or model of care delivery that includes an ongoing relationship between a provider and patient, around-the-clock access to medical consultation, respect for a patient's cultural and religious beliefs, and a comprehensive approach to care and coordination of care through providers and community services

Medical staff bylaws. A formal document of the governance procedures for physicians and others who provide care in the organization; approved by the governing body

Medical staff organization. The organization of an HCO's staff members that provides a structure to carry out policies, expectations for quality of clinical care, and communication from physicians to the governing body

Mission. A statement of purpose—the good or benefit the HCO intends to contribute—couched in terms of an identified community, a set of services, and a specific level of cost or finance

Needs assessment. A process for identifying and quantifying opportunities for improvement

Net revenue. Income actually received as opposed to that initially posted; equal to gross revenue minus adjustments for bad debts, charity, and discounts to third parties

Nonoperating revenue. Income generated from non-patient-care activities, including investments in securities and earnings from unrelated businesses

Nurse anesthetist. A registered nurse who has advanced education and certification to administer anesthesia without direct physician supervision

Nurse midwife. A registered nurse who has advanced education and certification to practice uncomplicated obstetrical care, including normal spontaneous vaginal delivery, without direct physician supervision

Nurse practitioner. A registered nurse who has advanced education and certification to carry out expanded healthcare evaluation and decision making regarding patient care; boundaries of independent practice are set by state laws

Nursing diagnosis. A standardized statement about the health of a client for the purpose of providing nursing care; identified from a master list of nursing diagnosis terminology

Nursing process. A system of assessing patients, diagnosing individual nursing care needs, planning care, implementing plans, and evaluating care

Operating budget. The aggregate of accountability-center expenditure budgets and the corporate revenue budget

Operational measures or operational scorecards. Six dimensions of measurement that include three measures of inputs or resources and three measures of outputs or results

Opportunities for improvement (OFIs). Result of comparing actual outcome against goal and goal against benchmark; also arise from qualitative assessments, including listening

Palliative care. Treatment to manage and reduce pain, discomfort, and other uncomfortable symptoms of life-limiting diseases or conditions with no known cure; services are provided in a holistic manner to include the patient and her family

Patient care plans. Expectations for the care of individual patients based on an assessment of individual needs

Patient care protocols or guidelines. Formally established expectations that define the normal steps or processes in the care of a clinically related group of patients at a specific institution

Patient ledger. Account of the charges rendered to an individual patient

Patient management protocols. Formally established expectations that define the normal steps or processes in the care of a clinically related group of patients at a specific institution

Peer review. Any review of professional performance by members of the same profession

Performance improvement council (PIC). A formal coordinating structure composed of representatives from all major activities or activity groups; the PIC's first job is to prioritize OFIs

Position control. A system of payroll control that identifies specific positions created and filled

Primary care practitioners. Initial contact providers, including physicians in family practice, general internal medicine, pediatrics, obstetrics, and psychiatry; nurse practitioners; and midwives

Procedures or processes. Actions or steps that transform inputs to outputs

Process improvement team (PIT). A group that analyzes processes and translates OFIs to actual performance improvement

Pro forma. A forecast of financial statements, establishing the future financial position of the organization for a given set of operating conditions or decisions

Programmatic proposals. Proposals for new or replacement capital equipment or major revisions of service

Protocols. Agreed-on procedures for each task in the care process

Providers. Institutional and personal caregivers such as physicians, hospitals, and nurses

Quality improvement organizations (QIOs). External agencies that review the quality of care and use of insurance benefits by individual physicians and patients for Medicare and other insurers

Rapid response team. Caregivers with training in critical care management and emergency treatment protocols; deployed when a patient's condition suddenly deteriorates

Reach. In advertising, an estimate of the number of people who will see or hear a specific advertisement

Referral specialist physicians. Doctors who care for patients referred by primary care practitioners on a limited or transient basis; likely to m nage episodes of inpatient care

Reserved powers. Decisions permanently vested in the central corpo a multicorporate system

Residents. Licensed physicians who pursue postgraduate educatio who pursue advanced study are also called *fellows*; resident are also called *house officers*

Root causes. The underlying factors that must be changed t tently better outcomes

Scenarios. Alternative approaches to improving the profile of opportunities reflected in the environmental assessment

Segmentation. The deliberate effort to separate markets by customer need and the message to which the markets will respond

Sensitivity analysis. Analysis of the impact of alternative forecasts, usually developing most favorable, expected, and least favorable scenarios to show the robustness of a proposal and to indicate the degree of risk involved

Servant leadership. The leader's obligation to be sensitive and responsive to associate needs

Service excellence. Associates anticipate and meet or exceed customer needs and expectations on the basis of the mission and values

Service lines. Operating units designed around patient-focused care for related disease groups and similar medical specialties

Specification. A statistical analysis that identifies values for a measure by defined subsets of a population, to measure the extent to which the values change across the sets

Stakeholders. Individuals or groups (buyers, workers, suppliers, regulators, and owners) who have a direct interest in an organization's success

Standing committee. A permanent committee established in the bylaws of the corporation or similar basic documents

Statistical process control. A method of identifying significant changes in measures subject to random variation

Strategic measures or strategic scorecard. Four dimensions of measurement (finance, operations, customer relations, and learning/human resources) appropriate for service lines or the HCO as a whole

Strategic opportunities. Opportunities that involve quantum shifts in service capabilities or market share, usually by interaction with competitors, large-scale capital investments, and revisions to several line activities

Strategic partnerships. Commitments with long-term obligations

Strategic positioning. The set of decisions about mission, ownership, scope of activity, location, and partners that defines the organization and relates it to stakeholder needs

Strategic protection. Safeguards the assets of the organization

Strategy. A systematic response to a specific stakeholder need

The Joint Commission. A voluntary consortium of HCOs and professional provider organizations that ensures a minimum level of safety and quality in HCOs

Transaction costs. The costs of maintaining a relationship, including the costs of communication, negotiation, and so forth

Transfer price. Imputed cost revenue for a good or service transferred between two units of the same organization, such as housekeeping services provided to nursing units

Triage. A method for sorting patients according to needs for various levels of resources

Trustees. Members of the governing board of not-for-profit HCOs who volunteer their time to the organization; their only compensation is the satisfaction they achieve from their work. The title reflects their acceptance of the assets in trust for the community; also called *directors*

Unexpected event report. Written report of an untoward event that raises the possibility of liability of the organization

Values. An expansion of the mission that expresses basic rules of acceptable conduct, such as respect for human dignity or acceptance of equality

Vertical integration. The affiliation of organizations that provide different kinds of service, such as hospital care, ambulatory care, long-term care, and social services

Vision. An expansion of the mission that expresses intentions, philosophy, and organizational self-image

Working capital. The amount of cash required to support operations for the period of delay in collecting revenue

INDEX

Team members: CSS, 265-66; internal consulting, 482

Teamwork, 175

Technology, 510

Terminology: standardization of, 321-22

Tertiary prevention, 164, 290

Testing: diagnostic, 146

360-degree survey, 58

Toxicologists, 407

Training: clinical support services, 255, 258, 261; components, 43-44; environment-of-care areas, 407-8; evidence-based management, 27; types of, 81

Transaction accounting, 419, 421-22

Transaction costs, 506

Transfer price, 410-11

Transformational culture: CSS elements, 261; dispute resolution, 66-67; ethical foundation, 64-66; goals, 48-49; improvement of, 52; negotiation, 66-67; nurse manager and, 231; operational foundation, 64; path to, 63-64

Transformational management: communication, 18; empowerment, 18; listening, 18; modeling, 22; negotiations, 21; power of, 16-17; reward system, 23; service excellence, 22-23; shared values, 17-18; supervisory training, 363; teaching, 22

Transparent performance review, 34

Treatment: goals, 163; specialists, 146

Trends: CSS, 278-79; goal setting, 115

Triage, 402

Trustee: definition, 106

Unexpected event reports, 365

Unified operations, 262

Uninsured patients, 258

Unit budget, 428

Unit operational measures, 58

Unit performance: evidence-based interventions, 236; improvement, 234-35

Unmet demand, 291

Upcoding, 455

Utilities management, 394

Utility systems, 404-5

Vacation/holiday pay, 368

Values: of Baldrige Award winners, 19-20; core, 166; definition, 17; goal setting and, 115; governing board establishment, 110; review, 509

Variability indicators, 326-27

Vertical integration, 15, 85-86

Vision: of Baldrige Award winners, 19-20; definition, 17; governing board establishment, 110; review, 509

Voluntary payroll deduction, 357

Volunteer Protection Act, 126

Wage/salary administration, 366-67

Waste management, 394

Work policy changes, 355

Work processes, 80-81

Work reports, 412

Workforce: benefits administration, 368-71; compensation,

ABOUT THE AUTHORS

Kenneth R. White, PhD, MPH, MSN, RN, FACHE, FAAN, is the Sentara Professor in the Department of Health Administration at Virginia Commonwealth University (VCU), where he holds a joint appointment as professor of nursing. From 1995 to 2008, Dr. White served in leadership positions in the graduate programs in health administration at VCU. From 2006 to 2009, he served as VCU's first Charles P. Cardwell, Jr. Professor. Dr. White is also visiting professor at the Luiss Guido Carli University in Rome, Italy, and the Swiss School of Public Health in Lugano, Switzerland.

Dr. White received a PhD in health services organization and research from VCU, an MPH in health administration from the University of Oklahoma, and an MS in nursing from VCU. He has more than 38 years of experience in healthcare organizations in clinical, administrative, governance, academic, and consulting capacities. Dr. White is a registered nurse and a Fellow and former member of the Board of Governors of the American College of Healthcare Executives.

He is coauthor (with John R. Griffith) of *The Well-Managed Healthcare Organization*, 5th, 6th, and 7th editions; *Thinking Forward: Six Strategies for Highly Successful Organizations*; and *Reaching Excellence in Healthcare Management* (all published by Health Administration Press). Dr. White is a contributing author to the books *Human Resources in Healthcare: Managing for Success* and *Evidence-Based Management in Healthcare* (both Health Administration Press), *Advances in Health Care Organization Theory* (Jossey-Bass), *Peri-Anesthesia Nursing: A Critical Care Approach* (Saunders), *On the Edge: Nursing in the Age of Complexity* (Plexus), and *Introduction to Health Services* (Delmar).

Dr. White has received ACHE's James A. Hamilton Award (2012), Exemplary Service Award (2011), Distinguished Service Award (2009), Edgar C. Hayhow Award (2006), and two Regent's Awards (1999 and 2010). He has also received the Virginia Nurses Association's "Virginia's Outstanding Nurse" award (1999), the VCU President's Award for Multicultural Enrichment, and numerous teaching awards.

John R. Griffith, MBA, FACHE, is the Andrew Pattullo Collegiate Professor in the Department of Health Management and Policy at the School of Public Health, The University of Michigan, Ann Arbor. A graduate of the Johns Hopkins University and the University of Chicago, he was director of the Program and Bureau of Hospital Administration at The University of Michigan from 1970 to 1982 and was the chair of his department from 1987 to 1991.

He has served as chair of the Association of University Programs in Health Administration (AUPHA), as a commissioner for the Accrediting Commission on Education in Health Services Administration, and as senior advisor to the board of the National Center for Healthcare Leadership.

The 7th edition of *The Well-Managed Healthcare Organization*, with Kenneth R. White, PhD, FACHE, has been called the "definitive resource" on the subject. The first edition won the ACHE Hamilton Prize for book of the year in 1987. The fourth edition was recognized by the Health Information Management Systems Society as the 2000 book of the year. He authored two articles in the *Journal of Health Administration Education* on the implications of competency assessment in graduate education, titled "Improving Preparation for Senior Management in Health Care" and "Advancing Education for Evidence-Based Healthcare Management."

Professor Griffith was awarded the Gold Medal Award of the American College of Healthcare Executives (ACHE) in 1992. He has also been recognized with the John Mannix Award of the Cleveland Hospital Council, the Edgar Hayhow Award (in 1989, 2003, and 2006) and Dean Conley Prizes of ACHE, The Filerman Award for Educational Excellence of AUPHA, and citations from the Michigan Hospital Association and the Governor of Michigan. He received the Excellence in Teaching Award from the University of Michigan School of Public Health in 2009. He was an examiner for the Malcolm Baldrige National Quality Award from 1997 to 1998.